THE NEW YORK DIARIES
1950–1969

THE NEW YORK DIARIES
1950–1969

**THE NEW YORK DIARIES
1950–1969**

CHAPTER TWENTY FOUR

CHAPTER TWENTY SIX

CHAPTER TWENTY FIVE

AFTER-WORD

by Anne König

CHAPTER ONE

... Was I born a Displaced Person?...
My life in Brooklyn...
First impressions of America... Writing saves my sanity...
Leo... The weaknesses of Civility vs. Strength of Barbarism... On American Pop songs...
A weekend in Stony Brook... A DREAM... Searching for work... Peggy... We buy a Bolex camera...
Beginning of filming... Novels into movies?... Letter from Robert Flaherty...
People in rain... Adolfas writes from Paris... On James Thurber... I am a bad patriot... On Julian Gracq... A STORY... On Jean Renoir...

January 11, 1950

I seem to live on moods, ups and downs. And I seem to be repeating the same mistakes over and over again. Some mistakes are beautiful. There is a beauty in mistakes that you can't find anywhere else, maybe that's why. And I keep avoiding any definite ties with anything and anybody. There are places and moments during which I feel that I would like to always remain there. But no: next moment I am gone. I seem to enjoy only brief glimpses of intimacy, happiness. Short concentrated glimpses. I do not believe that they could be extended, prolonged. So I keep moving ahead, looking ahead for other moments. Is it in my nature or did the war do that to me? The question is: was I born a Displaced Person, or did the war make me into one? Displacement, as a way of living and thinking and feeling. Never home. Always on the move.

February 18, 1950

I have been living all my life dreaming. Between me and the world there is always a space of un-reality. I don't want—or maybe I don't know how—to dissolve, to submerge into reality around me totally, unconditionally.
I see, I feel all the time this dream distance, as if I was from another century, maybe somebody who strayed away in time, from the times of Cervantes maybe. I am trying, with all that I know, to escape it, to throw myself desperately into the thick of daily-ness, in order to feel "the blood of reality." But I keep bouncing back, again and again, into the dreamland.

March 8, 1950

Dear Leo:
Do not reproach me for writing so seldom and so little. Don't send the cover. I don't want to publish anything now. Everything is cinema.

My inner state is like this: like never before.
Seven knives, seven thorns.
I can't understand any of it myself.
The earth has lips of rose bushes.
Every touch draws blood.

March 19, 1950

Films seen recently:
The Great Beginning
Panic
Nanook of the North
Louisiana Story
The Spanish Earth
Song of Ceylon
Window Cleaners

March 25, 1950

Three weeks ago we put $150 deposit on a Bolex camera, at Peerless. We have to pay another $150. We could take the camera right now, but we need a guarantor.

At first we thought it will be easy to find a guarantor. But now three weeks have passed, and we are still looking for one. Today we gave up the idea of finding a guarantor; instead, we decided to borrow some money and pay.

We went to Tysliava, the publisher of a Lithuanian weekly paper in Williamsburg. But he didn't show any enthusiasm for our dream. Instead, he gave us a long lecture on film-making. He said, "Ah, there is more to film than filming: there is also editing. And what do you know about that? Of course, I could guarantee it for you. But suppose you are killed by a car, or something—I'd have to pay for you, no?"

We left him, angry. We expected much more understanding from him. I don't know why we did. I guess, it's our foolish idealism. Anyway, all he did, he advised us to work in the factory.

So we went to the Lithuanian Catholic priest. He said, come tomorrow, the secretary will guarantee it for you. Next day we come—he is a mask. He says, I can't help you, I have no money. So we say, no, we are not asking for money, we are asking for trust. So he says, he spoke with Tysliava, and Tysliava advised him: don't do it, Mekas brothers are not practical, they are idealists, they do not know America—you'll lose your shirt if you go with them.

So now we are walking through Brooklyn angry. Ah, not even the priests have faith anymore.

No date, 1950

When I stepped out, or rather stepped on this island, I still carried in my hair the winds of Lithuania and the winds of the years of wandering through Germany.

The winds of America? I am only beginning to perceive them, very barely. But I want to feel them deeply—to feel them, to live them. I want to experience America to its very bottom. Then I can continue further, to somewhere else...

My greatest pastime and entertainment and happiness these days is to walk through New York, for hours and hours I walk drinking it all in.

No date, 1950

I am looking at my fingers. During the last few weeks my nails broke out in white spots. And more are coming. I don't know where my luck is stuck, but it's not here. But my nerves are all here, stretched like strings. The other night I tried to sleep. I couldn't. I was trembling all over, every atom in me. I wanted to get up, go somewhere, anywhere. But I was unable to even get up. So I just lay there staring at the room.

For a month or two I've been in peace. But now I have entered another of my recurring periods of depression. I keep trying to persuade myself that this is only temporary, "this happens only during the rain periods." But that doesn't answer all the questions.

Now that we both, Adolfas and myself, have been firmly branded by Lithuanians as communists—any meeting, any time spent with them is only a further wrecking of nerves. The family of Prof. Berentas and Algis are about the only Lithuanians we still see.

Williamsburg (Brooklyn), 1952. One way of describing the various geographical stages of my life would be to follow Dante and Milton. Semeniškiai, my home village, was Paradiso. My life in Germany, in the Forced Labor camp, and the post-war Displaced Persons (DP) camps, was Inferno. My Williamsburg/Brooklyn period was my Purgatorio. The day, in Spring 1953, when I escaped from Brooklyn to Manhattan's Lower East Side, I was entering the Paradise Regained.

THE NEW YORK DIARIES
1950–1969

13

Old Lithuanian immigrants, Williamsburg, 1952. They came here after the First World War. They told me they had never been in Manhattan. "How is it there?" they used to ask me.

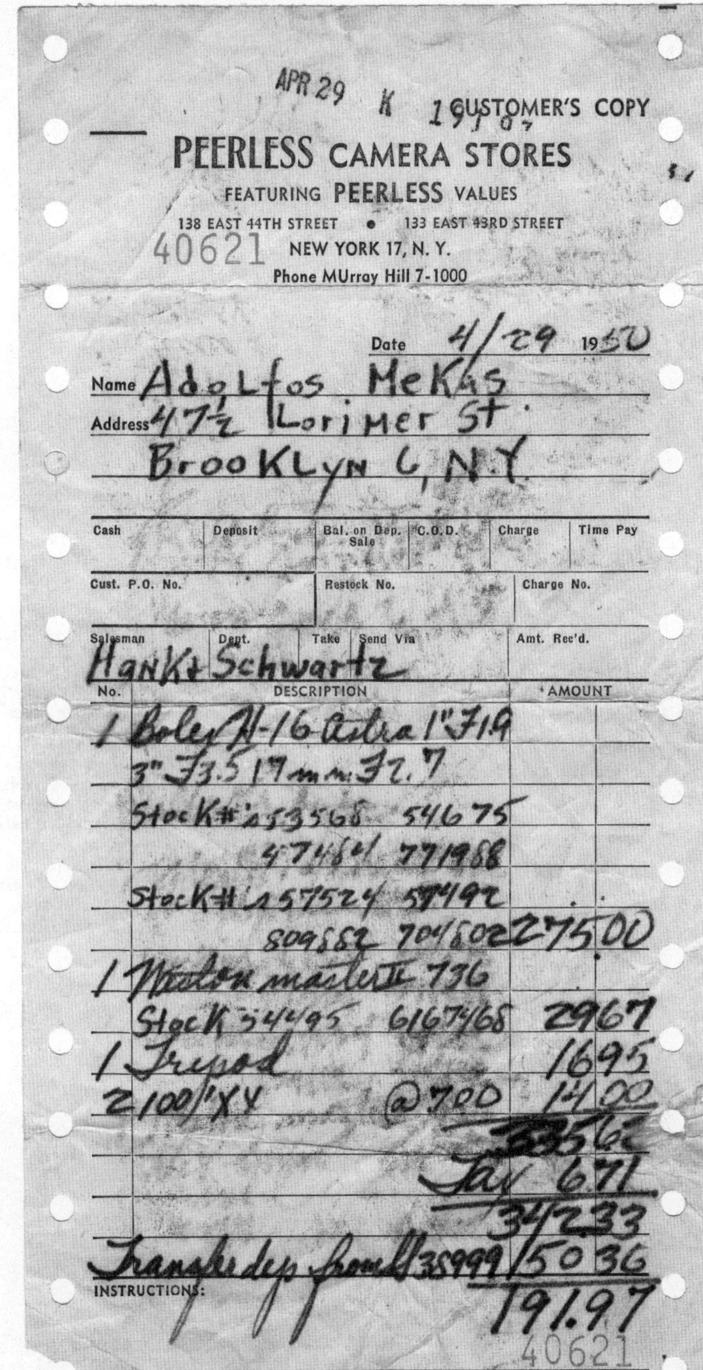

PEERLESS CAMERA STORES

K 19587 1 CUSTOMER'S COPY

FEATURING **PEERLESS** VALUES

138 EAST 44TH STREET • 133 EAST 43RD STREET

40621 NEW YORK 17, N. Y.

Phone MUrray Hill 7-1000

Date 4/29 1950

Name Adolfos Mekas

Address 47½ Lorimer St.

Brooklyn 6, N.Y.

Cash	Deposit	Bal. on Dep. Sale	C.O.D.	Charge	Time Pay

Cust. P.O. No.		Restock No.		Charge No.	

Salesman	Dept.	Take	Send Via	Amt. Rec'd.
Hank & Schwartz				

No.	DESCRIPTION	AMOUNT
1	Bolex H-16 astra 1" F19	
	3" F3.5 17mm F2.7	
	Stock # 053568 54675	
	474601 771988	
	Stock # 257524 58492	
	809552 704502	275 00
1	Weston master II 736	
	Stock 34495 6167468	2967
1	Tripod	1695
2	100'XX @ 700	1400
		33562
	Tax 671	
		342233
	Transfer dep. from #35999	15036
		191.97

INSTRUCTIONS:

40621

C1 All claims and returned goods must be accompanied by this bill. $

THE NEW YORK DIARIES
1950–1969

15

The family of Klybas, Brooklyn, 1950.
Klybas, Mayor of Biržai, a small town
of some 5,000 people where I went to
Gymnasium, managed to escape the
Soviets and ended up in Brooklyn, like
ourselves. Thanks to the persuasion
talents of their daughter Vida, they acted
as guarantors for the purchase of our
first Bolex at Peerless camera store.

No date, 1950

I look at these people and I am terrified. And I ask myself: Do I really want to be like everybody else? Do I really want to belong to this kind of world? Here are the everybodies. But are they happy? Do they feel happy, these Jedermanns? Maybe they are living in pain, inside. It's like when you really suffer, inside, you become oblivious to it, you live like a somnambulist: just like these people now on these benches this Sunday afternoon.

On our way here, to the park, we crossed Fifth Avenue and it was full of a different life... All the cars... Ah, they, too, every weekend they are driving their big cars same way, going to the same beaches for maybe thirty years, and they'll bake in the sun (they have to look tanned!). Yes, they like to have certain regular places where they can always go, like all animals do, all animals attach themselves to a place, to a habitat. They'll drink beer, "Coca-Cola" maybe, and will munch on crackers, will wade into the water, and they'll talk the same talks, and then they may go to some dancing somewhere, and then maybe this and maybe that. Then Monday will be here and they'll all go to work, the same work, the same faces, every week, every month, every year.

Ah, yes, they have memories, reminiscences—driving a car, going to the beach, drinking "Coca-Cola" etc. etc.—and the memories of one of them could be easily exchanged with those of any other—they are all alike—their lives are alike—one or two love adventures, maybe one secret (wife doesn't know it yet, not yet), a trip to Florida, etc.

Ah, I thought, it's good that I fall into those ravines of desperation—they open me to the other, different reality which I otherwise wouldn't see. Desperation, pain—ah, I can profit from them all.

June 7, 1950

Midnight. I just finished writing the short story, "In the Park." Now I am free, and I am ecstatically happy. So much lightness inside. Radio is playing Handel's Concerto Grosso in E Minor.

June 29, 1950

Sometimes writing saves me. And then, sometimes, I think, I hate it. Because nothing that is really fully lived needs to be written down. It burns itself out totally.

Does a tear need to be written down? Or a prayer? Or holding hands? I would like my life to be like that.

But now I have to compliment my life with writing...

A full life is like a fruit, it reaches its ripeness and it falls down.

Now, it sits under my brain and it keeps eating me, wants to be born.

July, 1950

It's three in the morning as I am writing this. Everybody is sleeping. Middle of the night. But I woke up and my eyes were suddenly completely open, with no trace of sleep. No, I couldn't sleep. And I know I'll stay awake the rest of the night.

Like many other nights.

No, I didn't live at all, no. I haven't given anything to anybody; and I don't have anything to give. Yes, I have been living on stolen bits of happiness.

I have even taken alms, yes, I took them too. I lied to myself, I said it was love...

No date, 1950

Leo says, his life is a theorem which can be proved only with one's heart, with one's (his) own life.

No, there never was an age of arts. Whistler says so too. In any given age there are only a few great, individual artists.

Pope Julius paid Michelangelo with his own personal monies. Cardinals didn't approve of him (Michelangelo).

Concedo Nulli—I don't belong to anybody (to anything). Like Erasmus, like Rilke. No attachment to place, ideas.

No date, 1950

Ideals? I don't know. They asked me a lot about them.

I am more interested, now, in the concrete everyday reality. Colors, feelings, voices, faces. I crave for a direct confrontation with reality, with nothing in between. No abstractions, no philosophy. And I don't feel that I am any weaker by refusing to make preconceived choices. I change my opinions very often, these days, about objects and people, and this upsets my friends a lot. What I am going to say tomorrow may be completely opposite to what I am saying today. I am tasting everything anew. Growing. Learning about the New World around me.

Everything is in flux and for that reason, every place I see, everything I hear now has such a real fresh vividness.

Yes, the world is fantastic!

Yes, I am a blank book and I am permitting the world to write in it... But if you think that to try to be that open doesn't take any effort—ah, you are wrong. With all the efforts that I am putting into it, into being an open book—I am only a little tiny bit open.

"If God didn't give you anything when He passed by, He'll give you on His way back."

"Stop working if you don't want to perish."

There are books for the average reader, with the average scale of experience and average emotions and average feelings. And there are books for the reader with a wider scale of experience and thought and feeling—for a reader ready for subtle tones—the 600 variations of yellow of the Old China.

Man didn't fall away from God: man fell away, is falling away from man.

They say there are no nights in New York, it's only illumination, neon lights... But ah, I have seen beautiful nights here... Humanity went through the periods of a) nomads, b) settlers. They have retained those characteristics even today. I, for instance, in many areas such as religion, ideas and my lifestyle, am a nomad. While most of the people around me are settlers in all those three areas.

July, 1950

We spoke last night about the endlessness of the cosmos, its ungraspable distances. Later I was walking home, I was lying in my bed and I couldn't sleep. I kept thinking about the equally ungraspable inner spaces.

Happiness, pain, fear, despair, Mozart— they all have their spaces. Life, dagger, poison. Again different spheres and circles and spaces. Their own gravitations. Every touch of hand, every word, look, glimpse, sunset, rain, kneeling in church, the smell of a rainy evening...

"The smell of a rainy evening." Say it, break it down into spaces. "Smelling flowers in Alley Park." Their smell dissolved, spread into invisible spaces, disappeared in the inner orbits with all their tiny satellites.

Sometimes by chance you touch a tone, a note—and everything reverberates through all the spaces with incredible nuances. One touch of hands, lips—and ah! Or maybe just a silence—and everything begins to sound, the incredible inner music.

As Dostoyevsky said, we live only through the glimpses, seconds, when the souls really speak, really meet, really see.

No date, 1950

Maspeth

Leo is climbing upstairs. Towel on his neck. He is singing in the bathroom right now. In the upstairs living room—radio music.

Ginkus, an old Lithuanian immigrant, in front of his Ginkus Candy Store, corner of Union and Grand Streets, Williamsburg, 1950. Ah, how many times he fed us and treated with beer during our first miserable months in Brooklyn! His bar was the hangout of the newly arrived Lithuanian immigrants. He had a big, generous heart, Ginkus.

```
              F I L M O S   L A P A S   1 9 5 1  M.

No.      Title          by         with                    Country

S a u s i o  men.

 1.  The Thief of Bagdad by Raoul Walsh,& Douglas Fairbanks      Amer. '24
 2.  Devil's Doorway                                             Amer. '50
 3.  Two Weeks with the Love                                     Amer. '50
 4.  The Land by R.Flaherty                                      Amer. '42
 5.  Industrial Britain by R.Flaherty                            Amer. '32
 6.  Moana by R.Flaherty                                         Amer. '25
 7.  Manon by                                                    Frac. '50
 8.  Long Voyage Home by Distant Journey by                      Chec. '48
 9.  Under the Sun of Rome by                                    Ital. '49
10.  David Copperfield by Zuckor                                 Amer. '35
11.  Mr. Trull Finds Out by Joseph Krumgold                      Amer. '40
12.  I Walked With a Zombie by Jacques Tourneur                  Amer. '43
13.  King's Soloman Mines by  Zymbalist                          Amer. '50
14.  He's a Hocheyed Wonder                                      Amer. '50
15.  The Invisible Man by James Whale                            Brit. '33
16.  Your Children Sleep by Brian Smith and Jane Massy    C16    Brit. '47
17.  Flugten by Albert Mertz and Jørgen  Roos             C16    Denm. '42
18.  Legato by Henning Bendtsen                           C16    Denm. '4
19.  Aybervilliers by Eli Lotar                           C16    Frnc. '49
20.  The World of Paul Delvaux by Henri Storck            C16    Belg. '4
21.  Waverley Steps by John Eldridge                      C16    Brit. '4
22.  Carmen by Lotte Reininger                                   Germ. '33
23.  The Band Concert by Walt Disney                             Amer. '35
24.  Mickey's Grand Opera by Walt Disney                         Amer. '36
25.  The Old Mill by Walt Disney                                 Amer. '37
26.  Water,Friend or Anemy by Walt Disney                        Amer. '43
27.  Swooner Crooner by Leon Schlesinger                         Amer. '44
28.  Musical Poster #1 by Len Lye                                Amer. '

V a s a r i o  men.

29.  Passion of Joan of Arc by Carl-Theodor Dreyer &Falconetta   Frnc. '28
30.  Mutiny in Odessa by Zecca,Ferdinand                         Frnc. '07
31.  Patemkin by Sergei Eisenstein                               Russ. '25
32.  The March of Wooden Soldiers                                Amer. '34
33.  Mr. Music                                                   Amer. '50
34.  Born Yesterday  by Cukor                                    Amer. '50
```

A list of movies we saw in January,
1950. A list of the plays, ballet evenings,
music was not much shorter.

Later, in the kitchen:

Leo: "See, I washed out the plate, I put it on the table—and it fell to pieces."

Ignas: "Bad luck. It will cost you ten dollars."

Leo: "Only ten dollars? Can I break a few more at that price?"

Ignas: "Stop! Stop! He's crazy. He says ten dollars is nothing. He'll break all my plates. What am I going to do then."

Leo: "You are right."

Ignas: "If one is married, even if one's crazy, they take him for a sound, normal man."

Leo: "I am running right now, I am marrying."

Ignas: "After twenty-five, even if you aren't married, you are taken as a serious man."

Leo: "In that case, I am O.K. as I am."

"Ah, how should I begin to tell you what happened to me…"

"What happened? Tell us, tell us…"

"Wherever I go—there is a road. Wherever I live—there is a house… Nobody's waiting for me… Wherever I go—everybody's younger than me. They call me a bachelor…"

"So why don't you marry?"

"Ah, that time passed away. I missed it."

"So why do you dance?"

"From spitefulness."

"Don't tell me. I saw her, she was *très sympathique*…"

"In the name of Son, and Father, and Holy Ghost…"

"Ah, I remember them all, those that I kissed."

"I don't remember any."

"Look, look, she doesn't want to admit that I kissed her."

"I really don't remember."

"But we kissed, no?"

"I guess we did."

"Ah, she is lying now."

"She doesn't recognize kisses."

"How can a woman catch you?"

"Difficult, difficult. I am a difficult one."

"Salt on the tail."

"I don't think you could catch me, I am too fast."

"No, no, no girl ever escaped me yet."

"You'll step on your own tail."

"I myself, I am not very fast, but I caught Vale."

"It looks that you are fast, you ran after me all the way from Europe."

"You should all marry, what is this? You'll become bachelors."

"Before we marry we want to have a good time…"

August 18, 1950

Yesterday evening, at 6 PM, the three of us, we agreed to go to Manhattan and meet at 3 AM in the morning in Times Square, and report on our adventures.

For hours I wandered through the city. I dissolved into it, I got drunk on it. I drifted deeper and deeper into it, without any control. I permitted myself to drift any direction.

I walked from street to street. I stood in the crowds, I sat in the cafeterias, in pokerinos, amusement parlors, jazz bars. I drank the rhythm of Times Square. I felt I was part of it, part of Times Square night. Then I took a subway and I rode for another half an hour. I had nothing to do. I was drinking the night, the emptiness and the loneliness of the sleeping city.

No date, 1950

Sometimes I think that the innocence, naiveté, idealism and blind faith of the Americans—as opposed to the unscrupulous cunningness of the Soviets—is a natural characteristic of higher civilization and cultures. That's why they go down.

A healthy, young (but stupid) animal or human, at the peak of life, feels the surroundings with its (his) nostrils and every pore of the body: is very careful, awake. But America is losing its animal (or call it fascist) energies, its sense of self-preservation. Its tools are culture, civilization.

But here I am. I have chosen culture and civilization vs. barbarism, fascism, and communism (the way it's practiced today).

I listen to the songs on the radio, and they all have a very special kind of unreality about them. A veil of unreality. There is no realism in them, neither in their melodies nor their lyrics. Everything is covered with a certain color of unreality, like the neon lights in Times Square. You look at the moon and you ask, is this the moon or neon lights. The artificiality is so strong that it makes even the real look unreal.

We were driving through New Jersey the other day, and we looked at the fantastic, almost surreal maze of factory chimneys and wires, electrical towers. The mist was hovering over it all, and I didn't know, was it the morning mist or the industrial, artificial, poison mist.

The other night we stayed up late. We couldn't sleep. We talked and talked, about America.

Yes, America is the first country which has succeeded to *forget*. It has mastered the art of forgetting in order to gain happiness. I read in some newspaper that 85 % of Americans consider themselves "happy." Take it easy! Not to think, not to worry about anything. No existential tremblings. Just glide through the surface of the clouds. Live on top of the clouds, on the silver lining.

I was very surprised, at first, when people here called me by my first name just after one meeting. But, of course, in the land of forgetfulness and surface one believes that one can know a person from one meeting: there cannot be anything of importance beyond it, the surface does it. The movie screen... And they tell me their intimacies and I feel suddenly like I am their psychoanalyst or something. Even their openness and intimacy is not really felt, it's full of neon lights...

No date, 1950

I went to church, to the midnight mass, and listened to a boring sermon. Behind me a couple was talking all the time, whispering. The choir sang, and the singers kept looking at the people in the church, in a hurry to finish, because people were already leaving the church, and they wanted to meet their friends, and I found it very human, something miserably human in this otherwise very abstract and artificial set up—the girls want to see their boys, that's real.

No date, 1950

the drizzle on a muddy hill town street
and the docks & dark banks and piers
drizzle on blue night trees, street lamps

to watch the rain, listen to its sound, how
it falls on the leaves, fragile wet drops
and listen to Chopin
—like in an old poem—
as the rain falls on grey houses, reflections
of evening lights.

Yes, New York.
Ah, to sit here on this pier and gaze into the
muddy dark waters
with the never ending music
of the city behind me—like a huge
cathedral organ
played by Messiaen.

There are times when I want to make them mad, so that at least once, once in their lives they'd shout it out, honestly and passionately, from their very heart. But I do not believe that they are capable anymore of getting mad. Their "education" doesn't permit them to get mad.

This bum. I respect this bum. He is cursing this man, and I am not sure what for. He expresses himself clearly. I respect this bum's curses.

Notify at Once any Change of Address

NOTICE: This book must be carried by the member at all times and be ready for inspection by any authorized person.

Members are requested to p r e s e r v e this book in good order. If lost, a new one can be had at a nominal price.

Members when paying dues should see that the month for which they are paying is officially cancelled.

Without Fail Take a Withdrawal Card When Leaving the Craft.

48 REGISTERED

This is to Certify, *That in consideration of Application for Membership duly signed and filed*

Jonas Mekas
(Name)

072-26-9970
(Social Security No.)

was granted membership by

General Warehousemen

Local Union No. 852

New York, N. Y.

Date Initiated

April 1950

Card Number

76127

Members when paying initiation fee should see that the above space is officially cancelled with the date they were initiated.

They didn't even ask me if I wanted to belong to it. A guy from the Union came to me when I was working at Bebry Bedding, and told me that now I was in the Union and that I'll have to pay Union dues.

Christmas 1952, Stony Brook.

The Pranė Lapė family Stony Brook Lodge was one place we occasionally used for the weekend escapes from Brooklyn. The Lapė family took a special liking to us and treated Adolfas and myself as part of the family.

STONY BROOK LODGE
STONY BROOK, L. I.

Nėlė Lapė, daughter of Pranė Lapė, with Adolfas, during one of his leaves from the U.S. Army, summer 1952.

Marija Gimbutas, the archaeologist, Stony Brook Lodge, 1952.

No date, 1950

A STORY

I am carrying this strange secret. It keeps eating me but I can't tell it to anybody. The thing is, this secret cannot be told in words: it can be only transmitted through laugh. It can only be laughed out, so to speak. But whenever I tried to laugh it out, my friends thought ah what a strange laugh. This laugh resembles a child's laugh when you tickle a child's neck with your finger, gently gently. When, as a child, I used to walk along the village street and laugh by myself. It probably sounded a little bit strange, maybe even idiotic. But I was trying to communicate it. So the farmer neighbors used to say: Why are you laughing? Maybe rain is coming?

No date, 1950

They tell me: "Don't destroy it if you have nothing better to put in its place."
But I say: "Eh, destruction is destruction. Shit is a shit, what's the difference?"
The Spring.
Farmers walk out into the fields.
They return home drunk with happiness.
"You know, women, they are like a knife under your neck, a burden..."
"But what a knife, what a burden! I would like to have one under my neck... a knife like you."

September 10, 1950

Stony Brook
The house was still sleeping. I peeked into the children's room. The door was open. I tiptoed to the door and looked in. Jonas, the little boy, was sleeping peacefully, with his face in the pillow.
I descended downstairs and walked out into the garden. Now the mist was really heavy. The bay had disappeared. The beach cottages lined along the bay looked like grey fuzzy blurs in the mist.
I stood on the steps leading to the water. There was dew on the sand and on the green blades of beach grass.

Ah, what a pleasure to feel the morning dew on your feet. There was a wedding in the neighboring house, all night I could hear music and dancing. From the bay came the sounds of motor-boats, the night birds shouted in the trees around the house and the grasshoppers played noisily their incessant music, the night was full of their instruments.
I walked to the water's edge and stared into the bay, at the weeds. It was very, very quiet, nothing moved, nothing. Only a distant motorboat could be heard somewhere in the mist, distant and muffled.
Then, suddenly I heard a horse neighing. I found it very strange to hear a horse in these surroundings, in this place, although I knew that the lodge was full of horse riders this weekend, and now they were all getting up, I could hear them bang the doors, and they talked loud, and the woman in the rider's pants was eating her breakfast, and the young punk jockey, he couldn't have been more than fourteen, unless he was a midget, he was leading his horse towards the bay—and everywhere I went—on the beach, in the woods, around the lodge—I could see the signs of horse hooves.
Adolfas was sitting high on the shore, on a bench, very still. He had been sitting like that for an hour already, since he got up, at seven. He couldn't sleep either.
Ah, how strange—I thought—ah, how could one ever live *seriously* here. It's too quiet. These trees, this beach. I stood looking at the bay, Rembrandt-like sketches of the shoreline, and there was a mist hovering over it, the fishermen were returning home. No, I couldn't live here. Too picturesque. I thought about my ten months of Brooklyn, and I tried to compare the faces, and the movements, to place them into these surroundings, into this rhythm, and it was very difficult to do so. No, there was a different life going here, a different rhythm, a different mood. Here you could see the

separation between morning, and day, and evening.

We stood for a long time near the water's edge watching the children dig out crabs, and how later they throw them into the air for the seagulls—yes, the crabs, how they dig in with their tiny little legs, they dig themselves in, and soon you don't see them at all.

Nėlė was already waiting with breakfast, and she walked around so lightly, so without any sound, I have never seen anybody walk so softly—and we sat and we talked, watching how the mist turned to drizzle, and by noon it was a real rainstorm and water ran down the window panes and it was good to listen to it how it was beating over the roof, the trees, the porch.

I sat in the chair and didn't want to think about anything, I just wanted to listen to the rain, to look at it without any words, I sat and watched the raindrops.

I wanted to forget all the books and all those conversations at home, those long evenings. I wanted to live now with what I saw, what I heard around me, right now. I didn't know what was happening with me, and what will remain from this weekend.

I sat in the chair and watched the rain and it was all the same now. The rain was real. From inside into the porch and into the woods the radio carried the sounds of the city.

September 11, 1950

I spent two days in Stony Brook, with the Lapė family.

This evening I took a train home. It was late, it was ten o'clock, and the train was full of returning weekend outers. Teenagers, girls and boys, cuddled close together, talking silently. Women and men with very serious faces and tiny suitcases under their legs. They were all rushing back to the city.

The train was rushing through and past the empty dark fields. Here and there a house, a light. Past the towns and woods, occasionally making a long, vibrating nervous toot.

I sat leaning on the window and stared into the darkness, listening to the clanking of the wheels. With every turn of the wheel I felt the city coming closer and closer. And then the first New York outlines appeared and the first neon lights star-spangled all over the skyline tearing the mood of the past two days to pieces.

I was still full of the weekend, and as I walked from the station, I permitted memories to return and take over and pass through my body cells like a movie, to replay it again—and I felt good.

But as I was approaching Linden Street, I was suddenly hit by the reality I suddenly saw the dirty street, Brooklyn, and I thought about the next five days, the five days that I'll have to spend in the factory, the boredom, and, ah, all those faces again. I'll surely see them all tomorrow.

No date, 1950

A DREAM

I dreamt:

I found myself in a royal court. There were members of royalty there. My hair was disheveled, my clothes dirty, heavy, my shoes old. I had just come from moving manure from the stables.

We came here as a continuation of an old tradition of early settlers: not for the sake of a better bread, or in search of adventure, but as exiles, outcasts.

Yes, we have seen and tasted life already before we came here, and we can look at everything with an open and sad eye.

My Yugoslav neighbor is drunk.

He says, he can't sleep because he keeps hearing voices of all the people who have been killed and tortured.

He says, how could he sleep with all that whispering going on in the world.

Even today, when I pass Warren Street, I see vividly all the hours I spent in its smoke-filled waiting rooms together with many others, desperate, waiting for any job, any.

... somewhere in Queens, a small boiler repair place where I worked for a few months... drilling... drilling... I can still hear the sound...

On subway:
A woman with white leather gloves, a knitting needle, black hat, black coat. A bum reading a newspaper, brown coat.
"Nowadays everything in modern homes is operated by switches, everything except the children," says the bum.
Silence. "Is there much snow in the streets?" he asks. Silence.

Oscar Wilde to André Gide:
"Would you like to know the great drama of my life? It's that I've put my genius into my life; I've put only my talent into my works."

"Only the work of art itself can raise the standard of taste."—Diego Rivera.

And now, after
I have crossed the shores of death and sadness let me
dream utopias.

Nėlė:
"When I finished college, my first job was in a bank. Ah, what a great feeling, the first job! And a room, an apartment of my own! Freedom, life."
"But the fourth day, I sat among the papers in the bank, and I cried."
"Four days of the same boredom, monotony. It seemed to me I had been there for half a year. Endless. Will I have to work like this all my life? Is this what I was dreaming, going to college, to do this?"
"I sat and I cried."

No date, 1951
Some are lying in their beds for months, trying to die, and can't die. It's a terrible thing when you want to die before your time has really come.
Others—they just fall asleep. From old age, or an illness takes them away.
To kill oneself?
No, it's not easy to kill a man.

We went through the war, we saw everything and we are alive. And then there are others, they cut them to pieces, they burn them, they skin them, they peel their nails off—and they are still alive. They cling to life with every cell of their bodies.
They live. Without eyes, without legs, without arms—surreal lumps of flesh, on wheelchairs, they live, they cling to life—maybe the mouth is still left, nourished through a rubber pipe—in bed for twenty years—but still: life!
They live like corals in the seas, clinging to some rock, like sponges, attached to the shores of life.

No date, 1951
"China's Religious Heritage" by Y. C. Yang: "He who can come to know the new, through reviewing the old, can be a teacher of others."

Confucius: "If you know not life, why speculate about death?"

The society doesn't need artists. To some artists, such a society seems unnecessary.

I only opened my mouth twice or thrice—and they already tell me: you are not necessary!
So now I feel very free.
Since I am not necessary to the society, I can write any way I want.

No date, 1951
I was walking today, looking for work. After sitting five hours in the Warren Street employment agency, I got lost among the downtown streets. People, streets, shops. Strangely, for the first time in two years of my New York life, here on these streets, I could perceive a touch of memory, of something familiar, here, on this corner of Chambers Street and Broadway. I have spent so much time around Warren Street that there is now a little

part of myself here, too, in these dingy rooms, luncheonettes, bars. I passed a place where I had worked as a plumber's helper. In another place I had stopped once on some delivery trip. There was a familiar smell coming from the corner frankfurter stand and it was sticky and hot. I continued walking. This was my New York. I almost felt as if I was at home. Like a cat being stroked.

No date, 1951

"There is something about that smile of yours. You have almost a morbid mind," said Earl.

"I am not a stone. Do you think one can live half of his life in hell and forget about it?"

"But you should be strong."

"I am strong. But I ain't a stone."

We passed by a butcher shop. For a minute we stood and looked into the window, at a line of dead pheasants displayed in the window.

"But you have hope?"

"Even in the KZ* they had hope. Hope is a fool's mother."

"Are you happy?"

"I don't know any longer what it is, happiness. Years ago I knew it clearly, but now I have lost that knowledge, like you lose a word you don't use."

"Do you feel free?"

"Sometimes I feel I am free. I am not bound any longer to anything. No country, no community."

"You never talk much."

"You know, I'm afraid of people. I am very shy. I learned to be silent, ever since I saw German soldiers beating up my brother for walking across the railroad tracks to get a drink of water. I get silent, when I hear talking about community, or humanity, or the nation. The only ties I can have now are with single individuals, friends, Peter, John, *Marty*. No abstract groups of people, humanities."

We stop at the corner of 23rd Street and Sixth Avenue. Earl is always very respectful of red lights.

"Don't believe me. Don't believe a word I say," I say. "I am always lying. I learned it in Europe, to lie. Why do you think I am walking now this street and not somewhere else, let's say, in Siberia? Because I lied all the time. And it wasn't the Sartre lie, no. It simply was that I had eliminated the word NO from my dictionary. Now I am always saying yes. Because those who said NO are dead now, long ago. I am here with you, now, because I didn't use that word."

Now he looked at them, dead now, friends of his youth, and their faces seemed so young and so relaxed, now, ten years younger, without the lines of the last ten years.

No date, 1951

Damnation! I am condemned to write everything down. My lips, they have conspired to be silent, in collaboration with the typewriter.

No date, 1951

Peggy joined me for lunch today.

We were walking down the 23rd Street, crosstown. We were walking slowly. We kept stopping and looking into every window. I stared, she looked.

"I like suburbs. You can see further there," said Peggy.

"It's too open for me," said I. "I like backrooms, backstreets, dark corners, where you can see things that are not openly displayed. Discoveries. I don't even listen when people talk loud, I listen only when I hear whispers… All interesting things are said silently. Have you ever heard anybody saying I LOVE YOU loud? Only the

---

* KZ, German abbreviation for Konzentrationslager, concentration camps.

Myself, in Maspeth, Queens. This photo was taken by Adolfas.

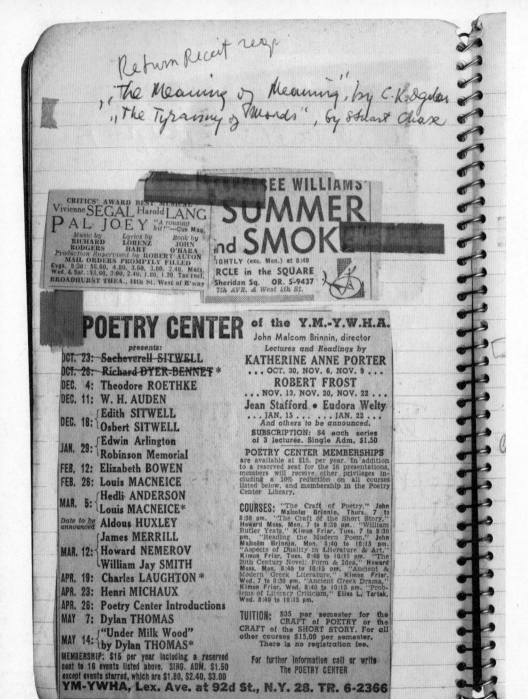

CRITICS' AWARD BEST MUSICAL
Vivienne SEGAL   Harold LANG
PAL JOEY   *"A rousing hit!"*—Cue Mag.
Music by   Lyrics by   Book by
RICHARD   LORENZ   JOHN
RODGERS   HART   O'HARA
Production Supervised by ROBERT ALTON
MAIL ORDERS PROMPTLY FILLED
Evgs. 8:30: $6.60, 4.80, 3.60, 3.00, 2.40, Mats.
Wed. & Sat.:$3.60, 3.00, 2.40, 1.80, 1.20, Tax incl.
BROADHURST THEA., 44th St. West of B'way

[TENNES]SEE WILLIAMS'
SUMMER and SMOKE
[N]IGHTLY (exc. Mon.) at 8:40
[CI]RCLE in the SQUARE
Sheridan Sq.   OR. 5-9437
7th AVE. & West 4th St.

POETRY CENTER of the Y.M.-Y.W.H.A.
John Malcom Brinnin, director

presents:

OCT. 23: Sacheverell SITWELL
OCT. 26: Richard DYER-BENNET *
DEC. 4: Theodore ROETHKE
DEC. 11: W. H. AUDEN
DEC. 18: { Edith SITWELL / Osbert SITWELL
JAN. 29: { Edwin Arlington / Robinson Memorial
FEB. 12: Elizabeth BOWEN
FEB. 26: Louis MACNEICE
MAR. 5: { Hedli ANDERSON / Louis MACNEICE*
Date to be announced: Aldous HUXLEY
MAR. 12: { James MERRILL / Howard NEMEROV / William Jay SMITH
APR. 19: Charles LAUGHTON *
APR. 23: Henri MICHAUX
APR. 26: Poetry Center Introductions
MAY 7: Dylan THOMAS
MAY 14: { "Under Milk Wood" / by Dylan THOMAS*

MEMBERSHIP: $15 per year including a reserved
seat to 16 events listed above. SING. ADM. $1.50
except events which are $1.80, $2.40, $3.00.
YM-YWHA, Lex. Ave. at 92d St., N.Y. 28. TR. 6-2366

Lectures and Readings by
KATHERINE ANNE PORTER
... OCT. 30, NOV. 6, NOV. 9 ...
ROBERT FROST
... NOV. 13, NOV. 20, NOV. 22 ...
Jean Stafford ● Eudora Welty
... JAN. 15 ... ... JAN. 22 ...
And others to be announced.
SUBSCRIPTION: $4 each series
of 3 lectures. Single Adm. $1.50

POETRY CENTER MEMBERSHIPS
are available at $15. per year. In addition
to a reserved seat for the 16 presentations,
members will receive other privileges including a 10% reduction on all courses
listed below, and membership in the Poetry
Center Library.

COURSES: "The Craft of Poetry," John
Malcom Brinnin, Thurs. 7 to
8:30 pm. "The Craft of the Short Story,"
Howard Moss, Mon. 7 to 8:30 pm. "William
Butler Yeats," Kimon Friar, Tues. 7 to 8:30
pm. "Reading the Modern Poem," John
Malcom Brinnin, Mon. 8:40 to 10:15 pm.
"Aspects of Duality in Literature & Art,"
Kimon Friar, Tues. 8:40 to 10:15 pm. "The
20th Century Novel: Form & Idea," Howard
Moss, Mon. 8:40 to 10:15 pm. "Ancient &
Modern Greek Literature," Kimon Friar,
Wed. 7 to 8:30 pm. "Ancient Greek Drama,"
Kimon Friar, Wed. 8:40 to 10:15 pm. "Prob-
lems of Literary Criticism," Elias L. Tartak,
Wed. 8:40 to 10:15 pm.

TUITION: $35 per semester for the
CRAFT of POETRY or the
CRAFT of the SHORT STORY. For all
other courses $15.00 per semester.
There is no registration fee.

For further information call or write
The POETRY CENTER

c. 1975, revisiting 47½ Lorimer Street, where we lived in 1950. The trees we filmed with our first Bolex, which I used in *Lost Lost Lost*, were still there, but the house was gone.

Oct	Nov	Jan	Feb	Feb	March	
	30			15	1	

Special Events: at 9:30 pm on dates above
Central Needle Trades Auditorium, 225 W. 24th St., bet. 7th & 8th Aves.

1954/55

Cinema 16 175 Lexington Avenue, NYC MU 9-7288
Membership card *Complimentary*
Tuesday series *Jonas Mekas*
name of member

Regular Performances: at 9:30 pm on dates below
Central Needle Trades Auditorium, 225 W. 24th St., bet. 7th & 8th Aves.

Oct	Nov	Dec	J	March	April	May
9		14	11	15	12	10

	nov.	jan	feb.	feb.	march		may
8	16				7	21	10

special events (9:30 pm on above dates at the
Central Needle Trades Auditorium)

cinema 16 membership card 1953/54
issued by cinema 16, 175 lexington avenue, nyc, mu 9-7288

wednesday series — 9:30 pm

Jonas Mekas
name of member

regular performances (9:30 pm on dates below at Central Needle Trades
Auditorium, 225 west 24th street, between 7th and 8th aves., nyc)

oct.	nov.	d	n.	march	a	may
4			7	1	1	2

this certifies that *Mr. Jonas Mekas*

is a **member of the**

**cinema 16
film society**

OCT 1951

signature of member

Amos Vogel
president of cinema 16

cinema 16, 59 park avenue, new york 16, n. y.

generals do. Or when someone is dying? These are silent matters. How can you find anything good in a brightly lit window?"

An elevated train rattles over our heads, drowning for a minute everything in its scream.

"I like the elevated trains," I said.

"I hear they are taking them down."

"But I like them."

"You like everything that is not like everything else."

"You know, there are slaughter houses at the end of the 14th Street where the blood runs into the streets. Do you know? They kill sheep there. White sheep. You don't believe me? Yes, I am lying all the time. But it's true about the sheep. I am not lying. Their white wool is full of blood, I saw it."

No date, 1951

NO EXIT, says Sartre. NO EXIT, because he's trying to get out through the wrong door. There is another door for EXIT, on the right, and it says EXIT.

Did Sartre heroes ever try the right door? I bet, they, like all Aristotelian heroes, felt that it was not DRAMATIC to do so. No resistance—no drama… So they all act from blind passion… Or perhaps, some joker mixed up the signs? In real life there are many exists (I misspelled, but it's O.K.). Sartre's philosophy says NO EXIT not because there is no exit but because Sartre likes that idea, NO EXIT. It sounds heroic, desperate, and tragic. The word existentialism sounds tragic and heroic too… and beautiful…

Every businessman is arrogant, believes in himself, and will defend his bag of money with whatever means he can.

Politicians are the same. They are arrogant, they believe in themselves only (not in the people), and they'll defend their chairs by whatever means available.

That's why we have wars and revolutions.

A STORY

He left a big fortune, but it's all in writing pens. He used to buy writing pens and stack them in a special room. About the time he died he had many thousands of them and people couldn't understand why he did it. Besides, he invented a pen that could write under water—but nobody wanted to buy it: they didn't think they'll ever have an occasion or need to write under water…

Rejuvenation of language also means a rejuvenation of one's view of reality, man, objects.

At Graphic Studios.

"The girl I married…"

"What happened to the girl you married?"

"She cleans the house, makes everything happy, oh!"

"You know, a good girl can change a man. She changed me. She says I am an orderly man now, that's what she says."

At Graphic Studios.

He sweeps the floor. Uses "Green Dust." Then washes the coffee pot, turns the flame on, and goes to buy the rest of the stuff—milk, coffee (Martinson), danishes. Hot cross buns, jelly doughnuts, pecan rings, sugar doughnuts, coconut danishes.

A STORY

The secret that the alchemist came to, finally, after many centuries of trials and experiments, was that, in order for the gold to succeed, after everything's done, the alchemist had to throw into it himself, his own self. The alchemist quit.

No date, 1951

At Graphic Studios.

"Well, well."

"No cake for Don."

"I'll give him half of mine."

"Man is sick anyway."

"He was never a hitter."

"Yankees would like to have a hitter like him."

"Robby was in a tougher spot than he was."

"Robby never got as many as he got."

"Never heard."

"What do you mean?"

"Never heard."

"It was in the papers."

"Even if he did not hit—he is a great player."

"But when he will hit you'll find the ball in Washington D.C."

"Baah. It was far from it last night."

"Hey, look, Lom, don't start talking."

"I'm not talking. It's you who's talking."

Howard picks up a tray and closes himself in the darkroom. He is still mumbling, you can hear him behind the closed door.

No date, 1951

I recognize this street.

That's why I am here again. I have been here before, and to have been somewhere at least twice is more than I can say about most of the other streets. That's why I am here. Craving something familiar, some memory of this place, home…

Ah, this goddamn desperation of a DP, that's what this is, I said to myself.

I walked out of the subway and started walking down 50th Street, west. The street must have an end somewhere, I said to myself. I'll walk until I see its end, that's something, and this is Friday evening and I have nothing else to do and nobody to see.

No date, 1951

When he stood that evening, in Bremen, and a day before, when he looked at the passing Northern Germany planes—no, he didn't regret anything. But he knew he'll miss this landscape.

Objects always caused him the most pain, not people. All the cruelties, all the pain that people had caused him—he forgot it next day. He had an inexhaustible capacity for forgiving. The girl—he suddenly re-

membered his last day in school, after the exams, the two of them went for a walk, and they sat under the bridge and watched the river, and he offered her honey and bread, but the girl picked up a handful of sand and threw it on the honey and on the bread and ran away and he was left alone sitting by the river holding the sandy bread and honey. But he wasn't angry, no, as he looked at the sand, he was only amazed, and even now, when the face of the girl had vanished from his memory completely, he remembers very sharply the color of honey and bread, and sand, the greyness of dry sand.

Later, on the train, during the last months of war, and during the miserable postwar weeks, he remembers the crowds on the train, and the thirst, and the hands, hundreds of hands, eyes stretched towards one miserable cup of water. And the smell of sweat, hot air. No, he never felt thirst as desperately as they. He stood by the wall, pressed to the wall, and watched them, almost from the outside.

August 19, 1951

Did some filming in Williamsburg. Mostly close-ups of people, filmed through the window of Donatas' Austin. Shot 115 feet. Yesterday I filmed in the harbor, a ship arrived with a load of DPs, the name of the ship "Muir." They permitted me to film, they thought I was from TV. Even the police ignored me. Shot 180 feet.

Saw *Four in a Jeep*. A jeep is a good subject.

No date, 1951

Can a film replace a novel? We have already forgotten three *Quo Vadis?* films, but the novel keeps inspiring new versions of films—and we are talking only about *Quo Vadis?*, not Joyce.

A novel, a book, enters the world, and contributes, brings something new into it, to our understanding of the world we live in,

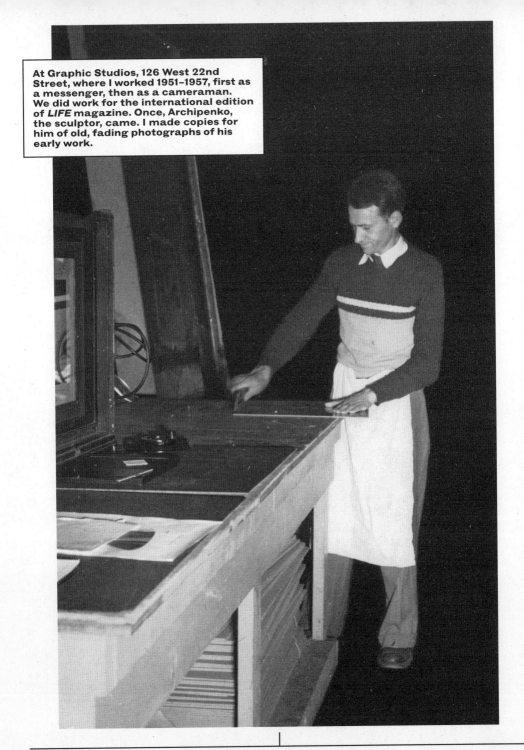

At Graphic Studios, 126 West 22nd Street, where I worked 1951–1957, first as a messenger, then as a cameraman. We did work for the international edition of *LIFE* magazine. Once, Archipenko, the sculptor, came. I made copies for him of old, fading photographs of his early work.

ROBERT FLAHERTY FILM ASSOCIATES, INC.

333 WEST 52nd STREET
NEW YORK 19, N. Y.

PLAZA 7-8466-7   March 9, 1951

Mr. J. A. Mekas
58-85 Maspeth Avenue
Maspeth, L. I.
New York

Dear Mr. Mekas:

      I owe you many apologies with regard to your
script, "Lost, Lost, Lost, Lost". I have been out of
the city a good deal of the time in recent months;
however, I have read your script with much interest.

      The idea behind your story is most interesting,
and your script has been written with great feeling. I
do not feel, however, that it is in my line; and because
of other commitments I am unable to consider it.

      Accordingly I am returning the script herewith,
and wish you every success with it.

          Sincerely yours,

          Robert Flaherty

In our Maspeth period (58–85 Maspeth Avenue, 1952) we shared the apartment with Leonas Letas, one of the most important modern Lithuanian poets, with whom we also shared our room in the Displaced Persons camp near Kassel. We grew up literally and intellectually together. We wouldn't have been what we became, without each other. He was an essential part of my own, and my brother's, life.

Adolfas Mekas.

changes it—while the film, based on it, has nothing new to add to it, the book has said it all, done it all. So the film goes through the same ground once more, without a life of its own, like a shadow, truly like a shadow.

No date, 1951
A poet like Brâncuși, he takes a chisel and chops out all the unnecessary, superfluous "words," emotions, images—leaves just what he needs.

No date, 1951
A MEMORY
On his clothes, in his hair he could still feel the ocean.
A strong wind blew from the Hudson River.
He walked away from the pier, and along 23rd Street.
Scraps of newspapers flew in the air around him, the dust was getting into his eyes. He always had weak eyes, he was afraid of wind and dust, from childhood.
He walked but he was still drunk with the memory of the sea, the smell of salt, the sound of rolling waves.

No date, 1951
Some guys are fighting in the street. So the old man decides to call the police. He goes to the corner and pulls the fire handle. What does he know.

Fire truck comes, the captain is angry, tells the old man he'll have to pay fifty bucks. He says, I won't. So they took him to jail.

Later:
"They wrote down everything, a police car came… I say, give me a cigarette. No, they said, no cigarette."
"It's O.K. to smoke."
"But they gave me to eat."
"They all steal. Such thieves sitting there, doing business…"

No date, 1951
He stood in the Rockefeller Center. A girl, surrounded by a crowd of tourists, was explaining, telling them the dates, numbers, about the building.
He stood there, behind the crowd, looking at them. The girl rattled so fast, much too fast for his still slow English, he couldn't follow her.
He still felt a total stranger here. How did I get here, he thought.
He tried to project himself into the crowd, be one of them.
No, it doesn't work.
He walked through the Rockefeller Center underground passage. He touched the wall. The wall was thin, empty, like in a theater, not very real, he thought. He hit the wall with his knuckles and listened to the empty sound.
Bright lights fell into his eyes. Postcards with the city views. A woman shouts from inside the stand:
"Take your change!"

No date, 1951
People in the rain. In the car, on the road. Rain, rain, rain. They stop by a lodge (Stony Brook), they run in. Rain, rain. We see them inside, more people, wet, standing in the door, looking at the rain, waiting for rain to stop. But the rain keeps pouring, over the pine trees, over the road, and over the roof of the lodge, it sounds like music. They talk, inside, drinking "Coca-Cola", couples, wet, waiting. A record is playing, a sweet voice is singing something. Everybody's speaking in low voices, a young man kisses his girl, and an old man stands in the door, looking out. There is another car, just came, and more coming. Complaining about the rain. Somebody starts playing piano. The young couple leaves the house, and walks along the road in the rain. The old man is still standing in the door, looking out. Rain. The young couple walks along the wet road, in the rain. Radio inside, singing. Voices. Rain.

January 13, 1952

Two girls, thirteen, or twelve, with red socks, white ballet shoes, waiting for the train, in the subway, home from the class, still immersed in dance lessons, are doing their steps, on the subway platform, very very excited, bubbly. They repeat their class exercises, very very lightly, very involved, completely oblivious of the people, subway reality, noise. They are totally in their own dream. Who cares about the people, there is nothing in the world but the two of them and the Muse of Dance.

Went to Whitney Museum, on 8th Street, saw Sloan's retrospective. I liked his dark style. His flesh, his city, beaches, streets. His paintings of streets, subways have something of America that is gone. A record of times past. Round fleshy women, mountains of flesh, full canvas of flesh.

In the Museum of Non-Objective Painting I found piles of Ney, Rebay, Bauer, and a couple of very good Moholy-Nagys. A couple of very weak Kandinskys. I liked the tar blackness of Ney.

They were lying there on the ground, with their faces close to Mother Earth and, goddamit, they didn't learn to understand it, to know it, to love it. Even then, with their faces pressed to the black earth, bullets zooming past their cars, they thought only about their lost properties.

"Some Vietnamese wonder if Americans still believe in the right of all men to fight for self-determination, as Americans did themselves."
—David Duncan, *LIFE*, Dec. 30, 1951.

"In Malaya's capital city, Malayan and Chinese children are not permitted near when English youngsters play." (ibid.)

No date, 1952

There are times of harmony, of digesting the past, when architecture quietly is spreading across the cities—and the poetry—and music—and painting—Bach—Mozart—.

And then there are periods when everything collapses. The harmony falls to pieces. Perspectives disintegrate. The monsters of Goya appear. Van Gogh's nerves tremble. Rimbaud abandons poetry and chooses life. Art for life. Dogmas, truths, measures collapse. The search spills out with streams of rejuvenating words, forms, colors. Until, one day, there is so much, too much of the new, so many splinters and pieces fall all around, that it all exhausts itself, tires out, and slows down. Somebody begins to polish all the exciting sharp fragments thrown out by the bursts of temperamental volcanoes of human spirit. A new classic period sets in, another "blossoming" of culture…

No date, 1952

Adolfas is writing from Paris. He is walking through Paris in the American army uniform. He is in the army now.

He says, for the first time he understood the depth of the hatred that French have for the Americans. When he hears steps behind—he steps to the side, to the wall, and permits them to pass by, everyone that comes from behind: he doesn't know which one of them has a knife in his hand. Every night Paris leaves a few American soldiers dead, with knives in their backs. Nobody advertises this fact.

April 5, 1952

Just finished reading Thurber's *Album*. The book is not like his short humorous sketches, stories, tales. As he says himself, he wrote it just to pass time. It started as little fragments from his childhood. Memories, portraits of people he knew, etc. Before he knew it, it grew into a book. He

In May of 1951, Adolfas was drafted into the U.S. Army. He was assigned to serve in Signal Corps division, stationed in Europe. Most of his time he spent in Verdun, Belgium.

In Maspeth/Brooklyn, during one of Adolfas' brief leaves from the U.S. Army.

Myself, 1950, with the first Bolex. It worked fine until 1958 when Ray Wisniewski, a good friend, borrowed it to film the protesters of a nuclear ship entering the New York harbor. During a skirmish with the police he dropped it into the ocean. Being a good swimmer, he managed to retrieve it, but it never worked well again. Around the year 1959 I bought the second Bolex.

In those years the Garden of the Museum of Modern Art, now gone, was a treasury of sculpture and a place where many of us spent many happy weekend afternoons. It was a perfect place for careless rendezvous.

writes with an amazing precision. He recreates the portraits of his parents, grandparents, and great-grand-parents, how they lived, what they did. All in his short, precise style. Like with a brush, so simply, right to the point. Such economy and precision of style is rare in the contemporary American literature—they all like, nowadays, to ramble and stretch, description after description, page after page.

Another virtue of the book, for me, is his respect for the objects, things. Things that at one or another time he or his grandparents used, touched, had around. He gives them as much attention as to the people who used them. Very very concrete.

July, 1952

I went to see Paulius at the Franciscan monastery on Willoughby Street. He wasn't home. I met Aistis. He was also looking for Paulius. So we stood outside and talked. Monks are walking around with books in their hands, their lips moving. Took a subway to Manhattan. Saw Lubitsch's *Trouble in Paradise*. Spent an hour at MoMA with Vuillard. Snooped through bookshops, went to Central Park, sat on the rocks, visited Shakespeare garden, the air smells of trees. Tried to read Joyce Cary's *The Horse's Mouth*, but it was too hot, and the eyes kept turning to the trees, couldn't concentrate. Nature doesn't tolerate art…

The difference between you and me, see, is that I don't save bills, receipts, checks. I don't care about the useful, practical things. But I get very excited about all kinds of unnecessary, useless things.

No date, 1952

Had a long walk through the city with Elena and Elisonaite.

When you walk through the city with women, you have to stop and stare at the window displays, so we did a lot of that. Then we went to the Modern. Elisonaite,

I knew her in Wiesbaden, she was only a child. Here she is a full grown woman, tall, beautiful, like a flower. Has a rough way of talking, a little bit cynical. When she says something, she says it flat and drab and to the point, doesn't mince words.

I knew her father, in Lithuania, in Panevezys, he was a very distinguished zoologist, a professor, a scientist, wrote the only serious books on wildlife in Lithuania.

Elena—very very different. A slow type. Elisonaite has a very fine, educated taste in art, and our tastes agreed. She has read the right books. We talked about Moholy-Nagy.

Elena, she is interested only in painting and nothing else. When she looks at a painting, she is only interested in what color was applied first, green or yellow, or… She is interested in purely technical matters. She says, she doesn't like Kokoschka, "there is no aesthetic in his work…" Which, of course, sent me into rage. She looks at every miserable painting, as long as it has "something interesting technically." If it's done well technically, she likes it, even if it's pure crap.

Her house is full of *nature morte* à la Braque, women and harlequins à la Picasso, figures à la Matisse. She has a few good canvasses of her own, she can paint when she wants. Only this terrible Lithuanian laziness and their eternal *nature morte*. The other day, at Almus, I began attacking all Lithuanian painters. They better begin searching for new things to paint. Take Elena: for two years she lived in Georgia. Travelled across the States. Saw all of Europe. And, goddamit, her room is stacked with the same *nature morte*! Landscapes, cities, people, rivers—she passed through everything and nothing registered. Nature, surroundings, do not exist for her. Leonardo da Vinci had to draw every newly discovered different shape, line, volume, object, color. You see Cézanne's life in his paintings and drawings—places, friends—

besides his forms. Or Picasso: fishermen, Seine, *Guernica*, he draws everything and everywhere, on sand, on paper napkins, doesn't put a price on anything, this is art or this is not art: his nature, his existence is to paint, to draw, it's his destiny, his life.

July 20, 1952

It was Niliunas who, when writing about *Idylls of Semeniskiai* said, that no, there is no mention of Lithuania in them, and no patriotic lines: but they are more Lithuanian than the openly patriotic poems.

No, I don't think I have ever been a good patriot. Neither is Adolfas, in the way my friends Lithuanians are. Others, they love their country, their patria. But we two are attached only to Semeniškiai, to our little village, to the countryside and the people and the objects there. It has nothing to do with nationalism. We are regionalists. Or the weather. Or the seasons of the year. Nature. Little nuances of nature. Nature, too, is always very regional. No rain, no wind, no snowstorm, no April is like that of our childhood, in Semeniškiai, nowhere. And I don't think it's only romanticism, sentimentalism. I really think it's a plain fact. Our movements, the way we walk. Our accents, the way we talk. Everything is determined, marked by the climate, landscape, sun in which we grew up, lived. No, it's not just a memory. I know, some day some clever scientist will prove very scientifically that I am right.

Shortcomings of the stars
living with the face of the guilty

I have no doubts about my beginnings.
I know my end.
But I have no idea where I am now.

August, 1952

Read Julien Gracq's *The Castle of Argol* After a few pages I was ready to drop it, but then I got caught and read it to the end. Lately there are few books that I can read from beginning to end. I cannot. *The Caine Mutiny*, *The Sea Around Us*, and several others—I read them in parts. Ten pages here, ten pages there—and you get it all. D.H. Lawrence said, somewhere, I don't remember where, that it's difficult to read contemporary writing in its entirety. In a few pages the author says everything that he knows, and later he just repeats it, because he has to write 300 pages. Gertrude Stein also said. No, no, it was Coleridge: "The reader should be carried forward not merely or chiefly by the mechanical impulses of curiosity, or by a restless desire to arrive at the final solution, but by the pleasurable activity of the journey itself..."—But when I was reading *The Caine Mutiny* the "pleasurable activity" ended, exhausted itself after twenty pages. And since the "solutions" were clear, I had no more "curiosity" to continue. The author didn't manage to make the journey pleasurable enough for me... I long for Victor Hugo, and Dumas, and Tolstoy, and Proust, and Kafka, Faulkner—those who knew how to make their (mine) journeys exciting.

You want to know how the face of God looks?
Look at these wood stumps in the sun
by the wall, the lumber.
Look at this dirty dung carriage resting
by the barn door.
Look at the little gooseberry bush there.
The fields. Ditches. Rivers. Drops of
sweat. The buzzing of bees. The fingers of
willow trees.
That's the face of God.

"direct" poetry (tiesiogine poezija)

Desperation is not truth.

Tina: "I am a superman. Give me some soup." (Tina is 5.)

The view from my 123 Linden Street apartment, 1952.

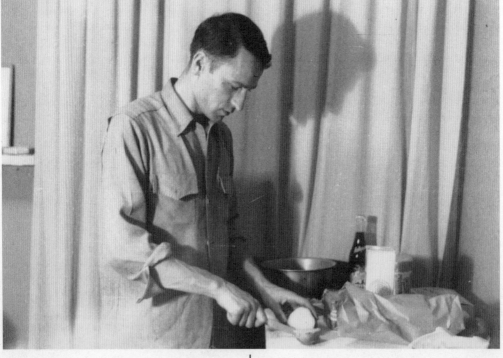

Why should one judge Orpheus?

They say, do not lose the road for the small path...
It depends where the road is leading to. It depends where one wants to go.
There are places which you can reach only through tiny paths. Only the dictators, armies, generals, and people without imaginations prefer wide, "strong" roads. Little paths take you to the gentle meadows, brooks, flowers, cool shadows. The roads are official, designed for going from one point to another. But I like to stop, to look— not only to travel and travel. My life is not a journey towards some destination that I know: it is rather a mysterious journey through the unknown and into the unknown and I would like to enjoy, I wouldn't like to miss any interesting side paths, patches of greenery. Because, at the end, at the end of the journey, there may be nothing but... a pile of rabbit shit.

There is this very popular attitude to poetry: poetry must be poetical... But my only desire is to clean myself from such poetry and return to the objects, words, the concrete senses and elements of our life.

A STORY
The world was so sane now, and he was the last madman on earth. And since he was the last madman on earth, they paid him great honors and kept him like a pet.
"Ah, what are we going to do when he dies, how are we going to live without the madman," said some.

December 15, 1952
JEAN RENOIR AT CINEMA 16
Jean Renoir spoke at Cinema 16. Screening of *La Règle du Jeu* followed. Even after eleven years in America he looks 100% French, in his short grey suit, his continuously gesticulating arms, and his whole body, moving and swinging when he speaks. He speaks freely and in an improvisational manner, a stream of consciousness of sorts. He likes to talk, just talk, simply and without fuss.
He didn't say this was his best film, only that he likes it very much. He said, his friends in Europe think this is his best. He spoke about the rottenness of life in France when he was making the film.
Some expressions I wrote down:
"In all my pictures I improvise much. Lines, movements, etc."
"This picture (*La Règle...*) can be considered a depiction of stupidity of a dying society."
"This is a normal picture about abnormal people."
"This film is about the ruling class of France just before the catastrophe. They don't feel any responsibility to others, like all classes of the catastrophe. In that sense, this film is an accusation. They (Vichy) understood the film best... and they banned it."

No date, 1953
I promised the old man to help him carry some things home. I walked along 22nd Street, carrying the bundles, and the old man walked beside me. The old man was talking and talking and asking questions. He was about to tell me all his life. But all I could hear was cars and the street noise and my own mind. I tried to be polite, occasionally burping a word or two, absent-mindedly, but it finally got on my nerves.
"Look," I said, "I can't hear a thing, it's too goddamn noisy."
The old man walked silent for a moment.
"I came to this city forty years ago, there is nobody to talk with," he said.

I tried to sleep, but it was like a nightmare. I tossed and tossed around in my bed. Only towards the morning I fell into an exhausted, deep sleep. But then soon I woke up again. I got up and I stood by the window. I looked at the street, the benches, lights.

January 29, 1953
To The Film Editor of the *New York Times*:
Limelight
When the Nazis came into the power, they burned the books of the authors who didn't think like them. Exactly the same did and are still doing the Stalinists in their countries. The art must serve the state. On the same tracks of fanaticism I find also the latest campaign against Chaplin's *Limelight*.
Even when the State peeled out the eyes of Riemenschneider and Stwosz for their beliefs, nobody dared to touch their art. Situation, apparently, got worse during the last five centuries. And it's difficult to tell, is our respect for people going down because we no longer respect art, or vice versa.
Jonas Mekas
New York City

March 5, 1953
Long hours of walking without sleep. I was angry about everything, the compromises I have made 'til now. I want only my work. To throw myself into my work. There is no other choice. The other choice is to go mad. I am not clear these days about the proper direction or the exact thing I should be doing. I have to burn the bridges once more. Their smoke will show me the new direction.

March 6, 1953
Had an appointment with Gideon, to go film Frank Lloyd Wright's building in Usonia. I called him this morning, he says he can't see anybody now (must be problems with his girlfriend). I have to call him in the middle of the week.

March 31, 1953
Circle in the Square, *Summer and Smoke*.
Reading *The Lottery*, by Shirley Jackson.

April 1, 1953
Harold E. Briggs' *Language, Man, Society: Readings in Communication*.
Shirley Jackson cont.

April 2, 1953
Was working at Graphic Studios 'til 8:30 PM.
Harold E. Briggs cont.
Was paid for last week, $115.

April 3, 1953
The Seven Year Itch, Axelrod.

April 4, 1953
Post office—script returned from Stanley Kramer.
Searching for an apartment.
"Picnic," Inge.
Club Cinema, *Kameradschaft*, sat twice.

April 5, 1953
Easter Parade. Took some pictures.
Édouard et Caroline, Jacques Becker. Good.
Magic Sword, Yugo stinker.

April 6, 1953
Looking for an apartment.
Went to the Nat. Film Board of Canada, got their catalogues.
Rented *Loon's Necklace* for Dorothy's party.
Spent couple hours in Gr. Village, snooping thru bookshops, drinking beer at the White Horse.
8:15 at the New School. Arthur Knight talking about art films & art theatres.
Hymn of the Nations, Toscanini film, made after the liberation of Italy (Verdi's music), beautifully done by Hammid.
Instruments of the Orchestra, made by B.I.S., directed by Mathieson.
Steps of Ballet, by Mathieson.
Henry Moore.

George Maciunas with his father
Aleksandras (on his right), and
his mother Leokadija (on his left), 1952.

Nijole Maciunas, George's sister, 1952.
She told me to meet her "crazy brother,"
that's how I met George.

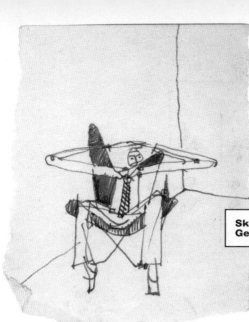

Sketches of myself and Adolfas by George, 1953.

Membership Card

For One Year From 3-14-53

CLUB CINEMA

430 AVENUE OF THE AMERICAS

Between 9th & 10th Sts.   GRamercy 5-8793

Issued to_____

209

Club Cinema was run by Howard John Lawson's "gang," American leftists and some American "communist" film enthusiasts. It showed mostly "workers"-oriented movies. After the screenings, usually attended by a very mixed group of people, there were drinks and discussions of films shown.

CHAPTER
TWO

... Escape from Brooklyn... Meeting Lilly... Moving into 95 Orchard Street... Getting drunk on New York... Adolfas comes home from U.S. Army... New friends, Gideon, Dorothy... Sneaking into the New School film classes... Working at Graphic Studios... New Jersey ... The Lubitsch "touches"... I begin to question direction of my life... Meeting Ian Hugo, Curtis Harrington... Coney Island... A trip to California, San Diego... No, I am not a patriot...

April 7, 1953

Shirley Jackson's *The Lottery*, cont.
Script notes for *Autobiography*.

Ten days ago I made my decision to ESCAPE from Brooklyn.
Thanks to Lilly, really. I met Lilly at Dorothy's screening, dancer and writer. She said she was in the middle of writing a novel. She had just moved out of her Essex Street apartment into one on Ludlow Street. "If you want it, it's still there, rent paid for another month," she said. She didn't have to tell me that twice! YES, YES, I almost shouted.

So now everyday for the last ten days I've been dragging my stuff from Linden Street to Lilly's Essex Street place. I am almost done. But this place is temporary, it has been already rented out. But I can stay here for a month until I find another place. Hello downtown! Hello Manhattan! Here I come! Goodbye Brooklyn!
Regrets not acceptable!

April 8, 1953

Cinema 16: Carl Th. Dreyer's *Vampyr*. Great. *Le Sang des bêtes*, *Fireworks*!

April 9, 1953

Letter from Adolfas, leaving on 16th of March for the States.
Letter from Adelaide Sims, with the article on McLaren.
Saw Lilly, got a tip for an apartment.

April 10, 1953

Brandon Films. *Encyclopædia Britannica*. "What is Communism," Milton Mayer, A. Schlessinger. Cleaned the house.

April 11, 1953

The House of Wax, latest 3-D, the best 'til now (Warner Bros).
Dorothy's party on Ludlow Street, I screen films.

April 12, 1953

Aidai magazine concert. Raining. Rouault exhibition!

April 13, 1953

"Language, Man, Society," cont.
Cahiers du Cinema, N. 3
Went to see Abe, Orchard 95, about an apartment. Then went to Lilly's. Met Jackson

MacLow. Also, Peter. Talked about poetry, Rouault, languages, Bismarck.

April 14, 1953
Cinema 16: *van Meegeren's False Vermeers*, *Form in Motion*, *Bop-Scotch* (Jordan Belson).

April 15, 1953
Took an apartment on 95 Orchard. Rent: $13.80 per month.
Cinema 16. Nothing very interesting. False Vermeers...

April 16, 1953
Raining. Working late at Graphic. Doing nothing.

April 17, 1953
American Dance Co. *Fantasy and Fugue* (Humphrey/Mozart); *Rites* (Lang/Bartok); *Visitation* (Limon/Schoenberg); *Deep Rhythm* (Humphrey/Surinach).
Took a few things to the new apartment.

April 18, 1953
Misalliance B. Shaw (theater). Beautifully directed (Richards).
Fear and Desire, Kubrick. Better than usual Hollywood stuff, but not enough.
Bought Hofmannsthal's "Reitergeschichte," *Stalin's Economic Problems*, S. de Beauvoir's *The Second Sex*

April 19, 1953
Reading Hofmannsthal.
American Dance Co. *Canticle for Innocent Comedians* (Martha Graham), very good. Visitation (Limon/Koner); *Dance Sonata* (O'Donnell); *Night Journey* (Graham), very good.
Saw nobody, met nobody.

April 20, 1953
Arthur Knight's film course at the New School. Saw *Two Bagatelles*, McLaren. Dots, also McLaren. *Notes on the Port of St. Francis*, Stauffacher. Soundtrack great.

Four in the Afternoon, Broughton. *Coney Island*, Sherry. Picnic, Harrington—simple, unity, strong mood. Harrington was present and spoke. Also met Peter Hollander, runs Kinesis now. Met also a strange character Donald Phelps, with a bunch of articles "on film criticism," he said. Arranged a meeting with Harrington next week, to discuss Film House idea. Reading Hofmannsthal's *Sebastian Melmoth*.

April 21, 1953
Packing my Linden Street stuff. Walking around the city, doing nothing.

April 22, 1953
Reading de Beauvoir. 30 pages. Hofmannsthal's *Briefe des Zurueckgekehrten*. Took a few things to the apartment. Mrs. Adams called and told that Miksys is in town. I should go and see him, but there is no mood to see anybody. Who is left? After so many years? Leo, Miksys?

April 23, 1953
Reading Hofmannsthal. *Utility, Beauty, Waste*, by Veblen. Met Gideon at Art Students League, sculpture class, we had lunch and talked about our film projects.

April 24, 1953
Die Moerder sind unter uns, Staudte, at Club Cinema.

April 25, 1953
The Love of Four Colonels, walk in C. Park, a beautiful Spring day. *Hunchback of Notre Dame*, and *Lost World* (with Pickford) at Steinway Bldg., 113 W. 57th St.

April 26, 1953
Reading *The Idea of a Theatre* Francis Ferguson, and *The Treasure* a drama in four acts by David Pinski. Cleaned the apartment. Open City and *Paisà*, at 55th Street Playhouse.

Lilly Bennett, on Orchard Street, 1953.
A dancer, she was writing a novel when
I met her. She helped me to escape from
Brooklyn by giving me her Essex Street
room—she was moving into another one—
until I found my own. She became my
"lead" in *Silent Journey*, a film I was trying
to make at that time. (Fragments of it
I used in *Lost Lost Lost*.)

Spring 1953, on the roof of 95 Orchard Street, with Adolfas just after his return from the Army, "a Korean war veteran…"

Adolfas, 1953, Orchard Street.

April 27, 1953

Spent an evening cleaning 95 Orchard apartment.

Sid Greif visited. Reading S. de Beauvoir.

April 28, 1953

With Ruthe at the Museum of Modern Art, Sculpture Garden opening.

A letter from Adolfas, he just left for Bremerhaven (on 22nd).

April 30, 1953

Searching for furniture, for the new apartment.

May 2, 1953

Painting walls. Adolfas came from Camp Kilmer.

May 3, 1953

We painted the ceiling, visited Leo, Zibuntas, Sidney Greif.

May 5, 1953

Critique of Pure Reason, Kant.

May 8, 1953

Art Student League ball. We go with Pytlak, Dorothy.

May 11, 1953

Theatre de Lys: Maya Deren show. *Meditation on Violence*. Maas, *Images in the Snow*. *Ritual in Transfigured Time*.

May 13, 1953

Cinema 16: *Coral Wonderland*. *Plague Summer*, by Kessler. *Maya Through the Ages*. Two UPA Magoo cartoons.

No date, 1953

Marcia. She has problems. At least twice a week she goes to the analyst. She is my Ludlow Street neighbor.

I pass by, just to say hello. We talk, then she suddenly covers her face with both hands and cries, loud.

I try to calm her, I put my hands on her shoulders.

"You go, you go now," she cries.

What do you do when a woman cries and when you don't know the reasons and she doesn't tell you?

"You go. Some people when they are crying they want to be stroked; some like to be left alone."

I leave. I close the door, which I found open, when I passed by, and I stand there, for a long minute, not knowing if I did the right thing. Inside, the subdued crying suddenly bursts into a loud crying, and I walk down the stairs, and out, and I hear it all the way down and out.

I walk down Ludlow Street, then to Orchard Street, and towards Delancey. Small drizzle over the dirty newspapers and Jewish shops.

Later, I go to eat with Henry. I get upset about the bread he leaves on the table. I talk to him about labor camps, DP camps. "You have a morbid mind," says Henry.

I wander for two hours through the downtown streets.

I am jumping and dancing, making a fool of myself.

Elizabeth: "What's wrong with you?"

Me: "I got my salary! I got my salary! What am I going to do with all this money?"

I sit down, staring at the floor.

"Aren't you going home?"

"What for? I don't have any. Every place is my home."

"You are a strange man," says Elizabeth.

"Yes, I feel everywhere like home."

"In this place too?"

I throw kisses all over the place.

"Yes, yes, right here, right on this spot I feel like home."

Elizabeth gives up and disappears into the darkroom.

I sit by the Hudson River. Evening.

"It's a beautiful evening."

"Yes."

"Are you a foreigner?"

"Yes. And you?"

"I am only studying here. I am from Ohio, my family is there."

"Ohio?"

"Yes, Ohio."

"I have no idea where it is," I say.

We sit silently.

She: "You see that barge? It's from Chicago. Do you see the letters on the cars?"

I look at her in amazement. How easily she can read all these mysterious signs on the crates, boxes and wagons, on the passing barges; names of companies, rivers, cities. I am amazed. It's poetry. She can read all the symbols and everything has a meaning to her, she is part of it all, this river is part of her, all these barges, these smoke stacks. I envy her. I am just a stranger sitting here and watching it all, just a stranger.

No date, 1953

There was one aspect of New York, which I couldn't grasp for a long time. The songs on the radio.

I thought it was all a dream. Like they call Hollywood a dream. But now I think that these songs and Hollywood are just a part, a very real part of a very real thing.

Yes, the voices of the singers are so dreamy. And so are the lyrics. Unreality…

I remember the first night in New York. Algis took us to Times Square. I will never forget the impact which hit us upon emerging from the subway, right smack into the very middle of the Neon Light maze. And in the middle of the sky, there was the moon. But I wasn't sure it was real or not. All reality had a veil of a dream here, the moon had no longer a reality of its own. It was just a prop in a huge opera of New York.

A week later, one early morning, we took a train to Newark. In the early morning mist we watched the fantastic maze of chimneys, wires, factories, bridges. I had read all about the workers, exploitation, strikes, capitalism, industrial miseries, but when I looked at it now, it didn't look like Hell at all, it rather looked like a scene from *1001 Arabian Nights*. In front of me there was a man reading a paper and there was a small headline telling that the Gallup poll had found that 85 % of American people think they are happy people.

So this is New York, our new home. A huge dream. And we decided to keep our own reality alive, in this dream, that evening, that night in Brooklyn, when we did not sleep, when we talked until the small hours, Adolfas, and Leo. We were trying to figure out the difference between the Veil of Veronica and the American Dream. Take it easy. Keep smiling. It will be all right. Fine. It's fine. Everything is fine, O.K. Go happy, go lucky. Lucky Strike. Smoke Cool.

We knew we were between Scylla and Charybdis. But we weren't sure at all, which of the two was Scylla and which one Charybdis…

And we have no maps. Blindly, blindly, we sail!

No date, 1953

Saw *So This is Paris*, Ernst Lubitsch, 1926. For Lubitsch the story is secondary. In every situation he finds a way of using his touches, be it tragic, comic or any other situation. Or just dancing, no situation at all. That's what circus comedians and clowns did for centuries. They took any simple story or anecdote or situation and built around it their tricks and people laughed their bellies out. They used their touches in right places and they timed them well. Everyone was known for his special touch. Comedy is 100 % touch.

Same, of course, with Hitchcock. Really. He knows that to thrill you he doesn't need thrilling situations: he needs thrill touches. Neither Lubitsch nor Hitchcock

PABLO CASALS

pose any big clear questions or "solve" or discuss any big "problems" in their films. Their films are made for touch's sake. If we are thrilled by Hitchcock's films we are thrilled by their thrill touches. Or, rather, by his touches. For these touches belong to him and nobody else, they are the essence of his art. Those touches are what makes those films his, what makes them recognizable as his. But since, as we all know, there is also an expression "touch and go," these touches are subtle and light, they are really touch and go, and if you miss them, you miss it all, it's all gone.

Isn't it the same with literature, with any art? Of course, it is. It's a very old thing, probably a stone age thing. The same stories are told again and again and again. How many situations Shakespeare counted there existed? What differentiates one from the other are always the personal touches. One hundred actors, one hundred Hamlets, different Hamlets ... Any work, if it wants to be considered a work of art, must have a touch of the artist's personality. If not, it won't touch anyone, it will be simply out of touch.

"Oh, those artificial lakes..."
"I just stopped, it was such a nice beautiful lake and a summer day. And then came my uncle. 'Come,' he says, 'come with me, in my car, and have a drink with me, leave your truck right here and come with me.'"
"And you know, they came and thought, Here is an empty truck and the town is so far away. They thought the man got drowned himself. And what do you think? They started draining the lake, they were searching in the mud. 'What the hell are you doing?' I say, 'Stupid, on such a hot day you are draining the lake.' 'A man drowned himself,' they say. 'You see, the truck is there.' 'What's the matter with my truck,' I say. And I was drunk, you know. 'We were drinking,' my uncle said, 'yes, we were

drinking.' 'What the hell,' they say, 'here is the truck, and the man drowned himself.' 'Stupid,' I say, 'it's my truck.'"

No date, 1953

How can I find myself again on a firm ground? This painful dead-end feeling? Everything is burning like a dry bush.
Today I feel that the only way out for me is the way of revolution. A radical change, a rejection of the whole way of life I was leading til now. Rejection of all I believed in. To doubt everything, to start again from nothing, from chaos. I have to abandon the idea of regaining the balance by conscious, rational search, evaluation of myself. I have to throw myself into the chaos of my own desperation, or crisis, and trustingly let myself be carried into what comes. By way of a revolution, by breaking away from it all, painfully, without pity. I know no other way out. And it's impossible to remain where I am now. I have to revolt. I have to shoot my ministers.
I run away from my work, without saying a word to anyone, and I walk and I walk for hours through the darkening city streets. I have to do something and I don't know what. The only trust I have now is in the spontaneous, unpredictable movements.

May 14, 1953

Visited Perry Miller, discussed the idea of Film House. Met Gideon at Art Students League. Saw Malaparte's *Strange Deception*.

May 16, 1953

Visited Ian Hugo. He lives in a tiny, very clean apartment. He had a projector in one of the corners of the room. He screened *Bells of Atlantis*, and showed some of his engravings.
Visited Curtis Harrington, he's in town. Discussed the idea of the Film House / Film Institute. He thought it was time for something like that.

Reading Mark Twain's *Life on the Mississippi* Hollingsworth's *Psychology and Ethics* Karen Horney's *Neurosis and Human Growth*.

No date, 1953

I went upstairs and sat at my table. "Goddamn it," I said. I looked out the window and I saw Orchard Street, like a heavy snake, moving in the summer heat. The buzzy noise of the crowd filled the air. There was the traffic of the market, traffic and rush everywhere.

I could not work. So I took the rotten core of an apple that was lying on the edge of the window and I threw it into the very middle of the crowd moving in the street below me.

June 4, 1953

Saw Duvivier's *Poil de Carotte*, at Club Cinema, on Sixth Avenue, in the Village. Poems by François Villon. Saw *Pastorale with Stokowski* by Mary Ellen Bute.

June 28, 1953

Went to Palisades Park.
There was a woman reading handwriting.
I paid my fifty cents.
Among other things, she said that I was
a) very skeptical
b) I like music very much
c) I am very observant
d) I have a great imagination
e) I am very moody
f) I am a man of extremes in every case
g) If I talk then I talk a lot; if I am silent then I am silent a lot—no golden middle.

No date, 1953

At Cinema 16, they sit there, and they watch Pablo Casals walking, in a documentary film, and in a beautiful peaceful landscape. Walking, alone, Pablo Casals. They watch it, and they applaud it, and then they return home to their dusty apartments, they remove dust from a piece of driftwood, and they continue living the same way as before. But Pablo Casals is walking in a beautiful peaceful landscape, and the sky is clear, so clear.

August, 1953

Carcerato (Doomed), an Italian film by Armando Zorri. A mediocre film, with all the cliches, a sentimental love story.
Ring Around the Clock (High Time), an Italian film. A social satire, makes fun of politicians and political parties. A small Italian city. The inhabitants have organized themselves into many different political parties. The parties don't agree on anything except the fixing of a tower damaged during the war. The communist, Porboni steals the clock and hides it in a coffin. Good use of music when Porboni visits his boss in Rome: we don't hear them talking, instead of words we hear music, and their motions are like those of orchestra conductors.
Congress Dances. The camera works wonders. I don't remember any other old movie where the camera was so mobile. From extreme LS to CU, back and forth, over the heads, any direction. Camera moves all the time. Set, by Meerson, reminds of *La Kermesse Héroïque* (also by Meerson), simple and clean. The story is weak, but the film is redeemed by the direction.
The Life and Loves of Beethoven, by Abel Gance. One of the best biography films I've ever seen. It does justice to the greatness of Beethoven. It's made of several sketches, scenes from Beethoven's life—his deafness, his life in the mill, his love for Juliette. The film deals with his later years. Clever use of sound and image. Harry Baur gives to Gance's Beethoven depth and reality.

August 15, 1953

"There are therefore necessarily six elements in every tragedy which give it its quality; and they are the Fable, Character,

Language, Thought, the Mise-en-scène, and Melody."—Aristotle

Water stopped running, the pipes are clogged or something, and the superintendent isn't home, he is at Two Guitars, down on 14th Street, playing mandolin, only his dogs are barking behind the closed door all alone.

September 6, 1953

Every year around this time, there are Mardi Gras festivities on Coney Island. A lot of noise, fireworks, and millions of people.

It was about 8 PM when I arrived. Every street was full. It was impossible to move through this noisy, hot crowd. It was like a big river flowing from one end of the main street to the other. Loudspeakers invited me to come and see a man with three legs, a woman with the hair of sheep, and, of course, the leopard man.

There were thousands strolling along the shore. Families, with children, and couples hand in hand, and lonely bums and women chasers. There were old men and women standing watching the parachute wheel, with their heads up. And then there were small groups of people on the beach, you could see them from the wooden shore floor, down on the beach standing in circles, sitting in the sand, singing, and dancing.

There was an Italian group, singing old Neopolitan songs. One was singing solo, and others sang in unison, repeating after him. They were so absorbed in their singing and so happy that they didn't see anything around them. They sat very closely in their circle, in a closed world of their own, and sang.

There was a larger group, another group, and in the middle of it there were four black boys playing drums, the same and the same rhythm, with their heads low, their eyes fixed on their drums, faces transported while the crowd around them rhythmically moved their bodies, back and forth, back and forth, making always the same and the same simple steps. Two black boys and two black girls, with their bare feet in warm beach sand and their screaming color swimming suits.

There were several other groups scattered around the beach, and the people standing and leaning on the wooden supports could hear the sounds coming from the twilight, the voices and the drums, and the clapping of hands of the Italian women. But those sounds were soon lost in the huge roaring that came from the other side—the shouting, playing, eating, drinking, dancing, attracting, rolling, rotating, flying, turning, all the burning and flickering lights and colors and loudspeakers inviting you to come and see the unseen, to touch the untouchable, to enjoy the unenjoyable—to be part of the river, part of the Mardi Gras in Coney Island.

No date, 1953

San Diego

He was eating, at this San Diego motel. Suddenly he stopped eating. Scrambled eggs. He looked through the window. A farmer stopped at the gas station, and a man in a combinezon was filling the tank. A woman passed by carrying a shopping bag and leading a small girl by hand. San Diego sun was hot and brilliant.

How strange, thought he. How unreal. As if the capital punishment didn't exist. As if the prison camps didn't exist. Concentration camps. And torture rooms, and nail needles, and cold water dripping regularly on your naked body.

He looked at the food and suddenly felt like vomiting. Suddenly he felt as if his mouth was full of sand. Or memory.

He put his fork on the plate and looked across the street. The farmer was still there, talking and gesticulating with the serviceman. And there was an old man standing and watching the car, as if he had

I always had a boyan. I never learned to play it, but I always played anyway. My brother Kostas played violin, had a band for some time. Petras played organ and accordion quite well. And my father was known for fixing musical instruments, he was born a carpenter but ended up as a farmer. But he never quit carpentry.

Adolfas with Lilly and one of my co-workers at the Graphic Studios.

After returning from the Army, for a year Adolfas was consumed by writing his first novel, *Diary of a Schizophrenic*, later submitted to Grove Press, but rejected. A copy of the original manuscript burned together with his house in Rhinebeck, in 1993, but a copy may exist in the Grove Press archives. I thought it was a very good novel.

never seen one before. Life was going on. How strange, how strange, he thought.

September 7, 1953

She worked as a secretary in an army publishing house. She was about twenty-seven, very thin, and with a boyish face. The way she spoke and the way she thought, her precision, her clarity and practicality gave him an impression that he was talking to a man and not a woman. She didn't have much to remind him that she was a woman. She had it somewhere, deeper, he didn't have any doubt about it, but he didn't have any wish, not at this time, to go that deep for it, it was not worth the trip, he thought. To him a woman, what a woman is, always begins with the surface, with the body, with the tone of voice. What the hell, he thought, what the hell, all her thinking is like that of a man. If she'd really be a man, that would be fine & easy, I'd talk to her like to any other man. Now, whenever he heard or saw her doing something that really belonged to the feminine part of her, it seemed to him a bit strange, it didn't fit her at all, it was a little bit surreal. Everything she said or did, the way she touched his hand, or the way she always said "Oh, I love it," her very body was to him pure surrealism, and her liking him was a cause of slight nausea to him, and he tried to hide it as best as he could. But whenever his eyes met hers, he was afraid that she may read him, he was very bad at hiding his feelings. It all ended with him trying not to look at her at all. But she sat by his side and talked, and he followed with his eyes the room, people dancing, drinking, eating tiny sandwiches. He wanted to leave her and go to the other room, where he heard some voices that he thought he liked, and as soon as she went to pick up a sandwich, he did so. But she came back and she found him, and she started talking to him, and he didn't listen now, he talked with Lilly, and Lilly looked into his eyes and she understood everything that was going on inside him, and she laughed. Then they started leaving, and they took a car, five of them, and they drove downtown. She left them somewhere midtown, and she said a loud BYE to everybody, and he was sitting on the side and looking at the city lights, trying not to see and not to listen, absorbed in lights, but she turned to him and said, "You can drop in, whenever you want, you know where I live now," and he felt the same nausea coming to his throat, and only when the car was several blocks away he opened the window and took a deep breath. The air was cool and fresh. It was very late.

November 8, 1953

For two months we have been waiting for rain and the rain didn't come. We had some ideas, with Adolfas, for a film sketch of sorts, and we needed rain. So we took several shots on the roof, using a gardener's can to make rain. The results were terrible.

Then the rain came. It came very suddenly, when we all had given up on it, one Sunday morning. Adolfas looked at the window and shouted: RAIN! So I grabbed the phone and called Sid, our "actor." He had an appointment, but dropped it and was on his way to Orchard Street. Lilly, our "star," was unavailable. She had a cold and couldn't go out.

Friday, suddenly, the snow started falling. By the evening we had winter. Good-bye to our autumn scenes, we said. But in the morning the snow was gone and we went to the Central Park to investigate, we found just what we wanted. The leaves are still half on, half off. We set a date for today, to shoot all our autumn scenes. I get a call from Lilly. "Look, I can't come today. Don't ask why, I'll call you tomorrow."—Clunk. Damn this neurotic city. She had another argument with Peter, I can bet.

No date, 1953

From my very childhood I was obsessed with colors, smells, sounds, moods. I never learned much in the school. I knew all the answers, I had read all the books. I used to sit, instead, and listen to what was going outside, trying to catch the sounds and smells that were coming from the nearby fields, the garden, the trees. The only thing I remember from the primary school is the smell of the lady teacher's hands, a very delicate odor of imported soap.

During the war, in the labor camp, the other prisoners, my friends used to say: Oh, you have no patriotic feelings, you have no sense of home, no sense of vengeance for the occupants and suppressors of your liberty. I lived on a completely different plane where nothing that was going around and affected so deeply the lives of all the others, had anything to do with my real life, it never entered or crossed my orbit. I lived in the world of my own senses, fantasies, moods, smells, images and towns and trees.

And when I stood on the ship and looked back at Europe, I felt no deep regret or sadness. Except, perhaps, I was a little bit sad about the landscape which I saw passing by, sad that it was passing by— and this had nothing to do with the past, this Verhaeren landscape, these windmills, gardens, this salty landscape. No, I had no sense of permanence of home, I wasn't attached to anything. Coming and going was in my blood.

No date, 1953

Places to see avant-garde and special films:
- Museum of Modern Art: classics
- Cinema 16 (Amos Vogel): "experimental" / new
- Theodore Huff Film Society (Bill Everson, Herman Weinberg): rare, privately available films
- New York Film Society (Arnheim, Weinberg): rare films
- 92nd Street Y: special films
- Dance Films (Livingston)
- George Amberg NYU film class (to sneak in): (with avant-garde film-makers present in person)
- Arthur Knight New School film class: same as Arnheim
- Artists' Club, 14th Street (Gjon Mili): never know, surprises
- Living Theatre (Becks): avant-garde
- Kinesis (Peter Hollander): good for California avant-garde
- Maya Deren screenings at Theatre de Lys (Deren, Maas)
- Hunter College (Perry Miller): films on art
- Club Cinema: left-oriented films
- Film Study Group (Bachmann, myself): avant-garde & rare
- Forty-Second Street: old and new Hollywood

CHAPTER THREE

... We make plans to start American Film House... New York independent film community... Searching for a building... George Capsis... I begin programming for Group for Film Study... On Josef von Sternberg... Searching, searching, searching for a building... A letter to Mme. Epstein... Frank Kuenstler ... Memories from childhood...

January 27, 1954
(Entry by Adolfas)

The American Film House is getting a more and more definite form. On this idea Jonas and I started to work early in 1953. We approached many names in the film art world after my return from Europe in May, 1953. No one was interested in it. Hugo, Deren, Jacobs, Harrington, Miller, Bachmann and others. We still didn't want to give up. We started to investigate some legal and practical questions. We prepared the working frame of the Film House. In that time two new film societies were formed in New York City: Group for Film Study (revival from last year) and Film Directions, Inc. Also Gallery East started film showings, whose film division was constituted of Jonas, me, and Brigante. Jonas also arranged programs and program notes for the Group for Film Study, and I did the technical work there.

Late in December 1953, after Capsis and Brummer organized Film Group (later: Film Artists Society) in New York, we prepared a written statement, and had a meeting with Brummer and Capsis. Brummer wasn't very interested in the project, due to his personal work. Capsis was very enthusiastic and jumped up on the idea, supplementing it with some of his own proposals.

Same day we decided that we need to have our own permanent theater. The same day we started to look around in Greenwich Village for a possible place.

A day later we talked with Bachmann again. Bachmann was still very skeptical, and said, "this can never be done the way you do." We (Jonas and I) decided that we will not talk to Gideon again about this but do it alone with Capsis.

A few days before we met Amos Vogel and we proposed to him our plan. He said, without $60,000 it's impossible such a plan. He was talking to us like some school kids. Brigante got interested in Film House and proposed an idea: to open it with a film bookshop and a reading room. The idea never got any consideration.

In the following week some of us check many possible places in Greenwich Village: all regular theaters, until we find one empty building on 91 Seventh Avenue S. We started investigating it legally.

During that time the Film for Industry went bankrupt. Capsis' friend Bob Campbell proposed to take that place together with his production unit. Same day we checked the 135 W. 52nd place. Price—about $200 a month. I wanted the place, George opposed, Jonas pro. George insisted on Gr. Village, as the most logical location. We had a long talk. I called Jonas to the White Horse. The 52nd Street place is already fixed for operation, while the place on 7th Ave requires over $3,000 for alteration work. Finally we agreed to stick to the Gr. Village place.

January 27th we found a lawyer and an idea to get three personal loans from a bank to meet the expenses.

Kinesis Inc. promised to help, but the decision has to come from California. Also Mr. Lewinson said something about financial help. Estimated expenses, taking the 52nd St place—$2,500. For the Gr. Village place we would have to pay over $5,000.

January 22nd I quit Bachmann's GFS.

February 2, Tue. 1954
(Entry by Adolfas)

After the second visit and a closer look at the 52nd place, we found that the place is too small, and our plans would greatly interfere with he Visual Transcription work.

So we had our meeting on Sunday, Jan. 31, and we decided to continue the investigation concerning the Greenwich Village place.

On Monday George called his father (real estate broker), asking for advice. It came out that George's father is the agent for that place and he promised to give us a better deal in rents, etc. Same day George had dinner with his father who promised an immediate action. He is willing to turn over to us the percentage he would get from the owner.

George's father also promised to give his lawyer and architect. Last night Jonas and I met Edouard de Laurot, who promised to give money, and be a representative in Europe.

February 9, Tue. 1954
(Entry by Adolfas)

George's father is negotiating with the owner. He wants that the owner would fix the place. He got the monthly rent down to $250. We spent a week trying to get a loan from a bank. It was very hard. We visited a Lithuanian banker (Valiunas) on Wall Street. Nothing. Today Jonas is trying to get a loan ($2,000) on his name.

GFS had a showing on Feb. 7. The attendance—120. A lack of publicity and a so-so program (*Roots of Happiness*; *Swain*; *Cops*; *Caravan*). Film Directions, Inc. last showing had just half of the auditorium. I am worried about the 7th Avenue place. George is very optimistic. Jonas thinks that George and I, we are too slow, and we don't do the right thing.

Kinesis Inc. (Calif.) is very interested in our project. They promised money. But at the last moment we decided not to take it, afraid that they would interfere with our policy, and it would be a stoppage to our operation.

February 14, Sun. 1954
(Entry by Adolfas)

On Thursday Jonas filed an application with the National City Bank for a loan of $2,000. Now we have to wait until Wed. to hear the results. We hope, as it was promised too, to get the money without difficulties. George and Brigante are co-makers.

Tomorrow we are meeting all three to discuss some basic statements and principles, to discuss the membership form and other operational problems.

In the meantime I have started the mailing list, which consists of 400 individual names, over 100 HS and Colleges and Drama schools.

February 21, 1954

Josef von Sternberg was the speaker at today's showing of Group for Film Study. We invited him to introduce *Salvation Hunters*.

He stood there, at the Irving School auditorium which we had rented for the occasion, there were some two hundred people, he was neatly dressed and prim, and he kept

THE AMERICAN FILM ~~ACADEMY~~ HOUSE

I.Information and Records Center
  for the use of film-makers, film-students,
  schools and the public.

a)books on cinema
b)film magazines
c)information on films
d)information on film directors
e)other film study materials

II.Publications

a)a film magazine, devoted to the practice an
  aesthetics of the contemporary cinema;will
  provide an international meeting ground for
  the film-makers, will discuss the current
  productions.
b)a monthly bulletin will provide the reviews
  and complete ceredits of all new films.
c)a Film Society Bulletin of current news and
  information on films and film-makers
d)Documents and Records; will publish materials
  of historical importance, documents, research
  data, etc.
e)books and monographs; detailed studies of
  directors, national cinemas, theoretical ~~mmmm~~
  writings.
f)will prepare the first Motion Picture
  Encyclopedia

III. Academy of Cihema
  will provide a platform for an advanced discussion of film theory and practice.

a) lectures by leading film directors, historians, theoreticians, and technicians
b) will provide an international forum for passing directors to discuss their work
c) will organize film appreciation courses for schools on various educational levels
d) will sponsor and conduct research projects such as the use of film in communities and civic programs

IV. Academy Theatre

a) retrospective screenings devoted to individual directors, countries, genres, historical periods
b) will introduce to the critics, distributors and the public, films of quality but which have not been adequately exhibited in this country
c) will provide a showcase for the work of the independent, low-budget film-makers, including documentarists and experimentalists

V. Film Society Center

a) will act as a national center for the co-ordination and assistance in the development of an active film society network
b) will assist in the organization of the distribution for films not normally covered by the standard commercial circuits
c) will assist Universities, Schools, Film Societies in the preparation of film programs and the obtaining of films

page 3

VI. Film Archive

to establish a center for the preservation
of films

VII.Festivals, Expositions

The Academy will organize a non-competitive
International review of the best films of the
year to be held annually in New York and
two or three other leading cultural centers.

VIII. Film-Makers' Center
a) will serve as a point of co-ordination
between The Academy and the independent
film-makers
b)will xxxxxx assist the independent film-
makers to establish a fund to aid the creative
film-makers in the realization of their
work
c)will assist the independent film-makers to
establish a workshop in order to continue
their work; studios; labs.

answering questions that kept coming from the audience, any question. What surprised me was that he seemed to be the only one in the auditorium who disliked *Salvation Hunters*. It was Sternberg himself who said the most cruel, negative words about the film.

Here are some notes I made from Sternberg's remarks:

"I was invited to introduce this film to you, but at the time I made this film, its sole purpose was to introduce myself…"

"I tried in this film to slow down the tempo of the film. Instead of fast cutting, my aim was to photograph a thought. At the time I shot it I thought I'll be able to influence the shallowness of the films of that time. But I did not…"

"All my work has been more or less a work of a poet. It has, if anything else, some poetical value, particularly in photography. But it doesn't have (in *Salvation Hunters*) any permanent value. It can be understood and appreciated only in relation to its time. This film is more horrible to watch for me than for you. I wouldn't show it myself anymore, but its showing, as you see, is out of my control."

"Its technique, cinematography, compared with other films of that time, is very good, I think. But the film itself is a very amateurish work."

Question from the audience: "What do you mean by permanent value?"

Sternberg: "I mean, that a work of art can be appreciated and enjoyed regardless of the time when it was made—like Shakespeare or Dürer. This film can't stand that."

"The film was made with non-professionals. There was in it only one professional actor, a star, who worked for $100 a day. He did not accept my check, so I paid him in silver and asked not to come any more. The girl that acted in this film impressed Chaplin so much that he took her for *Goldrush*. Some of the others became actors too, later."

"At the time I made this film I didn't put in it any symbolic meanings whatsoever."

Question from the audience: "But this film bears the mark of all your films, your style. I mean, the particular symbolism that is in all your films."

Sternberg: "Now I am being informed about myself."

Question: "Do the horns in the film have any symbolic meaning?"

Sternberg: "No. We rented the studio for $500 a week, and when we came, the horns were there. So we decided to use them in the background. The same way is with the dredge in the background. When we came, it was there, so we shot it, and the next day it was gone. It wasn't planned."

"To use the machine as the hero of the film was more a photographic contribution, idea, than a directorial one."

"I started as a splicer. I used to splice 50 films a year. So I got used to film."

Question about the inter-titles in the film.

Sternberg: "When Schulberg saw *Salvation Hunters* he thought I was the best subtitle writer in the world and gave me a title writer job. He said, my subtitles were so good that they saved him money filming some parts of the story."

February 24, Wed. 1954 (Entry by Adolfas)

I cashed the check from the bank in total of $976.40, and I put the money in my name on a special checking account, in amount of $970.

George's father is still trying to get in touch with the owner for the eventual lease contract.

Had a talk with our lawyer.

Met the architect.

Today I passed by the 7th Ave. place, and I saw that the sign in front of the building is removed.

My mailing list contains over 1,300 names.

7 Avenue A in 2013. Gallery East was located on the second floor, just above The Library.

The GALLERY EAST film showings are presented every last Friday evening of the month at 8:30 p.m. at GALLERY EAST, #-7 Avenue "A".
Monthly membership in the gallery entitles you to three other gallery events in addition to the monthly film showing.

****

NOTE: The 2nd program of this series will be given on November 25 and 26, and will include:

MOTHER'S DAY by James Broughton
FOUR IN THE AFTERNOON by James Broughton
GLEN FALLS SEQUENCE by Douglas Crockwell
RITUAL IN TRANSFIGURED TIME by Maya Deren
POTTED PSALM by Sidney Peterson.

The 3rd program in the series, set for December , will include:

OBJECT LESSON by Christopher Young
SAUSALITO by Frank Stauffacher
FIREWORKS by Kenneth Anger
AY-YE by Ian Hugo

Gallery East, 7 Avenue A, Lower East Side of Manhattan, was created by Joel Baxter, Louis Brigante and Storm De Hirsch in 1953. I discovered it after I moved to Orchard Street. Upon a suggestion of Louis and Storm, as an addition to art shows, I added a series of screenings of avant-garde cinema. That's how it all began…

February 27, Sat. 1954
(Entry by Adolfas)

We had an appointment to meet today and discuss some publicity problems. George called up and said that he can't make it today due to his promises to paint a girl's apartment. Meeting postponed until tomorrow.

February 28, Sun. 1954
(Entry by Adolfas)

George came to our place. George proposed the following: membership—$1.00 a year. Then the member can attend any of the showings by presenting his card at the door. He would be billed every two months for the showings attended. We thought that was the most interesting form.

Jonas is still sticking to our former proposition: to sell block tickets to the members. These tickets should be valid for any of the performances taking place within six months from the issue date. Or use both systems.

Then we went uptown to move some girl's stuff in George's car. The evening was spent at the girl's place.

March 1, Mon. 1954
(Entry by Adolfas)

George called up his father (who is negotiating with the people from the 7th Ave. place.) He said that they are looking for somebody to buy the stuff in the bar and are trying to find out how much it would cost to alter the place for us.

We are still not incorporated for George says he wants to have the place before we start doing anything. So, we just sit and wait.

March 2, Tue. 1954
(Entry by Adolfas)

Called up George's father. He did not have a chance to see those "crooks." He made an appointment to see them tonight.
So—we wait.

March 3, Wed. 1954
(Entry by Adolfas)

So we wait.
It's beginning to get on my nerves. George says: You can't do anything fast. Jonas is convinced that we will lose that place.

March 4, Thu. 1954
(Entry by Adolfas)

I called George in the morning—no news from his father. Then at 1 PM George says: "I got news." The place on 7th Ave. has been rented to somebody else since Feb. 18. So we are out on the street, after five weeks of negotiation.

I run to George's place and we sit looking at each other and blaming ourselves why we didn't grab that place at first sight.

We run through the Village streets. We checked 4–5 places—no one is suitable for us. The wind is very cold.

We went back, hoping that Bob is home. We want the place on 52nd Street. George gave in, and said: let's move out of Gr. Village. Bob went uptown and came back with the news that the place on 52nd Street got another customer and there is almost no hope to get it for us. He will check some other places uptown. In *The Villager* George found an ad for a loft 22 by 60 for $150. We jumped up. It was too late to see that place tonight. I went home after midnight.

March 5, Fri. 1954
(Entry by Adolfas)

I met George at the Minetta Street place (150). A very cold wind. We couldn't find the agent. We combed some more streets, until we found an entire three story building for rent on Jones Street. A big, empty place for $350 a month, no heat. I jumped up, and said YES. George was shaking his head and we still continued to search for the agent of the 150 place, but in vain.

We tried to sell the Jones Street idea to Bob and Dick. They are not interested.

With Leonas Letas, 1954.

Ever since I began screenings in Manhattan, I had confrontations with the Projectionists Union. They always picketed me for not using union projectionists. I could not afford them, I projected the films myself. Plus, they didn't even know how to operate 16mm projectors! Since I ignored their pickets, on occasion they used to sneak into the building in the middle of the show and disconnect the electricity.

FILM FORUM
A group for the advancement of the art of the film

PROGRAM No. 2   JUNE 12, 1954

FROM PAINTER TO FILM-MAKER

Lecture: DOCUMENTED SEEING by Sibyl Moholy-Nagy, professor at
Pratt Institute, actress, playwright, novelist, lecturer.

Program number 2 of the film forum will attempt to illustrate the evolution and character of the abstract and non-objective film. The abstract movement which started with the 20th century was a protest against
established concepts in the arts. The attack was mainly directed and
most apparent in painting. The revolting artists found the film a sympathetic medium to continue their search for new forms of expression. The
film had no traditions, no connections with the established rules of
technique. The film had further the exciting and compelling element of
motion. Motion had been already implied in paintings like Duchamp's
'Nude Decending Staircase'. It was very logical then, that the first
to begin experimenting with the abstract film were the painters themselves. Eggeling, Richter, Duchamp and Moholy-Nagy soon realized that
the forms, enclosed in paintings on a two-dimensional plane, in the film,
gained a new and the most dynamic dimension. Here line, form, color and
light, in their complex and varying proportions, positions and rhythms,
contrapointed or harmonized with music, produced a powerful aesthetical
and emotional experience.

The six films presented in this forum will attempt to present the most
significant developments in this movement.

Hans Richter: RHYTHMUS 21 (1921). One of the first experiments in this
direction. Rectangular forms occupy, modulate tonaly, and animate
the screen plane in terms of controlled middle depth.

Marcel Duchamp: ANAEMIC CINEMA (1927). In this film one of the most controversial artists of this century presents compositions of moving
spirals composed together with spiralic poetic sequence. Experiment
with roto-relief mobiles.

Moholy-Nagy: LICHTSPIEL: SCHWARZ-WEISS-GRAU (1929). The noted sculptor
and art theoretician creates a light symphony from shadows and reflections produced with his Light-Display machine.

Oscar Fischinger: STUDY No. 11 (1932). This is one of the earlier works
by the leading exponent of this new art of visual music. An abstraction to Mozart's Divertissement.

Norman McLaren: BEGONE DULL CARE (1949). An abstraction to jazz, an in-
formal approach to abstract rhythms.

Withney Brothers: FILM EXERCISES 4-5 (1944). A non-objective film experiment. Structure is based on canon form in music, using only the
basic geometrical forms, contrapointed or harmonised with color and
synthetic sound.

The forums are held at the auditorium of the Food Trades School, 208
West 13th St., New York City, every Saturday at 8 PM.

Persons wishing to attend film forums become members with their first
attendance. Admission $ 1.00. Attendance is limited to 200. Reserva-
tions are not required, but recommended.

For information and reservations call or write corresponding secretary:
Adolfas Mekas, 95 Orchard St., New York 2, N.Y. Tel.: CAnal 6-2245.

Executive secretaries: George Capsis, Adolfas Mekas.
Programs: Jonas Mekas

I am ready to sign the lease for the Jones place. George is very skeptical.

March 6, Sat. 1954
(Entry by Adolfas)

In the morning I and Jonas went to see the artist Bielskis, in Brooklyn. He agreed to do the trademark in two weeks.

At noon I, Jonas and George met at the Jones place.

We took another look at it. Then we saw the 150 place. Very small.

We talked and talked and we couldn't come to any decision. George is still opposing the Jones place. We, I and Jonas, are pro.

March 7, Sun. 1954
(Entry by Adolfas)

All three met at George's place to discuss the place, programming, and publicity. We definitely agreed to take the Jones place. Worked on publicity and programming. George saw his father, asking for money. His father said nothing.

March 8, Mon. 1954
(Entry by Adolfas)

Phoned the agent for Jones place. They are very kind to open the negotiation.

George filed the organization incorporation papers at the lawyer's. At 4 PM we (I and George) met Mr. Gorem who is interested in renting the top floor for a theater. He is willing to take from May 1st, giving us $300 security and one month in advance—$150 and sign a lease for one year. George is very skeptical. I am pro. I am afraid if George waits longer, we'll lose the Jones place too. I am pressing him to go tomorrow and start concrete talk with the agent.

March 9, Tue. 1954
(Entry by Adolfas)

We saw the agent. He wants two months' security, a month in advance, and a lease for three years.

Our proposition: one month security, one month advance, 3 year lease; he has to secure all necessary permits, and we take the place from May 1.

Agent agreed to everything except the one month security. He will let us know about that on Friday, after he talks with his boss. We check a few places uptown looking for some cheap theater chairs. The cheapest we found is $4.50 with installation.

Jonas is almost positive that we'll lose this place too.

George is very optimistic about getting the additional money. I just can't think where we could get it.

March 10, Wed. 1954
(Entry by Adolfas)

We found a place where to get theater chairs for $2.00 a piece. We'll do our own installation.

George stopped the lawyer from proceeding with the incorporation, motivating, that we have to be sure that we'll get the place. So—we are waiting for Friday, to hear from the agent.

Mr. Gorem called up this morning and he is willing to rent the top floor right now.

March 11, Thu. 1954
(Entry by Adolfas)

Waiting.

Today is three months since we started concretely working on our Film House project. We have some hopes to get one thousand dollars either from George's father or Brummer.

March 12, Fri. 1954
(Entry by Adolfas)

Had a look at Jones St. place again.

The agent still wants $700 security.

Bob and Dick are not interested to take the top floors.

Gorem wants to take the top floor but the agent fears that he'll never get the license from Fire Dept.

The final: we called up the agent telling that we agree with his terms, and we are ready to take the place, after he gets the Fire Dept. approval for ground floor.

We'll meet the agent on Monday 10 AM.

March 13, Sat. 1954
(Entry by Adolfas)

Nothing been done, the number is bad.

March 14, Sun. 1954
(Entry by Adolfas)

George with Bob came rushing to our place—they found a place on 15th Street. The place is closed.

We talked for a few hours. We were high in the clouds, as always.

Nothing accomplished—Sunday.

March 15, Mon. 1954
(Entry by Adolfas)

At 9 AM, George, Bob and I met and went to see the agent for 15th Street place. Three story building, $250 a month. 150 seating capacity, plus a nice basement for the lobby and coffee.

George is con, I am pro.

Called Jones place: The agent wouldn't rent it to us for he can't get a permit for public assembly. So, this place is out of question.

Visited a place on 58th Street, a huge four story building, with a hall, 30 ft. high. A most interesting building. $1,150 a month. We came back to George's place where we had pancakes and talked over. We were high in the clouds again.

George is still dreaming to find some arrangement with the new owner of the 7th Avenue place. I am sharply against it, for a thousand reasons.

We sent Bob again to see the agent for the 15th St. place. The place is available immediately. The trouble: two poles in the middle of the room must be removed, and a permit for public assembly must be secured. The agent gave his architect's

number, he would tell us how to remove the poles, in case the place gets the permit. We did not find the architect. We'll see him tomorrow morning. Tonight George is seeing the girl from 7th Avenue, will talk to her.

March 16, Tue. 1954
(Entry by Adolfas)

Couldn't find the architect.

Called up the lumber co. which was there recently. They say those two poles were put there without a permit, so they may be removed likewise.

George and Bob got an idea to go uptown and check the regular theaters and movie houses. After a few hours of visiting huge theaters, I insisted to go back to 15th Street.

Bob went to the agent. Just in time. The agent was writing the lease contract for another group of people.

I wrote immediately a check for $100 and Bob convinced the agent to give us the place, instead of the other party.

The agent said OK with him, but he has to get permission from the landlord. He doesn't think that he would object to give the place for our purposes.

He will check with the landlord tomorrow.

March 17, Wed. 1954
(Entry by Adolfas)

In the morning Bob called up over 20 different places trying to get something for us. The agent had no time to meet the landlord today. He will do that tomorrow. So, nothing could be done today, and I went to watch St. Patrick's parade. Today I made the first payment to the bank—$50. Paid in cash with Jonas' money.

March 18, Thu. 1954
(Entry by Adolfas)

The agent told Bob, that after he investigated me (he sent somebody to Orchard Street): "Nobody from Orchard Street could afford to rent this place."

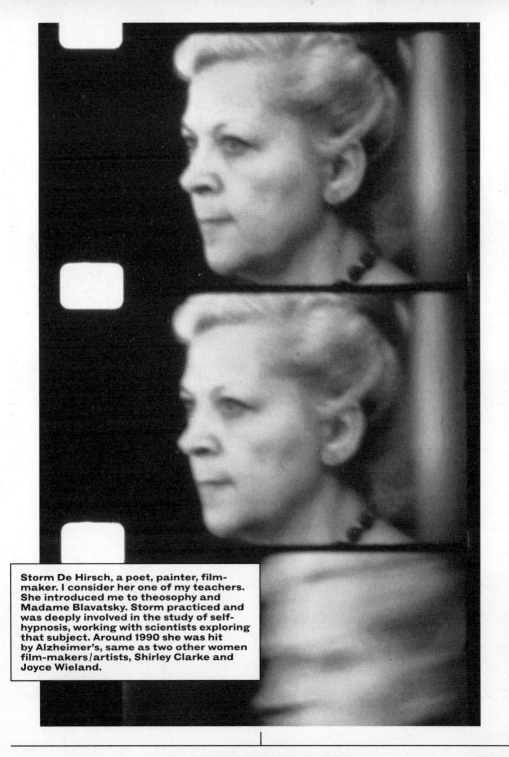

Storm De Hirsch, a poet, painter, film-maker. I consider her one of my teachers. She introduced me to theosophy and Madame Blavatsky. Storm practiced and was deeply involved in the study of self-hypnosis, working with scientists exploring that subject. Around 1990 she was hit by Alzheimer's, same as two other women film-makers/artists, Shirley Clarke and Joyce Wieland.

A painting by one of our young relatives of the farmhouse in which I grew up. I watched my father build it when I was six and seven. I think I could build one identical, anytime.

So, Bob did some nice talking. The results:
a) he wants that we send an architect to check the building;
b) we get an insurance first.

George did some phoning, is trying to get a building contractor.

March 19, Fri. 1954
(Entry by Adolfas)

Bob was busy with his own troubles until late afternoon, so I and George went through many streets again. We walked more than 8 hours, checking every available place.

We located one place: West 3rd, third floor. Two places on 13th Street and other places. In the evening we met Bob who said, he'll go and see the agent first thing Monday morning.

March 20, Sat. 1954
(Entry by Adolfas)

Nothing.

March 21, Sun. 1954
(Entry by Adolfas)

Nothing.

March 22, Mon. 1954
(Entry by Adolfas)

Called up the agent for 15th Street. He said he'll draw up the lease.

I picked up the art work from Bielskis. We do not like it very much. Jonas did some photo enlargements of it.

Now we are waiting for the agent to call Bob in regard to signing the lease.

March 23, Tue. 1954
(Entry by Adolfas)

No word from the agent. (He is investigating Capsis.)

Jonas did some photo enlargements of our logo done by Peter Hollander.

Waiting.

March 24, Wed. 1954
(Entry by Adolfas)

Got in touch with the agent. He is still stalling.

I checked streets for vacant buildings and lofts.

March 25, Thu. 1954
(Entry by Adolfas)

The agent wants us to get all licenses before we sign the lease. We (Bob and I) check the Building Department for violations, etc. Everything's clear on our side.

Called up the agent and gave him hell. He at last promised to draw up the lease and have it ready for Monday to sign it. The poor agent, he checked the telephone directory and found Film House listed. He investigated that firm thinking that it is the same one we are forming. After the investigation he was more willing to talk with us.

March 26, Fri. 1954
(Entry by Adolfas)

We all three signed the incorporation papers at the lawyer's. He will proceed with it on Monday.

March 27, Sat. 1954
(Entry by Adolfas)

Zero.

March 28, Sun. 1954
(Entry by Adolfas)

Zero.

March 29, Mon. 1954
(Entry by Adolfas)

The agent is not willing to give the house to us.

We sent a fake architect (Brummer) to check the building. We discovered a side door for exit. We called up the agent. Agent was very surprised, and told us he will check about that door. More stalling.

Called up the place on 3rd Street. Price

$225, two months' security. But not willing to rent to our purposes.

The lawyer filed the incorporation papers. I combed the streets.

March 30, Tue. 1954
(Entry by Adolfas)

I called up Bob asking for a show down with the agent. Bob is still trying to get uniformed firemen to check it. I'll see them in the afternoon.

March 18, 1954

Dear Mme. Epstein:

Some time ago, while visiting Benoit-Levy, I had an opportunity to read a little article, written by Jean Epstein. The title of that article was, if I remember right, "Le ralenti du son." It described his experiments with sound in his film *Le Tempestaire*. Because Epstein is not very known in the U.S., and because I happened to be one of his few admirers, I took the liberty to translate that article into English. Now the monthly film magazine *Films in Review* would like to publish it. But I was informed by Mr. Benoit-Levy that he received that article from you. So I decided to write to you and ask for your permission to print this little article in *Films in Review*. I am sorry to say that this magazine is very poor financially and it cannot pay for the articles. But I would like to see it printed anyway, the more that in the autumn, probably, as you know, we are organizing a showing of Epstein films in New York. To organize such an evening was my own idea, but it took months and months to persuade people to undertake it. Even now I have to suffer hard blames for persuading them to do it. Some people will never forgive me that, because they believe that it will be a financial failure. And you know very well how much importance to money people are giving here. I did not meet yet a person in New York who would show a film because it is good.

On the occasion of this showing I am preparing a little brochure on Epstein and his work. I have some material at hand, including the memorial issue of *Cahiers du Cinema*, but my sources here are very limited. If you would have any articles on his work, or notes on his films—in the case you happened to have more copies than you need—I would appreciate very much if you could send it to me. I would send it back to you as soon as I finish my brochure. Or, if you don't need it back, I would pay you what it costs to you.

I'll be waiting for your kind answer. (*Films in Review* would like to publish that article in their May issue.)

Yours,
Jonas Mekas
95 Orchard Street
New York City, N.Y.

No date, 1954

All my knowledge is through feelings. I can feel your past, your future, your wishes and your fears. You are closed to my mind but you are transparent—like a glass—a glass of pure water—to my feeling eye. I feel you through (like: I see you through) even if I don't know everything about you. My knowledge of you is of the other kind, not mind…

Me: What's new?
Frank: Oh, nothing. The autumn is dying.
Me: And who killed it?
Frank: Literary critics killed it…
(Frank Kuenstler)

"We should wake up and arrest the senseless trend toward materialism and begin to honor the uncommon man—the man of spirit and imagination. Quality, not quantity, should be our goal."
—Frank Lloyd Wright, in a speech

Map of the area of Lithuania where I grew up.

August 30, 1954

Frank Kuenstler came to look through his Washington Square footage, on the viewer, rushes. He was sweating for an hour—terribly hot today—talking with himself, happy if he came across a good shot and cursing when a bad one (that means most of the time) came & I continued reading Dos Passos' *The 42nd Parallel* only I don't know really why, and drank more sparkling water, soda, "Coca-Cola," and what not. It's 11 PM now but the heat is the same & merciless.

MEMORIES

In the corner of the living room there always stood a wooden cabinet. The cabinet was very old, drilled out by woodworms. It looked as if it had been painted long long ago, but the paint had fallen off almost completely through the years. On its door—also long long ago—our father had painted two birds, facing each other, their beaks touching each other, in white paint. It was the Family cabinet. At the very bottom of it there was a little box in which father and mother kept their wedding rings and the documents of the ownership of the farm.

On the shelves there were some old looking mysterious keys, and for years there was, on one of the shelves, a baby cap that one of us had worn, long long ago. Some old letters; father's sketchbook with drawings for the carriages—ah, our father made the most beautiful carriages, and he used to point them out to us through the window, Sunday mornings, when the neighbors were driving to the church. And later—I was about twelve—on the shelf the debt notes and loan papers began piling up—higher and higher each year. We were poor. The years were bad, and the house had to be moved to another place, and the tuitions for the children had to be paid—and the pile of debt notes didn't diminish from constant counting, checking, looking. That was the bottom shelf, the very bottom.

Right above it was the drugstore shelf. Tightly stacked next to each other were little bottles of all sizes and colors, most of them never touched. Nobody ever used them. It looked more like an archive, a record of all past illnesses. And nobody in the family knew what was in any of the bottles, or when to use them, against what. Only in one corner there were six or seven tiny colored flasks, with iodine, Vaseline, and some other items that were put to some occasional use, on the wounds or scratches, when one came home in the evening after a long day's work, plowing the fields, cutting wood, or digging out stones. Ah, there was a lot of work, after we moved to the new place. And a little bottle for the toothaches, with a goose feather for the application, a piece of cotton.

There were also three or four larger bottles, they belonged to our mother, mostly for her rheumatism and headaches.

Ah, the bleak days of worries and rains. Our mother used to sit most of the time—whenever she wasn't working in the garden or in the kitchen—she used to sit with her aching rheumatic back next to the warm stove, applying occasionally some of the medicine to her shoulders. I used to listen to her quiet complaints about the rains, autumn, the cold weather. Ah, my head my head, she used to say—my head is splitting, my head is splitting… This rheumatism will drag me to the cemeteries yet…

And then, the work, the pigs, the cows are calling, and she has to leave the stove and run to milk the cows, to feed the pigs, and cook the meal, and do this, and do that… to work for six growing children, to think about how to meet the debt payments, and how to give us all good lives—postponing her own life to the time when the children will grow up, in the future…

But we children we looked at her, and we understood nothing. We didn't understand why our mother, at the age of fifty, had such white white hair, as white as snow. No, we didn't understand it.

That was the second shelf.
The two middle shelves contained father's library.
These were the mysterious, intriguing shelves. Even today I do not know what turn my life would have taken without these two central shelves.
They contained some fifty large, thick books, all bound in leather. Their paper was old and brown, but still strong, with many many finger marks on the margins. Their letters were large—I do not remember any print in small type. Some contained mysterious drawings.
They were all holy books. The largest was the House Bible. Others: psalm books, sermon books, etc. There was one that described Hell and contained many Bosch-like pictures that frightened the hell out of us—the flames, and snakes, and daggers, and the lions tearing the sinners to shreds. I do not remember our father ever reading this book, but we children used to spend a lot of time in its pages. It attracted us immensely.
Then, there was the New Testament, two or three copies or versions, I am not sure now. They were set in different types, they looked different. Those were Confirmation Day presents to my brothers and sister. The oldest of them was in tatters, with the cover long gone—that one belonged to our father. The pastor who gave it to him, and wrote an inscription, it said "to my first Confirmant," he had died long ago. The brown ink of the dedication was now so thin it was barely readable, and had eaten itself through the paper to the other side. Next to it were the New Testaments of our sister and the oldest brother, Povilas. They were still new.
Somehow, by some strange privilege or right, on the same shelves were stacked old calendars, now all in tatters, all full of little daily entries, dates of when the cows were taken to the bulls, when the potatoes were planted, and such.
The Bible occupied a special place. Its last pages contained inscriptions, with our father's hand, in large and shaky letters, the names and birthdates of all of us—in that order: Elzbieta, Povilas, Petras, Kostas, Jonas, Adolfas—in three year intervals—one after another.
No, it wasn't only on Sundays, or Holy days—no; it was practically every regular evening, after the day's work was done, the cattle fed, the barn closed, and the supper eaten, the mother silently bent over the spinning wheel, buzzing whirring pleasantly, soothingly—and after the older brothers had established themselves in their respective places to work on weaving baskets, spinning ropes; and those who were attending school had dug their noses deep into their books, we two, the youngest, used to squat on the floor with our feet tucked under, and watch them; it's then that our father used to bring from the cabinet the House Bible, open any chance page, and read it. Ah, we used to press harder on our heels, there, on the floor, hypnotized by our father's voice, with our eyes focused on the white circle of light around the petroleum lamp. There he sat, our father, in the circle of light, at the end of the wooden table, and read. Slowly he read, word by word, with no hurry, occasionally stopping to think, repeating the lines, and the mother's spinning wheel was whirring, purring—and the familiar sound of the lamp—and when you closed your eyes a little bit you could see the rainbow colors floating from the lamp into the room—as we listened to the father's voice reading slowly about the life of Samson, and Samson was right there, in the room; and now in walks the good Ruth, and gathers the wheat ears; and Esther, and little David, and all the apostles—one after another they come into the room, as the large clock on the wall was ticking and ticking—late into the night until our eyes slowly closed—
and when we wake up again, after maybe a half of an hour or maybe just one minute—we don't know how long—we still hear the same buzz-buzz-buzz of the spinning wheel, and the crackling of the willow branches, our

older brothers working on the baskets, and the father's voice: "...and Samson took a bone of camel and..."

And then, finally, father used to close the book; very very carefully he took it back to its place in the cabinet, announcing that he's going to the stables for the final check up.

The sister puts down her knitting and disappears into her little sleeping room. The older brothers slink into their own cold room. Only the mother's wheel is still whirring and purring in the empty living room, and the windows are black.

There was another book that took a special place, our father's second most used book—a book of prayers. Sundays, just before sitting down for breakfast, or any day, late at night before going to bed—we all used to kneel down, each in our own usual place—myself at the end of a long bench by the south wall—and our father used to read a prayer from the book. Some of them were very long, we didn't understand them, they were mysterious, strange. Then we sat down at the table steaming with hot cabbage soup or we rushed to our respective sleeping corners.

Our mother was the first one to get up. We could hear her in the kitchen, working with pots and pails, as she tried to handle them very very quietly so as not to wake us up, as she was preparing to go out to milk the cows. Half an hour later we heard her again, back from the stables, singing silently in the kitchen. She always sang, very very silently, for herself all the time, as she was preparing the breakfast. The father was already gone to feed the horses, or into the field. Our mother sang and sang, and we could hear her sing, in our sleep—and she sang sweetly, and we never knew what she was singing, these were old songs, she used to say, she learned them from her grandmother; and others she just made up; still others were psalms and hymns sung in the church.

Ah, how beautiful was that music, that singing, that silent melody, when I listened to her, half asleep, just waking, barely awake, with my eyes still closed, the light trying to get into my eyes, a rainbow of colors crisscrossing on the eyelids.

CHAPTER FOUR

We start *Film Culture* magazine... Money problems ... A visit to Arthur Miller... We are sued by the primer... On Alban Berg and Anna Sokolow... Searching for money ... On rereading childhood books... On importance of "un-importance" in cinema... *Film Culture* N. 2... Editorial meetings... More on *F.C.* money problems etc.... We move to 109th Street... Anaïs Nin... In defense of avant-garde film-makers as "artists"... Bob Stock's poetry salon ... Meeting Ken Jacobs... On Edouard de Laurot... Working on *Film Culture*... Our visit to 14th Street Artists' Club...

August 31, 1954

Three weeks ago, to pay his TV school, Adolfas borrowed $100 from Leo. Now Leo is buying a house on Lake Erie, needs money back immediately. He was always like that, friend or no friend, he will cut your throat for a penny. So I borrowed $50 from my boss, added another $50 from my own this week's salary, and mailed it to Leo. But today I am facing a crisis. I have to return $50 to Perskie; the rent is due tomorrow; there are two electricity bills on the table; Video Lab bill is not paid; and I still owe ten dollars to Abe, our neighbor. Tomorrow is also the payment day for the bank loan I took for *Film Culture*. I went to another bank, Chase, and applied for another loan, but they don't want to give it without a co-maker.

This week we are cutting down on food, eating only in cheap Horn & Hardart automats. When I came home today, I had only four cents left. If not for Abe, I would have been kaput. Dorothy is broke too, she has sixty cents left, she said. During the lunch hour I saw Sid counting his money in the corner, and there weren't too many pieces. I alarmed everybody at the Graphic Studios, where I work now. One or two dollars I may get from Phil or Charles, they are the only ones who are willing to help out when it comes to a matter of lending a dollar.

Visited our neighbor on the second floor. I was passing by and he invited me and introduced himself. Puerto Rican, has lived here for thirty years, likes horses, good food, women. He put it in that order. He said he is leaving tonight for two months, going on business, to some place. I didn't ask him on what kind of business, but he expects to make a lot of money and have a good time. He doesn't have any steady job, he lives just like that. I was (still am) reading Dos Passos and Kafka's *Tagebücher*. On the street the voices of children playing baseball, cars passing.

The heat is the same, killing. I have a good idea: to construct an air-conditioned chair. That's what I need now.

December 4, 1954

Visited Arthur Miller, in Brooklyn Heights. The aim: to raise money for *Film Culture*. We still need $500, by next Tuesday. He was very happy about the first issue and said he will try to get money from some people he knows. We spent a long afternoon talking. He was complaining that nobody wants to stage his plays anymore. "My plays are tabu now," he said. "They still think that my plays are plays à-la-thèse. I thought that that argument was discussed and closed in the early thirties. But I was mistaken. What can you do with people like that?"

He was depressed and angry.

"They can't understand that an artist could be engaged in his times, problems. The best writers, the ideal writer of today has to be completely detached from the social themes. Complete un-engagement. In the novels and in theater you see laborious reproductions of every detail as it is in life, details, but nothing behind it. Emptiness, in all plays you can see on Broadway or elsewhere."

He said, he thinks that the only intellectuals are to be found not among the so-called intellectuals or artists, but among the industrialists, manufacturers who know that culture, arts must go together with the production. Culture, he said, in America, is detached from politics. Politics mean campaigning, elections, etc., but no cultural-ethical integration. America is where Europe was 75 years ago. Victorian age here has just passed, and after a great confusion in every section there is a great wish for the returning to the point of departure back to Lincoln, Franklin, constitution. They can't understand the relativity of history. They are taking it without adapting it to the changing times.

He expressed his great interest in existentialism, especially in Sartre's plays, such as *Devil and God Almighty* wondering why nobody has produced it here yet.

December 10, 1954

Still looking for money. Last week our books showed that we had only $120. The sum needed to pay for the next issue of *Film Culture* is $700. During the last few days I've approached at least thirty people in "film business," for sponsorship. I got names but no money.

While preparing the first issue, I was mostly concentrating on the contents. Money seemed such a secondary thing. But now I am facing the song.

I reported on the sad financial situation to the Editorial Board. I simply proposed that each of us come up with $100—and the problem is solved! The idea didn't work. George is going to South America and doesn't have a single dollar extra. Louis said he is willing to give any help to the magazine except the financial. Gordon said he has money but he wouldn't give because of his principles. "Why," he said, "why did you start the magazine at all, without money! You can't start a magazine unless you have money for at least three or four issues." If he'd known that we didn't have money he wouldn't have helped from the start. So I said, if we'd all think that way, *Film Culture* would wait for another two centuries. There are thousands of people with money and business brains, but it had to be us, without money and without business brains to do the job. Gods are cruel… I didn't dare to tell him that this morning we received summons to appear in court. Pacific Printing is suing us for the printing of the first issue. We have seven days to pay $723.91…

December 11, 1954

I am continuing the money Odyssey. Perry Miller said she spent all her money on a

FILM

CULTURE

JANUARY, 1955   Volume I   No. 1

ERICH VON STROHEIM / Queen Kelly; Walking Down Broadway
ORSON WELLES / For a Universal Cinema
HANS RICHTER / Film as an Original Art Form
EDOUARD L. DE LAUROT / Towards a Theory of Dynamic Realism
HERMAN G. WEINBERG / The New Films
GEORGE N. FENIN / Motion Pictures and the Public
WILLIAM K. EVERSON / A Family Tree of Monsters
        also articles by GORDON HENDRICKS, FRANCIS BOLEN, ROGER TILTON,
         JOSE CLEMENTE, RICHARD KRAFT. and others

THE NEW YORK DIARIES
1950–1969

103

'Reno, Nevada' (Marilyn Monroe and Arthur Miller Dancing During Filming for 'The Misfits'), 1960.

secretly laughing at you because she's a step ahead of you, and knows it.

A picture of Abraham Lincoln hung on one wall of her apartment. Among the books scattered around the living room were "The Philosophy of Spinoza," the tales of Edgar Allen Poe, a volume of architect Frank Lloyd Wright, and a smaller one entitled "Film Culture," which may have been a mystery.

Then Marilyn entered, as ever, and said:

"I'd rather not be asked whether I'm pregnant or not, or to discuss anything political or religious. Otherwise, I'll talk about anything.

trip to Europe, she owes money to her mother. We called dozens of people without any results. I tried to see Marlene Dietrich but was thrown out by the doorman.

So now I have to work full-time, and often overtime too, at the Graphic Studios, on West 22nd Street. We walk around hungry, live on coffee, saving money to pay the printer.

December 18, 1954

ON ALBAN BERG & ANNA SOKOLOW
We went, with Elizabeth, to Kaufman Auditorium for an evening of modern dance and music. *L'Histoire du Soldat*—despite the fact that I like this work very much, this tasteless, mediocre production made me almost hate it. I still remember Stroux's beautiful production, in Kassel, six years ago.

But on the same program there was *Lyric Suite* by Alban Berg, choreographed by Anna Sokolow. It was impossible not to be pulled into its music and dance, its atmosphere of complete desperation, loneliness, frustration. The man here is helpless, a tragic puppet, without a will of his own, performing agonizing, hopeless movements to the rhythms of equally sad, agonizing, hopeless music. If this is the essence (and art deals with essences) of the world we live in; if the world of Alban Berg and Anna Sokolow is also our world—and what other world could it be!—ah, how sad we must be, deep deep inside!

Elizabeth said that although this production is true, it is only partially true; it shows only a small part, only one aspect of reality (truth) and therefore I shouldn't make wide generalizations from Berg and Sokolow: "There are other parts and aspects to life, more happy, more optimistic," she said.

"There was no protest on part of man, no struggle against his morbid fate, the struggle which is the basis of all classical moral drama; there was nothing but helplessness," she said. "Yes, but then," I argued, "if this is only one part, then this part must be very big, immensely swollen." I thought about dozens of experimental artists, films made by the young artists today, those desperate, sad films of Harrington, Anger, Markopoulos; or those many painters and writers, New Directions, etc. etc.

"But look," I said to Elizabeth, "if we begin to call a particular period black or desperate or lost, or whatever word we choose, this word has two edges: with one edge it cuts into the past, with another it cuts into the present and future, it acts upon us. Words have magic powers, just by their sheer presence, and today when we read them—yes, the words, the names act upon us, they cut into us. That's what I am thinking about. It is not that these works aren't true. They are true. What counts, however, is what we do about it, once we know the truth. You see, today we are so badly lost that although the truth is shown to us by our artists we are no longer able to act, to do anything about it, to learn anything from that knowledge, from that truth. We are like children. The truth is there, like a rock, but we continue on the same disintegrating road. The terms we invent to describe our spiritual attitudes, states and conditions when they are correct, (even when our analyses are correct) boomerang back at us and we still sink still deeper. The words that describe our present (or immediate past) we take as our guides into the future. We confuse words with reality."

"Yes," said Elizabeth, "but isn't then the moral responsibility of the artist to create a more constructive, more optimistic art which instead of evoking or naming by name a ferocious dragon would evoke a more hopeful specter of the future? Can we say that Berg is using his moral responsibility? Or is he only a puppet expressing agonies of his generation without any will of his own? Although his music and Sokolow's choreography really express the spiritual state of a large segment of this generation, and although both artists have recorded and presented it very impressively—as far as their arts go—still, aren't they both performing negative acts towards their contemporaries because of their moral passivity, because of the magic meaning of arts, and because of man's inability to learn from art? What will this do to us, how will it affect us, the unengaged, uninvolved, 'objective' art of this century? And, further, are the artists themselves aware of this problem of morality, and the possible consequences of their art?"

"You see," I said, "it's here that the critics, philosophers, and the critic in the artist himself fail. The artist doesn't fail, but the critic fails. I am quite certain that nobody in the audience took *Lyric Suite* as a critical statement on human condition today; they were watching it only 'as an art for art's sake,' as 'modern art,' 'art experience,' without realizing that this is them, that they themselves are being mirrored on the stage. It isn't the work of art that fails; it is our attitudes to works of art that must be changed, how we look at works of art; the deeper functions of art have been forgotten, that's the real crux of this matter. We keep blaming the artist. This lack of understanding of deeper meanings of art has contaminated, sunk into the center of our artists, into their minds and souls, affecting the true meaning and function of their art. If we look at great works of the past, let's take *Prometheus Bound* or Milton's *Samson Agonistes*—there is always, in the work itself—the works which are true statements on the spiritual states of their periods—there is a thought planted, in these works, a critical mind is present; a thought that is always a little bit ahead of and above what's being described—a certain consciousness which makes us

know, while we are reading these works, or seeing, that these are us there, our natures are being discussed, these are not works for their own sake; really, there is always something Brechtian in them, but in a more subtle, subliminal, less obvious way than Brecht's estrangement business. It is this element, this consciousness, this inspiration, this realization that is missing in the work of Alban Berg and Anna Sokolow.

And the lack of it, or the lack of guidance to it, made us miss the very essence of the work. All that we saw remained an external movement, moods, desperations, with no meaning to it at all. Yes, beautiful, and strong, yes, but empty, like a beautiful shell: a magical word of desperation, a work of desperation acting magically upon us, upon the audience, upon its own creators—our critical spiritual powers were not awakened—the Cerberus is sleeping —a dragon is devouring its own creator by branding him with its flaming tongue right on the forehead with a sign of doom."

December 27, 1954

Like so many times in the past, I'm trying again to organize my confused life. That's why these diaries. They help me.

Decision was made by fate that English should become my new language. I have to write more and more to get this language into my blood.

So this is my training ground, my conversations with myself. And, of course, one must be a little bit looney to talk with oneself. Looney or lonely.

Anyway, I am not a very good talker and I'll never be one. I am a paper man. And I am one of the best listeners in the world. And a good listener is better, you'll agree, than a bad talker.

There were times, only a generation ago, when a boy of 13 or 15 was already earning bread. Edison sold newspapers at 10.

FILM CULTURE

Editor and Publisher:
JONAS MEKAS
Editorial Board:
GEORGE N.FENIN
ADOLFAS MEKAS
EDOUARD L.DE LAUROT
GORDON HENDRICKS

215 W.98 ST., NEW YORK 25, N.Y.   TEL.: CA 6-2245

PUBLISHED EVERY TWO MONTHS FOR THE ADVANCEMENT OF A MORE PROFOUND UNDERSTANDING OF THE AESTHETIC AND SOCIAL ASPECTS OF THE MOTION PICTURES.

Essays and articles on the aesthetic, technical and commercial problems by leading film writers, critics, directors, distributors and film-goers - offering substantial and stimulating content to the professional and layman alike.

64 pages, with illustrations.

IN THE FIRST ISSUE   Vol.1   No.1   December 1954

FOR A UNIVERSAL CINEMA, Orson Welles
TOWARDS A THEORY OF DYNAMIC REALISM, Edouard L.de Laurot
MOTION PICTURES AND THE PUBLIC, George N.Fenin
FILM AS AN ORIGINAL ART FORM, Hans Richter
A FAMILY TREE OF MONSTERS, William K.Everson
TWO SYNOPSES BY ERICH VON STROHEIM: QUEEN KELLY; WALKING
        DOWN BROADWAY
DESCRIPTION OF A NEW FILM BY HANS RICHTER
A DOCUMENTARY: JAZZ DANCE. Articles by Roger Tilton, Richard S.
        Brummer, Robert Campbell, George Marvin
THE NEW FILMS, Herman G.Weinberg
THE LETTER FROM BRUSSELS, Francis Bolen
THE LETTER FROM MADRID, Jose Clemente
THE SOUND TRACK, Gordon Hendricks
THE NEW MUSIC, Louis and Bebe Barron
JOURNAL OF A FILM FIEND, Richard Kraft
NEWS CHRONICLE; LETTERS

IN THE SECOND ISSUE

WHAT DO YOU THINK OF THE PUBLIC ? An inquiry made by George N.
        Fenin among leading motion picture directors - ELIA KAZAN, WILLIAM
        WYLER, JOHN FORD, CECIL B.DE MILLE, and others.
RICHARD GRIFFITH: Museum of Modern Art Film Library.
LEWIS JACOBS: From a Note-Book on Film Art.
HERMAN G.WEINBERG: Excerpts from his forthcoming book SIN AND
        CINEMA.
ARTHUR KNIGHT: It Happened One Night.
HANS RICHTER: N.F.S. (Not For Sale). Sequences from the script.
JONAS MEKAS: The State of Experimental Film in America.
        Also articles by Len Lye, Amos Vogel, Willard
        Van Dyke, Sidney Berkowitz, Ian Hugo, and others.

HOW TO GET YOUR COPY

Yearly subscription (6 issues): U.S.A., Canada and South America - $ 2.25.
Other countries - $ 2.50. Single issue - 40 ¢ (see your nearest art pub-
lication dealer).

For subscription please use the form below:

Enclosed please find my check (money order) payable to FILM CULTURE
for $........ to cover a yearly subscription commencing with the .... issue.

Name ....

....
        Street   City   Zone   State
FILM CULTURE, 215 W.98 STREET, NEW YORK 25, N.Y. TEL.: CAnal 6-2245

Q 334057

SUMMONS

CITY MAGISTRATES' COURT OF THE CITY OF NEW YORK

CITY OF NEW YORK

COUNTY OF NEW YORK .... LOWER MAN. DISTRICT MAGISTRATES' COURT .... Court, Borough of ....

In the Name of the People of the State of New York

To .... *Adolfas Mekas* ....

Complaint having been made this day by .... *A. Koetong* ....

that you did commit the offense of ....

VIO. 1292-A-P. L. (resck $60)

YOU ARE HEREBY SUMMONED to appear before me, or any City Magistrate holding this Court,

at No. .... 2ND. STREET & 2ND. AVENUE ....

on the .... 4 .... day of .... November ...., 19..., at .... 10 .... o'clock .... A .... M.,

to the end that an investigation may be made of said complaint.

AND UPON YOUR FAILURE to appear at the time and place herein mentioned a WARRANT

may be issued for your arrest for the crime or offense charged.

Dated, this .... day of .... OCT 14 1954 ...., 19 ....

Officer on Post Please Assist.

.... PAUL BALSAM ....

City Magistrate

We didn't have even one dollar in our pockets when we issued the first issue of *Film Culture*. Adolfas had no job, and I had only my Graphic Studios salary. But I knew a monk at the Franciscan Monastery in Brooklyn, on Willoughby Street. They had a small publishing house for religious pamphlets. I managed to persuade them to print the two first issues on delayed payment. We were absolutely sure that the magazine would sell like hot cakes. Since that didn't happen, I was left with my miserable salary money to pay the bills. The monks sued me... "You, people of God," I said, "how can you do that to us..." But no, I had to pay, in installments. You'll notice the address of the Court: it was the building—what an irony or joke!—which today is the house of Anthology Film Archives! I bought it in the City auction in 1979.

Editorial board of *Film Culture* magazine, 1957. From left to right: Andrew Sarris, Eugene Archer, George Fenin, Adolfas Mekas. Bottom: Jonas Mekas, Arlene Croce, Edouard de Laurot.

- Hartney Arthur   UN-55968
    299 Riverside Dr.
- Rudolf Arnheim, ~~Sarah Lawrence College~~
  ~~Bronxville, N.Y.~~ (35 Parkview Ave.)
- Margarets Akermark, M.M.Art
- Dr. George Amberg, University of Minnesota
    T. N. M. 213, Minneapolis, Minn.
- Leo Adams   50-89866 at work
  Humberto Arenal 334 E 51ˢᵗ Pl-58940
  Leo Adams 437 West Front St. Erie 2,
  Pansilvania Tel. 44944, Mr. Mrs. Hanks
- Anna Oddoy →
- Joan Abena EW-46999
    Pinga's girl-friend
- Eugene Archer MO-36,600, R.12-14 J.
- Artkino CI-56570 (RI-99708)
- McAgy - LY-65866
- James Agee 17 King 80.
- Actors' Studio   432 West 44 th So -
- Vincent Joseph Azzarelli, 237 Carroll St. B'klyn 31
- Max Ascoli, 136 E 52 MU-84033

A B C D E F G H I J L M N O P Q R S T U V W Y Z

What an industrious, practical, money-making generation! That's why they can't forget it, they can't stand it, to see that the current generation is not practical at all. Today, at 15, they'd rather dance rock 'n roll. Even juvenile delinquents are less corrupt than their parents and uncles. This generation, the rock 'n roll generation doesn't give a damn about money and all that.

Ah, their parents, they were such busy-devils, with the smell of money in their nostrils.

After my work at Graphic Studios, we had a small editorial meeting at George Fenin's. Edouard came too. Adolfas is still in Canada.

Edouard is still wearing the same black monk's shirt and people are beginning to believe he's either a monk or a priest. He encourages their confusions. He likes to create confusions around himself, he thrives on it.

I am reading *The Wind in the Willows* (Kenneth Grahame) which Elizabeth gave me. I read it so long ago, when I was twelve, that only small fragments remain in my memory. I can't recall a single incident, scene. But I can still feel the mood of the book. It comes to me all the way from my childhood, this book. And I can still see myself, reading it, cold winter evenings, sitting by the table, with my back to the cold ice-covered window, I can hear the wind howl outside, and my mother sitting by the fire, knitting. And the good hedgehog emerges before my eyes, his strange sweet adventures.

Sometimes I think I should not reread books I have read and admired in my childhood. Now, when I reread them, I find the fantasy worlds gone. I feel like an elephant walking through a china shop. The book is still the same. But I have become different, very different.

I am still thinking about last weekend's trip to Glenn Rock. I have been too long in the city, I am betraying nature, fields. I saw again the birches, and the woods, and the stones, and the horses, the road, the brook, and yes, the birds & the fresh air and the sun—this little break from the city made me drunk.

December 28, 1954

It seems to me that contemporary short stories, plays and films give more importance to the plot than the content. Plot short stories, plot films, plot plays. This exaggerated preoccupation with the external. What plot was there in my daily life, when I grew up in my village? But the content of the life there affected my whole being. Totally insignificant, plotless situations, details, actions, words, gestures; a walk, a laugh, a smile—all very "unimportant" & "bad plot." And there is no violence & no suspense. Nothing that makes a good movie…

I am dreaming about a film which would depict a period of a man's life, revealing his character and soul through little daily activities, without any plot.

Can an artist's work have more depth than the artist himself? No. That is, without divine intervention…

I went to 55th Street Cinema to see Fritz Lang's *Siegfried and Kriemhild's Revenge*. I have never seen these films before. Though presented in a mutilated form, both films, and Siegfried in particular, are masterpieces. There is no cinema like this today. Their visual poetry, compositions, it makes Hollywood look ridiculous. It was raining, on my way home. Winter rain.

Write a play about a man who refuses to work on immoral jobs. He sits home, with children dying of hunger, wife, etc., and talks to the neighbors who try to persuade him to give up and work.

He wants to take himself out of that society in protest against it. He declares himself dead. He doesn't want to leave any trace that he ever lived, he hates his society so much. The play or film should deal with this effort. How will it end? Probably, the more he tries to cut himself out, the more clear it becomes to him that he is too connected with other people. He becomes an activist anarchist.

January 29, 1955
(Entry by Adolfas)
The last manuscripts are being retyped for the 2nd issue of *FC*.
Edouard has difficulties of cutting his article "Critics and Criteria" to 8 pages (originally he wrote 26 pages.) He called this afternoon and said that instead of reducing the article to fit *FC*'s 8 pages, he enlarged it.
Mme. Fenin (mother) wants to investigate the members of our editorial board as to their political backgrounds.
Jonas is calling people, trying to get money for *FC*.
No word from Gordon since Jan. 26.

January 29, 1955
Adolfas made routine trips to Fenin's and Weinberg.
George Fenin is still in Uruguay.

11:30 PM: Andrew Sarris did not receive Gordon's article which was mailed to him on Wedn. Lost? Wrong address? Or?

"The world is a bridge; pass over it, and build no house."
—Moslem saying

"The thing to do with a good, but imperfect, organization is to improve it. The United Nations is the nearest thing the world has to a universal international organization and is therefore the logical place to begin working toward enforce- able disarmament through world law."
—John Henry Merryman, *The Nation*, Jan. 8, 1955

January 30, 1955
George Capsis promised to send $15.00 as his sponsorship money. He said, "I'm writing the check right now." A classic line.

7:30 PM – 10:30 PM: Editorial session with Edouard concerning his article and other matters.
10:30 PM: We go to Dr. James to pick up his review of Arnheim's book. Tea, a fantastic break!
11 PM – 1:30 AM: An editorial session at Brigante's place. Final checking of manuscripts, corrections on titles, etc.
2:30 AM: To bed. Terribly cold. *FC* needs more blankets. We may appeal to U.N. for humanitarian assistance.

February 1, 1955
(Entry by Adolfas)
Mailed letters asking for press tickets.
Hendricks' article arrived.
Did not succeed to make arrangements with Film Directions to sell *FC* at their shows. Mention in their notes promised.
Received $15.00 from Capsis (new sponsor).
Tried to sell advertising space to Camera Equipment, Reeves, Swiss Airlines. No results.
Could not find anybody at BIS to pick up the ad. I'll see them tonight at cocktail party (5:30).
Misplaced-lost-stolen my list of film magazines from all over the world.
Now I'm going to see more possible advertisers.

Later:
No food and nothing to drink at *FC* headquarters.
6 PM – 9 PM (entry by Jonas): Working with Ed on editorial.

Adolfas with Frank Kuenstler.

A. GARMAIZE, PRINTER
116 NASSAU STREET, NEW YORK 38, N. Y.

Municipal Court of the City of New York

Borough of Manhattan: 2nd District

PACIFIC PRINTING CO., INC.

Plaintiff's Address
37 East 18th Street

Borough of Manhattan

Plaintiff

against

JONAS MEKAS, individually and
d/b/a FILM CULTURE,

Summons

Defendant

Classification No. B-26

To the above named Defendant

You are hereby Summoned to appear in this action in the Municipal Court of the City of New York, Borough of Manhattan: 2nd District, before the Clerk of the said Court, at his office at 8 Reade Street in the Borough of Manhattan, in the City of New York, within seven days after the service of this summons, upon you, exclusive of the day of service, and to make answer to the complaint; and if you fail to make answer, judgment will be taken against you for the sum of $ 723.91 with interest thereon from the 29th day of August, 1955, together with the costs of this action.

Dated, New York City, the 3th day of February 1956.

Defendant's Address:

SIGMUND MOSES
Attorney for Plaintiff

Office and Post Office Address
33 West 42nd Street

Borough of Manhattan   New York City

After our troubles with the Franciscan monks who printed the first two issues, I used the same trick with the Pacific Printers. We were getting some donations, plus I was getting some overtime hours at the Graphic Studios, so I took another chance. But again, we failed... and again, we were sued... more time payments...

9 PM – 12 PM: King Vidor's *Hallelujah*, at Cinema 16.

February 3, 1955
(Entry by Adolfas)
I called Mr. Siegel. He will write an article on film censorship for the next issue.
Almus called. He wants his $20 back on Saturday. I promised. Yes, Siree. S.O.S.
Mr. Turner called. He'll send $10 for the magazine but doesn't want to be listed as sponsor. "Don't do that, promise me not to use my name anywhere. I don't know what will become of your magazine and I don't want my name to be mentioned in it." He was afraid that *FC* is a leftist magazine, etc.

February 5, 1955
(Entry by Adolfas)
A very difficult and delicate surgery performed: I had to cut 8 pages from *FC*. The printer found that we have material for 60 pages instead of 52 or 48. Took out Kraft, Kracauer, James, and a few small items.
8 – 10 PM: Conference with Louis.
Gideon Bachmann called. He wants to take an ad. Also said there is a half-page mention of *FC* in the new issue of *Educational Film Guide*.

February 7, 1955
(Entry by Adolfas)
Himlaspelet.
10 PM – 12 AM: in the lobby of Capitol, working with Edouard on shortening his essay.
$20 returned to Almus. George back from Punta del Este Fest ("trash").

February 9, 1955
(Entry by Adolfas)
General meeting at Fenin's. Present: Jonas, Edouard, George, Adolfas, Gordon Hendricks, Louis Brigante and Edgar Gunther, a new member of *FC*. He will take care of the advertising and business end, he said.

Gordon, after expressing a few dissatisfactions about copy-reading of N. 2, resigned as a member of the Editorial Board. He promised to help *FC* by trying to get sponsors. Mr. Hendricks resigned and left immediately.
Mr. Gunther pledged his support in advertising & business management. Business meeting set for Monday (14) at 8 PM at Gunther's.
Second meeting at Mekas'. (Louis, Edouard, Jonas & Adolfas)—preparing the dummy for *FC* 2 and other technical matters & notes for the printer.
Received all galleys except a few small items.
The meeting broke at 1:45 AM.

February 10, 1955
(Entry by Adolfas)
9:30 AM: I met Gunther and the artist from *Fortune* to discuss the cover for *FC* 2.
10:30 AM: Checked magazines & papers at NY Pub. Library.
11:15 AM: Talk with Pinga. He was very satisfied with the editing done on his review of *Gate of Hell*.
12 Noon: Meeting with Weinberg.
Business correspondence.
Compiled 2 lists: free copies; exchange copies.
3 PM: Meeting with Bachmann. He returned mimeo machine. Signed contract for an ad in *FC* 2 for $30.
4 PM: Visited UN. Spoke with the editor of United Nations Secretarial News. Promised to print a notice on *FC* in the coming issue.
6 – 10 PM: Working on the last technical details (Jonas & Adolfas).
Writing captions for pictures, content, data, etc.
Fenin called. Says, Edouard fucked up his article—rewrote, changed, added his own opinions.
Hendricks called asking to print his name as "contributing editor."

10 PM: meeting with Boris Kaufman.

11 PM: meeting at Brigante's. Final printing instructions.

Midnight: Jonas meets Bachmann, to discuss changes in his article.

February 11, 1955
(Entry by Adolfas)

8 AM: Office work, business letters, etc.

10 AM: Business telephoning & time out for tea.

11 AM: Post office, trying to get info about cheaper mailing of *FC*.

11:30 AM: Public Relations (Rosalind Kossoff, Emily Jones).

11:30 AM: Mail pick-up from Fenin.

3 PM: Advertising. Stop at BIS.

4 PM: Sorting mailing, classifying, answering.

5 PM: Time out for breakfast.

February 11, 1955

Visited Kaufman. He promised to write an article for us on the function of motion picture photography. Reading proofs.

February 12, 1955

Proofreading. Sarris picked up galleys for 2nd proof-check.

February 13, 1955
(Entry by Adolfas)

10 AM – 1 PM: Editorial meeting at Fenin's. Mr. Fenin described what he called "crookeries" of Mr. Joachim at Punta del Este. He stated that the use of Joachim's name in *FC* would bring us nothing good and he would resign as editor if we printed Joachim's interview with McLaren.

Dissatisfaction with Edouard having too much saying in correcting of articles. He tends to rewrite and put his opinions in. In the future all re-writing must be done together with the authors of the articles. Edouard grumbles.

3 PM: *El río y la Muerte*, Buñuel.

6:30 PM – 9 PM: Meeting with Sarris on Lex. Avenue, last checking of proofs. Edouard rewrote the first chapter of his (this time his own…) article. Must be reset.

"Arrest me, arrest me!" shouted the freckled boy. "Arrest me! I'm 65 years old!"— and he walked into the middle of the street, imitating an old man, to the great amusement and laughs of his friends on the sidewalk, on 42nd Street and Broadway.

The failure of the modern drama is not its rebellion against Aristotle, its supposed "untheatricality," but its triviality. Triviality. Whenever a drama reaches deeper, we don't care whether it is Aristotelian or not. It must be important to us, that is the first condition.

Sean O'Casey in *The Green Crow*:

"And let us realize that not one of us can mess up his life without messing up the life of another in one way or another. The saying 'He did no harm to anyone but himself' is out of the lower gospel. The man who can do no harm to anyone but himself is dead."

"A feeling for life rather than a sense of the theater is the first thing a man must have if he wishes to become a dramatist." p. 98, ibid.

June 7, 1955

We have moved our HQ to our place, to 16 West 109th Street. Siegel, he said he was a lawyer, called on behalf of some furious film-makers who felt insulted by my article in *FC* 2 ("Experimental Film in America"). The un-named film-maker, said Siegel, argued that my article could damage experimental film-makers' reputation in the country's universities. He referred specifically to my reference to "the conspiracy of homosexuals." He said, Maya

Deren University lecture series may be harmed by my article.

September 15, 1955

George said he overheard Anaïs Nin telling that she has proof that *Film Culture* magazine is sponsored by Moscow. Where else could the Mekases get all that money to publish the magazine and have parties at Waldorf Astoria? We fell on the floor laughing.

William K. Zinsser, in *Herald Tribune*, Oct. 2: "One day we were walking in a village in northern Siam, near Chiang Mai, a place where people make fine lacquer and ornate silver by ancient hand methods. It was a place of great tranquility, and we felt far removed from the strident tones of Broadway. Just then a sound truck came through the village advertising *Son of Sinbad*. Posters on the truck showed Dale Robertson triumphant—not only over his enemies but over a bevy of leggy beauties wearing almost nothing."

Kono, Japan's Minister of Agriculture: "The Japanese people would much rather see pictures than read. American films are very important in their lives and are responsible more than anything else for their ideas on America."

December 8, 1955

Meeting with Gunther. "Your magazine will never make money nor support itself. I don't understand why you should put your time or money in it. I just don't understand it. It has no future, this magazine, unless you change the content." (Gunther is one of the assistant or advising editors of *Fortune* magazine.)

December 9, 1955

A letter came from the attorney of the first issue's printer. He wants that we meet him to discuss how we are going to pay our bill.

December 10, 1955

Our new printer, Harry Gantt, is smarter than our old printer. He wants to be paid 2/3 of the costs before the magazine is out. That means we have to raise an additional $300. Brigante said: "I know you'll raise it, you always did." This is the only hope, old fool's blind trust. I called Herman. He did not have any advice. Edouard is making his calls, to his friends, or at least he says so. At the moment, or for a moment, I have nobody else to call. I'll go back to my notes, address books.

New York Times, Dec. 13th (from an article entitled "Creative Movies," unsigned): "...most of the serious amateurs are commercial artists, writers and painters who make films in their spare time as a means of recreation."

Oh, degraders of art!
The above quotation is typical of the thinking of many other writers (and speakers) on the experimental film, the avant-garde film.
On one hand, these writers are ardent crusaders for the art of cinema, on the other hand they are creators of a deep confusion. What with the endless flood of cheap and low movies from all over the world, it's an effort of Tantalian proportions to prove to anyone that film as an art exists and that a film artist exists too, and he doesn't create "in his spare time as a means of recreation" but from his deepest needs and from his concern for his art.
It is accepted that a poet or a composer creates from the inner need and passion and formal concerns; but it is still not understood that a Vigo, an Eisenstein, Anger, Broughton, or Deren are making their films from the same creative need, from their aesthetic preoccupations. It is not understood that a film artist basically isn't any different in his creative processes from any other artist. To make a film takes more

DIARY OF: MOTION PICTURES

By JONAS MEKAS

October 4—Finally, five years after its release in Europe, De Sica's *Umberto D* is opening in New York. Today, one can seldom see a more sincere attempt to depict day-to-day life on the screen. *Umberto D* is undoubtedly the ultimate expression of Zavattinian neo-realism—a meticulous description of a "slice of life." The film contains everything that is good in neo-realism—the engagement, the interest in everyday problems, etc. Inevitably, it also shows most of its artistic limitations—oversimplification and reduction of life to surface reality.

Though *Umberto D* is a successful work, one gets tired (both in films and the theater) of the continuous preoccupation with a detailed naturalism that lacks depth, imagination and vision. One misses the early Clair, Chaplin and Dovzhenko—all film creators instead of pedantic re-creators.

Intro Bulletin

A Literary Newspaper of the Arts

EDITORIAL DIRECTOR — Louis Brigante
ASSOCIATE EDITOR — Storm De Hirsch
BUSINESS MANAGER — D. Anthony Fusco

CONTRIBUTORS: Stan Baer, Alan Callahan, Eric Cashen, Scotti D'Arcy, Ed Diehl, Leighton Kerner, Lawrence Lipton, J. H. Livingston, Jonas Mekas, George Moorse, Joel Oliansky, John G. Randolph, Simon Vinkenoog, Eugene Walter.

Address all correspondence to:
BOX 860, GRAND CENTRAL STATION, NEW YORK 17, N.Y.

INTRO BULLETIN, 255 East Houston Street, New York 2, N.Y. Published monthly. Subscription: $1.00 per year. 10 cents per single copy. Copyright, 1957 by Louis Brigante. Printed in the U.S.A.

It was in *Intro Bulletin* that I began what three years later turned into the "Movie Journal" column in the *Village Voice*. *Intro Bulletin* was Louis Brigante's and Storm De Hirsch's heroic attempt to establish in the United States a newspaper dedicated to the arts, similar to some one could find in Paris. It had a brief, two-year existence before it succumbed under the piles of unpaid printers' bills. I usually keep my *Intro Bulletin* columns a secret from my friends because I wrote them before what I later described as my "St. Augustine conversion." My understanding of cinema, and especially that of the American avant-garde film, was still very academically and provincially oriented.

than "spare time," and it's far from being a "means of recreation." The film artist, like his colleague poet or composer, lives months and months with his film, like under a curse, trying to work out the right approach to the material, to find the right form, the right structure, to come to grips with it, spending all his time on it and with it and working for his bread in his SPARE TIME only.

No date, 1956

Sophocles about Euripides:
"He paints men as they are; I paint them as they ought to be."

(Re: Edouard): Who am I to judge how wrong or how right he is in the final consequences of his thought? I respect his almost feverish belief in what he is doing or saying, I do not doubt the sincerity of his intentions. The others, who are criticizing him, they are also making judgments and statements about everybody and everything, though they do this only in the name of themselves, just for the opinion's or ego's sake, for their self-contentment. Edouard, whatever he does or says, does it in the name of the society, he is always trying to relate his actions and thoughts to the society, to its highest ideal, to the dreams of humanity. No doubt, whatever he says is still personal, how else could it be! The difference between his critics and him is the purpose, the motive, the attitude behind his statements. The difference is between an unconscious selfishness and a fanatically selfless idealism.
One can do great things after one realizes one's own limitations.

February 9, 1956

Last night we three went to see Duvivier's *Return of Don Camillo*. Bad, except for a sequence with Fernandel playing in the frozen fields with the child. Duvivier revived for a minute.

Reading Maxim Gorky's *Reminiscences on Tolstoi*.
Yesterday, during my lunch hour met Jay Leyda, picked up his article on Richard III and Boris Godunov. Also met Melnechuck on 8th Avenue and 43rd Street, asked him to send his article on Hitchcock to Hitchcock himself for additional comments.
Met Arlene Croce, gave her to retype Brandon interview.
Reading Daudet. Working on my Pagnol review.
Roger [Tilton] called. One of his students, a Ukrainian immigrant, Listjenko, wrote an essay on Dovzhenko. Asked whether I want to read it. I said yes. He will mail it. Roger is re-editing *Jazz Dance* for the third time. He said he's searching for a script for a feature film.
8:30 PM Went to see a new German film, *Don Juan*, on Mozart. Good opening shot—camera pans and tracks revealing and establishing. Recently I have seen many bad films with good openings—*Man With the Golden Arm*; *Bad Day at Black Rock*; *Othello* (this one is O.K.). There is a good killing scene, death scene, where the count falls down (killed by Don Juan) on a red carpet. Camera on Don Juan, moves sideways like drunk, then in a sudden drunk circle pans in a blur over the blood-red carpet's close-up on the Count falling; and we see the red of the carpet only, like blood. The rest—just routine job.
Kracauer called. Said, it would be good to have some illustrations for his article. Wants twenty copies of issue N. 7.

February 10, 1956

Preview of Neame's *Man Who Never Was*. A military reminiscence thriller, slow-paced, unpretentious. Met Gideon, Suzy, and Dworkin. Dworkin said he is hearing many rumors about *Film Culture* which he doesn't want to say in front of others. I told him that I was not interested in stupid

Dovzhenko is dead..

people's comments or rumors. He is a dumb, plump, stupid film reviewer, and is becoming fat.

We went to the Artists' Club, 20 East 14th St., "cream of New York's art world," said Francis Lee.

We came about midnight. A large crowd of artistos drinking cheap wine and talking in small groups. There was no life at all, but you could feel something dead, like someone dead was lying somewhere in the corner. We could almost smell the corpse, it had been there for too long, unburied. "Where is the coffin?" asked Adolfas.

We spent an hour with a voluminous woman painter who said she painted abstract and is reading about India where she wants to go to "discover herself." I tried to persuade her—we all tried—to paint New York, what she knows, but she said that wouldn't be good for art (I was sure of that!), she wants to be "more universal," she can't bind herself to a place, she said. So, we said, certainly we can't bind ourselves to THIS place for too long, and we walked out into the night.

February 11, 1956

All day working on manuscripts for *FC* 7. Sarris came with Eugene Archer to help. Later Arlene Croce dropped in. Sarris was working on his review, we left him at midnight, locked him up in our room, so he wouldn't escape. When we came back, at six in the morning, from Stock's, he was still writing.

At Stock's a very young man showed his first documentary footage, random shots of Orchard Street.* Edouard hated it and started attacking him. The young man insisted that Edouard had missed all the subtleties of his footage. Later we read poetry. Fitzgerald was lying on his stomach on the floor and was murdering Shelley,

---

* As I found out, a good many years later, "the young man" was Ken Jacobs. He still remembers the occasion well.

with a tragic and weeping voice, Bob read Lorca, and Jerry read a good ballad by Bob, Jackson MacLow also read. It ended, as usually, with Edouard attacking America. To Edouard attacking America is a mantra, he repeats it at every beginning and closing.

Received summons from Pacific Printing, $723.91 unpaid, for the first issue of *FC*. Seven days' time to pay.

"There is no civilized or coordinated civilization left, only individual scattered survivors. Darkness and confusion as in Middle Ages."
—Ezra Pound (from a letter)

February 12, 1956

1:30 PM: Met Weinberg, went through all the corrections of his manuscript. He was happy with our corrections.

3 PM: At the Museum of Modern Art, saw Capra's *Mr. Deeds Goes to Town*. It's better than I expected. Grant is perfect for the part, does a perfect job.

Algis called. Said, Czeslaw Milosz translated one of my poems, was printed in *Kultura*, a Polish cultural magazine published in Paris. Algis started working for the Free Europe Committee. For money. Almus called, wants to meet, to discuss a TV program he wants to do.

10 PM: The three of us went to see *Boris Godunov*, at the Cameo.

Edouard said that all the talk about him being promoted at the Brooklyn Public Library was his invention. He fooled everybody, he played a big boss there for a few days, and everybody believed him, including his supervisor. You never know when he's telling truth or is just inventing. He is an actor, basically. He read today my poem on rain, in Milosz's translation, better in Polish than I did in Lithuanian.

All evening spent working on manuscripts. Earlier in the evening had a meeting with Weinberg and Fenin. Fenin said, Dworkin is gossiping to everybody about *Film Culture*, attacking it.

Called Richter. He criticized me for printing the essay on experimental film. He was also unhappy that I did not give him enough space.

February 13, 1956

It's getting cold again. And I thought the Spring was coming!

Reading Gorky's *Reminiscences* and Ortega's *The Dehumanization of Arts*.

Frank Kuenstler came with a bottle of whisky. Wants *FC* to publish his collection of short stories dealing with movies he collected from various sources. Said, he is ready to start his novel.

February 15, 1956

Saw Dratfield. He promised an ad for *FC*, for $20, in each issue, a good man. Told him about Frank Kuenstler's review of Picasso film, attacking it for its "leftist" commentary. Leo said: "Today the most intolerant and fanatic people are those who call themselves liberals." Frank called himself a liberal, the other day.

Rest of the day spent working on MS, selecting typefaces, etc. Sarris with Archer came. Went to bed at 2 PM, dead tired. Marie [Menken] stole from Luce's (*Time*) office a memo on us, four pages. Harmless.

February 16, 1956

Saw Pacific Printer's lawyer. Made an agreement to pay $25 every month starting this week. The debt is $750.

Called Leo to help with the layout of *FC*. He refused. Sick, has a cold, too busy, no time. Pranas is in the country, could not get to him. I have to do it myself again.

CHAPTER FIVE

... Leo and Edouard clash... Humberto Arenal... The sadness of American Pop songs... The case Lucy... Should I close *Film Culture*? ... Existential questions... I am lost, I am searching... A rendezvous with FBI agent... Plans to make a movie on the situation of the Black People in the South... The plight of a movie "critic" as compared to the literary... Themistocles Hoetis ... An idea to create an association of small lit. magazines... A drunk actor... Hannelore's aunt... Benefit at MoMA for *Film Culture*... Why I am doing what I am doing... I am in doubt of my life again...

Train ride to L.A.... A psychic foretells my future... About why I am keeping this diary... Donald Phelps analyses my handwriting...

February 17, 1956

Made three payments: $25.00 to Pacific Printer, $22 & $25 to the City Bank, against the loan we took for *FC*.

Got a terrible cold. Can't even speak, all kinds of sensitive spots in the mouth again. SNOW SNOW SNOW. But it's melting, wet and dirty.

A letter came from Vaičiulaitis, about *Idilės*. He wants to print them all in *Aidai* magazine.

Had to work late at Graphic Studios, came home after midnight, could not work on *FC*. On the way home, 59th St., Adolfas came into the same train, on his way home from a screening. At 110th St. we got out of the train, and Leo stepped out from the same train! Some coincidence, all three of us, the Blue Room!

We sat til 2 AM rambling.

February 18, 1956

10:15 AM: Delivered *La Strada* script to Weinberg.

11 AM: Screening of *La Strada* at the Museum of Modern Art, for *FC*. After the screening we sat a couple of hours with Jay Leyda discussing it (Leo was with us). Edouard did all the talking, Leo just sat there and listened without opening his mouth, and Leyda pronounced every two minutes or so one or two wise sentences, or syllables.

6 PM – 9 PM: Working with Leo on layouts. Leo got into a shouting argument with

Edouard. Leo accused Edouard of insincerity. He said, Edouard had no respect for the others. His attitude to him, to Leo, was insulting. Not that he minds what he says—he minds only his attitude. Leo was shouting with his face red, which he doesn't do often. Edouard tried to be cold and rational, but because Leo was right, Edouard felt a little bit uneasy. From the very beginning, when Leo came, around 6 PM, Edouard was teasing him, and there was a put-down in his attitude. Leo is too sensitive not to notice such things. We have always arguments with Leo, but we always treat each other as equals, as friends. Edouard thinks that Leo is much inferior to him and looks and talks to him as if Leo were a degrading object of some kind. With all his logic he so often underestimates the sensitivity of others. No respect for human beings. Humans are only means to spread ideas, for him.

10 PM: We went with Adolfas to Fifth Avenue Cinema to see Fairbanks in *Don Juan* and *Catherine the Great*. Boring, sleepy, except some sequences in *Don Juan*.

Francis Lee showed a telegram from Langlois in which he tells that Bardem was arrested and asks American film-makers and film critics to protest to Spanish government.

Bardem is the young (33) Spanish filmmaker who wrote *Welcome Mr. Marshall; Cómicos; Felices Pascuas; Muerte de un ciclista* and other films in which he takes social stand. He was also editor of a film magazine in Madrid. Magazine was closed two weeks ago. I happen to be the only one here who knows him.

February 19, 1956

I called Humberto Arenal at *Vision* magazine about Bardem. He will send me some material on Bardem. He said, he is not a communist but belongs to a leftist anti-Franco group.

Working on next issue of *Film Culture*. Arlene Croce came to help. At 10 PM we went to see *Umberto D*. The best sequence, to me, was the sequence in the early morning, when the young maid gets up, goes to the kitchen, puts the water on the stove, begins grinding coffee. The silent, lonely early morning hour, and her situation, the coming of a child, and no husband, ants on the walls, the sound of the leaking pipes— it all worked for me.

February 20, 1956

During the lunch hour I went to see Amos Vogel. He was very cautious about writing or signing a protest letter in support of Bardem.

Leo came. We were talking until two in the morning.

February 22, 1956

6 PM: Eugene Archer came to help proofread the next issue of *Film Culture*. Later came Sarris and Arlene Croce. We all worked late into the night. We all got into a long discussion because Andrew insisted that cinema is "not suitable to express loneliness." I argued against it, but I don't think I won.

February 26, 1956

After the war, people were wondering: how an intelligent nation like Germany could follow Hitler so blindly, etc., commit all the cruelties, to become a mob. You could travel through Germany, as I did, and talk with the same Germans in 1948 or 1949 and you wouldn't be able to believe (as I couldn't) that these same people were running crematoriums.

Now, these days, we are reading about the Autherine Lucy case in Tuscaloosa, Ala. The same community which just a month ago was an example of good interracial behavior, whites and blacks comingling and working brotherly together, this same community, suddenly, in the span of two

"I am not a civilized person — I shall never be a civilized person". Jonas Mekas

7 I. 1956.

Jonas Mekas

Jonas Mekas, Adolfas Mekas, Edouard de Laurot.

Photos staged by Eduoard de Laurot to publicize *Film Culture*.

NAPAPIIRI
POLCIRKELN
ARCTIC CIRCLE
CERCLE POLAIRE

weeks, became blind, racist, demagogic, unpredictable mob. How is that possible? America, Germany—it's the same. There is no stable, strong inter-living among people. Life is based on competition, business. It is a politeness for business sake only. If you give it a chance, if you dig deeper, you find hatred and selfishness: you find a wolf.

We drove to Usonia, with Gideon. Filmed Frank Lloyd Wright's house. Gideon said: "You can't use black and white & color one after the other because the audience will think about it, the audience will be conscious of the color."
I said: "Editing or shooting, b&w next to color, will work only if it's done not as an accidental thing but as an integral expressional means. Sure, the audience will be conscious of tricks, if color and B&W are used as a trick only."

February 28, 1956
A man sits in a luncheonette and gives a complicated order. He can't eat this, he can't eat that, he wants exactly such and such. The man refused the sandwich because it was on "whole wheat" and not on "white bread."
A nation of babies. A mature normal person can eat everything that's food (except mayonnaise, of course, which is NOT food…). What made his fuss really ludicrous to me was that there was absolutely no difference between two ersatzes!

Vicarus homini…
"creeping socialism"
Good people are seldom courageous here; only crooked politicians are.
Subway wisdom: "A cheap woman makes a better wife and you get the same thrill."

Listen to the sadness of the pop songs, on radio, played in factories, stores, in the streets, homes. There is a resemblance, in their sad melodies, to the sadness one finds in the folk songs of all countries, East European or Latin American songs. They go much deeper than just the words which often are sentimental and banal. The words may lie, but the melody doesn't. When I listen to the American songs, on radio, as I work—and at Graphic Studios the radio is always blasting—I almost tremble, how sad, somewhere very deep, the whole country must be.

Spring, 1956
I've always permitted myself to become deeply involved in all kinds of public projects (activities) which take more of my energy, time, attention and whatever else you can name, than my aesthetic activities. My aesthetic activities take place on the very margins of my life, on the very edges of my orbit.
My friends keep asking me: Why don't you just write, or make films? Why do you waste yourself!
How can I answer them? My life has been giving a different evidence of my character and my fate. The idea of being "just a writer" is a Utopian idea. It's in my character to give a great part of myself to the public activities, however useless they may prove to be. Maybe this is the only thing that gives me the inner peace and good conscience to devote the rest of my time to writing.
If life would only consist of yeses and nos! My life would be easy. The problem is that yesses and nos are only on the surface; deeper, they both come together. In the deepest depth, where Yes and No come together, there is almost no conflict. But I am not there yet. That's why I can't make clear decisions, Yes or No decisions. I know, some day I'll be able to make them. All my life will be a journey towards this single unanimous Yes vote. But it will come only after all the years of split vote of indecisions. This is not the question of dropping *Film Culture*—this is a question of my

whole being, my whole life, past and future, the question of HOW TO BE, and WHO I AM.

But today I am in doubt of everything. I lost my balance and everything is in motion again, all my beliefs, purposes, directions. What til now was GOOD and BAD, the very sense and purpose of my life is in motion. It's election time again. I stand alone.

September 30, 1956

A certain Mr. Kinney called. He said, he's from FBI. Wants to ask me some questions about somebody, where could he meet me. "Could we meet at Grand Central?" he said. "No, no. A man can get lost there. Let's meet in front of the Museum of Modern Art."

October 1, 1956

I met Mr. Kinney in front of the Museum of Modern Art at 12:30 PM. A man of about 35 of age, in a brown suit and a straw hat. Showed me his card, FBI. Wants to ask some questions about Jay Leyda. He asked if I know if Jay Leyda has made any trips to foreign countries since 1955. No, I said, I don't know, because I've met Jay Leyda for the first time only in 1956, and I never ask my writers about their personal lives or their past.

"Would Herman Weinberg know it?" he asked.

"I don't know," I said.

"Could you give me Weinberg's address?" I gave him Weinberg's telephone number.

"Is Richard Kraft also one of your writers?"

"Yes," I said, "he writes occasionally, he is a specialist in silent cinema."

The agent laughed. I don't know why.

"Would he know about Jay Leyda?"

"As far as I know they do not know each other. The reason is that Jay Leyda is the first class writer, and Richard Kraft is a second class writer…" I said.

The agent laughed again.

"Could you give me Mr. Kraft's address?"

"I don't have it with me," I said, "but I have it at home. I can give you all this information because it's no secret, it can be got in many ways. I have no problems doing this."

The agent looked at the paper sheets in his hand, scribbled with ink pen, and said: "Where is Edouard Laurot in this city?"

"He is at the moment in Europe."

The agent said nothing. He scribbled down Weinberg's telephone and made a couple of small notes.

"Can I help you with anything else?" I asked.

"No," he said, "That's all. Are you editor in chief?"

"Yes," I said.

He smiled, we shook hands, and he walked away.

You opposed the electrocution of Rosenbergs. But permit me to ask you a few questions.

Tell me, why did you oppose the electrocution:

1. Because you did not believe that they were spies?
2. Because you are against any death penalty?
3. Because he was a Communist, as you are?
4. Would you do the same if an Anti-Communist was condemned to die?
5. Would you do the same for a man condemned to die for killing another man?
6. Because you think that nobody should be sentenced to die for spying?
7. Why don't you protest against death sentences executed for spying (or other reasons) in Argentina, Spain, Russia?
8. Because these things don't happen near to where you are? Or because you don't care much about what happens further from your nose (what you don't see seems to be OK, even death executions?)???

Some of the happiest times we had that summer were during our jeep escapades into the Upstate New York and Vermont forests, together with Gideon Bachmann. That jeep later became the key protagonist in Adolfas' film *Hallelujah the Hills*, in which many of Peter Beard's adventures were based on our escapades. The original script of *Hallelujah...*, now lost, was actually made up from photographs we took during those trips.

In the woods, by a lake, I suddenly felt like a farmer boy again, jumping around, and climbing the trees.

October 19, 1956

Met Mr. Morsel from the National Association For Advancement of Colored People (NAACP). 20 W. 40. He pledged full support to our film on the South today; he will provide information on the South; we can use his name when we need. Gave us addresses of some helpful (he thought) people.

Mr. Emmanuel Muranchk (?), from Jewish Labor Committee (just came from the South). Unions which are sympathetic to Negroes: automobile workers (best bet), Fund for the Republic, Inc.

October 20, 1956

Hollander—TV rights, write to him.
- Get stock footage on Negroes available in NY.
- An advertisement in papers looking for backers.
- Get stock footage from the local (the South) amateur cameraman, etc., from the police.
- Contact that man from New Jersey.
- Get a letter from Dr. James etc. that we are on a trip to photograph materials for the University…
- Contact Van Dyke. Equipment???

October 21, 1956

Presented the idea of my film to Fenin. Jackie Robinson. Restaurant workers. Arenal. Negro churches. National Council of Churches of Christ; Black Eagle; Ebony (Allan Morrison; Amsterdam News, C.B. Powell; James L. Hicks; Jesse Walker; Southern Baptists; Urban League; William Faulkner; Oxford; Mississippi; Elia Kazan; Salvatore T. Covino, Boonton, NJ.)

October 22, 1956

Letters sent to Hafela, Covino.

No date, 1956

I am reading Coleridge's *Biographia Literaria*. Again, like many times before, when reading literary criticism, I am thinking of those great works of literature of which we speak with awe and admiration, and of critics who have such high standards to go by. There are always great literary works which serve as comparative landmarks, in perfection of form, style, language, construction. The long tradition of drama and poetry (same could be said about music and painting) help the critic to keep standards when discussing new works.

Oh, the poor film critic, wading through the Everglades, snake pits and junkyards of cinema! How poor he is, when compared with the writers on the other arts, how poor he is in his means & tools. His toolbox is not loaded with wrenches or rulers or other such things; no, instead, his tool box is full of ends and bits, fragments of future tools. So that, not having anything to go by, a film critic has to keep his eyes and his feelers and his intuitions wide open and wide stretched for anything that comes his way. There is not much hope for a literary critic to discover anything new while going through old literary magazines or books; but by re-seeing old movie classics, or just any old movies, a film critic each time is embarking on an adventure. A movie "classic" which at the time of its release was acclaimed as a masterpiece suddenly falls to dust and becomes just an historical footnote in the evolutionary chain of film art; and again, he sits and watches an old movie the title of which nobody heard before, and right there before his eyes a unique work of art unfolds itself.

Oh, maybe, after all, we are not in such a bad state, when compared with the literary critics! What is there for them new to discover? Only dust. I can bet they are envious of our excitement, of our adventures, of our Frontiers, where all kinds of treasures lie buried, waiting for us…

No date, 1956

The other day, after seeing Olcott's *From the Manger to the Cross*, W. S. Hart's *The Return of Draw Egan*, and St. Clair's *Are Parents People?* (1925), we had a long evening of rambling. Sarris found that these films, particularly Olcott's, were more than ridiculous—their acting, their directing, their simple (he said: uncinematic) construction, etc. The evening before, he had seen *Death of a Salesman*, the film version. He had many comparative arguments to back his opinions. I was sort of surprised and pleased with all three films. What is the secret, I thought, that the acting in all three films is still so real, and powerful, despite the space of time between them and me? I didn't find the films naive at all. I was watching them same way I'd be reading some old letters or memoirs, or an old book from the 17th century. I did not approach them with an expectation of art, but as pieces revealing the feeling and thinking of the time, in this case, *From the Manger*, the period of 1912. I did not reject or judge these films because of their "outdated" techniques as I wouldn't reject a medieval novel or an early work by Matisse.

January 15, 1957

Themistocles Hoetis: he lives by abstract principles of "individualism" and "independence," too weak to test them, to apply them to life, afraid to lose them. He is afraid of others, he really does not know what he believes in nor what he wants.

He laughed at us. He said we are "noble" and "courageous" and we are "with a mission."

Brigante and Themistocles were strongly opposed to my idea of calling all independent magazines to discuss the creation of an association, to help each other, to create a distribution center. No, they said, that would violate the principle of independence, that would take our independence away!

Who can take my independence away! I want to make business, he said (Themistocles), I am thinking in big terms, not small. I said: We are not interested in business, we are not interested in money, things must be done from passion and with passion, not money. They laughed.

It was refreshing, after they left, to see Fitzgerald, an actor with the Living Theatre, drunk, sick, beaten. He came in and collapsed in the chair, unshaved, hungry, sick. But he was human, he lived, he spoke the essence of life, a miserable essence that he was, but no business. It is hard to say to him anything now. He sat there silent, we understood each other perfectly. As a matter of fact, he said: "I have said already too much" although he spoke only five words since he came in. "Ask me some questions," he said, "how I live." "I am afraid," I said, "I am afraid I know how you live, I don't want to ask and hear what I think." "Yes," he said, "I know you know." "Where are you going now?" "Home." "Where is your home?" "Nowhere." "Where are you going, then?" "When you have nowhere to go you go nowhere," he said, "you just go."

February 20, 1957

for the PLAY—Hannelore's conversation with Mrs. Kaufmann.

"Is there any news in your relationship with your father?"

"No. Everything seems to be as it was. No worse no better."

"I think it is your own fault. I think you don't know how to talk and act with him. I think it is very easy, only that you don't seem to be able to do it."

"I spoke with him…"

"But you haven't shown him that you can stand on your own feet. You know, parents want…"

"On your own feet? Haven't I worked right after my divorce as a waitress in a restaurant? Then I worked in films, but there

Adolfas with George Fenin and his boy. Fenin served as one of the editors of *Film Culture* beginning with its first issue. He was also one of the editors of *Oggi*, the Italian language daily in New York, and served as the secretary of the Overseas Press Club. Thanks to him the Club threw a party at their Waldorf Astoria suite for the presentation of the first issue of *Film Culture*. Since it cost us nothing, we invited to it the entire New York film community. It was a big party with wine and stuff. Knowing that we barely had money to pay for our coffee next morning it was a good joke, we thought... but the joke was also on us: since it was at Waldorf Astoria, everybody walked away with the impression that the magazine had a rich backer, which made it more difficult for us to ask for money to pay our bills...

**I SEEM TO LIVE, VOL. 1
CHAPTER FIVE**

niW bnp yplↄ ot ɘtidW

Look through from other side against light

8x8

Rudolf Arnheim, Luis Bunuel, Rene Clair, H. G. Clouzot, Jean Cocteau, Carl Th. Dreyer, Marcel Duchamp, N. Gabo, Fritz Lang, Norman McLaren, Jean Painleve, Herbert Read, Mies van der Rohe, Jose L. Sert, James Johnson Sweeney, Josef von Sternberg, Herman G. Weinberg, Cesare Zavattini

invite you to THE FIRST PRIVATE PREVIEW OF HANS RICH-TER'S NEW SURREALIST FILM POEM **8x8**

in the auditorium of the Museum of Modern Art, on March 7th, 1957, at 8:30 p.m.

8x8 will be introduced by
SHELLEY WINTERS
BOSLEY CROWTHER
SALVADOR DALI
HANS RICHTER

for the benefit of FILM CULTURE, America's independent motion picture magazine, devoted to the aesthetic and social aspects of the cinema.

8x8 is a fairy tale for grownups, mixing Freud and Lewis Carroll with Venice, Venus and Old Vienna.

An impromptu art film by Gjon Mili on Salvador Dali will precede the screening of **8x8**

- -

Please send _____ tickets to the address below. My contribution ($5 minimum for each reserved seat, payable to FILM CULTURE) is enclosed.

NAME _____

STREET _____

CITY _____

ADMIT 1 P M 8:30

8x8 THURSDAY, MARCH 7, 1957 IN THE AUDITORIUM OF THE MUSEUM OF MODERN ART 11 WEST 53RD ST., N. Y. C.

PRIVATE PREVIEW OF
HANS RICHTER
FOR THE BENEFIT
OF FILM CULTURE

To help *Film Culture* pay its bills, Hans Richter premiered his new film, *8x8* as a benefit for the magazine. The screening took place on March 7, 1957, at the Museum of Modern Art.

Marcel Duchamp, Hans Richter, Robert Flaherty's widow Frances, Elsa Maxwell at the premiere of _8×8_.

Frederick Kiesler, Hans Richter, Lilian Kiesler, Alexander Calder at the premiere of _8×8_.

was no more work. You know. Is that not enough?"

"I don't know, Hannelore, but I wonder sometimes about you. You know you are already at the age when one half of your life is over. And you don't know what to do with your life…"

"But, Tante, I know it very well. I can't take any job. Don't you think they are very unhappy people? I need them. But they do not seem to be able to need anything, they are very unhappy. I want to help them. It's more important to me at this time than anything else. I thought that now, when they are separated also, they could need me at least. Or maybe they would find happiness in giving. Happiness through giving, to their own child."

"Look, Hannelore, so now I'm beginning even to doubt your sanity. I don't know what you are talking about. You want your parents to GIVE YOU! Instead of proving to them that you can stand on your own feet."

"Oh, Tante—don't you see that I can stand on my feet and alone. But it's not that that is important, at this moment, not me. It's they that I care. Don't you see that… What proof do you want? Does a woman have to prove herself that she is a woman? I will never ask my own child to prove herself. She is there, she doesn't have to prove me anything."

"Oh, Hannelore, I don't understand you. You are missing something, you are a dreamer, an idealist."

"No. I am very practical. Is there anything else less dreamy than to want to give your father or your mother happiness? Happiness through giving. It's only money. But money can be a medium through which they only can approach now, to change now perhaps themselves—nothing else exists that they can really understand. But they seem to turn away even from that, they want their unhappiness, I seem to be of no use to them, their own child. They do not know me, they do not understand me, they do not want to understand me nor…"

"Today my father said: it's your ex-husband who should give you money. He should be punished for that. You should do something.

No, I said, I don't want to dirty my hands. Someone else will do it. I just don't want. They will do anything just not to help me, just not to GIVE, just to keep in themselves, closed, with no opening to the others, to their own daughter. No communion. Oh, if you only would know how much that hurts me.

March 7, 1957

Introduction to *Film Culture*'s benefit screening of Hans Richter's film *8×8* at the Museum of Modern Art:

Good evening, distinguished guests, ladies and gentlemen. I welcome you in the name of the editorial board of *Film Culture* magazine.

First, I have to make a correction in our program. Unexpectedly, Miss Shelley Winters had to leave for the West Coast to participate in a new production. She regrets not being able to be present this evening and sends her greetings to you, to the distinguished speakers, and to Mr. Richter.

Just a minute ago, Miss Winter's telegram arrived, which I would like to read to you: (text of telegram)

This evening we are celebrating a double occasion: the first screening of Hans Richter's new film poem *8×8*, and the second anniversary of the magazine *Film Culture*. We have worked hard during these two years to create a publication worthy of the young and dynamic art of the cinema. I believe, we have done something in that direction, and we shall continue also in the future to serve as a free ground for the outspoken and constructive analysis of ideas, achievements and problems in the domain of the film.

KEREN KAJEMET LEISRAEL TRÆ-FOND
genplanter skovene på Israels bjergskråninger til
minde om Theodor Herzl, zionismens grundlægger.

With many good wishes

for Christmas and

the coming year

1959

With sincere greetings

Carl Th. Dreyer.

I want, further, to express my gratitude to Mr. Hans Richter, who has donated this evening's proceeds to the magazine. And I also want to thank those present here, who may want to assist further in the growth of *Film Culture* magazine by making use of the check you will find enclosed in the complimentary copy which you have received this evening.

We are privileged tonight to have with us the creator of *8×8*, Mr. Hans Richter. Today, when so many of our film-makers seem to be losing their individual personality in the making of their films, we need more than ever to appreciate those who do keep their creative individuality intact. Mr. Richter is one of these.

Now, it is my great pleasure to introduce to you the distinguished lady, known to all of us, our Mistress of Ceremonies, Miss Elsa Maxwell.

April 20, 1957

Saw Mr. Powell and Mr. Hicks from Amsterdam News about making a film about blacks in the South. Their suggestions:
Dr. Kenneth Clark, EN-9646, just returned from the South, was sent by a church group; Philip Randoff, 217 West 125th Street; Belafonte's agent: Mike Merrick.

"La culture naît sous forme de jeu, la culture à l'origine est jouée."
—Johan Huizinga

Spring, 1957

SCRAPS
"That is, I should never act in such a way that I could not will that my maxim should be a universal law."—I. Kant

IV.438: (categorical imperativus)
"Act according to maxims which can at the same time have themselves as universal laws of nature as their object. Such, then, is the formula of an absolutely good will."—I. Kant

"Thus the first proposition of morality is that to have moral worth an action must be done from duty. The second proposition is: An action done from duty does not have its moral worth in the purpose which is to be achieved through it but in the maxim by which it is determined."—I. Kant

No date, 1957

Hollywood (America) is emotional & "stupid," and therefore is more open to the image language of cinema. The brainy Europe is de-visualizing cinema, it's all literature there.

"If you are idle, be not solitary; if you are solitary, be not idle."
—Samuel Johnson

Found text:
This typewriter must receive special care in deference of its great age and culture!!! fuck you all this is a good language for an old machine like this a no place no place for poets said the old man and died he was full of age and shit so it was OK but this machine has only age plus it can't talk but it will do I guess that ripper Harry bless his balls if he has any I mean

September 3, 1957

We need more Puerto Ricans to destroy the efficiency.

"What is your name?"
"My mind is slowing down a little. I don't remember names too well," said the old woman, in the bar.

Thomas Moore condemned John Frith to be burned alive at the stake.
Then Thomas More wrote UTOPIA.
And then the King stuck his head on a pike and exhibited it on the London Bridge.

"Non si debbe desidere lo impossibile"—L. da Vinci

deserts burn without fire, without flame

"A writer must be close to madness when he dreams, and close to reason when he writes."—André Gide

"You have changed your mind!" said Edouard.
"Will the clock 'change its mind' because in an hour from now (we have 1 PM now) it will show (be at) 2 PM?" said I.

"false problems"

Leonas Letas: "It's easy to exploit someone who is in a state of trance."

"L'homme sensible moderne ne souffre pas pour tel ou tel motif particulier, mais, en général, parce que rien de cette terre ne saurait contenter ses désirs." Sartre, *Baudelaire*, p. 40

No date, 1957
Am I doing them (my social activities) only from sheer lack of will power? Am I only a powerless instrument of the others, going where the stream carries me, driven by chaos?
Is it all really coming from me or am I a puppet? Shouldn't I turn back to myself and look for the real self? But how will I know it! How can a self see oneself? I am doubting everything now. To begin with a doubt. How true it is. Cogito ergo sum.
I say, I have to continue *Film Culture*, despite all the problems, all the debts; despite the fact that I have to work full-time, and often overtime too, at Graphic Studios, to keep the magazine going; despite the fact that we walk around hungry, live on coffee. We say, the art of cinema needs it! Isn't it true that probably we ourselves need it more than the art of cinema.
So I am writing again. But it has always been so in my life. My writing is part of myself, an inseparable part of my existence, it's all in the stars. The writing is a voice through which I can read & see some of my inner directions, voices which otherwise I neither see nor hear—directions and decisions of which I have little control. All my life has been a debate between me and the typewriter, it is the only way I seem to be able to move ahead. But today I am in doubt of everything. I lost my balance, my inner balance, and everything is in flux. All my beliefs, all that until now was "good" or "bad," even the very sense and purpose of my life. I stand alone, trembling and insecure.

I have no love anymore, no understanding, and no compassion for the society as it is. I am driven to some other society, some future dream. I have to find myself or else nothing has meaning what I am doing and any act of destruction would have more positive content than any so-presently-called positive action.

We were riding on the Fifth Avenue bus, I and Frances. I said: "Yes, I could drop everything. But wouldn't that be an easy way, an escape? Couldn't I grow stronger by embracing what it is?"

"For salvation
cannot be planted like a tree.
And the Heart's Mirror
hangs in the void."
"Satoba Komachi," by Kwanami

December 30, 1957
Rest.
Find a new apartment.
Get a part-time job for the summer.
Get a teaching job for the winter.
Get a suit.
Publish Lotte H. Eisner's book.
Finish *New York 57* script.
Publish *Nusiraminimo Gėlės*
Visit Mississippi and Red Mountains.

Organize a FILM HOUSE in New York for 16 mm and classics.
Try to settle finances.
A used car?

No date, 1958

I stood by the window. I looked at the chimneys across the street, at the people. No, I can't reach them. I can't place myself into their place, feel how they feel. Where am I? In what dream?

I want to be like them! How foolish.
I am reaching into the emptiness. For what? Communion? Communion with emptiness is impossible.
Or am I exaggerating?

The noises from the street are coming to me. Voices from the garage across the street. The Puerto Rican children kicking paper boxes along the street.
I am sitting, sad, beaten, lost, and I do not know what to do. I just sit, with my eyes open to the window.

March 24, 1958

New York Times
"The deterioration of large numbers of young people robs the city and the nation of priceless human resources vitally needed in this critical era. The cost to the country in crippled skills and destroyed talents runs to countless millions if not billions of dollars each year."

Money!

Kirillov: "Everyone who wants the supreme freedom must dare to kill himself. He who dares to kill himself has found out the secret of the deception." (*The Possessed*, p. 115)
Kirillov, ibid: "Everybody thinks and then at once thinks of something else. I can't think of something else. I think all my life of one thing."

1958 *Atlantic Magazine*
Berenson: "The fruit of my life was my loafing, not my work—when I was woolgathering and satisfying useless curiosities. I didn't prepare myself for anything but my voracious appetites for the useless, such as reading anthologies of Greek and Provençal poets. I never feared wasting time."

"Never discuss works of art except in their presence," he says in repeating Goethe's dictum.

Someone sitting alone in his empty tiny Brooklyn flat and playing harmonica or mandolina, like Brody.
Yes, there was no war!
Leo looks at his hands: he can't play violin anymore. We all look at our hands, not knowing why Leo is looking at his. He didn't tell us why he was looking, he told me that later. Yes, there was no war!

April 2, 1958

Dear Mr. McMillan:
Adolfas Mekas of *Film Culture* has asked me to answer your recent letter. Midway in the production of *Swamp Water*, Darryl Zanuck removed Jean Renoir as director and substituted the late Irving Pichel. However, Renoir's contract required that he be listed as director, hence the credit you saw. Renoir probably shot about two-thirds of the picture.
This was the famous occasion when Renoir, in parting, said, "Well, Mr. Zanuck, it's been a great pleasure to work at 16th Century-Fox."
Sincerely yours,
Richard Griffith
Curator

April 30, 1958

Pittsburgh
With everything behind him now, he looked at the passing landscape. It was flat and

PAUL ROTHA.

Cliffords Inn
London E.C.4 England

March 23rd 1958

Mr Jonas Mekas
Film Culture
215 West 98th Street
New York 25, N.Y.
USA

Dear Mr Mekas

On receipt of the February issue of FILM CULTURE, I am more
pleased than I can adequately express by your appreciative review
of PATHS OF GLORY.

Kubrick's magnificent and brave (in these days) anti-war film,
couched in the most deeply-felt human terms and loaded with astringent
irony, surely ranks alongside Renoir's La Grande Illusion and Pabst's
Westfront 1918 in its denunciation of violence as a means to an end.

Technically---by which I mean its use of the camera, microphone
and editing process---I find the film perhaps the most brilliant to
come to us from the United States in these post-war years.

I am glad that FILM CULTURE, too, praises without stint this major
work which I have not ceased to do in public and in private since I
saw it three months ago, when it held a 5-weeks run at one of London's
main West-End cinemas.

Whatever Kubrick does next, he has by this one film secured for
himself a place alongside the world cinema's most worthwhile directors.

Sincerely,

Paul Rotha.

boring. Bushes, empty fields, stores—the same and the same.

Once he saw four horses standing in a green field. Their heads were lifted. A flock of sheep grazed on a hilltop.

In the morning he passed a river. It was covered with mist. He felt a longing for the river of his childhood. Later, as the train cut through a town, he saw the same river again. Now it was murdered, crucified in the maze of factories. The sewage pipes were running down into the river, vomiting poisonous yellow contents.

Ah, the river of my childhood, he thought. The river of my childhood was cool and abandoned, it lay in the stillness of the forests.

At night, there was some rain. Now, as he passed through, the trees and the grass were under water. There were also a few large yellow flowers.

On the train, at midnight, six hours from Chicago.

The monotonous sound of the train has numbed and exhausted me. When I am on the train, or in a car, I slump into a half-consciousness, totally withdrawn.

I let my eyes glide, not looking but simply keeping them open to the landscape as it passes by without really looking at it. All seems very mysterious to me, not very real—the cars passing by, faces, the trucks, the heavy sound, everything moving from somewhere into somewhere.

I sit there, numb, tired, feeling the perspiration on my face, drinking coffee in the bright silent roadside diners, half-dazed.

I am on the train now and I think about all those hours and nights spent in buses, cars, trains, drinking black coffee—this late night, on another such train, carrying me further and further away.

I put the light out and I try to sleep. I cannot. Emotions and thoughts pushed out of their routine orbits, keep coming up from the deep, swelling up, as the train is cutting deeper and deeper into the Iowa night. I look at the black landscape, flat, grey and dark.

This tiredness, this monotony, this being nowhere makes me feel a part of something else. I dissolve slowly into the Iowa night, I become almost one with it, undistinguishable, unthinking, only vaguely feeling my own being—as the train keeps cutting through the sleeping cities, forests and rivers.

May 1, 1958

Today I have understood that my responsibility, my engagement should be, primarily, to myself. Only through myself can I be responsible to others. This realization relieved and freed me. It relieved me from the constant tensions caused by a never ending, never satisfied abstract sense of responsibility to others.

I know where I come from (New York).
I know where I am going to (L.A.).
But I don't know where I am now.
That's Zen for today.

Who in this city of light and sadness is searching for salvation, truth, final answers? Is there anyone who doesn't sleep nights thinking about the meaning of this city, this night, the sadness, himself?

May 14, 1958

Los Angeles
From: Rev. Jeanette Bradtke, 11425 Elliott, El Monte, California
You have been working too hard until now, on many things. Don't PUSH so much. Saturn caused your life—until now—to go up & down, like the stock market. But with August your life begins to go suddenly UP and will go so for 9 years (that's how far I can read one's future). To get the most of this you have to develop more—and I advise you like a mother, since you don't have one here—to develop your masculine

side. You have it in you, but people do not see it. Let them see it. You have a face of the actor Leslie Howard. You are a book worm. Until now you were getting books into yourself, and now you'll begin to get them out. You will be a great writer, you are a born writer, although you equally could become a great painter, also. Top temperamental character suitable for an artist. There are books of verse, plays, philosophy and religion that I see. Many of them, many.

You are always learning, schooling yourself, growing. You will be very good in research work, exceptional talent for research in science. Your books will live on forever. You will be a very happy man.

May, June, July will be very busy months, you will start many things, important things, and then will come the harvest, from July on.

You will have a better place to live. You will settle down during these three months (?) in your home, happily.

You'll be invited soon to a large house. There will be a discussion, probably business discussion. Be masculine, be strong and you will win luck.

Also, there is another business meeting soon, probably with MGM. There are many businesses going in your future. Get your body ready for the 9 years cycle. Take exercises. Your mind is 30 miles (years) ahead of your body. Your body is very young. Work on it now, it will bring you success among people.

I see in 3 years from now a patent, and idea, an undertaking, that will come into focus. You were working on it, and you are working on it now—but in three years you will get it out and it will be a very important thing that will make you very famous. There are also 3 people connected with it that I see, in this situation.

Also, in 3 years, you will create a work that will be so great that it will shake the world, and I really mean it, it will shake the world and it will be a great work of success. All this will require from you great strength, get your body ready.

You are a very ambitious man. All your ambitions will come through eventually. Because you have a great confidence in what you create and what you do. This confidence comes from the fact that this is not your first life. You have brought with you the experience of several other lives which helps you do what you do and make you confident. Your creative power came with your birth. It is UNIVERSAL therefore FOR EVERYBODY. You will have two more partly pioneering years. But then the fruits will begin to fall.

You will have a very good health, there will be no accidents in your 9 years (that's how far I can read one's future)—the only health trouble you'll have is with your teeth. You have very strong feelings towards someone at this moment. Your wishes will come through.

I see you very clearly in my circle. If you ever need help, think of me, I will catch your thought and I'll give you advice.

I will never forget you. More than anybody else. You are a very wise man.

Saturday, May 17, 1958

Los Angeles
INSERT
ONE can be beaten by the sun, monotony, and boredom. The flowers, trees, and hills can become a threat. Faces you once dreamed about—the idyll!—become a burning desert. A desert that burns without a fire.

NO illusions … no illusions … And don't renounce old friendships! And look into the eyes! No more illusions. The flowers have always betrayed me, always in the middle of the heart!

SO I pick up the stick and I begin to swing it, left and right, across the blue petals and the green bushes, right and left, swinging over the sun-beaten landscape, the hills and the valley, beating again and again—the peace!

—blue sky! The flowers fall broken, and the leaves... But I stand and I can feel how the hills and the sky breath the same tired monotony. A bird whistles in a tree. There is no wind.

NO, it is not me that needed them, no. It was always the flowers and the landscape and the hills that wanted me, my life. They have always exhausted me to the last drop of my life—and I have stuck to them—fool's fidelity!

PAUL lifted the broken stick of wood and he threw it angrily into the green peace of the trees. A few broken leaves fell silently on the burning summer hill.

May 19, 1958

With Adolfas, we went to James T. Farrell reading. Mostly he talked about Murray Kempton's book, what a good writer he was. Gave him *Film Culture* N. 2, asked to write, he said he'll think about it.

Me: "Your book, *Studs Lonigan* is a great piece of literature. What do you think Hollywood is going to do with this book? I heard it was bought for a film."

Farrell: "I don't know... I sold it to Hollywood because I have to live."

I keep writing. I feel this is the only thing I can do now. I cannot talk to anybody now. Or, more truly, I don't feel like talking to anybody. I sit in the corner, looking at them, and no thought comes to my mind, no feeling. They are there, but they mean nothing to me, nothing. Only when I sit down by my typewriter, I am able to begin to concentrate, I begin to talk, even if it is only myself that I am talking with. But this is the only way to break this deadly status quo, to try to get myself out of this mess, out of this night. As I talk with myself, things become clearer to me, I begin, if nothing else, at least, to get some courage to make another step, be it what it may, blindfolded.

Spring, 1958

Art? Subtlety? Their minds work only on 14pt. bold, and caps.

The construction and style of *Madame Bovary* grew out of, was necessary for the exposition of the bourgeois mores of the period. The young angry men of London and New York have to work out their own style and the most effective approach, even technology, if they want to make a dent (not talking about destroying) the royalism and capitalism of 1958.

Ortega y Gasset on yellow, drugstore literature: People read it in subways, etc., they are so engrossed in it because this literature, these books are full of action and very little description, these books have the true approach to writing, he says. But do they have the right approach to life? Is the hypnotist the best artist? Not everything that is effective in itself, on its own terms, is good for man in the wider human context.

There are those who entertain, and those who want and crave to be entertained.

There is nothing wrong with seeing any film or reading any book, good or bad. Unless one has something else to do. When you have something to do, no book or film is worth anything.

No critic has right to advise one not to read a book or not to see a film or play.

Charm, June 1958, editorial:
"...And, if instead of holding back you move into one of our new free-form silhouettes, you'll move into This Day and Age. If you make the decision to be not the age you are, but the age you're in, you can make a generous person-to-person impression, live your own summer of 1958."

Spring, 1958

Analysis of my handwriting by Donald Phelps
Ambition under effort. Inner strength and enthusiasms push him forward rather than

will power. No original will power drive. His talents push him. No great working ability and probably difficulties in first half of life. Tenacity.

Impairment in right eye. Something of a sacrificial nature. Decency and certain selflessness.

Tendency to overpowering emotions. Music, poetry, tone, sound. Highly intuitive, sometimes even up to psychism. Humanitarian ideals. Healing faculties, benevolence, interest in the occult.

Romanticism. Be careful with scandals and intrigues, also through women. Unfavorable for political activities. Aspect of getting involved.

Lack of emotional discipline. Tendency to sex or emotional bondage. Getting under the domination of a woman and losing his own will.

Irritability, great nervous tension, sometimes exposed to unexpected and violent incidents as accidents (?), violent fever (?). Opposed to all tradition, lack of emotional discipline.

Personal charm, dynamic personality, idealism, faculty to make valuable contributions to groups. Creative faculties, music. Very original and independent ideas. Quick of association, good memory. Faculty to express himself in writing and speaking.

Decisiveness in acting and success aspect. He could reach a very high position in his field. Desire for quiet life in later years may lead to renunciation, substantial success and moving.

Teaching abilities, intense mental abilities. Knows his inner values. Verbalizes well. Occasional lack of self-confidence and courage. Slight tendencies to resentfulness. Too many projects and unjust of his evaluations of people and situations.

Great creative powers. He is exposed to intrigues. Aspects toward female sex not too good. Women in his life not too good friends. Can get obsessed with a woman. Highly sexed.

CHAPTER SIX

... Beginning of filming of *Sunday Junction*... I don't dream anymore... On bad Hollywood movies... Synopsis for a movie on escapees from a Dictatorial Country ... The happiness and the movies of the Twenties... Edouard vs. America ... Recording highway sounds... Poetry of the highway nights... Adventures in trying to film in gas stations... Police... About books for Miltinis... Kuenstler's party... Diane Arbus... More problems with locations... On Lindsay Anderson... We are broke and hungry... Edouard and Pamela Moore... Dos Passos on James Dean...

I am a regionalist... On Lithuania... Peddling my play around... I begin working at Cooper Offset... Mary Frank...

May 29, 1958

From 9:30 AM – 11:30 AM I work at Cooper Offset.

Delivered Adolfas' manuscript—*Christmas in Toronto*—to Grove Press.

For two hours sat on phone making calls for Edouard's film. He says, I don't take enough initiative for *Sunday Junction*, his film. So now I am making all these calls. Spoke to Nathan Zeller, about editing facilities. I met him in my Hans Richter class, at the City College. Now he has his own editing studio. Also spoke with Leo Seltzer. He's teaching at Columbia. Asked if he has any students who could volunteer to help Edouard. Instead, he offered himself...He said, he wants to work on something interesting, is bored with what's happening in New York cinema these days. We are meeting on Monday.

Mary [Frank] called, apologized for last evening. We visited them on Wednesday evening. The place was full of drunk poets and I don't know what. Tried to talk to Robert, but he showed little enthusiasm. Maybe it was Edouard's very "socially minded" and "intellectual" tone that set him off. Anyway, the time was wrong, the place was full of jokers, semi-Freudian jargon, and beer. So now Mary wants me to come and eat with them, she's very embarrassed, she said, the evening went out of control.

We are intensively looking for a new apartment. Made many calls. Too expensive, in

most cases. Met Weinberg at the screening of *Parisienne*. Bought Sartre's *Nausea* and *Evergreen* N. 4.

A sign in the bus: "Three / 3 / out of five / 5 / fires are caused by a careless cigarette or a careless match." Underneath somebody wrote with pencil: "and a hot ass"

June 2, 1958

Edouard is trying to get a helicopter for the aerial shots. The N. Y. police don't want publicity, they are still delaying permission.

Writing letters to film producers and directors, asking if they have any access to film equipment that we could use—sound recorders, lights, dollies, tripods, etc.

"Your inner strength is masked by your outward gentleness," said the woman, who asked for a sample of my handwriting.

Studying "Farms for Sale" in *NY Times*. Decided to buy a farm of 2 – 3 acres, near New York. There must be a brook or a lake. And a BIG house. Many good offers in the paper, from $1,300 to $130,000... Met Glushanok.

Perfect films:
Casablanca
The Burglar
To Have & Have Not
Naked Dawn
Slightly Scarlet
Horse's Mouth

Academy of Nothing:
Dr. Minto, The Cosmic Barber, Joe Jones, Dick Higgins, Storm De Hirsch.

The Kingdom of the Gods, Geoffrey Hodson
Thought Forms, Annie Besant

"All Americans like to steal." Herman Weinberg

No date, 1958

Sometimes the horror grips me:
I haven't dreamt lately, I don't seem to remember my dreams any longer.
I am afraid to walk barefooted even in the room, as if some terrible microbes were waiting for me—or I'll step on glass splinters.
Television voices outside; the window open all night—
Am I really losing, slowly, everything I had brought with me from the Outside? The touch of the grass?

June 2, 1958
(Entry by Adolfas)

Writing letters to film people:
"We are writing to you as a person who is not interested in art or culture. We don't want to advance the art of cinema, we don't believe in social significance. We are interested only in business. We want to make money," etc.
Bachmann had a head-on collision with his motorcycle. Today he got out of the hospital.

June 11, 1958

Nathan Zeller insists on written document, made by a lawyer, signed, which should be given to each of the participants on *Sunday Junction*. He can't understand our objections to it, the uselessness of it and senselessness of it. "It is like with marriage," he said, very seriously and very honestly, beating us with his very honesty. "If you go and look for a ring, if you buy a ring, it means you are serious about it, you really mean it." And he meant it. Our unbusiness-like attitudes were beyond his understanding. He loudly exclaimed his surprise when we told him how Peter Weiss is making his new feature, reel by reel, how we are sending film rolls from here, and how he shoots whenever he gets some more of our stolen film stock, etc., and how we never count our change. Zeller

- Weegee (Arthur Fellig) 250⁶? W.47th St
- Silvia + Alan White   1135 First Ave., N.Y.C.
- Elizabeth Van Blarcon White
  171 Harding Rd, Glen Rock, N.J. R.1407
  GI-56659   The Coliseum House N.Y.23
- Weinberg 228 W.71st St. TR-3-1000 N.Y.23
- x Williams - SU-77714 ; 213 W 66th
- x Dr. W.C. Williams, 9 Ridge Rd, Rutherford,
  N.J. WE-90669
- x Orson Welles, Motion Picture Center, 846
  N. Cahuenga, Hollywood, Cal
- x Herbert Wolfe, NYC AT-94483 48
  48 105
- x Orson Welles 1027 Chevy Chase Dr.
  Beverly Hills, Cal Calif.
- x Richard Watts Jr. 920 Fifth Avenue, N.Y.21
- x William Wyler, 1121 Summit Drive, Holl., Calif.
- x Ray Wisniewski , 18 Spring 80
- x Orson Welles ,1144 Tower Road, Beverly
  Hills, Calif.   1958. March.
- x Shelley Winters TR-41504 27
                     271 CRWest

kept wondering. What was beating us, really, when we later talked about it, in the car, was that Zeller's surprise and exclamations were real. It was unimaginable to him, he hadn't met till now anybody who dealt with people in any other way but business. He thought that that was the only working relationship possible between people. "This is a new world to me," he kept repeating.

June 14, 1958

I hate mamies, Mamie Eisenhower & all mamies—those plump, stupid, round businessmen's wives, political wives, tourist's wives. I hate their plump mamie-bodies, their fruit-tomato-hats. I hate the ideal good American wives, flat, moon-faced, as they look at the camera, cutting into the birthday cakes, stepping down from the airplanes, caressing the cows.

July 2, 1958

It was too hot so we went to 42nd St. movie house, air-conditioned. Saw *Marjorie Morningstar* and *Badman's Country*. *Marjorie* is a mawkish film based on Wouk's mawkish book. It's supposed to be a typical portrait of New York Jewish life, but there was none of it. Direction and acting amateurish. They could have explored visually the camping scenes, but they didn't. Gene Kelly seemed enjoying himself with a few lines directed against producers and America. Otherwise, film did not go anywhere and it's hard to tell what's all about. One thing was clear: it advocated to young people to engage themselves in successful businesses and make money instead of letting yourself be guided by your imagination and drives. A typical conformist theme. Don't rebel.
Badman's Country got our spirits lifted up a little. Edouard liked Montgomery's black shirt—it's well designed, he thought...
Had an Irish stout at the bar, and went home.

Edouard to Sarris: "You are a case of those few American intellectuals who are able to rise above the system and who reject that system, they see its inhumanity, find it insufficient, etc., but are caught in the constant dialectic: on one hand he rejects it, on the other hand he wants to be accepted by it, he wants to prove that he can be successful also on its terms."

Exupéry said that real friends are not those that give to you but those who demand from you.

No date, 1958

"American people... are so unforgivably mercenary they worship any one who makes money, no matter how it's made."—*Tribune*

INSERT
A radio calling for help.
They are being followed.
In the plane, inside, three men.
Unshaven.
One is wounded, talking in fever.
They escaped from a Dictatorial Country
after several years of imprisonment,
war prisoners.
Finally, free!
The stars, the stars of their childhood,
in the sky. Free.

They talk. But they are tired. They talk
about the dreams of their youth,
when they were students together.
Intercut: Gaudeamus Igitur.

They are calling free countries. Calling for
help. They are being followed by the planes
of the Dictatorial Country.
They listen to the radio. They hear about the
books being burned in their own country.
They hear about the Atomic bombs stacked
for a new war.
They are just coming home, finally, from the
previous war.

They hear on radio talks about possibility
of another war.
Eh, boy, from the prison camp into the
army again…
The radio speaks, they listen. The man on
the radio asks:
Should we risk to endanger our good
relations with the Nation X (The Dictatorial
Country) because of these three men on
plane?
They listen to the angry discussions of some
senators. We want peace, they say. Why
should we risk our peace? We have a good
peace going.
They talk. Not much. They are tired and
disgusted & disillusioned.
They are being followed. They are calling
for help. They appeal to humanity, to the
whole of humanity.
The wounded man is in fever.
The pilot is tired and sleepy. The other man
takes the wheel away from him and
turns the plane upwards, into the sky,
into the stars,
into the stars of his childhood.
The pilot wakes up, he gasps for air. He
realizes what is happening. No, he says, no!
You have to face reality. Someone has
to face it and tell the truth, every day.
Such is reality of reality!
The other one succumbs, exhausted.
The plane is turned to normal position,
homewards.
The senators are arguing, on the radio.

The pilot speaks to humanity.
They are being followed.
They are calling for help.

An idea for a short documentary:
PRIVATE INITIATIVE IN A COMPETI-
TIVE CAPITALIST SOCIETY
to show, just simple documentary scenes,
a blind man selling pencils in subway entrance
the whole film could end right there, after
that one long, long, maybe 2 minutes, shot.

or add: a blind musician with accordion on
the street.

July 6, 1958

Sunday
Saw *Yankee Doodle Dandy* (Michael Curtis)
and *Sergeant York* (Howard Hawks), with
Cooper.
For years now, when watching old movies,
those of the twenties and the thirties, I
was wondering about the strange charm
they have. Even if they are badly made,
you can look at them and they still make
sense and have something to communicate. Now, if a contemporary film is badly
made (and most of those which are well
made)—they turn your stomach.
I think I am coming close to the truth now.
When watching these two movies—far
from the best—I could feel a certain balance of mood and purpose—a certain
balance—clarity—of happiness. It is a
naive, childish happiness, but it is undisturbed, innocent. That's what America was
in the twenties, and it is reflected in its
arts, that simple naiveté and innocence. It
has a certain charm because, basically,
there is no evil in it. Now, when you watch
a film like *The High Cost of Loving* or
Marjorie Morningstar, there is no more of
this innocence. There is a pretentious,
neurotic blabbering, with no balance or
happiness, it is 100 percent America of the
1945–58, the innocence fell to pieces
when the Naive Child fell into the illusion
that he has to lead the world, give the
ideas to the world, pronounce big truths.
The arrogance, vulgarity, ignorance,
banality, tastelessness, pretentiousness,
ugliness.

Edouard: "Immigrants to America do not
'adjust' to America, they rather resign to it.
They live in a state of resignation."

Reading V. Yermilov's *F. M. Dostoyevsky.*

A Poem Welcoming Jonas Mekas To America

This night's first star, hung
high up over a factory. From my window,
a smile held my poetry in. A tower, where I work
and drink, vomit, and spoil myself for casual life.

Looking past things, to their meanings. All the pretensions
of consciousness. Looking out, or in, the precise stare
of painful reference. (Saying to the pretty girl, "Pain
has to be educational.") Or so I thought, riding down

in the capsule, call it elevator lady, speedless forceless
profile thrust toward the modern lamp, in lieu of a natural
sun. Our beings are here. (Take this chance to lick yourself,
the salt and stain of memory history and object.) Shit! Love!

Things we must have some use for. Old niggers in time on the
dreary street. Man, 50 . . . woman, 50, drunk and falling in the street.
I could say, looking at their lot, a poet has just made a note of your
hurt. First star, high over the factory. I could say, if I had any courage

but my own. First star, high over the factory. Get up off the ground, or
just look at it, calmly, where you are.

A Poem Welcoming Jonas Mekas To America, by LeRoi Jones [Amiri Baraka].

Arlene Croce at a picnic, 1957. She was barely 22 when I met her. But she knew and loved cinema and ballet, and she was a very good writer. I immediately drafted her into *Film Culture*. Satyajit Ray wrote me that her review of *Pather Panchali* was his favorite of all. Later she became the dance critic for *The New Yorker* (1973–98) and wrote a definitive biography of Fred Astaire and Ginger Rogers.

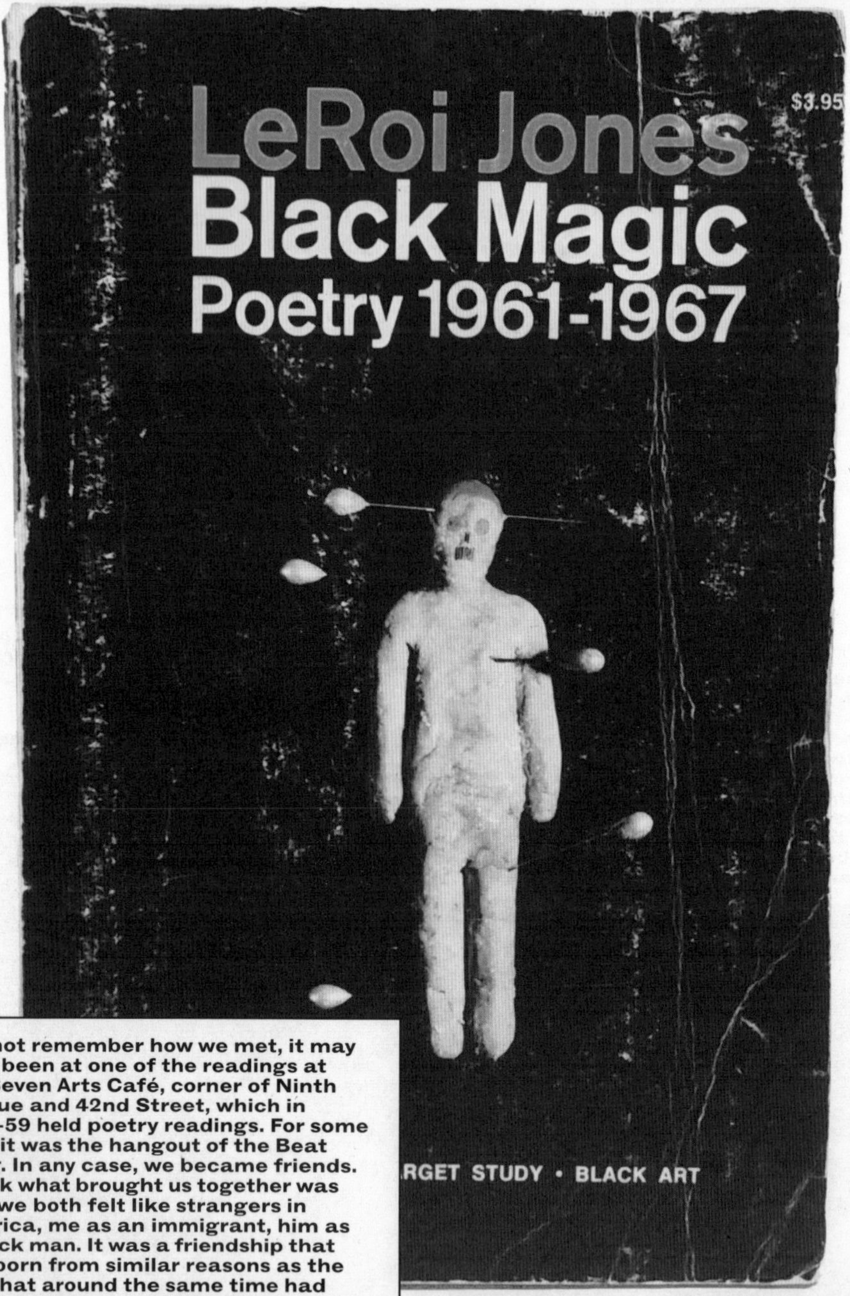

LeRoi Jones
Black Magic
Poetry 1961-1967

$3.95

RGET STUDY • BLACK ART

I do not remember how we met, it may have been at one of the readings at the Seven Arts Café, corner of Ninth Avenue and 42nd Street, which in 1957–59 held poetry readings. For some time it was the hangout of the Beat gang. In any case, we became friends. I think what brought us together was that we both felt like strangers in America, me as an immigrant, him as a black man. It was a friendship that was born from similar reasons as the one that around the same time had developed between Maya Deren and myself. We were both (Maya and myself) from Eastern Europe, with only a couple hundred miles separating our child-hoods.

At some point LeRoi came up with the idea that we should make a film on William Carlos Williams. We visited the good doctor of Paterson and talked about the idea. Williams found it of some interest, and during the following weeks I had several phone talks with him, and so did LeRoi. But I got somehow distracted by *Film Culture*, which was demanding more and more of my time, and the project sort of faded. There may be some notes on it in Williams' archives.

LeRoi Jones

PHOTO BY DANIEL DAWSON

TELEPHONE WISCONSIN 7-6266 EDWARD FISHER, LICENSEE

STERLING EMPLOYMENT AGENCY

251 WEST 42ND STREET, NEW YORK 36, N. Y.

DATE 6/24/57

EMPLOYER'S NAME Yale Transport

EMPLOYER'S ADDRESS 460-12th ave

REFERRED TO Mr. Sullivan or Mr. Juliano

INTRODUCING Jonas Mekas

FOR ~~TEMPORARY~~ PERMANENT POSITION AS Helper - 1-5 PM

SALARY $1.50 hr

KINDLY REPORT: EMPLOYED YES_____ NO_____ _______________

EMPLOYER'S SIGNATURE

TO FACILITATE OUR SERVICE. PLEASE INFORM US WHEN POSITION IS FILLED.

In true arts the quest is always for a new form-content relationship, and not for a new form.

Infernal adjustment…instead of internal adjustment.

Edouard: "Today emotions replace spirituality."

Jonathan Baumbach, GE-6-9786

Edouard in "Atlantic Gap":
"The culture cannot be 'transferred' onto the next generation through 'cultural' activities, works of art, or even the artists as such, but must be inherited as a manner of giving life a meaning: the way in which a whole people lives and expresses its conception of human destiny. The profound significance of cultural unity is that, not only each work of art, but each human life, has a meaning that transcends its own existence towards the universal, and thus may be apprehended as at once individual and universal. Now if in a given society the meaning of a particular existence, of its actions or the objects of its actions, is not translatable into the terms of a cultural universal, such an existence will tend to seek its entire significance in its own fleeting appearances: man will vainly strive after self-realization through anarchic individualism; there will be attempts to seek the truth of actions in the immediate products of activity; and, in art, form will recede from content."
"Cultural heritage, then, is primarily a condition of the soul, a way of 'feeling' the world…"
ibid: "To the degree then that the Salesman understands the Saint, he ceases to believe in salesmanship as a credo of life."

July 10, 1958
We placed an announcement in *Show Business* telling that we need actors for *Sunday Junction*. Now they are calling and calling, there is no end. They all want to act, they are all unemployed. It's hard to be hard on them. They persecute me wherever I go now, I hear their voices, I hear the telephone ring, desperately.
Last night we went sound hunting (as I closed the door, I heard the telephone ring—it rang when I went out, too, and I could hear it through the open window: THE ACTORS!)
We stood over a bridge, upstate New York, at midnight, listening to the poetry of the highway. The big, heavy trucks, approaching, thundered by, the tires singing, the red back lights glaring into the night. The gasoline trucks, and trucks carrying cars, other cars. Then a silence. Then a stream of light slowly lights up the rock, on the bend, as the car approaches, from a distance, a lonely, single car, fast and alone it passes the night.
We climbed on the rock and looked at the road stretching to the right and left of us. We submerged into the mystery of the night road, of lights and sounds, and our own thoughts.
A police car stopped and checked what we were doing. The man was good and didn't bother us too much. Adolfas calmed him down with a few phony papers. Show them a paper with a signature, letterhead, etc., and everything looks serious and proper. You can go and dynamite the bridge.
We screened the rushes at U.N. Hammid, a good man, arranged it for us. First break we got in a long time. What was most amazing and strange, was the dead silence, a feeling of sterility that pervaded the whole place, and the badly, outrageously designed ground floor. Your own voice sounded dead. How can one work in this atmosphere? I don't know. So—the results! We were glad to leave the building. We took a fresh breath of air when we got outside, hurriedly. *Mertvye Dushi!* (Gogol)

July 11, 1958

Edouard: "Did you buy the plug?"

Jonas: "No. I said I won't buy it today. I have no money. Perhaps tomorrow."

Edouard: "How much does it cost? Ten cents?"

Jonas: "But I don't have even ten cents. I only have one token to go to work tomorrow."

(Silence.)

Edouard: "If somebody would hear this conversation!"

July 14, 1958

Edouard (on phone): "What happened to you? You said you'll call us."

Sarris (on phone): "Oh, I could not. I have problems, you know, girls, women…"

Edouard (on phone): "Yes, in America love is always a problem!"

Later that day:

Garage attendant: "Is this a diesel car? Don't you have difficulty getting oil?"

Edouard: "Look, you Americans are always so afraid of everything."

Attendant: "What do you mean? We are not."

Edouard: "You are always making 'problems.' If I have a diesel engine I'll always get oil, one way or other way. There is no problem. I was in Poland, in Czechoslovakia with this car, and I got oil. If there was no station nearby, I put the car across the road, blocked the road. If it wasn't enough, I put also a girl beside the car, or two girls—and I got oil from the trucks. They always helped. Or I drove into the army barracks—they had to give—what can they do? But you always make problems of everything."

Epimenides, poet and a prophet, slept 57 years.

"I do not search, I find." (Picasso)

POE:

"The Poetic Sentiment, of course, may develop itself in various modes—in Painting, in Sculpture, in architecture, in the Dance —very especially in music…"

"…to attain that pleasurable elevation, or excitement of the soul, which we recognize as the Poetic Sentiment."

"…this certain taint of sadness is inseparably connected with all the higher manifestations of true Beauty."

August 7, 1958

I was wondering, when I came back from work, where they were. Now Adolfas called. They went to New Jersey with Sarris' brother and took his plane, for some air shots. Now they are stranded somewhere in Conn., in some marshes. Something went wrong with the plane, not enough gas, or something. Adolfas is sitting in the Atlantic Airport waiting for them.

Adolfas signed contract with Criterion Labs. They will develop and make work prints and final prints, etc., for a 75 min. film, 40,000 feet of negative. Without any business talks. The owner said, Oh, I am no businessman, just give me some paper to sign. So Adolfas wrote a contract and he just simply signed it. How many people like that are left in America?

August 14, 1958

Yesterday at Paris theatre we screened our rushes. Harrison Starr was not too happy, complained that he does not know enough about the film, how can he feel a part of it. Harrison: "I am as great a director as you are." (to Ed) Very insecure, always trying to be on even. ("I can fly, too" —after Ed said he took some air shots.)

Maya, with her big beautiful eyes, came to see rushes. She said she wanted to be in the film, but she is leaving for L.A.

We thought, last Sunday night, driving home through the heavy rain (there are no windshield wipers on Edouard's car, we could see nothing, so we stopped in a gasoline station and waited till the rain subsided a little)—

we thought we will write letters to some of the better writers inviting them to contribute one sequence to the film: give them a chance to tell what they really want. And then we thought, there was no one that we could ask. Nobody seems to want anything to say. The names that came to our minds —Farrell, Steinbeck, even Nelson Algren, Miller, R. Wright, belong to the other generation. And what about our generation? We felt quite abandoned in the rain.

Edouard: "There is nothing better than a perfectionist."

August, 1958

Got up at 8:00. At work (Cooper Offset), 9 AM – 1 PM: Went to NY University, to see Dr. Gargen, tried to persuade him to get N.Y.U. to sponsor *Film Culture*.
1:30 PM: went to see Ed Manelli, at Gaevert, he wasn't there.
2:30 PM: Letter to Lotte Eisner.
Went to Post Office.
Bought some fruit.
Retyped "Iskusstvo Kino" article.
8:30 PM: saw a stupid British comedy, *The Truth About Women*, walked out.

"Our film," said Edouard, "is like that drop of water that runs down the dry roof: it selects the lowest, easiest places, and it changes its course as it runs down."

August 18, 1958

Gideon: "I wanted to ask you something, maybe I shouldn't ask it, but…how are you getting along with Edouard?"
Me: "One has to understand people in order to get along with them. Edouard? I am willing to pay a price to work with intelligent men, to speak once in a while with an intelligent and uncorrupt man, living in this desert. Sure, I disagree many times with him, and we argue all day long —but so what?"
Gideon dislikes conflicts, like all Americans. Any disagreement (personal) is taken as a disaster, break-up, separation, kaput— because of them they give up friendships, marriages, etc. etc.—they run from life into their tower of "personality."

Last night, returning home late from shooting, found Leo's family. They were visiting some friends in New York, but could not find a place to sleep. We gave them our beds. We sat with Leo late into the night, and we rambled about our lives and old friends. He said he received a letter from Miksys with two words: BIM-BAM. As we grow older, we thought, it is the truth that becomes the most important thing. To be truthful, to live truthfully, to support truth. Maybe I make mistakes, but I do what I feel I should do, no more time for compromises.

I watched gas station attendants, in the early morning, standing in the empty station, leaning, looking at the empty road, in the early sun. There is great poetry in this early morning image, something that one can experience only in a country gas station in the early morning—the largeness of the space, the silent gas pumps, a truck parked on the side of the station, the horizon, a passing car, the smell of the wet gravel, sound of the gravel, the morning.
We were shooting the gas station sequence. As Edouard drove, with Adolfas sitting on the hood with the Arri, against the traffic, a police car came, they were waiting, hiding somewhere. "I am arresting you," said the cop. He took Edouard to the police station. It took half an hour to clear up the situation. "They could not understand why we are making a film without being paid, just for the love of making it," said Edouard later. "The policeman even called his superior on the phone and told that to

... somewhere in Upstate New York...
Adolfas recording highway sounds...

I SEEM TO LIVE, VOL. 1
CHAPTER SIX

him, asking, if such a thing is possible, that someone would make a film without being paid."

Excerpts from the conversation with the cops:

Cop: "Film is like fiction, you know, it's not necessary."

Us: "But fiction is necessary. Do you ever read books?"

Cop: "I read once a fiction. I did not like it. A book on geography, yes, it's necessary. The food is necessary. Or a telephone book. But not fiction. Everybody can write fiction —idiots, even communists can write fiction."

Edouard, later: "It's very hard to be anticapitalist."

August, 1958

We took a few shots from the Motel on the Mountain, the highway web north of us.

We were hunting sounds all night long. But now, suddenly, something went wrong with the tape recorder. Edouard and Adolfas are using their ingenuity trying to fix it. "You can never trust these delicate machines," says Adolfas. "I knew it would happen, it always happens when it's borrowed," keeps repeating Edouard.

We left town yesterday around 11 PM. Two hours from New York, in New Jersey, we started recording sounds. On the roadsides, in the gas stations, from the car windows; trucks, gas pumps, tires. Adolfas is in charge of the machine, and Edouard is just jumping around, as always. I, myself, I am mostly an onlooker.

There is a great poetry in the highway nights. The sound of the passing trucks, and cars. The moon high above the trees. The lights. The crickets in the grass. The hugeness of the landscape, the constant stream of cars, singing of the tires.

Around 5 AM we reached Harrison's shack in the woods. The forest night was full of mysterious noises. The morning birds were shouting like hell. And there was a deer or some other animal walking close by in the bushes; we could hear it walking over branches. A cricket was singing very loud in a crack by the shack's door (we recorded him)—and we spent some time trying to catch him, or just to see him, sneaking on him with flashlights and trying to lift the piece of concrete under which he was hiding. No, you can never catch a cricket, that's clear. We got his singing though, we got his voice, all right. But as soon as we got out the flashlight—he was suddenly silent.

They are still trying to fix the damned machine. The cars are beginning to light their lamps, and the sun went down half an hour ago behind the hill. It's still bright, though. But it's cooler now. The cars are zipping by. Occasionally one stops for gas, and the old man, in white shirt and white pants, gets up from his stool and goes to the car, attends it, changes the money at the counter, and sits down again on the stool, by the door. He sits there silently, watching the highway, looking at the hills North.

August 20, 1958

For some time now, for more than a month perhaps, I am carrying in my pocket a letter from Miltinis, asking to send him two books to Lithuania, an art encyclopedia and Reisz's book on editing. Occasionally I send him a few books. He, no doubt, thinks that we are rich by now, or at least rich enough, editors of a film magazine, film people, you know, and in America! But I am carrying this letter for weeks now and have no money to buy the damned books. How could I explain to him that we have no money? Knowing me, he, no doubt, would believe me, but I feel ashamed to tell him this. I don't know why, though.

Today I went to Holliday Bookshop, 119 East 54th Street. I displayed the letter of Miltinis to the owner of the Bookshop and asked him if he couldn't donate the books. "How could I sink my money into Soviet Lithuania," he said. "Ford is making money, and so do the whiskey stores, but I barely survive." "Not Lithuania, but Miltinis," I said. "It's the same. I can't." "You see," I said, "because I am in America, they believe, there, that I can afford the money to buy them books. The more that they need them, it isn't easy to get them there." "Why don't you say to him so, why don't you tell him that this country is no good for books, that bookstores are starving, and that you have no money, and that this is America!"

Still, I can't pull myself together to write him the truth. Am I ashamed for myself or for America? I don't know. To buy books… I passed a food store, I saw apples, and plums, ripe, in the window. I have been dreaming since my childhood: "Someday I'll eat plenty of fruits… I'll eat and eat and eat until I will not want anymore…" It's still a dream.

A few years ago I had illusions that this is all temporary, that we'll be able to eat whatever we want, someday. Today I have no such illusions. I know very well that whatever money we'll have we'll sink it all into the films, magazines, and what not, walking with gurgling stomachs. Such is our nature, and our fate. We are not businessmen, we are artists and this country, they say, is not for artists—or is there such a country at all?—But I realize this, and I know this, and I have no regrets and no reproaches… It is my own choice. I don't really envy those who eat grapes, or plums. I have a different calling in life, and different duties, different pleasures, dreams. My life is made of different dream stuff, I guess.

August, 1958

Late evening, beautiful summer night. A beer party at Kuenstler's girl's place. A lot of poetry talk, beer, music (from the radio through the open window, loud, from the apartment across). With Diane [Arbus], sitting in the window, on the window sill, where some wind, some draft was coming in with some night cool. Ah, how beautiful are the summer nights of New York, we said. There was something very special, to sit in the summer night window and see lights in the apartments across, and not too much car noise tonight, so quiet, except the radio from the window across, night music.

August 25, 1958

The manager of the Texaco station on the New York Thruway (fifty miles from Albany) said, "No, you can't film here." He wouldn't take any responsibility, he wouldn't give us a permit. "What if something happens, if somebody is hurt or…" So we packed up and left.

We got through the toll gate without paying. Adolfas went to the gate and displayed a pile of various signed papers. They meant nothing, most of them were negative answers to our requests. But they looked important, the signatures and the stationaries. It's amazing how much this means in America. I thought it was part of the Gogol's Russia, but no. Oh, the power of a piece of paper, of a meaningless piece of paper!

Joe's joke for today: "There is a new car this year: a pervertible."

We looked at the landscape, the hilltops, the mist floating over the dense woods. A picture from Fenimore Cooper. And then we looked at the mechanical, hostile faces staring at us, the servants of the New York Thruway gate boxes. It is almost impossible that they can keep their hostility and business-mindedness in face of all this breath-taking nature—but they do! It doesn't affect them, they are immune to nature.

We drove, Saturday morning, to continue our gasoline station sequence. "When I

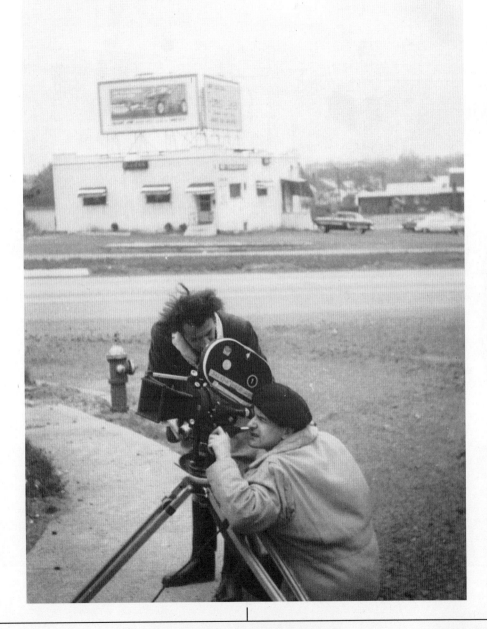

Edouard de Laurot, Adolfas during the filming of *Sunday Junction*.

arrived," said Adolfas, "they didn't want to give the station any more. They became suspicious about the film. That was expected. It is a pity that the bad weather prevented us from finishing it sooner. No words can persuade them now." Adolfas spoke with them, and nobody wanted to take any responsibilities. We made calls to several officials, with no results. O'Connor himself came finally, a fat slob. From him we found out the amazing stories that are going around about us. We're supposed to be shooting a film in which girls are sucking at the nozzles of the pumps; men are walking all made-up (!); it is an indecent film; girls were seen walking in bikinis; etc. "Why was one of the attendants sleeping?" he asked. "He had a spell of respite," said Edouard. "What is 'respite'?" asked O'Connor. "Rest," said Edouard. "Oh."

"They are primitives," said later Edouard, "there is no way of communicating with them. They meet everything with hostility and suspicion."

Edouard: "The definition of barbarity is that barbarity destroys all established human values, goes against those values. And that's exactly what Americans are doing. Wherever they go they bring their ersatz and destroy the true values."

We were driving along 14th Street. We had to suddenly stop the car. A well-dressed man, in his fifties, was walking across the street, and he jumped back. As we stopped, he continued walking safely, then stopped, looked back and said to us: "You scared shit out of me."

"And I thought you are a gentleman," said Edouard. He meant his language.

It is always like that: you look at somebody here, at a face, and you think: yes, perhaps, yes, here is an intelligent face. It can't be that everybody thinks about money only. But as soon as he (or she) opens the mouth, the gentleman and the intelligence and the hope is gone, the shit comes out. It's always the same story.

Last Thursday we met Collins, the British film editor. We talked with him about our film which he wants to edit. Then he began to give us advice about the business side, since we knew "about it so little." When we told him that we hate contracts and that nobody who is working on *Junction* has any contracts, he said, "I think you should make a contract among you three. Just to protect yourselves. You never know what can happen, even among friends." We started laughing. It was so ridiculous. As if money would be of any importance if the friendship would break. "Our friendship is tested," I said. "It cannot break because of arguments simply because we have arguments every day." Edouard said: "You see, the trust depends on the degree of intelligence. Only among people of minor intelligence contracts are needed."

Collins jotted a few notes on paper, what he would like to have in his contract. Among others, he wrote that he would like to have "a single frame credit." "Fine," said Adolfas. "Write this down." And we all laughed, but Collins could not get it. "You see," said Adolfas, "if we would be businessmen, we could get you by this contract and you would get nothing from us: you would get only one frame credit—that means literally one frame—and one frame on screen is invisible for all practical purposes."

August 27, 1958

After this weekend's unsuccessful attempts to find a friendly Texaco station, yesterday, Adolfas and Edouard went to see a certain Mr. Appay, the head of the Texaco publicity department, in the main office in New York. He didn't seem to know anything about our filming in Conn. and was on the cooperative side. He thought that this will be profitable to Texaco, publicity-wise.

He said, Texaco will cooperate, will give a station, etc. Last night Adolfas wrote a special script for them, a gas station sequence the way Texaco would like to see it, which had nothing to do with what we were shooting. A sweet script. Mr. Appay liked it. He even said that Texaco may give some money.

Today Mr. Appay called, in very official and brisk voice. He said that he got in touch with the Boston office and that we have to present to him the complete script, etc., he has to know what we are really doing. He said, he had informed all Texaco stations to keep us out. Mr. Appay was angry. "I didn't know you were shooting for weeks already," he said.

August 30, 1958

The story of making *Sunday Junction* is becoming more complicated and more enlightening than the film itself.

Last Friday, after Mr. Appay's call, in which he forbade us to use any Texaco station for filming, we thought that that was it. While waiting in the car on 43rd Street I got into talk with a gas station attendant, a German, a certain Hans. He got interested in Edouard's car. "Do you know anybody who runs a Texaco station?" I asked him. "Oh, yes," he said. "My good friend Kelly is an assistant manager of a Texaco station in Tarrytown." After more talking, der gute Hans called his friend in Tarrytown and made arrangements for us to shoot in his station. We went to check the station, and it was O.K. So we came home, got lost somewhere in Queens—got the wrong directions across the bridge, those signs are so goddamn confusing, we spent a whole hour, at midnight, in dirty, sad, desolate streets.

Saturday morning we packed up and with all our actors arrived in Tarrytown, at the station. The manager was already giving us the uniforms, when there was a call from the district manager. The manager was making his routine check, without any intention of finding us there, but the manager was so proud of the fact that we came to shoot a movie in his station, that he couldn't resist the temptation of telling the district manager about it. And that did it. District manager gave him real hell. What, those guys are shooting again? He told him to throw us out.

No breaks. The manager, though, happened to be sort of human. At first he resisted. "All I can do is to send you to another Texaco station," he said. "Look, give us only the uniforms. We'll go somewhere else and nobody'll know that you helped us. Look, we are also working for a company," we lied, "and if we come home without the footage we'll be fired, that's for sure." This did the trick. We got the uniforms. "Only don't shoot close here, because the district office is right here," he said. He gave us the address of a friend of his who had a small private gas station, also Texaco. So we went there. The station was miserable and small, and a tall big tree was standing in front of it, blocking the sun and throwing shadows, was difficult to match the previous footage. We were tempted to cut down the tree. Anyway, it was quite a problem. We shot most of what we shot in close-ups and from the roof.

Friday evening, when scouting for locations, we stopped at the Thruway police offices and we found a very good spot for long shots that we needed to end the sequence, so we went right there, since we couldn't get any long shots in the small Texaco station. We shot the whole series of shots right under the noses of the Thruway police, with the protection of two policemen, real jokers, and good men, comparatively. If Mr. Appay would see this, we thought, he'd fall dead. Under their very noses, and with the police protection! Tomorrow, we bet, they will meet the Texaco people and they will say: "Oh, there were some guys shooting a movie here

Edouard de Laurot in an argument with the Highway Patrol...

yesterday, with Texaco uniforms and all, and we helped them." We'd like to see their faces and the faces of the Texaco people!

Finally, finally we completed this sequence, if that can be called a completion. We were driving home and singing like crazy.

September 2, 1958

In the evening, yesterday, we stopped at Adventure Restaurant, in N. Jersey, a place we call the J.D. [Juvenile Delinquents] Breeding Farm. We took a few "establishing" shots, surrounded by a threatening crowd of J.Ds. They were shouting, jumping in front of the camera, making funny remarks, and demonstrating their hot rod cars equipped with six carburetors and other such things. When Edouard picked up one soft looking young James Dean for a small scene, they almost beat him up: why him, why not us! Immediately there were half a dozen James Dean-looking J.Ds., with jackets and with their necks pulled in, in a typical James Dean attitude, unshaved. It was amazing.

As we were finishing the scene, a heavy big hulk of a man (I thought he was drunk but maybe he wasn't) squeezed to us and said: "I am the father of the star," (pointing at James Dean...) "I want the footage back, or you sign a contract with him." He started talking big talk, big money. Edouard said he couldn't care less, he will reshoot the scene with any other boy. The big hulk continued grumbling and shouting and pushing around, while his son, who was a gentle, soft boy, stood on the side, seeing his hopes being demolished by his greedy father. I tried to console him, telling, that we won't listen to his father, that we may still use him. Meanwhile, the Big Hulk got into a fight with the policeman whom he accused of not protecting his child, and with the jadees who were making jokes about him from sympathy with their pal James Dean. Police had to break up the crowd several times. This time we were really happy to have the police protection. And we were glad to get out as soon as we could.

Edouard thinks that Finland is the only country in which you can take any pictures any place today and nobody'll ask for your passport.

Edouard: "When you are torn between two choices, take the most difficult one, and you'll never make a mistake."

Edouard: "Lindsay Anderson was sneering at people in Oh! Dreamland. He should have had sympathy, compassion."

Yesterday we went to New Jersey, to take some air shots. A certain Jerry, from Tarrytown airport, agreed to help us out. He wanted $12.00 per hour, but we got him down to $10.00, because that's all we had. Our expensive money! We are carrying some bread in the car, we break it piece by piece and we eat it, when we are hungry. I always thought this to be true: as long as one can be happy just by eating plain (impure American) bread, one is all right, one is not lost yet.

The plane was small and rickety, a two-seater, just enough to squeeze in with an Arri and the battery. The plane took great pains to lift itself into the air, but it managed somehow, although it went right and left, up and down, quivering and ricketing. I was waiting by the car, in the airport. First time in my life I forced myself to drink coffee from an Automat, I was so thirsty. With sugar, and hot, in the machine —bloody machines, they have, as one of the workers said, "a whole bunch of them in that room," soups, sandwiches, hot...

Again the theme of trust came up, as every day, it's Edouard's pet subject. "You can never know how much you can trust an American. I still haven't met a single one I could really trust. In Europe, I know: there is a man's honor, or tradition, or religion, etc. The four poles are always clear. But here, there is no base for any trust. He will come to you tomorrow and he'll say, 'I have changed my mind.' Just like that. Because for him there is no firm basis inside not to change his mind. One never knows what he'll do tomorrow."

Driving out of New York Edouard hit me suddenly on the back with his hand, wakening me from some dreams. "You look as if all terrors of our recent life got suddenly reflected on your face." Then, after a while: "I think we shouldn't have any reproaches to ourselves. We have done everything we could, nobody could have done more in our place—we risk our health, our youth, everything, on *Film Culture*, and on this film. And we haven't had any breaks, no breaks at all. These last two months have been really tough to me, one letdown after another, one betrayal after another. Someone else in my place would have committed suicide or ended in the asylum."

September 7, 1958

Something terrible must have happened to Edouard.

He came Friday evening all shaken up.

"Terrible thing has been done to me. It's impossible, it's impossible," he kept repeating. We never go into the privacies of our lives, we have always kept a certain distance to some parts of our lives, we always respected each other's privacy, and so it remains now.

We went for a ride, just to move. We bought some vodka and we stopped on the Riverside Drive and drank some.

He started talking, but stopped and started to cry.

"I know, theoretically I know that I should be strong and keep it inside, all inside. But my body refuses. An ignoble thing has been done to me. Years of my life ruined. It's always the trust to people that betray me, my idealism. I am like your wolf, in your story." The tears were rolling down his face.

It's amazing we reached the house safely. He felt a little better by the time we reached our apartment.

"I had to do it. I could not hold it any longer," he said.

He went to sleep but I could hear him all night walking.

September 8, 1958

I dropped a note to Pamela Moore telling that I have to see her. Tonight, it must have been around 3 AM, telephone rings.

"I am Pamela's husband," the man on the phone said.

"I want to talk to Pamela," I said.

"You can tell it to me, whatever you have to say," the man said.

"No," I said, "I want to speak to Pamela personally."

The man got suddenly very angry and started shouting.

"This is a democratic country of liberty. I will give you Pamela, but I order you to tell everything, you hear me? Everything! This is my order!"

The man sounded like a mixture of an hysteric army general and a boor.

He finally connected me with Pamela. She sounded tired and low. Her voice was kind and without anger. I told her that Edouard's state is horrible and that maybe she could help him. As I was saying that, the telephone was pulled out from her hands and the man's voice came again, in same hysteric tone.

"I know you want more money from her, you and that idiot Laudanski. He has terrorized her long enough, the immature girl. He got from her already $20,000. This is the end. If he'll continue bothering her I'll take some measures. There is a law in this country." And he leaped again into a long tirade about democracy and freedom. Then he lapsed into a series of curses, first English, then in Polish. I hung up.

September, 1958

One should never trust an ex-... who instead of joining a more revolutionary (progressive) idea (movement) retreats to the conservative, accepted ideas and movements. Never trust an ex-communist, ex-Trotskyite, any ex-.... There is little faith in a man of that kind in anything, he can be easily a traitor of any cause and of anything.

"What will you have to drink with your main meal?" Do I divide my meals into "main" and "secondary?"

"A rat can't throw up," said a worker in Central Park who was preparing a little poison-breads for rats. I was questioning his labor. I thought, rats aren't that stupid: if they feel that stuff is poisonous, they will vomit it out. But he said no, they can't do it. But so it is with man, when it comes to ideas.

"My objection to the royal symbol is that it is dead; it is the gold filling in a mouthful of decay." (Osborne, quoted in *Encounter*, Oct. 1957)

"And God said to Jonah, Doest thou well to be angry for the gourd? And he said, I do well to be angry, even unto death."

September 15, 1958
(a note I left with the doorman)
Dear Pamela:
I have decided to make one more attempt to reach you. You have to meet with Edouard, you have to talk to him. You might be able to help him. During the last three months he has gone thru a very deep emotional crisis, practically, a nervous breakdown. And I don't know how to help him. Thus I want to meet with you and see what could be done to help him. I am making this last appeal to you.

No date, 1958

"Pour un réalisme socialiste," par Aragon, p. 50:
"Cependant, au milieu du brouillard d'idéologies et de contradictions où nous nous débattions, de Dada au surréalisme, il fallut des années pour que la conscience me vînt, et à la plupart de mes amis, que ce n'était pas la simple affaire d'exaltation, mais une part de notre tâche propre d'écrivains, que de travailler à renverser ce monde qui nous révoltait."

"Autrement: La poésie doit être faite par tous, non par un."

Napoleon, from a letter to Cambacérès, Arch. Chancellor, Berlin, Nov. 21, 1806:
"I hear a complaint that we have no literature. It is the fault of the Minister of Interior."

John Grierson, in *Film Forum*, Oct. 1952:
"I once told Mackenzie King, the Canadian Prime Minister, that we absolutely needed a lunatic school of cinema on the wing (the right wing, the right wing) to keep documentary from getting too sober-sided."

E. M. Forster:
"It has never happened to me that I've had to choose between betraying a friend and betraying my country, but if it ever does so happen I hope I have the guts to betray my country."

Maurice Baring:
"If you would like to know what the Lord God thinks of money, you have only to look at those to whom he gives it."

September 26, 1958
"I am not weak. And I don't want to look weak. Have patience with me. Although my body is giving up, my mind is very lucid. One should always try to give a form to his emotions and feelings, even in the times of

Adolfas and Edouard ready for an air filming.

A1630

BANTAM BOOKS
35¢

The astonishingly candid first novel by the eighteen-year-old girl whom the New York Post called "America's challenge to Francoise Sagan"

PAMELA MOORE

CHOCOLATES for BREAKFAST

The story of a young girl's sudden
urgent awakening to love and desire

September 26th,1958

weeks expenses:

Friday:
Malted Milk - 0.3o
Vill.Voice   o.1o
Phone call   o.1o
tokens   1.15
bananoes   o.15
plums   o.3o
buses   o.3o
NYT   0.o5
              _____
               2.35

Sunday
  food   0.25
              _____
               0.25

Monday
NYT,Mirror   o.1o
Breakfast   o.65
Token   o115
food   o.18
photostat   o.62
food   o.44
tokens   o.15
milk   o.54
tokens   o.45
boxes   5.oo
              _____
               8.38

Wdn.
Breakfast   o.45
NYT   o.o5
Boxes   2.75
tokens   o.45
stamps   o.5o
food   o.5o
              _____
               2.70
               4.7o

Friday
Breakfast   o.5o
haircut   155o
loun dry   o.65
Dr.Panetiere 1o.85

Saturday
Food   o.78
garage   2.oo
News   o.o5
Mirror   o.1o
Paterson   1.52
Tokens   o.9o
NYT   o.3o
             _____
              5.65

Tuesday
Tokens   o.45
tokens   o.3o
food   o.24
breakfast   o.45
stamps   o.7o
NYT   o.o5
             _____
              2.19

Thursday
Tokens   1.6o
breakfast   o.45
NYT   o.o5
food   o.3o
food   o.75
mags   o.4o
             _____
          m 3.55

tragedy. It would be a weakness to commit a suicide, and it wouldn't solve anything," spoke Edouard, as we were driving thru the city today. He's still going thru his emotional crisis.

His Slavic part constantly drives him into danger. He can't stand waiting, suspense. He has to jump into it and resolve it one or other way, immediately. The Romanic part of him, with all its lucidity, is not able to stop him.

I think it was Nietzsche who was talking often about giving form to emotions, life. That makes art. But now I am thinking, I am wondering, if one can grasp & create forms of art, in art, if one is not conscious of them in life, in one's own life. A certain climate, a certain degree of sophistication is needed for aesthetic creation.

Anyway—this striving after the form makes Edouard's words sound—at least to strangers—insincere, posed. They see only the outward form of his feelings and thoughts. He is always preoccupied with HOW he does and says it, and this HOW becomes very often too conscious, artificial, or too familiar—hence the suspicion of insincerity, of mimicry.

I lack that conscious form. I seem to drift through my life effortlessly; Edouard swims, by his conscious effort.

"He will generally be found [the Saint] restoring the world to sanity by exaggerating whatever the world neglects, which is by no means always the same element in every age. Yet each generation seeks its saints by instinct; and he is not what the people want, but rather what the people need." (From *St. Thomas Aquinas* by G. K. Chesterton.)

Thursday, October 9, 1958

"The Death of James Dean,"
Esquire, Oct. 1958:
"Kicks are big business: the sallow hucksters needle the nerves. Through radios drumming rock'n roll and blurred girls crooning on TV
they hammer on the wracked nerves
buy,
buy speed, buy horsepower, buy chromium,
buy happiness in a split-level ranch house,
elegance in shocking pink lipstick,
passion in a jar of Parisian perfume,
or that portable transistor set
you can take along on your vacations
so that even beside the thunderous ocean,
or camping out in some hidden inter-
vale green in a notch of the hills, you'll
never be free
from the clamor of salesmen.
Why not resentful? There's more to life;
the kids know it. Their fathers won
a war, but weren't men enough to keep
 the peace; they let the pundits and
the politicians wheedle them into defeat;
they let the goons pilfer their pay checks,
too busy watching TV to resent oppres-
sion… (Freedom, What good is it? Let's
have social security
and welfare and tailfins on our cars
and packaging)
… There's no cellophane can protect
the glory of life when you've lost it;
the kids know it.
Dean owned a horse, but racing cars
was his public hobby. He'd won a race for
novices at some meet. His racing had
given the producers fits. He teased
them by telling them that racing was a
glorious way to die. (Life can't be all
Social Security and safety first. The kids
know that. It's glory a man has to have.)
Some friends furnished him with a
St. Christopher medal, but the studio had
written into his contract that he wasn't
to race a car until the picture was ready
for release."

October 12, 1958

Where are the Maecenas and hosts of art today?
"The hostesses are far too busy at the sink." (*The Times Lit. Supplement*, Aug. 1952)

With the beginning of this century everything seems to go faster, so many changes, everything is in flux. How do you want a writer to concentrate and write a novel with a "leisurely" elaborate, patient plot of a Tolstoi or a Flaubert or Stendhal? Today the poetically constructed novel (à la Joyce or Stein) is the only possible novel. Epic novel, poetry in prose; poetry and prose lose boundaries, reach for truth in new dynamic configurations.

Goethe: "Ein Kuenstler nicht die Natur wiedergibt. Er arbeitet wie die Natur."

"Politics I would rather not be quoted on. All the contact I have had with it has left me feeling as though I had been drinking out of spittoons." (Hemingway, in an interview, *NY Times*, Sept. 17, '50)

America needs "demoralizers"
(such as A. Gide)
"Il faut être *absolument moderne*"
(Rimbaud)

Me: "I have a good idea for you, for another anthology: 'The Best From *Close-Up*', the old film magazine."
Frank: "Why not from *Sight and Sound*, it's still being published, more people know it?"
Me: "That's the point, it's still being published."
Frank: "You mean, it's not dead enough..."

The secret of Dietrich is that she never fools herself about her age: she fools others.

November 8, 1958

I am a "regionalist." That's what I am. I always belong somewhere. Drop me anywhere, in a dry, most lifeless dead stone place where nobody likes to live—and I'll begin to let my roots into it, like a sponge. No abstract internationalism for me. Nor do I put my money on the future! I am now and here.

You see, Lithuania is a very small country. There are many other small countries. Everything is small in Lithuania. The rivers, there are no rivers that begin in St. Louis and end, you know, three thousand miles away or that go through thousands of miles of jungles or deserts or through the plains, like Volga or Amazon or Mississippi. There are no mountains that reach the clouds, there are only small hills and small lakes, you can see from one side to the other; and there are no songs that really go, you know, big big songs for open wide spaces. Lithuanian songs are small and they are directed inwards because there is nowhere else to go, it's a very small place, so you sit by yourself, you know, and you sing to yourself, two, three friends, maybe—

And then we have the big countries, and big rivers, and big mountains and big histories and big armies and big wars, and they always get together, like at the United Nations, and they proclaim themselves the Big Three, or the Big Four, or the Big Five, and they always think they are the only ones, and others, you know, others should be only a part of them, or speak their language, & when they speak about One World, if the Russians speak about One World, or the Americans speak about One World, they imagine that that whole One World will speak Russian, or American.

So you know why I am for small countries, and small rivers, and small mountains, and for a world in which there are languages which nobody understands outside the people who speak it.

November 9, 1958

"You have your mind in the gutter."
Overheard in the street.

Our films and theater are too verbal. Inflation of words.

"I will do what I have dreamed or I will do nothing."—Antonin Artaud

Pamela. Basically she has no faith in men. She thinks all men are here to harm her. She is not against Edouard, not against what he does: she is against his character.

Bridge on the River Kwai is not an anti-war film: it's a glorification of the army discipline.

November 18, 1958

"Write us a letter," said the secretary at the Phoenix Theater, "write us a letter describing the play, what's all about. If we like it, we'll ask you to send the play in." "A synopsis?" asked I. He looked at me, he thought I was crazy, they way I said "synopsis." He was still looking at me when I was closing the door.

I called the 4th Street Theater. A secretary answered, a man. "Do you read new plays?" I asked. "No," he said, "but you can send us a synopsis, a summary." "Synopsis?" I wondered if I got him right. "Yes," said the voice. "Is this the 4th Street Theater?"

I asked again. "Yes," the man answered. I said: "I thought I had a wrong number." I hung up.

"I can't accept it. First you send us a synopsis of it," said Whitehead's secretary. "But this is not a film script. I thought only the Hollywood studios ask for synopses. I could send you a synopsis of some Shakespeare play, perhaps," I tried to joke, but the secretary did not seem to appreciate my cheap ironies, she was very serious about her job, so I left her, and I heard her typing as I walked slowly down the stairway.

I came to pick up the play from Kazan's office, I received a note to pick it up. The manuscript was on the corner of the table, and I picked it up. "Did Mr. Kazan see it?"

I asked. "No," said the secretary. "I usually read the manuscripts myself before sending to him. I think your play is too short for an evening's performance, so I didn't even give it to him." "Thanks anyway," I said. There was no use arguing, the more that she seemed to be working—reading a manuscript of another victim, although, this time, the manuscript seemed quite fat and long.

I called B's secretary. B is not in, and he doesn't know when she'll be in. She took the manuscript home with her, he can't do anything. For three months now I've been trying to get the manuscript back. Good black covers, I paid $1.75 for those covers, and I spent a good two weeks, on my spare time, typing the blasted thing—and now I have to start from the beginning, to type another copy. Perhaps I should call her tomorrow again, who knows.

November 18, 1958

"Who is the producer here?"
Everybody turned to the young man, in his early forties.
"I am the producer," he said.
"I have a play for you to read," said I, giving him the manuscript.
He opened the manuscript in the middle, closed it fast.
"No, it's not the play I want."
"How do you know it?" I asked.
"I know. I have been a professional play-reader for years."
"There is no such thing," I said.

Village Voice offices, 1958, corner of Seventh Avenue and 4th Street.

November 12, 1958

movie journal

by Jonas Mekas

"PATHER PANCHALI" is still the most inspiring film to see in the Village (at the Fifth Avenue Cinema). It is most simple, most down to earth, and from the very heart. Specifically it is about India, but actually it is about everybody. The poetry of the film transcends its locality and speaks to us all. Constructed as an epic poem, it works on two levels: transfixing the eye with the sheer beauty of its images and gripping the heart with the sublety and truth of its drama. It is realism with a tear in it, but never sentimentalized — which is something not easy to achieve. It is so fresh that it caused some of our daily reviewers to lift their brows: "It has no structure!" "It has no plot!" (as if the art of the film could be equated with that of the novel); what's more, it's "unprofessional" (Crowther)! However, after seeing so many "professional" films one longs for the freshness of the "non-professional," one who (in the words of Thomas Mann) has not yet become "a traitor to his wild and lonely youth."

"MY UNCLE," which just opened uptown at the Baronet, is another very good example of the uncorrupt, "unprofessional" film. Tati, whose "Mr. Hulot's Holiday" and "Jour de Fete" we admired a

JONAS MEKAS has written many admirable reviews and articles for Film Culture, edited by him. His "Movie Journal" begins this week as a regular feature in The Voice.

few years ago, makes it again in this critique of the modern life. An amateur at heart, working outside the conventions of film acting and film "art," he has given us a comedy that is subtle, biting,

observing, and above all, personal. It is not a comedy of gags or funny lines (the only kinds of comedy left in Hollywood); here tragedy and comedy go together, enriching each other, contrasting and balancing between laughter and tears, as does all good humor in theatre (Chekhov) or in film (Chaplin, or Fernandel and Raimu in the early Pagnol films).

"NEW YORK, NEW YORK," made by Francis Thompson, who will be speaking on experimental film making at the Museum of the City of New York (Fifth Avenue at 103rd Street) on November 15 at 2.45 p. m., further illustrates the curse of professionalism. The most ambitious of the recent experimental films, it was awarded a prize at the Brussels World Fair and praised by many here. However, it is really only an honorable failure. Although it contains more craft than many films seen lately, it has little more to offer than that, unless one takes lens-trickery for art. But even the trick itself is too simple and too old: take a distorting lens, shoot around, then multiply your images optically. If you want to make it still more gorgeous, shoot it in color. To reduce New York to nothing but multiplicity is a pretty dead thing. It is very often that our craftsmen lack thought and heart, and their manufactured products begin to bore us after the first two minutes. If that is the price of it, then give us less finished but more alive, more imaginative films—films that still contain some adventure. No dry, dead academic professionalism!

November 19, 1958

movie journal

by Jonas Mekas

"AROUND THE WORLD IN 80 DAYS," after playing for two years on Broadway, is now at the local theatres. Jules Verne's book was an adventure story, and the

film, when it is good, is an adventure film and nothing else. Adventure at its simplest, however—for those who like to watch without reflection. And why should one avoid, once in a while, an innocent adventure? The film catches, in a number of scenes, the atmosphere, the fantasy, the youthful exultation of the book. There is no depth, no psychology, no symbolism in this adventure; it is the kind of film that has died out almost everywhere. One wishes to see Fairbanks jumping into the frame again, careless, smiling, radiant—or perhaps even Rin-Tin-Tin again!

"THE SEVENTH SEAL," which is coming to our art theatres soon, is just the opposite kind of adventure. Ingmar Bergman, maker of this film, is a young Swedish writer who has already a dozen films to his credit, although few of them have been shown abroad. Those who have seen more of his work consider him one of the two or three most intelligent film directors. His is the mental adventure. However, in "The Seventh Seal," as in "The Naked Night" and "Smiles of a Summer Night," he is not too anxious to arrive at any definite conclusions. His strength is (as Virginia Woolf would say) to find adventure in the journey itself. Obsessed with the ideas of love, life, death, good and evil, he meditates as he goes, talking in symbols, in parables and images that often are of breathtaking beauty. There is more cinema in "The Seventh Seal" than in the entire Hollywood production of 1958 (with the exception of Orson Welles' "Touch of Evil"). It is being said that Bergman is bringing Paris intellectuals back to the movies. Eisenstein was the last one to have that honor.

"ANOTHER SKY," presented in this month's program by Cinema 16 (office: 175 Lexington Avenue), pulls us into a very different kind of adventure. Made by Gavin Lambert (who was for several years the editor of Sight and Sound) it is an inner kind of ad-

1

CHAPTER SEVEN

THE NEW YORK TIMES
1980-1989

... In defense of Bresson... In Defense of Perversity... End of the year 1958 ... Cassavetes reshoots *Shadows*... Anice... My letter to the Department of Taxation... Letter from Maya Deren... Letters to Edouard... I am trying to cope with *Film Culture*, etc... About changing sensibilities in the arts... Meeting with Ron Rice... On Pop music and highways... Robert Frank... With Allen Ginsberg we visit Storm De Hirsch... About drugs and self-hypnosis... A STORY... Letter to Edouard... A PLAY...

FIGHT FILM ART MUTILATORS
Two films, shown at the 55th Street Playhouse, were severely cut by the distributor. *Les Visiteurs du soir* was cut by 30 minutes or 2,700 feet of film, distorting the structure and the meaning of the film.

This film is distributed by Brandon Films Inc., 200 West 57th Street who made the above cuts for commercial reasons: to cut down the running time, to gain more runs. *Diary of a Country Priest*, shown at the 5th Avenue Cinema, was cut by 15–18 minutes or 1,400 feet of film. Cuts were made by the management of the theatre with the approval of distributor, Brandon Films Inc. The director of the film, Robert Bresson, writes:

"My picture has been entirely mutilated by the distributor... it is impossible to cut out even one scene of the film without making it absolutely ununderstandable. I had built it with the utmost care and precautions. And every little detail is indispensable."

Both films are distributed by Brandon Films Inc. Please write protesting letters to the distributor and the management of the 5th Avenue Cinema and the 55th St. Playhouse. Boycott the theaters. Be watchful of other films distributed by Brandon. A distributor who has no respect for films should be boycotted.

FIGHT THE FILM ART MENACE;
WRITE LETTERS;
WRITE THREATENING LETTERS;
BOMBS; ETC. FIGHT FILM ART MUTILATORS!

November 21, 1958
In Defense of Perversity
In a bastard standardized conformist sick society perversity becomes a force of liberation. Horror and degradation for the professors, guardians of Morality, it is a drop of Holy Spirit, a ray of salvation.
One has to hit on the very head. The time has come when the action of the silent wisdom, when the truth takes the form of anarchy, and exaggeration, and negation. This is how the subconscious, in its organic protest against the dehumanizing tendencies, spouts and bursts and spits out its venom.

Young Angry Men are necessary not because they are bringing a new philosophy. No—others will bring it at the right time. Their function is to destroy. They came against their own will, to begin to clean the rotten swelling of their age. They are the subconscious of their (our) age.

The Beat and Angry generation is a protest. Not everybody in this generation is angry and beat. Generations get their markings from a few who express their generation clearest. They are being forced by the total subconscious of their generation to utter, to shout, to cry, to beat out their truths, suspicions, hopes, lonelinesses, warnings, prophecies. They are the true voices of their generation. Those are sensitive voices. They are perverse—they are not normal. Normality is conformist, money-minded, dead, Eisenhowerized, and Mamieed, and Fortunized, Harperized, deodorized. To be beat today is to be abnormal, to go against the normality, conformity, to be immoral, to be perverse.

Even the sexual pervert today is an innocent and helpless protest against the bourgeois morality and unsensitivity. Better a pervert than a businessman. A pervert is an innocent, crying, beating himself, not the others.

When the society is unlivable, the brave will die. The innocent will jump out the window, cut their innocent veins, soak in their innocent blood, or dream themselves out in the leaves of marijuana. The unsensitive ones will survive and become Mamies, salesmen, atomic pirates, Dullesses, professors, Wouks.

Listen to the songs, on radio, jukeboxes, cheap songs, true songs. Popular American songs are the saddest thing in America, or maybe in the world. Listen to their sacred sadness. There was never such sadness in the songs of a large strong nation: they always came from the trampled small nations, poor, beaten on the paths of war, famine. Now it is in America. An anguished sadness, a suicide sadness, a loveless sadness. Or listen to the jazz. It is a kind of silent, hidden, sad crying out, for oneself, somewhere very deep. Or look at the paintings of de Kooning. There is the same suicide sadness, and cry: he paints his heart out, the heart of his generation. The businessmen do not realize that these songs, and jazz, and de Koonings are also perverse: they demask their dead happy *Peale's Reader's Digest* smiles. The popular art and the modern art sing the truth, as all perversity today does.

Isn't it then that the Mamies, the Eisenhowers, the salesmen, and the atomists, and the Wouks, and professors who are the real perverts? Aren't they the ones who go against the truth of life, love and death? Aren't they the ones who smear their Old Age in *Mademoiselle's* fashions and wilt without tasting it, in anguish? Aren't they the ones who made love into dating and partnership? Life into business? The true perversity of our age? Aren't we the holy ones?

Isn't Elvis Presley a half-saint, who showed the absurdity of his parents' generation by exaggerating their ideals, by buying two three four cars? All ideals and truths of our fathers become fake and lie when lit up: rotten, evil, yellow puke.

So let us be beat, and angry, and perverse: if that helps to dethrone the falsity and rottenness of morality and puked way of living. It is more honest today to be confused, than to be sure (when the time is for dethroning). It is more honest to destroy than to build (there is not yet a clean place for building). It is more honest to be delinquent (and juvenile) than to learn and accept the ways of living of the governing generation, a way of living in lies and pukes and garbage.

Holy are the delinquent thoughts and deeds and insubordination, disrespect and hate for their ways of living, for their philosophies, for all work (for the perpetuation of the dump); Holy is beat and Zen and angriness and perversity.

This perversity doesn't deny the need of moral values. It only shows the corruption of the existing moral values. It is the first anxiety in which the new moral values will be born, in suffering, and in angriness.

Let us then deny and destroy so that, perhaps, some of us will find again and keep, until it will be needed again, the truth of life, the spontaneity, the joy, the freedom, exultation, soul, heaven and hell. Let us free ourselves for perversity, become James Deans, and Presleys, and Parkers, and Osbornes, de Koonings, Kerouacs, Bernard Shaws, and Millers, Genets, Villons, Rimbauds—to learn the dynamics of the holy perversity, not to be buried in the dump of the XX century normality.

Thus I spit on the generation that has produced me, and this is the holiest spit of my generation.

MILLION DOLLAR POETRY FOUNDATION endorsed by Walt Whitman, Hart Crane, E. A. Poe, Vachel Lindsay

The Million Dollar Poetry Foundation was created to enable to publish the work of contemporary American poets. Why should a poet wait until some pity-feeling publisher will offer him his presses? A poet respects himself and his work and he wants it to be thrown into the world— a part of himself that is his testimony, his gift, and his knife.

Send your contribution today.
All correspondence and checks should be addressed to:
Million Dollar Poetry Foundation, G. P. O., Box 1499, New York 1, New York.
The names of all contributors will be listed in the published books.
Among the books scheduled in the MDPF series are works by Tuli Kupferberg, Frank Kuenstler, Allen Ginsberg, Bob Stock.

Karl A. Menninger, M. D.:
"It has been shown, however, that many accidents are not accidental, but are brought about by a more or less unconscious wish on the part of the patient. 'Accident prone' individuals have been shown statistically to be the victims of ninety percent of all accidents."
(for literature on the subject, see: Flanders Dunbar: *Psychosomatic Diagnosis*, Karin Stephen: *Psychoanalysis and Medicine*, Karl A. Menninger: *Man Against Himself The Human Mind*, Alfred A. Knopf, 1957.)

To you everything is clear. You live on the surface, by the surface, and for the surface. As far as you see it, beyond the surface begins nothingness.

And that frightens you. How many times you have been given a chance to die—but you are holding stubbornly to the surface.
"Wer unter die Oberfläche dringt, tut es auf eigene Gefahr."
(One who ventures beyond the surface does so on his own risk.)

"Aber Gott hat mich hinangefuehrt wie einen Gaul, dem die Augen geblendet sind, dass er nicht sehe, so zu ihm zu rennen, dass selten ein gutes Werk aus Weisheit oder Vorsichtigkeit vorgenommen werde, sondern es muesse alles in einem Irrsal oder Unwissenheit geschehen."—Martin Luther, *Saemtliche Werke*, Erlangen: Bd. LVII 31f

"Der Glaube fordert nicht Kundschaft, Wissenheit oder Sicherheit, sondern frei Ergeben und froehlich Wagen auf Gottes unempfundene, unversuchte, unerkannte Guete."—Martin Luther

No date, 1958

"It's not cold today."
"Yes. And before Christmas."
"I wish it would snow instead of raining," said I.

A woman at the other end of the bar lifts her head.

"Where do you see snow?"

"No, I said I wished it would snow."

"And I thought it snowed…"

They stand behind the bar looking at the window.

"Sam, take my umbrella."

"Thanks, it's not raining very hard."

"No, it is not."

"Merry Christmas."

"Merry Christmas."

Notes kept New Year's Night as I became drunker and drunker:

1. The sky is very beautiful.
2. The night clouds.
3. Godam, I'm weak in my ankles.
4. Godam.
5. The hand is heavy. I breathe like a fish. Sleepy?
6. Three guys came in. No girls—so they look around, not interesting, they leave, hands in pockets.
7. Happy New Year! Tililil!
8. Retrace, retrace. Disappear. My hands dance as they move.
9. How are you?
10. I hope Elizabeth won't drink.
11. As close as your lips are to me.
12. Celebrating New Year's alone? Yes. When I come back you'll buy me a drink.
13. She smiled at the same time at me and at him. All three drunk.
14. Another Manhattan!
15. She wants to meet her on 47th & 8th Ave. at 4 AM.
16. Don't feel my face.
17. Ladies and Gentlemen, Picadilly wishes you Happy New Year.

January 10, 1959

Spent an evening watching Cassavetes reshoot some scenes for *Shadows*. Met Lelia.

"The reason why old men like young women," said Lelia, "is that young women do not think too much, they do not worry if they are right or wrong. They will deny something violently, from sheer passion, without caring if that is true. Their judgments are always extremist, and that is what old men do not have, and that is what attracts them to these young women."

Saw Anice.

"I see everything in black and white, there are no in-betweens for me," said Anice.

Extremes of youth? There is nothing youthful in Anice's endless talking. Her extremism has a quality of dry, old, dead. Lelia was talking about emotions. Anice's talk is cerebral, dry. Mostly she speaks in clichés, cerebral clichés.

I spend my life, most of it, in grey. Intellectually, my life is in those in-between subtleties that do not exist for Anice. But my emotions and judgments of those greys shoot into extremes. It is therefore that Anice bores me to death, as do many other people who talk in clichés. She continuously goes, like a machine: I like this, I like that, I don't like that.

Her Black & White way of thinking and talking is really a result of her poor past. She had an unhappy life. Her life habits are in black and white. Oh, damn the misery! Oh, damn the poor life!

She gets angry if somebody interrupts her at breakfast: she has to have her breakfast alone and in peace, no nuances, no changes, no variations. She shouts GO TO HELL! to a young man who interrupts her by saying HELLO when she is looking, enjoying the "architecture" of a New York street. She is difficult to push out of her pre-set frame of mind. Her clothes are also plain, tasteless, in extremes. She cannot understand why Hannelore allows her child certain things—she would forbid them. Tina must be forced to do this, to do that, to sit quietly when she eats, etc. She does not understand small nuances of freedom.

**Cliff Carnell, Erich Kollmar and
John Cassavetes during the filming of
Shadows, 1957.**

FOR THE PRESS
for immediate release
December 12th, 1958

from:

Jonas Mekas
Editor-in-Chief
FILM CULTURE
G.P.O., Box 1499
New York 1, N.Y.

The first INDEPENDENT FILM AWARD, established by "Film Culture" magazine
                    "to point out original and unique American
                      contributions to the cinema,"
and to be given once every year, has been awarded to John Cassavetes' feature film SHADOWS, independently produced by Maurice McEndree and Seymour Cassel.

The statement, issued by "Film Culture," follows:

"John Cassavetes' film SHADOWS, more than any other recent American film, presents contemporary reality in a fresh and unconventional manner.
"Our 'dramatic' feature films today suffer from an excess of professionalism. As a consequence, improvisation, spontaneity, and free inspiration are almost entirely lost, with little if any gain in their place. Attempts at new cinematic forms and new ways of seizing life are rare on the screen. Cassavetes in SHADOWS was able to break out of conventional moulds and traps and retain unusual freshness. The situations and atmosphere of New York night life are vividly, cinematically, and truly caught in this film. It breathes a modernity and immediacy that the cinema of today needs so much if it is to be a living and contemporary art."

The official presentation of the Award will be sponsored jointly by "Film Culture", and The American Federation of Film Societies, at a date to be announced later this month.

SHADOWS: Producer: Maurice McEndree; assistant producer: Seymour Cassel. Director: John Cassavetes. Cameraman: Erich Kolmar. Editor: Len Appleson. Music: Charles Mingus. In the cast: Ben Carruthers, Lelia Goldoni, Rupert Crosse, Hugh Heard, Tony Ray, Tom Allen, Dennis Sallas, David Pokitelow, and others.

                              "FILM CULTURE" magazine

Despite the fact that the publication of *Film Culture* depended a lot on my income from work at Graphic Studios, by the Spring of 1957 I had no choice but to quit Graphic Studios: the time *Film Culture* demanded from me was just too much to cope with. So I quit. During the next several years my survival depended much on part-time jobs for various small printers. By then, thanks to Graphic Studios, I had become a professional in several small crafts demanded by the printers, so to find a job for me was not too difficult.

January 28, 1959

I needed to make a call. We were just passing an Irish bar.

"No, I am not going into a bar," she said, with that I-am-a-lady tone. "Let's go into a drugstore."

She preferred a commercial, stupid drugstore to a real, human bar.

"Next time when we go out you should walk on the street side," she said before we parted. And I could hear seriousness in her voice, it wasn't a joke. And it annoyed me that she was so petty to tell it to me that way. In my mind I promised to myself never to see her again.

Is she destroying my intuition? Is she making me accept bad food, to praise bad clothes? I am a weak man when it comes to influences. I do not understand regular life, people's life, so I am a victim for anyone who wants to influence me on that level.

Disseminators of information, of wrong, unnecessary information. Nobody informs us about a lot of things that should be known.

Arthur Miller: "A man like André Breton, who is the father of surrealism, walks about the streets of Manhattan practically unknown and unrecognized."

Overexposure in cinema, scratched film, negatives, splashes of images as you move the camera fast—it's not much different from what Jimmy Giuffre is doing in music, his scratchy notes, sounds.

From Paracelsus:

"Throughout his life, a man cannot cast off that which he has received in his youth. My share was harshness, as against the subtle, prudish, superfine. Those who were brought up in soft clothes and by womenfolk have little in common with us who grew up among the pine trees."

"No man becomes master while he stays at home, nor finds a teacher behind the stove. Diseases wander here and there the whole length of the world. He who would understand them must wander, too."

"Evil is that which is finite."—Kabbala

"In experiments theories or arguments do not count. Therefore, we pray you not to oppose the method of experiment but to follow it without prejudice… Every experiment is like a weapon which must be used in its particular way—a spear to thrust, a club to strike. Experimenting requires a man who knows when to thrust and when to strike, each according to need and fashion." (source unclear)

"So I have traveled throughout the land and was a pilgrim all my life, alone and a stranger feeling alien. Then Thou hast made me grow into Thine art under the breath of the terrible storm in me." (source unclear)

Too much simplicity becomes banality, distortion.

Today, when we say "intelligence," we mean "the secret intelligence," FBI, CIA, etc.

No date, 1959

Notes for myself:
to do things that make no sense
to engage in useless activities
to undermine the respectability of myself
to be absurd
to lose my mind
react, say immediately, don't think
a new proverb: Never think twice
—think once
Do Before You Think

March 1st, 1959

New York City
State of New York

Department of Taxation
Albany 1, N.Y.

Dear Sirs:

I have received from you a notice (enclosed with this letter) in which I am asked to pay $500 penalty for the "failure to file New York State tax returns for the years 1952, 1953, 1954, 1955, and 1956."

I would like to have some clarifications concerning this penalty.

I remember some correspondence between us a year ago or so. I was asked to file the taxes for a few years. I did not understand at that time, and I don't understand now, why don't you simply bill me, or whatever the procedure is, for a specific and exact sum that I owe you, instead of asking me to pay the penalty. Since I am not keeping any office, I have no records of my income for those years, but you could very easily check that with the Federal Government and find it out, since I have been paying Federal taxes ever since I came to the States. I hadn't paid State taxes during the first years of my staying in this country for a simple reason that I didn't know about their existence. Later I didn't pay because I have never received (not even this year, 1959) any forms from Albany for filing my taxes.

On the other hand, even if I would have received the tax forms, I wouldn't have been able to pay them. For a few years already I have been giving all my money left from the basic expenses of living to *Film Culture* magazine, of which I am editor and the unquestionable need of which for our Universities and film students can be testified by any university. Since the magazine is not supported by any foundation and its existence depends mostly on me (it loses about $300 with each issue) and since I owe still over $2,500 to the printer, I feel that at this moment it is more important to give whatever money I have, to the printer and keep the magazine alive, than to pay taxes. The more, that my weekly incomes for over a year now have been only $18 (from my work at the Cooper Offset, New York).

In any case, I consider this penalty an unjust act. At worst—or at best—at least you could figure out the correct sum that I owe you. That is easier to do for you than for me, since you must have some contacts with the Federal Government. However, I would ask you to cancel my taxes for all past years. You wouldn't be doing a favor to me you would be helping America's arts and education.

If it comes to the worst—let me know the exact sum I owe you, and the smallest amount of money that I could pay you monthly (considering, that means, keeping in mind my weekly $18 income from Cooper Offset, 814 Broadway, N.Y. City).

Waiting to hear from you,

Jonas Mekas

use this address:
Jonas Mekas
G.P.O., Box 1499
New York 1, N.Y.

April 7, 1959

(retyped from old scrap pieces)

The temperament of our age does not permit passion, or anger—the life and arts are full of young old men who do not want to risk their ideas, jobs, images of themselves—or to risk even their friends—they are people of status quo.

Edouard: "Can't think when I drive. Man is what he does." From last summer's scraps.

The progressive ideas meant progress when they originated. The "equality" idea today has become a dead weight, brake to progress.

I can still feel the horror of unemployed actors, calling and calling, calling and

FOR SALE

MEDIUM-SIZED PRINTING store. 1 Vertical V45, 12x18 Kluge, 8x10 job press, also type and stock. Box 413, PRINTING NEWS.

LINO MATS 8, 10 and 12 point Vogue light with bold; 10 and 12 point Garamond light with italic; 10 point Memphis light with bold; 18 point Vogue light; 18 point Vogue bold. LEhigh 4-4340.

2 MILLER 2-COLOR presses, 27x41, late serial number, perfect condition, completely rebuilt. Each has dual spray and dust exhaust equipment. Also 10 Blatchford chases (without honeycomb). Available immediately. Reasonable. 5th floor, 257 West 17th St., NYC. Phone CHelsea 3-4515.

ATF CHIEF 17½x22½ DE model; ATF Little Chief 14x20 MP model; Harris 22x34 EL; Webendorfer 20x26; Miehle horizontal 22x28; Rosback 22" rotary perforator; 14x22 C & P press. Frank J. O'Neill, 8 Spruce Street, NYC. BEekman 3-7425.

INVENTORY CLEARANCE SALE 14x20 Multi recently rebuilt $895. 1250 Multi excellent condition $795. 1250 Multi rebuilt $1,395. 1200 Multi, tip-top condition. Kaminer, 30 Ferry Street, NYC. WOrth 2-1670.

SITUATIONS WANTED

CAMERAMAN with long experience in line, halftone, offset. Part time (afternoons or evenings) only. Write J. M., Box 1499, New York 1, New York.

LETTERPRESS, ESTIMATOR, production man. Experienced in all phases of estimating, purchasing, scheduling, costing, billing. Complete plant preferred. Box 465, PRINTING NEWS.

Dear Jonas Mekas:

Ever since your wonderful review appeared I have been wondering how to Thank you.

It's also been delayed by being very busy and also out of town to lecture (in Vermont).

But I thought perhaps you would enjoy having a good print of The Primavera moment from "Meshes".

Once more, Thank you so much —

Maya.

calling after we announced that we need actors for *S. Junction*. It was horrible.

Edouard: "If a person, whatever his occupation, does not actively defend anyone who is not given a fair trial, then, ethically speaking, he loses his own right to fair trial."

"We'll give him a fair trial, and then we'll hang him." (From an old Western.)

Oh, fire and energy of youth, millions of youth over the country—energy wasted without outlet, directed only to the pursuit of a practical profession, security. At 14 or 15 they are already like little grown ups, without idealism. There will be no "Ode to Youth" from them nor about them. Only old age. It frightens me just to look at them.

Go to Savoy, in Harlem, 125th St.

Simone de Beauvoir about a Washington museum: "This museum derives from a mausoleum and a Turkish bath."

He says to a 10 year old girl: "You have emerald eyes." Immediately: suspicion of perversity. What an age!

One should turn away from the society only when it helps (Rimbaud!) to bring it to self-realization, to show it its bad faith.

April 8, 1959
"After all, I am a poet, and they are not going to shoot poets." (Federico García Lorca)

"Visible distinguishing marks or features ..." When answering this question, I feel ashamed that I have none.

I have watched my American friends go through crashes and crises, but never, they are never really shaken. Yes, they will commit suicide, anything—not to go through anguish.

Will there ever be a real desperation (creative one, fertilizing) in American arts?

Language, Thought, and Reality by Benjamin Lee Whorf. Published by the Technology Press of MIT and John Wiley & Sons, Inc., New York.

"I don't like your lips; they're straight, like those of someone who has never lied. I want to teach you to lie, so that your lips may become beautiful and twisted like those of an antique masque." (Oscar Wilde)

Spring, 1959
I am not interested in interpreting life, world, others, myself, etc., but in transforming it. Yes, yes. But maybe I am, after all. Interpretation can change the world also, so it comes to the same.

April 12, 1959
Brother Edouard:
Two days ago I air-mailed to you some materials which you could use for your articles or lectures. One is the text of my "Iskusstvo Kino" article, the other (with a few pages missing) is an article on experimental film which will appear in a film book published by Grove Press. I will send you the book when it's out (in 2–3 weeks). Sometime this week I will send you more materials—some notes on recent pseudo-realist films, a few photos, etc.
I saw "Schermi" at Fenin. He writes for them, he knows the editor very well, he said.
FC distribution in Italy: I wrote to Pocket Libri, Piazza Bertarelli 4, Milan, asking if they would distribute *FC* in Italy. I don't know any other addresses or names. I didn't receive an answer yet. Can you contact someone in Rome? You can show them a copy, and if they are interested,

they can write us. It is a fifty-fifty deal (they get half of the money). I think they could sell at least some 50 copies there. In France I wrote to The Olympia Press, 7 rue St. Severin, Paris 5. It is a shame that we have no distributor in France. Partly the blame is on you, since you have spent so much time in Paris without getting a distributor for *FC*.

If you will go to Milan, some day, you can see that distributor perhaps.

Concerning *FC*, next issue: The deadline for the next issue is the end of May, approximately. Maybe even the middle of June. The earlier the better. I think that *S. J.* should be printed in a complete version, not in excerpts. It is true—and I think it is a very good idea—that an article could be written about writing a poetical film based on reality, using excerpts to illustrate the points, etc.—but that article would only introduce the script itself. I insist on printing it complete. As I see, I think better of the script than you do yourself. I consider it a small masterpiece of scriptwriting. About the introductory piece: Naturally, we don't want to complain, etc. All we have to do is to list certain facts, a very documentary introduction. This I could do, or perhaps still better, Adolfas, using his own memory and my notes that I was taking during the shooting (I have some 20 pages of notes on the adventures of *S. J.*)

S. J. is still resting in its cans. Any editing would become a full-time job, and I can't afford it. On the other hand, something must be done about it soon. The lab is becoming skeptical about our continuing the film. And they are a little bit angry that there was not a single word about the situation from you or Adolfas. They consider you a responsible man, director, etc. because you did all the talking, negotiations, etc. Three months ago I calmed them down by telling that this is only a temporary interruption, that the film will be continued later in the spring. But what am I going to tell them in June? Unless the footage is edited. I wrote to Adolfas as long as he has to come to the States to renew his passport, maybe he should come to N. Y. and edit the footage during that period. I did not receive his reaction yet. I see very clearly now that I will not be able to do it myself. I cannot use the cutting room during the day, and there are only two or three hours in the evening that I could devote to it. And not every day, since I have other duties, for the *Village Voice*, *Film Culture*, etc. So it depends on Adolfas. I have the right to complain: I have been left alone here in this blasted city to cope with 100 things at the same time:

to publish *Film Culture*

to appease the labs, etc.

to maintain the respectable name and the idea that we are alive and existing, not dead, *FC*, Bi-Continental Films, etc.

to meet young experimentalists from the city and from out of town, to introduce them, to encourage them, to lead them to some direction (after this issue came out, I received many letters from various places of the country thanking *FC* for taking a firm stand for their efforts; actors, directors are writing and asking about *Shadows*, and etc. etc. Fordham University wants me to come to them to help to work out the format etc. etc. of a film magazine they want to start, for the new generation; there are letters and calls coming in, and I have to cope with all of this alone.

Besides this, there is a very good chance these days, I will see what I can do alone —of starting a series of new kind of newsreels for the NY art theatres—5 minute long portraits of poets, painters, writers, and places, etc., like cafés, nightwatchmen, newspapermen, etc. etc.—short poems on New York. Village House of Commerce is interested but it needs pushing. What we could do together I cannot do alone. However, I'll try. etc. etc.

and then, I have my Lithuanian poetry, my *Village Voice* column which takes time (see films, write), I am organizing a Million Dollar Poetry Foundation to publish contemporary American poets (it is a very good idea, I will explain it later some day); this Tuesday I have the editorial meeting, plus a few other people, to start a supplement to *Film Culture*: 8–16 pages every month devoted to reviews only, and nothing else. Strictly a record of New York film openings which could go to subscribers or be sold on newsstands, and serve very well other countries to decide what films to import. I got this idea when I had to spend a whole week preparing a report for Poland's Ministry of Culture on American Films in 1958. They wanted my advice of what films to import. So this supplement would do all that. And then I have to go around with Adolfas' manuscripts, and have to do 100 other necessary things.

So, as you can see, I have a right to complain that I was left alone here to do the work of three. But I can do it. At least until the other two members of Bi-Films will come back to their nests—because I have no doubt—as we have said many times before—that America is the place for our work. We can test our wings and our claws in other continents—but the flying must be done here, there is nowhere else so much space!

Your brother,
Jonas

"All artistic activities are magical operations and music is the mystery of the universe exerting the all uniting power in nature. A most powerful conceiver // It allures the celestial influences. That the planets whirling in their orbs produce sounds is a discovery of Pythagorus. The spheres produce tones of the nucleus of all that exists // and men who can imitate this celestial harmony have traced their way back to this sublime realm // where moving according to these ideal figures // They then capture the magical meanings of the earliest sacred rites // movements that cause the gods to rejoice and echoes to haunt the planets // creating great curative forces."—Heinrich Cornelius Agrippa von Nettesheim (1531)

May 2, 1959
IRVING LERNER films:
Murder by Contract
City of Fear
Man Crazy
Edge of Fury
The Wild Party
Anna Lucasta

It is through SCHOOLS that most of the nivellization, dehumanization is being done. Humanity is being corrupted in the kindergartens already, in its most important period of growth. And how proud they are of their schools! They know how to write and read, my god!

Rock and roll as a slumber, an antidote against dehumanization. A slumber during which the subconscious can regain its balance, by itself, without outside effort. The subconscious (the private one and the total subc. of humanity) always regains it, if it is provided with such slumbers, if left alone—in African rhythmic dances, rituals, or Negro spirituals; religious ceremonies of Catholics (Protestant ceremonies provide only a little bit of it, they are too "sober," too intellectual, mental—an area which is of little help to the soul when it comes to the moments of regaining equilibrium); rock and roll does it. Strange how the Total Subconscious is able to take care of itself, against the laughs of the intellectuals and everybody—in a simple craze. The craziness is antidote, the millions in the asylums are antidotes. On the one side we have complete mechanization,

drying out of the soul and imagination—in America more than anywhere else because of the most progressed technical civilization—and on the other the ecstasy of the rock-and-roll, and beats, Zen-buddhists, abstract-expressionists, anarchists, asylums—the sensitivity, subconscious pops out, as a reaction, a protest. And the more extreme is the technical civilization, the more extreme is the relationship of these two poles, the more split, the more schizophrenic—but it is not sickness, this schizophrenia: it is a cure, it is a positive, saving force: force that comes from the very core of human existence, as a reaction, as a warning, as a manifestation, as a stating of fact.

On the article by Kracauer in *Film Book* 1: To talk about "audience" only as "vulgus," is the same as to discuss literature, poetry, drama from the point of view of a kitchen maid or a subway reader of a novel-romance. The experience of a work of art is not always "dreaming" or "slumber." It is also a conscious, physical experience. And then, again, not all dreaming and slumber are negative or empty. Compare contemporary films to the contemporary prose—Kerouac, Burroughs—or to painting—de Kooning. That is what I mean by bringing our cinema up to date. How can we "catch" modern reality with our outdated vocabularies, syntax, outdated tools and methods? Every age has its syntax, its rhythm, its style. We are in a period of gropings, of fleeting statements, outlinings, searchings, but no summaries. We are in the beginning of something, but not at the end. The end is still going strong, it's a long end… The form and style of our art must grow out from the attitude and character (essence) of new life if we want our art to be "new." We cannot "catch" it with dead, formalist, royalist, capitalist plots, petit bourgeois attitudes. Much of our written poetry has already escaped it, but our

cinema is still at the very very beginning of its escape and doesn't know where nor how to run away.

I refuse to go into serious discussions with Maya unless she abandons her metaphor of Bank Robbery which she equates with the creative process. Since I consider her equation a simplification of life processes—it reduces life to scheming—I really can't go into any further discussion on the subject unless Maya rethinks her metaphor.

Further, I can't discuss the new cinema with Maya unless she stops equating spontaneity and unconscious, as also Bosley Crowther does, with "catch-as-it-comes." Maya should know that any planning can go wrong, even IBM machines make mistakes, but there is an iron rule when it comes to the creation from the depths: no mistakes there, our unconscious makes no mistakes.

Further: I do not understand, why Maya ascribes to me a nonsense such as "crying for Freedom" when I have stated in my writings that I don't even believe in freedom; that an artist doesn't need freedom, that freedom is an invention for which I have no need; freedom is an invasion.

May 4, 1959
Richard Griffith said: "I read your essay [in *Film Book* N.1] and I liked it, the way you write, with real fire. But I disagreed with every word you said."
How could he agree! He, and all my older friends deal with the past, history of film, and I deal with the living cinema, with the future (not even present…). I am a police dog, and they are the hunters, killers. It is my nose that leads, it is their noses that follow.

May 5, 1959
Ron Rice called. We met at the Cedar bar, had a few beers. He says, he read my *Voice*

column, got all excited, wants to make movies. Did some painting, but decided it wasn't his metier. But now everybody's scaring him about the movie making expenses. Asked, what film school he should attend. I said, I don't believe in film schools. He agreed. I told him about the 8th Avenue outdated stock place, he said he'll go there. He said he wants to start by filming some paintings. I told him it was all wrong, he should leave painting to the painters. He agreed, and we had a beer to that.

A DREAM
I dreamt:
I am in a room, number 4. A big long room. I am running.
I run into another room, with a big number 5, then into room 3, and then I run back to room 4. I don't know which room is mine, which door to enter. I am dying but I am uncertain about my life. Then I stop in the middle of a corridor and permit the rooms to run past me. I wake up.

No date, 1959
Saw Truman Capote at the 92nd St. Y.
It is easy for Capote to talk, abstractly, about the purity of art, the art of literature. When the times are not clear and transitional, as they are today, it is a betrayal of humanness to ask for purity and clarity in art—it means only upholding of a status quo of life, escapism. And you, great Sean O'Casey! Your stupid remarks about the angry young men! Why do you want them to be peaceful and content with something that is unclean, dirty, something that stinks to heaven? Only because you made it? It is this stink that begins to bother heavens, so the angels send angry young men to do something about it—the beats, the angry young men are Hermeses, messengers of gods. It may not yet be clear to all, their function, their doings—they may seem like working in the negative—but where else can we be in times of corruption if not in the field of the negative, the opposing, in order to begin undoing the wrong doings of those who preceded us?

Improvisation and the use of accidents we find in *Paisà*, in *The Little Fugitive*, in Humphrey Jennings, Vigo, in Lumière's *L'arrivée d'un train en gare de la Ciotat*— There is always "small" poetry, and the large poetry; Brakhage's or Vigo's or Anger's poetry.

De Kooning: "There's no way of looking at a work of art by itself; it's not self-evident— it needs a lot of talking about; it's part of a whole man's life."

May 9, 1959
The popular tunes, songs, music pieces, when listened to in a closed room, seem often banal, trite, uninteresting. One has to put oneself into the right mood to listen to them, to like them. However, they blend perfectly outdoors, in wide open highway spaces, when blasted from the radios of the speeding cars, when heard from far away, or even in the car itself, in a windy convertible. Then they have a unique beauty, color. It is a space music. Highway music. Car music. American music. Folk music of the XXth century. It is not a music to listen to, like "serious" music, but part of the environment, background music, music to live with, nothing great, nothing "uplifting," but something that goes very well with—becomes an extension of—the landscape, open spaces. Even in the factories, it sounds better, among all those strange machines, wheels, tables, workers, the muffled voices of the workers. In any spacious place it goes well, where the listener cannot pay all his attention to it, where it can receive always only a small part of our attention, when we can't be critical listeners, where we are absorbed into something else: work, landscape,

driving, etc. I will always remember the beauty of Harry James' trumpet across Lake Edersee, resounding into the sunny hills on the other side of the lake, and coming through the spaces of the lake, the almost heartbreaking atmosphere created by it on a hot summer day, midday, and the raspberries are so red, so red, on the hillsides!

May 24, 1959

Notes on films
Saw:
The Cosmic Man, science fiction, written by Arthur C. Pierce, directed by Herbert Greene.
A "space" scientist comes to visit Earth, to teach the earth's scientists their science, to exchange knowledge, etc. The army wants to destroy him, as dangerous. A scientist saves him and he leaves earth.

The Silent Enemy, written and directed by William Fairchild. With Lawrence Harvey. Ltn. Crabs biography. A competently done British undersea war thriller. Crabs fights Italian underwater saboteurs in Gibraltar. Simple straight action film.

May 25, 1959

Robert Frank: realistic detail, but the feeling behind is dominant. Realistic detail plus feeling.
Alfred Leslie: His paintings are abstract. But when I look at them, to me, they are all feeling, very very strong emotion, in every stroke. Emotion in broad strokes.
De Sica is a craftsman all right. But *The Roof* is bad not because of its craft: it's bad because De Sica has a wrong attitude to life and to his art.
The New Film-maker (*Shadows*, *Pull My Daisy*) is starting a slow revolution. But it is a revolution of attitudes, not techniques. When the attitude is right, the rest will happen by itself. Even if one is wrong, technically, even if the film is "bad," like

many new low budget off-Hollywood films are, at least there is right attitude, they are not phony. Phonyness is what I can not stand.
Find Fernand Léger's quote: 14th Street windows, neckties, etc., are the only honest art, achievement that he can accept as honest, not phony, in America: people created these displays, signs, they made them without pretensions to art.
Alfred [Leslie] said he saw *Lonely Sex* on 42nd Street. It was a bad film, but he enjoyed it better than many of the phony art films. And it was made with love. There were many shots, situations that were honest, real, although not realistic. At least this man tried, even if he got it only once or twice.
Robert [Frank] got so mad during *The Roof*. The film was so stupid, he thought, so naïve, so bad. And how the critics got fooled by it is hard to understand.

SHORT STORY
A man fell in love with a crane.
"But you are a man," wondered his friends.
"Nevermind," he said.

June, 1959

Storm De Hirsch is a poet. A part of her subconscious wants to be expressed, wants to have an outer form. So she writes, in signs, intuitively, half-hypnotically, or she paints. Some fragments of her inner life emerge as words of long forgotten languages, some fall into more recognizable patterns of images of poems; others become paintbrush strokes, colors, lines, revealing invisible spaces, dimensions. What De Hirsch cannot say in words, she has to say in colors and shapes—nothing unsaid can stay long inside her without causing pain and even destruction. So she has to get it all out. These paintings are the patterns of her soul. They are lyrical. Her soul is lyrical, one part of it. But her poetry is all mind. Blake was all mind too. One part of

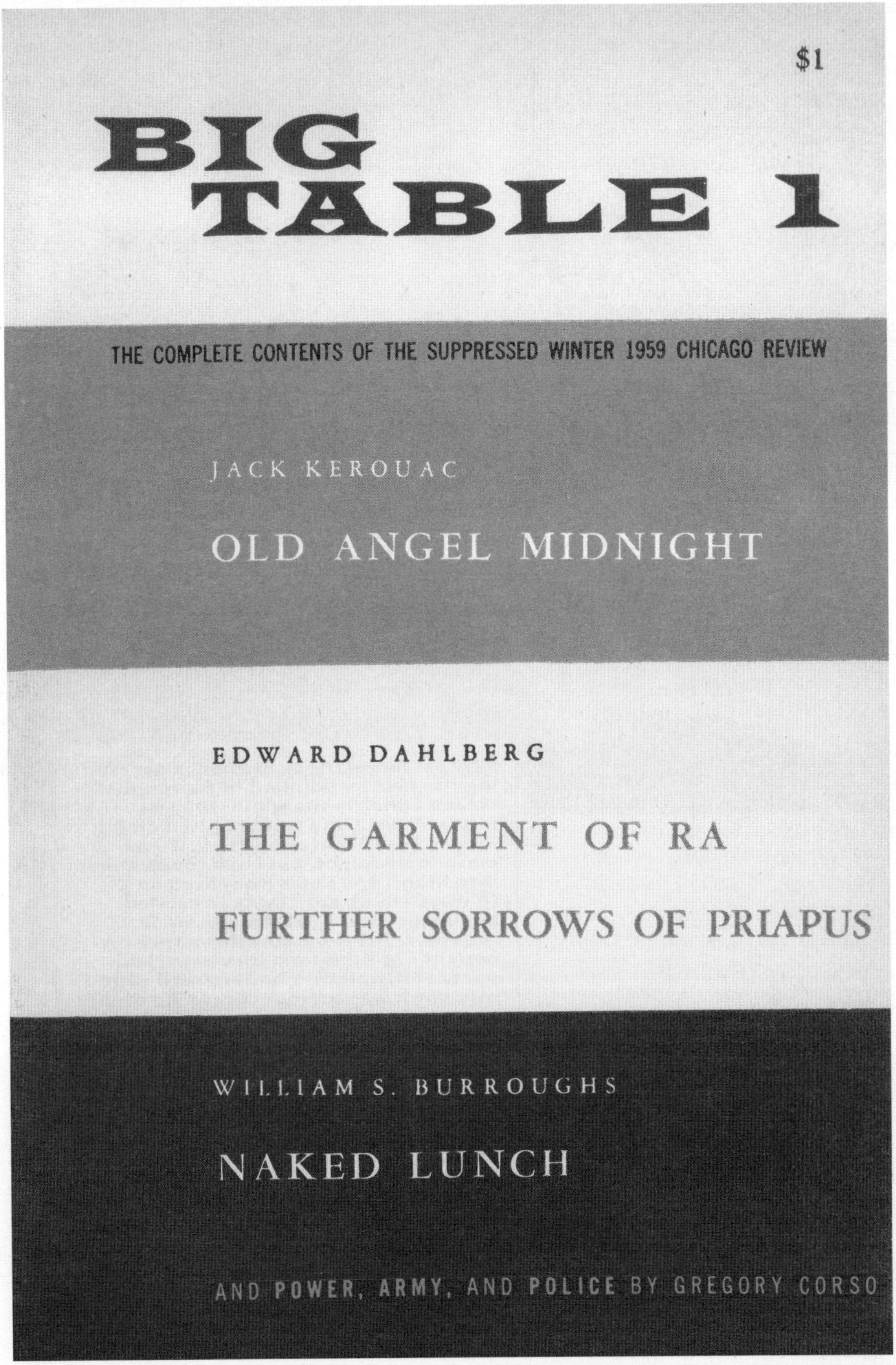

$1

BIG TABLE 1

THE COMPLETE CONTENTS OF THE SUPPRESSED WINTER 1959 CHICAGO REVIEW

JACK KEROUAC

OLD ANGEL MIDNIGHT

EDWARD DAHLBERG

THE GARMENT OF RA

FURTHER SORROWS OF PRIAPUS

WILLIAM S. BURROUGHS

NAKED LUNCH

AND POWER, ARMY, AND POLICE BY GREGORY CORSO

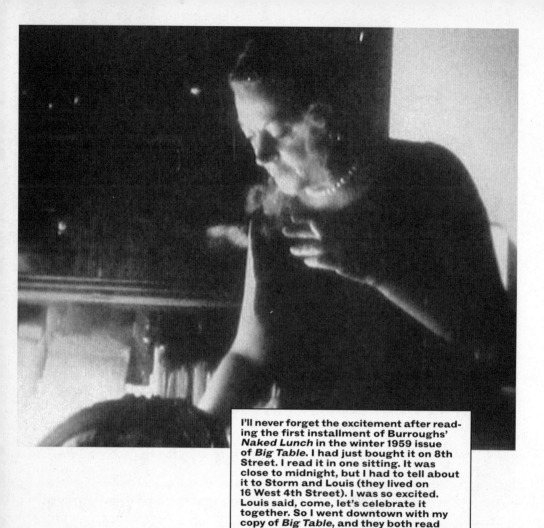

I'll never forget the excitement after read-ing the first installment of Burroughs' *Naked Lunch* in the winter 1959 issue of *Big Table*. I had just bought it on 8th Street. I read it in one sitting. It was close to midnight, but I had to tell about it to Storm and Louis (they lived on 16 West 4th Street). I was so excited. Louis said, come, let's celebrate it together. So I went downtown with my copy of *Big Table*, and they both read parts of it, and they both agreed with me that it was a groundbreaking event and an occasion for celebration. Storm pulled out a bottle of wine, and then another, and we talked and talked, in excited voices, late into the morning hours.

Storm's soul is all mind. There are many different compartments, mansions, in Storm's soul...

Dear Mrs. Althea Borden,
In response to your letter of Sept. 21st, regarding the character and abilities of Miss L. Storm De Hirsch, I can only express my unreserved recommendation. During the 7 or 8 years that I know her, I had many occasions to watch her and work with her under various circumstances. I have always admired her endurance, her social and private tact, the subtlety of understanding. Although with definite artistic vocation, she is not one of those emotionally loose personalities, but highly controlled, self-confident, sociable.
If you have any concrete questions, you may call me at OR-5-5142, I will be more than happy to be of any assistance to you.
Sincerely yours,
J.M.

August 9, 1959

The feeling when you are thirsty, when in the middle of August, and the sun, and the dust, you have no money for a good cool drink, and you are tired, and hot, dreaming of cool white waters, or the rain—
The smell of sweat, and the faces, perspired and red, wet, with salty eyes, and tired, the city dust, heat and soot—
And yet as I child I dreamt white bread, and candies...Or in Germany, in the barracks, when we used to say: AMERICA! To eat, to eat, at least one good meal! A simple dream which I am still carrying with me, in this summer day, perspiring, and hungry, and stealingly drinking cold water in sad Automats—

"Yesterday I passed a Mexican village. People here still die from malaria, lack of food. I haven't seen such misery before." (Adolfas)

October 15, 1959

"Who knows what the songs of the birds do to the earth during the spring?"

I had an impression, during Kerouac's drunk improvisation session at Robert's, for *Pull My Daisy*'s narration—that drunkenness did not affect his words, his tongue —just the opposite: it opened him even more. Allen told me, Jack told him that he, Jack, hears words when he writes, his ears are almost in pain, when he writes, he says.

October 19, 1959

With Allen [Ginsberg] and Peter [Orlovsky] we paid a visit to Storm. Storm said that Rimbaud is closer to her "subconscious poems." Yeats's visions, she thought, were too cold. She also said, that she used to smoke marijuana, and she has nothing against it, but she stopped because she found that self-hypnosis does the same as the drug. Plus, it "doesn't do any harm to the body," she said. She thought that Allen should also, perhaps, turn to self-hypnosis.
But Storm's poems, in "translations" from the "language of the subconscious" have the same coldness as Yeats's *A Vision*. There is the same metaphysicality.
It seems to me, that drugs like marijuana which affect body ("do something to body") & senses, they work more on flesh, on senses, and the imagination is much richer for that (like *Illuminations*); the senses are deranged, but the feeling for form, and rhythm and language are even more intensified, united. Whereas self-hypnosis (and hypnosis in general) seems to disconnect the senses, the flesh, and the mind is naked like steel, the symbols and archetypes come out, and although they are rich in meaning, they lack the rhythm & language of the drug (senses) poetry. No sensuality in mind...

No date, 1959

Living Places:
- October 29, 1949 – November 1949:
  Meserole Street, Brooklyn
- November 1949 – January 1950:
  South 3rd Street, Brooklyn
- February 1950 – May 1950:
  47½ Lorimer Street, Brooklyn
- May 1950 – Spring 1952:
  58 – 85 Maspeth Avenue, Brooklyn
- Spring 1952 – Spring 1953:
  123 Linden Street, Brooklyn
- Spring 1953 – April 1955:
  95 Orchard Street, Manhattan
- April 1955 – …:
  16 West 109th Street, Manhattan

Work Places:
- Nov. 10, 1949 – Dec. 10, 1949:
  GM Manufacturing Co.
- 13 – 08 43rd Ave.; "assembly worker"
- Dec. 23, 1949 – June 9, 1950:
  Bebry Corp. 21 – 22 40th St. Brooklyn;
  "riveter"
- Dec. 15, 1949 – Dec. 20, 1949:
  Emerson Plastic Co. 537 3rd Ave.,
  Manhattan
- June 1950 – June 30, 1950:
  David Altman Co., 320 E. 4th St.;
  "plumber"
- July 1950 – August 23, 1950:
  L.W. Machines, Johnson St., Brooklyn;
  "machine operator"
- August 23, 1950 – September 5, 1950:
  Bancelli, Maspeth; ironing in a
  laundromat
- December 1950 – May 1, 1957:
  Graphic Studios, 126 W. 22nd St, NYC
- July 1, 1957 – July 1958:
  Moss Photo Studios, 350 W. 50th St, NYC
- August 11, 1958 – summer 1959:
  Cooper Offset, 814 Broadway,
  Manhattan

October 25, 1959

The fear (angst) which can be seen today everywhere is not caused by the mecha- nization & atom; it is caused by man's dishonesty with himself and towards the outer world, including the bomb. He blames the bomb for things he should blame himself. We keep marching against the Bomb. We do not march against ourselves! But people used to, they used to go to a desert for 40 days and get rid of "themselves," of all the crappiness. They went on 40 day strikes against (or for) themselves.

They think they are free and honest and sincere, but they are so only within the small outside circle, like children, not knowing that the bottom of their small circle is only the beginning of the infinite circle.

A STORY

There was a man who knew everything. He was that wise. Then, again, he didn't know nothing, like everybody else. Until, one day, he knew everything again. After that his mind fell again into darkness as in the beginning (or was it the beginning?—the tale doesn't say it)—and he stumbled and grappled in the not-knowing. And so he was able to see and to know everything again, in a different way, perhaps, but it was as good and true as any time before. I wonder sometimes, so the tale goes, what is the man now: does he know or doesn't he know? As if that would matter. Sometimes he knows, sometimes he doesn't know; he knows it again, and he doesn't know it again.

November 5, 1959

Dear Brother Edouard:

Forgive me for not writing for such a long time. On one hand, there is nothing new in my life, on the other—too many things are bothering me at this time.

For some time now, for a good 2 – 3 months, I have been going through one of my "periods," to which I return every two years or so, to re-evaluate my life, to take new directions & make corrections.

With Robert Frank, on last day of filming
Pull My Daisy.

Many times during the last weeks I have been tempted to leave everything and run to some far and lost desert, and live there for at least 40 days. I understand why all saints chose deserts at one or another period of their lives, to find, or redefine themselves. Not that I am confused. I need a desert just to help myself. I have been cutting many unnecessary ties, engagements, involvements, passions, trying to return just to myself, to my own core, to free myself from the American dust, from my own false dreams. Jokingly I call this period my shrinking period. Like a dog that before jumping, before making a leap, bends his legs, pulls himself together into a small ball of latent concentrated energy. I feel that the time for my own real work is coming, I have to get ready for it. Reviewing, writing on films, etc.—I had enough of it.

Adolfas came back and has no money and no job, and no room, and has to live on nothing, since my only weekly income is $19 and $15 of these go to pay for the room! So I am going down into new debts. My mother is writing letters to me, asking for medicine, one of our brothers needs desperately medicine, a bad TB case, and I am helpless and have to wait until a miracle happens, not being able even to explain to my own mother the situation in which I am.

I haven't thought much about *Film Culture* these days. New issue is being printed, finally, after a long delay, and it will be out sometime next week. Definitely, there will be another issue, despite everything that I am going through, and I will write to you about it later in December or so.

Together with my various decisions and shrinkings and cuttings off, I am returning slowly to my own piles of manuscripts and papers and notes, and for two weeks now I have been working very hard on a script for a feature film, with a work title *Fragment of a Century*. The decision is to have it ready before the end of the year. We have a pile of scripts here, but they always were too experimental, not finished enough. I think that I have or I'll have something that will be a good basis for an important film. I want to make my own film, and I will come to it. I want to use this winter for raising money. Everybody, any stupid dope is able to do it, I don't see why I couldn't do it with my persistence and insistence. The more that these coming 12 months will be about the best months in perhaps 30 years for a new and unknown film-maker in America to start his own film. There is much talk here now about the new French wave, new Polish film-makers, etc. with a certain envy and desperation, the climate is ready, for those who are willing to push, to persuade, to get backers. I will make my film this coming summer or I'll go crazy.

So that's where I am. I am entering a very busy and crucial period, and you will understand my long silence. You have just passed—or are passing now—through a very important period, too. I can feel that we are very close to our aims—I can feel it from the strange tensions in the air, and from our own desperations. Adolfas feels the same, walking like a closed wild animal in our small room (where there isn't even place for walking) brooding angrily in himself, cursing his publishers and everybody.

Brother Jonas

No date, 1959

A PLAY

First man: Where are we going?

Second man: Just riding.

First man: Riding, riding. I'm getting bored. Let's do something.

Second man: See that house? There lives a lady with jewels. Let's get them jewels.

First man: I'll get the lady.

Second man: Don't mind the lady. Jewels.

First man: Let's go.

Act Two
Lady: What do you want?
First man: Keep quiet, lady.

SCRIPT
He leaves the Monastery.
Has to take over his father's business.
Comes home, finds out that his father was in banking.
So he gives out the money to the poor.
Gets arrested.
When it's cleared that money isn't fake, and his own, he is released.
Gets swindled out of all his money by politicians for a "governmental election," for the election of "the government of the people, for the people."
Disillusioned with Public Activities, retreats to private pleasures, women, etc.
Is tricked by a Lesbian of his last money.
Is taken to mental hospital.
Is cleared of all mother-father-etc. business, comes home sloppy, blank, flippant.
Now he's ready to live just like everybody.
Gets a job as a salesman.
Cannot sell anything. Works in a sewing machine store, Singer.
Gives the machines away, for nothing, to the poor, is fired?
Meets a woman. She is a "beatnik."
Finds out, she lives with three husbands.
He kills them all?
Or: he gets a corner for himself, in her "flat," as one of four.

Films I saw recently:

High School Big Shot, by Joel M. Rapp
An exemplary student becomes a sort of Raskolnikov, wants to steal the narcotics people's $1,000,000 for his girl. Son-Father relationship is more original.

T-Bird Gang, by Richard Harbinger
A boy whose father was killed by the gang joins it to betray—revenge it.

These and similar films are like a rehearsal, breaking the ground of contemporary themes, locales, new faces.

Lost, Lonely & Vicious, Karl Meyer.

CHAPTER EIGHT

... Frances... About self-containment... Mescal... I decide to make my first "real" film... A DREAM... On *Shadows* as projection of myself... Letter to Edouard re. *Film Culture*, N.Y. film scene, etc... Adolfas returns from Canada... Notes made on train to Chicago... Detroit as image of Hell... I try to change my life... The unreality ... Close to another of my "nervous breakdowns"... An unpublished *V. Voice* column... Brakhage at the Living Theatre... From a letter to Edouard re. *Guns of the Trees*... On Peter Orlovsky... Broke... Desperate... Search for a job...

November, 1959

Sunday night.

Dear Frances:

Here is the address of the Archdiocese of New York, which should have all information on convents, monasteries, etc. around New York: 451 Madison Ave. (PL-91400). The Franciscan Brother in Brooklyn, whom I mentioned to you, is Brother Andriekus, GL-5-7068. Just tell that you are my friend. You should talk sometime to him, on the phone at least. He may come up with some suggestions. He himself is a poet, and I have no doubt he knows Hesse. Or, at least, he should...

So much on practical matters... as for the unpractical matters, here is an excerpt from my diary:

November, 1959

Frances called and said she is leaving for the country this afternoon, to see the autumn. The autumn! I was envious, I was angry, I was jealous.

In some part, in my heart's corner, I felt happiness about her freedom. She was strong enough to go and spend a day alone by herself, to look at the autumn. On the other hand, I wanted to make her a slave of my own desires, to limit her freedom. My love wanted her free, independent and happy but my desires wanted to limit her, to keep her close to myself, to reduce her to a part of myself. I sat there, fighting myself, fighting my jealousy, and looking at a lone tree behind the window, my only sign of the autumn. My desires, my emotions refused to obey my mind and heart.

November, 1959

..."self-containment"... ideas... Hermann Hesse... *Narziß und Goldmund*...

Didn't I myself go through long periods of self-containment? Wasn't I myself who had hurt other women with my self-containment? Always self-scrutiny, always the intellect...No, it's not hate, it's all nonsense about hate being love's opposite. One can love and still hate. The opposite of love, its denial and its enemy is the intellect, the mind. When the mind begins to work, it possesses the body as much as love does. The thought is also a passion, the mind is a passion, and we cannot be possessed by two passions at the same time. Where is the devil, asked Marcia last night. Yes, that is so: God, devil, love, mind, they can all take over the body, and they master our every movement. So that when I touched her hand, that evening, there was no response, it was cold. I am so self-contained today, she said. The intellect was not only in the mind. It was also in the flesh, in her hands, in her walk. And I hated it that moment, I hated it. Because it was me who wanted to be the master of her mind, her flesh, and her tone of voice, and her walk. I wanted to be her devil. But I was helpless. She was in her own church. I was beaten. She had a magical circle around her which my ego was not allowed to cross, my passions froze.

So I shrunk back into myself, I pulled myself into a small bundle, a small ball, into a small center again, like a wild animal preparing for a leap, and all night long I was leaping up, all night long, all night long my ego was trying to break through the circle, beating itself each time unto the invisible line of the circle, again and again, until, late in the night, I fell asleep, exhausted, in my own desperation, anxiety, helplessness, jealousy.

Factual information as a form of criticism. 16 mm. Color. Ektachrome. Original. Reversal print. Kodachrome. Film stock year 1971. Print stock year 1973. Print made in 1974. Etc. Etc.
A project for a university film course: Collect data on color etc. film stocks, when they came into existence and when they went out of existence, etc.

November 6, 1959

Adolfas was showing a bottle of mescal in Dratfield's office.
"Oh, go away," shouted Leo's secretary, almost in fear, "Don't drink this, Leo," she said, "this is that drink that makes you see images, you see visions."
A poor woman, I thought. I saw her in that office three years ago, and two years ago, too, and today. The same boring monotony, office ugliness. And now, when that rare occasion (supposedly) comes when she could see visions and beautiful images— she runs away in panic, she shouts in fear: "No, Leo, no, don't drink this, I don't want this, you'll see images!" And this is an image (movies) distribution place! Could one fall deeper than this into the everydayness? She has lost even the desire for visions, for glimpses into the other... Once you have left Paradise, don't look back, don't look!

November 10, 1959

For five years now I have been actively engaged in film criticism. However, at this stage in my life, I feel that what I want and what I have to say I can no longer say through film criticism alone.
There are changes going on in the world, and there are changes going on in me. There are secret changes which nobody can see but me. It was not long ago that Frances reminded me of Nietzsche's *The Birth of Tragedy*. I re-read his introduction, to me the most tragic statement he ever wrote: "This new soul should have sung, not spoken. What a pity that what I had to say, I did not have courage to say as a poet —through poetry, perhaps, I could have succeeded in saying it." ("Sie haette singen sollen, diese neue Seele!—und nicht reden! Wie schade, dass ich, was ich damals zu sagen hatte, es nicht als Dichter zu sagen wagte: ich haette es vielleicht gekonnt!")
It shook me again, this statement. It shook me out of the illusion of a critic. I know now

that my only chance to achieve a better understanding of the world and myself, and to help others to understand themselves and their worlds, is by saying it through a film of my own.

November 11, 1959

I had a dream. I saw the planet Earth, and one side of it was burning. It burned slowly, like incense, and burning chunks were falling into sort of a holly plate, and the pieces continued to smolder and smoke on the plate.

When I suddenly woke up, with this image still in my consciousness, my world had collapsed. Everything that I believed in, everything that I was doing had no longer any meaning. My inside, my brain was on fire. I felt I had to make burning decisions, I had to change my whole life, to make drastic corrections in the parallaxes, angles and directions in my life.

I tried to sleep again. I wanted to escape the thoughts. For a few seconds I fell back into sleep. But now I dreamt, and it was very very sharp and very very real, I felt I was holding a hand grenade in my palm, a small grenade, and it was ready to explode. I woke up.

I was lying with my eyes open all night, with the pieces and splinters of my life floating all around me, in the middle of New York night, burning, falling to ashes, in order to start from the ashes again, like in a desert, somewhere between insanity and ecstasy. I was burning, burning myself, like incense, burning, for some unknown purpose—

Fall, 1959

Why, why now, at this stage in my life, why do I feel this burning necessity for a drastic change? I feel I do not have any other choice but to burn myself out completely, in order to regain some basis from where I can begin to rebuild myself anew.

During last five years I have neglected poetry. I had turned towards the criticism. But now, suddenly I am full of anger and gathering emotion.

I have reached the line where criticism, science and philosophy stop. The regions into which I am driven to and pushed and tricked in, are no longer those of a critic.

The realization that I was betrayed by *Shadows* was only the last stone. It helped me to realize that what I was talking about, what I really saw in it, in the first version of it, was something that nobody else saw. What it was, I was pursuing my own ideal. Cassavetes had no idea of what he really had. And since he didn't really know what he had, it was very easy for him to destroy it, to change it. When I was trying to explain it to Nico and John, there was no real response: they didn't seem to understand what I was talking about. And I suddenly felt, in horror, that I was talking, most of the time, to myself, and about the things that mattered only to me. The ideas and the desperations that I was breeding deep inside myself and which I wanted to exchange with others—none of it ever really reached anyone. And so, now, now I have come to this conclusion, that only through art I can reach the others, through my work as an artist.

My last few meetings with Frances have brought all of this into a stillsharper focus. I became aware, more than before, that my own generation—Frances is only nineteen —has already begun to show all the signs of a dying generation. This is my last minute to escape before the bridge falls down. Frances is still full of uncompromising idealism and dreams, everything that was still so much part of me before I got submerged into all the "adult," "useful," "society," "cultural," etc. etc. activities, which involved me into associations with many dull, very very dull people who make the popular art, films, all the dull conversations, dull ambitions, dull eyes.

Now, suddenly for the first time in five, six years I am breathing freely again. I am exchanging the good company of smart friends, and social recognition—into the vague, uncertain landscape of the new, unborn, trembling existence—throwing myself back into the doubt, searching, desperations, dizzy grounds, swinging abysses.

November 12, 1959

Like a prism, like a magnifying glass, she helps me to see myself in a different light, from different angles, and more clearly. I see myself through her. The exultation with which I receive her every word, every reaction becomes double-edged and they cut both into outside and inside.

November 20, 1959

Brother Edouard:

Adolfas came back three weeks ago. He spent most of his time these last three weeks looking for a job. We are completely broke, and I don't earn enough money even to support myself. But there are no jobs. So, the same story. Last weekend they went hunting, somewhere near Canada, Adolfas and Gideon. Came back cold, hungry, and with no deer! (They saw one dead on the road.)

I don't know if Col. forwarded you my last letter. In that letter I described in a few words my spiritual situation at this moment. To sum up that letter and to bring you up to date:

I have been trying to clean out my house. Had enough of the old and the same New York friends, film snobs, and all kinds of snobs. Sitting much home. *FC* is in the bindery, after a long delay finally will be out next week. I have decided as soon as the issue is out, to close it. At least, to disband the editorial board. If we want to continue, and we definitely will, we'll continue just by ourselves. No phony editorial boards. This is just part of my house cleaning. There are many other, more personal matters.

I hope something concrete will happen in Yugo., with your script etc. Still, I feel angry on the world that you have to waste your ideas and scripts and time and energy and everything always on somebody else's films. Experience, yes, but of that you have already enough, more than Eisenstein had when he made his first film! As for any credits, they will not help much in America. At a time when Orson Welles himself cannot get an American producer to sponsor him, what does it mean—a man who worked for Orson Welles?

Still, that is the only way, to work for the others first—what else there is, at the moment?

We have run, we have thrown ourselves into various directions and with various projects, but I don't regret much, we didn't make too many false steps in our lives, I think. Only that the goddam world is so stupid, so blind, so businesslike everywhere.

You asked me about when I think your return will be necessary. It is not easy to answer. But I have good hopes. As always, perhaps too optimistic. But I think that I will get my film produced. So when that will become a reality, then it will be the time for all three of us to start working. Nothing concrete and useful for you in America at this moment. I think you are getting more experience and more done, at this stage of our lives, in Europe. So let us wait, hopefully, for the Spring. I will be working hard these months on *Guns of the Trees*, which is the title of my script.

Let me know where to write, what address to use.

Wednesday, November 25, 1959

On the train from New York to Chicago.

It is night now. Only the lights of the towns, the bridges and the lamp posts are scattered across passing landscapes.

November 2, 1959, at the Living Theatre.
Ray Bremser, Frank O'Hara, LeRoi Jones
[Amiri Baraka]. From *Lost Lost Lost*.

My mind is finally at rest. The decisions have been made. I have only to move now; at least until Sunday night. I look into the night, through the train window.

It would have been easy to give up this trip. But I thought I should end one phase of my life with a certain geographical displacement note. Chicago. This will be the last effort, my last drop into the cup of the so-called "public" life. From now on there will be only the work on myself, going out of myself in other ways—to give myself to my own work, to give myself to more personal, even obscure irrational impulses and drives—

Not to criticize, not to rationalize: to love.

The true beginning of this new period began that night, when I saw you, suddenly, standing there, leaning in the doorway, lost in a sort of cosmic gaze upon the room. "An angel is warning me," I thought.

Oh, the idealism of youth!

It's all Maya's doing.

I believe nobody came into my life unnecessarily. I always met the right people at the right time, at a certain turning point: Leo, Edouard, and now you. I became their fate and they became my fate.

The train just stopped. What is the station? Someone shouted out the name, but I missed it. A man walked in selling "Coca-Cola." Outside I can see patches of snow.

November 26, 1959

When I woke up, in the morning, we were passing the endless plains running from Lake Erie, to the North. Snow patches, and scattered trees, now frozen, stood out in the huge, peaceful vastness stretching to all sides. And as I looked at this landscape, it had such a strong personality, style, that it was difficult not to respond to it, not to get lost in it. It overcame me, its cold, wintry purity and truth. A deep peace and serenity came from it and it was purifying, it forced me to abandon all pretense, all officialdom, and be just myself—just as

this landscape was its bare self, it's bare itself, in this early winter morning, with its bare cold trees, and snow sheets and frozen water patches.

A man just walked in, at a small station. "Snow is ahead of us," he said. And it seemed to me as if he meant: Oh, snow is more pure than we; the snow is still more itself than we are; the snow is ahead of us in its it-ness, in its pure whiteness, its cold, crystal destiny, on the wintry plains of the Great Lakes—the snow always is what it is, it always fulfills its destiny uncompromisingly with such a peace that I look out through the window of the rushing train and I want to shout, as I used to do in my childhood: OH, SNOW, SNOW, SNOW!— and be again with it, be again!

Detroit. We stopped in Detroit. A stream of cold air oozed in. Some people got up to leave. What an image, suddenly! What an ugly collection, what an ugly crowd of spitting, crouching, cursing grumbling men and women. They all seemed to be grim and angry, for some dark reason. Angry to come back to their city? Or angry just to come to it? So that suddenly, without even seeing the city, without even looking at it, I had before my eyes its soul, in its ugly nakedness. The soul of Detroit. These grim people, men and women, even this invalid on crutches, spitting on the floor, as if the broken leg would permit him now a revenge on the living whose legs aren't broken—and this woman pulling her little child, a girl of four, crying—and all the men and women in those tasteless hats and grim faces and dirty suitcases—they were the soul of Detroit, Detroit that I never want to see. It stood now before my eyes, like a disease, and I, unconsciously, pulled myself closer into my seat, into my corner, making myself smaller and smaller, retreating, trying to make myself invisible —but I wanted that it would spit fire— drawing a circle around myself to protect myself from this image and the vapors it exuded. I could feel its presence around me and I remained in my position of invisibility and retreat for a long long time, until the train moved out, through the black piles of car scrap and thistles, and patched-up and ugly workers' houses and soot black even under the snow—until the first landscape appeared again.

The bureaucrat at the ticket office in New York refused categorically to sell a ticket because I wanted to pay with a check. Cash he wants. He needs identification. So I showed him all kinds of documents I had, all my membership cards to museums, film societies, and my social security card, and the library card, and the bank booklet. No, that is not enough, the bureaucrat said. So, I said to myself, I'll show him the most important paper I have—and, before the by now angry and pushing people, I pulled out, like in that poem by Mayakovski, MY AMERICAN PASSPORT! The bureaucrat did not even laugh anymore—he got angry. This is not a document, this doesn't identify you! Don't you have a driver's license? No, I shouted, NO, I don't even drive, man. I got so angry, I shoved all my cards and papers back into my pocket and left the ticket window. How could I forget the simple fact that an American passport is his driver's license! Since I have no driver's license, I have no identity.

Still angry and not able to think clearly, and I had only three minutes left until the departure of the train—I decided to act my own way. I simply walked to the Chicago train, and took a seat, without thinking about any tickets. The men who check the tickets on the trains, I figured, should be different from the city people: they live with passing landscapes, there must be some kind of different feeling for life and people in them. From my childhood I have liked train conductors and ticket men.

I was right. The ticket man just took the number of my Museum's Press Pass, wrote it on the check, gave me the ticket to Chicago, and continued further down the line, talking to children. It was very good of you, I said. He didn't even hear me. A landscape full of trees was passing by.

A flock of huge white birds, sitting on the edge of the thin ice on a half-frozen lake, near Ann Arbor. A small wind was rippling the surface of the water into which they gazed meditativly.

An apple tree, by the road, with frozen apples still on its cold branches, covered with blotches of snow.

A tree lying in the cold river, as it fell in, days, weeks, months ago, sideways, half of its branches and trunk in the water.

The snow covers so much of the ugliness of the industrial cities that some of them look like decent places.

A dozen or so horses all black standing in the snow, near a farm, on the very top of a hill we just passed, like a painting of Grandma Moses.

Again I see snow, the cold purity of the landscape. After four days of boredom, monotony of Chicago.

What a difference! And how a man can live like that!

What a fool I was to go to Chicago in the first place.

Serves me well!

He is right in details, but poisonous in his totality.

This man thinks that he can revive dead ideas, religions, etc. Leave the dead in peace!

December 15, 1959

To hell with self-improvement, as far as my character or my behavior concerns. I will stay what I am, or I'll change as I go, indirectly. But no special attention—I have too much to do anyway. In other words: to hell with myself. I am too busy for such egoistic concerns!

James Broughton, Julian Beck, Marie Menken, Parker Tyler. In the background, the Invisible Man... If I am not wrong, it was during the opening of Willard Maas' film, *Narcissus*, at the Living Theatre, 1958.

I guess I am the worst man when it comes to explaining myself. I should never try it, really. I'll never try it again, at least not until next time… It is stupid. It is ridiculous. It is pitiable. One gets you or one doesn't get you. One sees what you feel or one doesn't. If one has to explain oneself, that is the end of it anyway: doesn't matter which one of the two is wrong. Like a bad novel. Flowers do not explain themselves. I always confuse the issues when I begin to explain myself, that is a fact. Even my horoscope says that I am wrong in my judgments of myself. Nobody should believe a word I say about myself. My explanations of myself are really reactions to the others and to the environment, and nothing else. I will be taken for what I am, for what I am worth, even if I am a fine mess, I don't care any longer. Even my shyness, etc.—why the hell should I try to erase it completely, or worry about it? I have enough to do and enough to enjoy in life anyway. My mistake until now was always this minderwertigheit's complex… Now, I just don't care…(Is this the beginning of I-don't-care period?)

No date, 1959

There is wisdom in waiting. One has to know how to wait, you can do nothing about it. It will either come or not, the answer, the cowboy, the flash. But this is the wisdom of a transitional period. It's almost ready. We are anxiously sitting through a period of waiting, of dread, before the flash of destiny shoots through our blood. And we can do nothing, absolutely nothing about it. Those who do, they make bombs or engage in similar destructive activities.

This is my Review of *The Connection*.

December, 1959*

A huge crowd is milling outside. No more tickets. In the auditorium the screen is almost dark. A few reflections, a beam of light. Suddenly, a doorway appears, a cup, a hand, a shadowy face. All reality broken, destroyed, no realism.

"Bravo!" shouts a man. "Boo!" shouts another voice. "My bravo was louder than your boo!" retorts the first voice. Again a silence. Now the shadowy figures are embracing, in the huge, animal darkness.

There is a man on the stage now, before the screen, talking something, half drunk, half inspired. "Willard Maas…" a voice whispers. "He was not drunk when he made his two films," whispers a youth leaning by the wall. He came from New Jersey to see the films.

In the lobby a man pulls from under his coat a huge can of film and passes it to a young man with a mustache—this is a free exchange market of the avant-garde, both ideas and stock. Boultenhouse, whose first film poem was just screened, is surrounded now. He has to answer questions about cameras, someone is in the middle of making a film, another one is searching for a cameraman.

On the screen: A dark blob is eating a yellow blob. "What cute things!" shouts a mountain of a woman from the back. "Marie Menken… she made the film…" a voice whispers. The black strange thing finishes devouring the yellow thing, and creeps on the window.

* In December of 1959 a screening took place at the Living Theatre, corner of the 14th Street and Sixth Avenue, New York City. A program of five or six films was projected. One of the films was Stan Brakhage's New York premiere of *Window Water Baby Moving*. Stan was the projectionist for the evening. After the screening of Stan's film Maya Deren came before the audience to declare, very emphatically, that giving birth was a very "private matter" and it shouldn't ever be filmed. "Even the animals, when they give birth, retreat into a secret place," said Maya. I do not remember Stan replying to Maya. He was in very low spirits that evening. He was hungry, broke and depressed. What follows is a piece I wrote for my *Village Voice* "Movie Journal" column. The piece, however, was misplaced at the *Voice* and it was never published. I found it some years later (2014). Down the stairs stumbles a policeman. "Avant-garde films!" he curses angrily. "I felt there was something queer going on."

On the screen: A young man looks at his hand. It trembles. It jumps. A hand of inspiration, not a real hand. A hand of a poet. A fist. "Cocteau!" shouts a bearded man. He tries to walk out, in protest. He steps over the heads, gives up, cannot pass, sits on the floor. In the back, by the wall, somebody applauds violently the birth of a new film poet.

On the screen: a wild party. A few youths, drunk, exulted with adolescent nonsense, stare at a couple kissing. One jumps up, and runs to the couple, sticks his face close to them. "Ha! Ha!" he laughs loudly— and he runs wildly around, laughing, with a face drunk and crazy and ablaze.

On the screen/probably for the first time ever in film history/: a woman gives birth to a child. We see it all. The woman is ecstatic. And so is the father. The audience is totally totally silent.

In the backstage, high upon the ladder, the projectionist, author of the film, Brakhage. It is cold there. A cup of stale coffee besides the machine. "It is bad. I have ten more films ready. But no money for printing. This is the end. Nobody wants to help experimental film," he talks to another man, sitting on the end of a garbage barrel —at the Living Theatre, last Monday.

December 30, 1959

There is always that feeling of unreality around me. I feel like I am in a constant flight, and without any controls, without any steering wheels.

I see my older friends, and some who are much younger than me: I see them already settled, already so earthly, almost in the very center of the earth's gravity.

Like Teiji [Ito]: he is so young, but so earthly. Only I am still in flight. I haven't reached yet the point of gravity, of still-stand. I am so far off and out, even when I am so close to what's called reality.

Kisses of reality! Short moments when my lips and the lips of reality meet. Love?

Betrayal? Covering something up? Kiss of a prostitute? What?

But then, because of the smallness of the contact area, & because of its brevity—because my contact with reality is always through these thin wires—these brief moments become so painfully, so unbearably real, when they come! How many watts & volts of reality are burning the wires?—as if everything that I had missed during my space (dream) flights, as if all this, now, suddenly, were coming to me, in a short fusion, in such an impatient concentration that it consumes itself, cannot stand itself, and it burns under the pressure of its own force, before the happiness arrives, before the stillness arrives, and I am thrown again into where I was before, even more painfully—brother of Sisyphus.

Agrippa von Nettesheim. *The Philosophy of Natural Magic*

Agrippa. *The Vanity of Arts and Sciences*

Agrippa: (in the above book) p. 187, an essay on "On Prostitution, or the trade of Whoring" and page 197: "Of Procuring"

Agrippa von Nettesheim. See: Arnold, Ignaz Ferdinand, 1774 – 1812

February 9, 1960

From a letter to Edouard:

Here is the script, the first version. There will be many changes and, perhaps, drastic revisions, but the main idea will remain more or less the same, as outlined in these pages.

I am quite certain that this is not what you would like to make. I know that you would take a more positive attitude, with a more dramatic plot, characters, situations, etc. But that would be your film, not mine. I may introduce changes and accept suggestions, but only those which will go with my conception of what I want to do. As you'll

Robert Frank during the filming of
The Sin of Jesus, **May 1960. At George Segal's chicken farm in New Jersey.**

On the set of *The Sin of Jesus.*

see, when you read the script, it is reduced to the simplest scenes. I knew from the beginning that it wouldn't make any sense writing a script which would require more than $10,000 to make into a film.

Here is a statement, or a note, on the formal aspects of *Guns*:

Formally, *Guns of the Trees* is conceived as an episodic, horizontal film. There is no apparent direct plot-story connection between one scene and the next. The scenes will act like fragments of a larger mosaic, each contributing to the total idea and mood of the film.

More on formal aspects. As you see, the film is divided into six sequences. These six sequences very possibly will be indicated on the screen by numbers, words (One, Two, etc.), or blank screen, like parts of a book. Each sequence is divided into smaller scenes, which will be also separated by very short visual breaks (a few black frames, or some other such device) —like taking a breath before beginning a new chapter of a book. Each scene shouldn't last more than 2 minutes.

Acting will be spontaneous, half improvised. Photography will also be very much improvised. No obvious, formalistic framings. I would prefer a hand-held camera throughout the film.

March 29, 1960

From a letter to Edouard:

Guns will definitely go into shooting, if not in June then in July. I have $6,000 in the bank. It is not easy—nobody wants to invest money in the first film of somebody they do not know. The money I got until now was from someone who knew me from my writings. He didn't even ask me what kind of film I want to make. He simply trusted me. A man with a heart of gold.

The script for the Canadian film, *Hallelujah the Woods*, is ready. Adolfas wrote it in 4 days. He will also direct it. It is his film. He just came from a meeting with one of his Toronto sponsors. They are interested in the film, they may throw in some or, if we are lucky, all necessary money (the budgets for each of the films we put at $13,000 – $15,000.) It will be decided when they see the script, which will be sometime next week.

If Canadians won't sponsor it, we'll try to raise money ourselves. La Salle, of Bresson's *Pickpocket*, may play one of the two leading parts, he wants it very much. The script of *Hallelujah* is very good. You'll get a copy as soon as we have one extra.

About your coming to help us: Again, I have to stress, that we have no money for living. But since we are used to living on nothing, we'll manage. So, you have to make your own decision. Also, if you'll bring back the Arriflex, it will save us some money.

No date, 1960

A FILM: He sits under the tree, in the park, listening to the leaves in the wind.

March 30, 1960

Guns will not lift itself "above" its material. It will have more to do with naming the areas of anxieties than providing solutions. This is still a period of darkness. I am part of that darkness myself.

Periods of darkness, however, are really periods of birth. The anxiety, the trembling of this generation is really the first condition of re-birth, of a more conscious existence.

We feel that somewhere deep in us there are roots of truth, but we are not able—not yet—to reach them, even if we listen very hard. We burn, we tremble, we search and we search, never arriving. But we try ceaselessly, with a faith in our own desperation, the only faith that will lead us somewhere, we follow it without questions. ...In a sense, *Guns* will be an autobiographical, first-person film—at least in its own general feeling.

...You don't have to be a Communist to be an anti-capitalist: it's enough to be a poet.

Marian, when typing the press release, made a mistake in Adolfas' title: instead of *Hallelujah the Woods* she typed *Hallelujah the Hills*. We decided that her mistake improved the title. "Hills" is lighter and more joyful than "Woods." And the possibilities of shooting and monkeying around on tops of hills, and singing at the top of our voices: terrific.

"On apprend beaucoup plus de chose importantes en tournant un film en 16 mm, dont on fait le montage soi-même, qu'en étant stagiaire ou assistant."—Truffaut

May 11, 1960

"Is this your first film?" This is the question I hear again and again. No! This is not my first film—it is my 100th! Have I finished all of them? Yes, most of them, in my dreams, in my imagination. Some of them were quite beautiful, some of them were very beautiful, and some of them were very very beautiful.

Since the rumor about the film spread around, I am being approached by many who want to make their own first films. "Why don't you make it?" I ask them. "How? We don't have money." "Do you have a script?" "No," they say, "We want to be sure first that we have money." Blast them all! They still think that films are being made with money. I don't think they really believe in what they want to do, it is not part of their blood.

Guns, as it looks now, will be sponsored entirely by my friends. I am borrowing money wherever I can. I said to myself: I will test their friendship with the most difficult test of all: money.

May 23, 1960

Why do I do this, why do I do that? Why do I write for *The Voice*, why do I publish *Film Culture*? Why don't I just make films? Why do you do so many things at once? All those questions!

It's like being on a swing. To swing, first I have to move the swing; then I swing with it, and then it swings me, and then I am also swinging the swing. Where does the swing begin and where does it end, and what is, really, the swing?

June, 1960

Yes, Peter Orlovsky, as he walked down the Third Avenue, gesticulating with his long arms, freely, and with his blue striped farmer's shirt, in large steps, and singing, singing just for himself, in a very high high voice, in a voice that seemed to be coming out from some very deep inner regions, very personal, very fragile.

Yes, Peter Orlovsky, as he walked along the Third Avenue, 13th Street, singing in that strange voice, not seeing anything, anybody, just singing, completely relaxed, and happy and careless, gesticulating with his arms, in a happy exuberant stride as if he had been walking like this many thousands of miles, perhaps all the way from Mexico City or all the way from San Francisco and is now on his way to somewhere downtown and all the way to the South Pole.

Yes, Peter Orlovsky, a mysterious walker singing his weird mysterious song, in his blue striped shirt and a child's smile on his face, Peter Orlovsky as he walked that day, early in June, along the Third Avenue, 13th Street, not seeing anything around him, singing at the very top of his voice.

And as I stood there, looking at him, somehow, mysteriously the whole street, the rush of the people, the open bar doors

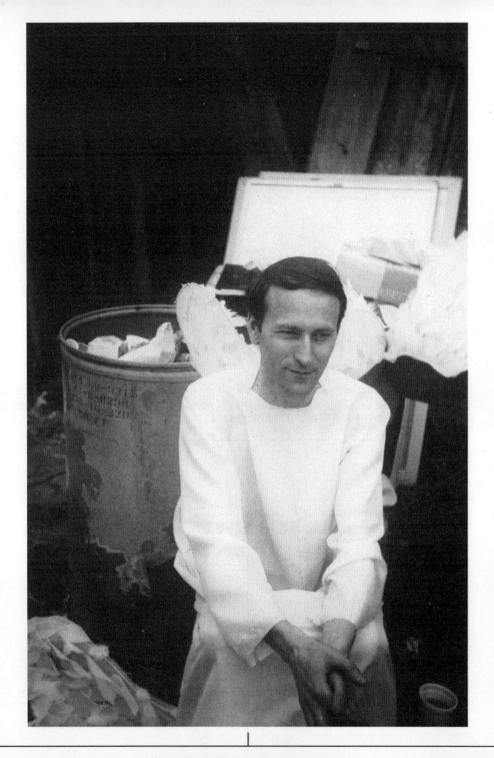

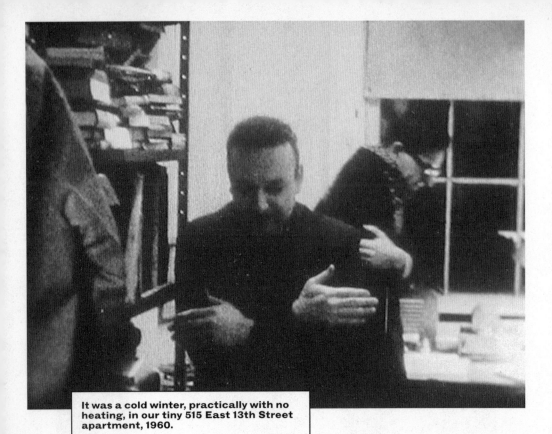

It was a cold winter, practically with no heating, in our tiny 515 East 13th Street apartment, 1960.

seemed to suddenly acquire, for one short moment, an importance, a certain intensity of life, a certain meaning of being; their drabness and their sadness suddenly, for a brief moment, seemed to gain a certain human perspective, in the shadow of this mysterious traveler who seemed to disregard and forget everything around him, at the same time casting upon the surroundings he passed through a shadow of his own life, casting a meaning upon the rest of the street—

as he walked in his long stride, singing, as he walked thus, gesticulating with his long arms, as he walked that summer day down the Third Avenue, yes, Peter Orlovsky.

June 3, 1960

I was walking today along the street, looking at the food displays in windows. It would be good to have all that food. I thought about all my old friends, from Germany, and from Brooklyn, who were more practical than myself, who became doctors, and architects, and businessmen, and many other things. I visit them sometimes, and they have houses, and lawns, and families, and summer vacations, and I, stupid, I chose my freedom, I wanted to be a poet. What an idiotic thing to be. And so I got it all, including my freedom, and I shouldn't complain about the price, no, I shouldn't. Wasn't it me, no, who used to say that you have to pay for your stupidity? Or that other saying: for the stupid head the feet must pay?

The Unlearned Lesson
The new film directors have learned nothing about film acting from the classics.
They could learn a lot from Lumière, though.
The acting style in Delbert Mann, Lumet films, is stagy and stiff.
The 2 kinds of acting possible in modern film:

1. Improvised, free (Brando, *Shadows*) (neorealists, Lumière, Flaherty) and
2. Stylized, for action films musicals (non-realist films)

June 12, 1960

Yesterday I went to the employment agency, on 42nd Street. Black, dirty. A line of people waited in front of me, mostly Puerto Ricans, Negroes, and students. I had little hope, but I was lucky: a helper on the truck was needed for the Yale Delivery, Garment Section. I was working today for four hours. It was a hot day, humid, sweating. I was thinking about how much work I have to do this afternoon, on *Film Culture*, and I'm dirty and tired now. On my way home I stopped at the agent and told him that I won't be coming tomorrow. I was desperate, I said. Yes, people come here from desperation, he said.

CHAPTER
NINE

... I begin filming *Guns of the Trees*... Filming in the Catskills... Hunger ...The curse of the *Private Property*... Arrested... Disagreements with Edouard... Notes on the young generation... On Howard Hawks... Rossellini, Renoir ... Against Nouvelle Vague... Edouard against *Pull My Daisy*... Fulton Fish Market... Equipment stolen... Out of money... Hungry ... We learn to steal food... A drink with Lionel Rogosin ... Robert Frank... On physical fitness...

June 25, 1960

Frances said: "When you look, sometimes, your face has the determination of a heavy truck."

All bad actors are so versatile when it comes to the analysis of their scenes! Fantastic detail work. They beat me on that. But they cannot act them. It is like with New Criticism. They all seem to be such good critics, going thru pages and pages—but they cannot write a goddam thing themselves. Nothing but brain equilibristics.

Sheldon told me: "I cut my hair for the *Guns*. My father told me that my hair was too long. I told him I spent my money on film—*Guns* needs money more than G. M. So he says: cut your hair and I will buy a share. So I did, without waiting to hear it twice."

So now we have $500 to continue the shooting.

July 14, 1960

Every day a dozen envelopes with photographs, credits on the other side, etc., come in, from actors, sending their pictures. Do they think we are making a movie about actors? They can't play anything but actors. They look like actors, they speak like actors, they behave like actors, and they are actors. And I hate actors!

Had two weeks of shooting. Today we were scouting for new locations in Connecticut. Got arrested, all six of us, for trespassing, at a public lake.

"I'll slap your asses all over the place," shouted the cop at the Police station. He was particularly tough with Adolfas because he thought he was a "beatnik." Adolfas had to grow a beard for his part, so now, wherever we go, we are treated as "beatniks." The cop became mild as a cherry blossom when Barbara told him that her brother was the Connecticut State Attorney General. He immediately ordered to let us free, law or no law. Barbara had been following us all afternoon. We didn't know her at all. Young, maybe twenty. She saw us filming and got interested and stuck around us. So she was arrested, too. Barbara's brother-in-law gave us a long lecture, after he bailed us out. He said, we shouldn't argue with the police. While he was explaining to us the usefulness of the police, he was broiling a steak, that phony outdoor barbecue cooking, or something like that. He was mad that Barbara, at the station, told to the cop that she was disgusted with his language. Swallow and forget, that was the lesson the State Attorney, upholder of the law, was trying to put into our heads. We left angry and disgusted.

No shooting since last Thursday. No sound equipment. No car. No money.
$6,000 with which we started shooting *Guns* is completely out. Luckily, we have all our film stock. But what about living, etc.

July 27, 1960

We were scouting for locations, in N. J. Our jeep suddenly refused to go, in the very middle of the State Forest. We pushed and sweated, but nothing doing. We decided to look for help, to walk to the highway. Since Adolfas and Roberts have beards, we hid both of them in the woods, not to scare the people away. We stopped six cars. They all said, "Oh, sure, we want to help you." But none helped. Here are their excuses:
The first car: "Can't help, because I have a new car. I would certainly give you a push, boys, but the car is new."
Second car: "I know, some boy scouts will be coming this way soon, they will help you."
Third car: "I would like to help you, but this is not my car, I don't want to push with it."
Fourth car: "I certainly don't want to see you boys stuck. But I am late for a date. You saw yourselves how fast I was going." He was going fast, he almost ran me over.
Fifth excuse: "O.K. I am going, but I'll be back with a rope and I'll pull you out."
Sixth excuse: "I can't, I am in a hurry. But I know some boys in town, I'll send them here."
None came back. No boy scouts, no ropes, no boys. After two hours or so, finally, an elderly man with a woman stopped. Although hesitant, he drove into the woods. Sheldon was running in front of them, like a good dog, leading them. Approaching the jeep, we saw that Roberts and Adolfas, with beards and all, were standing there besides the car. Sheldon said later: "I just kept running. I was afraid to look back to see if the car was still following me—they may get scared and turn back."
Just before the man was ready to push us, the jeep started by itself. So we laughed and left the bumpy forest road singing. Figure out the moral of this story for yourself, good man.

July 28, 1960

We reject all professionalism. Our techniques are improvised, our means are improvised. We are working without a budget (they are always asking us: "What's your budget?"), borrowing money as we go. If we had worried about budgets and unions and distribution, we'd never started the film. Now we are far ahead, and nobody will stop us now. Edouard, who repeats every minute that he is a professional, calls us "the beatnik productions." If that's what it is, so be it.

Stylists lie. Any perfected form of art begins to lie. As a matter of fact, the surest way to arrive at a style is to lie. *Shadows* and *Pull My Daisy* threw away style, went fresh. Their spontaneity is not style—it is part of their content. The style and polish will come next, the lie will come next.

Private Property got a pail of dirty water dumped on it. They all see what it borrowed from the old, but they all miss the new things in the film. Their immunity to the new, to the youth is amazing. They react only to what is old. What is the moral of this story?
We got a heavy gyro-tripod for sound shooting. The only trouble is that it makes

a grinding noise when you pan it, it is so goddam old and decrepit. So I told the actors to cough during the pans. At least that is how the joke goes.

Last night, scouting for locations in Long Island, we went an extra 20 miles to Almus, just to get coffee and cake, which we got only because one of his brat children happened to have a birthday—we even had to play baseball with the children, all for one small meal. I think I am going to Hollywood tomorrow!

Some bright young enthusiast will read these notes, hoping to find some subtle revelations, aesthetic discourses, thoughts on cinema. I can imagine his disappointment, when he'll find most of my notes devoted to dreams about a decent meal, or just a piece of plain good bread with butter.

Now even the weather is against us. We planned to shoot the Harlem River scenes and the street scenes with Gregory. Now it is pouring.

July 29, 1960

Mrs. S. said to me: "I hope your film is not a morbid film. There are too many of them." Most of the films are, when I think now, falsely happy. Not morbid. Was *On the Beach* morbid? It was simply a bad film, not morbid. Kurosawa's *Dirty Angels* was a really black film—but it was not morbid. Its blackness was healthy, that of life. Dostoyevsky had plenty of it, the same blackness. The gaiety of *Ben Hur* or some independent productions is a fake healthiness, sick. *Savage Eye* could be called, perhaps, morbid. But, again, it is so only because of its bad taste. Is it a really morbid film? Is this what Mrs. S. meant? I don't know.

Shooting the scenes with Gregory and Frances on the beach. We chose the Idlewild Airport beach. Forbidden for outsiders. We took two beat-up boats from Sarris' mother and transported the equipment

and actors. The weather was against us. Smog eating our eyes. Visibility—zero. Still, we managed to get some footage. In the evening we found our boats stranded deep inshore by the retreating tide and it took us some work to get them back into the water. All wet, full of salt and sand, Adolfas and Sheldon took the boats back to Sarris, with Alice riding on the bow. The waves were too high, and we didn't want to risk our equipment. The rest of us, we smuggled ourselves and the equipment out of the airport with the help of a friendly truck driver, hiding on the floor of the truck.

In the gas station an attendant asked Sheldon, pointing at our jeep:

"Is this a beatnik car?"

During the shooting on the beach, a group of truck drivers stopped their trucks and came to watch us work. One said:

"You are either Communists or beatniks." Sheldon's mother called from Baltimore. She asked what he had for dinner tonight. He said, "I am fine, mother, I just had a good dinner—a big steak." He was finishing his "Coca-Cola," and we had a real treat: a frankfurter each.

August 3, 1960

In fifteen minutes we are leaving again for shooting. Last five days have been hectic. This is, more or less, the account of the last few days:

We left for Catskills on Saturday. Willys started heating up. We had to stop every mile on the mile. Instead of three hours, it took us 12 hours to get to our destination. In a small village, on a hill, the jeep finally stopped for good. The hill saved us. We coaxed the car backwards down the hill, against heavy traffic, all the way to the gas station.

It was a strange gas station. The attendant was more interested in fishing than in cars. He showed us a bucket full of fish he had just caught in a near-by river.

At our 515 East 13th Street apartment, during the filming of *Guns of the Trees*. Believe it or not, in those times, when Adolfas came back from the U.S. Army, he was allowed to take home with him his rifle (the second rifle in this photo is Edouard's). We had it around for several years until one day Adolfas left it in his jeep over night and it was stolen. Many times he went hunting to Adirondacks. Never shot anything, but once was almost stampeded by a bear.

He introduced us to his wife, and to his children, and we had a long talk, and then, sitting there, in the station, in the woods, near the river, we all watched the sun set, silently.

Tired, hungry, the jeep fixed, after midnight, we arrived at the Druskoniai, a place the address of which someone gave us in New York, "a good place to stop." Instead of the expected hospitality, idyllic country farm, etc., we found a tourist trap, where we paid our last money ($1.50 each) for a meal that we'd have paid 75 cents in New York. The owners were hiding behind the door watching us, afraid that we'll steal something, so we decided to steal some food, which we did, stuffing our pockets with ham, and we slept in one six dollar room, all six of us, on the floor, scaring our hosts and their guests. Sheldon's patched-up jeans, with half of one sleeve missing, the knee sticking out; Adolfas' and Roberts' beards, like two Saints from Azerbaijan, black and tired, Edouard alone was trying to keep the clean front, well dressed. But he limped and jumped on one foot, the other bandaged and sticking out, and feverish, so that didn't help the image at all. We slept somehow (Danny in his Yogi position), and continued shooting near a lake where we were helped by a local farmer who fed us with fresh milk still warm from the cow. We had a rifle shooting contest with the farmer's family, shooting beer cans in the trees and things.

While scouting for locations, overlooking a lake, deep in the woods, we found a beautiful place, just what we needed. A sleepy woman came out, looked at us and, before we had time to open our mouths and say Hello or Good Day, she shouted at us:

"Get out of here! I'll call my husband, he is a police officer in New York!"

Goddam, we said. At the end of every road there is a cop!

"O.K.," we said, "call him, we'll talk to him."

A long distance call which cost our last three dollars ended in disaster. We told the cop we would like to take some pictures on his grounds. So he started asking us questions, interrogating and cross-examining us, taking down all possible numbers of all possible and phony papers we had with us.

"No," he said. The woods are his property, after all. By our very being there, on his property, we have already made criminals of ourselves. It is an illegal act, a trespassing, etc. It is a crime.

"O.K.," he said on the other end, "I'll let you shoot on my property, but how much will you pay?"

This was the last drop. With money, we are O.K., no more crime, even for a cop. So we shouted a few curses at him, hung up, and sped out, since we suspected that the cops were already coming to get us. On our way out we saw a few strange people walking near-by, old parents of the cop or his wife, walking into the woods, stopping, meditating, going back, and going into the woods again. They looked like some prehistorical animals going into the woods to die, trapped, sad and lonely in this place of Law and Decency.

We dragged our tired and hungry actors for half of the night looking for a place to sleep. We even got into a prog camp. We told them that we were making an anti-capitalist movie, and things like that, just to get into bed. They threw us out. They were either too careful or too square. They acted very businesslike.

We dropped Danny and Roberts at a motel, Hilltown or a place like that, and at 2 AM, we continued our search for a place to sleep in the woods. We found another camp, children's camp, with everybody asleep. As we walked across the camp, with flashlights, through the dormitories and bunks, the place looked like Belsen, or some Polish village raided by Germans, with everybody dead.

We slept in the woods, with mosquitoes singing around us, the smell of fresh leaves and forest flowers.

We set up our cameras by a small lake, in L.I. Just when we were about ready to start shooting, a cop came and told us to move. *Private Property*. He told us the place belonged to a movie theatre chain owner.
Got terribly hungry. No bread, no nothing. Stopped at Almus, in Great Neck, but he himself had nothing. Bought some food in a store and ate it in front of a synagogue, late at night. A rabbi came out to check, so we fell on our knees, pretending we had come to pray, shouting lines in five different languages, including Latin, which, as we later realized, had nothing to do with Hebrew anyway. In any case, we finished our meal in peace. Sheldon went to the houses nearby for bread, and succeeded in getting some: they thought he was one of the college boys, trying to do something crazy to get into one of the fraternities, or something. They did not believe he was really hungry.

August 4, 1960

Edouard keeps harping that Sheldon, our cameraman, needs more discipline. He has to do what he is told, he has to obey without questioning, etc. And it is very true. Still, I believe, it is all wrong. It wouldn't be wrong in Europe, but it is wrong here. Because one of the main characteristics of Sheldon's generation (he is 21) is their disobedience, their anarchy, their disrespect for the officialdom. This generation is by necessity a generation of irresponsibility, disobedience. More than that: I think that these "negative" characteristics should be encouraged, developed further. The official system is too strong. It will take plenty of disobedience and "irresponsibility" to knock it out of balance, to rejuvenate it. Edouard says we should have chosen a German cameraman!

August 5, 1960

Late at night, searching for locations, we found ourselves in Hoboken. What a sad place to be at night. I wondered who lives there, in this black city. Long monotonous streets. A bitter Hoboken smell floated in the air. We had a cheeseburger for 35 cents, which tasted much better than New York 60 cent cheeseburger.
It's raining, morbid, dark. This is the second day without shooting. Depressing. Time wasted. The days drag. We are far beyond our schedule. I am trying to organize actors for tomorrow, in case rain stops.
Still no money. The footage shot during past three weeks is piled up on the floor, undeveloped. I don't know what I have there. Every time I hear the word money— and it happens at least ten times a day— my chin drops, and I look for a chair to sit down.

August 6, 1960

Q: What is your film? What's all about?
A: What is your life all about?
Q: What does it say? Got a synopsis?
A: Have you ever read a synopsis of a poem?
Q: Is it an experimental, or a commercial film?
A: Commercial? When was truth commercial? When was poetry commercial? And why should it be commercial or uncommercial? Who started all this "commercial" business anyway? I am making a film, I am painting a painting, I am writing a poem, etc. etc.
Q: This sounds very exciting. Could I help you? I am one of those who like to invest in anything that is different. I believe in the new.
A: There is too much talk about the new cinema, the different cinema. There are people who say they want to invest in this "different" cinema, "off-Broadway" cinema, etc. I meet them every day. I talk to them and I find that all they want is to invest in

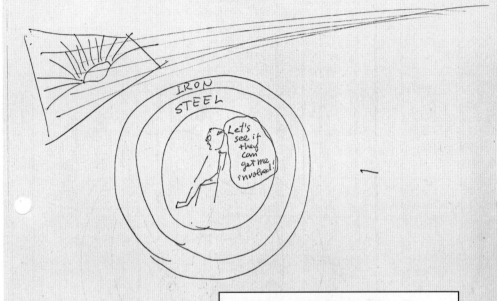

My critique of Bosley Crowther, film critic of the *New York Times*.

safe, old-fashioned cinema. Their "different cinema" is really not so different at all. The truly independent film-maker will always have a difficult time, let's not fool ourselves.

August 7, 1960

Shot air-raid scenes with Gregory, in the empty downtown streets, at 6 AM. Sunday morning is the only time one can film in the streets. Empty, nice. Only a few bums here and there, sitting in the shadows, invisible, or peeking around the corners. Cops came, looked at us. We told them we were shooting an amateur movie, on weekends. They left us alone. Yesterday Sheldon went to get a permit for shooting in the street. They asked for $35! Crazy bastards.

Again out of money. We couldn't even go check our next week's locations, no money for the gas.

We cannot do anything until tomorrow, and it's only 4 PM. We'd get drunk if we'd had any money. So we lie on benches and just wait, with our eyes open, staring at the ceiling.

August 8, 1960

The *NY Times* is reporting the disbanding of 11 gangs in East Harlem.

Gangs! They still uphold some independent spirit, some disrespect for the officialdom, parenthood. And how could one consider the abandoning of alliances a positive act, a virtue? It's a betrayal of friendships, it's a complete loss of honor, it's giving up the independence, it's becoming a sheep. Society without thieves, robbers, hooligans, or gangs, is a dying worthless, sissy society in which all theft and murder is legalized, done from above.

This is a black day for East Harlem.

"Painting, any kind of painting, any style of painting to be painting at all, in fact is a way of living today, a style of living, so to speak."
—Willem de Kooning

Curtiz *Casablanca*, Hawks' *To Have and Have Not*—it's strange how Hawks, and Kracauer, and *Cahiers du Cinema* come together here. Truffaut informs us that in *400 Blows* he used Cinemascope and very long takes (without cutting) to minimize any conscious (obvious) stressing of the main centers of interest in the film. He submerged them, he wove everything into a pattern of action, movement, observation, mood, detail. Instead of catching with our eyes (and minds) a few singled out points of attention (like in *Caligari* where all lines run into one single point, one dot, and you're supposed to look at it—and why, then, tell me, why all the rest of the image is there if you care only about that one dot?) (which later would create blocks in our mind, presuppositions, preventing us to perceive freely the images, obscuring other subtle details and levels of movement) (but surely, *Caligari* did not have any other subtle levels, it had only that one dot and those lines!), we absorb (in Hawks) everything equally, everything is important here, no close-ups here, no morality of the selected virtues or wisdoms: the morality of Hawks' style (approach) is open, all-embracing.

Hawks, Rossellini, Renoir plant their views, morality not like herrings on a plate, but much deeper, in subliminal regions. Welles is out of balance, extremist, paranoiac, a shocker. Hitchcock is a very subtle, polished Welles, too, a sophisticated Welles. We organically resist herrings, obvious propaganda, moralizing—but we are helpless against the subliminal indoctrination, one which acts like life itself upon us, slowly. We cannot resist our unconscious which has better eyes and ears than our flesh. It is here that the power of *Shadows* is, the power of *Zéro de Conduite*, and the power of Hawks—all three different in content, form, style. And here is the power of Star Cinema. In Hawks Bogart becomes a human being. He is not making any points, he is not tailored to sell anything but himself. We don't look at him as "Art." If Bogart would appear as a stylized Citizen Kane, we would resist him, we would take him as art. But now, we say, Bogart is playing Bogart, he is not creating a character. He is only a Hollywood star! So, we say, there is nothing behind it, this is not art, so let's just watch him, relax and watch him—this is only entertainment. And there we are, fooled completely, and we sit and we watch, cured from all art preconceptions (at least for that moment), we sit there, while all this time the sweet poison of the secret art of Hawks flows into our subconscious, without meeting any resistance in our "culture" shield. That's what Hawks' art does. It doesn't even look like art. It's so simple.

Hawks' style in his Bogart-Hemingway movies, to me, is the peak of American fiction film. "The purpose," "aim," "idea" was eliminated almost completely. No symbolism of any kind, unless by mistake or as a joke. His people simply proceed living on film, as we watch them, they live on film. They seem to be creating the film as they go. Director steps aside (so to speak). *Air Force* moves almost like a documentary. It takes several viewings to realize that its construction and artistic logic are as strict—and, I'd say, even more strict—than that of *Alexander Nevsky*. Really, the logic of Hawksian creation is a whole level deeper—two levels deeper than that of *Nevsky*.

August 11, 1960

What I want to achieve—ideally—with my film: is to overthrow the government. All governments. So that we could begin from the beginning. That's as good an aim as any other.

Nouvelle Vague… They are so bourgeois, all those N. Vague films. It is not Nouvelle Vague—it is Nouvelle Bourgeoisie.

On one hand, we say that we are free to criticize the government; on the other hand we tell the citizen to do nothing "against" the government. We say that to advocate the overthrowing of government is a crime. Now, it is a sacred duty of a human being—and a citizen—to do everything in his power to get rid of the government that he believes is corrupting the citizens. It's in the Declaration of Independence.

"Recent history is the record of a vast conspiracy to impose one level of mechanical consciousness on mankind and exterminate all manifestations of that unique part of human sentience, identical in all men, which the individual shares with the Creator. The suppression of contemplative individuality is nearly complete. These media are exactly the places where the deepest and most personal sensitivities and confessions of reality are most prohibited, mocked, suppressed."—Allen Ginsberg

August 13, 1960

Our jeep broke down again—trouble with the engine. It took Sheldon twelve hours to get back from Baltimore where we had sent him as our ambassador to raise money. He came empty.

Today is dark and drizzling.

More troubles with sound equipment. Doesn't sync. We'll need great ingenuity to save some of the recent footage. In most of the downtown places the current is too weak to run camera & sound & lights.

August 19, 1960

No shooting for the second week. Complete reorganization. Our sound equipment is a disaster. And we ran out of money. The only man who helped was Dan Talbot, with a $750 loan. All others found excuses and had no understanding of what we are

Filming *Guns of the Trees* by the Harlem River, 1960. Adolfas, Frances Stillman, Sheldon Rochlin, myself.

Argus Speare Julliard and Ben Carruthers during the filming at Fulton Fish Market.

doing. The most depressing visit was to P., in Newark. A Lithuanian immigrant, a post-war DP but now a garbled version of a cheap nouveau riche. He insisted on showing us his "swimming pool with a flower garden," and kept repeating that "you only live once." The same man, thirteen years ago, wrote the constitution for a student organization called The Light, in Tuebingen, full of idealism with big words...Now he is a fat Newark snob with a swimming pool. He examined me carefully, playing a businessman, and found me a bad "investment," he said. I almost vomited right there on his hamburgers.

In America, cinema has finally caught up with the literature. Modern cinema (*Pull My Daisy*) is not much different (I mean, not behind) from modern writing (Burroughs, Kerouac). The same temperament. I don't see this is N. Vague films. They go a few steps behind their literature. Literature inspires them, not life.

August 22, 1960

The stack of exposed film is still in the corner, not developed. No money for the lab. Arriflex broke down. It is in the repair shop. Mercedes stopped in the middle of the street. A new battery is needed. Adolfas with Edouard just called, they said they will be delayed. They are trying to put the battery in by themselves, the garage people refused to help them.

On Sixth Avenue I met Panna, the Hungarian girl who a month ago went to L.A. with a mission to get money for our film. She came back very ashamed. She went to L.A., and then she rushed immediately back to New York, because someone wanted to marry her here. When she came back, the man backed out; he found out that she was not as rich as he thought she was. Now, she said, she feels bad. She betrayed the film for a man, and, what's worse, for a stupid man.

Adolfas and Edouard just came back with a new battery. Adolfas shook from a bag a pile of tools he stole from the garage, as a punishment for not helping them.

August 25, 1960

Today we went to shoot Ben and Louis scenes, in the demolished ruins on 9th Avenue, near 28th Street. As soon as we set up our camera, two henchmen from the Garment Union came to us. Private property. One square mile of bricks, a field of nothing. One, in a black funeral parlor suit, a typical gangster movie type, was the speaker. He meant every word. Tough, short words, faces with no pity, Brute Force, a black Chevrolet. "I'll push you through the wall," he said. We believed him.

When we looked into their faces, there wasn't a drop of any feeling. It was a concentrated toughness. Black, like their suits, like their Chevrolet with air-conditioning and two-way radio. Ignorance, stupidity. Go to Union Square, we know your type—one said. What he meant—a horrible thought—was that only they represented America, the true America. What a demented image of America they must be carrying in their butcher heads.

We packed up and left.

Edouard saw *Pull My Daisy* finally. I was postponing the screening, I knew that the film will mean nothing to Edouard. It was like showing a book to a horse. He is as stubborn in his Europeanism, and as smart, as a horse. The film went in through one end and came out through another, without leaving anything or doing anything, that's what he said. Only a bad taste in the mouth. That's what all America does to him, he said. Comes in and goes out. He gets ulcers from it, but no understanding and no vitamins—he cannot live on it or with it, it angers him, he vomits and spits it out.

I am giving up. I stopped arguing with Edouard about our different methods of work, different aims, different films, etc.— all discussion proves a waste of time and a waste of nerves. He has no respect for other people unless they agree with him. And then, I am not in the mood of explaining things. I am going through a period of work, something that has been piling up in me for a long time. I have no time for explanations. Take it or leave it. Edouard constantly drags me into puddles of rationalizations, motivations which distract me and confuse me in the very middle of work. When I tell him this, he doesn't seem to understand a bit. I give up.

Shooting again.

Yesterday we shot the scenes with Ben and Argus at the Fulton Fish Market. We got there 7 AM, the busiest morning hour. What a jungle. We moved fast. We got our shots in three minutes, shooting from the jeep window. But there was immediately a crowd of tough looking men, with hooks and knives all around us. One tried to push the camera down, and there was a fat butcher pushing the sharp end of his knife into Adolfas' back. Someone pushed a fish down Edouard's neck while he was standing there, watching us disapprovingly: it's not a professional way of doing things, he said. As we moved fast to the other end of the market, fish and crabs came flying after us. A mounted cop rushed to our side, pushing around with his horse, so we sped away.

In the Bronx, we were chased twice today by the police and by the owner of an oil factory. We found beautiful railroad tracks, old, not used for years, grown up with grass, weeds three feet tall. Peace everywhere, beauty. We were shooting in the grass, with Argus and Ben, both beautiful, when we saw a police car driving straight at us across the flowers: *Private Property*. We had five minutes to get out. We did.

Since we had to finish the scene, we drove around until we found another abandoned railyard. This time we decided to be smarter. We prepared the shots, outside of the yard, got the camera ready in the back of the car, behind a fence, then we moved in swiftly, like the Normandy invasion, and shot everything, one-two-three, in five minutes. As we sped out of the place, we saw cops moving into the yard. We sped the hell out of the place.

August 26, 1960

Edouard said: "Films like *Pull My Daisy* were made by dozens in Europe in the twenties by the Surrealists, and are being made by dozens of amateurs in France and Italy today." He can't see the difference in styles and content. His thinking is literary, or, perhaps, ideological, despite all his talk about cinema. He just doesn't like the style of *Pull My Daisy*. Edouard, every movement he makes, every word is weighted, controlled, calculated—like his clothes. So that on the end, I don't know when he is just mechanically making up words and when the words come from deeper, from the heart. It's all mechanical. Edouard said: "A work of art, a film has to lead, to be conscious of its time, its people, etc. *Pull My Daisy* is a useless film, it doesn't do any of that. At best," he admitted, after three hours of arguing, "it sums up its times, but doesn't lead."

I said, *Pull My Daisy* is alive! Any film that wants to be alive and fresh and is made after *Pull My Daisy*, will have to go further than *Pull My Daisy*, or it will be of no value, it will have no life of its own, it will be a dead thing.

August 28, 1960

More troubles. This morning, Sheldon left the tripod in the car. Everything was stolen. The window broken. Hammid's tripod, and Edouard's Arri tripod were gone. Our gun, and the loading bag, and our tools went too. Total $1,300 or somewhere there. I am making calls now for another tripod, and Adolfas is out to steal some tools from the hardware stores, things like small screwdrivers, pliers.

Yesterday, we were shooting downtown. "Humanity does not deserve my picture," said one old bum when we wanted to use him in the background. He stood up and walked away. Right he was!

Edouard is grumbling why I gave to Seymour Val the script of *Guns* in the form I have it. He said, it should have been rewritten in a professional way. To impress. I don't care any longer about businessmen, I don't have any wish to impress them. They must take me as I am, with what I am doing, or not. I did not make any compromises till now, so why should I make them now? They will have to accept me as I am, and my film, and my notes, and my script, the way it is. *Esquire* asked for excerpts from the diaries. I told this to Edouard, so he says, we should work on them, to prepare the excerpts "professionally," the way *Esquire* people are used to. So I say, to hell with them. I don't need *Esquire*. If they need me, they'll have to print it as is. I am not interested at all how they are used to see or read things. I am fed up with it.

August 31, 1960

For the second week now we are living on one meal a day. Once every day we all go to the 77th and Amsterdam corner restaurant to get our one dollar meal. The rest of the day everybody's on his own—to steal, to get from friends, girlfriends, or live on water and air.

Sheldon walks to the icebox every ten minutes, opens it, and closes it again. He knows damn well that there is nothing in it. Still, he keeps doing it.

We are moving ahead, somehow. The lab deal was signed, finally. We rented a new Arri blimp. Everything is set to go. Last night we shot Ben and Argus night con-versation scene, on Perry Street, the most humid evening of the summer.

Just now, when, finally, we are again all set to go—we have to starve. Called Capsis. He wants to help, he said, but his wife forbids him: they have a baby, a family, she thinks they shouldn't risk their money. There you are—babies! Today, I called him again, at work, where his wife cannot hear him. It may work.

Meanwhile—I have fifty cents in my pocket, and I had my tea with a slice of old, green bread that I found forgotten in Sheldon's icebox. This should last until the evening. It's 11 AM now.

September 2, 1960

All our money sources exhausted. Last three days I've been calling everybody, humiliating myself. Good friends have no money. Those who have money are businessmen. Yesterday I had one coffee and one ice-cream. Frances bought a few cookies.

Capsis said: "The fact that you ran out of money, that you are in this situation today shows that the production was badly organized. How could you start a film without enough money to finish it?" It made me mad. That's why they never do anything. They are always working on their budgets. For ten years he has been working on his budget, getting grey hair.

We started *Guns* without money and we'll finish it without money and without budgets.

Capsis said: "You are a true artist. You want to finish your film at any cost, with no consideration for the others. I have a family." What a nonsense is all this about the artist working without considerations. Went to Rockland State mental hospital. We wanted to get a permit to shoot there. We parked near a cage-like building peopled with elderly women. One woman kept talking all the time, and the words she kept repeating were cash, money, cash and cash again. To go through that horrible state, time, place, to no end, talking about money, cash, going again and again through that horrible dictionary in her head! What a terrible way to be insane! The money doesn't leave her even in her darkness.

September 10, 1960

Called Gutman for money. He said he can't do it, he doesn't have any. He put everything in *Pull My Daisy*, Robert's film. I said, maybe then you know who has. No, he said, I don't know anybody.

Last night I spent three hours with Lionel. He got drunk. Was in one of those moods. Talk, talk, talk, about the New American Cinema. Both got drunk. We were cursing all the businessmen, and Seymour Val, and film-makers who sell themselves out. After another hour of drunk talk, Lionel said he will invest in *Guns* $250, I should meet him later today, at six, to pick up the check, if he doesn't forget it when sober. So, at least that much for the New American Cinema.

Got $75 from Amos. Bleibtreu said he is sending a check for $100, a short loan. Things are improving!

The head spins, the legs are weak. Getting tired fast. Blast the entire world.

Yes, Lionel remembered. Bless him.

September 11, Mon. 1960

Raining, for the second day. Saturday night we re-shot the Party scene. Planned to move to Brooklyn, for Ben & Argus morning scenes. And then the rain came, hurricane Donna, and all hell broke loose. Today it's still raining hard and the wind slashes across the streets. Took a few rain shots, with the lenses full of water, by the raging Hudson, spilling out of its mold, swelled, inhuman. Now sitting home and listening to the rain beating on the window. Sheldon should be here any minute. Got to return the sound equipment to Columbia University. Then, meeting Harrison, for money, and at 3:30 screen rushes for Wayne Howell and some of his schmuck friends, to get some money.

Another delay. The screening is canceled. And so was the Harrison meeting.

Called Ben. Their spirits are low. They are as anxious to go ahead as we. Cursing the weather.

If you find too much anxiety in the artist's work, while you are so happily and normally healthy—I warn you: you are very mistaken about yourselves. The anxiety of the artist indicates that there is an anxiety in the subconscious of America & the world today. The artists are forecasting the approach of a bad weather. There are visions and warnings in the theater of Happenings, in the action painting, in the assemblage sculpture, in the new cinema. Don't criticize the artist: it is useless to criticize him. Try to listen to him, try to understand his secret, incoherent messages. Learn to read the Morse code of Art!

September 15, 1960

Sheldon wants to know clearly what I want in this scene. The actors want to know, too. And Edouard insists on working out everything carefully and clearly before we arrive on location, he keeps harping on it, "Let's discuss it, let's discuss it. You are making a fool of yourself in front of people," he says. Oh, how many scenes have been killed by discussions! Hell. If everything were that clear what I want to do with this or that scene, I don't think I would need to do it at all.

Where Edouard and all the official cinema works by plan, with clarity and Ordnung, the new film-maker works through "ignorance" and "confusion." It isn't easy at all to stick to this ignorance—everybody wants a clear plan in advance, everybody wants order, I have to fight it every minute. Ordnung doesn't interest me. I know that through confusion and derangement I have a chance of arriving somewhere, of catching some secret movements of the unconscious, or Life, or Myself—but I have no trust, no trust at all in clarity, in pre-planning, where everything is predictable, everything is written down.

September 16, 1960

Just when we are in full swing again, catching up with the lost time, the rain comes. The day's shooting is ruined. Pouring like hell everywhere.

And then Sheldon calls: the jeep doesn't start. Wet, dripping, with my shoes full of water, shlurping—holes like bull's eyes—got uptown, to get Edouard. Nobody else knows anything about cars. Still, the car doesn't start, we'll have to wait until tomorrow.

Met Mary Frank on Avenue A. Lent her 50 cents to buy some fruits. Robert is still editing *The Sin of Jesus*, and out of money. So I stood on the corner, overlooking the wet park, waiting for the bus, and cursing the brown trees same way as Robert was cursing the rosy spring buds in April, those bloody fragile green buds. He still needed some winter footage.

Art, art, art. Always GD art. Who needs it! And who said that Kerouac is not literature? Always the same art bull talk. Maya Deren wrote that piece in *The Voice*. Brain creation, intellect, culture, tradition, and all that. They are going to teach Frank and Kerouac art! They are going to teach me, me, who went through labor camps of their culture and tradition! I put a match to it, pow! Culture & art is O.K. as long as it's not used as a club to hit life on the head.

September 17, 1960

Last night Panna invited us for a supper, a real meal. We ate and ate and ate, for three hours, like pigs, with our stomachs aching, and drinking wine, and ending with Csárdás. We didn't even know how to eat.

Re-shot all Brooklyn Heights scenes. Shot the beach and park scenes with Gregory and Frances. Again in full swing, trying to finish the summer scenes. The ground is covered with leaves. Leaves, leaves, leaves, I see nothing but leaves. From the middle of August I see nothing but brown leaves everywhere. The first thing I notice when I see a tree are the brown leaves. I kick them wherever I see them, on the ground, on pavements, on the streets, I step on them, with anger and disgust.

Got stuck with Barron's baby. We needed a baby for Argus & Barbara scenes, and this one cries and cries and cries. He waits until he hears "action," patiently, then, on the word "action" he starts howling. After listening to his uninterrupted protest for two days, we had to give him up: he doesn't like cinema, it's clear. Had to re-shoot the scenes with another child.

Sheldon. What Americans lack is the intelligence of the body. Their bodies are completely underdeveloped. I don't mind if one is underdeveloped in mind. But since my childhood, since my farmer's days I hate, I can't stand, I look with disgust on people, young men, who have no intelligence of their bodies, who are sloppy, ungraceful, uncoordinated, cannot adapt themselves to different and unexpected positions, etc. etc.—and I cannot look at Sheldon, it makes me sick, his clumsiness with the camera, dollying, etc. We are giving him up as our cameraman. He cannot bend himself, nor swing to the side, nor shift the weight of his body from one leg to another. As he swings the camera, the whole ground—not talking about the camera—shakes. The only thing he can do is to stand straight, or bend in a 90 degree angle, at his stomach. A complete mess.

Frances said to me: "I do not know what I should really do in that scene." But this was part of my plan-less plan, I chose her for the part to play just herself, not to create someone else. It is her confusion and tension that I want in my film. And, until now, despite the constant subversion of everybody, it worked, and only because she didn't know what she was doing. I tried to explain this several times, but as any actor should, I guess, she thinks she could act greatly if she'd only know exactly what I want. But I don't want her to act: as soon as she would begin to act, she wouldn't suit the part any longer. She is not an actress.

September 25, 1960

Had three days of good shooting. The insane asylum scenes in L.I., with the farmer chasing us across the cabbage fields, because we stepped (he thought) on his budding rye fields; fire-escape scenes; insurance agency scene; mother's scenes. Making progress.

The city is full of big men of U.N. Krushchev, Castro, everybody, getting in our way, blocking the traffic, and making nuisances of themselves in general. Thursday night, coming home from shooting, with Frank dressed as a monk, we stopped, from curiosity, in the Soviet Embassy street to look at the crowds. Immediately got surrounded by the police, put against the wall, searched, interrogated, cross-interrogated, cameras and the car practically dismantled, every piece taken apart, fuck them all. They thought we came to kill Krushchev. And no wonder, the way we looked. Adolfas' beard, and a "fake" priest, and Sheldon with Edouard in their crazy sweaters—craziest bunch you ever saw. You had to see us there lined up against the wall, with the crowd, and the detectives and the police around us, and the photographers and everybody. They wanted to take Frank to jail. Somehow, in his monk's cloak he looked very suspicious. You cannot impersonate a priest if you are not a priest, they kept repeating,

it's against the law. "But I am not an actor, I am a poet," kept saying Frank, which contributed still more to the general suspicion. I don't know how, but I managed to pull Frank out of their hands. It was simply by pulling, the cops pulled him their way, and I pulled him my way. Somehow the cops gave in, Frank almost fell on me, cops let him go. Or perhaps they just got bored with us. I don't know what—they could not understand what we were at. To complicate the matters, Sheldon (later he told me, it was a joke!) told them that he was a Russian Jew. So they pushed us back into the car, and ZOOOOM we went, as fast as we could.

CHAPTER TEN

... The New American Cinema Group... The First Statement of the N.A.C. Group... Robert Frank, De Antonio... Filming in Brooklyn... Hunger... On new cinema techniques... New imagery... What do we mean by anti-Hollywood?... Advice to a "beginning" film-maker... About our eating habits... Hunting for money... About Sheldon's generation... On film acting... On improvisation... My working practices vs. those of Edouard's... Europe vs. America... George Maciunas saves us... Manifesto on improvisation... About asking for money...

September 28, 1960

Who is Miss Estelle Costa?
I saw that name in my dream last night.
Wind across the Central Park.
The Venetian blinds clank in wind. She can't sleep, she watches the window, its blackness. It's night, a windy night.

Another rambling meeting of the Group, at Allen's office (165 W. 46th Street). I offered to end the rambling by officially declaring that we exist. We voted on it, and my suggestion was approved by the majority. So now we are the New American Cinema Group. Later we met at De Antonio's place, I collected their ideas for a manifesto of the Group, which I suppose to write. Lionel failed to show up.

September 30, 1960

The Group met in the basement of the Bleecker St. Cinema. Lionel is the owner, Adolfas is the manager. I presented first draft of the Manifesto, which was approved. Doc Humes suggested we have two manifestos. I was for it. He said he'll write the second one.

THE FIRST STATEMENT OF THE NEW AMERICAN CINEMA GROUP

On September 28th, 1960, a group of twenty independent film-makers met at 165 West 46th Street (Producers Theatre) and by unanimous vote bound themselves into a free and open organization of the New American Cinema.
In the course of the past three years we have been witnessing the spontaneous growth of a new generation of film-makers —the Free Cinema in England, the Nouvelle Vague in France, the young movements in Poland, Italy, and Russia, and in this country, the work of Lionel Rogosin, John Cassavetes, Alfred Leslie, Robert Frank, Edward Bland, Bert Stern, and the Sanders brothers.

September 28, 1960: at the inaugural meeting of the New American Cinema Group. Sam Val, Robert Frank, Ed Bland, Ben Carruthers...

... Argus S. Juilliard, Peter Bogdanovich, Adolfas Mekas, Shirley Clarke, Marvin Karpatkin...

... Seymour Val, Ed Bland, Adolfas Mekas, Lionel Rogosin, Alfred Leslie, unidentified, Sheldon Rochlin (with glasses), Shirley Clarke (back to us), others unidentified.

THE FIRST BULLETIN OF THE NEW AMERICAN CINEMA GROUP

On September 28th, 1960, a group of twenty independent film makers met at 165 West 46th Street (Producers Theatre) and by unanimous vote bound themselves into a free and open organization of the New American Cinema.

Among the motions agreed upon during the meeting were the following:

1. The Group (gathered by invitation of Lewis M. Allen, stage and film producer, and Jonas Mekas, film critic and film maker) will consist temporarily of those who were present (or invited) at the meeting of September 28th, 1960. The admittance of new film makers into the organization will be decided by the group's executive committee.

2. A committee of four -- Lionel Rogosin, Emile de Antonio, Edouard de Laurot and Jonas Mekas -- was selected to prepare a written statement on the main aims of the group.

THE SECOND meeting took place on September 30th, at the Bleecker Street Cinema. The first draft of the statement of aims was read, discussed and approved.

THE THIRD meeting of the Group took place on October 8th, at the office of Emile de Antonio, 66 West 53rd Street. It was decided to detail most of the practical activities of the Group upon various committees. The following were elected:

1. Officers of the Group, with equal rights: Shirley Clarke, Emile de Antonio, Edward Bland, Jonas Mekas.

2. Chairman of the meetings: Lewis M. Allen.

3. Committee to explore the situation of film-licensing and shooting permits in the city: Harold Humes, Alfred Leslie, Don Gillin.

4. Anti-Censorship Committee: Don Gillin, Emile de Antonio, Jack M. Pearlman.

5. Committee to explore the financing of films: Lewis M. Allen, Alfred Leslie, Jack K. Pearlman, Guy Thomajan, Walter Gutman. One non-member, John N. Bleibtreu, was drafted into the committee.

6. Distribution matters: Emile de Antonio, Don Gillin.

7. Publicity: Peter Bogdanovich and Jonas Mekas, working together with the Executive Committee of the Group.

THE FOURTH meeting of the Group took place on October 11th, at the Bleecker St. Cinema. The main purpose of this meeting was to discuss legal matters. Upon the recommendation of Jack K. Pearlman, the Group's temporary attorney, it was agreed that, to be more effective, the Group should be incorporated.

The official cinema all over the world is running out of breath. It is morally corrupt, aesthetically obsolete, thematically superficial, temperamentally boring. Even the seemingly worthwhile films, those that lay claims to high moral and aesthetic standards and have been accepted as such by critics and the public alike, reveal the decay of the Product Film. The very slickness of their execution has become a perversion covering the falsity of their themes, the lack of sensitivity, the lack of style.

If the New American Cinema has until now been an unconscious and sporadic manifestation, we feel the time has come to join together. There are many of us —the movement is reaching significant proportions—and we know what needs to be destroyed and what we stand for.

As in other arts in America today—painting, poetry, sculpture, theatre, where fresh winds have been blowing for the last few years—our rebellion against the old, official, corrupt and pretentious is primarily an ethical one. We are concerned with Man. We are concerned with what is happening to Man. We are not an aesthetic school that constricts the film-maker within a set of dead principles. We feel we cannot trust any classical principles either in art or life.

1. We believe that cinema is indivisibly a personal expression. We therefore reject the interference of producers, distributors and investors until our work is ready to be projected on the screen.
2. We reject censorship. We never signed any censorship laws. Neither do we accept such relics as film licensing. No book, play or poem—no piece of music needs a license from anybody. We will take legal actions against licensing and censorship of films, including that of the U.S. Customs Bureau. Films have the right to travel from country to country free of censors and the bureaucrat's scissors. United States should take the lead in initiating the program of a free passage of films from country to country. Who are the censors? Who chooses them and what are their qualifications? What's the legal basis for censorship? These are questions which need answers.
3. We are seeking new forms of financing, working towards a reorganization of film investing methods, setting up the basis for a free film industry. A number of discriminating investors have already placed money in *Shadows, Pull My Daisy, The Sin of Jesus, Don Peyote, The Connection, Guns of the Trees*. These investments have been made on a limited partnership basis as has been customary in the financing of Broadway plays. A number of theatrical investors have entered the field of low budget film production on the East Coast.
4. The New American Cinema is abolishing the Budget Myth, proving that good, internationally marketable films can be made on a budget of $25,000 to $200,000. *Shadows, Pull My Daisy, Little Fugitive* prove it. Our realistic budgets give us freedom from stars, studios, and producers. The film-maker is his own producer, and paradoxically, low budget films give a higher return margin than big budget films. The low budget is not a purely commercial consideration. It goes with our ethical and aesthetic beliefs, directly connected with the things we want to say, and the way we want to say them.
5. We'll take a stand against the present distribution-exhibition policies. There is something decidedly wrong with the whole system of film exhibition; it is time to blow the whole thing up. It's not the audience that prevents films like *Shadows* or *Come Back, Africa* from being seen but the distributors and theatre owners. It is a sad fact that our films first have to open in London,

Paris, or Tokyo before they can reach our own theatres.

6. We plan to establish our own cooperative distribution center. This task has been entrusted to Emile De Antonio, our charter member. The New York Theatre, The Bleecker Street Cinema, Art Overbrook Theatre (Philadelphia) are the first movie houses to join us by pledging to exhibit out films. Together with the cooperative distribution venture, we will start a publicity campaign preparing the climate for the New Cinema in other cities. The American Federation of Film Societies will be of great assistance in this work.

7. It's about time the East Coast had its own film festival, one that would serve as a meeting place for the New Cinema from all over the world. The purely commercial distributors will never do justice to cinema. The best of the Italian, Polish, Japanese, and a great part of the modern French cinema is completely unknown in this country. Such a festival will bring these films to the attention of exhibitors and the public.

8. While we fully understand the purposes and interest of Unions, we find it unjust that demands made on an independent work, budgeted at $25,000 (most of which is deferred), are the same as those made on a $1,000,000 movie. We shall meet with the unions to work out more reasonable methods, similar to those existing Off-Broadway —a system based on the size and the nature of the production.

9. We pledge to put aside a certain percentage of our film-profits so as to build up a fund that would be used to help our members finish films or stand as a guarantor for the laboratories.

In joining together, we want to make it clear that there is one basic difference between our group and organizations such as United Artists. We are not joining together to make money. We are joining together to make films. We are joining together to build the New American Cinema. And we are going to do it together with the rest of America, together with the rest of our generation. Common beliefs, common knowledge, common anger and impatience binds us together—and it also binds us together with the New Cinema movements of the rest of the world. Our colleagues in France, Italy, Russia, Poland or England can depend on our determination. As they, we have had enough of the Big Lie in life and the arts. As they, we are not only for the new cinema: we are also for the New Man. As they, we are for art, but not at the expense of life. We don't want false, polished, slick films—we prefer them rough, unpolished, but alive; we don't want rosy films: we want them the color of blood.

October 1, 1960

Marvin's case shows very clearly that when one works with non-actors, only after you secure one unrehearsed take, you can try to improve it. In most cases, particularly the tone of the voice degenerates with every take and every dry-run. Only an actor can improve the dry-runs.

Robert Frank came in the morning, we gave him 4,000 feet of outdated film for leader. He is tired, angry, beaten down by work, by businessmen, by contracts. "I'll never make a film like this again," he said. He was tired, he was almost talking to himself, unshaved, black, hungry.

Edouard said: "You are egoistic, you cannot accept other people's ideas."
It's not that I don't want to accept other people's (he means, his) ideas. It's only that in creation one cannot give form to what's not entirely assimilated, what's not

- 2 -

His wht. — work print.

Will be going to Cape Cod next week.

Hope all is well with your own production.

Yours, Gregory Markopoulos

Toledo - 8/10/60

Jonas,

I am on vacation — getting closer to completion of "Serenity" —

Enclosed are clips from the film, but

entirely one's own, what didn't grow out of your own deep experience.

We lived another day on bread alone. Edouard said: "They say, a man doesn't live on bread alone. We can!" We were sitting in Brooklyn and breaking pieces of bread, and eating, and there was nothing that could taste better. Argus, and Ben, and Frances. The hostess whose place we used for the scenes, did not offer even coffee to us, she was too much involved in her own sick self.

De Antonio said: "When they were organizing the American exhibition in Moscow, State Department screened a 4-hour long version of *Jazz on a Summer's Day*, and immediately rejected it. They said, we cannot send to Russians a film in which blacks and whites are shown together. Besides, they said, the Russians hate jazz. So they rejected the film."

Still shooting our summer scenes. Today we shot Frances & Argus conversation on the porch, with our teeth chattering, cold like hell.

The goddam battery fell on my foot, swollen, blue, like an avocado.

Now we are waiting until 7 PM, Panna is taking us to her father's house, in Conn., to feed us a little. We are dead tired, and all we want is to sleep.

Came back late, driving through the Connecticut night, and it's getting cold already. The long journey was not worth the meal, I mean, the reverse.

October 2, 1960
Shot Frances-Gregory scene in the Newark airport. Got very good cooperation from a lonely field guard. He was bored, Sunday, he took us right under the noses of the taking-off planes. The only trouble —mosquitoes. Got bitten everywhere, like death, even on the lenses. On our way out, we wanted to take a shot of Frances walk-

ing in the reeds—we turned into a small road leading us deeper into the marshes. Had to turn back immediately. Got into the very middle of the mosquito nest, the car was full of them immediately. We sped out, with all windows open, beating them out, with hands and necks all bitten. United Nations should come to New Jersey, instead of going to South America, to kill the mosquitoes.

Frances fed us well in her mother's house. Mother was out of town…

October 3, 1960
Shot the bar sequence, with Argus and Ben and Frank, after a night of adventures. The last minute we had to change the location. We planned to shoot at David's, on MacDougal Street, but then we found out that the place was too small. So we went to Brooklyn, to Williamsburg, Grand Street, the verfluchte Platz where Adolfas and myself spent two years of our lives— old, dusty, sooty memories, factories, gipsy windows.

It took us some time to find a bar. Talking with drunk waiters, old men. They are all so good, but they do not want to take responsibilities without their bosses, and their bosses are always either sick or somewhere out in the country. Finally, half lost, and writing crayon signs on the sidewalk for the second car, somewhere on Grand Street we met a strange man, half drunk, who seemed to recognize us from our old Williamsburg days. He came to our help. He succeeded in finding a place, on Union Street, a Lithuanian bar with three drunken men. They were glad to see us, they were so drunk and bored with themselves and with drinking that they let us in and helped us. It was not easy to keep them silent during the sound takes, but they were O.K., and we got what we wanted. Then all the wires burned out. By the time we finished shooting it was dark in the whole house. But they all said, drunk as they were, "Don't worry, don't worry, the owner is not in, what do you care, just pack up and leave, we don't know anything," and they kept on drinking, in the dark. So we packed up and sped away through the midnight Brooklyn, through our old South Third Street, and Lorimer, and Meserole Street and gipsy windows.

We spent the rest of the night at the home of our Grand Street man, who took us home, and fed us with beer and herring and some old cheeses and insisted that we sing on the phone to his girlfriend, "a German whore, Elizabeth," he said, at three o'clock in the morning, so we sang, and drank more beer.

October 5, 1960

Last night, in my sleep, I worked out a theory that stealing food is no sin. I was working on it all night. When I woke up, I lost some of its fine points. Still, it sounded terribly true and made plenty of sense. If anyone is starving in the world of plenitude, no doubt someone is stealing food from people. We, the people, have to TAKE back what belongs to us. Now, I remember also reading in some of the old books, some old religion, I don't remember which, was preaching the same.

October 6, 1960

No shooting since Monday. Out of money again. Sent Sheldon to Baltimore, to comb his relatives. Borrowed $50 from Talbot. Projector broke down, we can't screen our rushes. Adolfas has been fixing it for last two days, machine parts are all over the place—screws, bolts, springs, wheels. To change one small part he had to take the entire machine apart. The repairman wanted to charge us hundreds for the job. De Antonio called. Said, he found somebody with money. Always, those people with money!

Eugene Archer read the Group's manifesto. He said, it was not for the *New York Times*. It would be good for the *Village Voice*, but not for the *NY Times*. A fool! A manifesto which would suit the *NY Times* wouldn't be a manifesto anymore: it would be a Press Release!

The last meeting of the Group was terribly disappointing. Half of them are ready to lick the *Times*' feet and Wall Street floor. So where will they be in a year from now? Humes and Leslie seem to be the only ones who do not give a damn what anybody thinks about them.

Cutting down on our milk rations. Sheldon and Adolfas were drinking milk instead of coffee until now. Today we decided to switch to coffee, cheaper. With thirty cents that we spend on milk we can buy a loaf of bread.

Meeting with Eugene and De Antonio, for the *NY Times* piece. He is becoming more and more square. No manifestos for Eugene.

In France, the new critics and the new film-makers stick together, they are not ashamed to praise each other. Now, Eugene says: "I can't quote you, we have been involved, you know." He meant, we worked together on *Film Culture*, therefore he shouldn't quote me. He should be "objective" and keep me out. Doesn't want to be accused of friendly propaganda. What, then, about Truffaut, Chabrol, etc. etc.? What a difference! How difficult it is to get any enthusiasm here from anybody. Objectivity! It's capitalism, not objectivity. Even Edouard kept harping that I should rewrite the manifesto. It's not serious, he said.

Eugene said: "You have been writing about *Shadows* for two years. But we (*Times*) could not write about it because the film was not released here, nobody could see it here." But isn't it the *NY Times* that is responsible for the delayed release of this film in America? With its silence? It's getting cold. Winter time. Sheldon came back—no money, no nothing. Hitch-hiked back from Baltimore. Has no place to sleep, no money to eat.

That coffee is eating our mouths and our stomachs. Acid wounds in the mouth. We are going back to tea. But the tea one gets here stinks, simply stinks, all those rose leaves and pekoe oranges.

Received $25 from Wingate, from Baltimore. With a note: "Enclosed is a long-term, no-interest loan. Please do me the honour of accepting it." Richard Wingate. "No reply expected." We met him four weeks ago, came to visit Sheldon and helped for a couple of days on shooting, he knows how we live. How well timed, bless Wingate.

October 7, 1960

Were stopped by the police twice. We placed our camera by the East River, near Fulton Street, to catch the river and the sun. We turned around: we were surrounded by the police cars. "What are you doing? What pictures? Don't you know you can't take pictures here, the Navy is right here, on the other side?" Some crap like that. "Hell," Adolfas said, "how can we know that the fucking Navy is there, we heard no shooting, there are no signs, nothing." All this time, I was trying to connect the camera, the godamn cables got entangled around the cops' legs, no current. And the sun was just right for what we wanted. Adolfas turned his back to me, covering the camera, and kept arguing, shouting loudly, and I got the plug right, and ran the camera for ten seconds—all we needed, without the cops noticing anything. O.K., we said, we are going away from your ships, right now. They kept us in the car for half an hour, though. They took all our numbers, they called their HQ a dozen times, then they let us go.

Second time we met the cops at the yacht club, on 76th Street and West Side Drive. Ben and Argus scene. I was ready to press the button, when a cop, all smiles, walked to us and said we had to move or show the permit. So we went.

Checked the list of scenes to shoot. I have at least twenty summer scenes left. And the godamn wind is blowing the leaves off, they are falling down like hell, the leaves, everything is getting black and dark and disgustingly tragic, ready for the burial scene—even the sky is full of October, full of wind.

No date, 1960

A play about a man who refuses to work on immoral jobs. He sits home, with children dying of hunger, wife, etc. and talks to the neighbors who try to persuade him to give up and work.

The Delinquents, directed by Robert Altman, U. Artists
The Delinquents has good visual taste, an eye for simple locations and characterizations, well acted. The plot has no particular structure, loose.

Danny, who was helping us for a few days, left in a hurry. The army is after him, for desertion. The banks are also after him, for a car that he bought on time payment. And the police are after him for selling marijuana, or something. So out he went, just in time. A good man.

It was 3 PM and I had only a malted milk today, and I had only 60 cents, and, like the last bet on a horse, hopelessly, I used it for a taxi, since I was late for the appointment with Jerome, and there I sat, voiceless, and without a penny. My 60 cents ran out on 48th Street and I said to the driver, stop when it reaches 60 cents, and he did—and I walked the rest, 15 blocks, and was dead and tired when I reached Jerome's office.

Oh, man of gold! I could not believe my eyes when Jerome wrote the check for $1,000. He should have a monument, I thought, not those generals and horses.

October 10, 1960

We screened an hour of our rushes to a few invited friends and investors, for money. It reminded me again that I have to stick strictly to my own intuition. I cannot trust these people. I am not making respectable, safe films. And that's what they cannot understand.

Edouard said: "It lacks precise meanings. Any poetry has to have precision." And Herman said: "I miss compositions. Cinema is painting with images, compositions." That kind of crap. Precision. Clarity. Planning. Complete control.

The difference between my approach to film poetry and the approach of the thirties (Herman, Maya, and Edouard) is the same as between an abstract painter like Stuart Davis, and Alfred Leslie. Whereas in the thirties the lines, compositions and colors stood in the foreground—the first stage of abstract art—now all that is far in the back of the mind, in the back of the hand muscles that lead the brush. Like Joyce and Burroughs. The techniques are mastered—it's the emotion that is again in the foreground, the deeper content.

Clarity and precision… you have it or you don't have it. It doesn't make a bit of difference. A shaky movement, a hesitation, a flash of self-consciousness can carry more truth and life than a cleverly designed and calculated composition. If Stuart Davis was only form, Alfred Leslie is form plus content. It's my emotion that is the content. The movements of emotions. And these emotions and these movements are reflected in the rhythms and movements and hesitations and embarrassments and uncertainties of the painter's hand, of the film-maker's hand, the poet's words.

It's so clear, no use even talking. Anybody who is 18 or 20 gets it immediately. That's why Sheldon understands me so well, or, today, Marcia's young man, Joe Brown, or whatever his name is—he got it immediately, and he got almost mad on Weinberg, just listening to him with one ear. Bamboozled Peter Bogdanovich into buying a meal for us (Sheldon, myself, and Adolfas). Checks are bouncing back.

Yesterday shot Tina's scenes, and more Gregory downtown. We are down to our last three reels of film. We'll shoot until we run out of film, then we'll start editing. The film stock will dictate the script and the length of the film. That's something new in cinema aesthetics…

"Would you call your film a positive film?" Weinberg asked. Edouard: "There are three steps in every revolution: 1) when people are against something, rebelling against something; 2) when people are rebelling for something; 3) when they are willing to sacrifice for something." Which is true. At least it sounds true. Disagreement comes only from Edouard's impatience with America. He wants that *Guns* show people of the last stage of revolution, if not the third. Whereas I feel that America for at least another five years will be going through the first stage, and that *Guns* has to contribute to that stage, to the stage of against. Discontent. And it is the stage through which I am going myself. Only my next film may reach the second stage. America needs more anarchy and destruction, and that is what I want to give it. Destruction of the status quo. I say, America! But Europe needs it even more than America. America is beginning to be against something, the younger generation, at least. But Europe is still wallowing in a graveyard of dead bones. Europe is a cultural necromaniac.

Yes, my film is a positive film: it is the most positive film of all at this place and time: it is destructive.

October 12, 1960

Yesterday we reached another all-time low. Again on coffee alone. Sheldon didn't even get his coffee, as a punishment for long sleeping.

Shot Ben's scenes in the railroad yards. No cigarettes, no food. We kept stealing cigarettes from everybody. Artists in that. Humes' crew is working (on *Peyote Queen*) without budgets, as we do. The same troubles. So we sent Sheldon to his friends, and we three went to visit Hammid, with food expectations. We revived after a cup of tea and a piece of cake. Later, Hella brought some bread and cheese, so we had a feast.

Today, the first thing was to get some money, and some fuel for the jeep. Called De Antonio. He helped us out. The jeep, with its belly full, pulled us across town bouncing.

Spoke with Movielab people, and with some of De's friends. Trying to get a loan from Movielab.

Sheldon's millionaire, who came to see the rushes, left for Baltimore. Not interested. Still, he fed Sheldon, so he ate and ate enough to last three days. No wonder he didn't complain too much yesterday.

Making arrangements with De for the distribution of *Guns*. Planning, dreaming. The New American Cinema needs not only new film-makers: it needs also new distributors, and new publicity people, younger, more daring, different. You cannot sell a new film with old methods. We have to start everything from the beginning, and work everything out by ourselves.

October 19, 1960

A week without shooting. The best days of autumn are going by, the sun and the leaves. Hungry, angry, frustrated we drag our days somehow or other.

Last night we invaded Peter Bogdanovich, he had to pay for our meals again, the second time this week.

Movielab spoke about lending us $2,000 to finish the shooting but nothing came through. Humiliating myself, I listened to them, telling me that they didn't like the footage, that the film makes no sense, etc.

Listen to him. Teaching me, only because I need his stupid money.

$50 from Hannelore and $35 from De. That will push us for another week.

October 20, 1960

When the New American Film-Maker says that he is "against Hollywood," "against technique," etc., he doesn't mean that he is against cinema techniques, against knowing one's tools! What he means is that Hollywood has made a god of tools; that there is nothing left but tools; that Hollywood is blind to the new surroundings, new imagery, new emotional content, new intellectual content. They are blind even to their own tools. They use them mechanically.

Today when all Hollywood imagery is invented on the sets, recreated artificially (with the independents imitating Hollywood sets on locations)—it is enough to place the camera on the Lower East Side street or under the Harlem Bridge, and, without any cinematic techniques, the image will be so fresh in its never seen reality, that it will hold you with its immediacy, its presence, its photogeneity. That's what *Shadows* did. We don't say that a skilled craftsman, with a good visual sense, who knows cinematic language, couldn't improve upon this simple image by the right placement or the right movement of the camera, etc. Not at all! What we mean is simply: let's change the imagery, let's bring up to date the imagery. We exaggerate only to wake Hollywood up to the new imagery, new content. Who was it who said, the other day: Look at men who have children—they stay young longer!

ADVICE TO A BEGINNING FILM-MAKER
1. Mistrust every living film-maker. Respect dead ones.
2. Stay away from the advices of the professional editors. They are all "cutters," literally cutters.
3. Snarl at the criticism and advices of

From a fading newspaper clipping. Harold Humes was an active member of the original N.A.C. Group. Acclaimed for his novel, *Men Die*, and cofounder of the *Paris Review*, he left one unfinished film, *Don Peyote*.

With Adolfas, during the filming of *Guns of the Trees*.

professional cameramen, laugh at the "right" exposures, beautiful colors, sharp focus.

4. Ignore dramatic scripts with a lot of talk. Shuffle pages around, like Orson did in *Mr. Arkadin.*

5. Invent cinema from the beginning as if nobody did it before you.

Spontaneous cinema—by naming it "spontaneous" you kill it, you become aware of it. Spontaneity is a way of life, but not a way of art. As a method, yes, but not a form.

What I write is not (never) a result, but a process, the thing itself, plus the typewriter, fingers.

"With the conscious mind we are able, at most, to get within reach of the unconscious process, and must then wait and see what will happen next." (C.G. Jung)

October 22, 1960

Went to Westchester, shot one scene with Gregory and Frances, the birch scene. It took us three hours to find the godamn birches.

In one place, we stopped. It seemed a perfect location for what I wanted. Beautiful lines of trees. We stood there and admired the trees. Suddenly, we hear a voice shouting: "Move on! Get out of here or I'll call the cops!" There was a man sitting on the roof, fixing something, shouting at us. We were standing on the roadside, looking at the beautiful line of trees, and this fucking man shouts at us and threatens us with cops! The first thing he can think about is his Saint *Private Property.* He uses cops like dogs, to chase people out, just get the hell out of here. He got us really mad. "Let's get out the gun!" shouted Adolfas. "We'll shoot you, you bastard!" shouted Edouard, red with anger. The man, by now, was shitting in his pants, a perfect target on the roof, like a duck. His wife ran out, and his children, in panic, screaming their heads off. The man almost fell off the roof from fear. "We'll shoot you, bastard!" we

kept shouting. Then, suddenly, we had enough of the whole sick place, let him go to hell with all his birches, we said—and we sped away.

It took us some time to find another place. Frances is going through another of her breakdown periods, nerves, tears. Everybody sulky. Frances was talking this morning about suicide again. It's that bad. It is terrible how her part and her life are the same. Which is following which I don't know any longer.

Sheldon later said that everything goes like that because of our constant hunger. We had our coffee in the morning, and we worked all day on nothing, and only on our way home, back in the city, at seven, we stopped in a place and had a bowl of soup each. The same was yesterday, with a difference that I managed a decent meal from De. The exhaustion, tension and hunger brought everyone to the point of exploding any minute about nothing.

October 25, 1960

Art? It is not a question of showing the world, the reality, the nature in a different or more revealing way. It is more a question of experiencing that nature, a new relationship. To show the nature in a different way, it is a matter of curiosity, novelty. Like those strange photographs of the leaves through the ultra-ray photography. There is a wonder, and amazement perhaps in it, but no direct emotional experience.

It is here that many abstract films, like those shot through various crystals, prisms, kaleidoscope lenses, colorful as they are, are often lifeless curiosities. They show the same objects distorted or differently lit, a game of boredom but not of revelation. Some Painlevé and Cousteau films have some of the wonder, because they reveal the unseen, unreachable. They have a touch of dream. But they never pervert it to "art"; they remain within the real.

It follows, that there are no important or unimportant, no big or small themes, subjects. There is no big or small way of living, no small or big lives, if they are lived deeply, essentially. It is the intensity, the attitude that matters, it is the intensity of rapport that makes the subject matter interesting, personal, that makes it big or small, important or unimportant. The surface approach deals with appearances; the deep approach deals with being, essence, truth, absolutes.

October 26, 1960

We went (Adolfas & myself) to the Absinthe House, to a reception for *Ballad of a Soldier*, a dinner arranged by Kingsley for a dozen film critics. Now, thinking back, we laugh. Frank Kuenstler just came in. He called, said he had nothing to eat today. So I went out and spent my last dollar on some food and now we are eating. So Adolfas says: "Yesterday, at the Absinthe House, I looked at the menu and I saw the ten dollar prices. Somehow, automatically, we went to the cheapest order, something about three dollars, an omelette, and ordered it. The others were ordering expensive hams— you know, on Kingsley's pocket. We did not care about Kingsley, but we could not change our habits! We did not order even an appetizer, although everybody else did. However, we did not realize what we were doing, at that moment. Only now, thinking back, we realize it."

October 31, 1960

The question becomes that of timing.
When does one have to stop and readjust one's sight and perspectives?
Which stars are real and which ones are false, mirages?
When should one throw away Parker Tyler?
One will never know.
Yesterday we shot the scene with Argus, Ben and Frances in Prospect Park. Also,

Frances' suicide scene in New Jersey. Our summer scenes... The wind was blowing from the river, ice cold, like for Annabel Lee.

Another screening for possible investors. Again polite praises and no money. Ben had some luck: in the flea market he bought a winter coat, a black coat. And what a surprise: in one of the pockets there was $100 in ten dollar bills! So they bought plenty of food and we all ate sweet potatoes and listened to Miles Davis.

November 1, 1960

Came home from a walk. Raining, night, morbid. I was sitting home and going out of my mind. I was walking around the room and beating the tables, the icebox, walls, with my fist. Had to take a walk, to clean out the system.
I thought I will sit and work. Cannot. The mind is too cluttered with money. Edouard called. Says, while we wait, we should work on the script. It's impossible, I said, or shouted. Until I settle the money problems, I can't work on the script, I can't work on anything. Just can't. So I walk around the room, surrounded, squeezed into the middle of the room by the pieces of equipment, cameras, reels, cables, lamps, and I walk and walk, in that small circle, beating everything with my fist.
The street is not much better. Particularly now, when it is raining, and cold. It looks morbid, dark, grizzly, poor, miserable. Almost a Selbstbildnis.
Allen said he sunk all his money into *Connection*. Those who promised to invest, backed out, politely, waiting for "his second film," then they will invest. The same story. They all mistrust, they all want to wait and see. They wait and see how you starve your way through and how you walk the raining night streets beating the walls with your fist—they are waiting to jump on you, if it CLICKS. To hell with all of them,

Eugene Archer, Adolfas, Sheldon Rochlin, myself, and Emile De Antonio, by Dan Talbot's New Yorker Theatre, Broadway and 89th Street. Next to the New Yorker's projection booth, upstairs, De Antonio, or as he was known, De, had his office. Many an evening was spent in that office, and many bottles of beer, with De, Dan, and Peter [Bogdanovich] (who did the programming), talking, talking, dreaming.

I SEEM TO LIVE, VOL. 1
CHAPTER TEN

to hell with all those who wait. Let them burn, let Dante put them into the right place, into the right compartment where they can wait and wait and wait with an eternal fear of losing their godamn money. Had oatmeal, five of us. Argus bought some oatmeal with what money was left from the find, and we were jumping happily, except Sheldon who has a stomach that is good for nothing.

November 7, 1960

I think that Sheldon is half asleep even when he is most awake. His normal state of living is sort of half-sleep. And that is what his generation is. He is sensitive, receptive. Many things can be projected upon him, many ideas. He catches them, always, though sometimes slowly. But it works like with a hypnotist's medium: he is almost will-less. And one wonders, what's going on in this half-sleep generation, in this amoeba existence. Why the laws of life wanted it that way. One thing is clear: it is not a dead or dying matter. Just the opposite: it is a bundle of potent, sleeping energy, very alive. Is God using them, projecting into their sleeping consciousness something, something that will save America? Something that cannot be projected and bred anywhere else—not in the minds and hearts of the businessmen, generals, Nixons?

Again, Edouard. I have to watch constantly my actors from his dramatics. He pumps European drama into them, always talking about drama, meanings, conflicts, ideas. As if cinema had anything to do with any of it.

Today I said: There is no money for the fuel. Edouard says: We would have, if we wouldn't waste so much on film. I said: But that's exactly where I want to waste it, on film. No, he says, the scenes must be prepared in advance. I say: It is not my way. I search from the situation; I begin with ignorance; I better will shoot more without

a plan than less with a plan. He says: That's amateur, that's not professional, etc. etc. And so day after day, always the same, and always from the beginning. Anybody else in my place would have gone out of his mind by now.

November 8, 1960

I always seem to be going to extremes…
Once the pattern is set, one can begin to work on subtleties.

Film-makers are more irrational than any other artists today. Maybe that's why cinema is the most prophetic art today. It's through their irrationality that deeper contents & movements are grasped & revealed.

Poor Carruthers. Still without a job. No acting for the best film actor of America. Starving, living on nothing. And Argus expects a child. They say, it happened because they were talking so much about it in the film, they got used to the idea, and wanted to have one of their own. There we are.

De's friends bought one $500 share, so we returned some burning urgent debts and bought enough film stock to continue the shooting. We are coming to the very end now. Ben's loft scenes.

I'll be damned if I ever ever again take Edouard—or any close friend with directorial ambitions—on any of my films! He continuously drags me into the European mud puddles of drama, meaning, and all that fucking stuff. Stage acting, formalism, hell. And he has nothing to do. So he boils, boils, thinks and invents in his mind, then, without even knowing it, begins to impose it on others, all those concocted ideas, through his sheer will power of which he has tons and tons. He continuously confuses my actors, particularly Frances. By now she is irretrievably gone. If I'll get anything from her, it will be a miracle. On Ben he has no power, he is too conscious of his own method. He laughs Edouard away. But Frances, not being an actress, and being full of intellectual ambitions, all confused, is often impressed by Edouard's intellectual flights, she is constantly hanging between both of us. I want her to be just herself, no acting; Edouard keeps showing her poses, and going through intellectual interpretations and explanations of the scenes, confusing her; he wants her to make "meaningful movements" instead of just doing that or that; "meaningful" expressions; always trying to create something else of her than what she is, whereas my conception of the Frances character is she as she is, confused as she is. He wants to make her clear, determined, one dimension. One can do that with an actor and achieve results, but Frances, like all non-actors, becomes just more confused instead of clarified, and finally gets completely lost in "acting" the scene, and starts crying for guidance, which is usually the end of everything. I keep saying: Leave my actors alone, I trust my actors. I always begin with my actors. Let's see first what they do by themselves, and then let's try and improve upon what they do, from there. Edouard says: No, I never trust actors. You have to tell them exactly what you want, that's directing. Hell. At least he should have sense to realize that our directing ideas are opposed, and stay out. But no, he keeps poking in. Edouard is still trying to persuade me to change the title of the film. Now he suggests *Even the Trees*. He still doesn't understand what I'm trying to do.

November 11, 1960
Still shooting at Ben's. Various improvised bits, Frances-Gregory "love" scene.
More arguments with Edouard. Whenever I come to improvised, unplanned shooting, he lies down and sleeps. "I am not interested in this type of cinema," he says. So we had another argument about what cinema is. A slight change: He admitted that his approach may not be best for Frances. Also, he admitted that he may use some of the "new" spontaneous techniques in his film, to destroy the theatrical acting, since he will work "only with actors." It took four months to arrive at that, at least.

E: "Filmed images have to transcend the reality, to be art."
Me: "I am not interested in art. Cinema has nothing to do with art."
E: "Nonsense."
Me: "Cinema shows. It is not a literary art."
E: "I say this about this kind of shooting (referring to my spontaneous camera explorations): It is television."
Me: "Not everything is bad about television."

Etc. Etc.

Had another screening, to Frances' mother and a Hollywood producer, a certain Mr. Brown. Frances' mother wants to organize a screening for Park Avenue women, for investing into *Guns*. As for Mr. Brown, he is a schmuck.

Method? Improvisation? Spontaneity? Yes, half of our scenes are improvised.
Today we seated our actors around the table, eating, in real life. I wanted to record and shoot a few conversations while they ate. Nothing much came out. Then, later, Argus had some vodka, and loosened up, and got into a discussion with Frances, telling her about her past. They sat there and talked and talked, forgetting us. So I grabbed the camera and started shooting. They did not even notice me, or just didn't give a damn. They touched upon something that interested them more than our film. What I got on film was no more improvisation of a scene but living itself.

November 15, 1960

This Sunday we went to New Jersey, for the "guerrilla" shots. In an hour's drive from New York we discovered a little side road, with signs on the trees PRIVATE PROPERTY, KEEP OFF, KEEP OUT, in an ever-increasing number. So we just drove in, and kept going past all the fuckin' signs. They became more and more threatening with every turn of the road and with each tree. We went deeper and deeper into the woods, a Conradian darkness, until we hit a sign: STOP. DEAD END. STRICTLY FORBIDDEN. We continued further beyond the dead stop, all dead by now, kaput, and arrived near a house. An old man came out and asked what we wanted. We said, we want to take a few shots in the woods. The man happened to be the keeper of the place, the guard. We couldn't believe our ears, we thought it would never happen to us in America: there was not a single mention of the words PRIVATE PROPERTY.

The woods and the huge lake, miles of woods around, quite wild, belong to a group of rich execs from New York, they spend their vacations here. The old man, he said he was 72, but he looked like 60, was bored to death alone in the woods. So he gave us wine, and we took our shots, and we blasted with our guns. The man said the woods were full of rattlesnakes, and he was sorry when we left him alone with his bottle of wine.

A pile of autumn leaves was burning on the roadside. I thought it was just what I wanted. We jumped out, put the camera on the roadside and started shooting. Suddenly, from nowhere, I swear, a cop appeared. They are like mushrooms. An argument issued. He insisted that we needed a permit to shoot there. So Edouard says to him: "Don't you see what we are doing? We are shooting Frances, the smoke, and the sky. From whom should we get a permit to shoot the sky and the smoke?" Still, the cop insisted that we need a permit, although he was confused from whom. He ordered us to leave the place. Luckily, during the argument I managed to get the shot, so we left the cop with his sky and his smoke.

November 20, 1960

More on Edouard versus myself theme: Frank just called. He said, talking about today's shooting, that he was constantly distracted by Edouard. He said, he would prefer to work tomorrow without him. When I am thinking now, I remember all those times when Ben and Argus said the same, Edouard confuses them, shies them off.

Edouard's method is that of imposing his own form, shapes, his will upon others. He believes (and he stated today in the car, on our way home, that he has ten times more imagination than I—something that I have heard from him many times before) in his intellectual superiority and he uses others only as mediums, as means to project himself, and is unhappy when it doesn't work. I begin everything from weakness, from zero, opening myself completely. Any outside force can easily bend me at such moments. It is here that the presence of Edouard during the shooting is most destructive. I have to be completely in control of everything, work alone on the scenes, with nobody advising—otherwise I begin to lose control, I begin to want to be "strong," I lose my weakness, my naturalness, my truth. Again, today, on my way home, I felt that I fell into Edouard's trap. I had to shoot the scene, Gregory's line "I don't believe in false solutions," with a smile on his face. But the dead seriousness which Edouard always instills in Gregory and Frances situations misled me, and I shot the whole godamn scene seriously.

They all hate New Jersey. I like it. More than any other state. They say, it's ugly, rough, shapeless, vulgar. That's why I like it, because of its strange shapelessness, Stankiewicz plus Leslie plus Kaprow landscapes of living plasma, shapeless woods that look like blotches of emotion, formless but alive. You hate them but you can't be neutral to these towns, dirty little towns like Paterson or Hoboken! How can you be neutral to Hoboken? It is so expressive in its own ugliness, it is almost sad, it is like we, ourselves. I like this piece of unfinished America, this amoeba, this sad sad place.

We stopped at the New Yorker (Theater). Dan [Talbot] gave us a few bucks, to eat something. Oh, how many times he has fed us, saved us, always smiling, like Buddha, and Peter [Bogdanovich], both there, among millions of frames, little pictures, moving, moving, through long evenings, drinking millions of containers of black coffee. That's Dan.

Edouard's method, I think, wouldn't be as disastrous in older cultures. Let us say, majority of Europe. The inside of a European is full of grooves, moulds, forms; there are many basic things that they all have, moulded by the same culture, tradition, past. So when you ask an actor to do this or that, he will do it that way without much argument, his Being is not pushed out of balance, he is not threatened. The differences of degrees do not matter. He will take the order, he will paste it on his face, it will stick, and he will take it as his own, adapt it, readjust it, because, in a sense, it is his own.

Now, the American, specifically the younger generation, lost and searching, groping, fragile, in an uncertain landscape, responds differently. It is very easy to impose upon it something, on this soul, something from outside, and ruin it for good. This soul is not yet sure of itself, it has to find its own way, it is still budding—the most dangerous, the most sensitive time; even the animals, insects hide themselves before giving birth. They are supersensitive, they hear through the wall…The same with the soul of a country, of America, a continent, a race—which is painfully going through its birth pains: the American culture, the American. Nonsense about the "American way of living." There was never an American way of living until now, it's only coming. And nobody can blame the younger generation for being oversensitive, even fearful, too concerned with itself, not trusting any other will but their own (which is still so weak), no will at all, only distant, deep inside, waves and motions and voices and groans of a Marlon Brando, or almost no voice, just a motion of a mouth of James Dean, or Ben Carruthers for that matter—waiting, listening—or Kerouac's spontaneous prose; or jazz; or Pollock, de Kooning. As long as the "lucidly minded" critics stay out, with all their form, art, structure, style, clarity, content, importance, and all that crap—crap, that is, at this particular moment in history in this particular place—everything will be all right, just keep them out, for Chris' sake.

November 21, 1960

Saturday morning we picked up some food, plenty of it. George Maciunas saved us this time. He gave us boxes and boxes of food samples, from France. So we loaded the icebox, and gave some to Edouard, and there are still stacks all over the place. So now we are eating and eating and eating. All we need is bread.

I have been walking with fever since Saturday. I am beginning to feel my strength returning. Last night as I lay in bed, with my eyes open, I thought: What a waste of life, what a waste of life have these past few months been to all of us. Now I feel full of energy. My imagination is beginning to work. I want to work. The thoughts and feelings, emotions are flowing. And I was going through all these months of work

Picketing the Women's Prison, corner of Sixth Avenue and Greenwich Street, today the site of the Jefferson Market Garden.

half starving, on bread and coffee, and butter—feeling, how my body is weak, how my imagination is drained.

I open my mouth, and my voice disappears, from weakness. I have to repeat the sentence twice. And then, there is that strange sound in the ears, and I barely hear my own voice, it sounds so far away. Day after day we drag ourselves hungry, through the summer and through the fall. What a waste of life! The film, I feel, is also dragging, and is also losing its voice, and hears strange sounds in the ears—just like me. While all the godamn millions of pounds of meat and bread and scrambled eggs are flowing down the drains of time.

I want to shout, and beat the walls, from anger, from madness, from helplessness, as I sit now alone, this dark New York November night, thinking about my wasted life, humanity, scrambled eggs, and *Guns of the Trees*... And my mother, there, far in a small village, waiting for my letters, waiting.

November 22, 1960

THE SECOND NOTE (MANIFESTO) ON IMPROVISATION
It's in his quest for inner freedom that the new artist turned to improvisation. It was the silent suffering of the blacks under the whites' slavery that provoked jazz improvisations. Now it is the turn of the white man in America to improvise, to free himself. He uses his art not to entertain, but to liberate. The young American film-maker, like the young painter, composer, actor, he resists his society. He knows that everything he has learned from his society about life and death is false. He cannot, therefore, arrive at any true creation, creation as a revelation of truth, by reworking and rehashing ideas, images and feelings which are dead and inflated—he has to descend much deeper, below all that clutter, he has to escape the centrifugal force of everything he has learned from his

society, its people and its textbooks. His spontaneity, his anarchy, even his passivity are his acts of freedom. The new artist cannot be blamed for the fact that his art is in a mess: he was born into that mess. And he is doing everything to get out of it.

The same reasons underlie the new artist's mistrust of plot and formal dramatic structures. This is not a time for telling stories, but for expressing attitudes. Dramatization and plot are possible only when the society is going through periods of peace, where the aims and ideals are very clearly defined, crystalized. No clear values or ideals can be found in America or, for that matter, in the rest of the Western world today. Therefore, no effective dramatization is possible without betraying the truth in process. It would come to imposing on people another structure of lies (artificialities). The only possible form —as we already have seen in jazz, abstract expressionism, or modern theater (Happenings), and now, finally in film—is the registering, documenting (or reflecting, if you want) of the desperations, moods, outcries against the enemy, who is not always clearly definable but always present. It is no accident that so many Happenings contain scenes in which the actors throw themselves violently against the wall with their bodies. Like Kafka's protagonists, they do not know the real name of their enemy. All they can do is lash against it with emotional and irrational expressions of frustration.

The fragile, searching acting style of a Marlon Brando, a James Dean, a Ben Carruthers is only a reflection of their unconscious moral attitudes, their anxiety to be—and these are important words —honest, sincere, truthful. Film truth needs no words. There is more truth and real intelligence in their "mumbling" than in all the clearly pronounced words on Broadway in five seasons.

November 26, 1960

Only two more scenes to go. Then, there will be only small bits left. Wednesday we shot the Monastery scene, with Frank and Frances. The head of the Franciscan monastery on 32nd Street offered us all help we needed without asking a single question. Just come and shoot, just like that. We are not used to such cooperation anymore.

We shot in the garden, in front of St. Francis shrine. A few monks came and stood watching us. Brother Jean Bosco helped Frank with clothes, and helped us in other ways, lighting candles, organizing tools, and things. At one time, the sun came out from across the buildings, just when we were ready to shoot, and changed all our lighting. I asked Brother Bosco how long it will take for the sun to pass the gap between the buildings. "I don't know," said Brother Bosco, "I have never been here, I never come out. I am always in my room. This is the first time I am here. I wanted to see St. Francis." He meant, our actor. "We have no St. Francis," I said, "nobody has a right to play St. Francis." "Then I want to see the monk," he said. He stood there until Frank came out—the good monk Bosco.

Ray Wisniewski bought a truck, is preparing to leave for California. He will make a film about a group of pacifists who will walk across the country. Last Monday a group of pacifists were protesting the launching of the Navy nuclear submarine, Polaris. Frances wanted to go, too, but overslept. She is going through a period of engagement, participation. Influence of the scenes we are shooting. She wants to do something for humanity. With her moods of desperation and depression bordering on suicide, she is ready for anything.

Today I read a report in the *Post* on the arrested pacifists. New Haven sheriff J. Edward Slavin was quoted as saying: "They've got to stop preaching non-violent resistance to the other prisoners. Some of the inmates are getting stirred up. This isn't India. We aren't staffed to cope with this sort of thing."

Should they preach violence, instead?

In any case, I think all those pacifists are schmucks. I wish they would do something violent instead. You cannot fight business-men with passivity. Hit them on the head. Pacifists have no guts, at least most of them.

From home and abroad, we are accused of nihilism and anarchy. The new artist could sing happily and carelessly, with no despair in his voice—but then he would reflect neither his society nor himself, he would be a liar like everybody else. With the soul being squeezed out in all the four corners of the world today, when governments are encroaching upon us with the huge machinery of bureaucracy, war and mass communications, the only way to preserve the soul is to encourage the sense of rebellion, the sense of disobedience, even at the cost of open anarchy and nihilism. The entire landscape of human thought, as it is accepted publicly in the Western world, has to be turned over. All public ideologies, values, and ways of life must be doubted, attacked. "Smell it & get high, maybe we'll all get the answer that way! Don't give up the ship!" exclaims Allen Ginsberg. Yes, the artist is getting high on the death of the civilization, breathing in its poisonous gases. And yes, our art definitely suffers from it. Our art is "confused" and all that jazz jazz jazz (Taylor Mead). But we refuse to continue the Big Lie of bastard culture. To the new artist the fate of humanity is more important than the fate of art. You criticize our work from a purist, formalistic and classicist point of view. But we say to you: What's the use of cinema if man's soul goes rotten?

December 1, 1960

"Natural processes are uncertain, in spite of their lawfulness. Perfectionism and uncertainty are mutually exclusive." Wilhelm Reich, *An Introduction to Orgonomy.*

Any living art is imperfect. Down with perfect art.

We came yesterday on the set. The first thing Sheldon says is, Where to place the camera? How would I know. First, I have to throw myself into the situation, to walk in the room, around and around, and try to catch some of its life, and then reject everything, and begin again. I cannot work out all that on paper, at home, like Edouard. I have to start not with myself, but with Gregory and the monk, and their room. Walk in, I say, how would you walk in, what would you do? Only from there we can begin, however imperfect that is. I know, it would be nice, visually, mechanistically, if the monk would sit right there, compositionally. But will that go with his other movements and his feelings at that moment? So, down with that beautiful dead composition, any composition. Let the compositions grow out of the situation, from their movements, however primitive. Primitive, but alive. Life, truth is what matters.

December 3, 1960

It is time to make up our minds. The film artist still lives with his inferiority complex. A business promoter wants to make a commercial film, so he goes out and shouts loudly and makes a lot of noise. For what? For a basically dull purpose: for more money.

Again and again, I catch myself feeling ashamed, whenever I have to ask to invest in *Guns of the Trees.* As if I wouldn't have the right to do so. It's O.K. to make a commercial movie but there is something sinful in wanting to create a work of art... Should a film artist feel inferior to a business promoter, to one whose actions are motivated by personal profit alone? Why should I feel so?

Our creative intentions are selfless; we know that there are things which man should know and experience.

Why should we say our truths only to the walls, to the trees, to the blue sky? Why should we ground our energies? Let them loose! Let them strike man right in the center of his heart!

We need money to make our films, so let us say so. And let us say it clearly. We are not fooling anybody with any false promises of money. Our aim is Beauty and Truth.

It is the old guard that is confusing us. They say to us: "Don't tell your investors that you are making an art movie. Don't tell them that your actors are unknown. Tell them you are making a commercial movie and that it will make lots of money." I had enough of this. I am neither making a commercial film nor am I going to write any synopses any more. Basta!

I believe that there are enough people who will support art, who believe in the necessity of revealing subtle aspects of human experience, who believe that only the singular artists, only a personal creative expression can bring the ecstasy and Beauty. And it is through these people that the best of the New American Cinema will come into existence.

Long live the New Investor and the New American Cinema.

CHAPTER ELEVEN

... Editing *Guns*...
Frustrating screenings for investors
... On dubbing...
On Rossellini... On Chayevsky's *Marty*...
About "unpretentiousness"... About stealing food...
Shelley on poetry...
On function of a cameraman in New Cinema... Tautrimas visits... Working on "ourselves"...
Notes after reading *Naked Lunch*...
On unimportance...
di Prima, MacLow...
The Connection...
Pull My Daisy...
More on Hawks...
In praise of Star Cinema ... On Richard Leacock... Orson Welles... Stealing food at SAFEWAY...
Film acting in Europe and America... On Brando, James Dean and Carruthers...

On Marilyn Monroe...
A note to academicians... On dubbing... sounds... The poetry of the highway nights...

December 10, 1960

Beginning of the second chapter of our work on *Guns*. We started editing. Last night we screened three hours of rushes. Now Sheldon is sitting and learning how to splice, with Adolfas supervising, he likes supervising things.

Met with De. He just came from Boston where he had some hopes for money. More promises, and no meat. We bought more beans.

Adolfas and Sheldon, they are arguing about food. Wingate is a vegetarian. Adolfas says, no vegetarian was ever good for anything. He just opened another can of George's liver paté. We have been eating nothing but the godamn liver for the last month, we can't even look at it any more.

Today, waiting outside by the Movielab, on 54th Street, I saw a man, one of those paranoiac cases, a man of 55 or so, walking, and talking to himself. He was counting and recounting money! Talking money all the time. The Hell on 54th Street, New York, 1960, Anno Domini.

December 12, 1960

Now even the weather turned against us. For a month I was planning a screening for today, for possible investors. But yesterday it started snowing. Today New York looks like Alaska, the snow is all over the town. None of the seven investors showed up from their seven hideouts. I spent my last money to pay the projectionist—who came... Then we all got into a bus, paying only for three, and went to 87th Street, to Diane's place, to see if there is anything in her icebox. There was nothing in it. We collected between all of us 45 cents and sent Sheldon out to buy some bread and tea. He came back with ham and eggs and butter. He managed to steal it all. So we ate and then went to the New Yorker, our last refuge, to see some old Hitchcocks. Dan gave us five bucks to begin life anew. So we walked through the cold, snowy New York streets shouting and singing.

December 13, 1960

Mrs. S. let me down badly. She promised to get the Park Avenue ladies to the screening. It was partly for them that the screening was set up. Then, yesterday, she backs out: had no time to call nor talk to anybody! It made me sick. No more screenings for any Park Avenues, no more fooling with any Avenues. It makes me sick just to think about showing the film again to some schmucks. I was listening today during the screening to the comments in my back by some Madison Street lawyers, businessmen, and I kept repeating to myself: stupid, stupid, stupid, why the hell did I invite them here, who are they to judge me, why should I expose myself or my film to these dead, humorless, bored people. No more, no more.

December 14, 1960

For the fourth day we sit inside, winding, rewinding, checking, screening, trying to see what we got. Adolfas with Sheldon is splicing the last reels of footage. We are reaching the end of the first stage, familiarizing. Not even familiarizing, just looking, like somebody else's work. Some we didn't even recognize, didn't know we had. On the radio: Charlie Parker.
Like some bad dreams, sometimes bits of Edouard's sentences return to my mind, bad dreams: "Do you know what you want with this image? What's the meaning?"

whenever I see bad footage. How better is the footage, when it went by itself, without meanings, without planning, without all that "what's the meaning of this?" shit.

There was a big discussion going last winter, to dub or not to dub. I remember, Bosley Crowther was for dubbing. One of his strong arguments, I remember, was that in France, most of the foreign films are dubbed and they like it.
I was reminded of this recently, while reading an article by a French critic, Jacques Siclier. He was writing about Capra's *Arsenic and Old Lace* and Paulette Goddard's *Ideal Husband*. The dubbed films are difficult to sit through, he writes. Particularly Capra's *Arsenic and Old Lace*, that example of typical Anglo-Saxon macabre humor, the dubbing destroyed everything. Did Crowther ever check what other critics said about dubbed films in France? So, go to the Bleecker and see not dubbed *Arsenic*.
Markopoulos screened *Serenity* last Tuesday midnight at The Charles. It is still unfinished, says Markopoulos, he is making changes all the time. I have never seen such blue sky in cinema! And yes, it was so quiet, so serene.

Now, why does Rossellini exert such a strong influence upon the new generation of French film-makers? We know that his later films have fared quite badly in the States. And several of them—in fact, those which *Cahiers du Cinema* admired most, were not even released here, or, if released, then in badly mutilated versions and in second run theatres. Even in Europe he has been completely misunderstood. This year, when Rossellini came to Venice with *Il Generale Della Rovere*, he was crowned, blessed and awarded the top prize—for a film that clearly retraces his postwar steps, for a film which he himself considers inferior to his other more recent work. After the success of his post-war films—*Open City* and *Paisà*—Rossellini, against the confused voices of his devoted followers, declared that the changing times asked for different themes and different styles. So he turned to new themes. Beginning with *Stromboli* and *Francesco Giullare di Dio*, he began a search for a more life-like, unrehearsed and natural style that would reflect more faithfully his new feelings and the new, changing world. He began eliminating strong and obviously stylized plots, his films became more episodic. So the commercial distributors ran away from him and the critics declared Rossellini dead. However, Rossellini was more alive than all his critics put together. He continued his experiments until, in *A Voyage in Italy* and *India*, he succeeded fully in achieving his aim. His *India* is a very personal notebook—a fusion of facts, subjective observations, recreations and interpretations that completely reflect modern India. The film could not have been made by anybody else but Rossellini—it is so subjective. Although the film was shot in real situations and places, it is not a documentary, but a highly personal film of fiction in which the new, free form, plotless structure begins to emerge. It is here that Rossellini joined hands with the youngest generation of France, becoming their young father.

However, it is not only the stylistic and formal aspects that separate or bind the Nouvelle Vague from/to their predecessors. There are other equally important differences. The most obvious of all is the very fact that these films are made by a new generation, and thus, very naturally, they reflect new temperaments and new ideas, those of the cold war generation. These ideological and temperamental beginnings go deeper than the Cannes film festival. In fact, the real birth of the Nouvelle Vague should be dated with the appearance of Françoise Sagan, Roger Vadim, and Brigitte Bardot. Sagan, or Vadim, whatever their work is worth artistically, were the first ones to sum up the mores and dreams of their contemporaries, and, by pushing them into an irrational extreme—the same way Elvis Presley pushed to the extreme the lust for materiality by purchasing four cars—made their contemporaries realize the absurdity of those mores and those dreams. In a true existentialist manner, their more sensitive contemporaries became conscious of the pretension.

Hollywood is eager to buy plays which proved successful on TV screens. Some of these TV-plays are small budget local dramas which, on the whole, are a great improvement over Hollywood wide-screen productions. They introduce new themes, new locations, some new faces. Nevertheless, these so called "unpretentious" films contain one great weakness, namely, their "unpretentiousness." They undergo a thorough cleaning before they are put on the screen. Even a seemingly innocent film like *Marty* was trimmed (see the interview with Chayevsky, *N.Y. Post*) to fit Hollywood moulds, as were stage plays like *The Shrike*, *Big Knife*, *Seven Year Itch*. The face and character of the play is erased to please the largest number of public. Themes, characters, problems are reduced to this "unpretentious" simplicity so that they become anemic to comply with the false assumption that the public will react only to easily recognizable patterns and shapes. What the public should get for its money, how the audience should react, how life in the U.S.A. "ought" to appear—is calculated in advance, an important selling point being to protect the public from any possible "unknowns".

For Tina film:
"... repelled I ran away from the city traffic & faces & all the sadness. I sought out, I

found most silent & quiet corners in the city where no one else ever came… I was thinking: It depends entirely on me what I am, what I look at, where I am, what I do to myself, to my soul…"

December 17, 1960

Spent an evening with Hughes, Renata Adler, Polidoro, LaSalle. Had to defend our food stealing. Polidoro, he understands. He even said, that he would steal from his friends, after which Hughes looked around at his things. Driving home, Renata bought four dollars worth of fuel, had a pity or a good heart for us, or for the jeep. The jeep had a full belly again. Poor Willys, we dug it out from under a mountain of snow today, it still doesn't believe it can run free…

The sun is out, the snow is melting. Went out, looked at the sky—the children are laughing loud, playing in the streets, the sun, everything sounds like a bright Spring day, with snow melting, the cold retreating—almost an Eastern European Spring day. I almost saw the icicles melting, hanging down from the roofs, dripping down, and the lumber stacks burning in the April sun…

The sparrows are chirping gaily on St. Mark's Place, and the old men are out again, sunning on the benches, all wrapped up in their winter coats—and it's cold, it still is, no use fooling myself. So, it is better to sit home, and work.

"I never explain anything to actors. Because I never know myself exactly what I am going to do. Besides, actors, especially professionals, when they know in advance what they are going to do, study their roles and get them completely wrong. I prefer to tell them what they are going to do just before they have to do it."—Federico Fellini, in interview, *Esquire*

"A poet is the combined product of such internal powers as modify the nature of others; and of such external influences as excite and sustain these powers; he is not one, but both. Every man's mind is, in this respect, modified by all the objects which he ever admitted to act upon his consciousness; it is the mirror upon which all forms are reflected, and in which they compose one form. Poets, not otherwise, than philosophers, painters, sculptors, and musicians, are, in one sense, the creators, and in another, the creations, of their age. From this subjection the loftiest do not escape. There is a similarity between Homer and Hesiod, between Aeschylus and Euripides, between Virgil and Horace, between Dante and Petrarch, between Shakespeare and Fletcher, between Dryden and Pope; each has a generic resemblance under which their specific distinctions are arranged. If this similarity be the result of imitation, I am willing to confess that I have imitated."
—Shelley, from the preface to "Prometheus Unbound"

December 24, 1960

Again arguments about Sheldon. Edouard says it was a mistake to take him as a cameraman, he is no cameraman, he is no good. There are so many good cameramen around, he doesn't see why I should defend Sheldon. I said, if America would have 15 cameramen like Sheldon, things would begin to move. It is absurd, says Edouard, any cameraman is better than Sheldon. What are they, who are they? I ask. Kaufman, for instance, or Schuftin. But they are old, I say. It's like *New York Times* hiring a journalist who writes in 1914 style. Nobody will do that. Or a novel written in a nineteenth century style. We need new cameramen. O.K., Sheldon is not really a technician, he is really quite bad, he ruined plenty of our footage. I know all that. Kaufman has technique, but he is from a different generation, and he is brilliant. But who wants him in the New

Cinema? What Sheldon has, they do not have: Sheldon understands the contemporaneous. He needs help on technique, but he never failed in understanding what I wanted. Edouard failed all the time. Even when Sheldon didn't understand, he was able to swing with me. Let the camera be shaky, and uneven! This is not time to write perfect books and make perfect films. This is time to break loose from the overused techniques and names, subject matter, forms—and you cannot do it by polite respect of the established techniques and names, but by simply ignoring and even laughing at them! I have sent many people to see *High School Caesar*. They all later thought that I fooled them. It took Sheldon to see its real youthfulness, its real virtues, no matter how banal the film was.

And then: what is the function of a cameraman in the New Cinema, author's cinema, personal cinema, my cinema? Yes, in the old cinema, which is a mish-mash hodgepodge of 100 people, the cameraman has to be a technician and nothing else. But in my film, it is me who choses the locations, it is me who choses the angle, the spot, the movement of the camera—and only a cameraman who is not a technician can follow all my personal whims. It is not the "proper" exposure, not the steady pan that I am after. I am after my dream. This asks for a more subtle and more unpredictable movements and speeds than those of Hollywood, and to read all that, to guess all that, to get into that part of me— or, let us say, director's creative personality—is much more than to be a technician. The New Cinema needs new cameramen. The New Cinema needs cameramen who have feeling for the new reality and who have the temperament of the new life. In a period of rebellion, of search, the new cameraman has also to be a rebel and a searcher. We'll find our own movements and rhythms and lighting and techniques.

We don't have to borrow anything, we are that arrogant.

Not that I have succeeded in the filming of *Guns*. Probably I failed 90 percent. Probably, to really achieve what I want, I have to take the camera into my own hands totally and completely, and speak through the camera alone, which I swear I intend to do from now on. This has been a bitter experience for me, the filming of *Guns*. I didn't DARE to escape it totally, I didn't. The snares of Edouard prevented me from it. But that period is over and over.

December 26, 1960

Met Tautrimas, the Lithuanian documentarist. He came here with a few other Soviet artists, writers, to look at America. He wanted to see our "studios," to see how we work, our film, etc. I didn't know what to say. We are against studios, I said, and I am working without money and with nothing, and nobody helps us, we are stealing even our food. It was very hard for him to understand this.

We went to a bar, for a drink, and I had nothing, not a single cent in my pocket. So he bought all our drinks and coffee. Suddenly we felt so godamn poor. So we talked and talked, until morning, and drank Lithuanian vodka, and dreamed our cinema dreams.

We planned to meet again, today, but they called from the Bronx, somewhere in the Bronx, completely lost, and drunk, from a telephone booth—lost in the Bronx, with nobody speaking English, mad drunk Lithuanians.

We interrupted the editing for two days, to celebrate Christmas. Today we had a jamboree at the New Yorker, in the office, upstairs, with De Antonio, Dan, Peter, Sheldon, Diane, drinking vodka, singing, eating kielbasa, and making so much noise in general that the projectionist called and asked to keep the place quiet—and Peter Bogdanovich was imitating Dylan

Thomas and Orson Welles, and all that—until De got completely drunk, and we all spilled into the street.

We tried a new method of editing. We have cards for every scene all laid out on a huge reflector. We caught a roach, and followed him on the board, walking through these cards. But, somehow, the roach chose a very straight line, not interesting at all.

We managed to cut the first sequence down to 20 minutes, which is about one tenth of what we had shot. It breaks our hearts to chop it. We would like to screen a four-hour version just to bore everybody to death.

Since it's Christmas time, we decided to suspend our food stealing activities for two days. The more that we managed to line up, for the Holidays and even deep into the next week, a few dinners. That should keep us well alive. So, peace to the SAFEWAY!

December 31, 1960

A few hours of the fifties left. We just finished the first rough cut of *Guns*. Got down to ten reels, 20 minutes each. On that occasion Adolfas pulled out a bottle of vodka, and we had a celebration, the five of us—Sheldon, Chuck, Lynn, his girl-friend, and ourselves. Chuck has been helping us for the last few days on splicing, with Lynn and Diane sitting around, bored to death. Shirley Clarke just finished her own rough cut, 2 hours long, and with the sound. It took her two weeks.

It is not easy to keep our four—often five and six mouth kolkhoz alive. The major part of our meal supplies we still have to steal. Much of it comes from the SAFE-WAY food store, next door, mainly because we like its name. Chuck took out some pans and a coffee pot—the big things. I have to provide with smaller items such as coffee, butter, cheese. We buy only bread and potatoes.

Louis called. Money. He could use one token, he said, has to get uptown. I went to see him on 4th Street. We laughed both about it, but it wasn't funny, somehow. Do you want 25 cents? I asked. I could give you 25 cents, that's all I have left. No, he says, very seriously, 15 will do.

January 1, 1961

Creative film, film auteur, personal film, private vision, film as an art, etc., etc.—now they are all talking about it. Leave the film-maker alone, let him create, they say. As if true authorship can come just like that: suddenly, just by giving a director more freedom, a personal art will bloom in the middle of California.

What nonsense!

The artist is always alone, nobody can "leave him alone." True creation is the same at all times and in all the arts: the work always begins with the artist himself. Call it a total involvement, call it a derangement of the senses, call it a madness, anything—but it must be there. One will not arrive at "art" by merely perfecting his technical tools or by means of "more freedom."

Tolstoy asked: "How much land does a man need?" I ask: How much freedom does an artist need? How much freedom did Howard Hawks need to create his work? Or Dovzhenko? And the men who made those clay masterpieces, those anonymous potters?

And then, who cares about freedom! Who invented freedom! We are always talking about wrong freedoms. There are meaningless freedoms; and there are sweet prisons of the hands that you love.

What have we been doing with ourselves, these last fifteen years, myself, and Adolfas, and Leo, if not continuously working on ourselves, on our sensibilities, testing ourselves, throwing ourselves into unexpected directions, dangerous curves, diving deep and blindly, at the cost of our nerves, our flesh. All these years! Sitting late into the Maspeth and Williamsburg nights, dreaming, talking. Our endless walks in Wiesbaden, and Kassel, postwar trains, nights unslept. And always greedy for more, never enough, greedily going through every new book, every old book, painting, music—the hours of discoveries, disappointments, always working on ourselves. It is these years of work on ourselves will grow into everything, it will eat into everything like acid, into everything we touch.

It is this content, it is this *ourselves* that will be visible, and not the technique, not the technical details. We are so full, that we can go into the studio, into the street, and make an "author's" film without knowing anything about how Hollywood or anybody does anything, how they light, or how they dub, or how they do this or that. And we are going to do it. And nobody will fool us: There can't be an author's cinema, there can't be any personal work of art without the first stage, without the work on oneself. Brakhage was able to do it in his first films, Kenneth Anger was. They were free and ready, and open, with no truckloads of Hollywood techniques. Robert Frank and Alfred Leslie were able to do it in *Pull My Daisy*. They just did it. Their sensibilities were ready to explode any time, and they exploded. And go and tell them about techniques, and film schools, and form, and content, tell them. Yes, and Cassavetes did it in *Shadows*. It is the new sensibility that is at the heart of the New Cinema; people who are free and breaking out, who are full to the breaking point, point zero—not techniques. When it breaks out by itself, it traces its own content, its own form, style, shape, rhythm, pace, texture and tone that no 100 scriptwriters or producers would ever be able to dream or arrive at it is the curve of life itself.

Improvisation? Spontaneity? Wasn't that the only method of creation any time, anywhere, for any true artist? Improvisation comes from real need, from ripeness. Any birth is an improvisation. Techniques? The basic vocabulary of filmmaking is already lodged in our subconscious. The new generation of film-makers, of film poets—if they are ever going to be poets—now, for the first time in film "history" can begin creating from within, which is the condition of any creation, including the creation of Eve. The film-maker as a specialist is dead.

Burroughs (W. S.), very possibly, is the first to write *absolument moderne* (in "The Naked Lunch") in America. All techniques of modern writing are perfectly integrated here: they came already from the deeper subconscious. Joyce is already dissolved. Hence, the unhampered, spontaneous flow of Burroughs, the unpredictability of form, freshness, aliveness of Burroughs—the nakedness of an improvisation as a method.

Those who respect Joyce, the classicists and academicians (what a paradox: Joyce was made into a stick to stifle experiment!) will cry red blood: the "formlessness" of Kerouac, of Ginsberg, Burroughs; the "formlessness" of Pollack, de Kooning, and now, Leslie, Frank, Brakhage, Cassavetes. Form! Form! They cry, not realizing that it comes to more than form: they want form at the cost of life itself. And the only form they can see and perceive is the old, overworked, 1,000 years old form.

What does it mean, "new form?" It means a new content, a new experience. That means that Burroughs, that Kerouac, that Ginsberg, that Leslie could not create any other way: they simply exploded, they were too full. They were carrying too long their experiences, long nights, long walks, long drives, long evenings of conversations, their confrontations with all the works of art they deeply experienced—their need to express grew and grew like a river, they had no choice.

It is these explosions, more of them, that we need, irrational, without choice—only they are worth anything in art, any art. Only this cinema is truly "author's" cinema. The cinema of essences, blotches of emotions, explosions of energy, life as it's felt and experienced in 1961, by a man who is embracing his times. By a man who knows that the condition of being *absolument moderne* is the same as the condition of being *absolutely alive*—that it means to be very, very open, absolutely self, and listening, absolutely uncompromising. When we are caught in a continuous automatization, a drying out of all soul, all senses, and all real touch with reality, we have to balance it all and to counteract it all with an ever-increasing ecstasy, be it rock-and-roll, beatitude, Zen, even anarchy, even insanity: bursts of irrationality. And the more extreme this technical civilization (or truer: bureaucratic civilization) grows, the more extreme will be (and must be) this relationship: the more split, the more schizoid. But this poet's schizophrenia is not a giving up: it is rather, a "sickness unto death" that comes from the very core of human existence, of human desperation, as a reaction, as a warning or preventive fact, or act, a positive force, probably the only true saving force or act that man has left for himself. But even that one act is involuntary.

When the life is perverted and made unlivable, the innocents will jump out the windows, soak in their innocent blood, will dream themselves out in the ecstasies of drugs. The insensitive ones will survive and will become Mamies, salesmen, atomic pirates, Nixons, professors, Wouks.

The creation in 1961 must be like action painting, like a Jazz improvisation, like Kerouac's prose, like Brakhage's and Anger's cinema. Like every art, cinema had to explore its limits, its other side, its abyss, it has to look down, it has to become dizzy. And you begin to sing, but without knowing and maybe without even wanting to sing—but you do it, from anxiety, from loneliness or maybe from an unexplainable ecstasy that you are still here and that earth is here and flowers are here and the sun—from your own unwanted happiness.

January 5, 1961

"Yes, I have a Moviola. Who is the editor?"
"I am the editor."
"But you directed the film?"
"Yes. Therefore I am editing it."
"Hmm?"
"Yes."
"But it's not done like that professionally. This is not professional. Is this a professional film?"
"Yes, the film is professional, all right."
"But you don't have a professional editor."
"But I told you, I am the editor."
"You directed it, no?"
"Yes."
"It's not done so, it is not done so. It is not professional."
"Oh, hell."

I just spent two hours with Unger & Elliot manager Mr. Woods, trying to get a Moviola. Didn't work. He wanted to talk us into giving our film to his editors, to edit it!
He said, we can't do it ourselves, it's not professional.

It is always so: when art (and life) becomes stale, there comes a fresh wind of youth from some downtowns carrying gusts of uncontrolled, rough life that threatens to sweep away all official art: barbarians of the arts. Life or art, this is their choice (and Joyce). Rimbaud-like. And by choosing life they gain art.

And so it is with the New American Cinema. The official cinema is splitting apart from its own boredom; the dead syntax, the dead image, the overused routines are becoming so obviously ridiculous (the only time when one feels like laughing at the dead)—and so 1,000 years old. Cinema that is 1,000 years old, that's what we have today!

Any return towards the self, therefore, any tendency towards improvisation and spontaneity, any debunking of the mechanical approach to arts, should be considered a true direction for any and all artists today. We must strive towards a cinema where we begin, as in all true art, with certain centers of emotions, attitudes, experiences; and around these centers we then create, improvise, develop. It is a means whereby we can escape the clichés and molds and retrace lost originality of the eye, whereby we can search for the very essence of life that would lend our work an uncorrupt truth and depth. In "artistic" or "artificial" cinema this depth is achieved through consciously placed symbols and their conscious juxtapositions; here, just the opposite occurs: it is achieved by destroying or displacing all conscious plots, all importance, all seriousness, all symbolism. There are times when one can trust one's deeper unconscious more (or, let us say, our dreams, our imagination) than one's conscious reasoning. I'd say further, when the truth is lost, it is better to trust a throw of dice than your mind.

Thus, *Marrying Maiden*, *The Connection*, or *Pull My Daisy*, in which nothing "important" seems to happen, reach deeper into the contemporary reality than any pseudorealist film or theater piece. They reach into the truth of an entire generation, revealing not its surface actions but its very spirit, its poetry, its joys and its sadness.

12 Angry Men will always stay on its dreary naturalistic detail plane. We can analyze the mentality of the people who made it, but then it will end right there, it will never lead us into anything else. Whereas the makers of *Pull My Daisy*, by loosening their sensibilities, through flights of spontaneous improvisations, or by simply abandoning their minds, entrusting their minds to the dice throw—have succeeded in descending into those depths where there is no lie and no contrivance, where there is only the trembling of life itself. If sometimes it sounds like a cry, or it pains, like an open wound—it's so only because the life itself is like a crying open wound.

How much freedom does an artist need? Take Howard Hawks. He is almost a saint. A man with no pretensions to art whatsoever. By renouncing the artist in himself, and by devoting himself to craft alone, he purified himself and his work: his work became a song to friendship, one of the purest friendship songs that there is in the entire cinema. He works like those unknown potters and weavers. In the distant places of France and Chile and Azerbaijan, anonymous, with no pretensions, they weave and they make their pots, a pure craft, a pure objectivity, a renunciation of themselves as "artists." And their work sings. The clay sings, the linen sings, the film sings.

Hawks undermines our pretentious talks about art. If Bogart, for instance, would appear in Hawks' films as a stylized Citizen Kane, we would resist him, doubt him, we would take him as art. But now we have to face Bogart playing Bogart. What a dirty trick. So, we say, there is nothing behind it, this is not art, so let's just watch it, relax and watch it—this is only entertainment. There you are, fooled completely, and you sit and watch, cured from all art preconceptions, you sit there, while all this time the sweet poison of the secret and sacred art of Hawks flows into your subconscious, without any resistance. That's what Rossellini does, that's what Renoir does. That's what art does.

It doesn't even look like art. It's so simple. Like a rosary, or a prayer wheel. No good director, no Rossellini, no Hawks, no Renoir will point with a finger and say: look at this image, look at this image, look at this camera movement, look at this symbol. Close-ups, and all that. No more. Now it's you who have to work on the film, to figure it out for yourself. Now it's the image itself that, without your knowing it, steals into your subconscious and begins to work on you.

But we have been terribly confused all these years, always looking for "art." We developed a whole genre of "art" films, they play at "art" theatres and they're supposed to be serious, deep, intellectual and all that. But it's this "art" cinema that is the most false cinema of all. It's literature, not cinema. It still circles in the domain of literature, verbal ideas, verbal imagery.

I will be the one to laugh some day, laugh at all the serious critics and serious "art" films. One day everybody will suddenly realize that the so called "star" cinema, the cinema which supposedly had nothing to do with "art," a cinema that just simply followed a Monroe, or a Jean Harlow, Gable, Cooper, Elizabeth Taylor, Bogart—decried by everybody as cheap entertainment—this cinema will prove to be more true than any pretentious "art" cinema.

And it will be on that day that the pompous critics will realize it was these films that used cinema in a proper way. They didn't give a damn for "content" and "ideas" and "important" subjects. Instead, they concentrated on the human face, human movements, followed this one man or this one woman and, almost in a documentary fashion, recorded their movements and their expressions. Not a Jean Harlow or a Gable or a Bogart playing, impersonating some other character, no: that would be theatre. These films recorded Bogart and Gable and Harlow as they were, playing themselves. It is Jean Harlow and it is Gable and Bogart that is the true content and meaning and idea of these films, and it is here that they differ from any other art, literature, theatre, painting. It's the human face, Garbo's face, or the movements of Douglas Fairbanks that is the content and the plot. The story plot is of no importance at all. And whenever a director, by listening too long to the stupid gibberish of the critics, decides to make actors of his stars—they become theatre, dramatic figures illustrating some words of literature or some characters of a play. No more cinema, no more MM, no more BB.

When the world is confused, when aesthetics are confused, when nobody knows any longer what is good, what's bad, what's beautiful, what's ugly, what's important, what's unimportant, what's craft, what's art—the most humble and most right is to say: I don't know anything, so I'll be just an open eye, watching everything equally, there is no good and no bad and everything is important.

It's Ricky Leacock who is one of the humble saints of cinema, creating the true cinema: not trusting himself, but his camera. Living amongst strangers—becoming one of them, recording faces, movements, and the words as they happen, and the laughs—he himself being only the camera. He is not directing, he is not telling them what to do or what to say or where to move, he is not doing anything: he is only faithfully following the motions and sounds, be it President Kennedy (in *Primary*), or a poor Venezuelan family high in the Andes (*Cuba Si Yankee No*). The camera has never caught life with more authenticity. He is creating cinema, not theatre, not literature, this man. This is what the star cinema did, too: the star cinema was a documentary of the star. You cannot direct a star. You watch a star, you follow a star.

Helping George Maciunas fix up his A/G Gallery, 925 Madison Avenue. We had to chip away the thick paint and plaster, to expose the original brick wall. Hard work, a lot of nasty dust…

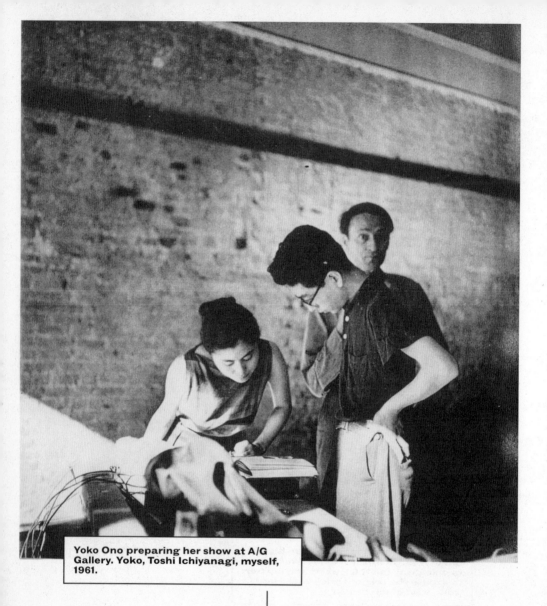

Yoko Ono preparing her show at A/G Gallery. Yoko, Toshi Ichiyanagi, myself, 1961.

PAINTINGS
&
DRAWINGS
BY
YOKO
ONO
JULY
17-30
1-6 PM
EXCEPT
FRIDAY
AT
AG
925
MADISON
AVE
(74)
PREVIEW
3-5 PM
JULY
16
SUNDAY

Since the days of Lumière, since *Nanook* the film-maker was trying to push the theatre and painting out of the film. The film-maker wanted man's insignificant actions. Man's mind is man-made, man's motions, expressions, man's insignificances are God-made. And this is the domain of cinema. One domain that no other art can register that perfectly. Cinema is the only art that lives through insignificances; cinema is the only art that needs no meanings, no ideas; that is, in it's very essence, it's an anti-art.

So they say: this is not "art," there is no "intelligence" here. There is no "content," it's too simple. Man must create.

When the truth is lost, it is better to trust a throw of the dice than your mind. Diane di Prima's or Jackson MacLow's chance poetry, the chance theatre is closer to true creation and truth than any "serious" contemporary art, hundreds of "serious" contrived plays, experimental films, poems. Both di Prima and MacLow, with the help of a pair of dice, purified and cleaned their work from overused ideas, overused, contrived imagery, overused molds and patterns so that their work would again regain the purity, innocence and power of a newly born word.

It is the same with cinema. By forgetting art, Leacock, Hawks and the star director entered the territory of the true cinema.

And all this talk about plots, and content, and social messages in cinema, all that pretentious literary nonsense.

There are no important or unimportant subjects; there are no big or small plots in art. And what is the plot? The plot is only a piece of rusty wire on which to attach the flowers of the festivity garlands.

Orson Welles, for instance. He took this (as Frank & Leslie did in *Pull My Daisy*, as Gelber did in *The Connection*) this "stupid" plot of *Touch of Evil* and he started swinging. This man exploded into images. His sensibilities started bursting (what is the meaning of Rimbaud's title *Illuminations*? Explosions!)—taking dangerous and reckless curves. And what was banal becomes beautiful, begins to swing, to grow. Not from the hands of 100 technicians and writers, but from the very depths of this man, Orson Welles, from the depths of all his years—every image, and every shade, every detail is full of it, crawling out in an enormous mass, a fugue, a baroque fugue of imagery that can be only his, Orson Welles, and the characters begin to move and behave and talk as only his characters can behave and talk—and Orson Welles himself, no more himself—a dirty, sloppy, sweating slob, all sin and dirt and evil, walks there, no more himself, but something that crawled out of his soul, his subconscious worm.

When we come to truly personal art, to the true "author's" cinema, we enter the territory where the creation, the only creation, happens out of an inescapable, involuntary inner necessity. Creation, which is like sickness, or a cancer, perhaps, where one doesn't have a choice at all.

Until now, when the critics said that you cannot make a film "unprofessionally," they always meant that Hawks or Hitchcock couldn't make *Air Force* or *Psycho* with a 16 mm camera and bits of film. And they were right. And when Cocteau says that you don't need all those lamps and crews, that the only thing you need is a 16 mm camera—he meant *Fireworks* and *Desistfilm*, and he was right, too. It is time to realize that there are many cinemas, that the content of Brakhage or Maya Deren is of a more intimate nature, of a more private nature, that it needs a different form, different technology, different technique. Nobody will ever make *Air Force* in a Fourth Street loft, spontaneously. Different experience, different content, different techniques.

But it is the personal, private, poetic cinema of Brakhage, Maya Deren, Robert Frank, that has the most unexplored possibilities, that is free from the burden of equipment, of crews, budgets, unions. And it is this cinema that deals with those areas and depths that interest us most at this moment. The spontaneous cinema, the cinema of explosions, illuminations. Unlimited possibilities. The cinema of essences. Through the cracks of the old withering official life, through the ever increasing cracks in the official arts, one can already perceive—though still frail and weak—the movements of a fresh, new, April wind. And when we listen to it, sometimes it sounds like a song; sometimes it is like a breeze in the reeds; and sometimes it sounds like a cry, like a crying wound.

Listening to Jimmy Giuffre's music, I thought about "overexposures" and "underexposures" in sound and image, "scratched" sounds and "scratched" images, "random" sounds and "random" images.

"Listen carefully to first criticisms made of your work. Note just what it is about your work that the critics don't like—then cultivate it. That's the only part of your work that's individual and worth keeping."
—Jean Cocteau to a young artist

"happenings:"
1. Kiss your neighbor on the left. Kiss your neighbor on the right. Then the neighbor kisses his neighbor, etc. (Kiss Chain Game)
2. The audience holds hands.
3. Each member of the audience comes and stands in front of the audience for a minute.
4. This could be part of the SCHOOL (or CHILDHOOD): Each one in the audience is asked a question from the First Grade textbook, on various subjects. No laughing or smiling; if somebody smiles, ask why.
5. Ask if they know poems by heart.

Clarity doesn't interest me. I know that through confusion I have a chance of arriving somewhere, of catching some secret movements of the subconscious, or Life or Myself—but I have no trust, no trust at all in clarity, in pre-planning, where everything is predictable, everything is written down. Those are one-dimensional films and they bore me.

January 14, 1961

For a change, we went to New Jersey. Adolfas, myself, and Sheldon. Shot some road footage. But mostly breathed the winter air, looked at the scattered snow patches. Stopped by a frozen lake. Got crazy on the ice. For ten years haven't been on ice like this. So we fell on our backs, we skated on our shoes, did crazy things, like dogs let loose from a leash. Some people were fishing through the ice holes. The day was warm, clear.

Got the film down to about 160 minutes. Still trimming. The projector began breaking, every few days we have to stop everything and Adolfas takes the whole machine apart to fix it. We are trying to get a Moviola. Shirley said she will have one next week, maybe. Jerome offered his own, next week. What a difference between people and people. Here, no strings attached. And then, there are those who say they are your friends, and they want to see the whole footage before giving their old Moviolas for one single day.

Visited Storm and Louis. Storm is studying early 18th Century writings, originals. Louis jokingly said that he doesn't want to read anything that was written after the Bible. Everything is so twisted, corrupt, in later writings. One has to go to the originals always. The farther back you go, the more truth you find. It seems to me that's the same with the people around me: the lower you descend to the people like Sheldon's generation, and farmers, and simple Brooklyn dock workers, the more hope there is to find some life, direct life. The idiots have more truth, more direct contact with life today than the so-called intelligentsia.

January 17, 1961

That gold woman, Shirley [Clarke], she arranged that nights, when she is not working, we can use her Moviola. She is still working on *The Connection*, shuffling and reshuffling again. "You know where the key is," she said. Just like that. "Come and work." So we brought our footage and worked all night. We'll be continuing tomorrow night. Bless Shirley.

Our poor old jeep died. The trip to New Jersey killed it completely. The winter weather, the cold. First the pistons broke, then the clutch, then the radiator. We were still driving for a couple of days. Then, Sunday night it stopped for good, poor thing. It looks so sad there. Had we known, we'd have left it in the country, on some frozen lake, to die in nature, like Tolstoy. Now, tomorrow, the junkyard people are coming to pick it up. Only a memory—the seats, the windshields are left. It served us good, the poor Willys, the Papacar, as Hammid's children used to call it.

Since we cannot live without a car—too expensive to travel by subways—we bought a 1951 Ford from Daniels, the writer, Louis' friend. It is a real beat-up thing, we bought it for $75. But it runs fine. It makes all sorts of noises, it has a bad personality, but it works OK.

Sheldon has been searching for a job all week long. Nothing. He has nobody to borrow money from. Our resources drained out two months ago. Every morning I am risking the film and everything by stealing from the SAFEWAY a piece of butter or instant coffee, or a piece of cheese. (WE STEAL ONLY SAFEWAY, is our slogan.)

ABC
How to Live With Artists and Have Respect
ETC
(Mostly for Edouard)

1. Never impose on the artist's time. He never knows when he works. He may give you his time, if you press, but, without knowing it, he will hate you, eventually, for it.
2. You can have respect of an artist only when you are able to live as an equal with equal, when you don't deride him or his work but take it as a different creation from yours. If you can force yourself to recognize the creation of other, even if it's not your own creation —you'll have his respect.
3. Always return borrowed books, if you borrow them from a poet: books are his only property, they are part of his life. He will forget if you don't return his horse, but he'll never forgive you if you don't return his book.
4. Don't act like a pompous ass.

January 19, 1961

Last night, with Diane, Sheldon collected one dollar in the street. Panhandling. They got a penny from one. A Chinese could not believe that they were asking for money. Do they do this in America, he asked, and gave fifty cents. Got a dime from another. Diane was luckier. She held on to Sheldon's hand, and looked sad and embarrassed. It worked better.

January 22, 1961

From today's *Greenwich Village News*, Sheldon brought in:
"Action must be taken soon, a prominent Villager stated, or else the Village runs the risk of inundation by a flood of panhandlers, with the corresponding lowering of property values and loss of regional prestige."

Almus Salcius and George Maciunas, Great Neck. For several years Almus ran a gallery in his Great Neck house. In 1960 he joined George in his 925 Madison Avenue A/G Gallery venture.

At nights, in Shirley's editing room, during the day at the New Yorker, the Forgotten Cinema cycle, two new films every day, a feast of Hawks, etc. Rossellini's *Voyage to Italy* is a masterpiece, Aldrich's *Kiss Me Deadly* is a masterpiece, and so is Hawks' *Air Force*. That Hawks is great, no joke. *Cahiers* guys were right. How he creates the mood, even in not such a great film, like *Dawn Patrol*. There is no triviality or sentimentality in a bad sense, no melodramatics in Hawks. He is almost documentary. Direct relationships, no fussing. Moods established, details clean, relations clean. *Air Force* is as good, or maybe better than *Alexander Nevski*. It is a heresy, but it is a fact.

FILM
Show a little stone
Title: This was the stone that killed Goliath

Whenever I mention *Shadows* or *Pull My Daisy* I can hear groans from the best minds of the last generation. This is not art, there is no conscious creation here! This is a spontaneous mess! Maya Deren (*Village Voice*, July 21, 1960) summed up this attitude for everybody: this spontaneous creation, she said, "reminds me of nothing so much as an amateur burglar in a strange apartment, turning all the drawers onto the floor, cutting up the mattresses, ripping off the backs of pictures, and in general making one ungodly clumsy mess in a frantic search for a single significant note." Whereas in true creation, she said, "one begins with a concept, a magnet charged with conviction and concentration."

The modern American film, however, (like poetry and prose), is created by different sensibilities. It is not an academic acting —it is Marlon Brando, James Dean, Ben Carruthers who best express the new style of film acting.

In the old school of directing, the director imposes his own will upon the actor. "Charged with conviction," as Maya Deren says, the director takes an actor, like any other raw piece of material, and begins to mold it into a contraption of his own.

But it is this type of directing that is butchering our cinema, our theatre, and our actors.

You can still do things like that in Europe and get away with it. The European school of stage and film acting, compared with Brando, Dean and Carruthers, is antique. But we understand it: It is antique, but it is not immoral. The soul of a European is full of deep molds, forms of past cultures. He may even die without escaping them. That is his fate.

It is a different situation in America. Anyone, in any art, who perpetuates old styles of acting, or writing, or dancing, commits an immoral act: instead of freeing us, he drags us down.

But it is not easy to drag down the new generation (by which I mean a great part of post-wwII generation). A European director, working for the first time with a group of young American actors, immediately notices their constant questioning, soul-searching, always-watching sensibilities.

The young American, lost and shaky, searching, fragile, groping in an uncertain moral landscape, resists any attempt to be used in a preconceived, thought out manner, in any creation which begins with a clear conception of what one wants to do, because he knows that most of what we know is fake.

I have been watching Sheldon. I think that Sheldon is half asleep even when he is most awake. His normal state of living is a sort of half-sleep. And that is what his generation is (he is 21). He is sensitive, receptive. Many things can be projected on to him, he catches ideas fast. But it works like with a hypnotist's medium: he is almost will-less. And one wonders, what is going on in this half-sleep of his generation. One thing is clear: it is not a dead or dying matter. Just the opposite: it is a bundle of potent, latent, sleeping energy, very alive. Is there something being projected into this sleeping subconscious, something that will save America and mankind? Something that cannot be projected, cannot grow anywhere else, in the subconscious minds of businessmen and generals? Since this generation is least protected, most passive, it is most suitable for breeding the most fragile, most subversive secret flowers of good and evil...

Nobody can blame, therefore, the younger generation for being oversensitive, for not trusting anybody else's will, for being too concerned with itself, with truth, sincerity. The young actor of today doesn't trust the will of a director any longer. He doesn't think that the part he is playing is only a part and he is only an actor. He merges with his part entirely, it becomes a moral problem for him, a problem of existence. Thus, he doesn't trust any will but his own, which, he knows, is still very frail and, thus, harmless—no will at all, only distant, deep waves and motions and voices and groans of a Marlon Brando, James Dean, Ben Carruthers—waiting, listening (the same way Kerouac is listening for the new American word and syntax and rhythm in his spontaneous improvisations; or Coltrane). As long as the "lucidly minded" critics stay out, with all their "form," "content," "art," "structure," "clarity," "importance," and all that nonsense—everything will be all right, just keep them out. Because this new soul is still budding, going through a most dangerous, most sensitive time. Keep out all those strong wills with preconceived, worked-out ideas.

Even the animals hide themselves before giving birth. And women, they can almost hear through the walls. It is a highly sensitive and private matter. And it is the same with the 'total subconscious' of a country, a continent, a race, painfully going through its (re)birth: American culture began with the groans of James Dean and Brando and Carruthers.

It is true that the new man is in a mess. And so is his art. ("Natural processes are *uncertain* in spite of their lawfulness. Perfectionism and uncertainty are mutually exclusive."—Wilhelm Reich) But he is not in a frantic search for a "single significant note," he doesn't even care about "significance": he is in search of the meaning of life itself.

Films, most of the current films are repeating old imagery and thematics. Only slowly new imagery is coming in, and usually in 42nd Street films such as *Delinquents*.

It is the rhythm and feeling of life that are important, the inner life, not the action, and it is this that today's films miss. Suzuki: "To grasp life from within and not from without." So, although the *Delinquents* is a bad film there are more moments in it that catch the inner rhythm of today than, let us say, a more ambitious film like *Nun's Story*, etc.

"J'aime beaucoup *Une femme est une femme*, c'etait un essai très intéressant et sincere. Toute oeuvre d'art doit être un essai... Je n'aime pas les films achevés, j'aime ceux qui s'ouvrent sur l'univers, qui ne se prennent pas au sérieux et qui sont 'vrais.' *Une femme est une femme* fait partie de cuex—là, et c'est pourquoui je l'aime."—Jean Renoir

February 9, 1961
MARILYN MONROE AND THE LOVE-LESS WORLD
Marilyn Monroe, the saint of the Nevada Desert. When everything has been said about *The Misfits*, how bad the film is and all that, she still remains there, MM, the

saint. And she haunts you, you'll not forget her.

It is MM that is the film. A woman who has known love, has known life, has known men, has been betrayed by all three, but has retained her dream of man, love, and life.

She meets these tough men, Gable, Clift, Wallach, in her search for love and life; she finds love everywhere and she cries for everyone. She is the only beautiful thing in the whole ugly desert, in the whole world, in this whole dump of toughness, atom bomb, death.

Everybody has given up their dreams, all the tough men of the world have become cynics, except MM. And she fights for her dream—for the beautiful, innocent, and free. It is she who fights for love in the world, when the men fight only wars and act tough. Men gave up the world. It is MM that tells the truth in this movie, who accuses, judges, reveals. And it is MM who runs into the middle of the desert and in her helplessness shouts: *"You are all dead, you are all dead!"*—in the most powerful image of the film—and one doesn't know if she is saying those words to Gable and Wallach or to the whole loveless world. Is MM playing herself or creating a part? Did Miller and Huston create a character or simply re-create MM? Maybe she is even talking her own thoughts, her own life? Doesn't matter much. There is so much truth in her little details, in her reactions to cruelty, to false manliness, nature, life, death, that she is overpowering, one of the most tragic and contemporary characters of modern cinema, and another contribution to The Woman as a Modern Hero in Search of Love (see *Another Sky, The Lovers, Hiroshima mon Amour, The Savage Eye,* etc., etc.).

It's strange how cinema, bit by bit, can piece together a character. Cinema is not only beautiful compositions or well-knit stories; cinema is not only visual patterns or play of light. Cinema also creates human characters.

We are always looking for "art," or for good stories, drama, ideas, content in movies—as we are accustomed to in books. Why don't we forget literature and drama and Aristotle! Let's watch the face of man on the screen, the face of MM, as it changes, reacts. No drama, no ideas, but a human face in all its nakedness—something that no other art can do. Let's watch this face, its movements, its shades; it is this face, the face of MM, that is the content and story and idea of the film, that is the whole world, in fact.

March 16, 1961

The academicians shouldn't be afraid. None of the modern poets, painters, playwrights or film-makers want to touch them. This is a generation of artists who are interested more in life than art. The new artist realizes that nobody knows what truth is; nobody knows anything about what really matters. So he simply relies on himself, on his own intuitions to discover it in himself and through himself, by his own harmless innocent actions. Nobody is forcing you to follow him. You can stay with your art. Live a life doped by false philosophers, immoral politicians, ugly newspapers, television, radio commentators, mechanical professors, parrots and schools—and vast libraries of false, ignorant textbooks—they are all yours!

Faced with these legions of printed, shouted, screamed, projected ugliness, the artist feels that his spontaneous, improvised way of living and creating is the only way to discover any truth about what concerns him so deeply, so essentially, so existentially.

Yes, he is groping in a huge darkness. He goes into the blind alleys, and he tries again. He beats his head against the wall, against too many walls, he often bleeds, and he cries, but he is not dropping atom

SEEGER CONVICTED OF U. S. CONTEMPT

Jury Finds Folk Singer Is Guilty of All 10 Counts of Defiance in Red Hunt

By PHILIP BENJAMIN

Pete Seeger, the folk singer, was convicted of contempt of Congress yesterday by a jury in Federal Court. He was found guilty on all ten counts of an indictment charging him with refusing to answer questions by the House Committee on Un-American Activities.

Mr. Seeger had appeared before the committee Aug. 18, 1955, when it was in New York investigating possible Communist infiltration in the entertainment industry.

The 42-year-old singer could receive up to a year in prison and a $1,000 fine on each count. He will be sentenced next Tuesday morning at 10:30 A. M. The verdict will be appealed.

The jury, composed of eight men and four women, deliberated for an hour and twenty minutes before bringing in its verdict. Mr. Seeger was continued in $1,000 bail pending sentence.

Queried on Activities

The indictment was based on his refusal to answer ten questions at the 1955 hearing. The questions concerned alleged membership in the Communist party and participation in various Communist or Communist-front activities.

Mr. Seeger did not specifically invoke any Constitutional amendments as a basis for refusal to answer questions, but he said during a recess yesterday that the First Amendment, which guarantees freedom of speech, was implicit in his refusal.

During the three-day trial before Federal Judge Thomas F. Murphy, Mr. Seeger's attorney, Paul L. Ross, had attempted to cast doubt on the validity of the Congressional committee's investigation of the entertainment industry in New York, since no legislation had resulted from it.

In his charge to the jury yesterday, however, Judge Murphy

Associated Press

CONVICTED: Pete Seeger, folk singer, who was found guilty of ten counts of contempt of Congress.

said he had "determined as a matter of law" that the committee had conducted a valid inquiry and its questions to Mr. Seeger had been pertinent.

Irving Younger, the assistant United States attorney prosecuting the trial, said in summing up that the only issue was whether Mr. Seeger had been in contempt of Congress by refusing to answer questions.

Mr. Seeger did not take the stand. Yesterday Mr. Ross called four persons as character witnesses. They were Dr. Helen Parkhurst, an educator and founder of the Dalton School, a progressive school here; Moses Asch of Folkways Records, for whom Mr. Seeger has recorded songs; the Rev. Gerald Humphrey, a Protestant Episcopal priest from Beacon, N. Y., where Mr. Seeger lives, and Dr. Harold Taylor, former president of Sarah Lawrence College in Bronxville.

Two other persons indicted with Mr. Seeger will go on trial soon. They are Elliot Sullivan, 54, an actor, of 2 Peter Cooper Road, and Martin Yarus, an actor known professionally as George Tyne, 44, of 514 Central Park West.

Finnegan, Mediator, Resigns

WASHINGTON, March 29 (UPI)—Joseph F. Finnegan resigned today as director of the Federal Mediation and Conciliation Service after more than six years in the post.

KENNE
FOR (

WASH (AP)—P Congress to study oceans. hinge up

His re oceanogr sages ask increase priations the fiscal

These opment of port plan Federal and educa

Mr. Ke for ocean message of $23,4 merce De ment di ocean.

The Pr proposing or even oceanogr in a conti and apply a part o ultimately of life in

KENNE
1C R

WASH (AP) — wants a the price mail sta $318,000, from user third clas

Postma ward Day in a leter Robertson ginia. M the Senat son had i cated po posals for it.

Special to The New York Times.

WASHINGTON, May 22—The Senate subcommittee on constitutional rights is investigating the Post Office practice of intercepting mail from abroad that it considers Communist or subversive.

For ten years the Post Office Department has seized magazines, books and similar material coming in from Communist-dominated countries. The department has estimated that this amounts to more than 15,000,000 pieces of mail annually.

bombs, he is not suppressing books, he is not investigating anybody, he keeps files on nobody, he is purging nobody, he is "liberating" nobody, he is writing no constitutions, he doesn't impose anything on anybody, he is only a barefooted, hungry, singing, beat-up monk, drenched by unceasing rains. He knows: it makes no difference: you sit on the riverbank and you watch the play of the wind; or you plow the field; or you make a film; makes no difference at all. It's the intensity of your attitude towards truth or God or Soul that matters. It's YOU that matters. It's you that is the matter.

March 20, 1961

We just got back our sound transfers, and we watched surprised and with our eyes popping out, surprised that the lines are in sync. Everybody was scaring us about the sound, the dubbing studios, etc. We wasted a month making contacts, talking and bargaining with dubbing studios, and then, suddenly, one evening, we got mad, sat down by the Moviola, and started dubbing right here, in our room. A crazy thing to do, but we found that it works perfectly and that we had wasted one month of our lives, believing the professionals, studios, Edouard, and all that crap. So, now, we run the image on Moviola, several times, we watch it, we repeat it with the actor saying the line, then we stop the Moviola and the actor says the line again to the running tape recorder. It is amazing how much a man can master. Argus rattled through entire sentences, beautifully. She has one speed of speech. She is great, Argus. And she is mad, and persistent, she works like a horse to get her lines the way she feels they should be. Ben is having a harder time only because his lines, his pauses are more dragged, irregular. Yesterday we did all Frances' lines. So now we are almost through with the dubbing, and not a single cent spent. Harrison Starr managed to swing our tapes into Pathe, for a free transfer, so now we are listening and checking. I told about our dubbing method to Shirley, and she went crazy mad, that's the way to do it, she said, and everybody thinks so. Jerome's Moviola saved us. Shirley gave 40,000 feet of used 35 mm tape, so we degaussed it (again through Harrison Starr, bless him) and now we have plenty of tape. Jerome contributed another 10,000 feet of tape. We are rich, boy!

he is such a pig
couldn't be worse
Listen, we have to go. Really.
Rainy.
Raining flowers?
It's watery
& cloudy.
that fascist pig

I've found that my first thoughts, ideas are always best. I don't want to have anybody around to doubt, to criticize them, to doubt them on some logical grounds.

I have no pity for the older generation. They are finished, no good, corrupt forever and ever. They will all go to hell. The only hope is in the younger generation, if any, to keep the doors of Heaven from closing altogether. The doors are constantly continuously closing, and they are so badly closed by now that only by a sacrifice, by putting your own body, your own head between the door, at the risk of being crushed, the Door of Heaven can be kept open. It's a bloody job, to keep the door of heaven open, but it has to be done. And it's never too late. My film is a letter of solidarity, a motion, a gesture of solidarity to all those who think and feel as I feel—just to show that they are not alone—and the Door is Closing, closing...

April 3, 1961

All we are trying to do, these days, these weeks, these last few months, is to save somehow—no to make—to save the film. To save what was ruined by Edouard's presence, to save what was ruined by lack of money, food. Patching up, cutting, re-cutting. Half of the footage is still missing, has to be shot.

It's very clear by now, the whole film is a failure. From the very beginning, from the day Edouard stepped out of the plane. From there on the film began going down. And there we are, with the ruins of some-thing that could have been a film.

Since November, we have kept Edouard out. Whatever he touches turns into propa-ganda, stage, or shit.

CHAPTER TWELVE

May 16, 1961

This is my blue shirt period. During the shooting, June – October, I wore a red cowboy shirt. Never took it off. Then, sometime in October, I changed it to a brown khaki army shirt. When that finally became too heavy and too dark, in January, I changed to my blue worker's shirt, factory shirt. It still holds. The dirt is not visible because of color. Only the buttons fell off and there are holes everywhere. Anyway, no expenses on washing, no nothing.

Going through the Moviola tournament fever. Last night Peter [Bogdanovich] came and discovered a new method of turning the frame counter, he almost beat us. The thing is, who will spin more numbers in one turn. Adolfas keeps the record with 137. I come next with 133, which is still a good major league.

Gregory [Markopoulos] was editing his film *Serenity* the last few days at our place. He edited his entire film without a Moviola, without even a work print, he is working directly with the negative, original negative. Nothing is going to stop him from completing his film. After the last week's screening, he had to make more changes.

So now he's chopping like a madman. He hates his leading star, he keeps cursing her, and keeps cutting her out wherever he can. And I agree with him. She is the only heavy presence in the otherwise perfect film.

We are switching from beans to oatmeal. Gregory's discovery. He said he made his film (*Serenity*) on oatmeal. Our beans are popping out through our ears and eyes.

May 17, 1961

We were just waking up this morning when Louis [Brigante] barged in with a friend, David Stone. They said, they just quit their jobs. They were working in a publishing house, I don't remember the name of it, but it's one of the top publishing houses. They said they got so bored with their work there that they decided to quit, and they quit by destroying the entire office, by throwing all the papers on the floor, from the file cabinets. David looks small, punky, maybe 24, not more.

After a beer or two, David said, "Could I help you with something? I have time now. Anything in the movies?"

I wracked my head, trying to find something for him. That moment the telephone rang. Jerome [Hill] was on the line. "I just persuaded Menotti that this year's Spoleto Festival should feature the first New American Cinema Festival. So—go ahead! They are ready for it," he said. He is the main financial support of Menotti and his Spoleto Festival.

"But, Jerome, I am in the middle of editing my film, I have no time for organizing anything. In addition, do you realize that we have only three weeks to do it? It's crazy!" As I was saying that, I was staring at these two guys, Louis and David Stone. "Wait, wait," I said, "maybe I have somebody here who can do it for us." Then I said to David: "O.K., David, you want to do something in cinema? Here it is! I have a job for you. Here is your chance to organize a fes-

tival of New American Cinema in Spoleto. You have three weeks. I will help you, but it's your baby!" David did not even blink. "Yes, I'll do it, of course!"

I gave him a list of all films and filmmakers to be included, contacted. Crazy. But I think it will happen.

May 18, 1961

One of the belts of the Moviola broke. Work stopped. Adolfas is trying to fix it, making a belt of a piece of string, spitting on it, and twisting it. He did it! It works. At least for a while.

Chuck is watching my cabbage-potato-meat meal with great suspicion. He thinks it will turn my stomach green. Once he ate it, and then had to rush to the toilet every two minutes. But it's a good, healthy farmer's meal! Boiled potatoes, cabbage, and fat, good pig fat!

Went to see Francis Lee, need his help in filming the titles. Professional... You can't do this, you can't do that... Again!

All those taboos. We are breaking a dozen of them every day. You can't use an old film for leader, they say. We shot the whole film on outdated stock, and they are talking about leaders! You can't edit your negative yourself! We did it ourselves. And we know every frame of film.

A STORY

Now, there was a man who did nothing. So people used to laugh at him: What kind of man are you, you do nothing. What have you done in your life, they asked.

Having enough of this, one day the man made up his mind. He went and he did something, and came back to the people. However, by the time he came home, he had completely forgotten what he did. The people asked him: What did you do? What did you accomplish today? But the man couldn't remember, although he knew he did something. So he spat and said: Oh, the hell with it. MORAL: What's the use of working, sometimes.

May 18, 1961

Screened the new version of Gregory's *Serenity*. Splices falling apart. We could hear every goddamn splice on the soundtrack. It's shorter, and maybe better than the first version. Actually, it looked great. Gregory sat there and jumped up in his seat with every splice. And all this because there is no money to make another print.

Went for a walk to kill some time. Cold like hell, the seasons got mixed up. While we sat in our cellar, last five, six months, the trees became green, the Spring came and passed everything. Now it's green, but it's winter, icy. So I circled around the block, and ran back into the hole.

It's bean time.

May 19, 1961

Here I am again at it, making stupid calls, trying to raise some money. *Film Culture* is still at the printer, and Harry is pressing for money, and I have nothing. Calling everybody, De Antonio is trying to find something. Not even beans left, living on coffee. Again, mouth full of acid wounds. Called Art Ford: he said he'll think. Zero. We are rechecking the reels from the beginning, polishing here and there, a cut here, a cut there. It will have to stay as is.

1. There is no such thing as "non-action." Everything is action.
2. Everything has an effect.
3. Everyone can be affected, is affected.
4. There are only degrees, weaker and stronger actions.
5. And then, there are useful and harmful actions to the society today.

We are afraid to sound and look stupid—that's what's wrong with us.

Don't misunderstand me about Hollywood. When I speak about how bad Hollywood is, I speak about Hollywood today. I like many of the old Hollywood classics. But styles and themes outdate. When someone imitates someone else, it's bad. When NY imitates bad Hollywood, it's bad. Hollywood is dead, as far as I am concerned, as far as the new cinema is concerned. Nothing new has come from Hollywood in at least 10 years. Anything that we have new in cinema has come from experimentalists, from the independents.

May 21, 1961

Musicians! I have to pay them in cash. Any other artist would ask first what we want to do etc., but all they want to know is if I'll be able to pay them $4.00 per hour. I can't get a penny from anywhere. After half a day wasted, running around, calling, now, when every minute counts, I gave up. I will have to do something about those stupid musicians.

Lucia [Dlugoszewski] is great. She did the entire score in two days. Practically in 24 hours. Last night we screened the film, she made notes, we timed every spot she needed, and now she is sitting home and figuring out everything. We are recording this evening.

Everything is mounting, piling up, a feverish climax. We are living in a fever, our sleep is feverish. Exhaustion, tension on the very ends of the nerves. 'Til now we were working piece by piece. But now the entire film, with all its millions of details, sounds, images, frames, question marks, pauses, everything is there before our eyes. I have to see it as a whole, no more pieces; think about every little spot, but always in the perspective of the whole. We are working in a state of trance. When I answer the phone, they ask: Are you sleeping? The concentration, this trance changes even our voices, it numbs the physical senses, so that we live only in the *Raum* of the film, with its millions of frames, half in this world half in another.

JAM (jum-jummm) Received your nice manifesto & still have time to include it. In fact I have 2 more weeks time to print anything else → so please call up Stan Vanderbeek & others telling them to send goodies. Stan sent me a nice batch already which I am including, but I could use more from him OK?

Regarding japanese films — by young makers — no commercial official avant-garde. very nice. but I must pay for prints. If you desire desires let me know or write to Toshi Ichiyanagi.

Oh yes — Vanderbeek should send films for festivals here (films with sound tracks) WE WILL PAY FOR PRINTS!!! With printed $$ TELL HIM, PUSH HIM TO SEND ALL NICE FILMS AT ONCE !! I will write him too, but you must push him OK?

I am getting a house here in the farm land where we will have a gang of bandits established. will print fluxus, dollar bills, false postage stamps, write & perform music (NOVA ET ANTIQVA) etc. You should join us with your apparatus. we will cross border when our work becomes troublesome to authorities here. By then maybe we will get wagons for a caravan & move about continuously so no one can catch us, while we give fluxus festivals and generaly throwing fluxus about. With next mail I will write about VERY BIG PROJECT I AM COOKING. VERY BIG.

Best regardfull regards regarding regardant-ant-and guard against gard-ard-ga-ga-george-ge-ge

P.S – Wiesbaden festival goes as planned – with mayors blessing ↓

A letter from George Maciunas, from
6 J.-S.-Bach-Strasse, Wiesbaden,
just before his inaugural Fluxus Festival
took place there.

May 24, 1961

Last night we recorded Lucia's music. Harrison Starr helped us again with the CBS studio where he is shooting *The Miracle Worker*. So we did everything in one session. The musicians, the whole stupid bunch of them, snickered and laughed and giggled and shuffled at Lucia's score. They thought this was a ridiculous thing to play simple notes. Every little pause, they immediately went into their stupid musical bits, melodies. They do not know how to play single notes, they hate sounds. "Listen to the sounds," explained Lucia patiently, trying to get through their thick heads, "listen to the flutes, oboe, play to each other as if you'd never heard the sound of a flute, an oboe, a piccolo."

May 26, 1961

Mixed our sound at Pathé. Upton did it for us for practically nothing. A golden man. I still don't understand him. The first idealist I have met in America, the first human being in film "business." Or maybe he is crazy, to do that for us. In any case, bless him. And he still laughs and jokes. I have never seen anybody laughing or joking in film "business."

May 29, 1961

Saturday we locked ourselves in on 43rd Street, with Chuck [Silvers] and Dan [Drasin], and in one marathon that lasted until Sunday noon, we edited our negative. Hungry and without sleep, after holding bravely until the last minute, Chuck fell asleep in the car, on our way to Panna, for a lucky meal that we managed to hunt, and stayed asleep.

Doc [Humes] dropped in. Later, Bob Kaufman came. He walked around talking poetry until six in the morning. Doc just came from Cannes, bored with it, telling jokes about Allen and Corso, there, in Cannes, walking around with garbage bags under their arms, in that huge splendored crowd, searching for a garbage can to dump it out. Then, Nico [Papatakis] telling me how Shirley didn't get the award at Cannes, even when everyone agreed that *The Connection* was the most interesting film in the goddamn festival. Only because Cannes squares thought that the film was propaganda for drug addicts.

Doc promised to do something about money, to blackmail someone. We need $500 this week for *Film Culture*.

June 1, 1961

Screened our first answer print, needed a few light corrections, otherwise it was perfect. Perfect, that is, as light goes. That's all we could say. We sat there, and we looked at it, and we didn't react to it at all. Blank, nothing. Until three weeks ago, I could still feel that I was master of my film. I could maintain a certain perspective to it. I could look at it objectively, from a distance. And then, during the last crazy weeks, sleepless nights, it started fading out. Now it is out completely. Just a blank space.

We sat, late at night, on 4th Street, with Frank [Kuenstler], and Adolfas, looking at the street, and we were happy. We walked towards Sixth Avenue and, we said, it's amazing, now we are walking this street, damp, humid, grey night, all these people, voices, and we can enjoy all that. It's simply beautiful. No more film. Maybe it must be like that, maybe it's good that it faded away, said Frank. That's how it must be. So now you are free. The only thing left is that terrible one-year inertia. We can feel it, when we stand still, or when we sit at home, the tension, the wheels still rolling.

Adolfas put on the radio. A cello piece. We can listen to it. And it's amazing, we can listen to it without thinking of anything else. Not even money, although I made dozens of calls today, to borrow for the last payment, for the mix. Got $50 from George, stealing from his children. Doc is hunting around town, too. But even money, loans we do it now automatically, from inertia. Robert [Frank] dropped in with Martin LaSalle, returned rewinds, etc. He said, this borrowing money etc. is part of our life now. There will be another film, more borrowing, hunting for money. That is our way of life, don't worry, I don't worry anymore, just make my calls, the hell. The hell, we said, and went out into the street. Nico [Papatakis] just called. Back in New York with all his projects, wants to direct a film himself, etc. etc. Meeting him tomorrow at 5.

"These sewers in Wajda's *Kanal*," said Robert. "You know, they are symbolic: those are the sewers through which independent film-makers are crawling in America. We are still in the sewers," he said.

50 % of film-making consists of rewinding; the other 50 % is splicing.

Only those who make films either for money or pleasure are film-makers; I am a moralist.

What is *Guns* all about?
What's your life all about? Eh?

"Reprocher au film de ne pas être clair, c'est reprocher aux passions humaines d'être toujours un peu opaques."
(Robbe-Grillet, à propos de *Marienbad*)

My film has no *time* plot, *Blood of a Poet* had no *time* plot. *Hiroshima* has time plot.

Shirley: "I'm again where I started."

Idea for an ideal film distribution: chop the film in pieces.

Unnumbered reels, to encourage "creative" projection...

June 16, 1961

Film Culture got out, finally. But it's still sitting in the bindery, I need at least $500 to get it out. I made many calls today, humiliating myself, but nothing, zero. Gutman just gave somebody money to go to Europe, but no money for *F. C. Guns* isn't doing any better.
The print is sitting at the Movielab—they made another one, with the corrections—and we can't even look at it, we have no money to take it out, $300, and we don't know when we'll have it—and, as it is now, I wouldn't care less, let it lie there until doomsday.

I just want to go out, somewhere, and sit under a tree, and look at the blue sky, and do nothing, and see nothing but that blue sky, look at the eternity—everything seems so senseless—what for, why, what—and thanks to Francesca for those chocolate breads, the good woman of MacDougal Street.

June 19, 1961

Guns is still in the lab. Went to the New Yorker, to see *Othello*, walked out. The only films I can watch these days are Westerns and gangster movies. Can't keep my interest. Too tired.

Came home, walked along 14th Street, feeling heavy in the legs and shoulders, hungry and tired.
Put on a can of beans on the stove. I'll eat a can of beans by myself. Usually, we split, but Adolfas stayed at the New Yorker, so I'll have a full can for myself. Got frightened. Did I fall so low that I think like an animal, only about food? This can of beans suddenly put me in horror. The hunger can sink so deep into the flesh that it reaches, it touches the unconscious. Have you thought about that? So I left the beans and went into the street again, to roam through Avenue B.

Gregory Markopoulos helping hang posters for our Spoleto show.

IL NUOVO CINEMA AMERICANO

FESTIVAL OF TWO WORLDS
FESTIVAL DEI DUE MONDI

**A New Film Exposition
presented by David C. Stone**

**Rassegna di film
presentata da David C. Stone**

CINEMA-TEATRO SPERIMENTALE — SPOLETO

PROGRAM

JUNE 16 & JULY 3
Jerome Hill's *The Sand Castle*
John Korty's *The Language of Faces*

JUNE 17 & JULY 4
Jonas Mekas' *Guns of the Trees*
Dan Drasin's *Sunday*

JUNE 18 & JULY 5
Graeme Ferguson's *Downfall*
Richard Preston's *Nightscapes, The Maze, The Candidates
& Conversations in Limbo*

JUNE 19 & JULY 6
Robert Frank's *The Sin of Jesus*
Robert Frank & Alfred Leslie's *Pull My Daisy*
Edward O. Bland's *The Cry of Jazz*

JUNE 20 & JULY 7
Curtis Harrington's *Night Tide*
Ralph Hirshorn's *The End of Summer*

JUNE 21 & JULY 8 (matinee)
Ron Rice's *The Flower Thief*
Jerome Liebling and Allen Downs' *Pow Wow*
James Broughton's *The Pleasure Garden*

JUNE 22 & JULY 9
Peter Kass' *Time of the Heathen*
Hilary Harris' *Polaris Action Pilot & Highway*

JUNE 23 & JULY 10 (matinee)
Stan Brakhage's *Anticipation of the Night, Daybreak & Whiteye*
Robert Breer's *Recreation, Man and his Dog Out for Air, Jamestown, Cats,
Inner and Outer Space, Blazes, Homage to New York*

JUNE 24 & JULY 11
Allen Baron's *Blast of Silence*
Joseph Marzano's *When They Sleep, From Inner Space & Changeover*

JUNE 25 & JULY 12 (matinee)
Gregory J. Markopoulos' *Serenity*
Stan VanDerBeek's *What Who How, Ala Mode, Mankinda, Science Friction*

JUNE 26 & JULY 13
Erich Kollmar's *Changing Tides*
Madeline Anderson's *Integration Report 1*

JUNE 27 & JULY 14
Lionel Rogosin's *On the Bowery & Come Back Africa*

JUNE 28 & JULY 15
Sidney Meyers' *The Quiet One*
Michael and Philip Burton's *Journey Alone*
Helen Levitt, Janice Loeb & James Agee's *In the Street*

JUNE 29 & JULY 16
Morris Engel's *Weddings and Babies*
Warren Brown's *A Light for John*

JUNE 30 & JULY 10 (evening)
Ben Maddow, Sidney Meyers & Joseph Strick's *The Savage Eye*
Richard Leacock, Donn Alan Pennebaker & Albert Maysles' *Primary*

JULY 1 & JULY 12 (evening)
Bert Stern's *Jazz on a Summer's Day*
Stuart Hanish, Barbara Squire & Russ MacGregor's
Have I Told You Lately That I Love You

JULY 2 & JULY 8 (evening)
John Cassavetes' *Shadows*
Michael Blackwood's *Broadway Express*

**Daily at 5:30 & Midnight
Tutti i giorni alle 17:30 & 24:00**

PANETTO & PETRELLI - SPOLETO

New American Cinema In Spoleto

Dear Sir:

At the Spoleto Festival this year there are two film programs—those of the Festival proper and those of the "new American cinema" with which I am involved. I thought some of you at home might like to hear of what's been going on.

Our program opened with "The Sand Castle," by Jerome Hills, which was received very well. The following day there was a showing of "Guns of the Trees," by Jonas Mekas. Gian Carlo Menotti left. A countess fainted. And the

clergy banned it to its members. It literally drills into the spectator. I think it lacks aesthetic sense, but Jonas does get his message across in a rather Dada fashion.

Jesus Unbanned

Curtis Harrington's "Night Tide" —he had all the means and time, unlike most of the other filmmakers—is very disappointing. Six people were in the audience. Today "The Flower Thief," by Ron Rice, is being shown. Tomorrow: "Shadows." Some others in our exhibit: "Pull My Daisy," "Come Back, Africa," "On the Bowery," "The Quiet One," and Robert Frank's latest work, "The Sin of Jesus." Based on a Russian tale, Frank's film was at first banned here, but finally the Catholic censors passed it. It is excellent.

My film "Serenity" is being premiered on Sunday. It was made in Greece in Eastman color, a seven-years' project. The narrative is in four languages. It is the story of an idealistic refugee, a physician who attempts to grow a rose in the wilderness, as his forefathers had done in Smyrna, from where he had been expelled. Few today know of the 1 million people who were interchanged between the Greek and Turkish governments in 1921.

By Himself

We have had little help from the Festival proper, and David C. Stone, who was responsible for this effort, has done it mostly by himself.

I return next Wednesday.
Best to all,

—Gregory Markopoulos
Spoleto, Italy
July 21

The Village Voice.

XXIIª **MOSTRA INTERNAZIONALE D'ARTE CINEMATOGRAFICA**

LIDO DI VENEZIA - 20 AGOSTO - 3 SETTEMBRE 1961

SERVIZIO STAMPA OLIVETTI

Dear Jonas

Last night iwas really inspired to write a masterpiece to you
about film and festival and italia ns and french and all that
but now 16 hours later . I am softer and not cooking from intelllect
tual heat anymore nl only my bowtie makes me sweat.
Jonas i have respect for you I still have not seen yor film
last night showing of french film La fille aux yeux d'or
finished my last doubts about any honesty of anybody connected
with festivals. have never seen such shit projected anywhere.
all people with bowties and evening clothes swallow shit for 3hours
don't eveen burp afterwards. Journalists equally aphathic and only
seem to be interested to get free food and some cunt whatever natio
nality. I write this letter to you because i relly appreciate only
now the honesty and conviction you showed by writing the way you
did, Good night Jonas whistle while you work when i am going to see
your film que voulez vous ? j'aime cette machine a ecrire

Sieg Heil Berlin oder sterben!!

Robert

P.S. I'm working for
SHOW Magazine

Just saw Wadja's Film Samson—
it is best film they have shown here, last half hour of film political romanticism—Shit,

Today I managed to steal two lumps of butter from SAFEWAY. Sweating through a terrible flu. Some variety in our bean-oatmeal-coffee diet. Butter.

Last Sunday Panna took us to her home, to sit in the sun and eat. Suddenly we sat in front of a full table, and I could not eat. Nibbled this and nibbled that, a little bit of this, a little bit of that, and I couldn't. I went into the habit of nibbling, not eating. Can't eat anymore. I eat often but little. Can't take a big meal any longer. There must be terrible things happening with my body. I don't even want to think about it.

July 12, 1961

What is this obsession with the "new," they ask me. Last time I met Maya [Deren], she attacked me for my insistence on the "new." I said I am for the new because anything that is new is young and youth in itself is a virtue. Anything that moves forward is new and is a virtue.

It liberates, it frees, it sweeps away the dust and dirt that piles upon our emotions, thoughts. Not everything that is old has value. The oldest wisdoms sometimes are brought back, refreshed by the new.

Today I am putting my bets on the young and new.

From a newspaper clipping:
"In addition, the Communists hope to repeat the success which they achieved on the West Coast last May in spearheading mob violence against a committee of Congress."

(The reference was to the riotous student demonstrations in San Francisco against the House Committee on Un-American Activities.)

A STATEMENT

Guns of the Trees deals with the thoughts, feelings and anguished strivings of my generation faced with the moral perplexity of our times.

It has no plot just as a poem has none, and, like a poem, it cannot be summed up.

Conceived as an episodic, horizontal film, there is no apparent direct story-connection between one scene and the next. The scenes act like pieces of a larger, timed, emotional mosaic.

When we come to more essential things, the indirectness of the poet will seize the essence and the truth.

July, 1961

Not that I know what I am doing. I know and I don't know. What I know, really, is where I have to stop. The same I do in poetry. I don't know what I write, but I know when to stop. So, what happened with *Guns*, is that I was still going, this crab speed, and I know that it wasn't time yet to stop, not exactly—but if I would continue further, polishing some technical things, in the emotional state that I am in, I would run into a danger of destroying the whole thing. What happened was that it went too long, it went over the border of time. So it has to stay unfinished.

October 26, 1961

Dear Robert:
Here is my list of the better films I have seen during the past year (1961):
In alphabetical order:

Anticipation of the Night, Stanley Brakhage
Ashes and Diamonds, Andrzej Wajda
Blazes, Robert Breer
Breathless, Jean-Luc Godard
King of Kings, Nicholas Ray
La Dolce Vita, Federico Fellini
L'Avventura, Michelangelo Antonioni
Leda, Claude Chabrol
Prelude, Stanley Brakhage
Sunday, Dan Drasin
The Flower Thief, Ron Rice
The Sin of Jesus, Robert Frank
The Young One, Luis Buñuel

November 1961

AN INVITATION TO GENERAL STRIKE
Julian Beck and Judith Malina are calling
for a General Strike against the nuclear
testings. The date for the GS is set for
January 29 through February 4, 1962.

I voice here my support for the General
Strike and I am calling all film-makers,
film critics and actors to join Becks in a
gesture of anti-war solidarity.

The governments have taken too many liberties with the fates of the people.

The peace movements are growing all
around the world. They are scattered and
uncoordinated. But, wherever we are, we
have to speak out.

The gap between hand and hand is larger
today than ever before. But no matter how
much they are trying to prevent the hands
of the world from joining together—we
should keep reaching. Artists of China,
France, Soviet Russia, Algeria: know that
the other artists wherever they are, are
stretching their hands to join with you,
are reaching for the same: happiness,
beauty, truth, peace.

During the days of January 29–February 4,
join us in the movement of solidarity, join
the Strike for Peace, in whatever country
you are.

Rimbaud wrote *Illuminations*.
I have a big book of eliminations.

"However, everyone in this world has someone else whom he can look down on, and
I must say, from experience of both trades,
that the book reviewer is better off than
the film critic, who cannot even do his
work at home, but has to attend trade
shows at eleven in the morning and, with
one or two notable exceptions, is expected
to sell his honour for a glass of inferior
sherry."—George Orwell, "Confessions of
a Book Reviewer"

January 7, 1962

We had a meeting at 414 Park Avenue
South (my loft), we voted to establish our
own cooperative distribution center. The
only opposition came from Amos [Vogel].
He said, why do we need a new distribution center. Cinema 16 will distribute your
films. I pointed out that recently he had
rejected several important films, one being
Brakhage's *Anticipation of the Night*. Amos
said, it's up to him to decide what films can
be distributed. He insisted that there is no
place for two distribution centers, for the
independent film. At which point some
became pretty angry. Ron Rice was shouting at Amos, with Amos trying to be very
rational. In any case, we have now a center
of our own. No film will be rejected from
it—that was the first point we all agreed
upon. And we are going to run it ourselves.

All independent Film-makers Unite

WE are creating the Film-makers' Coop to
help ourselves to continue our work as
independent film-makers. We are dissatis-
fied with the conditions under which our
work is presently being distributed.

WE are not in business to make money.
We are here to make films. But we cannot
afford to be played-out of the monetary
compensations either. There are not
enough funds for our work. The independent filmmaking needs all support it can
have. Together, we can support each other.

For this reason we are creating the Film-
makers' Coop. These are the conditions
under which we are binding ourselves
together:

I.
1. Film-makers' Cooperative is a film distribution center created by the New
   American Cinema Group Inc. (a free
   organization of the independent film-

1962

NEW AMERICAN CINEMA GROUP
414 Park Avenue South
New York 16, New York
telephone: MU 5-2210

January 7th

8 pm

414 PA Sout

First meeting.

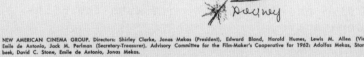

NEW AMERICAN CINEMA GROUP. Directors: Shirley Clarke, Jonas Mekas (President), Edward Bland, Harold Humes, Lewis M. Allen (Vice-President), Emile de Antonia, Jack M. Perlman (Secretary-Treasurer). Advisory Committee for the Film-Maker's Cooperative for 1962: Adolfas Mekas, Stanley Vanderbeek, David C. Stone, Emile de Antonia, Jonas Mekas.

P.S. /July 1999/: The list above is the record of
the film-makers who attended the inaugural meeting of
the Film-Makers' Cooperative on January 7, 1962.
                                    -- Jonas

-69-

April 25, 1962

ANNOUNCEMENT No. 1

In September 1960, the independent film-makers of
New York met and bound themselves into a free and
open organization, the N.A.C. Group.

One of the aims set forward by the Group was "to
promote and/or create a film distribution center."

We are now announcing the creation of such a center to be known as

FILM-MAKER'S COOPERATIVE

--a cooperative for the distribution of films made
   by independent film-makers, including 35mm and
   16mm, both features and shorts
--a non-profit cooperative organized and operated
   by film-makers
--all income from film rentals and sales will go
   to the film-makers

The Cooperative will distribute films, organize
national and international traveling exhibitions,
and work closely with film exchanges in other
countries.

We urge the independent film-makers throughout
the world to establish similar cooperative distribution centers in their respective lands.

We suggest that all art theatres, film societies
and other film users keep in touch with the Film-
Maker's Cooperative.

Write for our catalogue of available films:

> Film-Maker's Cooperative
> 414 Park Avenue South
> New York 16, New York
>
> Tel.: MU 5-2210

makers) to assist the distribution of films made by the members of the Group.

2. The acceptance of films into the FM Coop will be decided by a special acceptance committee chosen by the NAC Group.
3. Films by non-members of the Group will be accepted into the FM Coop if approved by the Acceptance Committee.
4. Film-makers of other countries are invited to join the FM Coop for the distribution of their films in U.S.A.

II.
1. All policies of the FM Coop will be decided by the NAC Group. Once every year the policies of the Coop will be reviewed by the NAC Group and the necessary changes and adjustments will be made.
2. The FM Coop will have four main divisions:
a) 16 mm theatrical distribution
b) 16 mm non-theatrical distribution
c) 35 mm theatrical distribution
d) 35 mm non-theatrical distribution
e) The emphasis in the first year will be on the 16 mm non-theatrical distribution.
3. The FM Coop will operate primarily in the U.S.A. But it will also act as an agent for the distribution in other countries, if the film-maker wishes and if the Coop feels that it has the necessary power to do so.
4. The FM Coop will also advise the theatres and film societies on programming the films distributed by the Coop. It will organize film and lecture tours. It will program special series of screenings to introduce the work of the independent film artists.

III.
1. Films will be accepted into the FM Coop for a minimum period of one year.

After one year the film-maker is free to extend his contract for another year, or take the film out of the Coop.

2. No advancements will be paid by the FM Coop to its members for the films accepted into the Coop.
3. The FM Coop will have a uniform mailing piece for all films in the Coop. This doesn't exclude an increased attention in special cases. Also, if the film-maker feels it necessary, additional publicity materials will be prepared at his own expense.
4. From films distributed by the FM Coop the film-maker will receive 75 % from the net/gross if he is a member of the NAC Group and 70 % if he is not a member of the NAC Group. The rest will go into the fund of FM Coop.
5. The incomes of the FM Coop will be divided between:
a) The operating costs of the FM Coop
b) The Film-makers Fund (operated by the NAC Group to assist film-makers to complete their work etc.)
6. The film-maker is free to make his own screening dates with his personal prints. In those cases the Coop will have no part in his income. However, as long as the film is under the contract with the Coop, it cannot be handled by any other film distributing company, unless given a special permission by the FM Coop.

It is under these conditions that we are joining together into the Film-makers' Cooperative

February 8, 1962
At the screening of *Open City*, at the Museum of Modern Art, there was a woman with a child, in the audience. The child was laughing, talking. Not much, just enough to hear it if you are listening. He sat silently, until the middle of the movie. Then, you could suddenly hear his voice,

Film still from my 414 Park Avenue South loft (between 29th and 30th Streets, third floor), which between 1962 and 1967 housed *Film Culture* and Film-Makers' Cooperative.

ON UNIONS ETC.

FILM-MAKERS SHOWCASE IS RUN
BY FILM-MAKERS ON A COOPERATIVE
BASIS, WITH ALL INCOMES GOING
TO THE FILM-MAKERS TO CONTINUE THEIR
WORK.

THE PEOPLE WHO WORK AT THIS
THEATRE ARE FILM MAKERS WHO CONTRIBUTE
THEIR TIME FREE.

WE ARE ASKING THE UNION TO CON-
TRIBUTE THEIR WORK FREE. ALL FOR THE
GOOD OF THE CINEMA + BEAUTY + LOVE

+ TRUTH.

UNIONS THINK WE ARE NUTS.

" BE POETS OR FANATICS "
                    John KEATS

FILM-MAKERS COOPERATIVE

The Short Happy Life of the Charles

J. Hoberman

For a few short years, one theater on New York's Lower East Side became the cradle of a cultural revolution.

Two decades ago this spring, a new sort of film community was born in a moldering movie house on New York's Lower East Side. In late 1961 a pair of young film buffs—Walter Langford and Ed Stein—acquired the Charles, an ancient seven-hundred-seat theater located on Avenue B, a few blocks north of Tompkins Square Park. Economic necessity forced the partners to relinquish their theater barely one year later, but by that time the Charles had become a landmark of sorts in the creation of an American counterculture.

Like the programs of the handful of other revival theaters—the Thalia, the New Yorker, the Bleecker Street—that then catered to the rising interest in offbeat movies, the Charles's program was an eclectic mixture. Astaire-Rogers rubbed shoulders with Italian Neorealism, Edgar G. Ulmer was celebrated along with the Marx Brothers, *Touch of Evil* was advertised as Orson Welles's masterpiece. In addition to staking out a position at the radical edge of the auteurist spectrum, the Charles defined its personality in other ways. On Sundays there were jazz concerts, in the lobby hung paintings by local artists, and once a week, in a bid to attract neighborhood senior citizens, there was a special Ukrainian-language double bill.

Looking to further expand the boundaries of their grass-roots Lincoln Center, Langford and Stein recruited Jonas Mekas, then the film critic at the *Village Voice*, to organize some additional screenings. Significantly, these were to be on weekends at midnight, giving them a ready-made aura of cultish exoticism.

Mekas was then in the early stages of his passionate commitment to American experimental cinema, and—educating himself a step ahead of his readership—he scheduled a series of one-person shows for avant-garde filmmakers whose work was still relatively unknown in New York. These screenings were later followed up with articles in the *Voice*.

For some time, "underground movies"—a term apparently coined by the experimental animator Stan Vanderbeek—had been surfacing sporadically at various venues around what would soon be known as the "East Village." Vanderbeek's own American Underground Cinema was a peripatetic exhibition center that floated from storefront to storefront, and experimental films were occasionally screened at Amos Vogel's film society, Cinema 16, as well as the Living Theater. The Charles, however, provided the under- ground with its first, semipermanent base of operations.

Among other things, Mekas's screenings served to unite a number of divergent or isolated strains of avant-garde film. Between October 1961 and June 1962, he gave one-person midnight shows to Colorado filmmaker Stan Brakhage (whose most recent work at the time was deemed too radical for Cinema 16), animator Robert Breer (recently arrived in New York after a decade in Paris), Gregory Markopoulos (another expatriate who had just returned to the United States), and San Francisco animator Larry Jordan, among others. Mekas's sense of the avant-garde was extremely broad. He also scheduled programs of works by independent documentary filmmakers of the thirties (Willard Van Dyke, Lewis Jacobs, Herman G. Weinberg), as well as contemporary social satirists like Vanderbeek and Richard Preston. Suddenly, a sense of an ongoing alternative American film tradition began to coalesce.

Mekas had an eye for new talent, too. At his suggestion, the Charles began holding monthly open screenings, where admission was ninety-five cents or one can of film. According to Langford, these open houses were initially a stopgap measure precipitated by the exhaustion of available Ukrainian talkies. Their astonishing popularity—the first had a crowd of filmmakers lined up around the block—took everyone by surprise.

Among the hundreds of filmmakers who had their first public screenings at the Charles were Warhol associate Paul Morrissey, director Brian De Palma, cinema-
Continued on page 34

March 1982

EXPLORATIONS

from page 22
tographer Nestor Almendros, hard-core porn pioneer Fred Baker, video innovator John Reilly, Robert (*Putney Swope*) Downey, and Ken (*Tom, Tom, the Piper's Son*) Jacobs. "The Charles screenings were wide open," recalled filmmaker Jack Smith, whose own *Flaming Creatures*, soon to become the most notorious underground movie of them all, was, he says, specifically made for the Charles. "People brought their own films and saw them on the huge Charles screen—a truly surrealistic experience—and they looked damn good."

The mainstream critics who began to visit the Charles were apt to review the audience as much as the movies. "Madison Avenue types mix among the beards, black leotards, and sloppy sweaters," wrote the *Daily News*'s Sunday magazine. "Half the audience juggles paper cups of coffee. Some pull sandwiches or chicken legs from pockets or bags." The Charles screenings were social events, and one *New York Times* reporter was as struck by the intensity of the discussions that arose during intermissions as he was by the exhibit of sculptures resembling "Easter Island monoliths" up in the mezzanine.

More than anything else, outside observers were struck by the Charles's uninhibited patrons. "Audience Adds Sound Effects," the *New York Post* headlined their piece on the phenomenon, anticipating *The Rocky Horror Picture Show* cult by some fifteen years. "Booing, hissing, and applause were all permitted equally," one habitué recalled. Indeed, expressions of disapproval could be particularly severe. "After showing some of my rushes there, I felt like committing suicide," a tyro filmmaker remembered.

Six months of open screenings had their climax in July 1962 with a single, grand Filmmakers Festival, cosponsored by *Show Business* magazine. *The Hard Swing*, a twenty-four-minute cinema verité account of a San Francisco stripper, won first prize; and Ron Rice was named the most promising filmmaker. (Rice, then twenty-seven, would have little time to redeem that promise. A bit more than two years later, he died of pneumonia in Mexico.) The success of the Filmmakers Festival inspired another first: Starting in mid-July, Rice's feature *The Flower Thief* began playing a continuous engagement. (The short on the bill was Vernon Zimmerman's *To L.A. With Lust.* A onetime associate of sculptor-happenings artist Claes Oldenburg, Zimmerman would later break into Hollywood to make such eccentric exploitation films as *Unholy Rollers* and *Fade to Black.*)

The Flower Thief was the beatnik film par excellence. Characterized by the use of outdated raw stock, minimal editing, a casual sound track, and an arbitrary chronology, it featured Taylor Mead as a kind of holy innocent absurdly wandering through the fleshpots of San Francisco's North Beach. Unexpectedly, Rice's film got something close to a rave review from the *New York Times* critic Eugene Archer, and, despite the Charles's lack of air conditioning, *The Flower Thief* played to full houses for three weeks. Even more amazing was the follow-up: Brakhage's ultrasubjective *Anticipation of the Night*, a harshly lyrical film that identified the protagonist's eye with that of the camera, ran for two weeks along with *Lemon Hearts*, another short by Vernon Zimmerman.

That September, the Charles management announced another Filmmakers Festival, as well as ambitious plans to open a second, all-underground movie theater deeper on the Lower East Side. The festival came off, but it was to be the Charles's last hurrah. The theater went dark a month later, and when it reopened in January 1963, it was under the more conventional ownership of future porn mogul Radley Metzger. Apparently, Langford and Stein just ran out of money, although Jack Smith put the situation a bit more colorfully. According to him, the golden age of the Charles "ended when the ecstasy got out of hand and it became difficult to collect admissions because of the confusion of filmmakers and audience."

Although the creative period of the Charles lasted less than a year, the theater's legacy has been impressive. As the first of the dozen or so avant-garde showcases administered by Mekas before the 1971 establishment of Anthology Film Archives, the Charles effectively put underground movies on the cultural map. Not only were its high-spirited, youthful audiences the precursors of the midnight movie cults that flourished during the seventies; but, as the theater that invented the avant-garde tradition of the open screening, the Charles was the spiritual home of a particular utopian ideology, a place where the audience was not just the passive recipient of mass-produced fantasies, but an active community, producing movies for itself. ◼

J. Hoberman is a film critic for the Village Voice *and a contributing editor of* American Film.

WESTERN UNION
TELEGRAM
®

The filing time shown in the date line on domestic telegrams is LOCAL TIME at point of origin. Time of receipt is LOCAL TIME at point of destination

UDA 133 (44)(34) SYA 144

NP033 HTM2 DL PD WUX NEW YORK NY FEB 28 1968   1968 FEB 28 AM 5 00

FILMMAKERS COOPERATIVE ATTN LESLIE TRUMBULL

175 LEXINGTON AVE

NEWYORK NY

COPY OF CABLE SENT HENRI LANGLOIS PARIS QUOTE:

LET US KNOW WHERE WE CAN PICKET FOR YOU HERE IN NEWYORK.

FRENCH CONSULATE? STATUE OF LIBERTY? ALL NEWYORK FILM MAKERS

WILL BE THERE. LET FILMMAKERS COOPERATIVE KNOW OR ME

      MARIE MENKEN 62 MONTAGUE STREET BROOKLYN

417A EST/28.

SF1201(R2-65)

12TH STREET & AVENUE B ● GR 3-6170

"New, different, and imaginative..."
— *Village Voice*

"The home of new American cinema"
— *Scenario*

The Charles is a new and different kind of theatre, a movie house that offers a unique variety of film programs and entertainment. Among the many films you will be able to see at the Charles are some of the finest recent releases, revivals of the great classics, new films by independent film-makers, and the most daring experimental works of both American and foreign directors. Besides its regular program of films, the Charles has matinees every Saturday planned for children, weekly live Jazz concerts, and a continuous exhibition of paintings and sculpture by New York artists. Also, personal appearances of important film personalities. Come to the Charles and see for yourself. You will find it the most informal theatre in town.

FILM-MAKER'S FESTIVAL

(April 4, 1962)

The Film-maker's Festival is held the first Wednesday
of every month by the Charles' management. Films are
gathered through an open invitation to all film-makers
everywhere. No limitations of length or finish afe
placed on them; all that is required is that in each
case a serious attempt to create a film has been made
and that this attempt is evident in the results. The
Charles hopes through the Film-maker's Festival it will
bring to light valuable work being done right now, whether
the film-maker is known or not. It is also hoped that
the film-makers themselves will benefit from the effect
of having their work shown on a large screen before a
large audience.

1) Reverie - John van Gonsic

2) Jazz Glints - Hardy Keck

3) Point of View - Jerry Gold

4) America on the Move -
                  Stan Russell

5) Skater's Circle -
                  Herman Landau

6) To L.A. with Lust -
                  Vernon Zimmerman

7) The Year the Universe Lost
        the Pennant -
                  Bhob Stewart

    * COFFEE BREAK *

8) The Family Fallout Shelter -
                  Edward English

9) Poor Little Sam -
                  Chris S. Kasaras

10) Rhythm City - L. Marinelli

11) Forms - Adolph Attianese

12) Unedited Rushes - by G. M.

    * COFFEE BREAK *

After the break, any unscheduled
films will be shown.

Ed Stein and Walter Langsford, the
owners/managers of Charles Theatre.
Theatre logo: George Maciunas.

```
                    THE CHARLES THEATRE
                    12th St. and Ave. B
                        GR 3-6170


                  FILMMAKERS FESTIVAL PROGRAM

                         WEDNESDAY
                       July 4, 1962


     1.  Madeline Tourtelot and
         Ed Bland                  REFLECTIONS        (5  min.)

     2.  Ed Corley                 SOLO               (30 min.)

     3.  Barry Harvey              FINFIDELITY        (2  min.)

     4.  Joseph Marzano            THE INNER SPACE    (5  min.)

   √ 5.  Joseph Marzano            CHANGEOVER         (5  min.)

 √√ 6.  Ed Corley                  UP THE AVENUE      (12 min.)


              Intermission of 15 minutes

     7.  Fred von Bernewitz        SILENT NEWSREEL    (13 min.)

     8.  Joseph Blanco             THE NEW WORLD      (5  min.)

     9.  Richard Preston           NIGHTSCAPES        (10 min.)

    10.  Brian de Palma            ICARUS             (30 min.)

    11.  Stan VanderBeek           WHAT WHO HOW       (10 min.)


              Complete Shows at 3, 6 and 9
```

careless, full of life. "Get the child out!" Shouted angry voices, men and women. Why the hell are they watching this movie, I thought. Here is a humanist film. Deeply touching. Real. And these goddamn people sit, watch it, and it does nothing to them. They watch it abstractly, as some abstract product, and when they hear a child's voice, they can't stand it—they can't stand the most alive thing in the world. How terribly bad things have become in this town.

No date, 1962

Recently there hasn't been a day that I'm not angered by some new article, written by another British, Italian, American, or Russian film critic. Their number particularly increased after the New American Cinema exposition in Spoleto.

The more I read that the New American Cinema is senseless and confusing and anarchistic, etc., etc., etc. the more I realize one thing: they keep talking about art. The horrible fact, or call it a sad fact, is that the film critics, all over the world, simply stopped living. They don't look forward any longer. They just sit there, protecting their own bags. Yes, you sit there, eating your breakfast peacefully, content—at your young age! You refuse to admit that in fact, in the world around you, in the whole world, the Hell is going.

I pity your guts. I pity your art. I pity your countries. I pity your births. I pity your cinemas. I wish your death.

You say you are for art. You say, you are for morality, but I tell you, that the dance, the music, the cinema which continue the perpetuation of old forms perpetuate also the old ideas, moralities of yesterday, forms and ideas which sustain the capitalism and wars—that these are immoral, poisonous. So don't talk to me about art without morality. The only art without morality is the art of yesterday: the art to which you devoted your lives and 99.99% of your magazines. You are part of the wax museum of horrors of the XX Century.

May 15, 1962

Totentanz, at the Judson Church. It could be called a Happening. A young man, Peter Schumann, is behind it, I found out later. None of the participants were dancers. They were painters, just anybodies, nobodies. And it worked. It worked as an experience of anti-dance, anti-ballet, anti-theater, a cleaner of the mind. Moving freely, playing music, without knowing music, without knowing dance, or if knowing, forgetting it, beginning from scratch.

This is not art, someone said. What is this business of looking for art everywhere? Can't one even spit without the accusation that spitting is not art? Sometimes I wish I could burn down the theatres and art galleries. I think we should introduce an annual day on which we'd perform ritualistic burning and destruction of established works of art.

Anyway. We are opening ourselves, we are loosening up, everywhere, little by little. Did the man who asked about Art give any thought why something like *Totentanz* is being done? At this place, this time? Or what it means, how it reveals us, our needs—I mean, the needs of our souls, a need for still more opening, more unpretentiousness, humility, almost humiliation? It is not for the effect's sake that *Totentanz* was performed. The reasons were more real. It was a spontaneous, inevitable action, like a movement of the hand that betrays something inside or a word that slips out, in sleep. It was a necessity and a fact. And don't ask for the reasons.

To understand the reasons, we know, it may help us to understand ourselves. But perhaps, it is too early, we are not ready to understand the real reasons of what's happening today, both in life and art. Let it happen by itself a while longer, before we put our clumsy minds to it, before we begin to analyze it. For our lives, in this decade (and, possibly, for one more) are mysterious, uncontrollable happenings. Not our rational, intellectual, bookish inquiries that will reveal the path (philosophy, religion, ethics, etc.) which we will take or are taking; rather, in the happenings such as *Totentanz* (and which come from nobody knows where and which say and express something nobody knows yet what or why) that the seeds and the keys of/to our future are hidden, sometimes more, sometimes less open to the eye of the outsider, or for that matter, to the insider's eye, too.

These strange voices, the actions of *Totentanz*, these men and women, coming in, walking out, these masks, clumsy movements, fragments and hints of trance states, bodies and voices, falling, mingling, or sitting quietly—are our reachings for new inner states and motions, a part of the inner revolution which is beginning to release energies and truths that we have in ourselves. There is sacredness in this foolery.

May 16, 1962

Went to Erick Hawkins and Barbara Tucker dance recital.

Only once before I have had such a strong experience at a dance evening. It was a few years ago, at the Anna Sokolow's group performance of Alban Berg's *Lyric Suite*. For very different reasons, it provoked me, it changed me, it made me rethink many things about life, myself, art.

I had seen Erick Hawkins dancing before, but it was never like this. This was a perfection from beginning to end. This was one long, uninterrupted masterpiece. And it was a dance that had nothing to do with little stories, jokes, or pseudo-intellectual symbolism, which I see in so much of modern dance. It has something big about it. This was a dance at once serious and joyful (who was it that said: the natural state

of mind is joy); at once abstract and humanly warm; there was feeling in it, but there was no sentimentality; there was an emotion in it, but there was no emotionalism; there was a meditation in it, but there was no intellectualism.

It had still more, and I haven't seen this anywhere else before, or I have seen only glimpses of it here and there: a dance that touched, just barely, like a bird's wing, the very essence of something of which, I felt, the dancers and their motions and the audience and myself were a part. In the same instance, as they were dancing and as we were watching, we were tied up together, touching something very deep and very real and very luminous. Kabala says: Cry, and your crying will be heard through the entire universe. Here, I felt, I was witnessing the movements of such purity and perfection that they touched somewhere, through their baseness, the very heart of the universe.

It was a dance that neither left you sweetly empty, as the beauty of the classical ballet dance most of the time does; nor did it tire you inside as the raw emotionalism of the expressive, etc. modern dance does; neither did it put you into a trance, as the snake-charmers do. The dance of Erick Hawkins left me wide awake and thoughtful, like after seeing *Hamlet*, illuminated.

I was surprised by Barbara. I was amazed with the progress she had made during this one year that I saw her last. I could not recognize her. From an unsure, young dancer she had become a mature young dancer, with a complete mastery of her craft, although still fragile in her body, girlish, sort of, which added something special to the clarity and purity of the dance, her girlishness serving as a lyrical and warm counterpoint to the strong and pure choreography and movements of Erick Hawkins.

Lucia Dlugoszewski was standing there, besides her piano, like an all understanding,

With Joseph Freeman, writer (created *Partisan Review*, was editor of *The Free Masses*).

At the Film-Makers' Cooperative, 1962.

Fools Monestary

ENTER Hello &
WELCOME
FOOD, LOVE, SEX
WOMEN, MEN, &
LIQUOR or MORE Happy
ACCEPTED
LOVE & KISSES
A SMOCH, FOOLS, ASSES
LOVERS

In the Spring of 1962 Barbara Rubin became my helper at the Coop. One thing she introduced into the Coop was a bulletin board, which actually was our door, with daily changing, very often Zen-like, messages.

watching, listening consciousness, and, as the dancers danced, she punctuated, made periods and commas and parentheses with her sounds, and underlined and italicized, bringing still more order into the whole, or opening it up, when necessary, and leading those among us who were still outside of the dance, not yet exactly with the dancers, into the very center of it, so that we sat there, silently and engrossed into this huge and almost sacred happening, an experience, which we have been given as a gift.

I did not see a single line in NY papers on the recital. A fact which, for me, adds to the greatness and the purity of the occasion.

May 17, 1962

Spent evening with Joe Freeman. He talked and talked. All about what's happening in America, France and everywhere. "It's more interesting for me to snoop in college magazines, student publications, the raw, young magazines, than in all those *Partisan Reviews*, serious big magazines. They are not in touch with life." His best memories were from the Smith and Vassar colleges—meeting with students. These experiences were small turning points, each time.

The Method of Zen
By Eugen Herrigel. Pantheon Books.
"... For this reason it is in the highest degree questionable whether the peculiarities we are endowed with by nature do really possess any 'personal' value at all." The Masters deny this—quite rightly, it seems to me. "All the twists and turns of character of which we are so proud are perhaps, at bottom, impersonal." p. 24

"Even those who have gone through much suffering are in danger of missing the right way. For the meaning of suffering is hidden and is revealed only to him who knows how to accept and bear it.", p. 123
"The Japanese theatre, No as well as Kabuki, is based not on words, but—here we can discern its Buddhist roots—on silence, so that the story can only be suggested, not told."

"A Japanese play is not meant to be read, like a European one, which may reveal all its beauty, or brilliance, or profundity at the first reading; it 'becomes' a play only through the genius of the actor, who adds to it precisely that element which cannot be expressed by words."

"There is in existence a theatre record begun several centuries ago, whose central feature is a pedantically accurate description of the dumb shows performed by great actors. This was felt to be the main task and purpose of theatrical criticism. Every actor could then learn how this great predecessors played his particular role and how to work towards a truly timeless form of acting." p. 64 chapter "Remarks on Japanese Acting"

Willard Maas writes: "If I do not care as much for Stan's present work, find it long-winded and find much of it borrowed from Marie Menken and McLaren, rough and unfinished even when most beautiful. It does not mean I am mourning the loss of a talented film-maker... I know I helped Stan become the fine film-maker he is, both Marie and I and Parker and my friends, and we have every right in the world to criticize him when we think he does not come up to our standards. We all love Stan very much and he loves us and we understand each other, and we do not care to be misinterpreted in print."
(He wrote this to me in response to my remarks in the *Village Voice*, that some of Stan's earlier friends who liked his early films, seem to dislike his later work.)

June 25, 1962

After a long night of thought, I decided to leave the *Village Voice*, to end my journalistic stint, and go further. It begins to interfere with my development.

I went to the *Village Voice* today with this idea. But the first thing I heard, when I walked in, was: Jerry Tallmer is gone. He went to the *NY Post*.

I thought there was a small warning of fate in it. I should stick around a little bit longer. I cannot leave them today. That wouldn't be kind at all.

Then I thought, later: it was me who didn't sleep last night and made up my mind to leave *the Voice*: but it was Jerry who left. I guess I did the thinking for him…

(Unpublished column for *V. Voice*)
This is a farewell note.

I have been thinking of giving up my "Movie Journal" for some time now. But kept finding excuses.

My excuses have run out.

There is no doubt that I can be of use to independent film-makers. I am a fanatic and I can do much. But it is my fanaticism that is also my danger. I have a tendency to impose my own dreams on others. Some of my observations and fantasies have been blown up out of proportion and have become directives pulling others in their winds. I have become a force, a leader, even a saint…

It is time to dissolve all forces and all illusions and all saints.

Even art can enslave men, take over them, take away their freedom.

I feel today that only that art is sacred which has no "ideas," no "thoughts," "meanings," "content," but is simply beautiful; serves no other purpose but its own beauty; it just *is*, like trees *are*.

Underground cinema will not get anything from going into the wide public. Popularization drags beauty down.

I am tired of force and action.

It is very easy for a man, and I am talking about myself, to begin to feel that he is needed and is important. Which is an illusion.

It is unimportance that I am after.

My argument for continuing this column went like this:

But shouldn't I simply be a humble servant of the film-makers and do my duty, do at least some good to my fellow humans? Are you telling that your freedom is more important than to serve men? Aren't you like one who leaves people and retreats to Himalayas, busy with himself? It's your egoism that is guiding you, not the sense of freedom.

It is so easy to think that what you are doing is needed.

Really, nothing is needed.

That includes this column.

June 28, 1962

Ask John Wilcock what happened with Stan Russel's movie that he was making with Bill Manville.

Buddha's sayings:
Down with J. P. Sartre! Long live Brooklyn Dodgers!
To hate is a waste of money and time.

ACADEMY OF NOTHING: Dr. Minto, The Cosmic Barber, Joe Jones, Dick Higgins, George Maciunas.

June, 1962

"The eye doesn't have to know—it has other compensations," said Sidney Meyers the other day.

A note on Commerce and Art:
Good oranges and good bread are commercial.
Good films are commercial.

Why should one *judge* Orpheus?

PRESS RELEASE
For immediate release

The Charles Theatre
12th St. & Ave. B
New York 9, N. Y.
GR 3-6452
Contact: E. Stein
          W. Langsford

SUMMARY: JAZZ AND JAVA PRESENTS LE SUN RA & HIS COSMIC JAZZ

    Sunday JAZZ & JAVA series--February 18th at 2 pm--presents
OUTER SPACE JAZZ with LE SUN RA and his COSMIC JAZZ SPACE PATROL
in NEW YORK DEBUT.

    LE SUN RA's music is a combination of MONK--ELLINGTON--
ORNETTE COLEMAN: HARD SWINGING JAZZ plus the NEW SOUNDS of
the ZEBRA DRUMS, JAPANESE FLUTE, FIREPLACE, FLYING SAUCER, and
the TOMORROW.

    $2 admission includes Jazz concert AND regular film program,
which follows right after.

    At the CHARLES THEATRE--12TH STREET & AVENUE B--GR 3-6170

                          *

    The CHARLES at 12th Street and Avenue B in the EAST VILLAGE
presents a steady fare of ART FILMS--film classics, revivals,
and foreign films. Dedicated to a policy of furthering the
development of American arts, it is the home of the New American
Cinema.

    In addition to its Jazz & Java concerts, the Charles pre-
sents experimental films on Friday and Saturday nights, and on
February 8th had its second FILM-MAKER'S FESTIVAL, which has
been called a JAM SESSION OF FILMS.

    To see and hear what's happening, fall by the Charles at
12th Street and Avenue B or call GR 3-6170.

                    0-0-0

FOR ENGAGEMENTS

CALL

4-9474

SON RA

During my visit to Chicago in 1959 a
young black film-maker Ed Bland (who
was making at that time *The Cry of
Jazz*) introduced me to Sun Ra. Later,
after Bland moved to New York and
found out I was doing programming for
The Charles, we were having a beer
one day and he suggested that it would
be great if Sun Ra would give a few
concerts at The Charles. We both got
very excited about it. That's how Sun Ra
came to New York.

August 19, 1962

Dear Jonas,

     Are you on vacation? Why don't I hear
from you any more? Please, do say something!
Just let me know that you're not mad at me,
or you are mad at me from some specific reason
or non-specific reason, etc.

We are now planning a symposium of Japanese
avan-guard film-makers on the condition of the
Japanese film-makers. We will tape the whole
thing and send you the translation so that you
may probably be able to put it on some American
film magazine as "Symposium of Japanese Film-
makers". I do not know just how you feel about
it. I do know that Japanese film makers are
eager to have this symposium since they want to
reach the American film-makers and others who
are interested in knowing the conditions of film-
makers in Japan. . . . .

How about the short shorts that we were going to get?
Are you objecting to the way it would be sent? Please
let me know as soon as possible since the Art Festival

is not too far ahead.

I'm coming to the end of my wits about staying in
Japan. This is horrible. New York is my only town.
But just today, I bought a beautiful plant spending
all my money. The plant looks so nice in my apartment
which is gradually becoming "my room". It is so simple
to get use to a room. That is how people wander and
that is how they settle down, I guess. It is rather
sad.

Kiss the pavements of New York for me.

                    As ever,

                    yoko

You not only have to learn (know) how to write poetry; you also have to learn (to know) how to talk about poetry. And then, the two are different things. You may know one of them and not know the other, and be very good in one of them or in both of them or in none of them.

Imagination? The Surrealists? Flights of fantasy are not the only sign of imagination. There is another kind, which is more earth bound, which is very rare—the *realist* artist has it, and you need it to understand the multiplicity of human experience. My kind of imagination is bound to reality in that special way, down to earth imagination, and it's not easy for me to go to the other kind—outward, dream —or surreal—imagination, switching the modus of imagination is like switching worlds, areas of experience, of knowledge—not only that of style.

Overheard: "If he would have the guts to knock mom out once."

"Rationality is only one aspect of the world and does not cover the whole field of experience. Physical events are not caused merely from without and mental contents are not mere derivations of sense-perceptions. There is an irrational mental life within, a so-called 'spiritual life,' of which almost nobody knows or wants to know, except a few 'mystics.' The 'life within' is generally considered as nonsense and has therefore to be eliminated; curiously enough in the East as well as in the West." (C. G. Jung, letter written in Feb. 1961, published in *Encounter*, Jan. 1961)

"True poetry can sometimes be acceptable to the mass of people when it disguises itself as something else. But in general ours is a civilization in which the very word 'poetry' evokes a hostile snigger or, at best, the sort of frozen disgust that most people feel when they heard the word 'God.'" (George Orwell)

"To inspect the invisible and hear things unheard, being entirely different from gathering up again the spirit of dead things." (Rimbaud)

Your image consists of:
A blue April sky
A sort of rich strong perfume (the origin of which I cannot detect), then, there is an earthy kind of trembling, an animal kind of trembling and repose and the sweetness and softness of the apple blossoms and the intensity of a panther ready to leap

August 20, 1962
Dear Yoko Ono:
Forgive me for this long delay. I was in the midst of various duties, there were too many unfinished things concerning the Film-makers' Cooperative and other matters. Now I can tell you something more definitive.
Film-makers' Cooperative is by now well-established, and is beginning to do its work. We pushed four experimental films programs into the first run theaters, which created a lot of talk in the press and in town. We feel that we are ready by now to invade the international waters, and to be able to help our friends from other countries. There are two films coming from Italy, which we'll help, and the film of Hiroshi, which you discussed in your last letter, sounds good and he should send us a 16 mm print (to the Cooperative's address, above).
I am enclosing the first edition (very poor, as you see, but we had to get out something fast) of our catalogue, and you should look through it with Mr. Igawa and select films that you would like to show at the Art Center. When you select the films, we'll check the exact prices of prints, and

In Central Park, with Debbie Feiner.

I SEEM TO LIVE, VOL. 1
CHAPTER TWELVE

we'll start thinking of how to get them to you. I don't think there will be any big problems.

The Connection people are waiting for an opening in NY this autumn and they are not willing to discuss any foreign sales for another month or so. If anybody is interested to buy the film for Japan, they could write to: Shirley Clarke, 372 Central Park West, New York, N.Y.

By the way, the premiere of *Guns of the Trees* is set for October 9th at the New Yorker Theater.

I hope you are as busy and as beautiful as ever—

Best wishes, Jonas

September 2, 1962

(from a letter to Louis Brigante)

I know you are hungry etc., in Venice. But you know I can't help you there. Unless you quit and go back to Rome. To hell with all those festivals.

Bachau, I heard from Sarris, is skipping Venice.

I will be editing *FC* in the woods. There will be nothing but green leaves, instead of pages. I don't mean money by green. I mean simply green. Deadline remains 15 – 17. Since I will be staying in town only about ten days, it will be a feverish editing. I hope I'll get the articles in time. S.O.S. S.O.S.

Did you get Talbot's telegram? If not, this what he wants from you: When you get back to Rome, contact Visconti and try to arrange for him—check under what conditions—screening deals for *Ossessione* and *Terra Trema*. He wants to show them. Check if they have English subtitles. Also, he would like to premiere the early films of Antonioni—*Cronaca di un Amore, I Vinti*, and *La Signora Senza Camelie*. Also, anything else that you may come up with. Write to him. Dan Talbot, New Yorker Theater, Broadway and 89th Street, NY. Today I am broke completely. Next time

I'll include a few bucks for mailing the festival materials, and a few more copies of *Cinema* with the script of *Guns*.

Ten copies of *FC* went to your Roman address. You should find them when you come back.

I don't think I will go to the post office before the 15th, our mail will not be forwarded.

Luck to both of you.

Jonas

Late September, 1962

In Vermont, with Adolfas, shooting *Hallelujah the Hills*.

We open our eyes: raining. We shoot a few scenes, trying to imitate a sunny day. Cold. Damp. Rain caught us on the lake.

Marty doesn't know how to run the motorboat. Circles around like crazy, with the scared actress.

Yesterday we set up the cameras in the middle of a pasture. We needed a shot near some cows. But where are the cows, I said. Oh, we can get them here, said the farmer, they are on the other end of the pasture.

So I went to one end of the pasture, David to the other. We crossed miles of mountainous woods, brooks, got wet like hell, crossing the woods that neither man nor cow ever crossed. No goddamn cows. Finally, from the top of the hill we scouted some animals, cattle. But instead of nice domesticated cows we found wild, scared beasts. At one moment, fifteen of them were running straight at me, in a wild stampede, they chased me into the woods. Somehow, I don't know how, we succeeded in getting the cows and the actors—twice we lost them—to the end of the pasture where the cameras were waiting. And there they stood, angry and wild, staring at the camera, camera-conscious, staring at us. As soon as we started shooting, they stampeded over the camera and ran into the woods again, nobody would have been able to keep them on the hill. So we gave up. Friday morning: cold like winter. We walk out: "Frost!" shouts Adolfas. Really, true. Everything is frozen, the windows of the cars, the ground, the grass white with frost. The air clear and pure. But cold, like I don't know what. We pulled out all our winter clothing. Apples on the grass covered with ice. Nothing better than a nice frozen apple on a morning like this.

We run our cars, and the smoke is rising, a huge mist cloud hangs around the cars. We shot our mist scenes, with David running like mad with the smoke bomb around the trees, and us shooting with two cameras, sort of DeMille style, the burning of Rome.

No date, 1962

Richard Gilman writes in *Theatre Arts*, July 1962:

"When Antonioni visited the studio of Mark Rothko he is reported to have told the artist that 'your paintings are like my films—*about nothing, with precision.*'"

From Buddha's Unpublished Writings:
"I tell you to spy. Steal the knowledge, if needed—it belongs to no man: it's God's —and distribute it through the nations."

We don't know everything about art. Really, we know very little about ourselves and art. But we know that there is beauty in art and in us, and that the beauty (art) does something to us, even if we disagree what beauty is and what we are ourselves. We also know what "anti-art" does, that we need anti-art. When art becomes too academic, come anti-artists.

One or two artists in every generation are given the intuitions of what art is; "anti-art" is Art even when it's just Nothing, a useless box, for example.

"The guy is perfect except his ass sticks out," subway scribble.

"Here I am
at 16, silly
walking,
around."

Found in the subway:
"1) the phone rings all day long
2) I have to come to the office early
3) I am writing just on my typewriter
4) I like to sit in the office and look at the people
5) On a hot day I like to order cold grapefruit juice"

Tina: "Picking flowers, unwrapping gifts— these are the peaks of experience."

BUY TRUTH BONDS

"Jack Smith is a perpetual adolescent but somehow he manages to overcome it; while Kuchars remain talented adolescents."—P. A. Sitney

One of the most horrifying expressions I've ever heard: "I'll beat your brains out!"

"I don't want to be caught in the movies tonight."
"He is all gone, man."
"He is the most."

September 25, 1962

Polish films, at the New Yorker

See You Tomorrow, by Janusz Morgenstern with Cybulski. Polish Beats, love story. O.K.
Panic on the Train, by Kazimierz Kutz. A thriller. O.K.
Bad Luck, by Andrzej Munk, with Bogumil Kobiela. Comic satire, second part seems too long?
You Clever Devil, by Maria Kaniewska. A weak family comedy about a smart student.
The Past, by Leonard Buczkowski. Polish "Nuremberg" film, so-so.

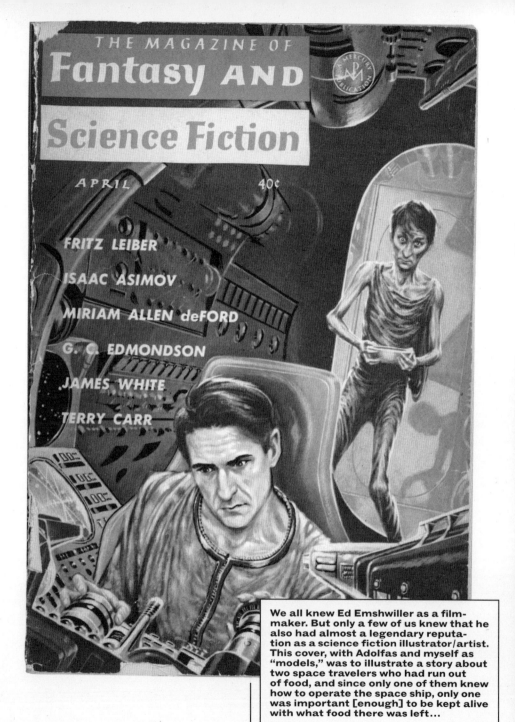

THE MAGAZINE OF
Fantasy AND
Science Fiction

APRIL   40¢

FRITZ LEIBER

ISAAC ASIMOV

MIRIAM ALLEN deFORD

G. C. EDMONDSON

JAMES WHITE

TERRY CARR

We all knew Ed Emshwiller as a film-
maker. But only a few of us knew that he
also had almost a legendary reputation as a science fiction illustrator/artist.
This cover, with Adolfas and myself as
"models," was to illustrate a story about
two space travelers who had run out
of food, and since only one of them knew
how to operate the space ship, only one
was important [enough] to be kept alive
with what food there was left...

THE NEW YORK DIARIES
1950–1969

November 1st 1962
South Londonderry

There is not much time
for thinking, one can not
think (I mean, I can not) in the
midsts, surrounded by nature, now,
in Vermont. Nature absorbs you, if
you are open and relaxed enough, and
thinks for you. It seems to be thinking for me. My own thinking
seems senseless and vain,
when I am confronted with
when I am looking at a
red Vermont sunste,
tops of the hills,or
even the trees. There is
much more wisdom, in them,
then in me. I try not to think,
I try to think tru them, become
one with them, see tru them,
and there is a good, large, vaste
feeling, when I do so,
when I suceed in doing so, in dropping, at
least for short moments, the fragments of
culture,intelligence, knowledge of the people.

Get:
J. B. Priestley's *Midnight in the Desert*
Read the part about time as the fourth dimension
Victor Zuckerkandl's *Sound and Symbol*, Bollingen series
Edited by Laslett: *The Physical Basis of the Mind*

A good idea: Collect money to send NY Censorship Board to the South...

Note on Spoleto show:
Chief of Police of Spoleto told Markopoulos to take out from *Serenity* an insert asking to help the Algerian Refugees
Teatro Sperimentale belongs to the Archbishop of Spoleto
Menotti walked out of *Guns* mad. He supposedly said, "How do you dare to show this film!"

film myself in front of a restaurant
film a loaf of bread
my obsession with "pure bread"
film my meals, what I am eating these days

September 28, 1962
Wind across Central Park. The Venetian blinds clank in the wind. She can't sleep, she watches the window, its blackness. It's night, a windy night.

THE GROUP
Meeting August 24, 10:30 PM, Bleecker (decided to push the short films)
meeting September 27, Lew Allen's office, 10 AM
decided to continue
collect members & dues

President: J. Mekas
Vice-president: Lew Allen
Finances, office, etc.: Jack Perlman
Membership committee: Stan Vanderbeek
A. Mekas
Ed Bland

November 1, 1962
South Londonderry
There is not much time for thinking, one cannot think (I mean, *I* cannot think) in the midst of all this, surrounded by nature, now in Vermont.

Nature absorbs one if one is open and relaxed; it thinks for you. It seems to be thinking for me. My own thinking seems senseless and vain when I am confronted with, when I am looking at a red Vermont sunset, the tops of the hills, the trees. There is much more wisdom in them than in me. I try not to think, I try to think through them, become one with them, and there is a good, large, vast feeling, when I do so, when I succeed in doing so, in shedding—at least for brief moments—the fragments of culture, intelligence, knowledge of people, of the world, and merging myself totally with nature, earth.

No date, 1962
The day turned out to be warm, warmer than any we saw here. Shot our lake scenes, swimming scenes. Somebody brought from town a copy of the *New York Times*, we glanced through the first page, decided that it was ridiculous to read the paper, and instead used it for wrapping, with nobody interested even to look at what movies were playing.

Saturday morning: A beautiful morning. Again small frost. Now, in another ten days, the leaves will start falling like mad. They are falling now already, one by one. Lines of fine silk mist circle the peaks of the hills and the forest heads.
This is the only way to shoot movies. To go away from the city, completely away. How much can be done this way, with nothing distracting. 250 miles from New York. Having fun. Film-making should always be fun, not dictatorship.

No date, 1962

"Research without mistakes is impossible. All natural research is, and was from its very beginning, explorative, 'unlawful,' labile, eternally reshaping, in flux, uncertain and unsure, yet still in contact with *real* natural processes. For these objective natural processes are in all their basic lawfulness variable to the highest degree, *free* in the sense of irregular, incalculable, and unrepeatable."—Wilhelm Reich, "Orgonomic Functionalism,", in *Selected Writings, An Introduction to Orgonomy*.

Isn't this a perfect description of the poet's approach to life, to creation, to work, to himself? It's therefore that the poet has his hand on the living pulse of life.

No date, 1962

MOVIE JOURNAL (Unpublished)
They say there is new cinema coming to America. Now, I saw this film, *The Connection* that everybody's talking about. I could make films like this myself, everyday. It's nothing. Besides, I don't believe that a woman can make a film. It's a man's job.
So she went and she made this dirty movie. I was ashamed, I almost blushed, the language they talk. And the fun they are making of the Salvation Army. I don't think it is fair. I have watched them often, on cold winter days, singing Christmas carols, they are nice, these sisters. I have also bought once a wicker chair at the S. Army, and they delivered it to my house, for free. You see what I mean?
I tell you: if you have any morals left, if you care for good, healthy life, stay away from this filth. It is for dope peddlers, beatniks, eggheads, communists, nihilists, anarchists, Negroes. What they are trying to do in this movie, is to corrupt our youth, to undermine our way of life. It shows people in a very bad light.
What do we see in this movie? A bunch of dope peddlers sitting and talking playing jazz, doing nothing. Is that how our people spend their time? It is disgusting. They say, it shows the world "the way it is" today. I don't think people are like that. We have a new government in Washington. Things are being done. We have never had such a high standard of living. Colleges are full. We may even have an Art Department in Washington. We have Lincoln Center. What is, then, the sense of showing our people as a bunch of dopes? We have been told, that this film is being shown even abroad! We are for positive films, films with ideas, drama—characters with heightened destinies. I think this new cinema, *The Connection* et al, ignores all that good cinema and good drama should be: tight plot, cleanly defined characters, drama which keeps your attention, ideas that move your brain. Nothing of this is in *The Connection*. They talk and talk and talk and walk and walk and walk. Camera keeps running around, with no purpose or plan. It is evident, that this girl Clarke didn't have any idea what she was doing. She is making alienated gestures in a void.*

November 11, 1962

New York City
To: Edouard de Laurot and Charles Sterling

1. Among poets and writers, if a magazine refuses to print a piece, that piece is either submitted to another publication, or, if the author is mad and talented and angry enough, he starts his own magazine.

---

* The unpublished review about Shirley Clarke's film *The Connection* is a satirical response to a public debate about her film. After the movie came out, the film critics of *The New York Times* called it "deadly monotonous" and "drab." Jonas Mekas instead considered *The Connection* the best movie of the year (*The Village Voice*, October 4, 1962). One week later he wrote for *The Village Voice* an OPEN LETTER TO THE NEW YORK DAILY MOVIE CRITICS where he blamed his fellow film writers for not appreciating the movie. He called them "deaf, blind, and dumb."

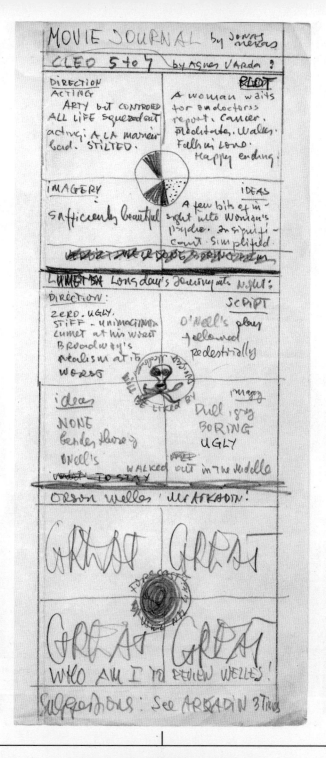

MOVIE JOURNAL by Jonas Mekas

CLEO 5 to 7 by Agnes Varda?

DIRECTION ACTING	PLOT
ARTY but CONTROLED ALL LIFE squeezed out acting: A LA marienbad. STILTED.	A woman waits for an doctors report. Cancer. Meditates. Walks. Falls in love. Happy ending.
IMAGERY	IDEAS
Sufficiently beautiful	A few bits of insight into Woman's psyche. Insignificant. Simplified.

~~VERDICT: WELL DONE. BORING FILM~~

LUMET's Long day's Journey into Night:

DIRECTION:	SCRIPT
ZERO. UGLY. STIFF – UNIMAGINATIVE Lumet at his worst Broadway's realism at its WORST	O'Neil's play followed pedestrially
ideas	imagery
NONE besides those of ONeil's verdict – TO STAY	DULL, gray BORING UGLY WALKED out in the middle

ORSON Welles: Mr ARKADIN:

GREAT   GREAT

GREAT   GREAT

WHO AM I TO REVIEW WELLES!

Suggestions: See ARKADIN 3 times

With Adolfas, during the filming of
Hallelujah the Hills.

Now, this is new to me, that someone, who insists that he is an intelligent man, and an artist (whose job is beauty and truth) is trying to push himself into a magazine by force, by threats. This is beyond my understanding.

2. Among artists, film-makers included, if a colleague is working on something, his privacy is respected, he is left alone to concentrate on what he is doing. If you are, as you insist, intelligent men, and even artists, why then, tell me, you don't show neither understanding nor respect for the other artist's work, why do you disturb him while he needs all his energy for his creative work? Why threats, blackmailing, threatening calls, imposed visits? Why don't you concentrate on your own creative work, instead of disturbing the one who is working? Tell me, where is your reason, intelligence, and self-respect, as artists and men? And you dare speak about friendship! Are those the signs of friendship? Or I am getting crazy?

3. People live together, then there are times they have to split. There are times when two friends who have been working together separate. According to reason, and according to friendship, they feel, that together they harm each other, that they can do more for humanity working separately, although disagreeing on their ideas. That's where we are. Why, then, try to paste things by force? Why not trust time, which perhaps will bring us together again? Why try to force friendship, when friendship can grow only from a free choice, from the acts of friendship—and not from the acts of force and animosity?

4. Did we ever use force, did we ever try to impose anything on you, did we ever show disrespect or animosity to *your* work?

These are the things I am trying—and I cannot—understand. Can you explain them?

Wishing you the best, Jonas

P. S. One copy of this letter I am sending to Mr. H. G. Weinberg since the circumstances have made him familiar with some of the facts and acts I am trying to understand here.

January 3, 1963

Stopped at the Jolas Gallery, to see a presentation of "photoscopes"—strips of motion and still film rotating slowly (projected slow speed with the plastic toy projectors.) I see more and more of the neo-Dada stuff happening etc., presented in 57th Street galleries, but lifeless, academic. These photoscopes had something academic about them. To a more square viewer they may look daring, imaginative, avant-garde. In the perspective of the living, changing art, however, they look like bluffing. I remember Cocteau's line, "You can't bluff while you go backwards."

I saw at Jolas many faces from the successful "avant-garde," official art. I thought I saw Harold Rosenberg's shadow passing on the wall. Later, Storm said, "He never got out of the fifties." Yes, they will keep repeating, imitating, reproducing the fifties until it will look like a dead potato.

January 13, 1963

Dear Marie:

Here I am, fifth day in Vermont. Since all our shooting is outdoors, our working days are short. We have only six hours of light. The dark comes early. Fantastic sunsets. Now we are sitting indoors (our crew consists of ten), with a fire going. We are trying to kill some time. There are only woods and snow around us, no neighbors in sight for miles. I went through the old books we found in the house (almost 200 years old),

old Longfellow volumes with yellowed engravings, *Book of Trees and Flowers*, and an old translation of La Fontaine with Doré illustrations.

I walk out into the night, I look at the moon, at the trees, all white with snow. What a silence. And it is snowing. It started snowing this evening, the trees all covered, puffy.

I brought my Kierkegaard with me. But I didn't open it. I cannot think when I am in the middle of nature. Nature doesn't like any other thinking but its own, which is vast and bottomless. I walk out, I look at the snow, the trees, the sky, and it seems to me that my own thinking is senseless and vain.

Like this morning. We got up very early, at six-thirty. Mists were floating above the cold forests, and the hilltops looked like 36 views of Hokusai. You stand and you meditate before them, you learn from them. I try to think through them, become one with them, to clean myself from the civilization which is eating my generation from inside and outside. There is a vast, good, almost a satori experience when I listen to this fantastic white silence. At least for short moments I feel free from culture, intelligence, knowledge and history.

In a sense, those moments resemble the moments when I am with you, those moments of flesh wisdom, when I abandon everything but flesh. One has to begin to build one's intelligence up from there (really, I am talking about myself). How right was Reich. The social revolution begins with flesh. When one is as disillusioned with the values of one's civilization as deeply as I am, one has to begin from the beginning. I am going backwards deeper and deeper backwards.

I took one shot for my own film today. White snow, nothing else. Nothing else seemed to be worth filming. And then, I don't even know why I filmed the snow, it is there to look at, to walk upon, to be white. I felt almost foolish filming it. Still, I felt, it is a beginning, I have to begin somewhere the dialogue, from a white scratch, from almost nowhere, from the snow as white as a belly. The whiteness of your shoulders.

A dog with black spots came from somewhere and started jumping around and licking my hands. So I put the camera aside and spent most of the forenoon talking with the dog. We became good friends.

Mists were still hanging around the tops of the hills. Further, on the left, I could see the very beginning of the gathering snowstorm which reached us later in the afternoon.

End of page… I am thinking about you (we are both runners…) Love…

CHAPTER THIRTEEN

... Film-Makers' Coop memos... Fund-raising for Ron Rice ... Letter from Joan Crawford... I am trying to change my life's direction again ... the Third Report of the N.A.C. Group ... Filming Dalí... How to stage Shakespeare... Notes from the ship FRANCE... Paris... Notes from Cannes ... On cinéma vérité ... On human voice in cinema... Ricky Leacock on cinéma vérité... More notes from the ship... On train to Avignon... Letter to Brakhage re. "monastery of fools"... From the ship... On Jerry Jofen ... Zen of Splicing... On film distribution ... On Storm De Hirsch... Notes from the Coop...

January, 1963

Sign on the Co-op door:

THIS IS THE MONASTERY & CONVENT of the
ORDER OF FOOLS
&
THE ACADEMY OF NOTHING

Observe Rules
Respect Silence

Remember
You Can Always Turn Back From This Door
Work is Being Done Here

SO GO AWAY

Enter only
if absolutely necessary
or if you're bringing food & drinks.

OFFICE BULLETIN
Dear Workers:
Please Please Please don't make this place into a business place. Let's do our work, but let's not make it like work. Let's organize, but let's keep things loose. Each of us has to go on our own way. Let's help each other go our own ways. Let's keep the beginnings and the ends loose.

January 28, 1963

WHILE-U-WAIT, remember that this is a benefit screening of a film in progress, unedited, incomplete.
Usually it is the big commercial film that is after money. Ron Rice is engaged in the creation of art. Art is so different from money that the artist is ordinarily ashamed to ask for money—it's the commercial film that goes drumming shamelessly about money. But I don't see why it should always be so. The creation of art needs money too, and no one needs be ashamed of it. Thus, this benefit screening. Some of you will be shocked by Ron Rice's

footage. Some will be enraged. Angered. Confused. Insulted. Post office types will call it pornography; Great Art types will call it non-art; others will call it obscene and perverse. I don't know what other nonsense will be pronounced about this film.

Such states and pronouncements will describe the pronouncer's psyche but not Rice's movie. For *The Queen of Sheba Meets the Atom Man*, even in the form you will see it tonight, is the most unconventional, most liberating, most shocking movie since Buñuel's *L'Age D'Or*, not to mention that it is bursting with Newborn Beauty.

Rice's movie is no more shocking than our lives. The state of man's soul today is more shocking then any of man's produces or creations. Rice undertook to expose us completely and totally with the radar of his creative imagination. Enough playing craps with the half-baked bourgeois etc. Nouvelle Vague etc. art. We have only one life so let's see what we really are, let's look into the mirror of absurdity.

Meanwhile, the film has to be completed and it's you who have to help complete it. There are enough people who help the commercial movies. But what about poetry, what about the visionary and liberating imagination of man?

In short: I am inviting you to join the friends of the Muses, to join the friends of Beauty. Put your money into art today so that man may live Tomorrow. I tell you —and I am understating it immensely— that man is in bad shape. You don't have to think twice about this—think once.

—Jonas Mekas

P. S. Drop your contributions into the Contribution Box at the Living Theatre tonight or mail it to Ron Rice at Film-Makers' Cooperative, 414 Park Avenue South, NYC.

January, 1963

The other day I stared at the white nothingness of snow. I dissolved myself into it. I tried to start from there, I am trying. To start again from nothing, from nowhere. It cleans me out, this whiteness, this space, this silence. I don't know what will come into this emptiness but every try is worth, I consider.

Like being with you. It was the same feeling, beyond reason, beyond thought-memories, making love to you, beginning again from somewhere deep, uncontrolled intelligence. I felt clean from culture. Like in this snow whiteness. It pulls me in, there is such a secret pull, strength in it, my thoughts go blank, I get completely pulled into the physical presence of the white falling snow like into the soft whiteness of your flesh.

January 23, 1963

Some good things that happened today: Received a fan letter from Joan Crawford. Letter from *Journal of Social Issues* for an article on Absurd. Good news on money for Storm's film ($3,000). Good on Co-op *FC* deal for Monday. Peter got $4,000 for *Hallelujah the Hills*. Co-op and Festival texts finished. Bleecker deal for Coop midnight screenings closed. *Guns* booked at Cornell. Raining.

No date, 1963

Things to do:

Critics' Junket: Get all movie critics in one place (conference of something, a $10,000,000 movie production in Poughkeepsie, for instance), then shoot them, with a machine-gun. Imagine the headline: Movie Critics Massacred in Poughkeepsie!

Her hand (CU) reaching for the blooming branch, or—in slow motion—only the act of stretching the hand, cut before reaching. Repeat it.

Hand, CU, holding apple, or other things.

Why do we use Christ's name as a curse? Christ, forgive us.

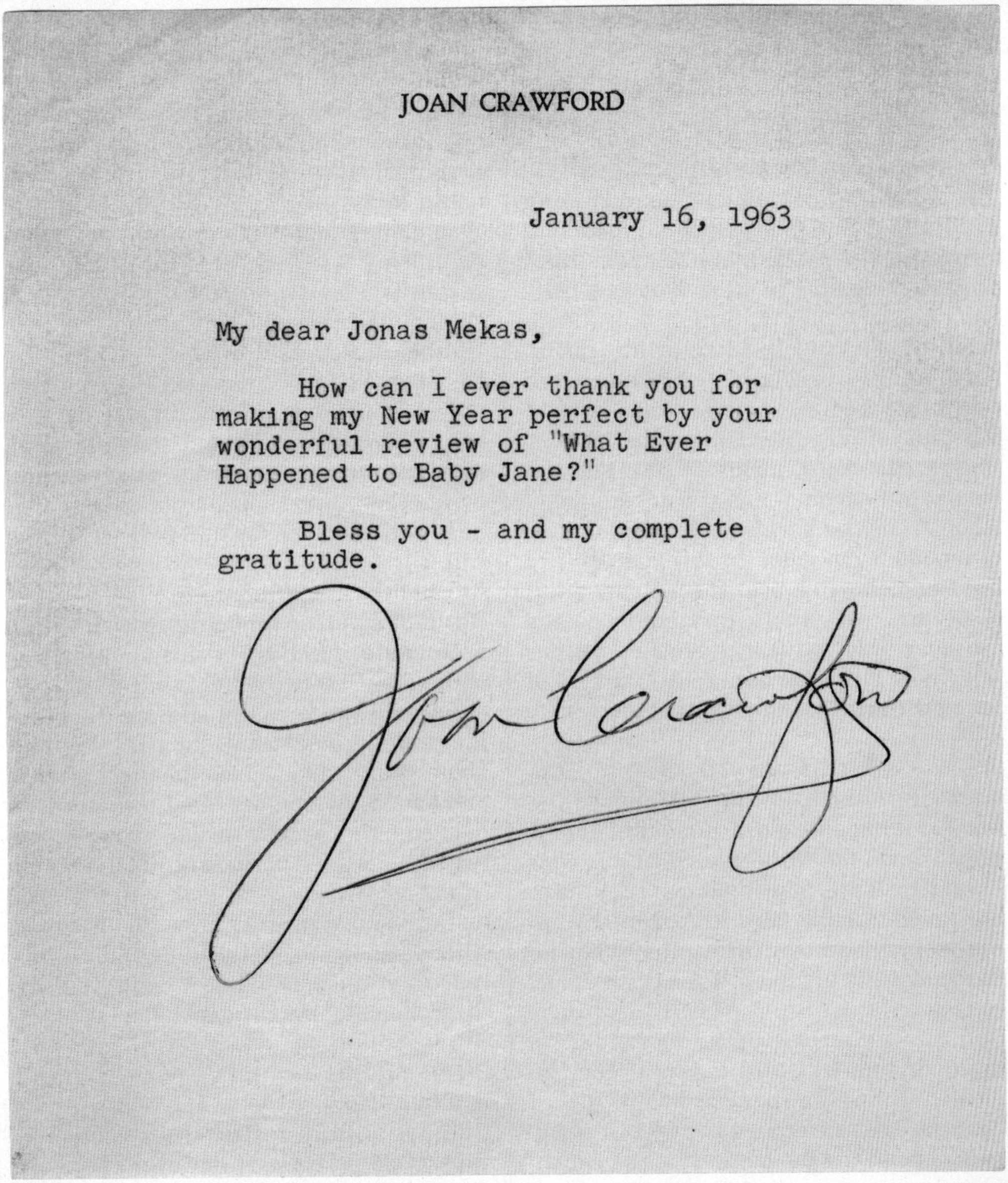

JOAN CRAWFORD

January 16, 1963

My dear Jonas Mekas,

How can I ever thank you for
making my New Year perfect by your
wonderful review of "What Ever
Happened to Baby Jane?"

Bless you - and my complete
gratitude.

Joan Crawford

CU of the moon. Then, move the camera to her face, looking at the full moon. Could be sun.
Defoliation.

"I am not writing for my own pleasure. It is like going to a psychiatrist against one's will—and trying to say something—something which might help him to understand, or gain some sort of insight on me. Only I sit and say things that really don't mean much to you, and you like a little bit to paint things a brighter color. Fluorescent —to promote a lively, happy train of thought. His type of thought—I mean he likes it. Fluorescent colors make me sick. You are not a schizophrenic—but you debate. Good —sometimes bad. This is mainly a matter of moods. I am going to tell you a bit of the fragments that pass through my mind. Some are real, others, imagination. They are ideas—words—without sequential order —for it is not a necessity—it is a sort of break-through."—Diana Hall

No date, 1963

There were times I wanted to change the world. I wanted to take a gun and shoot my way through the western civilization. Now I want to leave others alone. They have their own terrible fates to go. Now I want to shoot my own way through myself, into the thick night of myself. Thus I change my course.

Going inwards, through the door of flesh— the door that will lead me into other regions. A blind journey, no doubt, full of chances, and shreds—42nd Street of my being—but what the heck, what the heck.

I am destroyed, pushed freely somewhere, afloat, forms displaced, driven by the forces from much deeper, beyond my grasp, into these states of myself where I lose my own knowledge, where everything becomes open, flowing, uncertain, where the unknown & new take over me like a wave of heat, where I am like a feather swinging in a heat wave with no power of my own, where I begin to feel the rhythms and melodies around me, the rhythms of strange new light going through me, feeling through my first dance lesson—the first touch, the first taste, the first opening of the ear—.

Thus I am jumping into my own darkness, embracing it. There must be something, somehow, I feel, very soon, something that should give me some sign to move one or another direction.

Yes, I must be very open and watchful now... completely open... I know its coming... I am walking like a somnambulist, waiting for a secret signal, ready to go one or another direction, listening into this huge white silence for the weakest sign or call.

As I sit here alone and think about you and it's night and I am reflecting on everything around me... And I feel a certain kinship with you—like two lonely space pilots in outer cold space... As I sit here, this late night, alone, and I think about all this, and about you, and for a brief moment, I don't know for how long, we meet—somewhere between the words, images, spaces—between the words, perhaps, and I am happy, in my own way... As I look into the cold endless space passing by without sound without speed, a metal blue endless distance between us... But I know you are there, I can feel your heart beat.

CO-OP MEMO
n. 100001345
I do not want to restrict your "personal" "expressions" etc. etc. However, there are things in this place like films, sound tapes, etc. which MUST BE WHERE THEY ARE, in specific places assigned to them on the shelves, so that we can get them when we need them. We have, so to speak, certain responsibilities to some of the people (if you forgive me saying so) so that they can feel secure about their things, like for

instance Harry Smith said the other day: "I feel safe to leave the machine here with you."

But this morning I found an empty box and on that box was written "Taylor Mead Home Movie Tapes," only that the tapes weren't there and only the sad empty box was there.

Now whoever (I don't want to guess it here) took the tape and didn't put it back and left the tape in one place and the box in another, not giving a damn about it—I can't say that that was the most responsible action that human being ever did. So this is only asking for that much.

CO-OP SHOP MEMO
1. Wednesday morning, from 8 AM to 12 NOON Co-op will be at Naomi's disposition—to work in peace on her soundtracks. This means: EVERYBODY OUT AND KEEP OUT during that time. This is an order that has to be obeyed in this monastery.
2. LOVE YOUR NEIGHBOR EVEN IF YOU THINK HE IS WRONG ONLY THAT NAOMI HAPPENED TO BE RIGHT LIKE WE ALL ARE.
3. You can go into the fields.

CO-OP MEMO 2
Many of us come here, do something of great importance or of complete unimportance. Still, we all have to stick together and work somehow together without fighting in this place and without stepping on each other's heads. Each of us has a "horse," so let's try and live in peace with these horses. Sometimes I have to take "strong" "steps" to keep some kind of disorderly order in this monastery: but look at the flowers, what beautiful disorderly order they ARE (they have)—and since we all are flowers (Barbara says so), we have to tie our horses once in a while to the fence so they will not eat the roses.

February, 1963

You come to listen to Bach, to hear art for art's sake... But I watch & listen & tremble. I am all shook up, terrified with glimpses of the lost paradises, of how much we have lost, the meaninglessness of my life, how far I have to go, how far I have fallen back—.

I have tried, I have done everything to be like everybody else. I have tried to be (feel) REAL and be close to things (with things)—
touching the ground in the park; or stealingly touching the sand piles in the construction grounds; with my teeth with my mouth sucking on a tree, with my teeth deep in the wood—
but as soon as I leave it, I fall back into my fantasies, illusions and dreams, into my illusory world. Even the sounds I hear have a different meaning to me than to anybody else; street cleaning trucks, or boat whistles; or the movements of the people, voices, expressions; the shape of things and the uses of things, purposes—everything has a different meaning to me—a surreal meaning which I perceive but do not understand. There is no meaning at all in all this, it just happens, it just is.

"Today I realized that I am forty and that an immense emptiness surrounds me and my soul."

Filmed Anne on Eldridge Street. Kate was there too. Next day Kate attempted suicide.

Stan Brakhage said one thing at the Cinematheque, last Monday: the term "art" must be redefined; I am willing to stand behind that term, "Art," he said; "I like that term, I will stand behind that term with my work—art has always been redefined through the works of art," he said.

Suspense & surprise elements, adventure elements against your "NO." While to me (us) in Nazi & Stalin camps there was no surprise, all possibilities were eliminated.

No date, 1963

A DREAM

I had a dream. I was walking with somebody.
"Look," I said, "we are just where we started.
I seem to recognize this place from before."
"It's quite true," he said. "We have been here,
and we haven't. We are traveling thru the
same place but on another level."
I woke up.

Emerson, in his essay, I think it was called "Spiritual Laws," summarized:
"The more a man digs into his own experience, when he makes a work of art, the more different he will be from anybody else." And then, somewhere else, he has another statement, which, as most of such statements are, is rather paradoxical: "The more one digs into one's own self, the more universal one comes out."

March 1, 1963

I am in a complete darkness. Often I feel I am sinking. I'm reaching for air. And I feel today that the only way out, my only hope, is to submerge, perhaps, into this darkness completely, like into a coma. Not to run away from it, not to stare into it, but to embrace it, and thus go beyond it.

This feeling of going nowhere, of being stuck: the feeling of Dante's first stropha: as if afraid of the next step. As long as I don't sum myself up, as long as I stay on the surface I don't have to move forwards, I don't have to make painful and terrible decisions, choices, where to go, and how.

Because, deeper, there are terrible decisions to make, the steps to take. But I am still traveling thru the boredom. It's at forty that we die, those who did not die at twenty. It's at forty that we betray ourselves, our bodies and our souls, by not going

farther, by taking the easiest decisions, retarding, throwing ourselves back by thousands of incarnations.

I stuff myself with dailiness and I vomit my brains out and then I pull the chain. Day after day I am trying to break out. My god, for seven years, trying to "develop a mind which rests on nothing whatever" (written on my wall 109th St.) and I find myself again on zero. I don't want to be slaughtered by culture & civilization even if I have to go for another seven years. Seven years of hell or whatever is the name.

There are brief glimpses of clear sky, like falling out of a tree, so I have some idea where I am going. But there is still too much "clarity" and "straight order" of things, not enough shuffling, I'm getting always the same number, somehow, and I have had enough of it and I vomit out broken bits of words and grammars of the countries I've passed thru, broken limbs of slaughtered houses, geographies. My heart is poisoned, my brain peeling in shreds of horror. I've never let you down, world, but you did lousy things to me. So now I feel like I owe you nothing, like I can begin anywhere, go any direction—
But I have come close to the end. Now it's the question: will I make it or will I not. My life has become too painful, and I keep asking myself, what am I doing to get out of where I am? What am I doing with my life? The race is beginning. The race has begun.

No date, 1963

Here I am again, back in the city. And the pain is stronger than ever. I have seen bits and glimpses of lost paradises and I know that I will be hopelessly trying to return, even if it hurts.

And again I am vomiting my brains out. The deeper I swing to nothingness, the further I'm thrown back again into the regions of my brain, swinging always in

FILM-MAKER'S SHOWCASE
Every Monday Midnight at the Bleecker Street Cinema
Programs arranged by the N. A. Cinema Group

PROGRAM 2   February 11th, 1963

FUCKING MEKAS, DID YOU WRITE THIS?! YOU SOUND LIKE A GENIUS, YOU BASTARD. I'M ENVIOUS. —MARSHALL ANKER

ABSURD, CHANCE, ZEN ETC POETRY

These are a few examples of the new film poetry being created by the New York film underground today. A free, unforced, spontaneous, liberating, newborn poetry. No intellectual & formalistic & symbolist imagery, no forced act: they are light & careless & beautiful. They are made with utmost creative freedom, with no art, content, professionalism etc complexes. They have the freedom of the image of Brakhage, the "uncleanliness" of action painting, the freedom of Theatre of Chance and the Theatre of Happenings, and the sense of humor of Zen. Their imagination, coming from deeply "deranged" or, more truly, rearranged & liberated senses, is boundless. Nothing is forced in these films. They rediscover the poetry and wisdom of the irrational, of nonsense, of the insignificant, of the absurd -- they attack and destroy in us the false, the pretentious, the contrived, the phony. They open us for the poetry that comes from regions which are beyond the reach of intellect & reason. It is art in its most engaged & innocent & useless sense: it disengages us from false engagements.

I have no doubt that I am exaggerating the virtues & beauty of these film poems -- but that's how I am, a crazed maniac obsessed & dazed by the Newborn Poetry.

JONAS MEKAS

larger and larger circles, each time more and more frightening depths below me, gaping with black mouths, until my very being becomes dizzy. Then I close my eyes and I pray silently for you, that you wouldn't have to go through this.

But I know, I know very clearly it's hopeless. I saw your eyes. I said nothing. They betrayed the same dream. They looked familiar. And so did your hands, crisscrossed with signs and directions of pain. I thought for a moment that I should go on my own way—but here we are again, I couldn't leave you and you couldn't leave me.

March 16, 1963
THE NEW AMERICAN PORNOGRAPHY EVENING
Lotte Eisenhover, a striptease piece, *Crossroads*
excerpt from *Queen of Sheba*
Vanderbeek's *Black & White* film
Oldenburg's happening with Lesbians
Sculptures
paintings slides (ask Leslie)
During the Intermissions a special edition of *Fuck* magazine should be sold
Lenny Bruce
Jack Smith slides
Krassner
Norman Mailer

March 25, 1963
6:30 AM: UP
7:00 AM: the shop; film moved to the lab; *Voice* column written
8:00 AM: trip downtown, deliver column to *Voice*, walk in the Park, Post Office
9:00 AM: read *The Big Bite*, Mailer's *Esquire* piece, April
9:30 AM: back at the Co-op mail, accounting done for the day.
9:45 AM: pulling out the negs for *Haikus* the day is becoming hectic, can't keep track any longer, sorry—was well intended...

"In case of love, as in that of wills and testaments, the last is the only valid one, and it annuls all predecessors."—Pitigrilli

April 19, 1963
Filming Dalí at Ducrot studio

Brakhage: "She always insisted on keeping out of my asthma attacks, i.e. she wouldn't become my mother."
Barbara (to me): "You keep Debbie's things for her, like a father."

Concerning the above: This obsession with "mothering" and "fathering."
As if these feelings of "caring" would belong only to mother! This fear must come from a deep complex insecurity, or some other such shit.

read p. 205 *A Portrait of the Artist*... Joyce
read *The Sacred Mushroom* by Andrija Puharach
read *Sound and Symbol* by Victor Zuckerkandl, Bollingen Series
Yarrow (Achillea Millefolium)
Reading Laslett's (editor) *The Physical Basis of the Mind* & *An Introduction to Psychology* by Gardner Murphy.

April 20, 1963
Junk art. Oldenburg. Rauschenberg. Etc. We are longing for textures. Colors. Materials. Everything was (or still is) becoming monotonously uniform, simple, glossy. The most sensitive among artists start reacting against the simplification of colors, materials, surfaces. Abstract art was beautiful, but not rich enough, for the eye and the soul.

FIVE WAYS OF GOING BACK TO SHAKESPEARE
1. Announce the production of *Hamlet*
   put chairs on the stage
   seat two or three people on stage
   give a copy of *Hamlet* to each one

let them read the book silently
let the audience sit and watch
Performance will end when they finish
reading the book.

2. Some of the best Shakespeare productions I have seen were first readings of the play, with actors sitting quietly, reading aloud.

This should be a lesson to us.
Stage *King Lear* or *Hamlet* or even *Macbeth* with actors sitting or standing quietly on the same spot during the entire play. They say lines without moving.

3. A parody of current Shakespeare productions could be staged on another evening: Actors would pronounce lines, let's say, of *Hamlet* by standing on their heads, jumping constantly around, fuming, tired, rolling on the ground: "Shakespeare in action." (This is a critique of contemporary theatre.)

"How to cultivate nuttiness in myself."
—Ken Jacobs
"I'd like to die with an 8 mm film pressing to my chest."
—Ken Jacobs
"Wonderful! Everybody has the same ideas."
—Ken Jacobs

May 5, 1963
from the boat FRANCE

Dear Linda:
I have already reached the middle of the ocean, but I still haven't seen the bottom of the sea although I keep looking into it. I haven't even seen a fish. It's amazing.
It's very boring here. Texas ladies in furs sitting in the sun, French tourists. All stupid like hell. I am happy they stay out of my way, because I walk around like a bum, and I am sure they think I am an idiot (I hope they don't take me for some "extravagant" millionaire…) so I have plenty of space just for myself, and nothing to do at all—it is maddening.
Best to you and David—keep the fort

May 9, 1963
Standing in Notre Dame. Watching a kneeling man. Dark, unswept. I couldn't force myself to kneel. And I was so far from praying! I was holding a folded newspaper, conscious of my hands.

De Brocca: "Oh, technique, schools! The film-maker's school is to go to the movies three times every day for ten years. Only those who went through this school, have the real love of cinema. For those, who have worked their way up as assistants, cinema is nothing but a bread-winner."

Truffaut: "There is only one kind of bad spectator: the one who walks in, in the middle of the film."

René Clair: "It is absolutely anachronistic, in our times, to continue the film exhibition methods introduced 60 years ago. The electronics should be used to change the projection & distribution of images to the public—via TV & cables. What foolishness. What incomprehension of the tools that have been put at our disposal. Just imagine, all theatre screens connected to one another with one center of emission, be it by means of wires and cables—which is so easy to do & for so little money. Imagine, one print would suffice for the whole country and…"

Truffaut: "We have heard 100 times that cinema is an escape. We should remember this. For a good escape must be prepared secretly, & with much observation & thought. It can be done only as a sure thing, at night and in complete silence. So let's keep this in mind, when we prepare, shoot or project a film."

THE THIRD REPORT OF THE NEW AMERICAN CINEMA GROUP
April 15th, 1963

Our amorphous organization has survived another ten months.

Since our Second Report last July, we have devoted most of our
energies (those left over from film-making) to the development
and strenghtening of our film distribution center which is known
as the Film Makers' Cooperative. Film distribution remains our
main problem, second only to that of film financing.

THE CHARLES IS DEAD

One of our local outlets, which we helped to bring into life,
the Charles Theatre, has collapsed. Bad business on the Lower East
Side. Those evenings that featured the independent cinema, however,
were the only evenings which made money at the Charles. It was
the European Art Film and the Hollywood Film that brought on the
downfall of the Charles.

FILM MAKERS' SHOWCASE

Since last February, we have been holding weekly midnight
screenings at the Bleeker St. Cinema under the name of Film
Makers' Showcase. The Showcase gives us a chance to see the newest
work of the American Independents. Midnight is an ungodly hour, but
no theatre in New York is willing to give the independents a better
hour. That's how much we are loved.

THE NEED FOR OUR OWN THEATRE

Our aim remains to have a theatre of our own. Recently, through
Harold Humes, we have made a contact with the division of Cultural
Affairs, a branch of the Mayor's office. They assured us that the
City has decided to assist Culture and that it will help the independent
film makers, through the N.A. Cinema Group to acquire a building
suitable to accomodate a small theatre and the offices of the Cooperative.
We are checking up on these promises. We are not too optomistic, but
we believe that something may come out of it. At least, we would like
to see for ourselves how serious the City politicians are about the Arts.

SECRETARIES OF THE COOP

In February, "Film Culture" magazine managed to swing a small
grant for the Coop, large enough to pay for a new catalogue, to do
a mailing, to pay for a few urgent prints, and to employ, on a part
time basis, David Brooks and Linda Silber as the executive secretaries
of the Coop. They have their hands full with the rapidly expanding
activities of the Coop.

INTERNATIONAL FILM EXPOSITION

An important undertaking of the Group is the International Film
Exposition (see the attached Announcement), devised to satisfy the
constantly flowing requests for screenings of the independent American
cinema from other countrues. Of no less importance will be the First
Auction of Modern Cinema, which will take place later this summer, first
in New York and then in other cities -- an entirely new approach to film
distribution (read the attached Tentative Text of the Auction Announcement).

RELATIONS WITH OTHER DISTRIBUTORS OF INDEPENDENT CINEMA

Often, since the beginning of the Film Makers' Coop, questions
have been asked about the relationship of the Coop with other distributors
who distribute films similar to those we are making. The birth of the
Coop was a spontaneous happening provoked by the sick situation of film
distribution that existed at the time, primarily by the simple fact that
no distributor wanted our films (or they wanted them with "changex");
whereas we beleived, as we still believe, that we are making the living
cinema in America today. So we got angry and, instead of negotiating
or bargaining with the distributors, we decided to do it ourselves, in our
own "unbusiness-like" way.

Over the last year the extent of the publicity given to our work and
our "movement" has provoked and forced the distributors to take our
work more seriously. The distribution situation today is a little
better than a year ago, when we first started the Coop; nevertheless, we
don't beleive, and we really have no proof, that the situation will keep
getting better. We do know, however, that there will always be a new
cinema, and that it always will bemmet with mistrust and misjudgement.
The taste of our distributors, even the best ones, lags at least by two

or three years behind what we are doing. Keeping this in mind, and,
in general, being a sort of anarchic group of people, we feel that
despite certain disadvantages, we want to continue the idea of the
Coop. We don;t like to be judged by distributors. We know what our
work is worth, and it is up to the people, not the distributors, to like us
or to dislike us. We don't think much about the taste of the audience
either -- but we believe in a direct contact, with no intermediaries
pre-selecting what "pepple" should or shouln't see. Anyway, we
like the idea and we like the spirit in which we are working, and then,
who cares about the logic of it anyway.

We must stress the fact that the Coop never intended to embrace
all independent etc. film makers. We don't want anything of the sort.
We encourage and urge those among us who feel that their work at this
moment could reach more people through other disributors, to join them.
The Coop is an irresponsible and changing group where anything goes,
anything can be tested, and where we can get excited about anything
with no need to blush now or later -- we are the working frontier of
the independent etc. cinema.

Two meetings (one in February and another in March) took place to
discuss the possibility of merging the Coop with Cinema 16. Too many
contradictory opinions were expressed. It was decided to wait and see.
Some of us felt that Cinema 16 has not fully understood the real reasons why
the Coop was started in the first place.

A RECOMMENDATION OF THE COOP TO THE INDEPENDENT FILM
MAKERS. INSISTENCE ON CO-DISTRIBUTION

One decision on which we all agreed, and which we intend to recommend
to all independent film makers as part of our general policy, is the
following:

We are of the opinion that the more distributors who distribute our
work, the better our chances will be to reach the people interested in
it. There is no one single distribution set-up today which, by itself,
can reach all possible film users, and we don't think there will ever be
one. We don't even think that a dictatorship of one single distributor
would be a good thing.

Our policy is this: We insist on the right of the film maker to sell
or rent (co-distribute) the prints of his films to as many different
distributers as he can find (like an author has the right to sell his book
in a thousand different bookshops, or rent it through 10,000 different

libraries). There can be no monopoly of film distribution -- cinema
monopolies are part of cinema's childhood.

ORGANIZATIONAL MATTERS. GENERAL MEETING

During the last year we have had three or four small meetings.
We have learned from previous meeting that large meetings result in
much talk and no action. We can talk at home, in the bars, etc. So
we have been following, as our working method, an anarchistic
dictatorship. It has resulted in no talk and at least some action. We
intend to follow this policy in the future. The next large meeting, to which
all members of the group and the Coop are invited, will take place
later this Spring (for the purpose of electing new "officers" and having
plenty of talk.)

NEW CATALOGUE

A new catalogue of films distributed by the Coop is being prepared
for late April printing. I suggest to all those film makers who have
films ready for distribution to write or call the Coop before the end
of April (short discriptions of films-- length; black/white or color;
sound or silent; 35mm, 16mm or 8mm; one paragraph content
discriptions -- are needed).

> New American Cinema Group
> President
> Jonas Mekas

April 15, 1963

FEATURES IN PRODUCTION BY N.Y. INDEPENDENTS

Not long ago, VARIETY printed a report on N. Y. commercial
independents. They announced a record number of productions:
eight films were being made in New York. Now, we tell you:
the "uncommercial" independents are beating them 1:15.

Here is Our List of Films Completed Or In Production:

POINT OF ORDER, Emile De Antonio and Dan Talbot (completed)
THE NEON ROSE Barry Gerson (completed)
PEACOCK FEATHERS, Jerome Hill (completed)
TWICE A MAN, Gregory Markoupoulos (editing)
DIONYSIUS, Charles Boultenhouse (editing)
GOOD-BYE IN THE MIRROR, Storm De Hirsch (editing)
HALLELUJAH THE HILLS, Adolphas Mekas (completed)
THE COOL WORLD, Shirley Clarke (editing)
MAN OUTSIDE, Joseph Marzano
DANCE OF DREATH, Stan Vanderbeek (shooting)
FLAMING CREATURES, Jack Smith (completed)
THE QUEEN OF SHEEBA MEETS THE ATOM MAN, Ron Rice (shooting)
DOG STAR MAN, Stan Brakhage (editing)
LEWIS AND ALLAN GO TO MAINE AND MEET JANE, W.D. Cannon (editing)
Untitled Feature, Vernon Zimmerman, (shooting)
Untitled Feature, Robert Frank (editing)
THE SHOWMAN, Al and David Maysles (completed)
THE NIGHT SONG, Herb Danska, (shooting)
BLACK FOX, Clyde Stoumen (completed)
GREENWICH VILLAGE, Jack O'Connell (completed)
Untitled Feature, Willard Maas (in preparation)
Untitled Feature, Morris Engel (shooting)
STAR SPANGLED TO DEATH, Ken Jacobs (shooting)
LIME TWIG, Philip and Michael Burton (in preparation)
GOODBYE BEAR, Peter Kass (shooting)
Untitled Feature, Burt Brown (shooting)
THE FLAMING CITY, Dick Higgins (completed)
Untitled, Taylor Mead, (shooting)
SECRET LIVES OF SALVADOR DALI, Jonas Mekas (shooting)
Untitled Feature, Lionel Rogosin (shooting)
ROBERT FROST, Shirley Clarke and Robert Hughes

Also: features in preparation by Emile De Antonio, Adolphas Mekas,
Ed Bland, Ricky Carrier, Robert Frank, Clyde Stoumen, Nicholas
Webster, Kenneth van Sicle.

thomas TRAVEL BUREAU, INC.

130 WEST 42ND STREET, NEW YORK 36, N. Y. | WISCONSIN 7-0818 | CABLE ADDRESS: "THOMASTOUR"

To: Mr. Jonas Mekas
414 Park Avenue South
New York, New York

Invoice N° 12596

Date: April 29, 1963

File:

Passenger: Mr. Jonas Mekas

Ship, France Eastbound
May 2, 1963 New York to LaHavre
Tourist Class Berth C, Cabin B212
$260.50 plus $3.50 port tax

260.50
3.50

Ship, Queen Mary Westbound
May 23, 1963, Cherbourg, to New York
Tourist Class Cabin C145 All
$199.00 plus $3.50 port tax

199.00
3.50

$466.50

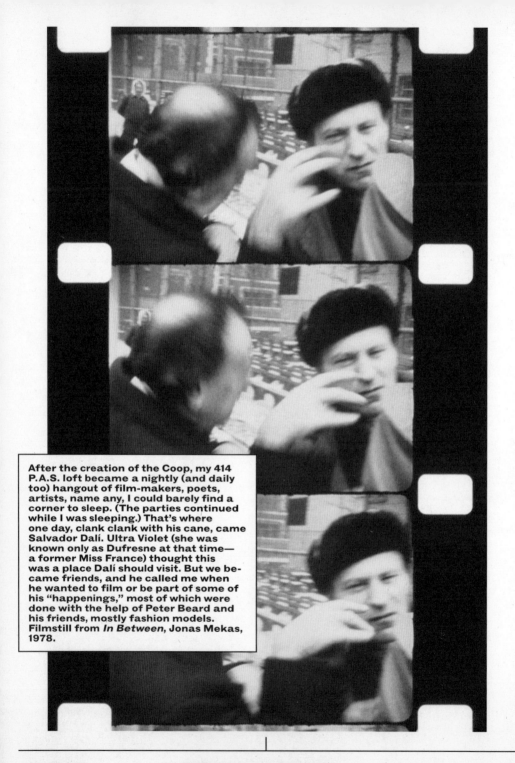

After the creation of the Coop, my 414
P.A.S. loft became a nightly (and daily
too) hangout of film-makers, poets,
artists, name any, I could barely find a
corner to sleep. (The parties continued
while I was sleeping.) That's where
one day, clank clank with his cane, came
Salvador Dalí. Ultra Violet (she was
known only as Dufresne at that time—
a former Miss France) thought this
was a place Dalí should visit. But we became friends, and he called me when
he wanted to film or be part of some of
his "happenings," most of which were
done with the help of Peter Beard and
his friends, mostly fashion models.
Filmstill from *In Between*, Jonas Mekas,
1978.

May, 1963
CANNES TRIP

"Il faut tout tourner, mais il faut avoir un sujet."—Pierre Juneau à propos de Jean Rouch

Leacock would say: "Il faut tout tourner, mais il faut avoir un homme." The difference between the French-Canadian school of cinéma-vérité & the American (Leacock & Maysles) is that where the French-Canadians start with subjects, themes, ideas —Leacock starts with people. It is people that come through strongest in *Eddie Sachs, Football*, or even in *The Chair*, and it is the same in *Showman*. They don't sell any solutions, any ready-made opinions about the people they show: they document them to the best of their abilities, and the rest is up to us, how we look at these people. In *The Lonely Boy*, from the very beginning, there is a snide view, there is the morality or moralizing of the film-maker, who looks down upon his subject. Maysles said to me, "In *Lonely Boy*, they have no respect for man, the film-makers are not humble enough." In Chris Marker's *Cuba Sí!*, we get an abstract idea of Cuba; but in Leacock's-Maysles' *Cuba Sí, Yankee No*, we come to liking & understanding Cuba in a much more real way, through the people, through their presence. Ideas we can doubt & reject; but we are taken by the faces, voices, gestures of the people.

It's becoming clear, that only now we have the first really "talking cinema." More than that: we have national, untranslatable cinemas. We all thought that cinema will break through the language barriers. We were mistaken. There is one cinema which is becoming as difficult to translate as poetry: Rouch, Marker, Brault, Jack Smith (of *Cobra*.) Leacock, Maysles. The word has come to cinema, or, more exactly, the human voice has arrived to cinema.

Cinema has used words since its beginning. But the human voice, its subtle nuances, inflections, timbre, were kept out, as if not worthy of cinema. If we'd make a graph of the voices of actors, and the voices of country people, we'd see the immense poverty of the former and the richness of the later. Now, suddenly, the richness and beauty of the human voice is being discovered. I remember our first screening of *Blonde Cobra* when we suddenly, with Storm De Hirsch, became aware of this new situation. We knew that we just saw a masterpiece; a work of art, a film of such poetic strength and richness that it left us silent. The cinema, for the first time was brought to the level of Rimbaud-Baudelaire. There was no question about that. But there was also no question that *Blonde Cobra* had integrated the voice so perfectly, so integrally, that the film became untranslatable; that it will never be the same to a Frenchman or an Italian, what it is to us; that in the future, people will painfully attempt to translate this film, & will fail, as all translators of poetry fail, Jack's voice will have to remain there, because it's the film.

So there we are: the national cinema. And what became of our dreams of "international" art? It was fine, as long as cinema stuck closely to the painting: compositions; or music. But now that is no longer enough. We have discovered the beauty of the human voice, speech, & we are beginning to integrate it into our work. One could still translate most of the cinéma-vérité films. Subtitles are imaginable for *The Chair* but *Moi, un Noir* or *Seul ou avec D'Autres* are untranslatable, because of the color of the language. The *Blonde Cobra* & the films of Jean Rouch, however, are the first totally integrated, untranslatable films not because of the "slang" etc. qualities & richness, but because of the complexity of the integration of the meanings & levels of the voices. The cadence, the color or the voices become part of the content and form of these films, new levels of meanings come in.

From a conversation with Ricky Leacock
Movie N. 8, April 1963
Q: There seems to be a difference in belief between you and Jean Rouch; he thinks that the presence of the camera modifies the action, and with your technique you say this doesn't happen.
Leacock: We find that the degree to which the camera changes the situation is mostly up to the nature of the person filming it. You can make your presence known, or you can act in such a way as not to affect them. Also, of course, it depends on the intensity of what's happening to them. But we don't think that it affects people very much, at least I don't. Let me add that, of course, it affects them in Jean Rouch's films, since the only thing that is happening to them is the fact that they're being filmed. There's nothing else to think about. How can they ever forget it?
Q: You've said that your relationship with your subject is a personal, equal relationship. Do you think that this is ideal, rather than attempting to be invisible?
Leacock: You can't be invisible. You're either an equal or a subordinate, to put it bluntly. Bob Drew pointed out at the meeting, if anything, the films of Rouch give carefully thought out answers to problems, and that we, if anything, attempt to give evidence about which you can make up your own mind. That's what we hope we're doing anyway.
We feel that if in a Rouch film you turned the picture off and listened to the soundtrack you would get the full contents of the film. If you turned the picture off in our case, the thing would be absolutely incomprehensible.
The other day I tried to write out a definition of what we know we can make film of relatively easily: A film about a person who is interesting, who is involved in a situation which he cares about deeply, which comes to a conclusion within a limited period of time, where we have access to what goes on—we can be there, in other words.

No date, 1963

1. LAUGHING BOXES
   make a few wooden & metal boxes
   place in them laughing devices (tapes)
   place them on stage
   place them in various places of the city
   (streets, dark corners of the waterfront,
   in the C. Park bushes, etc.)

2. HAPPENINGS FOR THE NOSE
   take a brown paper bag
   put it in water (preferably: street
   puddle after rain)
   take it out of water
   smell it

3. walk
   a
   wet downtown street
   after rain

4. buy
   LIP-ADE
   (first aid for sore lips)
   smell it

Confucius:
"Politeness is the basis of success."
Polite movies are also successful!

"Who ignores words ignores people."

On Cinéma-Vérité:
"Editing" must be eliminated.
It is in editing that cinéma-vérité movies are butchered.
There is so much hypocrisy in politics etc. that when we go to the movies we want an assurance that we're not being lied to.

When in Marker's *Cuba* 63 a series of images edited to music appears in the midst of authentic footage, we know that the author is selling something, perhaps a lie.

"Vérité n'est pas le but mais peutêtre la route."—Chris Marker

Picked up at Cannes:
"Un film n'est réélement bon que lorsque la caméra est un oeil dans la tête d'un poète."—Orson Welles

"Ideas which change the world come with feet on pigeons."—Nietzsche

Question: How come the birds in your film play so well?
Hitchcock: Because they were paid well.
Q: There have been many different interpretations of your film. Which is your own interpretation?
H: I wanted to show that if man doesn't behave well toward nature, then nature will turn against him.
Q: Why do your heroes never die at the end of your films?
H: Because I need them for my next film.

"Aujourd'hui un Descartes s'enfermerait dans sa chambre avec une caméra de 16mm et de la pellicule et écrirait le 'Discours de la méthode' en film…"
—Alexandre Astruc

Saturday, May 18, 1963
Picked up at Cannes, from interviews, overheard bits, etc.:

Hitchcock: "I have one minor weakness: paintings. I own Dufy, Paul Klee, Vlaminck. I keep them in my own house, for my pleasure, and not in L.A."

90 films were made in France in 1962. 21 of them were first films of new directors; 13 were second films of young directors.

May 26, 1963
It is true that I am despairing. But my despair is not the end: it is the condition, the route to the way out (or another beginning). I have come to this. It is here that my life has led me to. I am forty and I see no light. I am in a thick darkness. Often I feel I am sinking. I gasp for air. And I feel, today, that the only way out, my only hope, is to submerge perhaps into this darkness completely, like into a coma; not to run from it, not to stare into it, but to embrace it, and thus go beyond it, with or without *perhaps*.

I stared today into the endless mist. It has been surrounding us from the very early morning, tightly around us. The ship keeps calling, every two minutes, with its foggy voice.

I am calling similarly from the depths of my night & mist. Night & Fog is written on my back. I thought today, there must be a meaning in all this, for me, a meaning which I must grasp, somehow. Why am I here, in such a miserable state, & at forty, and in the middle of the ocean; my lot cannot be, cannot end like this. I have to take it as a terrible gift, this pain, or a warning, this doubt of my life, as something that, eventually, should push me further, polish me finer, inside—otherwise, Why? Why? Why? What is the use of all this? That was Frances' question, I remember now, the suicide room, *Guns of the Trees*, and I find myself asking the same questions.

I remember the morning I passed Avignon. I fell into a slumber, for a second, and I saw, I felt, I heard a voice: "Beautify your own soul—that is the best service you can do to others, that's what you should do" —and I woke up with a jump of the train, and I looked out the window. It was so fresh, bright, the hills, the trees, the fields —and I was asking myself: what am I doing, what am I doing with my life, why can't I be like that—those hills, those fields.

And I remember, I used to be like that. There was a time, when I used to be like that, like the morning landscape of Avignon, in those distant times of innocence, yes. I was like that. But now I am far away from it, and lost, and with no way out in sight, and I look out into the morning with envy & memories & painful sadness; something that is like a measure of the lost distances, or a reminder, I don't know. But the Nice express is running, and I can only look at it, for a moment, at the Avignon morning, and then I fall back into sleep, a tormented, bad sleep, painful, bits of broken dreams.

I am thinking now about that morning, today, two weeks later, closed in a thick fog of the Atlantic. I can still hear the ship calling, and each time I think the sun perhaps broke out, perhaps, & I look out & I see nothing but the thick fog, and the wind gusts throw small rain showers into my tired eyes.

"artists are the antennae of the race"
—Ezra Pound

May 27, 1963

I am sitting in the lounge, watching the passengers play cards. I am bored, terribly, painfully bored. I walked out, crossed the deck, and the mist is still here, and the wind, so I go back. Why should I be so bored, I keep asking myself. Don't I have enough in myself to keep myself busy? Or am I dying? In truth maybe I'm dead!
And then, I know it is not so. It is not. But I feel I am on the very surface. Not really in the ocean. Just on the surface of it. Like this ship. Afraid to descend deeper into myself. Why? Why? I keep asking. All these weeks, for months now I have been feeling like this, living not in myself, not with myself, but between the crust of myself & that of the earth.

No date, 1963

Dear Stan:
This is letter-writing time, which is very rare in my life. I just finished proof-reading your book and I am still full with it, even if I got it letter-by-letter, I got the letters but I probably missed most of what was between the letters. Still, I say: IT'S A GREAT BOOK.
I noticed you are using your letter on the Monastery of Fools. Ever since you wrote that letter I was planning to drop you a few lines about it. Because I felt (despite the truth of your observations on the subject) that you have misunderstood me a little bit, or you've misunderstood me "out of context."
You start with my line and then you go to talk about artists as fools in historical perspective, etc. etc. etc., while my Monastery of Fools, the Co-op, none of us and me the least, EVER meant this as a Monastery of Artists. What I meant was just the opposite: we are the ones who SERVE THE ARTIST. From this place, here, on 414 P.A.S., various invasions and attacks are constantly mapped out and executed. We are no cripples. We don't ask, we don't beg. We believe fanatically in it; we really don't know what we are and where we are going and we don't make any rules about it, leaving both ends open; etc. etc. We say "fools" only in the sense that everybody else is performing their duties and work for money. Even at the Co-op, David is working only because he is paid, and he just told me, that he will be leaving the Co-op soon because he needs more money. Ken Jacobs is running our shows at the Gramercy only because he gets some money from it—at least that is the determining factor. The only people who get no money from any of the activities, and refuse to do anything for money, is me, Barbara, and P. Adams (it's Barbara who paints those flowers etc. on your letters.) It is not that we don't need money or expect

alms for our survival: it is more an action against the business mentality and the practicality of the world where dedication and love and actions of faith are replaced by actions of and for money. We are active & fighting fools and nobody will put us into a cave. We are no fools in the true sense, we are fools in a completely different sense, in our own sense. We make fools of ourselves, working for other film-makers for nothing 24 hours every day. I made a rule here, I wrote it on the door that this place is a place of work & dedication.

I don't know if I am making myself clear at all. Whichever & whatever—Best to you all & Love.

May, 1963

I am sitting here in this small room. I lie in my bed. The ship is rocking heavily. A strong wind is blowing. I went out. I stood against the wind, and I could not breathe. So I am back in the room. I can feel the huge loneliness surrounding me. I am hanging in the space. No contact whatever. The room. The ventilation sound. I feel the presence of the ocean beneath me, very very close. This invisible presence is stronger than anything else. I can't even think or concentrate, although there is nothing in the room really distracting. It is as if a strange unfamiliar drug has overpowered my blood. I feel like such a nothing, myself. For two days I have been doped and loony. It took me two days to begin to get used to it. I am beginning to collect myself, to fight back, to resist its invisible presence. I can feel the lack of human presence. The space—air—is empty of human spirit. The huge mass of pure physical mass of the ocean is overpowering the space, is overpowering my presence, my spirit, my body. I remember now again Storm's room and the Blue Room, and what we said. We said: "It's so easy to talk here, to be here; ideas are in the air, the spirit is in the air." Here there is nothing

to help me. I am totally alone here. I have to find everything either in myself (thru myself) or try and make, establish a contact, to be my own radar, in this space, in this space which is bare of human (physical and mental) presence, the aether is surrounding me and the ship and the ocean. Everything depends now on me. Here only me and the unfamiliar spirits in their Atlantic retreat, rough, powerful, monstrous.

For two days I've been in this strange, somnambulist state. Only now, on the third day, I am beginning to be conscious of my fight against the powers & demons of the ocean; that this silence and passivity resembles the curled retreat of an animal, a dog when it is fighting a sickness, a wound. I reacted the same way. I retreated, in the presence of the Oceanus & Aether surrounding me, threatening me, me being an invader here. I am beginning to collect myself and fight back, perhaps. In my still somnambulist state—perhaps only because of it & thru it I am reaching now into the immediate vastness around me, attempting to make a contact with the unsubstantial dreamy forms of thought somewhere in the aether—the only conversation I can make now. Because, on this entire huge ship, I am entirely by myself, as if no one else was here. A lone, shipwrecked man, the rest of the passengers being zero, because they have been already consumed and nullified by Oceanus, as far as my being & fight is concerned—they are only ghosts.

No date, 1963

Revisited *Psycho*. It still holds. Maybe Hitchcock's best. Virtuoso filmmaking. I was so absorbed in it that I didn't have time to think about its moral or immoral implications. I will think about it when I get older.

Revisited Kubrick's *Killer's Kiss* and *Beau Serge*. Now I am burying Kubrick and

FILM CULTURE

G.P.O. BOX
NO: 1499
NEW YORK
N.Y., U.S.A.

Les Abysses — 45.000.000 old francs
Hitler connais pas — 30.000.000 " "
Seul ou avec d'autres — 45.000 New francs

> Je dis qu'a partir des récits que les journalistes en firent, un metteur en scène reconstituera un jour, avec des figurants, l'événement, et que s'il sait son art, c'est ce film qui sera « vrai ». Et que si nous pouvions voir aujourd'hui des bandes filmées sur la révolte du « Potemkine », elles seraient moins « vraies » que le film d'Eisenstein.

> Il faut bien voir ce qu'il y a, d'ailleurs, de vertigineux dans cette débauche de « vérité » qui a saisi notre époque, et aussi d'équivoque.

Françoise Giroud
in "L'Express"
9 Mai 1963

"Ce départ à zéro reflète une lassitude idéologique...

... • La ~~la~~ ~~caméra~~ caméra Brault et le magnétophone invisible
~~r~~ résolvent magiquement le problème de la mise en
scène et des décisions morales qu'elle suppose.

"Problèmes du cinéma-vérité" in Positif, N. 49, 1962
Raymond Borde

" Telle est l'ambiguité d'un cinéma documentaire qui veut en
faire trop ou pas assez. ~~Il~~ Il n'a pas défini un état
d'équilibre entre les lois de la prise de et la recherche de la
vérité. Il est écartelé. Il recourt à la maladresse comme
à un ~~ant~~ antidote du film traditionnel. Mais il ~~~~ devient
confus ou ennuyeux, alors même qu'il se veut simple
et direct. Il n'a pas résolu ses problèmes de forme
en dépit des caméras de poche... ... Il découle d'un
besoin sympathique de vérité en soi, d'une aspiration
vague, à fleur de peau, mais de rien d'autre, et
en ce sens il est naïf." ibid

David Brooks, film-maker, served as manager of the Film-Makers' Cooperative in 1962–63. His life was cut short in a car crash.

Chabrol. Two overrated directors. Kubrick began and ended with his first film, *Fear and Desire*. Chabrol was never any good. There are interesting moments in all of his films but those are the rare exceptions. His new film *Leda* started well, and in five minutes ended in boredom, in Eastman color. Color photography? If you admire his color and flower fields, see Markopoulos' *Serenity*, which has ten times more beautiful poppy fields. Chabrol's color is a tourists' color, which is O.K., if you like tourism. I hate tourists.

"Wer las nachts ueberm Rhein die Wolkenschriften der ziehenden Nebel? Es war der Steppenwolf. Und wer suchte ueber den Truemmern seines Lebens den zerflatternden Sinn, litt das scheinbar Unsinnige, lebte das scheinbar Verrueckte, hoffte heimlich im letzten irren Chaos noch Offenbarung und Gottesnaehe?"
—p. 51 *Der Steppenwolf*, Hesse

"Shelley saw reality as in process."
—Eli Siegel

June 2, 1963
A DREAM
I dreamt a sentence:
"and as they walked, they burned katurnia, which increased still more the mystic experience." When I woke up, I had a feeling that *katurnia was a plant, but I wasn't too sure any longer.*
Immediately after, I dreamt a tale:
"A man was riding a frog."
No, it starts like this:
A man said: "I'll ride on a frog to the city."
They said, his wife said, "Don't do it."
(or: "You can't do it.")
The man said: "I will."
They asked, his wife asked: "Why do you want to do it?"
The man said: "To prove that it is more difficult to listen to it than to do it."
Here I woke up.

The dream happened during a noon nap.

Cleaning bath
can't use bath when I need
her place is full of dog's lice
not safe for cameras, etc.
place full of ugly paintings and furniture
cockroaches

Edouard cannot accept the fact, hasn't enough either humility or wisdom, that we are living today in a transitory epoch and that no lasting culture, arts, no static qualities can grow nor be tolerated by life forces. Beats accepted this with great humility, like monks, renouncing their own ambitions and good life, and thus they are helping life forces to move faster out of the dead and sterile epoch into one of life—

Dry petals of dead flowers have secret cures in them; and so do the shreds of snake skin; anything under the sun, once touched by life (sun) is imbued with power over death.
Keep looking for things in places where there is nothing.
Whenever I touch earth with my feet—in Central Park—I feel suddenly so good. The earth in itself is our truest friend, medicine.

Agrippa: "It is [the Earth] the first matter of our creation, and the truest medicine that can restore and preserve us."
(*The Philosophy of Natural Magic*, V.)

The Lithuanians in their pantheist days kept an eternal fire, guarded by *vaidilutes* (young virgins)

June 9, 1963
Mailer evening: What other American writer today has an auditorium of Carnegie Hall size, for himself, to express his views? It was an evening beautiful and glorious, the way he was digging, painfully

into the depths of himself. *NY Times* & *Post* gave short funny notices, making fun of the evening and Mailer.

Jerry Jofen: "I am so deep in my own loft, with all the things, with everything, that even when I go out, I carry my loft with me, I see things through my loft, I see nothing else. Only once in a while do I see bits of the Outside World, bits. Yesterday, for the first time, I saw even SKY!"

Marlon Brando: "I have no respect for acting. Acting, by and large, is the expression of a neurotic impulse. Acting is a bum's life."

June 12, 1963

The Zen of splicing. Like the Zen of Archery. You have to do it and do it until it's like throwing pebbles in the water. Then you have mastered editing. Then you give up editing, like Ken Jacobs did, like Jack Smith, or Markopoulos did, which, really, is the true secret of editing. Like shooting without aiming—and hitting. After your nth splice you realize that, really, splicing is equivalent to editing; that editing is nothing but splicing. So you shoot your film beyond splices and beyond editing. You go to the other side of the consciousness of editing. You swallow it, you relegate it to your stomach or maybe fingers. The many become one again. You leave the camera and the eye alone. You screen your footage and you are amazed at the art of what you see, at the perfection of what you see, at the right-placedness of every movement, every camera stop, every accidental cutting. I mean, your mind thinks it is accidental; actually, you have been structuring your art inside yourself for years; the structuring occurred long before you pushed that button; the camera became the extension of your hand and your eye which became the extension of your aesthetic sense and your aesthetic

structuring senses. Oh, the uselessness and the futility of editing. I saw Gregory editing *Twice a Man* and *Serenity* without a splicer or a viewer. What does it matter? Or Ron Rice, building his fantastic set, for months, shooting with an empty camera, living on his set for days and days—and then he shoots *Chumlum* in one evening, all edited, all spliced, right there, in the camera. Such is the mastery of the masters; of Smith, of Ron, of Jacobs, of Brakhage, of Gregory, and other monks of the art of cinema. It is the camera that is their bow; their self is their targets; and they shoot beyond their senses with their two eyes closed: but there is the third one, wide open, unseen by the mortals—and they hit right into the heart of poetry. It is amazing, yes.

No date, 1963

Let us not worry about the limited distribution of our movies, small audiences: it is not part of art & beauty to force itself untimely (or even timely) upon the people. Our works are only shreds that fall away from our selves, in our continuous growth. There will be a few to whom our work will speak one or two words, will start something inside, some small movement. No, we are not underground. We are closer to the sun, throwing light into the sad darkness, joy & love & beauty into the dark undergrounds of human misery.

Storm De Hirsch is a poet. One part of her wants to "express" itself, wants to get out. Some fragments of her inner world come out in words of long forgotten languages; some come out thru more recognizable patterns and images of poems; others come as plastic strokes, bits of colors, and lines reaching after invisible spaces and dimensions with the tiny webs of their line and wire extensions. What De Hirsch cannot say with words, she has to say with color and shape—nothing unsaid can stay

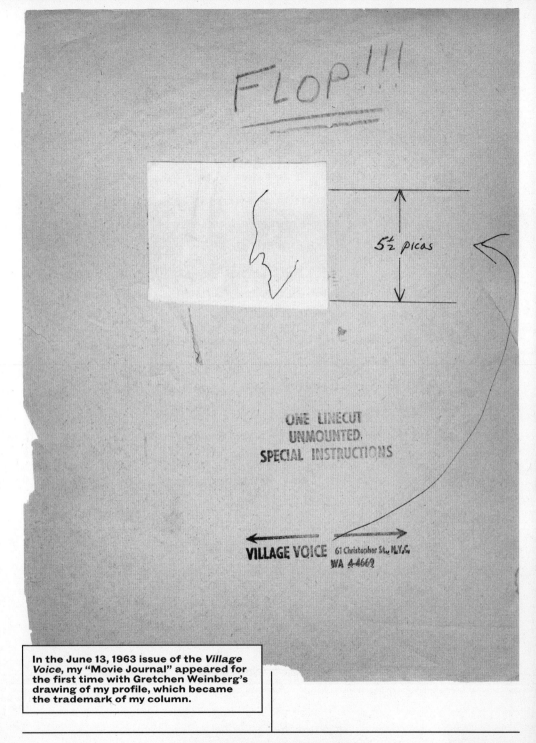

In the June 13, 1963 issue of the *Village Voice*, my "Movie Journal" appeared for the first time with Gretchen Weinberg's drawing of my profile, which became the trademark of my column.

To   THE EDITORS

From   ROSALIND CONSTABLE

Date   October 1963

OFFICE MEMORANDUM

UNDERGROUND CINEMA   (from Memo of August 1, 1963)

Jonas Mekas, who writes a disputatious Film Journal for the Village Voice, said not long ago (May 2): "Perhaps you have noticed that most of the time, lately, I have been writing about movies which you can't see anywhere. I think it is a very bad state of affairs when the best of contemporary cinema cannot be seen at all." Mekas went on to say: "The movies I have in mind are Ron Rice's The Queen of Sheba Meets the Atom Man; Jack Smith's The Flaming Creatures; Ken Jacobs' Little Stabs at Happiness; Bob Fleishner's Blonde Cobra — four works that make up the real revolution in cinema today. These movies are illuminating and opening up sensibilities and experiences never before recorded in the American arts, a content which Baudelaire, the Marquis de Sade, and Rimbaud gave to world literature a century ago and which Burroughs (Naked Lunch) gave to American Literature three years ago. It is a world of flowers of evil, of illuminations of torn and tortured flesh; a poetry which is at once beautiful and terrible, good and evil, delicate and dirty. A thing that may scare an average viewer is that this cinema is treading on the very edge of perversity."

These four films were made by members of the New American Cinema Group, founded by Mekas in 1962. Their films are distributed (if that is the right word for "movies you can't see anywhere") by the long within a poet without breaking out—or breaking her. These paintings—if one should call these works so—are patterns of her soul. They are lyrical outbursts of some ceaseless activities within her. They are simple statements, simple colorful shells of someone, perhaps in the process of becoming a butterfly.

Picked up at the Co-op:
"I just came back into town.
Ah, ah I see that will be the beginning of the next movie.
I can begin working right away."

"He is such a pig."
"Couldn't be worse."

"So, we have to move."
"I want to check St. Mark's Place."
"I don't feel like talking to him. I will talk to Dorothy."

"I work for manpower or something."
"I'll fast."
"Listen, we have to go, really."
"Raining."
"Raining flowers?"
"It's water."
"It's a cloudy day."

(silence)
"I'll go with the fascist pig next week."

"The sage is full of anxiety and indecision in undertaking anything, and so he is always successful."—Book XXVI, *The Texts of Chuang-tzu* quoted by Salinger (could be his own invention)

Whatever you do, do it as a prayer.
Does not matter what you do.

June 23, 1963
The *Voice* said:
"You don't have to go anywhere. You just have to make yourself ready. Prepare your-self. Know it's there. It will come by itself. Your work is here—it will come by itself. Just have trust & knowing & be open & ready. Don't worry, don't frustrate. It will come thru your smile."

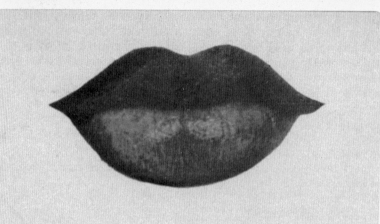

LOVE & KISSES TO CENSORS FILM SOCIETY
(Division of the New American Cinema Group)

1963 MEMBERSHIP CARD NO. 1547

SHOWINGS
Every Monday Evening at
THE GRAMERCY ARTS THEATRE
127 East 27th Street, New York City

CHAPTER FOURTEEN

... New aesthetics of cinema... On 8 mm cinema... THIS SPORTING LIFE... Jack Smith and *The Great Pasty Triumph*... Baudelairean cinema is born... On Brion Gysin, Jerry Jofen... Intro to the N.A.C. Exposition... Barbara Rubin on Jack Smith... The *Flaming Creatures* affair at Knokke-Le-Zoute... A letter to New York film-makers from Knokke... Letter to Barbara and Sitney on NY scene... Letter to Yoko Ono... Report on FM Coop meeting... Letter to Barbara... Letter to Jack Smith... Letter to Sitney on Marko-poulos, Brakhage, Harry Smith, *The Brig*...

July 10, 1963

New aesthetics of cinema?

MOVEMENT: Movement can now go from complete immobility to a blur, swish, to a million unpredictable grades of speeds and ecstasies. The classic vocabulary allows (recognizes) only the slowly, classically, respectfully paced pans, and immobility, and so-called clear image.

We have freed the motion. The camera movement now can range anywhere between a clear, peaceful & idyllic recognizability to a frenetic feverish etc. madness of motion. The full range of your emotions and sensibilities. You bend your words and your syntax to express properly your inner movements. There is no such thing as "normal" movement. Normal movement means what? It means going only by established, static values, norm and patterns of perception, thinking, etc.; it means living only in the past, not giving full consideration & respect to the present; it means going against Darwin's law...

LIGHTING: The image can go now from the "properly" lit (they mean: realistically; but in truth: it means according to the accustomed, "past" conventions) to a complete destruction of the "proper"; from a complete white (washed-out) to a complete black; that is the range of the lighting (see *The Dead, Flaming Creatures*). Oh, the millions of nuances that are open to us, the poetry and drama of shades of over- and under-exposures, of darkness. There is no such thing as "proper" or "normal" lighting.

The technical-aesthetic revolution that is going on in cinema today is doing to cinema almost the same what James Joyce did to literature, it enables cinema language to reach into our terrifying (&-ied) souls (Smith, Jacobs, McLaine, Brakhage, etc.).

We still hear talks about "shaky" cameras, and "bad exposures," but less and less. More and more we begin to realize that

FILM-MAKERS' SHOWCASE

Every Monday Evening at the

GRAMERCY ARTS THEATRE

138 East 27th Street (near Lexington Ave.)

there is no single way of exposing things; and that the steadiness is not an absolute (and not at all) a virtue & quality of the motion, that cinema language and syntax, like any other language and syntax, is in constant & watchful flux. (*Panta Rei*)

No date, 1963

8 mm camera freed the young film-makers. Because they don't think 8 mm is commercial, they do not imitate the commercial or any other cinema, they just make "home movies."
You don't have to understand the individual images, frames: you take (get) only the breath of them.

No date, 1963

It is the lack of love that, I may say, is at the bottom of the failure of Lindsay Anderson's first feature, *This Sporting Life*. He seems to hate his subject. How can one understand, or show to the others something that one has no love for? So he throws at the screen fuming close-ups, bits of action, exaggerations, makes plenty of noise, but everything stays on the surface, nothing essential or subtle is revealed, touched: it's too noisy for poetry. The piece is contrived, forced, made-up.
The angriness of a poet is love for truth. He says his truths with passion. When a naked truth is thrown into a corrupt surrounding it acquires a quality of anger. It bothers people by its simple presence. It bothers establishment. Ginsberg shouted some truths, they came from love. There is a great sadness in *Howl*. There was a great sadness in the *Book of Job*, too. There is no sadness without love.
There is no sadness in Lindsay Anderson, the angry young man of London. There is murder there. There is the fist. There are many other things there. But there is no sadness. So, where was I? Oh, I really don't know.

July 12, 1963

"Life is just one big splice."—Louis Brigante
"Sex is a pain in the ass."—Jack Smith
"Be sober. Keep all my commandments." —Revelations

In *Twice a Man*, Gregory Markopoulos uses editing in a new and intensified way to capture the unconscious & thought, the movements of nonliterary intelligence. He demonstrates, in a most beautiful way, that editing can be one of cinema's glories. His film, exquisitely beautiful, pulsates with subtle levels of sensuous sub-imagery, fountains of color burst in magnificent, glorious fireworks.

August 5, 1963

There are works appearing which are making a turn in the so-called "new American cinema," a turn from the New York realist & cinéma-vérité school (the cinema of "surface" meanings and social engagements) towards a cinema of poetry and truth.
Jack Smith's *Flaming Creatures*, Ron Rice's *The Queen of Sheba*, Ken Jacob's *Little Stabs at Happiness*, Bob Fleishner's *Blonde Cobra* —these works indicate the scope and direction of what's happening in cinema today. These movies are illuminations, reflecting & opening up sensibilities & intelligences never before recorded in the American cinema—the world of *Flowers of Evil*, of *Illuminations*, of *Naked Lunch*, of torn and tortured flesh, of flaming senses; a poetry that is at once beautiful and terrible; good and evil; delicate and dirty. A Baudelairean cinema is born.
Don't mind the fact that a great part of this cinema is treading on the very edge of perversity. Today there is a very concrete (dialectical) necessity to break down the walls of inhibitions, to tear off false, antic clothing. These are, as Ken Jacobs puts it, "dirty-mouthed" films. They are far and beyond the contemporary & temporary morality. They are innocent.

Gramercy Arts Theatre, 138 East 27th Street, New York. Between July 1963 and March 1964 it was run by the Film-Makers' Cooperative under the name of Film-Makers' Showcase. Among the films premiered in it were Andy Warhol's *Sleep*, Kenneth Anger's *Scorpio Rising*, Ken Jacobs' *Star-Spangled to Death*, Gregory Markopoulos' *Twice A Man*, Jack Smith's *Flaming Creatures* and *Normal Love*.

August 29, 1963

A DREAM

"What should I do?"

"Be humble"

"Should I do what I'm doing or leave it?"

"All growing depends on you, it is all in you, not only in what you're doing. It is how you are doing it. It's in what you're doing and in what you're not doing."

I dreamt this conversation.

September 8, 1963

What I heard this morning, while watching the sun rise upon Hoboken:

"Should I retreat, into some silent place, and work out all this by myself?"

"No, you should stay here and continue doing what you are doing and work it out the difficult way. The easy way will save your soul alone; the difficult way will save your soul and a few others. This is your choice: Salvation by/for yourself or salvation together."

"Sum up. It is a time for summing-up myself. See where I am, to look a little bit backwards, and all the way back, and see where I am, how I am. It is time to go further."

"Every action should be a prayer," the voice said.

September 13, 1963

There is pitiless law of life, there, in the Bomb. All "actions" of man are being unified here in one single "action" so that he can wipe himself out. The pitiless laws of life have been revealed to us many times by poets, saints and prophets alike; there can be only two directions for man: towards the sun, or towards the self-destruction.

Yes, we have an A-Bomb. But wait until we have a Z-Bomb.

...for these useless boxes, these paintings, these "senseless" movies resemble more the koans of the Zen monks, then art; for they are only pointing at instead of filling us with something.

We have Gysin's flicker machine. We have films made and projected only once. We have film-makers who are content to have their work shown to a few friends, leaving it at that, one-time experience, with no further ambitions. Harry Smith who works on his fantastic movies for twenty years, without anybody seeing them. Happening artists whose fantasy worlds disappear the same evening.

Which is unbelievable to the commercially minded who wants to commercialize even their fantasies, their pleasures. Anything for sale, reproduced into infinity until it costs nothing, is worth nothing, is nothing. Jerry Jofen who works, films and paints, and collects around himself huge masses of fantastic work wherever he settles down for a week or a month and then he leaves, moves somewhere else, and leaves everything right there in the room, not taking anything, and again starts from the beginning, and then leaves again—and only some of his friends drag some of his paintings or films behind him in big heavy suitcases, and Everngam digs his films from the garbage can of West 22nd Street.

It is time to sum up, to sum myself up, so that I could break out again

times of summing up are really times of breaking out

September 15, 1963

More Autumn Notes

Eh, what is the total sum of summer?

Eh, what is its contents, form, purpose?

(This is over the falling autumn leaves or a quiet autumn scene, landscape)

And me, in the middle of my life, where am I, what did my life amount to?

The summer explodes into the fountains of brown and red
that's what the summer green amounted to.

Borges relates that once upon a time there was a wise man who devoted his whole live to seeking, among the innumerable signs in nature, the ineffable name of God, the key to the Great Secret. After a life of tribulation, he was arrested on the orders of a Prince, and condemned to be devoured by a panther. While waiting in the cell into which he had been thrown, he observed through the bars the wild beast who was waiting to devour him. Gazing at the spots on its skin, he discovered in the pattern and rhythm of the design the number, the Name that he had been seeking for so long and in so many places. He knew then why he had to die, and that he would die only after his great wish had been fulfilled—and that would not be death.

"One sees buildings of a consummate silliness: buildings which are beautiful before they are finished, enchanting when they consist only of foundations and of a few great scaffoldings and cranes towering into the day or into the half-darkness. When they are finished they are a mass of curly-cues and 'futile adornments.' Because?"
—p. 101 Gaudier-Brezska

INTRODUCTION TO THE INTERNATIONAL EXPOSITION OF THE NEW AMERICAN CINEMA (1961 – 1963)

The purpose of this Exposition is to show to other countries that part of the American cinema which has the least chance of getting abroad.

In most countries during the last three years creative experimentation has been manifest in the dramatic film only. In America, the most interesting things have been happening in the poetic, non-narrative cinema.

It is this cinema that we want to show to the world: the cinema which you will never see at the festivals.

The significance of this cinema goes far beyond the context of the contemporary American film-making.

We feel that the dramatic cinema has come to a dead end; that the aesthetic questions raised by our work have to do with the essence of cinema, and with the state of modern art today in general.

The young American film-makers represented in this Exposition feel that the official Film Festivals which are mushrooming all over the world have become commercial projects—they no longer show what's really going on in cinema. We are speaking specifically about the American representations at Film Festivals.

There is too much emphasis on the dramatic narrative cinema. This emphasis has become damaging. The young American film-makers are sending this Exposition as a sort of artistic protest and manifesto.

We are taking a stand for the poetic and non-narrative cinema. We are taking a stand for modern cinema.

The critical publications are busy discussing "new" cinema. Most of the time we don't know what they are talking about, since they are still talking about the same old cinema in a new disguise. We are concerned with the experimental frontier of our art, where the things begin. It is not true that all of the cinema is an art for the mass audience. Cinema, like any other art, has works the appreciation of which requires more complex and awakened sensibilities and intelligences. After all, man grows in both limb and understanding.

Not all film-makers represented in this Exposition have realized their visions equally. Much searching and probing is going on. However, a few have reached the highest aesthetic development possible in modern cinema. They are creating works which illuminate man in a manner in which only the highest achievements of art have been capable in the history of man's creative expression.

The international discussion which is taking place today, asking what is new cinema and whether there is a new cinema at all, would be incomplete without the knowledge of the aesthetics of these film-makers.

This Exposition is our expression of solidarity with those few creative artists in cinema—in whatever country they may be—who are concerned with the subtler aspects of their art and their lives; who are concerned with the continuous growth of man.

Jonas Mekas
Program Director

October 20, 1963

Barbara kept filming Jack yesterday. She said, he is like a child: as long as you film him, he is happy. So, like a good mother, she kept filming Jack. Since there was no film, she kept rewinding and shooting five times on the same roll. Just to make him feel happy.

Ken screened all his *Spangled* footage. Will need money to make a print. Barbara said: "Oh, we'll get money for you." That means I have to get money for him. Where? I am sick of playing money daddy to all. Sometimes I have nothing on my mind but money. That is, most of the time, lately. Barbara says, I should let others raise money for film-makers. She doesn't know yet that NOBODY else wants to do that, that one either goes into the business of making money for oneself, or else one considers oneself an artist and feels that money will "destroy" or "corrupt" him/her.

Study the new art and it will reveal to you the new ways & forms of thinking and seeing—because our art(ists) precede philosopher(ies).

"On apprend beaucoup plus de choses importantes en tournant un film en 16 mm, dont on fait le montage soi-même, qu'en étant stagiaire ou assistant."—Truffaut

November 1, 1963

It is enough shouting.
No more shouting.
Silence now.
Silence.

November 2, 1963

O, Hell, Oh, hell.
What am I doing here?
What am I doing here.
Hundred miles from my home.

December 22, 1963

It took me long to realize that it is love that distinguished man from stones, trees, rain
and that love grows only thru loving
Yes, I've been so completely lost, so truly lost.

About Leo who goes searching for faces of ecstasy everywhere, looking into every face he meets. The happiest man has no shirt... remember that! He was that poor.

Ecstasy reflected in a face of a saint, a lover, a jazz player.

They were walking.
Asked, where they are going, a voice answered: Each one is walking separately, somewhere, but they are all walking to the same destination, separately, but together.

That day you wanted to come with me but you couldn't.
I went alone. But it wasn't the same.

You said, you had a feeling that in one of my lives I had something to do with the circus. You said you could see me in Spain.

NEW AMERICAN CINEMA GROUP
414 Park Avenue South
New York 16, New York
telephone: MU 5-2210

Oct.24th 1963

FILM-MAKERS' FIVE O'CLOCK TEA
At Mrs. Charles Murphy
Reception to Milton Sperling

1. Andrew Sarris (film critic, FILM CULTURE)
2. Robert Breer (film-maker)
3. Stan Vanderbeek (film-maker)
4. Ron Rice (film-maker)
5. Jack Perlman (film-makers' attorney)
6. Gregory Markopoulos (film-maker)
7. Ken Jacobs (film-maker)
8. Al & David Maysles (film-makers)
9. Jonas Mekas
10. Adolfas Mekas (film-maker)
11. Lew Allen (producer)
12. Storm De Hirsh (film-maker)
13. Louis Brigante (editor, FILM CULTURE)
14. P.Adams Sitney (Director of the Intern.Film Exposition)
15. Laura Bell (Life mag.)
16. Harriet Rohmer (Film-Makers' Coop)
17. Harold Humes (Filmwrights International)
18. Alfred Leslie (film-maker)
19. De Kooning
20. Frances Stillman (film-maker)

COOP MEMO   no372057 TO DOVE LEDERBERG

what the hell do I hear permit me to curse on this occasion
jack smith dropped your fan on the floor or something and
now you say you ain't going to do anything for jack because
how can you do anything for somebody who drops your fan on
the floor such a terrible crime such a terrible thing todo

in any case as Barbara says let's ask the fan what the fan
has to say about all this and then let's decide what is
to be done about it

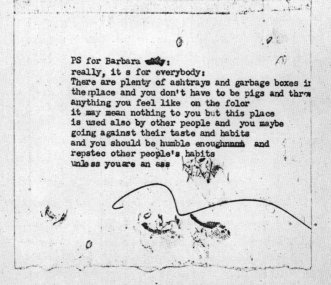

PS for Barbara   :
really, it s for everybody:
There are plenty of ashtrays and garbage boxes in
the rplace and you don't have to be pigs and throw
anything you feel like on the folor
it may mean nothing to you but this place
is used also by other people and you maybe
going against their taste and habits
and you should be humble enoughnnnh and
repstec other people's habits
unless youare an ass

200   12/5/63

PRESS RELEASE

December 5th, 1963

From: FILM CULTURE
414 Park Avenue South
New York, N. Y.

Tel.: MU 5-2210

INDEPENDENT FILM AWARD FOR 1963 GIVEN TO JACK SMITH
FOR HIS FILM "FLAMING CREATURES"

The presentation of the Independent Film Award to Jack Smith for his film "Flaming Creatures" will take place at the Tivoli Theatre (Eighth Avenue and 50th St.) this Saturday (Dec. 7th) at Midnight.

The Independent Film Award is being given yearly by "Film Culture" magazine "to point out original American contributions to the cinema." The Award became known first by bringing to the public attention John Cassavetes' low budget film "Shadows." Other past recipients have been Robert Frank for "Pull My Daisy," Ricky Leacock for "Primary," and Stan Brakhage for "Prelude."

"Flaming Creatures" is the first feature by Jack Smith, a young New Yorker, distributed by the Film-Makers' Cooperative, New York. The film has had only sporadic but much discussed screenings in Los Angeles, San Francisco and New York. It will be one of the American entries at the Brussels Film Exposition end of December, and at the International Film Exposition of American Cinema in Amsterdam this coming January.

FILM CULTURE
magazine

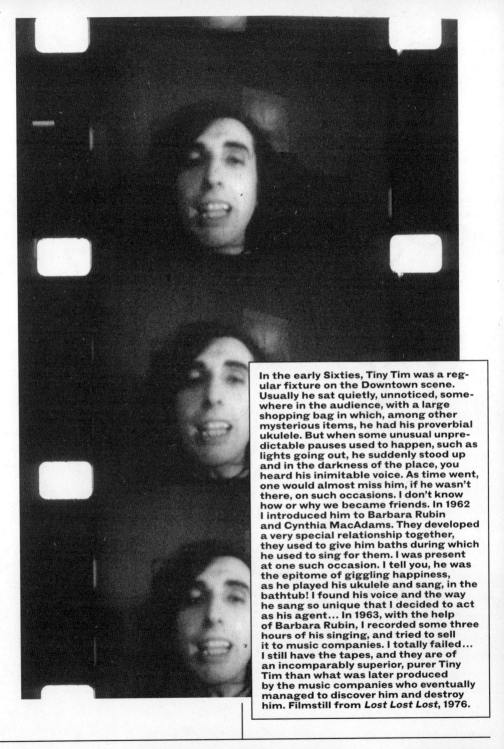

In the early Sixties, Tiny Tim was a regular fixture on the Downtown scene. Usually he sat quietly, unnoticed, somewhere in the audience, with a large shopping bag in which, among other mysterious items, he had his proverbial ukulele. But when some unusual unpredictable pauses used to happen, such as lights going out, he suddenly stood up and in the darkness of the place, you heard his inimitable voice. As time went, one would almost miss him, if he wasn't there, on such occasions. I don't know how or why we became friends. In 1962 I introduced him to Barbara Rubin and Cynthia MacAdams. They developed a very special relationship together, they used to give him baths during which he used to sing for them. I was present at one such occasion. I tell you, he was the epitome of giggling happiness, as he played his ukulele and sang, in the bathtub! I found his voice and the way he sang so unique that I decided to act as his agent... In 1963, with the help of Barbara Rubin, I recorded some three hours of his singing, and tried to sell it to music companies. I totally failed... I still have the tapes, and they are of an incomparably superior, purer Tiny Tim than what was later produced by the music companies who eventually managed to discover him and destroy him. Filmstill from *Lost Lost Lost*, 1976.

FLAMING CREATURES
SATURDAY MIDNIGHT DEC. 7TH

Plus: rushes from Jack Smith's Normal Love

ADM. 2.00

Tivoli Theatre
8TH AVE. / 50TH ST.

Why don't you work? They ask.
I am searching for the gold flower. Where the
gold flower blooms, there is my child playing.

Some important facts:
- I wrote a check to Bernewitz for work on *Flaming Creatures* soundtrack, June 13, 1963
- Lab TV for *Flaherty Report*, Sept. 4, 1963
- First payment to Lab TV on *Normal Love*, Aug. 29, 1963
- Harriet Rohmer, work at the Co-op, Oct. 14, 1963
- First lab payment on *Christmas on Earth*, Oct. 19, 1963
- First payment to Leslie Trumbull, Dec. 12, 1963

When artists organize themselves they become workers.
Not even craftsmen, just workers.

"The question is not what cinema could do to advance the feminist cause: the question is what feminists can do for the art of cinema."

Knokke-Le-Zoute, December 19, 1963
DEAR JACK
(& ALL FILM-MAKERS!!?????):
This is going to be a collective effort letter written on & off about "All the Shit" going on here.
There we are, sitting here, and there's no snow here, and there are almost no films here except what come from N.Y., and there are hundreds of phonies watching them, and perhaps five or ten good people, and they all want to see *Flaming Creatures*, and the Festival forbids to show it, so we are having late shows of *F.C.* in our bedroom, and also late late shows. Last night Godard was there, crouched in the corner, and Agnés Varda, Polanski, and most good people and now everybody wants to see it, because this is becoming an international scandal, really it has been a scandal since

we came here and made all efforts to get *F.C.* into competition and made a public protest, Barbara fighting with hair and nails, I had to pull myself out of the Jury because of this, and James Broughton is our only man in the Jury.
We had a Press Conference today explaining the position of those of us who are sticking together. We read the statements on censorship by Gregory, Stan Vanderbeek, Stan Brakhage, Robert Breer, and P. Adams Sitney made a beautiful speech explaining what *F.C.* is all about.
These are the facts now:
1. *F.C.* was accepted by the selection committee.
2. It was forbidden to show by the Minister of Justice
3. I withdrew myself from the Jury in protest against censorship.
4. We asked to take out the Fest films of Breer, Vanderbeek, Brakhage, Markopoulos, accordingly with their request.
5. We were refused this on the grounds that the film-makers gave their permissions to show their films by filling up the application blanks, etc.,etc., etc. "very complicated." We'll tell you when we come back.
6. No public screening of *F.C.* can be held here. We are planning to have one in Brussels immediately after the Fest. The law says, we should be arrested, together with all present.

Everybody liked *Scorpio, Twice a Man, Chumlum,* and they all have chances of winning and there is much talking about Stan's (B) work, and his screenings are noisiest (for silent movies!) & disturbing—the audience is snobbish & weird, and likes only documentaries from England. But Stan's work looks like gold here in this shit-Fest, and so did Kenneth's work—but there is also plenty of American-made shit here, we don't know where it came from and how it got into the Fest.

Hillary Harris is here, and John Whitney, otherwise no Am. Film-makers.

I don't know why I am writing these stupid facts here, in such a stupid way, because we are sitting here and eating, and this is no time to write letters and I do not like writing letters, I feel very stupid when I write letters—but we think that you must be anxious to know what is happening here—and so I am trying to do my best, because Barbara is sitting here and holding her "finger" at me, you better write a letter to N.Y., she says, you lazy "hypocrite," let them know what's going here—

(Barbara' s note:)
False!
It was a fork containing an enormous piece of meat and the statement was "you lazy—." To go into a little more detail, it was specifically (F.C.) not shown because of this Belgian law which was not stated in the applications you made out having any jurisdiction at an "Experimental (ESP) Festival." The judges here saw your film & the reaction was superb—blushing, red faces, delirium & came to the conclusion your film was not a film but a documentary. We will definitely have a screening, public one in Brussels, probably on January 3 & we will collect all information and send it to you. It is very sad that this festival which is supposed to be free & containing the most "new" & "different" etc. movies lacks depth, feeling & strength & that it has for the most part cockless, bigoted, sell-out people who make pretentious & outrageous statements like "I am a Marxist blah blah blah," "I believe in censorship & would you like to have films made on racism" (like one would say would you like your daughter to marry a nigger).
We are all running around & everywhere we enter a room everybody cringes HA! HA! HA! Sorry we couldn't show *Christmas* & hope everything is swinging & you did some great shootin'.

In Belgium they have a great law that everyone present at a screening illegal gets arrested & we are planning a Big Big screening (everyone seems to want to get arrested? Though we'll see when the time comes), Mr. Ledoux the head of the festival is a very good man & is helping us immensely as a matter of fact, he would love for this thing to blow up & when he showed the film to the jury he thought it would do good if we were raided & the jury was arrested. Unfortunately, being head of this festival he could not (for reasons we'll explain.) But I think he will be with us in Brussels perhaps in jail also.
Amos Vogel is "fighting" with us & brought applause with a very eloquent speech on "man's rights" & Jonas made every man at the conference take note literally & I don't think they will let him forget it, when he said, "It's on principle & I believe in liberty, justice—everything goes!" We are having daily screenings of *F.C.* Here & tomorrow we are having another press conference open to public & we will show *F.C.* Also there will be a chance that *F.C.* & all others will be shown at the Free University open to public in Brussels if not it will be shown elsewhere in Brussels.
Take care & we will try to keep you informed more often. Love to Stan, Bob, Ron, Amy, Francine, Jack, Jerry, Rene, Beverly, John, & all the other beautiful creatures,
Love & Kisses
Barbara
Jonas
P. A. Sitney

December, 1963
Everybody:
The fest ended in fiasco awards, although Americans got a good share. We'll stay in Brussels for two days, then we go to Paris. Barbara probably will stay in Europe, to work on the Exposition, to set up everything. We made many contacts for the

VARIETY, Dec. 11, 1963

LOCKED OUT, AWARD MADE ON CURB, 2 A.M.

Jack Smith, director of the New York avant-garde feature, "Flaming Creatures," was presented with Film Culture's annual award for his "most original contribution to the cinema" in an impromptu ceremony held on top of a car in front of New York's Tivoli Theatre at 2 a.m. Sunday (8) morning.

The open-air ceremony was necessitated when one of the co-owners of the Tivoli, ordinarily an Eighth Ave. nudie house, at the last minute cancelled Film Culture's midnight screening and award ceremonies, contracted for some days earlier. Concellation was explained by the fact that the picture has no N.Y. license, though one is not required for a private screening.

Ceremonies had attracted several hundred film buffs who, on arrival at the theatre, found themselves locked out. FC editor Jonas Mekas finally made presentation *sous marquee*.

N.Y. Post. Dec. 8

Jack Smith Gets Film Award

The Independent Film award goes to Jack Smith for his "Flaming Creatures," which will be entered at the Brussels Film Exposition late this month and at the International Film Exhibition of American Cinema in Amsterdam in January.

AMUSEMENTS

PRESS CONFERENCE

Date: Sunday, December 29th

Time: 1 p.m.

Place: SALLE DERRIERE LE MIROIR

Subject: THE WITHDRAWAL OF MR. JONAS MEKAS AS A JUDGE OF THE
PRESENT FILM COMPETITION

Mr. Jonas Mekas, who has withdrawn himself as a judge of the
Third International Experimental Film Competition, is holding
a press conference for the purpose of explaining his decision.

A propos his resignation, Mr. Mekas wishes raise in particular
the question of Belgian Law in relationship to the selection
and presentation rules of the International Experimental Film
Competition.

Film-makers and other interested persons are invited to
attend.

Knokke
December 30th 1963

Dear Jacques Ledoux:

I am handing to you the letters of Stan Brakhage, Stan Vanderbeek, Robert Breer, and Gregory Markopoulos, which delegate me to withdraw their films from the Festival. I hope you'll act accordingly to the wishes of the film-makers.

Our position is as follows:

Unless the decision of the selection committee of the 3rd Intern. Experimental film Competition, which states that the showing of the film "Flaming Creatures" is "impossible in regard to Belgian laws" is reversed and the film of Jack Smith treated equally with other films chosen by the committee as worthy of this Festival — in other words: unless the censorship is lifted from this festival, the film "Flaming Creatures" accepted into the Competition and shown publicly — the films of the above film-makers are being withdrawn from the Competition.

My own resignation as a judge at the Exposition I have already handed to you verbally shortly after my arrival at Knokke.

Jonas Mekas

Sur une nappe en papier, lettre de Jonas Mekas à Jacques Ledoux, annonçant la
décision de Stan Brakhage, Robert Breer, Gregory Markopoulos et Stan VanDerBeek de
retirer leur film de la compétition en cas d'exclusion de *Flaming Creatures*.

Exposition but it seems we'll have to arrive ahead of time to make various necessary arrangements. The case of *Flaming Creatures*, which went all over Europe, often on first pages, proves that we'll have troubles wherever we'll go, and we can't compromise ourselves, not after what we did and said in Brussels.

Fest refused to project *Flaming Creatures*. On the last day, we seized the projector, we held the projectionist, and we made an attempt to project the film ourselves. There was a big commotion, with Barbara mobilizing all the forces behind the projector, to defend the revolution. The Casino and Fest people mobilized their own resistance next to the light switch board. They disconnected the light. I was fighting a big bully man trying to force himself into the light room. House detectives came. The Minister of Justice was called and he held a speech promising to the people to change the law in Belgium concerning film censorship. Barbara kept shouting at him, and tried to project the film on his face, but the attempt failed. IN any case, it was a scandal. The press picked up the Minister's promises, and it seems that *Flaming Creatures* has accomplished in Belgium more than in New York, as far as the censorship goes.

I handed my own resignation as a judge immediately after my arrival. That's where everything started. From there on the fest became a suspense story, what's next. Moscowitz will probably be reporting this in detail in *Variety*. He thought it was one of the strangest and certainly historical festivals he ever attended. We held a huge press conference (Barbs, Sitney) with Paris, London, Berlin, etc. newspapers present, and we attacked the Belgian laws. We made several other attempts to smuggle *F.C.* into the projection room, to project it. Once I did it in a can of *Dog Star Man*. They discovered it just before it went on. The Second Festival opened in the basement

of our hotel where *Flaming Creatures* was screened at night to the people. Our hotel room, one night the audience consisted of Godard, Polanski, Agnés Varda, Marcorelles, etc., all crouched in the corners and on beds, just like at the Co-op screenings.

The films at the fest itself proved to be terrible, so nobody was really interested in the real fest.

Barbara became the main attraction of the festival. Ledoux said that she was the publicity trick of the New American Cinema. In any case, the New York cinema has boomed up tremendously and now everybody wants our Exposition show. There will be plenty to do after I come back. We'll need more money to bring here a few film-makers, maybe Brakhage, etc.

Stopped in London. Saw the theatre where *Hallelujah* is playing, a good snob place like Murray Hill, that type of crowd. The reviews were mixed. In Brussels they are all crazy about *Hallelujah*, they had a screening here at their film society, big success. Same in Paris, Marcorelles told me. It should do well at revival screenings, he thinks Brussels is boring. Leaving for Paris immediately.

I don't think I'll be writing before returning.

January 20, 1964

To Sitney and Barbara:

This will be a combined letter. Since you'll be working together, I feel I have to say certain things, and say them now, to avoid any confusion or misunderstanding later.

First, I ask both of you to be very very patient. I know you are. But both of you happened to have very different personalities. Both very obstinate. Both obsolutists. Both very self-confident. Very fanatic, in a sense. So you'll be clashing every day. Every time both of you will think that you are absolutely right. So please don't cut each other's throats. Because, looking from a third angle, you both are very needed, and most of the time you both are very right, although at two opposite ends. And either you manage somehow to combine the extremes for the growth and the good of the others, or the whole thing will be limping on one leg. I think, definitely, the Exposition needs P.A. Sitney's erudition and literary etc. knowledge, and also Barbara's blind and beautiful and unliterary and non-erudite idealism, which is an intelligence of a different kind.

By now it's clear that Brakhage won't be with you before the middle or even the end of February. That means, he will not be present at Munich, Brussels, and possibly Amsterdam shows. I don't see much possibility that any other film-maker from here will join you before that either. So the burden will be on you alone. So I want you to work out some kind of working understanding.

(...) We are having a meeting of film-makers on Wdn. night to discuss the Exposition and Brussels. I couldn't get them together for two weeks. But finally I gathered them together. I hope.

Jack is still shooting. He has one more day of shooting. It took him weeks to fix up his MOONLIGHT POOL. A fantastic set.

It was a really crazy week, really, two crazy weeks, since I came. Wherever we turned for money, we found nice words and nothing else. Meanwhile, the films were piling up in the labs. And Ron was crying. *Film Culture* got stuck in the bindery (N. 30 is still in the bindery, we can't buy it out). Telephone bills. And PA Sitney's desperate telegrams. Last Thursday, I gave up. What comes comes, I said. We divided our money in three parts, between Long John, Leslie and myself, and it came to a dollar each, and we said, let's see who will spend the money first. So Leslie went out and bought some coffee, and so his dollar went out. I threw out my own dollar through the window. Long John spent his on three bags of peanuts.

But things began changing on Friday. My old angel came back to town. I don't mean Angel Guardian—Barbara is my Angel Guardian & my love. I mean one of my money angels. So he saved us this time again. *Film Culture* will be getting out of the bindery next week, and I am getting some money for Jack, and just enough in time to get the prints from the labs to make today's shipment. Long John is running from lab to lab collecting prints, with post-dated checks. In any case, things are better than they were a few days ago. They will keep. They will keep improving, I know. We shouldn't worry, that's all. I was worrying too much, for a few days, that's why things stopped moving. Now I am giving myself and the film-makers and the Exposition into the hands of Fate, even if it be Fata Morgana.

You SHOULD FIND in one of the boxes Barbara's tapes and leaders. Also, printed materials & notes. Let me know if you need anything else.

It is a Spring day in NY today. The sun is rolling in the streets.

So this will be the end of my first letter to PAS & B.

Good Wind & Love

January 22, 1964

Dear Yoko Ono:

I received a mysterious telegram from Sogetsu which says: Prepared to Invite You Under Your Terms Wire the Availability.

I don't have the copy of the letter I wrote you. But I have no idea who or what Sogetsu is. Maybe I knew it, but my memory went blank.

The Exposition just opened last night in Munich, West Germany. Next it moves to Amsterdam, Stockholm, Wien, Rome, Madrid, Paris and London. We are heavily booked until at least end of July. It wouldn't be possible to go to Japan before middle of August. Just to be sure, we could plan Tokyo show last two weeks of August or first two weeks of September. The date could be left half-open, if possible. But it could also be set definitely, if needed. In that case it should be beginning September 1st.

We had so many expenses to get the show to Europe that we are completely broke. Forgive us, therefore, that we did not answer your telegram by telegram. We are saving money wherever we can.

Dear Yoko Ono: I hope your own life is going O.K.

Finally we got our own theatre in NY, where we can show movies or do whatever we want seven evenings a week. George will have his FLUXUS festival there in April or May. We are all excited about the things we can do now. There are many new films being made here. I saw the Japanese entries at the Brussels Film Exposition and they were BAD, really BAD. Sorry to say. Good intentions, but so derivative, and so heavy heavy heavy, and endddlessssss. The more reason to bring our Exposition to Tokyo.

I will be waiting to hear from you concerning all these matters—from you or whoever will take it from here on.

Luck—Greetings—& Love

January 23, 1964

Barbara Angel:

We had our meeting yesterday. Everybody was there, somehow. About thirty of us. I don't know how to tell you or what to tell you. It went the same way as it was all other times as far as I remember the meetings of film-makers. Everybody wanted to see Jack's new rushes. So we screened them. They were beautiful. Then we screened Genet's movie. It was beautiful. As long as there were movies. I asked for a quiet minute, and made an attempt to engage everybody into the Brussels and Exposition matters, and the Coop. I explained how necessary their presence in Europe is; I told that the Coop will do everything to help them to get to Europe. The only remark came from I don't remember whom, and it was "What about bringing European film-makers here, instead." Jack, meanwhile, got engaged into editing his film, in the corner; Jerry put on his coat and was leaving (I just caught him in the door, and he was in very bad shape, he said he can not concentrate to finish his movies, he has millions of feet but he has no place to edit. So I suggested Frances' place, and he said O.K. I was checking this morning with Frances again, if Jerry spoke to her; she was not in. I will try to arrange for Jerry to work in her studio. In any case, Jerry was happy to hear that he is needed in Europe etc.,etc., and said he will think, etc.,etc., but first is the movie.) Ron started talking about his own movie. A few left. Suddenly I felt that I was talking into an empty room, so I stopped, and I said: Oh, you have to finish your films first, anyway. Because, it became very clear, that whatever their films are, they are their real babies with which they are primarily concerned, and nothing else really matters. The next step for me was to forget group talks and just talk personally, one by one, as we are. That proved to be the only contact possible. Despite everything, they are very much concerned with the Exposition. I photostatted the newspaper clippings, and they were absorbed in them like children, almost like children, sorry to say.

I'll be having more smaller meetings, and more personal contact. To keep everybody informed about the Exposition and other matters, Coop, etc. we'll be mimeographing one sheet letter every week. So please, this goes for Paul and you, scribble a few notes, letters, which I will put into the newsletter, for everybody to read, just scribble down everything. This will be one of the ways of keeping us together and may be lifting everybody's spirit and moving everybody somewhere to some new planes. Everything counts at this moment.

FILMS | VIDEO | TV FILMS | RADIO | MUSIC | STAGE

VARIETY

PRICE
35¢

Published Weekly at 154 West 46th Street, New York, N. Y. 10036, by Variety, Inc. Annual subscription, $15. Single copies, 35 cents.
Second Class Postage Paid at New York, N.Y.
© COPYRIGHT, 1964, BY VARIETY, INC. ALL RIGHTS RESERVED

Vol. 233 No. 8 | NEW YORK, WEDNESDAY, JANUARY 15, 1964 | 72 PAGES

'FILM UNDERGROUND' EXPLOSION

BELGIANS BALK N.Y. 'CREATURES'

Knokke, Belgium, Jan. 14.
Belgium's "Experimental Film Festival" here last week refused to show a New York-made film of Jack Smith, "Flaming Creatures," on the grounds that the Americans were running experiment into the ground. Film is about guys who want to dress up like gals. It is plenty explicit. Some weeks ago the auspices rented the Tivoli Theatre on 8th Ave. in Manhattan for a post-midnight screening of the same film but the theatre cancelled at last minute.

"Flaming Creatures" divided the delegates, the critics and the Belgians. Comment ranged from terming the film a crude stunt, a stag film, a misnamed "artie." In any event the laws of the Kingdom of Belgium, a Catholic country, were invoked against it. This stirred a dispute led by Jonas Mekas, avante-gard film buff of Greenwich Village, who is chief spokesman for the so-called "New York Film Underground," now about to tour the capitals of Europe to show the continental brethren that Hollywood product is not all there is.

Mekas did what he could to dramatize a protest. He personally resigned from the festival jury. He tried to get the American contingent to withdraw all of their 47 films (shorts and features) on the fest schedule but the Belgians refused to release the films, the single largest registry of experi-

(Continued on page 15)

VARIETY

'Film Underground'
Continued from page 1

mental items. Failing his attempted boycott, Mekas unreeled "Flaming Creatures" in 16m version several times in his bedroom and once in the hotel auditorium. Thus practically anybody in attendance at the festival was able to see what the dispute was all about.

On the last evening, Mekas tried to take over the projector at the festival itself at end of the final official item. But a fest rep pulled out the projector plug. Followed a scuffle for it and much impassioned talk on "freedom of expression" by the Mekas group. It was believed the projectionist was fired for not trying to balk Mekas.

Finally, the Pre-Selection Committee put out a circular deploring the fact that this film could not be shown, reflecting on the liberty of expression in Belgium. It gave the film a special prize nod as the "Film Maudit" of the festival, literally the Damned Film of the Festival. It was felt a sufficient summing up of the affair.

Press and film people present were divided on the pic as was the jury, who also got a special screening. However many felt it was better than several shown and it should have been permitted with a special introduction to the general audience on what they were going to see.

And what was it finally? Smith had made a sort of high camp transvestite affair showing a group cavorting in a kind of 1920s setting. And the cavorting was seducing one woman among them, who was also somewhat hermaphroditic. There was manipulation of sex organs shown.

A sort of earthquake had Marilyn Monroe, played by a man, coming out of her coffin. General comment was that it was crude stunting and dull in spite of the carryings-on. On the "artistic" level there was perhaps the vamp feel of silent film days.

The undergrounders assert film is a pean to love and freedom. Consensus had it that it was too bad the film was not better done and more important to back the disagreement over "freedom."

Anyway, there was another pic in competition "Chumlum," of Ron Rice, that resembled "Creatures" curiously if genitals were covered.

The same transvestites were presented in latter film and rolled about frenzieldly. Pic had good color and some arresting compositions, if it all got repetitious.

One film by Kenneth Anger, "Scorpio Rising," was about black-jacketed American motorcyclists. It depicted them as budding bullies and Nazi types rather than criminally prone deliquents. It pictured some garish homosexual-like tussles. Also the holding of a sort of black mass. But no objections were aroused and it was felt an extremely well made individual film if not exactly experimental in nature. (Marlon Brando starred years ago in a motorcycle bums film, "The Wild One.")

Undergrounders own "Twice a Man," by Gregory Markopoulos, won a $2,000 prize. Mekas thinks uproar was worthwhile and that Belgian laws on film showings may be changed as a result.

He is now starting out on a tour of Europe to show the New York experimental film movement to European capitals.

THE NEW YORK DIARIES
1950–1969

For Jonas
David Pascal
Paris – La Coupole 1/64

Everything that will help us and others to grow and move ahead, out of the stale water in which we are now.

By now Paul must have received my telegram about Brussels. We felt, those few with whom I spoke, including Jack, that if Sitney gave his signature to Ledoux, we should not force or complicate matters further, this time. It is Sitney's mistake. But he would make another mistake if he would break his signature. That shouldn't be done. All we can do is avoid this in the future. NO shows in any place without *F.C.*, that is the simple rule. If they object, we move to another country. Or if there are ways of importing films without those ugly institutions, then a show or two could be arranged directly by you, in some rented place, Gallery, or no matter where. The problem here, I image, is the importing of films, the customs, bonds, etc. Whatever happens, we should remember that not the number of shows counts but how the shows are done. If we have properly done shows in three or four places in the whole Europe, that will be enough, the word will spread. That's why I will do everything to get a few film-makers to the Rome, Paris, and London shows. It is in those three places that we should concentrate without any compromises, even if they do not want us, we'll be there.

Brakhage called. His California engagement will keep him in LA until the 16th of February. He will not be in NY until the 17th or 18th.

Jack is shooting his last scene (he hopes) tonight. My Bolex is traveling constantly between Jack and Gregory, it proved to be a very useful camera. Gregory is in the middle of his *Prometheus*. I have no doubts at all, that after Ron finishes *Sheba* (he is working on it), and Jack finished *Love*, and they are working, although you can't push them, they will be ready for a change of air, and will join you. But it is almost useless, and it would be too disturbing to them, in the middle of their work, to plan any trips. We have to wait. The same with Jerry. Stan is the only one who seems to be ready and excited about it, at this moment.

We managed to get $100 for Kenneth Anger.

Ford Foundation became a big joke. After all the hopes and work, the NO answers began coming in yesterday. Gregory got NO. Jack got NO. Menken got NO. Mass got NO. I got NO. Boultenhouse got NO. There will be many more NOs. We have no idea who will get a YES, but it is a joke. So we can not depend on any businessmen.

A good news: I finally found a theater for us. On Christopher Street, near Hudson, two lofts on top of each floor. I am signing a contract in a day or two. We'll move out of Gramercy. We'll have daily screenings at the new place, on the ground floor, and we'll have a workshop for film-makers on the second floor. There are many ideas about what we can do there, everybody's excited.

Brussels, and the publicity about our Exposition is doing already its job here. 55th St. Playhouse came to the Coop yesterday, they are changing their policy, they want to become NY First Experimental Theater. Beginning Febr. 15, they will have weekly shows. Coop will prepare programs for them. First week *Twice A Man* with two Vanderbeeks; second week Robert Frank program; third week *Guns* and *Hard Swing* or something else; fourth week Ron Rice show; etc. etc. So with these films going UPTOWN (MIDTOWN), our Christopher Theatre can concentrate now just on the new, open to everybody, good or bad.

Sanders footage is still at the Coop, he disappeared, nobody can find him. I don't dare screen his original to look what he's got. Suddenly the place is too crowded with people. Naomi is cutting her negative here; and John is helping. Gregory just blew in (he spends more and more time here at the Coop, full of ideas); and a student (film) from Boston came two days ago and keeps doing things here and refuses to leave the place, is reorganizing things, wants to do something for filmmakers; Ken and Mel just left, they went to Bellevue hospital to visit, what's her name, the one who plays in *Normal Love*, with these red spots on her back, Miss Backus, I really forget her name right now —but she was committed by her mother to that inhuman place, for I don't know what reason, so Ken took a few pencils to her and colors;

So there we are
I have things to do, suddenly, and I have to end my letter here.
Please show this letter to PA Sitney, it was intended so.
I will drop you a shorter note soon, angel
My love to you, angel love

P.S. for Sitney:
I thought you should know this. I called Kathy, because she hasn't picked up any of your letters. She said, she can't pick them up because she is afraid, she has a block. I spoke with her for a few minutes, but it was of no use. That was about a week ago. I don't know what's wrong with her. I think she is simply silly. But what can you do about it. I don't know. I don't know what to do about that block. PAS: I don't think you should break your heart about that. Have a good time in Europe. Kathy will be here, exactly as she is, when you return. Nothing drastic will happen. So just proceed with your life, with the sails wide open, etc. etc., just as the old man said…

January 25, 1964
A COMBINED LETTER TO P.A.S. AND BARBARA:
Just received your (Paul) disturbing letter (and disturbed). A few things must be immediately clarified. Because the Exposition cannot be and should not be (although it can be) left hanging in the air. I wouldn't have started it if I'd thought that it is just a child's play. Exposition is important for the American and European film-makers, and we have to go ahead with it. (…) Don't blame Barbara for everything. It is very important to consolidate the viewpoints of both of you, one or other way. Because both of you are from the same generation, and you cover two completely different grounds, and they happened to be both very very important. Both viewpoints, Paul's and Barbara's, are exaggerated by idealism, but that has to be so, there is nothing without passion. But let's not be so unununderstanding, or so fanatic, that you begin to harm each other, that the work stops in a dead spot, each of you pulling it to your own, and only your own direction. No one direction is answer to everything, as you very well know. Important things, that should guide you, is your own honesty (but not obstinacy).
EZRA POUND: (CONFUCIUS): "Only the most absolute sincerity under heaven can effect any change. (…) The archer, when he misses the bullseye, turns and seeks the cause for the error in himself."
TO BARBARA: Please, do not misunderstand me. It is easy sometimes to exaggerate one detail and to miss the whole; although I happened to be with you, in your unending idealism and search for honesty, the search for honesty and non-compromising should never become a blind fanaticism, which, at moments, I have noticed in your words and actions and reactions. I know that fanaticism has also a function, and I am acting myself very often fanatically.
I have to interrupt my letter here.
A telephone call just came. Ron Rice was committed to Bellevue. He went there to visit Diane, who was committed to Bellevue three days ago, and pulled out his camera, and started shooting. Guards converged on him trying to get the camera

PRECISION FILM LABORATORIES, INC.

Telephone: JUdson 2-3970

21 WEST 46TH STREET
NEW YORK 36, N. Y.

Sold to
KEN JACOBS OF FILMMAKER'S CORP
414 PARK AVE SO.
NEW YORK, NY

Ship to

.00T

LAB. ORDER NO.	DATE RECEIVED		CUSTOMER'S ORDER NO.		INVOICE NO.	INVOICE DATE	TERMS	JN CODE
U 2273	12/12/63		PREC. ORDER		2356	12/12/63	NET CASH	2

QUANT.	UNIT FTGE.	TOTAL FTGE.	UNIT PRICE	DESCRIPTION	CODE	TOTAL
				'BLONDE COBRA'		
1 3/4 REELS			35.00 EA	RERECORDING	115	61.25
						61.25S
			4 %	NYC ST		2.45
						63.70T

Received Payment

DEC 15 1963

PRECISION FILM LABS., INC.

Paid with Coop check 371

All orders for printing are accepted by us on condition that the dupe negatives made by us shall at all times be our property and remain in our possession. IT IS AGREED that any film delivered to us, for any purpose, is held by us for accommodation of the customer and solely at his risk and that we shall not be liable for any damage, destruction or loss of any such film, regardless of the causes for same. If any motion picture film, negative or positive, is damaged, destroyed or lost in our laboratory through our negligence, it is understood that our liability is limited to the replacement of such film with new raw stock and that we assume no other liability, either expressed or implied, and provided the customer furnish us with written notice of claim within 30 days after knowledge of loss or damage.

FORM P128A 1/63 MP

At Overseas Press Club, New American Cinema Group announces Traveling Film Exposition. Top: George Fenin, P. Adams Sitney, Andy Warhol, Ron Rice, myself. Bottom: Unidentified, Stan Vanderbeek, Jack Smith, George Fenin, P. Adams Sitney.

from him. He refused. I don't know all the details but he was put under observation for I don't know how long. I just called a lawyer, we are going to the hospital right now. So I end here.

Love and Kisses

January 28, 1964

To Barbara and Sitney:

Just a short note: Concerning the purposes & nature of the Exposition. This is just to make my position clear, or clearer, if possible.

I say again, as I have said many other times before, that the purposes and nature of the Exposition should be left open, undefined, ready to take any route at any time. I am really tired of accusations, or whatever you call them, that I am avoiding or I don't know what, to define the aims of the Exposition; or that I am confused about it, etc. because it is all TRUE. Because that's how it should be, as far as I can see any truth. Because this is not the moment (or times) to be too sure about anything. Too many preconceptions, definitions, too many "sure" and "certain" people with too many "sure" ideas about things. Exposition can never be something "agreed." It has to search for its own life. Whatever I say now from NY or whatever any film-maker says from NY, can be changed according to the local necessities right there, by you. At this moment, Exposition IS YOU, whatever you are. It will change and it will be as alive only as you yourselves change and are alive. Don't look back at NY or me now, although do not lose us from your minds and hearts.

February 5, 1964

Dear Barbara:

We have a beautiful Spring day in NY so I said I will sit down and will write a short letter to my angel guardian who is keeping her eye on me. I just had a long walk, and it is warm and beautiful.

To bring you up-to-date:

Ron is out of Bellevue. They kept him there only for a day. They realized they made fools of themselves. But it was an ugly experience for Ron and for me. I went next day to get him out and had to listen to all the crap.

Jack did more shooting in his Moonpool, but he still has more to do. He has piles of new material. He is going his own speed. He planned to finish shooting last night, but then he said he had cold. One of those psychological colds.

We had a screening of *FC* last Monday at the Gramercy (without Love & Kisses cards) and a huge crowd showed up. No troubles yet. We are repeating the program next Monday, by which time the cops may be there.

Naomi is still busy with her negative cutting. She keeps losing pieces, and has a hell of a time, keeps crying, I don't know what to do. Frances screened her first print of *Body Trap* yesterday, and it looks like a movie, a small movie.

Ron spent all the $400 that I got for him to finish *Sheba*, he spent it on I don't know what, and has not a single penny left, and *Sheba* is as unfinished as before. Next time I will be smarter. I will keep money and will pay his bills. But I don't know when that next time will be. Some money I expect in a long run, later, but at this time the situation remains VERY bad. Some of my hopes did not come true. So all last week, I have been having screenings in various private homes around the Park Ave screening *Genet* (there is a tremendous interest in the film here, and it is a beautiful film), trying to raise money. Collected a few pennies, just enough to pay for Jack's rushes. A few larger checks are coming later this or next week. I will have to save for Stan's expenses.

We lost our Christopher St. place, about which I wrote you: Fire Department objected.

Saw Debbie. She was happy with your gift. And so was Barney (how do you spell?) with hers. Debby is still out, but she has to go back to Hillside Hospital next week. These are her last days out, for some time. We are planning to go out shooting snow tomorrow, upstate, if we get the car. I was shooting last weekend, in Springfield, but the camera I was using was defective (my Bolex is still with Jack) and all footage was ruined. So I am still far from the end with my *Haikus*.

So much on things and friends.

I hope you are not too angry with me for my previous letters concerning the Exposition etc.—I had to put everything, or as much as I could at that time, on paper, even if with mistakes. PAS wrote me about your fights in Munich—I mean, your brave fights with bureaucrats, etc., and he seemed to be very proud of you. So am I, angel. Don't think that I don't trust you. I trust you, angel. You know that I am not for perfection. Even if sometimes I become too strict, I try, immediately, to loosen myself out of the strictures. Sometimes I fail. But you are my constant reminder, your passion and your idealism, and your love. On the very end, we seek perfection, but perfection of ourselves.

Telephone keeps ringing, interrupting me every two minutes.

Adrienne sends her regards. She comes every Monday to the Gramercy. Just returned from Canada, and is blooming.

Milton Sperling hasn't been in town for weeks, since December. We keep checking with his hotel and they keep telling that he is coming soon. Nobody knows where he is. People are around me, and I can't type anymore. So here I end.

No date, 1964

Dear Jack,

I never expected this from you. I used to defend you with my nails and teeth when anyone said anything bad about you.

"Jack is the only one among the film-makers who never asked anything and did not expect anything." Therefore you were given everything, more than any other film-maker. At the time when Coop was doing very badly, during the shooting of *Normal Love*, it picked up every one of your bills for *Normal Love*, a good $2,000 in bills, without complaining, so that you could finish the film in peace. What it meant is me running around, persuading, collecting penny by penny, to pay your bills. Much of it I still owe to people, I took personal loans. I believed in you as a man and as an artist.

Until yesterday. You still remain a great artist, but I cannot have any respect for you as a man. You became, suddenly, as small as the rest. Petty, mistrusting, mistrusting me, the Coop, and your own luck. Accusing, where there is nobody to accuse. Making a big business of something where there is no business at all.

More than that. It became very clear suddenly that all the publicity, praises and assistance given to your work made you vain and demanding, it made you feel that you are the favorite and better than others. Instead of remaining humble and concentrating on your creative work, you became demanding, exploiting the goodness of the people who were helping you —helping not because they have money to throw away but because they liked your work. But now you are beginning to act like a pampered baby.

Isabel came to help you not from the great abundance of her money; she came to your help against the advice of her very husband, she is helping you with her own money. And you are playing a big man: everybody should help me! Fuck you, Jack. You forget that there are other film-makers who need help even more or at least as much as you; there is Gregory, and there is Stan, and there is Kenneth, and there is Jerry, and there are others.

I know I have made blunders myself. Coop was and still is a new and strange, not of this world, and as long as it does some good it should continue. It helped to bring us all together; it helped to complete a number of our movies; it did some other things. For you to come to the Coop and spout and shout and say very silly and thoughtless things is not helping the things in any way. And I really think it was stupid, and I thought it was my duty to tell you so.

February 12, 1964

A letter to Naomi Levine which I intend not to send but I may decide to send it out before I finish it. Anyway, it's all about everything, but specifically, it's about sort of a day in my life, which usually goes something like this:

8 AM, a beautiful morning. I go to the Co-op. Have a peaceful work on my movie until 9:30 AM at which time telephone begins to ring. Sherman is on the phone. Wants two programs of movies for the 55th St. Playhouse. I work on the program for 15 minutes. Then I go back to my editing table. 10:30. Louise comes. I stop working on my film. McCall calls. Needs stills from *Sleep*. Spend 15 minutes searching for one. Go back to editing. Joel comes. For an hour he talks about the trouble with Jack & crowd and money problems and *F. Creatures*. Have to listen. Promise to do something about it. Ron Rice calls. Needs money to finish *Sheba*. Needs tape recorder. I spend an hour on phone calling people for money and tape recorder. Another hour is spent on letters to Guggenheim about money for Jack's movie. Materials prepared. Joel and X. came. Again talks and complains about money, and troubles. Have to listen. Have to make peace. Stanley brings Jack's footage to develop. Gregory comes. Making calls to the labs to check Naomi's job. Someone calls, wants to "get into movies," a student. 15 minutes wasted. Again, calling Peter

and Robert arranging a screening at his place to raise money for the film-makers. Too tired. Going out for a walk. Had no time to touch *Haikus*. Gramercy owner calls. Complains about the theatre, we left it dirty, he says, etc. 15 minutes trying to quiet him down. He says Ken ruined the cooling system, left it running. The owner wants 300 dollars. Don't know what to say. I hang up.

I better stop right here. Because there is no end. Now, you remember, the day before, when I managed to make only five splices before noon and another five splices in the afternoon. Plus I had to run messages for you to the lab. And next morning too. And then, you left your "footage" and just asked me to "rush it" to the lab, you didn't even say anything about who will pay for it, you took it for granted that I WILL HAVE TO PAY for you, as if that were my duty or obligation. You took it for granted, without asking me if I had money. And then you shout that it's not ready, and etc. etc.—so I am beginning to ask if I am still sane. It's possible that I am mad. What is happening, what I am doing in all this mess of boorish impolite unmannered people, entangled in this insane net of egoists, and with no way out and with no more time for myself? It's not enough that I never ask anything from anybody for myself; not enough that I give all my days to others, with no energy left for myself, when the night comes —nothing is enough. A bunch of babies, that's what you are!

I really don't know why I am doing all this. Maybe, because somewhere deep I don't believe that people can be so inconsiderate. Here I am, like a rug on which they can step. It's all useless and senseless, whichever way you look at it, but sometimes it is sad, and I want to leave everything and run away and disappear. But then, again, I say, but who am I? Why should I be so proud about my own destiny? Because, who really does know one's

... there were also some lonely days at the Coop...

real destiny? It would be too pompous and too selfish, to run away. So I stay here and do what I am doing, even under these crazy conditions and act as the sounding board and the spittoon and the rug and the beggar for money, and the bank, and the judge, and the peacemaker, and the silent idiot, and a confession booth, and a "critic," and the scapegoat, and the dirt collector, vacuum cleaner, and often the dirt itself—I don't know what I am any longer. So forgive me, Naomi, that I sometimes fail you, and I fail many others, but it is really too much sometimes, and too confusing. I don't even know, often, which is the right direction, so I go blindly, going by the wind and the intuitions.

But it is late now and I am trying to clear my mind which was sort or more upset than usually and more drained out, and I want to go back and do some work at my editing table, for myself, before the night is over, to do something for myself, for a change; what a thought and what a temptation and what rare happiness: to do something for myself!

Goodnight then, good people.

I still don't know if this letter is really for you, Naomi, or it is just for myself, but I'll leave that undecided until tomorrow, I'll leave that to the fates to decide, they will take care of me—[The letter was sent.]

February 14, 1964

PAS:

Enclosed $150, of which $125.00 is loan returned. I will be speaking with Stan this afternoon, L.A., I will know more about his situation.

Are you alone in Amsterdam? I haven't heard from Barbara for ages, no idea where she is, or what address to write. I wrote to her Paris address.

When does Amsterdam start?

What program?

I will know about Storm's film only on Monday, will she make it or no. When does the show in Amsterdam end? When is the last deadline for Storm? I don't think there will be anything else ready. Storm can make it if it's very end of February.

Jack, finally, finished his shooting, after many heartbreaks, psychological sicknesses, emotional disasters, wars, breakdowns, storms, etc. etc. etc.—it's fantastic what it involves for Jack to shoot just one single scene, all that emotional etc. turmoil and the tears of an army of creatures. They keep coming here to me to the Coop to complain or to vomit their hearts out.

Anyway, Jack called early this morning (7:30 AM) to ask where he could find an editing room. So it sounds OK. Last three days he was hiding, sick.

Ron is hopeless. We had a benefit screening for him, really, two screenings. And *Sheba* looks great. I even got him $400 to finish editing. But he spent all the money, and did not do anything on film. Now he promises to finish it in two weeks, but I don't believe him any longer. He wants to go to Mexico. He has no intention of going to Europe though.

I still have more work to do on *Haikus*. I was interrupted by a new issue of *FC* (send please any materials, and soon, I still have one week time; notes on European experimental cinema etc.)—but I am very close. I may make Stockholm.

NO NEW FILMS OF ANY INTEREST

Fifty-Fifth St. Playhouse is opening now as an Experimental Film Theatre. We are doing programming. Every program will run a week. It's opening with *Breathdeath* and *Twice a Man* on 21 Feb, Friday. Big day for GJM. Week after that *Totem* and *Guns*. After that, Brakhage program. Etc. Not much money ($200 per week) but new possibilities, new public, national and international interest—in any case, a very important development.

This Tuesday we are starting a new showcase at the Poets Theatre, 4 St. Mark's Pl., every Tuesday and Wednesday night, and we are opening with a new epic by Warhol-Mead-Naomi, *Tarzan and Jane Sort Of*, a feature, sometimes good sometimes very bad. So now the city is full of exper. movies. What about collecting materials in Europe for a huge special issue of *FC*: EUROPEAN EXPERIMENTAL CINEMA ISSUE etc.? Engage good people in each country for articles, materials, filmographies, etc. —a huge job but could be very important. NOVELLLLL?

Did I tell you that *Sleep* must be accompanied by soft radio music?

I am making prints of Vernon Zimmerman's *Lemon Hearts* and *Scarface* and *Afrodite* for the Exposition. Will be ready for Stockholm. You don't have to show (if time limit exists) but they will be there. Hulten likes his films.

THIS IS VERY IMPORRRTANNNTTT:

I really can't read your LONGHAND. You scribble like a hen. Terrible. We couldn't figure out half of your letter. Try to get a typewriter whenever you can.

We have been running *FC* at the Gramercy for three Mondays now. It is old stuff, no one even blushes. But we still expect cops. If they come, we'll throw them out. *FC* "censorship" angle shouldn't be stressed without a need. It's only a movie like any other.

I have to end my letter here, because it's middle of day and there is too much business going here around the table.

February 23, 1964

New York Darkness
PAS:

Yr last letters (2) did not sound too happy. Don't let yrself be beaten by bureaucrats and ignorance. You will find much of it in the small countries. The smaller they are the bigger they think they are. Anyway, expect more troubles in other small towns. Don't worry too much about disorganization, incomplete shows, etc. As long as we can make a small dent into their ignorance, it's already a victory. I think we should concentrate our forces and energy only in the largest places, like Rome, Paris and London. Other cities will be only in-between stops. I don't think it's worth energy and nerves to fight all the ignorance: it will go away by itself some day. All we can do is try, and try hard. And you are trying hard.

I hope you received my check. There will be more money coming sometime very soon. If you have to pay yourself for some screenings, if nobody wants our movies —hire somebody to help you and screen— if it's within your physical reach.

(Gregory is sorry that he wrote about your "great sorrow" again, from Toledo. I just asked him if he wants anything to say, he just came in.

I still did not hear from Barbara—since she left Munich for Oberhausen. She must be very angry or "disappointed" with me, no doubt, probably I "betrayed her" or something, she thinks, which is all wrong because I never really betray my friends. There are plenty of misunderstandings that surround her, and I understand it, because she has her own world which is so strong that it is very difficult for her to understand other people's worlds, and it's ok as long as love remains in the world— Spoke with Stan, long distance. He is going (from L.A.) back home and he will be there for a week or so. Then he will start moving slowly towards NY, with wife, children, and everything. He said he has part II and III almost finished and all he wants now is to WORK, and he is coming to NY to work because he can't work there any longer, and he said he would prefer to stay in NY and work because he is in a working mood and he said he would go to Europe only if it was a very very urgent need. So I said to him, to make films is more important than to show them, no matter where or how, and that he should work on his films. So he was very much relieved. I alarmed

Gregory Markopoulos filming *Galaxy*, at the Coop, with my second Bolex.

Author with Nena von Schlebrügge in a Happening by Salvador Dalí. Filmed by Peter Beard, 1964.

everybody here to look for a place for him. I think I found one for $30 a month! On 12th st east, I am checking tomorrow.

What all this means is that Stan will not be able to join you in Europe, and that you'll have to continue pushing the SHOW with your own shoulders. My own plans are to come to Europe in April, for the Rome show, stay for Cannes Fest. (I will have a special show there, four programs, of NAC) and go with you to Paris and London. By the way, do you have anything definite in Rome? If not, I will try to do something about it.

Jack is editing *Normal Love*, but I don't know when he will have it ready. When he finishes *N.L.* I will ship him to Europe. He wants to go to Tangier, where Angus with Frances (Stillman) went (last week). Ron is—finally—working again on *Sheba* and he promises to have it in three weeks. I managed to get $600 for him for finishing work. I am a little bit closer to *Haikus*, I made sound transfers and I may have it in two-three weeks, but I am constantly being interrupted by other matters. We were thrown out of Gramercy, and we have police summons for showing unlicensed movies, etc., so I had to move fast to get another place, which we got, as you can see from the other side of this page, our new HQ.

Everybody on your list received Brakhage book.

I still didn't receive anything mimeographed from Ledoux, I mean, yr notes. Nothing.

What did you say about a new print of *Prelude*? Confirm.

Did you put a leader in the beginning of *Creatures*? It was eaten up a little bit, the beginning.

February 28, 1964

PAS:

Answer, point by point (I have a copy of the letter):

1. What is the situation in Rome? Anything definite? It's important to know. If nothing is set, I'll see what I can do about it.

2. Did you have any further correspondence with Spain? It may not be worth involving oneself with Spain. It may be better to concentrate on Paris London Rome. Unless you feel like seeing Spain. And unless they are taking the show seriously. When they were here, at the Coop, that time, they said they will show only the most innocent old movies.

3. While in London, check the Contemporary Arts Museum. It may be a good place for the show. They wrote inquiring about *Twice a Man*.

4. Don't rely too much on Solomon. He is OK but he is too much of a wheeler-dealer and his reputation in better places is not too high. He is good for the middle-areas. The trouble with him, really, is that he (on the very end) thinks only about himself, how to promote his own plans.

Sheba and *Pasty* in editing.

You will not believe, but between my *Haikus* and new issue of *FC* and etc. I managed to squeeze in a whole feature length movie. I saw the closing night of *The Brig*, and I decided to shoot it as a newsreel, cinéma-vérité movie. Next day I got the equipment, film, and I shot the whole thing, I have two hours long movie which I have to trim to 75 min, and it is a brutal piece. I shot it during the performance, with three cameras, changing one after another, without a stop, practically. I was walking with my camera and sound recorder on my back (I recorded sound directly on film) on the stage, I never left the stage—I covered the performance like a news reporter would, and it was the most exhausting evening of my life.

The Brig
Production Expenses

I.
FIRST STAGE: SHOOTING

equipment rental	$184.96
film stock 16 mm 2 hours	$489.44
striping (magnetic)	$107.64
protection sd track	$15.00
insurance of equipment	$20.00
developing & one print (optical)	$467.36
coding (edge numbering)	$42.75
transportation	$10.00
total:	$1,337.15

The film was shot with three Auricon cameras, "single" system (sd recorded directly on film, magnetic); protection sound was recorded separately with a Wollensack & one steady overhead mic; two hours of footage was shot. By the end of the first stage, we had one positive print with sd on film (optical) ready for projection and we did so at the New Bowery Theatre the day after shooting.

II.
SECOND STAGE: EDITING & BLOW UP

titling	$49.92
editing (moviola & space one month)	$300.00
sound (mixing, transfers, stock, transfer of both from film, and the protection tape) sd tracks	$914.67
to magno lab work (includes one answer print in 35 mm and one release print in 35 mm & negative splicing)	$770.45
blowing up from 16 to 35 mm	$2000.00
total:	$4,035.04

CHAPTER FIFTEEN

... Why FM Coop refuses licensing films... Summons issued to the Coop... Confusing laws... A letter to Naomi re. my average day at the Coop... Facts on seizing of *Flaming Creatures, Un Chant d'Amour,* and my arrest... Notes for TINA's film... Letter from Sartre... On Courts and Lawyers ... On censorship... A letter to Sitney on Brakhage, Markopoulos... Suggestions from Ginsberg... Notes on *Flaming Creatures*... Coop wall bulletins re. censorship... Women and *Flaming Creatures*...

WHY FILM-MAKERS' CO-OP DOESN'T LICENSE ITS FILMS
Film-Makers' Cooperative had some previous conversations with the Division of Motion Pictures. A letter was written to Louis Pesce in which Film-Makers' Co-op explained that the Co-op screenings were primarily of workshop character. At least two-thirds of the films at the Gramercy and later the New Bowery were screened in their unfinished versions, with soundtracks on separate tapes, etc., the purpose of that screenings being to raise money for the film-makers to finish the films. This is the only way the independent—avant-garde—film-maker can continue his work. Further, most of the films being short, and the minimum fee for licensing a short film being $3.50, the Co-op felt, and it was explained to the Division of Motion Pictures, that besides our objection to licensing on principle, it would be financially impossible, since that would come to approximately $30 expense per evening, a sum which would make the screenings impossible to continue. We felt, and still feel, that the Film-Makers' Cooperative shows, being primarily workshop screenings, should be beyond the "business" of laws.

A FEW FACTS ON THE TWO SUMMONS INVOLVING LICENSES
On March 17, the City Department of Licenses issued summons to Ken Jacobs for "Violating of the administrative code." The program was two Japanese experimental films, programed by the Film-Makers' Cooperative for the Theatre for Poets, at the New Bowery Theatre.

On March 18 for the same program (as above) of March 17, the summons were issued by Louis Pesce, director for the State Division of Motion Pictures, to Ken Jacobs and to the Film-Makers' cooperative "for exhibition of an unlicensed motion picture in public place of amusement for pay."

No tickets were sold that evening. There was nobody by the door. However there was a box near the door that said "contribute to the anti-censorship fund."

THE CITY SHOULD GIVE THE FILM-MAKERS A BUILDING FOR A THEATRE

The Group now feels that the best solution to all our exhibition problems would be to have an auditorium of our own, a small theatre where the independent film-maker could show his work to the interested audiences and exhibitors, stir interest, and generate more creativity in the low budget cinema. It is clear from past experiences that a commercial theatre, even if we leave the legal problems out, even one with the best of intentions, cannot give the film-maker the necessary freedom he needs.

This city should give the film-makers one of its old or unused buildings for this purpose. Rental expenses being free, film-maker could afford to show his films free, and thus avoid all the complications involved with the paid and public screenings. Ideally, such a showcase should have 100–200 seats and be equipped with 8 mm, 16 mm and 35 mm projectors. It could be operated very inexpensively and with complete independence. It would serve as a workshop-showcase for independent film-makers. In England, this work is done by the British Film Institute; in France by the Cinémàtheque Française. Both institutions are sponsored by the city municipalities.

ANOTHER PROPOSAL:
THE LAW SHOULD BE EXPLAINED

Perhaps under the guidance of the office for Cultural Affairs a series of discussions between the film-makers and the Department of licensing, and the Division of Motion Pictures could be organized, to discuss the laws involved. I have spoken to other film-makers, and I have found that neither myself nor they knew what this is all about; what is the real law here and what is not. There must be meetings held and the Film-Makers' Cooperative is ready to assist here, so that film-makers could ask questions and could get the right answers. At this moment, and I say this with true knowledge of the situation, the law is not known to film-makers. Both the laws and the people are operating in confusion, not knowing each other. The situation being as it is, the law cannot blame people for breaking it: the City and the State did not inform the people, or didn't inform them properly about the nature of those laws in the first place.

"This rapid domestication of the outrageous is the most characteristic feature of the artistic life, and the time lapse between shock received and thanks returned gets progressively shorter. At the present rate of taste adaption, it takes about seven years for young artist with a streak of wildness in him to turn from enfant terrible into elder statesman—not so much because he changes, but because the challenge he throws to the public is so quickly met. So then the shock value of many violently new contemporary style is quickly exhausted. Before long, the new looks familiar, then normal, and handsome, finally authoritative."—Leo Steinberg, "Contemporary Art and the Plight of Its Public"

No date, 1964

To P.A. Sitney

Good-Bye and *Haikus* may be ready for Amsterdam. Others not certain yet. I'll keep you informed about it. If I dig out any new film-makers you've never heard about, don't be surprised.

WHAT IS THE PROGRAM AT MUNICH? Let Munich show be test program for ourselves, concerning the length of programs, timing, order of films. A few things are sure:

– Brakhage films, or Menken, or Breer etc. must stay together, without interspersing anybody else's work in between. That is the only way of getting into the style and world of those film-makers.

STATE OF NEW YORK
EDUCATION DEPARTMENT
DIVISION OF MOTION PICTURES
STATE BUILDING, 80 CENTRE ST.
NEW YORK 13, N. Y.

TM 3443
Serial No.
(16mm-gauge)

ORIGINAL LICENSE

FILM-MAKERS' COOPERATIVE ....is hereby granted a license,

pursuant to the provisions of article 3 of the State Education Law and the Rules of the Board of

Regents adopted thereunder, for the exhibition of one print of a motion picture entitled

HENRY GELDZAHLER   (SILENT)

made and produced by.....ANDY WARHOL...and

consisting of....1,186.............feet of film, for and in consideration of the required license fee duly

paid in the amount of $.7.00.................... .

The Division reserves the right to revoke this license.

STATE EDUCATION DEPARTMENT
DIVISION OF MOTION PICTURES

DEC 22 1964

....
Date of issue

Director

It is necessary to preserve this certificate.

Form 2. Mp72-562-9000 (2A4-37)

- Gregory's unchanged position: *Blue Moses* and *Twice a Man* must be shown together.
- Low radio must be played with *Sleep*, which if projected 16 frames per second runs 6 hours, and if regular speed, 4 hours.
- Jack's unchanged position: NO *Cobra* with *FC* but OK *Scotch Tape*.

A FEW FACTS ON THE SEIZING OF *FLAMING CREATURES*

The screening of *Flaming Creatures* took place at the New Bowery Theatre on March 3. The theatre was leased by The American Theatre For Poets Inc., a foundation. Film-makers' Cooperative was asked to prepare a film program for the Theatre for Poets. Profits from screenings were split between the foundation and the Film-Makers' Cooperative (the film-makers). The Cooperative asked Ken Jacobs to be the projectionist at the New Bowery screenings: Florence Karpe was asked to take care of the contributions; Jerry Sims was asked that event to help at the door. All decisions concerning the screening and hirings came from the Film-Makers' Cooperative, through Jonas Mekas, who is the President of the New American Cinema Group and who is on its advisory board for the Film-Makers' Cooperative.

Under the instructions of the Theatre for Poets Foundation, the entrance was by "contribution $1.25" Those who did not have money, or not enough money, were allowed to go in free, or contribute what they wanted. The screening of *Flaming Creatures* was announced in the *Village Voice* as "a surprise program," with quotes from Dalí and Jonas Mekas, without mentioning the title of the film. Outside the theatre, there was a sign: "Tonight flaming surprise program."

The program was repeated two Tuesdays under the same conditions. The district attorney detectives saw the program on Tuesday, February 25. Tuesday, March 3, the detectives sat through the first screening and seized the film just before the second screening. Florence Karpe was arrested as "ticket seller"; Jerry Sims as "ticket taker"; Ken Jacobs as "projectionist"; Jonas Mekas as "distributor of obscene films." Jonas Mekas was not present at the screening. He arrived immediately after the arrest of the others, and asked to be arrested as the one responsible for the screening. The projector, the screen, the rushes (print) from Jack Smith's new film, *Normal Love*, and a newsreel on the shooting of *Normal Love* by Andy Warhol, were also seized by detectives.

The four were taken to the 9th precinct, fingerprinted, booked, and jailed. Next day they were photographed, taken to the Criminal Court, and charged with section 1141 of the Penal Code (showing and distributing "obscene" films). Upon the request of Jack Perlman, Cooperative's attorney, the four were released without bail. The trial was set for April 6th.

Flaming Creatures is one of the films distributed by the Film-Makers' Cooperative, 414 Park Avenue South, NYC.

FACTS ON THE SEIZING OF JEAN GENET FILM

Jean Genet's film, *Un Chant D'Amour* was given to the Film-Makers' Cooperative by Genet to help raise money for independent avant-garde film-makers in New York.

Knowing, that the film may be considered obscene by the New York police, Cooperative kept the film out of the public screenings. However, a number of people, admirers of Genet's work, mostly theatre people, expressed their interest to see the film, for private and professional reasons.

Two invitation screenings were arranged at the Writer's Stage, an Off-Broadway theatre. People were invited by telephone calls only. There was no advertising of any kind and no signs posted, not even at the theatre. Before each of the screenings, Jonas Mekas made the announcement that the film may be considered obscene by the N.Y. police, and those who did not wish to participate in something that may be considered a crime, could leave the theatre before the film was projected. No one left the theatre.

There was no admission charge. There was a box on the chair, with a sign next to it saying "Tonight's screening by free contribution to the anti-censorship fund," signed by the Film-Makers' Cooperative. Pierre Cottrell, a French film critic who came to see the film, offered himself to keep the eye on the box, which kept falling off the chair. However, he came to the box only a few times during the evening. Some contributed, some walked in for free.

Since the intention of the detectives was to incriminate the Cooperative on the grounds of "charged admission," and since the attempts to incriminate failed at the entrance, they tried once more on their way out. One of the detectives came to Pierre Cottrell, and, offering him a $2.00 bill, asked what should he contribute. Cottrell told him it was up to him what he wanted to contribute. The detective gave him $2.00 and said something like "Two dollars will do?" to which Cottrell answered something like: "Two dollars could be average contribution, that's what others gave." Upon which the detective showed his badge and charged Cottrell with selling $2.00 tickets.

The film, the projector, the screen were seized; Jonas Mekas (who projected the film) and Pierre Cottrell were arrested, taken to the 9th Precinct, fingerprinted, booked and jailed. Next day they were taken to the criminal court, and charged with Section 1141 of the criminal code. Both were let out on bail, $1,500 each, with trial set for April 13.

No date, 1964

I tell you to spy. Steal the knowledge, if needed—it belongs to no man: it's God's—and distribute it thru the nations.

Filmed with my Bolex in 1963:
Naomi Levine, *Yes*
Christmas on Earth
Ming Green
Walden
Normal Love
some of *Iliac Passion*
some of *Galaxy*

TINA'S SELF-EDUCATION (for the *Diary* film)
She sees the blackness of the city, that there is nothing in its essence that could help her to be happy, and that she has to build a center of light in herself and begin to change the city.

She is crossing the street with two other girls. They notice a strange girl, much smaller, standing and crying, nobody pays her attention.

They walk for a while, then they turn back and go to the crying girl and try to find out what it's all about. The street is dark, shadowy, busy. A few bums.

Nothing really works. Tina suddenly has inspiration. She says, let's go, I know a nice place—and they all run to a street next to them, where there is a backyard—and it's fantastic, the sun is falling brightly on a green tree, and a red flower, a real flower. She shows the flower to the girl, they touch it, they look at it, gently, and they forget everything else. The girl stops crying. She says, there was no real reason, only that she was afraid.

They take her back. They walk all four hand in hand, with their faces lit and bright and bravely facing the city crowd —and people turn around to look at them. End in a CU of Tina, with light falling on her face.

Next scene, next title: in school??

the village VOICE, March 19, 1964

movie journal
by Jonas Mekas

A few notes on my second arrest:

The detectives who seized the Genet film, "Un Chant d'Amour," did not know who Genet was. When I told them that Genet was an internationally known artist, I was told it was my fantasy.

I was called by the detectives "pink," and was introduced to other cops as "pink," because the covers of the two books I had with me, "Reviews of Modern Physics" and "Poetical Works of Blake," had red covers.

At the Criminal Court, before being squeezed into a 10-by-20-foot room in which 60 people were standing for three to four hours, I was told to leave the books outside. I put down the "Reviews of Modern Physics," but I kept Blake. The guard told me to put the book down. "The book could be used as a weapon," he told me. I told him that it was Blake, and that he would have to take it from me by force. The guard ripped the book from my hands by force.

Humanity Fades

During my Kafkaesque journey into the womb of the Tombs, the traces of civilization and humanity were fading out. While I was walking toward my cell, I was pushed on my back by the cop. I told him not to push me since I was not resisting. For this remark, the cop kicked me full force in the back. When I reminded him again not to use force, I was pushed again.

Somewhere in the process my name became "Mexas." When I attempted to correct it, since it was difficult to respond to another name, I was told to keep quiet, because my name really should be spelled "Schmuck."

When I placed all my belongings on the table and stood there, naked, the cop took my writing pen and threw it into the garbage can. "Why did you do that?" I asked him. I went to the garbage can, picked up the pen, and placed it back on the table. For doing this I was shouted at and threatened with beating.

Upon my release, on bail, I asked for my belongings, which included my keys, and was told to come another day. I am still sleeping in other people's places.

I have been shouted at, ridiculed constantly; I was told that they will make a statue of me in Washington Square; that they

TAYLOR MEAD in "Open the Door and See All the People," a new film by Jerome Hill opening on Wednesday, March 25, at the Fifth Avenue Cinema. Others in the comedy are Maybelle Nash, Charles Rydell, Susana de Mello, Jeremiah Sullivan, Ellen Martin, Lester Judson, John Holland, and Alec Wilder, who also composed the score. Hill's last film was "The Sand Castle."

will make "a mashed potato" of me by the time they are through; that I was "dirtying America"; that I was fighting windmills. One of the detectives who arrested me told me, at the theatre, that he did not know why they were taking me to the station: I should be shot right there in front of the screen.

The judge, mind, the judge himself was making snide and idiotic remarks about "art," with his tone of voice and grimaces implying that art was the most unnecessary, stupid, and low thing. It would be another matter if we'd been accused of murder!

This is just a small taste of Justice at Work, and it makes me puke. The time is here for a total change. But nobody really believes it will or can be done. The corruption is almost total, from top to bottom. Nevertheless, " 'Tis not too late to seek a newer world."

Cops Seize 4 In Raid on Village Film

By JERRY TALLMER and STAN KOVEN

Armed with an obscenity warrant, the police pounced last night on a public showing of an American "new wave" film and arrested four from the group. The East Village audience of 90 was dispersed.

The allegedly obscene movie was a widely-discussed avant garde work, "Flaming Creatures," produced by Jack Smith. The film had one previous showing last week at the same theater, the New Bowery, 4 St. Marks Pl.

Held for arraignment today were Jonas Mekas, a founder of the Film-Makers' Cooperative, which rented the theater; Kenneth Jacobs, 30, a film-maker and the projection'st, of 25 Ferry St.; Gerry Sims, 30, an actor, of 337 E. Fifth St., and Florence Karpe, 22, the ticket seller, 25 Ferry St.

Mekas, 41, of 515 E. 13th St., is a film critic of The Village Voice and one of the more successful experimenters in new forms of cinema. His "Guns of the Trees" currently is showing at the 55th St. Theatre and he worked with his brother, Adolphus Mekas, on the recently released "Hallelujah the Hills."

District Attorney Hogan's detectives, who interrupted last night's second performance and made the arrests, also seized the film, the projector, the screen and the sound track.

The detectives said they had witnessed last week's performance and saw a "newsreel" and the feature film.

Diane di Prima, head of the American Theatre for Poets, said her group had been renting the theater to show movies on an occasional basis.

She compared "Flaming Creatures" with the work of Jean Cocteau and called it "very beautiful . . . lots of nakedness . . . but nothing lewd."

The film's cast features La Monte Young, Francis Francine, Joel Markman, Shiela Bick and Mark Schlieffer.

Those arrested were booked at the E. Fifth St. Station, with Detectives Michael O'Toole and Arthur Walsh as the arresting officers. The charge was violation of Title 1141, a misdemeanor.

Film-Makers' Cooperative is an arm of the New American Cinema Group, Inc., established in 1961. Its stated objectives included an anti-censorship policy.

MEKAS RISKING JAIL SENTENCE

For the second time in two weeks, Greenwich Village film critic and filmmaker Jonas Mekas, who is also head of the New American Cinema Group, nonprofit distributor of experimental and avant-garde films, was arrested in New York for showing an "obscene" motion picture.

The second arrest came Friday (13) night at the Writers Stage Theatre in Greenwich Village where Mekas and French film critic Pierre Cottrel were showing "Chant D'Amour," a 22-minute homosexual fantasy about prison life made by French novelist-playwright Jean ("The Balcony") Genet. Audience was an invited group of writers, painters and theatre people who paid no admission though "contributions" were accepted. (Mekas risks a year in prison on each count.)

A week earlier Mekas and two others were arrested for showing the indie American-made pic, "Flaming Creatures," Jack Smith's 38-minute montage of a transvestite orgy which earlier had been named most important picture of the year by Film Culture, film buff quarterly which Mekas edits and publishes. Both "Chant" and "Creatures" contain a number of scenes prominently displaying genitalia, principally male. Case on "Creatures" is due to be heard in N. Y. Criminal Court, April 6, and the case on "Chant," April 13. "Creatures" hit the headlines early this year when Belgian authorities refused to allow it to be shown at the experimental film fest at Knokke-Le Zoute.

Apparent motive of Mekas and the New American Cinema Group is to get some kind of court acknowledgment that works of film "art" are above prosecution as pornography and obscenity. In a formal statement issued yesterday (Tues.), Mekas said in part, that "the new American filmmaker does not believe in legal restrictions placed upon works of art; he doesn't believe in licensing or any forms of censorship. There may be a need for licensing guns and dogs, but not for works of art. Likewise, we refuse to hide our work in restricted film societies, private clubs and membership groups. Our art is for all the people. It must be open and available to anyone who wants to see it. The existing laws are driving art underground. No legal body can act as art critic."

Last week, Mekas and the NACG held a series of private screenings of the films for various members of the Manhattan intelligentsia to recruit names to testify on behalf of the two pix, either to their merits as works of art or, barring that, simply to the effect that they are not obscene.

Rally Will Protest Raid on Film

Avant-garde film, theater and poetry leaders today were planning a rally to protest the police closing of a French movie and the arrest of the film's exhibitors and what they term a prevailing attitude of "repression" toward the arts in the city and nation.

Spurring the meeting was the arrest Friday of Jonas Mekas and Pierre Cotrell for exhibiting Jean Genet's "Un Chant D'-Amour," a 1950 film about homosexual love in prison. Police raided the Writers' Stage, 83 E. 4th St., closed the show, confiscated the film, and charged the two with showing obscene pictures.

Mekas was arrested on a similar charge last week when police closed "Flaming Crea-

tures," another experimental film with nudist scenes.

At the planning session today, Mekas, Julian Beck of The Living Theater and his actress wife Judith Malina, poet Allen Ginsberg, and poetess and playwright Dianne Di Prima will set the date for the rally, probably in April.

Beck, whose theater property has been seized by the Internal Revenue Service because of an alleged $23,000 owed in back taxes, charged the city administration with "trying to make the city look respectable for the World's Fair.

The Beck tax case will be argued today.

No Thin Green Line

Thousands of Marchers—Irish by birth or boast—will join the St. Patrick's Day Parade on Fifth Av. tomorrow. But the line they'll walk will be white.

Traffic Commissioner Barnes ruled long ago against painting the Fifth Av. line a different color each time a nationality group uses the street for a parade. He's promised that painters will stand by to repaint the line in case any ardent spirit tries splashing it with green paint.

N.Y. Post   March 19, 1964

Obscene Film Rap Now a Twin Bill

56

SUNDAY NEWS, MARCH 15, 1964

By WILLIAM TRAVERS

Jonas Mekas, 41, controversial film producer and critic, was arrested yesterday on charges of exhibiting an obscene film. Mekas arranged the showing to raise money for legal expenses in connection with his arrest on March 3 on charges of showing an obscene film.

A question in many minds yesterday was whether Mekas would risk court arrest again by showing another movie to raise

PHONE SUNDAY from 12 to 5

FASHION BASEMENT

defense funds for the new case, and so on into the distant future.

Mekas' new brush with the law took place in the early morning hours at the Writers Stage, 83 E. 4th St., at two showings of a French film entitled "Un Chant d'Amour" ("A Love Ballad"). The movie is a homosexual love story produced in France in the 1950s.

Audience Totaled 60

About 60 persons were in the small auditorium before the first showing when Mekas stood up and made an announcement.

"The police regard this film as pornographic," he said. "If they

come in here, they will consider it such and may arrest anyone watching. If you don't want to be involved, leave now."

Nobody left.

The law, represented by plainclothes patrolmen John Fitzpatrick and Walter Lynch, was in the audience and, after a showing before a second audience of 40, Fitzgerald approached Mekas and asked what sort of contribution was acceptable.

Pay As You Go

There had been no admission charge, but a "contribution box" attended by Pierre Cottrell, 18, of 70 Jane St., writer for a French film publication, was near the entrance.

Mekas suggested $2. Fitzgerald handed over the money—then arrested Mekas and Cottrell.

In Manhattan Criminal Court Judge Walter Gladwin fixed bond for each at $1,500 pending hearing on Tuesday.

Mekas, who lives at 515 E. 13th St., and three others were arrested on March 3 after showing a movie abounding in nudity in a lower East Side theatre. The title: "Flaming Creatures."

Mekas, film critic for the Village Voice, a weekly newspaper in Greenwich Village, and editor of the quarterly magazine "Film Culture," is president of the New America Cinema Group and producer of avant garde movies.

Variety, March 25

Village Closes Ranks

The recent arrests of Jonas Mekas and friends for exhibiting so-called obscene films has prompted the formation of a new organization. It's the New York City League for Sexual Freedom.

"Besides defending the freedom of expression, we defend the right to engage in sexual activity — including the exhibition and viewing of erotic films . . ." says the leaflet.

A STATEMENT

Like "Flaming Creatures," The Genet film "Un Chant d'Amour" is a work of art and like any work of art it is above obscenity and pornography, or, more correctly, above what the police understand as obscenity and pornography. Art exists on a higher spiritual, aesthetic and moral plane.

The new American film-maker does not believe in legal restrictions placed upon works of art; he doesn't believe in licensing or any form of censorship. There may be a need for licensing guns and dogs, but not for works of art.

Likewise, we refuse to hide our work in restricted film societies, private clubs and membership groups. Our art is for all the people. It must be open and available to anybody who wants to see it.

The existing laws are driving art underground.

We refuse to accept the authority of the police to pass judgment on what is art and what is not art; what is obscenity and what is not obscenity in art. On this subject we would rather trust D. H. Lawrence or Henry Miller than the police or any civic official. No legal body can act as an art critic.

Hollywood has created an image in the minds of the people that cinema is only entertainment and business. What we are saying is that cinema is also art. And the meanings and values of art are not decided in courts or prisons.

Art is concerned with the spirit of man, with the subconscious of man, with the aesthetic needs of man, with the entire past and future of man's soul. Like any other art, like painting, music or poetry, our art cannot be licensed or censored. There is no one among us to judge it. We have not only the Constitutional right but, more important, the moral right, to communicate our work to other people.

To consider "Flaming Creatures" or "Un Chant d'Amour" obscene by a few extracted images, taken out of context, and to make a criminal case thereof, without making an attempt to understand the work as a whole, or the true meaning of the said details, is indeed a narrow, naive and unintelligent way of looking at things.

The detective from the District Attorney's office, who arrested us last Tuesday with "Flaming Creatures," told us that he was not interested in the film as a work of art; he also admitted that he was not competent to judge it; he said he was looking at it strictly as a matter of "duty"; he was looking only for "objectionable" images according to his interpretation of the law.

That is O.K., as far as the duty of a hired man is concerned --
but what the hell does this have to do with truth or justice? The meaning
and essence of a detail in a work of art can be understood only if grasped
in the context of the whole.

You may ask why, with already one "obscenity" charge against
me, I am screening another film which in the eyes of the police is considered
"Obscene."

I am doing so because I consider the police actions unlawful,
unconstitutional and contrary to man's spiritual growth.

It is my duty as an artist and as a man to show the best work of
my contemporaries to the people.

It is my duty to bring to your attention the ridiculousness and
illegality of the licensing and obscenity laws.

The duty of the artist is to ignore bad laws and fight them every
moment of his life.

The duty of the citizen and artist is not to let the police and the
law abuse the rights of the people, both the Constitutional rights and the
unwritten, moral rights.

We say that the courts, by taking these decisions into their own
hands, are abusing man's basic freedom of expression as described in the
Constitution and gained by man in the thousands of years of his spiritual
development.

All works of art, all expressions of man's spirit must be permitted,
must be available to the people.

Who -- when even the best of our artists, the best of our art
critics disagree about art (and I am certainly a better authority on this
than any policeman or any court) -- who among you dares pose as judge
of our art, to the degree of dragging our art into the criminal courts?
In what times do we live, when works of art are identified with the workings
of crime?

What a beautiful insanity!

                                                    Jonas Mekas

March 7th, 1964
New York City

For the film:
About a man who is a refugee in a foreign country—an eternal refugee—but who left his beloved in the old country, and even as the years go, remains faithful to her—and sees her in every young girl young woman he meets—while, meanwhile, his beloved is getting old, and has grey hair, etc. etc. —only in his imagination she remains the same & eternally young—he is the chevalier in exile.

No date, 1964

Nonsense plunges us into the unfamiliar; it reaches into new perceptions. By disrupting the nets of the familiar associations it frees us, it opens our eyes to the wonder of a continuous & immediate living & experiencing & knowing.

March 5, 1964

Everybody keeps referring to lawyers, attorneys, legal organizations, etc. Are we really living in times when a man is not permitted any longer to defend himself by himself? The legal machinery is so complicated by now that once you're under arrest you don't know where to begin to speak and how and to whom. I was ushered through, from one stage to another, and then into the court, and with ten cops around, and the army of strange characters around the judge's table, and had not a vaguest idea of whom to speak nor who the judge was nor anything, all I know everything was settled before I opened my mouth and we were walking out. Donnerwetter!

March 24, 1964

A crime cannot be committed against the law; the crime can be committed only against people. If you say I've committed a crime, show me the people, the man, the woman to whom I've committed the crime.

Laws, like shoes, wear out.

Does art "appeal" to the sick or to the healthy?
what a question!

Licensors are clubbing us down again. Film-Makers: let us throw out the censors and the licensors. Our poems do not need licenses: they aren't dogs. We write them or we film them, and they are there for your enjoyment and for your good. Licenses are for dogs, because dogs can bite. Our poems are not dogs. Ah! but the poet can become biting if the need arises. We'll bite your balls off, censors. We prefer to live peacefully, though. We praise and sing the world around us and inside us. So love our art, love beauty, man-made beauty and God-made beauty. Leave us alone.

It is a duty of every citizen to contribute something to the betterment of the lives of his contemporaries. The improvement of the laws of the country is one of such acts. To improve the present law; to bring it up-to-date—this is what we are trying to do, this is what is implied in our actions. But we are considered criminals. How is that? How is it that we, who are concerned with the betterment of the law, meet the almost paranoiac resistance of the people of the law? Do our law people forget that besides protecting and guarding the law their duty is also the improvement and remaking of the law so that it wouldn't stand in the way of society's growth? The growth of the society is more important than the protection of the laws; the protection of people is more important than the protection of laws.

"You do not think common, lewd or lascivious thought just because you have read something in a book, unless it is your mental purpose to do so. Impure sexual thoughts or prurient interest is self-generated by a desiring mind which is disposed to lewdness and impure sexual thoughts."
—J. W. Ehrlich, p. 105 "Howl"

Justice Brandeis: "Moreover, even imminent danger cannot justify resort to prohibition of these functions [free speech, J. M.] essential to effective democracy, unless the evil apprehended is relatively serious. Prohibitions of free speech and assembly is a measure so stringent that it would be inappropriate as the means for averting a relatively trivial harm to society—the fact that speech is likely to result in some violence or in destruction of property is not enough to justify its suppression. There must be the probability of serious injury to the State. Among free men, the deterrents ordinarily to be applied to prevent crime are education and punishment for violations of the law, not abridgment of the rights of free speech and assembly."

Clayton W. Horn, judge, from the Decision on *Howl*:
"The authors of the First Amendment knew that novel and unconventional ideas might disturb the complacent, but they chose to encourage a freedom which they believed essential if vigorous enlightenment was ever to triumph over slothful ignorance."

ibid: "The Statute does not intend that we shall reduce our treatment of sex to the standard of a child's library in the supposed interest of a salacious few."

ibid: "Sexual impurity in literature (pornography, as some of the cases still call it) is any writing whose dominant purpose and effect is erotic allurement; a calculated and effective incitement to sexual desire. It is the effect that counts, more than the purpose, and not indictment can stand unless it can be shown."

ibid: "The United States Supreme Court refers to the various rules on obscenity by stating that: "sex and obscenity are not synonymous. Obscene material is material which deals with sex in a manner appealing to prurient interest. The portrayal of sex, e.g., in art, literature and scientific works is not itself sufficient reason to deny material the constitutional protection of freedom of speech and press."

HONI SOIT QUI MAL Y PENSE ("Evil to him who evil thinks")

Friday, April 9th (I think it is ninth…) 1964
PAS:
It seems you stirred a real storm in Sweden. Articles keep arriving from Nils HG, pro- and contra.
Very important: While in Paris, contact Miss or Mrs. Sonnabend, just found her real name: Illeana Sonnabend, 37 Quai des Grands Augustins Paris 6—she has a very important gallery (art) in Paris, she has seen *Flaming Creatures* and a few other films here, and wants to show some of them, maybe immediately after Cinematheque, in her gallery. Contact her immediately after you arrive in Paris, or you could notify her, perhaps, even before your arrival.
Also in Paris, this is important, contact Harold Stevenson, 28 rue du Faubourg St. Honore Paris 8. He is a very well-known pop artist, friend of Andy Warhol etc., and he will want to see *Sleep* no doubt, and maybe very helpful to arrange one or two special screenings of *Sleep* etc. to some selected artistic circles in Paris. He also promised to donate one of his paintings to help the Exposition. So remind him (he promised this to me in presence of Andy, he will remember)—and if possible try to GET THAT PAINTING FROM HIM and LEAVE IT with Sonnabend, for sale. Tell him that we need money badly.

When in Paris, contact: Nico Papatakis 41 rue de la Bucherie Tel. ODE 78.06 or ODE 24.52. He is a good friend of mine. He made *Les Abysses*. He also helped Genet to make *Un Chant D'Amour*, and it was thru him that I got that unlucky print of the film which is causing me so much trouble here. So tell him to do something for me. I need badly any possible clippings on film, I mean, on *Un Chant D'Amour*. I also need a statement on the film by Genet himself. Genet has to come out in my (or ours, I mean, independent film-makers) defense and support. The trial for *Flaming Creatures* is set now on May 18th. Genet will follow around the same time. I have little time to collect materials, but I need them.

Enough business.
So the old man didn't let you in, hahaha.
Stan is still in town. He is searching for a place near the city, to live and to work. They are OK, though confused—too many old friends dropping in constantly. But I guess they are in a transitional period anyway, so may as well.
Kelman drops in once in a while, snoops around, makes a few cracks, and sneaks out. Did he write you that he is now a film critic for *The Nation*? A big man, Ken. And L. John is still building his robots.
The place, I mean, coop is as busy, even more, than before. Much is going. But sort of sad, with all our showcases closed, with no movies to see anywhere. We still don't know what to do. We have been clubbed badly. Even Leslie is spending more time in the Courts than in the office these days.
But the spring is coming, I can see the sun outside, and some yellow flowers on the table, even Gantt's crooked sick flower has some green spots showing on its dirty stem. So we have some hope that the things will look brighter soon. Gregory is sitting at the other table is typing like mad with two fingers, claclaclaclacla, writing more letters for money, no doubt, or maybe to his *Serenity* lawyers.
oh. have a good time in Rome.

April 20, 1964

PAS:
Since my Roman Letters did not reach you, I mean, my latest letters, I have to repeat a few things:

1. On Cannes: We all feel that Cannes is not the best place to show Brakhage. Cannes crowd is very phony. It's like showing jewels to pigs. You could take *Scorpio*, *Chumlum*, *Tam*, to make one good program, perhaps. In that case it wouldn't go under the flag of the "new American cinema" but simply as one additional program of good movies for those who are interested to see good movies—casually, in other words. Two or three programs would become already a manifesto-ation and then the show would be looked at differently, thru distorted glasses. We think we should concentrate on Paris, instead. Storm is angry on Cannes and please DO NOT SHOW EVEN IF ASKED *Mirror* IN CANNES, this is an order from Storm. She has other plans for the film. *Tam*, I guess, is OK for Cannes, and so is *Scorpio* and *Chumlum*. That's my fair opinion. But you can also add something else, if you feel it will do any good. Maybe two programs. *Flower Thief*? and *Prelude*? You know, I guess, that there is no 16mm projection in Cannes, except the Petit Sale, in which the critics Section screenings take place. Insist on that auditorium, it is the best and easiest accessible to people place for movies, next to the main auditorium. Any small hotel etc. screening in town wouldn't do much good.

2. Don't ask x to help you. He is a good man, and we are good friends, but his reputation among the more serious film etc. people is not the best. He is too much of a playboy and Festival comber. Rochefort doesn't like him too much.

Criminal Court of the City of New York

PART __11__, COUNTY OF __New York__

STATE OF NEW YORK)
){ ss.:
COUNTY OF New York)

.... Det. Arthur Walsh ....

of No. .... District Attorneys Office ...., County of .. New York ....
City of New York, being duly sworn, deposes and says that on.. March 3rd, 1964 ....., at about .... P. . M.,
at ...... 4 St Marks Place   Inside .... in the County of .. New York .... State of New York,
the defendant, Kenneth Jacobs, Jonas Mekas, Gerry Sims and Florence Karpf .... did commit the crime of:
while acting together and in concert with each other

_____ OBSCENE PRINTS AND ARTICLES, in that said defendant unlawfully did sell, lend, give away, distribute, show and transmute, and offer to sell, lend, give away, distribute, show and transmute, and possess with intent to sell, lend, distribute give away, show and transmute, a certain obscene, lewd, lascivious, filthy, indecent, sadistic, masochistic and disgusting book, pamphlet, story paper, writing, paper, picture, drawing and photograph, and written, printed and recorded matter of an indecent character, having knowledge thereof, whereof a more particular description would be offensive to this court, and improper to be spread upon the records thereof, wherefor such description is not here given;

under the following circumstances:

That the defendant, Jonas Mekas, did supply and distribute lewd and obscene film entitled "Jack Smith's Flaming Creatures" for exhibition at the New Bowery Theatre, at the aforementioned location.

That the defendant, Florence Karpf, sold tickets to the public at the said Theatre at the aforementioned time and assisted in the projection of the said entitled film.

That the defendant, Kenneth Jacobs, with the assistance of the defendant, Karpf, exhibited the said film at the above time and place, and did operate the projector.

That the defendant, Gerry Sims, acted as the ticket taker and did accept the ticket at the der from the patrons.

Deponent further states that at the aforementioned time and place he did observe the said showing of the said gfilm and that it was indecent, lewd and obscene.

43 rue Piat Paris 20.

PARIS LE 16 AVRIL 1964

Monsieur le Rédacteur en Chef

La nouvelle est parvenue ici que le jeune
réalisateur Jonas MEKAS est l'objet d'un procès pour
avoir présenté une oeuvre de Jean Genêt, et nous en
sommes attristés.

Les oeuvres des poètes appartiennent à l'esthétique
et non à la morale; les faire connaître est toujours un
bien, et un acte honorable. Jean Genêt est un grand poète,
dont l'oeuvre théatrale est représentée à Broadway depuis
des années.

Nous devons remercier Jonas MEKAS d'aider à la
connaissance de Jean Genêt. Nous pensons que l'on ne peut
dans aucun pays, sans encourir le blâme de l'Histoire,
emprisonner un homme pour activité poétique, et nous
souhaitons tres vivement que Jonas MEKAS ne soit pas
condamné en Amérique de ce fait.

Simone de BEAUVOIR, Jean-Paul SARTRE,
Christiane ROCHEFORT

Cette lettre a été adressée au N. Y. Times.

1.

Christiane Rochefort, French writer, Cannes, 1963. Co-signer of support letter.

April 2, 1964:

Michael Kahn, owner of the Writers' Stage at
83 East 4th Street called to say he'd just
received a summons for:

exhibihing a motion picture for pay that had
not been licensed, etc.

"on or about the xx 14th of March"

(this was the contribution, invitation showing of
the Genet at which Jonas and Pierre were arrested.)

Asked him to have his lawyer check with Perlman;
told him Perlman has been retained by the Co-op.

He said he couldn't afford to fool around and lose
his license. Wanted to know how it is that the
Gramercy Arts Theatre is opening a new set of
plays, when they were suposed to have been suspended.

Later, Perlman called looking for Stone. Told him
above. He said that he would offer to cooperate,
and supply witnesses that it was free contribution
and invitational.

Kahn's hearing is on Thursday, April 9th, at 10:15 AM
at the Dept. of License Bureau, 80 Lafayette St.
L.

Do it alone, by yourself. Marcorelles and Rochefort and Eli (who works with her) are the best people to help you. Also, Gene Moscowitz. Contact him at Cannes, he is a VERY VERY GOOD MAN. (He went to school with Gregory, by the way)

3. In Paris: Ask Langlois to write a letter to French Embassy in NY (and a copy to us) asking them to ship to them FREE the following films: *Fool's Haikus*, *To L.A. With Lust*, *Lemon Hearts*, *Scarface and Aphrodite*, *Fleming Faloon* (there is new footage to add to what you already have), otherwise, the French godamn office refuses to talk with us or help us.

4. Did you write to Contemporary about the London date? Why don't you ever leave your European address to your European contacts? Contemporary keeps writing to us, asking for date. Keep direct contact. I shipped info kits to London and Langlois.

5. For Paris and London shows: it is very important for me that you have also retrospective, or whatever we call them, films shown at the Cinematheque, I mean, *Connection* and *Sand Castle*.

6. There are people here who have friends in Paris, London and Italy and are very anxious to know the dates of shows in those places, so that they could let their friends know about it. So inform me about the correct dates as soon as you know them.

I hope you received that one hundred in Rome. I am working on more which I will send you in a week or so.

April 30, 1964

DIARY FILM (Tina)

I prayed to be released from all the routines.

Looked at the early morning. Damp green bushes.

Touched the ground in the park, the earth.

May 12, 1964

Use any of the following three lines innocently and out of context when you speak with, for instance, Dwight MacDonald (or, we jokingly said, to the judge in the court) —this we figured out today with Allen Ginsberg:

1. "Your fly is open."
2. "Why you always so self-conscious?"
3. "Why you always so suspicious?"

Watch the amazing reactions, what it does to different people.

May 26, 1964

PAS:

By now I hope you have met Pierre Cottrell and you know about what happened with our film shipment. They are still sitting in the Coop. It is too late for Paris now. We'll try to get to London. We are searching for somebody who is going to London to take them with him. Those SOB at Cinematheque never wrote a letter to the French Embassy asking for the films, and without such a letter they wouldn't move a finger there (I mean in the fucked Embassy).

How are the FROGS taking us there in Paris?

I am trying desperately to get somewhere money to send to you before you leave Paris. We are so drained out. Tell David, if you see him, that Telestar people didn't send a check yet. I don't know where to turn to. *Film Culture* just came out and we have no money to mail it. In case you don't receive from me anything before you leave Paris, borrow somewhere or something —you should receive it in London, I'll get money even if I have to make a couple hold-ups. The show must go on, as the old Confucius used to say.

By the way, those interviews in all those German mags are very good (one in *Film*, and the other one in *Civis*), particularly the Angel interview. You are shaking them up OK. The trails (or traces?) of your beard will be left all over Europe, I hope it will do some good. Paris may not be ready yet for anything new, there the film-makers are too absorbed into their own navels to see what's going on in the world.

It is getting hot in NY. 95 degrees, blast it. But Gregory keeps shooting. I saw some of the *Prometheus* and I thought it was FANTASTICALLY BEAUTIFULLLL. It will be Gregory's best movie, I think. The color is simply fantastic. He has hours and hours of it. He is still shooting. How Gregory survives I don't know. Day to day, I guess. That's how films are made.

In the package that didn't go with Pierre, there was a new film by Carl Linder, *Devil is Dead*, which should reach you somewhere in London, I hope. Something for you to see.

Haikus were butchered in the lab completely. I am making another print. Now I can't promise it even for London. Forget it, strike it out of your mind—if it comes—comes.

Have you bumped into Barbara somewhere? What's becoming of Barbara?

I keep getting completely irrational incomprehensible letters, neither head nor tail—so that's how I guess she is, and I guess it's OK as long as she is going somewhere —some of us go nowhere—and I have not a vaguest idea where I am going myself these days, sort of in between something and nothing, or somewhere there, balancing on some kind of invisible line—

My trials are still hanging around my neck like a rope of shit and plenty of bulltalk.

I am ready for a desert, I mean, to go to a desert.

Stan, fate or obstinence, got back to Colorado and I think that is the best place for him anyway. In NY he was running around like mad, there is too much going here so much of nothing that he couldn't do anything but kept talking and talking and talking and bumping into things and people and it was, I knew, just a question of time before he packs up and runs out of town shouting and screaming mad, though he did it more quietly because it was a late night, really it was almost an early morning when they all left, after looking at some more films at the Coop sitting until three in the morning and then we went down to the street and we found the car was broken in and his viewer stolen, so that was the last memory of the NY, I guess, even his art tools being robbed from him, not only the soul attacked and sprayed with dirt—so we shook hands in the cool coming morning and they all crept in among and on top of their film cans, boxes and things and I stood in the middle of the street and watched him them driving off and I knew that was it anyway, Stan called two days ago and he said he is happy and he is working again on his film.

June 3, 1964

NOTES ON *FLAMING CREATURES*

1. Art depicts man both as he is and as he projects himself (read Jung, Freud, Reich, Marx).
2. and reflecting his soul and his unconscious
3. by way of artist's feelings, perceptions, intuitions
4. *Flaming Creatures'* techniques, its visual qualities and its content have reason in Jack Smith's unconscious.
5. It follows, that it doesn't reflect, say, judge's unconscious (or that of judge's generation) although it may touch it somewhere from a distance, since the unconscious of two different generations are never out of touch completely but they overlap (one develops from—and away from the other).
6. The social (?) values (significance) of *F.C.* is (at least one of the values) that it is a key (one of the keys) to the emotions, qualities, fears, needs or abundances of the soul of Jack's generation (matrix of the soul).

7. To really evaluate the social significance of *F.C.*, to really grasp its content, one has to dig into the depths of its content ("intrinsic content", Panofksy).

8. We cannot discuss the "artistic intention" in the courts or in general (see Panofsky, p. 12–13).

9. What is the "content" of *Flaming Creatures*? Panofsky: "Content, as opposed to subject matter, may be described in the words of Pierce as that which a work betrays but does not parade."

10. In *Flaming Creatures*, its content could be Jack's immense sadness, his sad thoughts about human conditions, sex, and life in general. Now, how can I begin to tell this to a judge?

11. The artist's intentions in creating a work of art can not be taken into consideration since one never knows one's real intentions nor do those intentions have anything to do with the meaning of the finished work of art.

12. Artists sum up their times, their "races." The meaning of *F.C.* should be taken as OUR OWN depth of meanings; as analyses and forecasts of things to come TO US ALL (our OWN things to come).

13. Really, all those things are HERE already, the artist is only more sensitive to see them first, he has developed tools to see them.

14. The sex-death equations; hermaphroditic dreamings (thoughts); sex fears; merging of sexes; etc. etc.—all that is already HERE (read numerous books, scientific studies on the subject; visit Kinsey Institute).

15. We should thank Jack Smith for being a forecaster, for bringing to our attention some things that we can't yet see but which are coming (our artists are our GREEN and RED lights). (Read Ezra Pound.)

16. Community standards? "I make community standards—new values, baby, for a younger generation, a generation with possibilities that glow with a pure celestial light—cosmic imagination. And the beautiful part about it all is that you can, my dear critics, scream protest to the skies. You're too late. The Musicians, Painters, Writers, Poets and Film-Makers all fly, and know exactly where its 'at'."—Ron Rice

17. Fast movement, flashes of imagery (from trains, jets or car windows) is part of modern visual experience.

18. These are experiences, perceptions so unlike the static experiences that, on occasions, they lead to mystical experiences, as demonstrated by the experiments of Gysin.

19. Flashes of color and forms etc. etc. as opposed to the earlier static scenes and shots in cinema (& a stable & content consciousness).

20. To grasp the meaning of *F.C.* techniques one has to grasp something of the film's content, which, on its own terms, reveals itself partly only through the techniques and plastic qualities (lighting, burned out qualities, trembling camera, shaky movement, etc.).

21. Washed out, burned out emotions? White light? What does it mean?

22. Our burned out emotional landscape where all sexes merge?

23. The burning of desires? Or the landscape after the desire?

24. Seen during a flash of an exploding A-bomb?

25. You can't discuss or criticize techniques separately from the film's content although film's plastic values by themselves could still please an educated, trained, used eye.

26. When Prof. Gessner denies *F.C.* techniques he does so because the content of *F.C.* escapes him; rejections of all NEW art comes, almost as a rule from being unable to grasp the new content; rejection of all new content begins, as

a rule, with the rejection of the new style & new techniques.

27. If you don't accept the techniques, you won't really see the content; the technique, in that case will seem to you hanging purposelessly and without reason.

28. Understandings of art can be intuitive, historical, and mental (intellectual).

29. Most of the understanding of the new art is primarily intuitive, its reason and its content being still too elusive to grasp with the analytical fingers of the intellect.

30. Reason and analysis cannot be applied to *F.C.*, not yet, or it can be applied only to some degree.

ON NUDITY AND SEX IN ART

31. *F.C.* nudity is not veiled, as opposed to the veilings on so many things (fear of facing them?) in contemporary world & in Hollywood films.

32. Veilings (read Reich and Freud) being part of the armored character of modern man (cause of his psychic disturbance).

33. The modern artist wants to open himself nakedly (sincerity is equated with nakedness) before the world without hiding behind symbols and veils—which means: he tells US to do the same, that we better open ourselves or else we are doomed.

34. He says, that LOVE, any love, homosexual, hermaphrodite, lesbian, any LOVE is better than NON-LOVE.

35. We see NUDITY and SEX "games": (male and female) in *F.C.* but neither nudity nor sex is new in art.

36. To properly evaluate Smith's successes and failures in use (depiction) of nudity & sex in *F.C.*, one has to be familiar with the history of nudity and sex in art, and in cinema specifically; one has to place *F.C.* in the context of art history.

37. One has to know the aesthetic problems that face the artists who attempt to depict human body in art, in all times—

38. "there is a high breathlessness about beauty that cancels lust"—Santayana, *Reason in Art* p. 171 (1934).

39. In a certain sense, or truly, *F.C.* belongs in the category of messianic (prophetic) works.

40. As in all messianic works, there are references, meanings, images, pertaining (referring) to hell, heaven, pandemonium, visions of the fall and resurrection of man.

41. Notice that Jack depicts almost a primordial, original man, beyond sex, as a hermaphroditic being (see Freud).

42. This hermaphroditic aspect is impossible to show fully without the use of the male and female sex organs.

43. "are you a man or a woman," is the key line.

44. Even the breast is shaken and abstracted in movement.

45. So that, together with the "shaking penis" they become almost one and the same organ, merging of sexes.

46. which comes to a "dramatic" climax when "Monroe" is revealed as a male.

47. HONI SOIT QUI MAL Y PENSE ("Evil to him who evil thinks")

ON GENERATIONS

48. Art of a given time is created (made) by the young, middle and old generations.

49. These three have different things to communicate to humanity of a given time. There are always at least three voices to listen to.

50. Not only the young generation has a dialogue with the world—the artists of the old generation continue their dialogue with the world.

51. Each generation has its wisdoms and knowledge to communicate.

52. There are always three voices to listen to, to learn from.

THE CHRONOLOGY OF WHAT HAPPENED

1. February 17, 1964: Film-Makers' Showcase at the Gramercy Arts Theatre was closed. Summons were issued by the City Department of Licenses for Ron Rice benefit show of December 9th, 1963.

2. Pocket Film Society screenings at the Pocket Theatre closed. Summons issued by the City Department of Licenses for Sidney Peterson retrospective show of December 9th, 1963.

3. March 3, 1964: Jack Smith's film, "Flaming Creatures"; Andy Warhol's film, "Newsreel"; Jack Smith's rushes for his new film, "Normal Love" seized at the New Bowery Theatre by the detectives from the District Attorney's Office. Kenneth Jacobs, the film-maker (who served as Film-Makers' Cooperative projectionist); Florence Karpe (who took contributions); Jerry Sims (who took care of the door); Jonas Mekas (as the representative of the Film-Makers' Cooperative) were arrested and charged with showing mfim and distribution of "obscene" films.

4. March 13, 1964: Jean Genet's film "Un Chant D'Amour" was seized by the New York police at the Writer's Stage, during an invitatiohal screening. Pierre Cótrell, French Film Critic, and Jonas Mekas (who projected the film) were arrested. Charge: showing of "obscene" films.

5. March ih 16, 1964: The Gate Film Club, at the Gate Theatre, was closed under pressure from the City Department of Licenses.

6. March 17, 1964: Kenneth Anger and Stan Brakhage show cancelled at the New Bowery Theatre. Screening harassed by the police, Fire and City Licenses departments, numerous detectives, and the State Division

53. No voice of one single age group or generation should be proclaimed over the other. Gessner proclaims the middle (his generation) and the judge proclaims the right (old) generation's views & dictatorship, when they impose their aesthetic and moral views on *F.C.* without listening to the other side (audiamus et alteram partem).

54. "The artist who creates new forms and employs new techniques—who develops, in a word, a new style—does so because he has something new to say; and in art, whatever is said needs its own language. The very newness is then felt as an attack on established patterns. The hostility to 'modern art' evinced by the pillars of church, state, and society is not a product of insensitivity. On the contrary, it displays a realistic awareness of the threat which art has always posed to sheer conformity. The charge of obscenity directed against the arts is strictly comparable to the moral depravity regularly ascribed to heretical religious sects. 'Thou shalt have no other Gods before me' and a new vision of God—so says the priesthood—can only be a visitation of the Devil."—Abraham Kaplan, "Obscenity as an Esthetic Category," Law and Contemporary Problems, School of Law, Duke University, Vol. XX, Autumn 1955, N. 4

55. The "old" generation shouldn't forbid the young generation to run to dance to make love to enjoy life only because its own bodies and bones are full of calcium and its mind is closer to the meditation on the coming death than on joys of life.

56. Each of the three groups (generations) has their own dominant existential themes.

57. One should be a child when one is a child—but not childish; one should be young—but not juvenile; one should be a man—but not a toughy; one should be old—but not senile.

58. All this must be remembered when "judging" *Flaming Creatures*.

59. And do not miss the humor, Jack's misanthropic humor behind it all.

CO-OP WALL BULLETIN

Temporarily, we have been pushed into the corner. We are descending underground, through the manholes. Now we have to look into our Mao manuals. Two steps back, three steps forwards; divide, disappear, then collect ourselves into small pockets, and then attack.

We'll have to retreat, temporarily, into the clubs and secret film societies. We'll increase our screenings across the country. We'll take New York via the country!

As long as we don't accept this as a way of permanency.

It is a question of tactics in a changed situation.

Imagine a rebel group, in Cuba, accepting woods as a way of living! The same with us. The film society card will be a reminder that we are in a fight. In a true sense, our joining into a film society must be considered and taken and kept in our consciousness as a subversive action.

Maybe it is true, maybe we are neither strong nor ready yet to bring the film liberation through our work to the larger public. We have to work more. To create more dazzling beauty, more free, uninhibited works. The freedom of our movies will infect with freedom the consciousness of those who will watch them.

We ourselves are worthless, if our art says nothing. We should make movies which should make the eyes of mayors and judges weep; that's what we need. That would set them free. A beauty that would pierce through ignorance and coldness.

of Motion Pictures. Summons issued by the City Department of Licenses
for "violating of the Administrative Code."

7. March 18, 1964: Kuchar program cancelled at the New Bowery
Theatre under pressures from the City. The theatre locked by the
New York police; posters confiscated; summons issued by Louis Pesce,
director of the State Division of Motion Pictures, to the Film-Makers'
Cooperative and Ken Jacobs for "exhibiting of an unlicensed motion
picture in public place of amusement for pay."

DECLARATION FOR THE FREEDOM OF THE BLACK
AND WHITE AND TECHNICOLOR SHADOWS

(2mm, 4mm, 16mm, 35mm 70mm, 150mm, 1,000mm, 1,000,000mm)

Moving pictures belong to the Muses-- like painting, like poetry, like music, like dance, like any other art.

Big or small, good or bad, expensive or cheap, "Cleopatra" or "Flaming Creatures"----they all belong to the muses.

They all are attempts to give man something beautiful.

Licensing of works of art is immoral, silly and unconstitutional.

Thats what we want people to know.

The main reason for licensing shadows is (they say) to ~~protect people~~ from obscenity in films.

That is very nice hypocritical reasoning.

We are grown-up people and need no civic and bureaucratic mommies and daddies to protect our morals any longer.

Do not baby the people.
It is beautiful to be a child; but it is pretty sick to be childish!!

Let all lives be free.

Let all art be free.

Let all life expressions be free.

Let man blossom.

                                      Film-makers Of The People
                                      May 23, 1964.   New York City

SATURDAY - MAY 23- DEMONSTRATION AT THE RADIO CITY
MUSIC HALL - 5 PM. (50th Street and Avenue of Americans).
EVERYONE INTERESTED IN ARTISTIC FREEDOM COME!!

No date, 1964

questions to Berman:

1. On what grounds will the case be fought?
a) *F.C.* is art and therefore not obscene?
b) *F.C.* maybe obscene but still it is a "speech"?
2. Is "cinema" protected under Const. as speech? If not, why not? We should fight for including it in "speech"

LETTERS FROM THE FOREST
a) Rabbit shit haikus
b) Reflections on life & Brooklyn Bridge
c) "My Childhood" in Brooklyn & Orchard Street
d) My questionings whether World War II took place
e) My dreams and visions of walking barefooted
f) From the secret notebooks of Unfulfilled Desires
g) Saint Mary of the Gates of Dawn

I still do not know how to pray. I still do not know how to pray. I still don't dare to pray. I am still afraid to pray. I still haven't been graced to pray. I am still wading thru the mind, crying.

Again I thought about my splintered, fragmented, single-framed world, with all monolithic ideas disappearing, the consciousness that is becoming more and more open, with many centers—where only occasionally there are islands of green peaceful patches, the rest being thrown in constant, anxiously searching movement, in a constant process forwards, something I don't know yet but which I desperately long for—

A DREAM
I had a dream. I was somewhere in a new, unfamiliar place. I looked, and in a not too far distance I saw an ocean, or a huge river. I walked towards it until I reached the sand, and I finally stood next to the water. I looked back and I realized that I was on an island, and that the tide was coming & water was rising & that I had no more time to reach the shore. As a matter of fact, the shore was already cut off by water. I was sort of worried, but before I began getting into a real worry, I suddenly noticed a tall handsome tree standing not very far from me, on the island, and so I started walking towards it, knowing that the water will never reach its branches, and as I was walking towards the tree, now quite peaceful, I woke up.

ON THE CO-OP WALL
After what I have seen of Justice at work —the politicians and the city bureaucrats, civic workers, my decision is very clear: the artist cannot integrate himself peacefully or lawfully into a corrupt and unlawful society.

We have to stay out of it or we'll be grinded by the wheels of conformity.

There is no doubt that a huge blow has been given us by depriving us of our rights to show our work publicly.

That does not mean we have to accept the licensing and the police idea of what obscenity or art is.

Our only choice is to change tactics and keep working. As far as I can see, we have to remain underground. We have to divide and invade homes, to "CORRUPT" PEACEFUL AMERICAN & WORLD HOMES with private home screenings.

Its not millions that count. The one big difference between our work and the Hollywood work is the privacy, complete authorship of our work, and perhaps the officials did us a favor reminding us that we should not nurture too much commercial ambition.

George [Maciunas] gave me some light on this, by starting laughing after I told him that all coffee houses film screenings and showcases are being closed. He said that was in perfect Fluxus spirit: a huge happening called Closing the Theatres, which is not easy to arrange, but when it happens, it must be taken as a Fluxus experience.

So there we are.

What all this suppression of avant-garde arts means, or could mean, in a longer run, is that it will change, transform into the germs of political action, even if indirectly. The City's (State's) war against artists should eventually and undoubtedly surely result in undermining politically their positions, and their eventual toppling down.

June 2, 1964

Flaming Creatures:

"The people," that is, police, District Attorney presented their case. Three judges. Presiding judge: Impelliteri. Detective Walsh and Detective Toole testified. Under cross-examination, detective Walsh admitted that three days or so before the seizing of *F.C.* he had a conference with the District Attorney about the film. However he had no warrant.

The film was screened in the back room of the court, for the judges, a few representatives of the Press, and the defendants.

At 5:30 the Court was adjourned until June 10th.

June 3, 1964

NOTES on *Flaming Creatures* screening att: Mr. Trager

An interesting fact, I think:

Elizabeth Sutherland (editor of Book section, *The Nation*); Susan Sontag; Isabelle Eberstadt (wrote article in *Tribune* in Jack's support); Shirley Clarke; Elaine de Kooning; Storm De Hirsch (poet and director or the film *Good-bye in the Mirror* which was shown at Cannes film festival this year, and was invited to represent America at the Locarno Film festival this coming July); Marisol Escobar (the Pop artist); Barbara Wise (Wise Gallery); Diane di

Prima (the poet), (and to a more limited degree Rosalind Constable) are among the staunchest supporters in public and in print of *Flaming Creatures* and are all WOMEN. They were not insulted by the film; they found it beautiful. Now, there is something in this fact that the women like this film almost more than the men!

June 12, 1964

Farmer's logic:

If something doesn't work in one place (if our public screenings are getting us in trouble with the police)—move to another place, or do it again in a different way.

Really, these are the underground techniques.

There are too few of us to waste our time in prisons and courts.

So we have to change our tactics.

It is not a compromise: this is a change of tactics.

We move deeper, where it's darker, and where we can work more effectively, and where our real work should be.

Nothing can be gained thru stupid martyrdoms.

We cannot fight police.

Our job is to expand the consciousness of the people (knowledge of the people) so that people would elect (or give birth) to better judges and better police.

In other words: why get in trouble with police if we can do more "damage" by other ways and by other tactics?

Coop   Memo   .r

Thursday July 9th 1964

att jerry joffen and everybody else, as a matter of fact

I received an undirect complain today ~~rom your~~ ~~eden~~
that some evenings lamps burn out (projector) and you
can't properly work at the coop.
coop is sort of cooperative place, and each of us has to
pich in. Since we have been badly broke last few
weeks, and lamps keep burning out after 5- hours pro-
jecion time -- concerning lamps, or anything else,
we all have to do something about HELPING OURSELVES AND
OTHERS. There is nobody to serve you or anybody else
here, that is important to understand-- but we all are
here to serve each other. In other words, no complains are
accepted. If there is something not perfect, whoever discove
rs that imperfection , has to do something about it,
to eliminate it -- not not by telling it to me, because
that is only evading the issue -- but doing something
about it
     I writ this down because it is a very typical
attitude,and I see it in other film-makers, and I think
it is time that I have e little sermon here on this
subject of COOPERATIVE working, so that we all know
or at least think about it
     and this is the end of my sermon for today
     t is can be reduced to one sentense:
     COOP IS YOU. IT WILL BE WHAT YOU ARE OR WHAT YOU DO.
TO COMPLAIN AGAINST COOP MEANS TO COMPLAIN AGAINST
YOURSELF.

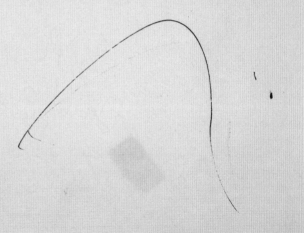

schedules: of trials:

Flaming Creatures : May 18th ~~June 2~~
Genet ———— ~~May 12th~~ June 2nd

Jacobs-Fernman June 8th
Naomi. June 2nd
Genet June 15
FC. '1 10
Aug 17th F.C.
19. June Genet
Joe Marxinson 30th
July 30th Jacobs
Aug 17th — Jonas
Aug 10th — Joel

FOR EVERYBODY TO READ

BEFORE YOU ENTER THIS PLACE ~~THEMM~~
you have to accept the rules of this place
because you are not alone, there are other people beside you

primarily, this is a place of work
complete silence is asked

if bed is given for the night, get up ~~early~~ EARLY and clean the place
so that not to make others angry who have work to do here

to use bacjk room and equipment, call Leslie in advance to
arrange for it, because there are many of us and
this place is becoming a tower of Babel already
we are trying to straighten things out

this is no place of playing ball   that is sure

if this is not good for you, turn back and GO
the world is wide

don't bring any more things here -- the place is loaded
with crap already
I,ll be throwing out everything soon anyway ~~cccc~~
                                    hear
you can complain to me -- but I can't hear/complains, that's all

i say all this because last few weeks this place has become impossible
for any work. Leslie has to pick up his things and run home to work
but that's ridiculous and impossible. The same with me. The same
with John Palmer, and Gregory, and Luis. There is a number of *and Naomi*
things to be done here daily and they must be done even if
we have to throw evrybody else, and we (or I) intend to do this
beginning right now -- unless the monastery rules are completely
obeyed.

You may think that WORK is or TO WORK is wrong or something like that
that one should only PLAY   a
which would show only that you are/pompous asses and you don't know what
          WORK or PLAY or ANYTHING is

July 26ᵗʰ 1964

[handwritten box at right:]
NOTICE
THE NEW REGIME
DOESNT APPLY ON
SUNDAYS BECAUSE
SANDAYS ARE FOR GOING

[handwritten left margin:] THE NEW REGIME DOESN'T APPLY ON SUNDAYS —

CHAPTER SIXTEEN

Why Jack hates Coop... I burn the bridges...

June 15, 1964

PAS:

Sorry I did not send the money earlier. Telling you the truth, I didn't have it.

Send me immediately your new address. I have a book for you, my promised surprise. I didn't mail it to London.

Flaming Creatures trial just ended. A true comedy. We were found guilty. I don't know yet what will be the sentence. No need worry, though. We are going to appeal—we are going to a higher court where we have some chances of winning. It will take years. I will send more detail on the trial in the middle of the week.

Barbara just appeared here from thin air. The bastards deported her from Italy back to NY. She was on her way to Himalayas.

Brakhage thought about the same as you about Linder's film.

Hello from David (St.)

Joel Markman was just arrested. Nobody knows for what.

David is walking out, so I am ending this letter to mail.

June 29, 1964

PAS:

I will start, as usually, lately, with a complaint: Where the heck have you been last 4 weeks, with not a peep from you, with no return address, with nothing? I hope none of the mail that I am enclosing is of any urgency—I did not have your address after London.

Number two: I have been swamped by filmmakers' calls about what happened in the London show, and all I can tell them is, "I haven't heard anything yet." That still remains.

End of complaint department.

Sorry about that check. I thought that bank checks are cashable all around the blasted world. I don't dare send cash, after Paris loss of $50.00 (the cash was in one of your Paris hotel letters). Best is to use American Express. I am very suspicious now about the hotels.

It is terribly hot here now. The summer is blooming red like a poppy and we are sweating and living on iced coffee and cokes, it is really beastly. Coop is becoming a real hell place with all the people and all the screenings going here all the time, with no other place to see movies —there are evenings when the place is so full that people are sticking out the windows, almost, I am amazed the place did not collapse yet.

These last few days Harry Smith moved into the Coop with his huge contraption— a wooden Trojan Horse with a projector, two slide machines, and various other windows and knobs and things for his square screen triple quadruple projection and he has been screening his fantastic cabalistic and superimposition movies and everybody is going nuts because these movies that he made 15 years ago are so fantastic, and his latest one, that he made just a few weeks ago, is no doubt the best of all superimposition collage or whatever movies, at least as good as *Chumlum*, but some will find it better—we have been overwhelmed here and have no real perspective yet, and he is crazy, evil, nasty, very brilliant, very learned in certain cabalistic and alchemist areas, like nobody else, and he has been insulting everybody, spitting around, I don't know how I managed to make him show his films here, but he moved in and he is going to stay here with his machines and films for some time now, he's OK despite all the strange things he does, one has to put up with him, although Gregory will never forgive him for making fun of him and his new film here one evening.

By the way, I have seen 15 hours or so of Gregory's new film, and there is no doubt that he has about the most beautiful 15 hours he ever did, there are fantastically beautiful parts there—with Jack riding high waves with *Normal Love*. I mean the crests of beauty now everyone is pulling themselves up by the ears to do better and better—there is a good competition now— so Gregory, too, I think, opened himself more than before and asked from himself more and is doing things he would never have done before (I mean, in a sense, before *F. Creatures*—*FC* has really opened a new era in a sense, despite all the fuss about it)—if Gregory will do as brilliant an editing job as is his footage, he will have a masterpiece. *Prometheus* may even prove to be a better film than *Normal L* for one simple reason: I am afraid, from what I see, that Jack may ruin parts of *NL* by bad editing. He is learning editing, but he doesn't know editing yet, and is making quite disturbing mistakes, and I don't want to go into details. Anyway, Jack has his first rough cut finished and is beginning to work on sound.

Stan is back in the Land and Gregory just called me. He said he spoke with Stan last night for 40 minutes and Stan is happy and blooming and just received his first 8 mm *Song 1*. He is working, that means, and that is better than many of us can say or be.

Andy (Warhol) is filming like mad every evening and has by now probably more footage than any other film-maker and he is really obsessed by film and is like a living reminder here to others not to fall asleep but move ahead into new adventures (he just finished his pimple sequence, for his new Soap Opera).

So the things are happening here.

Right this moment, Jerry Jofen—you wouldn't believe it—is in the back room of the Coop, although not working on his film but working on some kind of junky collage with Barbara, but yesterday Barbara spliced all his footage together and there are huge reels now and Jerry said he will now definitely finish some of his movies and will put sound etc. etc. One never knows anything with him what he will do or not.

Louis just called, he said Storm's film was just accepted. I mean she just received a letter that her film was accepted in Locarno Film Fest, in competition, so that is good news for Storm.

And *The Brig* went to Venice, they wanted to see it, so it is not far from you—it is all finished and it is a brutal piece for strong stomachs.

Now, tell me, if you have any decent answer, why you keep spelling-writing Hiakus instead of Haikus? But you are forgiven. *Fool's Haikus* are resting. Image was finished about two months ago but I got stuck with the sound. I just can't work it out properly. I destroyed three different soundtracks and I can't let it go silent, it needs sound, but I still don't know what sound, so I have to wait and see; the sound should eventually come one way or another when I least expect it perhaps.

That much of gossip.

Most of my life here is still consumed by running around, peddling films, trying to get money into the Coop, for Jack, Gregory, etc.,etc., and I have secured all the money needed to finish *Normal L.* You maybe interested to know that 12 film-makers, I mean, I persuaded Friends of New Cinema to give to 12 film-makers 10 dollars every week for a year, which is little or nothing but at least enough to eat (Gregory, Stan, Jack, Storm, Ken Jacobs, Naomi, Ron, George Landow, Peter Kubelka, Kuchars, Jofen and Jim Davis). Kubelka no doubt will be happily surprised, but I thought he should be honored at least in this small way.

Concerning Exposition:

Let me know exact date of Karlovy Vary, and where and when will you be after that.

There maybe some mail (enclosed in here) that may change your plans—maybe a booking in Germany or some other place —but your major stops in Europe are coming to end, unless Poland decides to invite you. After you are finished the films should be left, I think, packed, with Ledoux, I trust him most, until we know where they will have to go. Japan maybe next, but the date is not certain.

Working on a new issue of *Film Culture*. Anything? Get Peter Kubelka to write for us. Or I think you should tape an interview with him. See all his films. Do a piece on his work for the coming issue, whenever you are ready. Don't sit without doing nothing, don't spend too much time with those Viennese maids and cut down on your beer escapades before your belly begins to bulge and drip down from all that beer. And so this is the time for me like for all good men to close this letter and forgive me my rambling and disorganized manner and typewriter and fingers because it is really hot here and my brain is half melted and dripping down from the typewriter like Dalí's watches so don't wonder too much I hope you'll be able to get the meanings and facts if there are any.

Regards from everyone

We will survive, as Confucius used to say.

August 23, 1964

Dear Film-Makers:

This is to let you know that you'll be seeing me less and less.

I had enough of running around, running my ass off. I have been asked many times before, why I am doing all this; why I am not devoting my time to my own work. I always answered: I don't know what my real work is. I don't know what my function in this world is. I do what I HAVE to do. I always thought, and I still think that it's too pompous and egoistic to think that one should do something else than what one is doing even if that thing that one is doing amounts to nothing. But now the time has come for my own work.

And that's what I have to do: my own film work. Even if that "film work," my *Diaries*, will amount to nothing, like everything else that I have done in my life—I still have to do it.

Therefore this note is the announcement of the beginning, Phase One, of my leave of absence. Since it's in my nature to do 100 things at the same time and work on 100 different levels, visible and invisible, you'll be seeing plenty of me even when I don't want to be seen. But my first concern is now reversed: Until now YOU were my first concern; from now on my own film work will be the number one concern. I have been working on this thing for quite some time now—years, really—not knowing where to go and where to start and how to go about it. I am still not too sure. But I am ready to start. And it will be a long going. My *Diaries* calls for at least ten years of work. There are five different ends to it, and it is still very complicated, and no use trying to explain anything, although it is also quite clear to me—

So ahead I go, slowly, breaking myself away bit by bit from you & from many of my undertakings and workings—and since I am so deep in it, it will take me some time, quite some time to free myself completely—

total engagement—

but I am going

and I thought I will let you sort of know about it since we have been together for years, now, some of us—

October, 1964

WHAT IS "THE NEW AMERICAN CINEMA GROUP INC" UNDER WHICH AUSPICES *FLAMING CREATURES* AND GENET FILM WERE SCREENED
The New American Cinema Group Inc. is an organization that was created by the independent film-makers of New York in autumn 1960 to advance film-making. The aims of the Group are described in detail in the attached Supplement N. 1 and Supplement N. 2. The creation of this organization was a spontaneous effort of more than thirty of the most active New York film-makers.

SOME OF THE GROUP'S ACTIVITIES
Among the first major projects of the N.A.C. Group was the New American Cinema Exposition held in 1961 in Spoleto, Italy, under the guidance of David C. Stone. A similar Exposition was held in Stockholm in 1962, under the guidance of Alfred Leslie. In December, 1963, the largest Exposition of American cinema ever undertaken was shipped to Europe by the N.A.C. Group, under the guidance of P. Adams Sitney and Jonas Mekas. The fourteen programs will tour Munich, Amsterdam, Stockholm, Rome, Madrid, Paris, London, Bombay, Tokyo, Sydney, and other capitals. Much has been accomplished by the Group in working out and putting in practice new film financing methods for the low budget film production. A new system, based on Off-Broadway theatre investment practices, was adapted in the field of cinema. It proved to be a healthy asset to independent film production in New York. The Group's meetings with the motion picture unions have resulted in gaining concessions for low budget film-making in the New York area. The activities of the Group helped much to bring fresh blood into the N.Y. film scene.

WHAT IS FILM-MAKERS' COOPERATIVE
To assist the distribution of independently produced films a new division of the Group was created—the Film-Makers' Cooperative, a distribution center operating on a cooperative basis, with all profits going to the film-maker. Films are being distributed to theatres, film societies, universities, television, and other outlets.

Wednesday, September 30, 1964:

Jonas,

I'm putting this note in the first mailing of dailies which are
in the lab tonight for release about noon tomorrow. Two parcels
that had been delayed by the weather in Johnstown came in today.

Maya Deren's mother called for you today, and I told her I'd pass
her request on to you and that either you'd contact her directly,
or you'd instruct me to call her. Teiji Ito told her that you
were working on a biography of Maya Deren. If so, she would like
to offer any help she could give. Secondly, she believes you have
some of Maya's poetry, and she would like to see it. Her address
is: Mrs. Marie Deren, 62 West 93rd Street, New York, N.Y. 10025.
Her telephone number: UNiversity 4-6962.

Piero Heliczer wants to know if you're going to use his manuscript
in "Film Culture."

Jack Smith is talking about extending his trip to the L.A. FilmFest
to go down to Acapulco to see Ron Rice. (And what happens to NORMAL
LOVE?)

Isabel called me today to inquire about bills she can help with.
I told her I would send an accounting for Jack and Bobina tomorrow.

Barbara called me today to say that her case was discharged and
she wants to come up and collect her stuff, talk about what to do
with her film, and her plans to go to Tangiers. Probably will be
here Friday.

I'm still working on Ida Schenkman.

Storm's film is the American entry at Vancouver, according to Variety.

I think the Les Crane show over nationwide ABC-TV hookup will use
five minutes or so of Vanderbeek's abstract film study PHENOMENON #1
together with a ten-minute interview.

Bob Brown is beginning to get a little cooperation from film-makers
in helping to ready the "cinematheque." He is getting lecture-cum-
film-screening engagements for himself, to help support himself.
Not much of a self-starter, and a bit slow, but he's a good fellow.

I'm going to need a vacation of some sort, I think. So I'm thinking
of trying the lecture-road, myself! ...except I hate talking about
films. I'd rather see them, book them, and keep my thoughts to myself!

If I can, I'll pick up three rolls of film for you tomorrow and send
them off in the shipment of dailies, along with some copies of issue #33,
this note, VARIETY and the VOICE....

Best,

Leslie

To promote low budget features and shorts, the Group, through its right arm, Film-Makers' Cooperative, besides special screenings to the exhibitors, has organized and carried out several important projects. Its programming for the Charles Theatre made that theatre into an important outlet of independent cinema and brought the existence of the independents to the public attention. The Group also programmed and conducted a special midnight screening series at the Bleecker St. Cinema. In Spring 1963 the Group opened its showcase at the Gramercy Arts Theatre, which became internationally watched theatre of the independent cinema. After its closing by the Department of Licenses, the Group moved its screenings to the New Bowery Theatre, under the auspices of the Poet's Foundation—until that theatre was closed too, by the Department of Licenses. The Film-Makers' Cooperative did the programming also for the abortive venture of the 55th Playhouse in the field of the "avant-garde cinema."

No date, 1964

I sound like a disillusioned man. In a sense I am. My experiences of the last few months, my clashes with the police and with the law, my searchings and watching my friends going through the same, changed me a lot.

Today, I do not believe any longer in law, in achieving any justice in courts. I feel that courts are places where truth has become a joke. In courts the truth is mocked. The whole court procedure is a dehumanizing game.

Further, I have come to the conclusion that, in a sense, I was guilty. Guilty of stupidity. From my inexperience, I made a mistake. I wanted to expand man's consciousness from the top, instead of the bottom. Instead of working through changing the people, I attacked the law. Now I believe that the law can be changed only when

people are ready for it. And the people are not ready for it. People are tolerating the courts, the stupid laws, the police activities which are the mockery of human intelligence, dignity, and whatever is dear to man and culture. In fact, they are criminals. They are committing crimes and citizens are tolerating them. How to begin to wake up the people, that's the question. You beat a dog, and the dog licks your feet. The people behave like servile dogs. How to uplift men from their dog's state to state & dignity?

He (she) on stage.
Everybody's asked to come and touch her (him)
Listen to the heartbeat of next one to you
Look into the eyes
Say one word, line, "Who are you?"
Pronounce the first name of one next to you.

I used to sit in the restaurants, cafeterias, on gloomy days when the whole place looked like it couldn't be sadder & try to provoke one smile on the tired waitress' face by smiling myself—believing that the world, the city, would become brighter at least by one, even if artificial, smile—maybe that one smile will save it—afraid that the city may never come back out of the coma of grimness, gloom & mugginess in which it lay—hoping that even an artificial smile may warm it up, move the muscles of joy and happiness back to life—like they revive the drowned by artificial breathing, mouth to mouth—

No date, 1964

A note to Ford Foundation:
Jack Smith: The work of Jack Smith more than that of any other film-maker in America today, is free from conventional aesthetic and personal inhibitions and conventions. It is breaking fresh grounds in the "Baudelairean," deeply disturbed

and personal cinema. His work helps other film-makers to free themselves, to expand their own poetic content, to go deeper into themselves.

In *Flaming Creatures*, Jack Smith captures the forbidden pleasures & fantasies; he reminds us that we have bodies and senses; he opens the Pandora box of erotic mythology; he opens to other film-makers (and viewers) doors into their own private worlds; he expands our knowledge of ourselves; he adds something to the joy of living.

Jack Smith is part of that American cinema which is moving away from the realism of the early New York School, reaching deeper and deeper into the poetic and the irrational; broadening and clarifying our sensibilities; away from cinéma-vérité and closer to the poetry-truth. Jack Smith emphasizes the senses and the non-literary, intuitive intelligences; flesh is honored, pleasure joyfully accepted, life glorified.

In *The Great Pasty Triumph*, Jack Smith demonstrated that he is the supreme master of color in cinema today. He uses color like Rubens did, like Chinese masters did, like Max Ophuls did. It is a controlled, quiet, meditating & breathtakingly sensuous beauty of pink and yellow and blue. No one else in cinema today uses color as effectively and as aesthetically beautifully, as Jack Smith does.

No date, 1964

A STORY

He travelled a long way to arrive just where he had started. He had travelled ten thousand miles. He always wanted to know where the road really led to. But when he came to the end of the road, he saw nothing but a pile of rabbit shit. So he realized the foolishness of his wanting to know what's at the end of the road, and he thought about his long journey, the effort he put into it, and he laughed. He laughed with no regret, with no hard feelings. He knew he had been made a fool by some-

one who liked fooling. For a moment an understanding and communication was established with the absolute, even if just for a moment. And then he began his long journey back.

KEEP LOOKING FOR THINGS IN PLACES WHERE THERE IS NOTHING (from Buddha's unpublished writings…)

Dry petals of dead flowers have secret cures in them; and so do the shreds of snakeskin; anything under the sun, once touched by life (sun?) is imbued with power over death.

No date, 1964

MINI-MANIFESTO

Don't mind the fact that a great part of this cinema is treading on the very edge of perversity. Today there is very concrete (dialectical) necessity to break down all the walls of inhibitions, to tear off false, and antic, clothing. These are, as Ken Jacobs put it, "dirty-mouthed" films. They have no pretensions about themselves. They are far and beyond the temporary morality. They are in the fields of innocence.

I know that the "larger" public will misinterpret and slander our films. As there are poets appreciated only by other poets; or pilgrims understood only by other pilgrims; so there is, now, a cinema for the few, too terrible and too "evil" for an "average" man in any organized culture— but then, the organized culture has to be constantly disrupted.

The new content has developed a new, extremely subtle film language which enables artists to register and transmit their most subtle inner movements, intelligences and emotions, into images. The language of Brakhage, Snow, Jacobs, Menken, MacLaine, Jofen—this is the truly new cinema of today. Not the cinema of plots, stories, short stories, melodramas and morality plays, but a cinema which, for the first time, can deal with ideas, sensitivities, emotions, experiences on the level of the best of poetry.

MOVEMENT: Movement can now go from complete immobility to a blurred swish vision to a million unpredictable speeds and ecstasies (Brakhage's work, for instance). The classic film vocabulary allows (or recognizes) only the slowly, respectably, Brooks-Brothers-suit paced camera movements—the steadiness, the immobility which is called a "good," "clear," "steady" image. It is this respectability, this immobility of spirit that prevents the European cinema, even the best of it, from breaking out into the really new sensibilities, the new content. There is nothing in the new European cinema which hasn't been said by writers long ago.

Some American film-makers have freed motion. The camera movement can now go anywhere—from a clear, idyllic peacefulness of the image to a frenetic and feverish ecstasy of motion. The full scale of our emotions can be registered, reflected, clarified—for ourselves, if for nobody else. The camera can be as feverish as our minds. We need this fever to escape the heavy pressure of a heavy culture. There is no such thing as a "normal movement" or a "normal image," a "good image" or a "bad image." I don't have to tell you that all this goes radically against the accepted aesthetics of our classical and professional (commercial) cinema.

LIGHTING: Now it can go from the "properly" exposed and lit image to a complete destruction of the "proper;" from a complete whiteness (wash-out) to a complete blackness. Endless nuances are now open to us, the poetry of shades, of over- and under-exposures.

These new happenings in our cinema reveal that man is reaching, growing into new areas of himself, areas which were either deadened by culture, or not yet born. Add to what I already mentioned the complete disregard of censorship, the abandoning of taboos on sex, language etc. and you'll have some idea of what's going on.

More and more film-makers are realizing that there is no one single way of exposing (seeing) things; that the steadiness or sharpness or clarity (and all their opposites) are no virtues or absolute properties in themselves; that, really, the cinema language, like any other language and syntax, is in a constant flux, is changing with our own changes.

No date, 1964

To Naomi:
Just a note about why I didn't help you & stayed away from your picket on Saturday. There is already too much talk that I am imposing on other film-makers my own will, my ideas, my whims, etc. I'd like to stay on the side, now, as much as possible, not to impose anything, not to dictate, even unconsciously: let the will and wishes of other film-makers be seen. In other words: I felt, that this picket will have a meaning only if it comes from other film-makers (and other people).

No date, 1964

In *Twice a Man*, Gregory Markopoulos uses editing in a new and complex way to capture the subconscious & thought, the movements of unliterary intelligences. He demonstrates anew, in a most beautiful way, that editing is one of cinema's glories. His film, full of exquisite beauty, pulsates with subtle levels of sensuous sub-imagery. Bouquets & fountains of color burst in magnificent, glorious fireworks.

No date, 1964

AN ESSAY ON THE MORALITY OF OUR ART

What, then, about the "evil" in the world today? Do the artists approve of what's

happening in the world today?
Yes! Tell us, what's really happening?
A bomb fell on Nagasaki.
But Brakhage made *Mothlight*.
By his presence, by the presence of an artist, by the presence of poetry, the thinking and the actions of others are modified, changed, beautified.
That's what our "art" is "engaged" in.

No date, 1964

OPENING SPEECH
I was asked to open this Festival.
So this is an opening speech.
We have closed ourselves, the man has closed himself gradually during last 1000 years, and he is closed now to all mystery, to all the unexplainable, to the unexpected. Truly, man has closed so many doors to himself and around himself that he has locked himself OUT!
We think we know so much!
We think we know what art is.
We think we know what man is: what we are, what we should be.
We constantly close ourselves, we constantly keep drawing lines around ourselves, we sit behind them and we look at man and art from behind those lines, and we look very, very skeptically. We measure everything in many ways and we try to fit it all into what we already know, this side of the line.
But some irresponsible, unpredictable, unexplainable people have pulled all the doors off their hinges! Mama mia, mama mia!
Suddenly, our imaginations and our knowledge and our visions and all our measurements have been disrupted!
You are going to see many films at this Festival, and most of them are still carrying the seeds of the old.
But there will be glimpses, anxious glimpses, desperate and/or fragile attempts at something new and beautiful.
Because man is not easy to kill.

I am amazed how difficult it is to kill a man, both, bodily and spiritually.
He will go through the concentration camps, through the torture chairs; he will live with his hands and bones broken, without arms, without eyes—he keeps living, desperately trying to survive, endure, after centuries of death and materialism and industrialism and rationalism and false scientism—man's spirit has survived so many tortures!
So that tonight, at this opening, I am asking for your UNCONDITIONAL OPENING of yourselves.
Open all your eyes and all your mind circles and let the beauty whatever there is of it, drift and float and enter.
I am asking for an unconditional opening of your eyes.
I am asking for an unconditional opening of your minds.
I am asking for an unconditional opening of all the doors.
Because it depends on both, on those who make films and on those who look at films to keep all the doors open for the new so that the dreams could come in.
We have to open all the windows wide open to look out to see what's really happening.
Let's open all our eyes and let's look for things where man has thought for centuries that there was nothing there to look for or at.

No date, 1964

"You know to me not only films but all expressions of people should be shown, so as to touch all those aching to be felt & that no matter what the risks or dangers, everyone would be free to say whatever they feel & for it to reach as many people as possible legally or not. One can only constantly expose oneself, taking risks & plunging, for that is life. As far as the filmmakers themselves are concerned, they, too, need to grow & free themselves or else they too will die. Here as everywhere

there is a feeling of uselessness of the kind where people don't even bother anymore. These movies are new, different, freer; they will have an effect; if they don't grow (film-makers) then their movies will just pass on by to their own unfelt death."
—Barbara Rubin

No date, 1964

A DREAM
I was walking along the street. And people ran away from me, pointing fingers at me, an outcast
I came into a square—and pigeons flew away
Even a child runs away. A mother comes, she rushes towards him, picks him up and rushes away
So alone I walked the empty street
And I saw myself going in front of me so I tried to catch up with Myself
But Myself kept changing shapes, and faces, kept disguising, and dashing the corners and suddenly there is a large and wide and empty space in front of me; no more streets or corners—now I can catch up with My Self suddenly a cat jumps on my hand and begins to eat my right hand, and I try to move my hand but I can't move it I can't move myself

and I wake up

UNFULFILLED DESIRES SEQUENCE
Sailors, in the evening, drinking in a bar; women; music.
We all would like to roam the world free like sailors.

A DREAM
I saw a room. It said, "Another Room."
Every night at this time the dead (mad) enka-vedist (KGB worker) comes to repeat his crimes. He is the one who tortures and the one who is being tortured at the same time. He moans and cries alone.

Oh wasted years
Oh Siberia
Oh the prisons of the 20th Century
the anger
the inhumanity of man to man
it explodes your mind
what a man can do to a man
today

No date, 1964

To the Director, Venice Film Festival
I have to confess, that my original thought was to accept your invitation, to come to Venice, and make my resignation there. However, after another thought, I decided to dismiss this idea because it would be playing the destruction game. There is too much destruction already, I don't want any part in it. I want change, but I am against any destruction and any violence. Today more than ever. Those who have watched the growth of the New American Cinema, the Underground, should know by now that our spirit is to build, not to destroy. The things that we consider outdated, even harmful, we leave them to their own inevitable death by keeping ourselves out of it. We didn't waste energy in destroying Hollywood film: we directed our energies towards creating a new kind of cinema; we didn't waste any energy in destroying the competitive, commercial distribution systems: we created our own cooperative distribution center, Film-Makers' Cooperative; we didn't waste energy in fighting censorship laws: we created a cinema that is changing the censorship laws. The same thing, I believe, is with the Film Festivals. We stay out of them. Have you seen us at Cannes or Venice? If anyone dislikes Cannes or Venice or New York Film Festivals—let them create one of their own and show what a film festival should be.

Anyway, I wish you good luck—I wish everybody would leave you alone and in peace—

At the Coop, with Stan Brakhage and
P. Adams Sitney, 1963.

No date, 1964

Enough of the theatre of the absurd & horror & cruelty. We need a theatre of happiness. Happiness has no drama. So what?

No date, 1964

COOP BULLETIN

We have realized, suddenly, that because of the recent publicity, magazine articles etc., etc., fantasies have developed in our minds and hearts; some film-makers are beginning to think that the times have changed, that now everything is fine, that money is just around the corner, waiting, that we are darlings of the people, and everybody wants to help us to make our movies.

Nothing could be further from reality.

There are also those who think that many people now come to the Coop with money; that the Coop is monopolizing the financial assistance; etc. etc. What a dream! The truth is that during its two years of existence only two or three persons have come to the Coop with small contributions. Every penny that Coop managed to get from outside, to help to pay film-makers' bills, was a battle, a desperate running around the town from downtown to uptown to downtown.

The truth is that there was never—and there isn't today—money for the avant-garde arts. The articles and stories in the magazines are for the magazines' own publicity and sales purposes. And it's time that we come down to earth, wake up from our dreams, and face the same fight which we started two years ago so that we could create with the same honesty and the same intensity—

—or we have reached the end, a very sad end, before we have even started, before we have done anything of lasting Beauty—

No date, 1964

Every excuse and reasoning sounds reasonable and breeds more reason.

My decision, whatever my reasons, is more irrational than the impression I am trying to make here.

I open my wings and I fly.

And I disappear into warm summer sun.

The wind is blue.

It is easy to breath in the morning even in the city, at 6 AM—did you try?

Every man has his Himalayas.

Analysis breeds more analysis.

No date, 1964

What are USA, France, USSR, China etc. doing in Sudan, S. America?

By placing the idea that everybody can make movies, we want to liberate cinema. Which has nothing to do with politics. We want to liberate cinema from politics by putting it in people's hands. Cinema of the people.

Like with anything else that is vital, alive, and timely, the underground cinema movement has caught the imagination of the young Americans and from a small germ six years ago, it has become a movement that is changing cinema across the country and also, as I have found after two months of studying the European situation this summer, it's changing the cinema of Europe also. However, also, as with any such movement, there are also dangers. The danger in the first place comes from the press and mass media. During the last three years, the mass media caught to the underground movement, and began misusing it for their own sensational purposes. From my many dealings with them I can tell you that they have been willingly concentrating only on the sensational aspects of the artists working on the fringes of the avant-garde. So that a completely distorted image of the avant-garde has been created. Working with the Cinematheque, I often meet people, tourists, who come to the city and instead of going to

Venezia 10.9.64

Dear Jonas and Adolfas.

As I told you in the Post-cards-
your "The Brig" was the biggest
successe here. It was shown again and
again since, for buyers and journatists
that did'nt sea it.

Only one man was against it:
Mr Edouard de Laurot. He organized a
press-conference and then published this
page. He put in it names that had nothing
to do with him, and it looks like
his own privet' warka.

People did'nt even laugh at him,
but next time come along with your
films - to colect the glories.

Yours   Eli

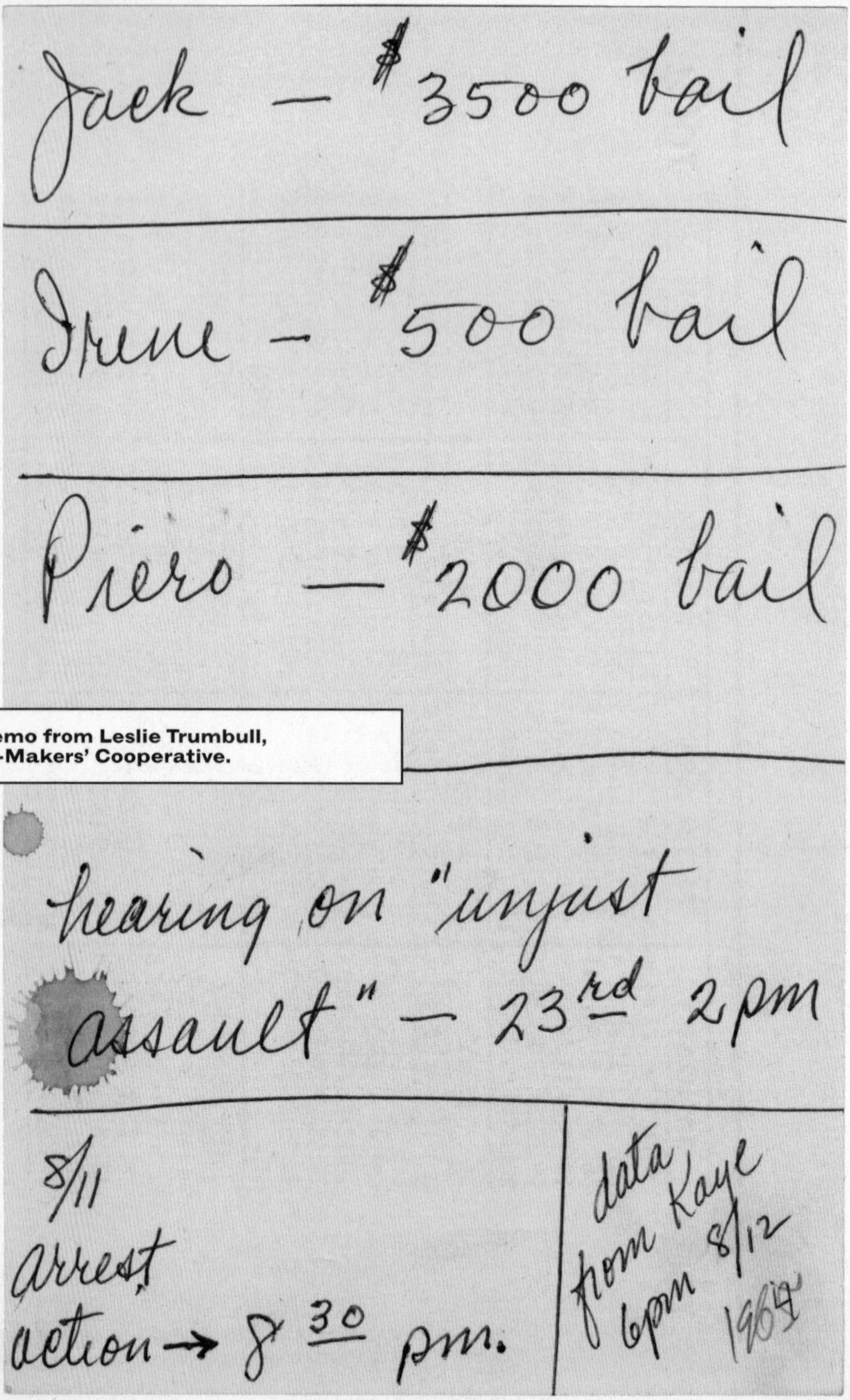

Jack — $3500 bail

Irene — $500 bail

Piero — $2000 bail

A memo from Leslie Trumbull, Film-Makers' Cooperative.

hearing on "unjust assault" — 23rd 2pm

8/11 arrest action → 8$\frac{30}$ pm.

data from Kaye 6pm 8/12 1964

the Statue of Liberty come to the Cinematheque to see "those dirty underground movies!"

October 29, 1964

Was passing a restaurant, the kitchen door open to the street. Suddenly a gust of hot food smells surged into the street. I stopped and drank the smells. It was almost as good as food. I remembered Bessie. She said, she is never hungry: she has enough of smells, during the cooking (she works as a cook in an Italian restaurant.) I felt suddenly much stronger. Even the weakness in the legs disappeared. For a while, at least. I stood there, drinking in all the smells. Then I continued.

"You look so drained out," remarked Long John at the theater. I did not think I looked that bad, that it showed so much. It was all illusion, my strength.

"I have to get my strength back," I said, and I went to the water tank and swallowed a few good gulps of good cold water. Water revived me for a while, or at least, again, I thought. John laughed. "With water?" he said. But water was good. I borrowed a penny from Jerry to make up 15 cents that I needed for a token to get home.

With Louis, yesterday, we delivered *Film Culture* to the post office and spent our last money on the stamps. We were crossing the town, walking, and I said, I'll treat you with a coffee, I still have a quarter in my pocket. No, Louis said, I will have a Coke. Later, we were walking, he said, "Coke has some cocaine, and on the empty stomach it is like drugs, it keeps you moving, so I prefer Coke to the coffee."

October 30, 1964

Seymour Stern showed up in town, from the blue sky. We had a long evening session, discussing the DWG *F.C.* issue which he is editing. We agreed on everything. He is ready to go.

This man, Seymour, he's amazing, his energy. The way he ran up and down the Coop steps, four floors. Like a boy. Even Gantt was amazed. Like a goddamn dynamo. We were eating, and he kept looking at the girls around. "Sex keeps me alive," said Seymour. "Harry should be a good friend of yours, he is also obsessed with sex." "Oh, great," said Seymour, "I am obsessed with sex." Yeh, that's what keeps him running up the four floors.

Like Chaplin. The same curve around the lip—both Chaplin and Seymour have them, I have noticed that two years ago.

Stopped at Bleecker Street where *Babo 73* is playing. Found Bob Downey there, happy and optimistic. Expecting another child (his wife, I mean…) "Only she keeps me alive," he said, "I can work in peace."

Last night, from the Bleecker (Gregory screened his rushes for *Prometheus*) I had to take Naomi home. "I want to have my own family, I want to have children, I don't want to make films. Really, I want, but family in the first place. That's what others can't understand. I am sick with the crowd. I don't even come to the Coop," she said.

I ventured, that Stan probably is an example. When you see Brakhages together, all of them, with children, it is a joy. How he manages to keep the balance between his art and his family, is amazing. Now, they say, you must be completely sick to be an artist, no family; you have to be completely sick…

"I hate this," I told Naomi. "Ginsberg runs in, at the Bleecker, he strokes his hand over my belly, everywhere, it is disgusting. I didn't grow up like that, I can't understand people like that, they have no respect for others, they are like pigs. I don't want anyone to put hands on my belly. What a messy bunch. No manners of any kind—a mess. I don't blame you avoiding them, I don't blame you at all."

November 1, 1964

Did some editing on Dalí footage.

Borrowed $200 (for two weeks) from Jane Holzer to pay Tek's rent. Need one more hundred by tomorrow morning. Sitting now by the telephone, thinking whom to call. Gregory promised to lend one hundred from his filming money, in case I get really stuck. Jane was almost crying. "Look what you did: I have no peace. Every nut wants to make movies now, that's what you did. The whole field has opened." Since her pix appeared in *Show*, on the cover, two weeks ago, she hasn't had any peace from magazines, newspapers and film-makers. While I was there, this morning, there were calls from the *NY Times, Journal American*; a film producer read half of his script on the phone, about witches or something like that. "Terrible," she said, about the script. She gave me the $200 stealing from her husband's money. "Let's hope he won't find out," she said. We made up a phony "loan" paper, in case he finds out.

Yesterday went to Met Museum, first time in three or four years. Looked at Velásquez and Vermeer. Goddamn good. It's good to see something old and good & beautiful. Had another session with Seymour Stern. Attended Kennedy campaign meeting at some student place near Columbia. A sad crowd. Met Marie.

Had a session with Dan Talbot about the NAC series at the New Yorker. Before meeting Dan, I stopped at Stone's and Barbara gave me two apples and a bottle of beer. I drank the beer on an empty stomach. I was almost drunk when I met Dan. From one beer bottle. I'd never believed that. But the irregular eating has weakened the organism so much that one beer makes me dizzy. That's bad, man, that's pretty bad.

November 2, 1964

David Stone left for Paris. Will be going to Rome, London, Stockholm, to close the *Brig* sales. Our only money hope.

Borrowed $900 from Lee. Lee! Plans big as ever. Has ideas for ten movies.

Isabel called. Asked not to tell Frederick [Eberstadt], her husband, that she is helping Jack to come back from Mexico. He is against it, she said.

Naomi called. Said she saw the most beautiful movie ever made: Ken Jacobs' rushes, summer rushes. Then, she proceeded to demolish all other films, Jack's, Ron's, Andy's, etc. I wondered: Why a beautiful film, an experience of seeing a beautiful thing should inspire one to demolish & attack other beautiful things? What kind of art sickness is that?

In the evening went to see Graciela dance at One Sheridan. She combines dance, Disneyland & Pop, Latin Rhythms, Spanish sense of macabre color, and Her Own Self (born Buenos Aires). As she danced, under silk costumes, deep inside, I was wondering what was going inside of this tiny creature, Graciela, and why she chooses to dance so, in these Disney colors & shapes, what is her soul forecasting? She stood there, at the End, for the applause—she bowed, very humbly, and one saw a glimpse of Graciela herself, as she truly was, yes, but I wasn't sure which one of the two was really real: this graceful woman, yes, a dancer—she could be one of the sylphides!—or the strange rubber, foam, and silk web creature, half amoeba, half Bosch of Disneyland.

November 2, 1964

Reduced to two daily tokens, I stay home now until late afternoon, and then I walk downtown, to the Tek, all the way from 89th Street.

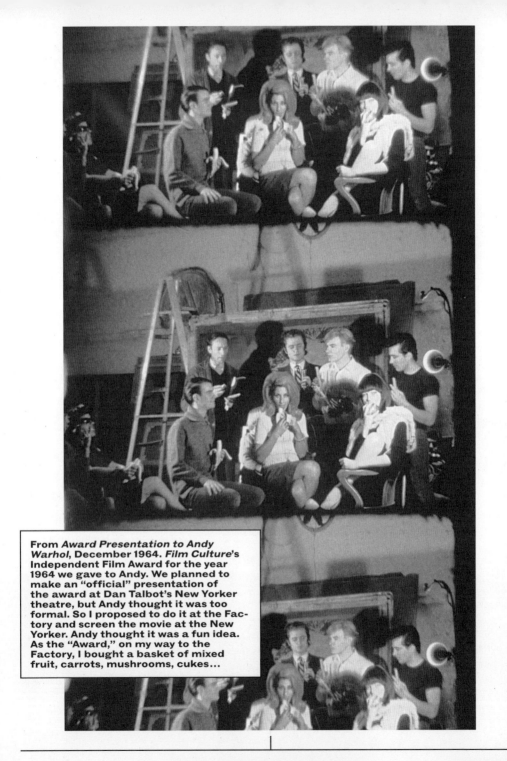

From *Award Presentation to Andy Warhol*, December 1964. *Film Culture*'s Independent Film Award for the year 1964 we gave to Andy. We planned to make an "official" presentation of the award at Dan Talbot's New Yorker theatre, but Andy thought it was too formal. So I proposed to do it at the Factory and screen the movie at the New Yorker. Andy thought it was a fun idea. As the "Award," on my way to the Factory, I bought a basket of mixed fruit, carrots, mushrooms, cukes…

Louis says #33 should be ready Wed/Thurs.

Monday, 28. September, 1964:

Jonas,

Time for a report from this end!

(1) No word since a week ago from Barbara. But there's always tomorrow, which is the day she's supposed to appear in court with the others.

(2) Washington Square Galleries received a summons for operating a theatre without a license, last Sunday week, the 20th. Harry Cropper (the owner) says his lawyer is going to fight it "all the way." Bully for him.

(3) UN CHANT D'AMOUR was seized by the San Francisco police department at its advertised, SRO screening by the S.F. Mime Troupe, according to a long-distance call from Saul Landau, who booked it from us. Charges were to be filed by the district attorney today. Bully for him.

(4) Items (2) and (3) are being communicated with full particulars to Perlman and Berman, respectively, for their information and advisement. Bully for them.

(5) Vogel is in for a jolt and will probably blame you and/or the Co-op: Ken Anger sent me a letter of authorization to pick up his prints and all file materials from C-16. Co-op will be distributor, and Vogel is asked to cease distribution, and account to Kenneth immediately. (In view of your recent negotiations with Vogel to program C-16 films for the Cinematheque, you may want to have me handle things in a particular way.) Kenneth refers to a registered letter sent to Vogel on September 19 that requires that a representative of the Co-op appear at C-16 on the 30th (Wednesday; day after tomorrow) to handle the exchange of authorizing letter for films and materials. Unless I hear from you by phone Tuesday (the day you should get this), I'll take the bull by the horns and follow Kenneth's instructions to the letter, so as not to foul up his arrangements. Bully for us.(?)

(6) Also regarding Anger; Brown today got a letter from him saying that he would like a program of his films to be held off until January, about. He wants to try to get a triptych print of INAUGURATION from France, plus footage of his early films, and something from his current project, all for a huge Kenneth Anger retrospective at the Film-Makers' Cinematheque. Bully!

(7) I'm still trying to get the bond money out of Schenkman. Bully-shit.

(8) That's all, Folks! (Bully for Bugs Bunny.)

Leslie

P.S. Sent checks to Perlman (for Sept.) and NY Telephone (for August) today. (....)

Jonas, Co-op is broke. Can you afford to send me another check? Bob

From *Award Presentation to Andy Warhol*, December 1964.

November 4, 1964

Yesterday, Election Day. Didn't vote. Saw Marzano's new film in raw cut. Bad.

Did more editing on Dalí footage.

Session with the architect at the Cinematheque.

Visited Yoko Ono. She just came back from Japan. To help her to come into the country, I had to employ her at *Film Culture*. She is ready to start life again. Told about her miseries. She brought a little film by Iimura, *Love*, 8 mm, very good, with touches of Brakhage and Andy. She brought with her Kyoko, her little baby girl.

A session with Perlman on legal matters of the Cinematheque.

Prepared first four programs.

Session with Talbot about the New Yorker series.

No date, 1964

Diary film

Sitney in N. Haven, early morning, Nov. 21st
Stan in the Park, Nov. 28th

HOW MANY LIVING POETS HAVE YOU READ?—P. A. Sitney

As the dog who ran away with the Saint's bread said, "You have to clean yourself from the supernatural as much as from the natural world…"

No date, 1964

Here are the names of a few film-makers whose work, I think, is breaking new grounds in film aesthetics and film techniques, and, therefore, in script writing practices: Ricky Leacock, John Cassavetes, Morris Engel, Lionel Rogosin (USA), Godard, Truffaut, Rouch (France), Bondarchuk, Kolotosow, Tchukrai, Tarkovski (USSR), Lindsay Anderson (England), Pasolini, Olmi, Rossellini, De Seta (Italy) etc. The list is incomplete. But if we look at the working practices of these directors, we shall soon realize that they have one thing in common: mistrust of detailed scripts. The degrees vary. But the general direction remains true. Even Wajda, after watching Leacock's *Eddie Sachs*, said he wants, in his next film, to explore the possibilities of improvisation.

It seems, that there is a growing necessity for improvisation, for loosening up the strict script. This is equally true for both, East and West. In Russia, it is coming as a reaction to the over-strict scripting of the personality cult: the reaction against the monumentalism. To quote Chukhrai: "None of the big and pompous words pronounced on the screen reached the heart of man… all my aesthetics developed as a reaction to that sort of cinema." Now I am absolutely against all defined, unchangeable positions in art. This decade will be marked by the explorations in improvisation.

In any case—Godard works with one page scenario on *Vivre sa Vie*. *Shadows* was made with no script at all; Morris Engel (*Weddings and Babies*, *Little Fugitive*) works without script. Rogosin never wrote a line of script. The content of their films is carved directly out of life, or improvised situations, life caught by the tail, so to say, at the moment of improvisation. Rouch uses no scripts, Pasolini uses no scripts, Truffaut's scripts are loose guides.

It is this cinema that interests me, since it's the only contemporary cinema capable of revealing the new truths about life today—old forms lead into old and over-used molds of thought and imagination. To start with a strict script means to start with a preconceived idea; no preconceived idea is a live idea (in art). What good poem was ever written with preconceived ideas? A poem is born during the moments of creating its content and its form, and its life. The same is true for cinema, although the old guard would like to persuade us that it is a mass art and therefore it is ruled by mass rules, which is pure nonsense.

A STORY

"I have nothing to hide from you,"—he whispered, and his lips were sticky in the heat and the sun and humidity, and he could hear the roaring of the crowd and he knew he had no other choice. This was the point of perspective, this was the infinity point, his whole being, his communion and his loneliness. So he stood there, in the middle of the anguished fields, with his wound painfully open, helpless and trembling, and he did not know how to tell them that it was real and it was bleeding. But then, he didn't even want to tell it, not any longer.

With his fainting eyes he could see the brim of the endless wall running far into the infinity.

"On the one side are produced private novels, with a readership of approximately one, which alone treated as Art, and on the other side popular novelists give up the struggle for any glint of truth and get read in millions at the price of surrender to the mass media, the condensations, films, television. It is arguable that such a polarization is the fate of all art in an advanced technological society. If it happens, and it may happen, we shall have committed cultural suicide."—C. P. Snow, *NYT*, Jan. 30, 1955

"I do not mean to suggest, nor, I believe, did Mr. Snow, that the findings, for example, of modern psychology were without profit to the novelist. But I do think it is true that they led him, in many cases, into the cul de sac to which Mr. Snow referred. They narrowed the path of experimental fiction, as Mr. Snow pointed out. Also, I would like to add, they distorted the picture of life that the novelists who took their cue from science were trying to present."—J. Donald Adams, *NYT*, Feb. 13, 1955

Sophocles about Euripides:
"He paints them as they are; I paint them as they ought to be."

Happening theatre like *Meat Joy* testifies a passionate wish to an immediate experience of reality. The verbal, conceptual arts disappear, step into the background. The flesh, the thing, the soul must be felt and known directly, through a different kind of knowledge. Like LSD experience, psychedelic experience. Like the whole beat way of life. The Western man IS undergoing the deepest change since Christianity began.

No date, 1964

I watch & listen & tremble, when I hear Bach. I am all shook up, terrified with glimpses of the lost paradise, of how much we have lost, of what we are, seeing the meaningless of my life, how far I have to go, how far I have fallen back—

As for Jack's hate of the Cooperative, it's very simple: Jack used up about $2,000 of other film-makers' money, but when the time came to return it, he simply said no and pulled out his films from the Coop. That's how much cooperation and understanding there is in Jack re: his friends and colleague film-makers. So he follows the capitalist methods and good luck to him.

Yes, I have definitely burned the bridges. I burned all the bridges with commercial cinema—its methods of production, distribution, exhibition, advertising.
I burned all the bridges with the Madison Avenue which is so dear to Jack.
I burned all the bridges with the second-rate independent cinema that imitates Hollywood, that wants nothing more than to get on TV, be it channel 13 or any other channel, under the pretext of independence.

No, I am not going to rebuild those bridges, not over my dead body—

If you believe in something, you have to believe in it totally. I believe in the art created by my generation.

This sense of *minderwertigheits gefuel*!

It's OK (Jack would be first to approve of it) for a commercial theatre to have a theatre, and an office, a couple of offices, and film storage spaces—and they have at least 1,000 such places in the country, that's OK, they are Jack's dream places. But when avant-garde film-makers dare to try to establish one, a single one, then Jack calls it an Institution, the end, etc. What perversion and what betrayal of the avant-garde!

Yes, and licking the ass of the capitalist cinema.

That's what Jack is doing, that's what all the free small press is doing—*Soho News, Villager, East Village, V. Voice*—just the same as *Time* and *Newsweek* and all the others.

That's why I am not going to rebuild any of those bridges.

Long live Avant-garde. Long live varieties of cinema undreamed yet.

No date, 1964

Matisse in 1908:

"My dream is to achieve a well-balanced art, all purity and tranquility and devoid of any unsettling or disturbing subject... something comparable to a good armchair."

CHAPTER SEVENTEEN

... Letter to Kenneth Anger... On Stockhausen and Cage ... More about money and myself... J.T. Farrell... With Shirley Clarke we review "history" of the Coop... Letter from Maciunas... About *The Brig*... Letter from Louise Brooks... Letters to Mark re. Poets' Theater... Letter from Ginsberg... Diane di Prima... About those who want to exploit us... Carolee Schneemann... Party at the Factory ... Looking for money... I cut my hair to raise money... On Lenny Bruce... On cinéma vérité... Art and Truth... Naomi... On Jack Smith... I visit Gregory... Friends of New Cinema... My answers to a Russian journalist... Visiting Beverly Grant and Tony Conrad... On Warhol's *Poor Little Rich Girl*... Ron Rice dies...

November 18, 1964

New York City

Dear Kenneth:

I thought I will surprise you: I will write a letter. To write a letter for me is like going on some big trip—I keep postponing packing my things and doing one million things which one has to do before going on a big trip. Even a small letter, like this. My friends have given me up long ago—they never expect any letters from me.

Anyway, I have heard by now so much about the L.A. happenings that I have really no idea what really happened. The only truth I can see—from distance—is the truth of the artists' temperaments.

I am more concerned, in this short letter, about your decision to withdraw your films from the Coop. And about the so-called Smith-Markopoulos Award to you.

A note on the Award: I have only one thing to say, whatever you make of it. When Gregory came back from L.A., he told the L.A. story the way he saw it, no doubt, and you have to believe me, he had not a single bad word about you. He said, you did what you had to do. The "Award" they gave you was meant to be their peace branch. They thought they were making a humorous but friendly gesture which you will understand and appreciate. As it turned out—as I see now—their gesture was misunderstood by you as another insult. It wasn't meant that way. It came from their hearts.

Maybe confused hearts, but hearts, nevertheless. That much about the "Award."

Concerning the Coop: Coop was created by film-makers to serve as their distribution center. To be a place where nobody bosses them, cheats them, or binds to 10 year contracts. And whoever finds, by luck or choice a better distribution, is free to try that other source. Coop has no contracts and the film-maker is free to join or go, for whatever time period he wants. The same with you. I don't think you should give a damn to whoever says what about your pulling out & collecting all your babies around you: you are the artist, you made these babies, and you have the birth and passion and temperament rights to collect them again around you whenever you feel like doing so. That's why the Coop was conceived as it is, a loose and contract-less center, and I defend this looseness even at the cost of some disorganization and chaos, sometimes, and a few dollars lost here and there: it doesn't matter, on the very end, a few dollars: it is the artist, it's you that matters. You have acted perfectly right and I will (and am) defending you. Telling the truth, none of the film-makers here really feel that you are acting wrong. They only feel that the reasons perhaps are not sufficient. But how big a reason should there be for anything? Who is going to decide that? Maybe the trouble is with people and with some of our artists that they are waiting too long, always for a reason to become BIG enough, until everything really dies.

I have nothing more to say, really. I just wanted you to know how I feel about it. And whenever you decide that your films should go back to the people, and they should go to the people through the Coop —Coop is always there. And please, don't identify the Coop with Gregory or Jack or with any one or two film-makers: there are seventy film-makers in the Coop, and even if only ten or so are really doing good work—nevertheless, no one is really the Coop: it's up to all of us to make it what it is, the total sum of us, of our films, our temperaments, and sorry to say, our mistakes.

I hope you are not letting yourself be sidetracked for too long or for too far away from your real work, your films. Your creations. I think that one single minute of your films is more important than ten Flesses or Cinema Theatres, and although you have to fight your fight wherever you go—you shouldn't let those battles make you into a soldier instead of a bard—let's hope, there will be some soldiers, who are born to be soldiers, to defend your cause— but you are a bard (or perhaps sometimes I fear there are no more real soldiers so that's why more and more poets are getting involved in the battles that are being waged for the sake of truth), so who am I to tell you anything but wish that you arrive home in one piece from your battles—put down your arrows, greet your children, and then make love—.

January 2, 1965
Music evening at 92nd St Y.

Stockhausen's *Kontakte* (for piano, percussion & electronic sounds, played by Max Neuhaus and James Tenney; John Cage's *Atlas Eclipticalis* with *Winter Music* (a version for kettle and drums and piano) played by Max Neuhaus and Philip Corner.

Stockhausen dramatizes sounds, melodramatizes. It bothered me all evening, and I tried to understand why. The piece was masterfully executed, and rich in sounds, etc., but it bothered me, it seemed almost a misuse of sounds; I wanted to hear the same sounds just as sounds, separated by pauses, and placed in space—with no dramatics.

After the first few moments of Cage everything became immediately clear. What a difference: here I heard sounds, or almost pure (execution sometimes seemed to

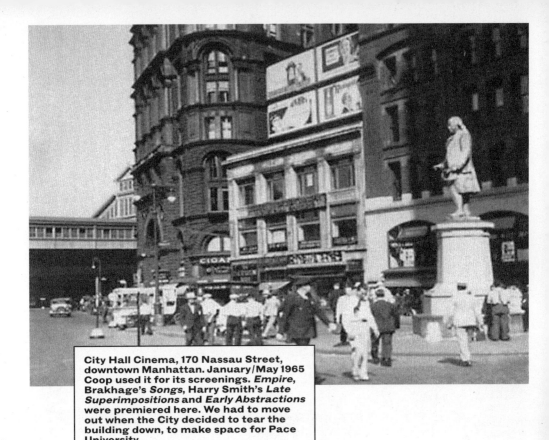

City Hall Cinema, 170 Nassau Street, downtown Manhattan. January/May 1965 Coop used it for its screenings. *Empire*, Brakhage's *Songs*, Harry Smith's *Late Superimpositions* and *Early Abstractions* were premiered here. We had to move out when the City decided to tear the building down, to make space for Pace University.

Needy

Dear Sir:

Help! Please add my name to the Jonas Mekas list of serious needy artists.

I had to have my right leg amputated last week and don't get around much any more.

I'm trying to scrape up enough dough to go to Kashmir to the fertile valleys in the south 'the Happy Valley' to feed chickens.

I try hard to put on a nice show once a year of my best work. Some folks dig it a d hang it on their waltz.

— Ray Johnson
Suffolk Street

Nov. 5, 1964 V. Voice

dramatize them, particularly piano, but not enough to destroy the purity or nakedness of the sounds)—the beauty of sounds left by themselves is enough to keep you in suspense, yes, almost in suspense, because of the tremendous tension and dynamics created by silences, because of the tensions between the sounds. I never realized until this evening the purity of Cage & how old fashioned and impure and melodramatic sounding Stockhausen is, when listening to Cage! I sat there in absolute suspense, completely caught by these sounds, on the edge of my seat, and I was myself like an instrument on which he seemed to work now, and things were happening inside, stirred & touched; things that were dormant, and experience so rich and so overwhelming, an experience which I got only from La Monte Young's 2nd Ave concert, four weeks ago: I was also sitting on the edge of my seat for two hours, and I wasn't the same when I left the place— I felt the same way now, listening to Cage, my own life became clearer to me somehow, illuminated in a new way. That is the secret power of great works of art that instead of enslaving you, envelop you in a dream, they wake you up to yourself, they open you up, they make you free. That's what Cage's music did to me. Later I was wondering—really, not even wondering, but just noting it, sort of, the fact, that only that art which is as intense and as pure as Cage's can reach our deepest depths. No impure, no half-art, no bastard art can do what Cage does, Homer does. I had a feeling that art is either great or it is nothing. There is no place for half-art. There isn't place even for almost-art. To jump a hurdle almost, to swim the river almost, means that you have drowned.

No date, 1965

"Images are not to be trusted. They help to transpose down to a lower level of consciousness an idea which could only sur-vive at another altitude. They deliver a corpse to the cellar. The only images capable of conveying a lofty idea are those which create in one's consciousness a state of surprise and insecurity calculated to raise this consciousness to the level of the idea in question, where it can be grasped in all its freshness and strength. Magic rites and genuine poetry serve no other purpose."
—Louis Pauwels and Jacques Bergier, *The Morning of the Magicians*

January 10, 1965

Friends:
This is a time for a letter to all my (our) friends. I have to get this out of my system. Because it makes me mad sometimes. It makes me feel, sometimes, when I have to ask you for $50 or for $100 and when I have to get it one way or other, because there are needs that cannot wait—Co-op is empty, Cinematheque is empty, *Film Culture* is empty. And then everybody says "Oh, maybe you are spending too much..." "No, I have already helped..." "No, maybe another time..." "Oh, I thought the Co-op is already on its feet..." "Oh, the Cinematheque must be making money..." etc. etc. Or just silences. So I go to some other friend and I make any kind of excuse, I beg, and eventually I pay what has to be paid, because things must be done, the Co-op must continue, *Film Culture* must come out, the Tek screenings must go on. But why do I have to go through all this begging, through all this running around, this scrounging, these millions of telephone calls, millions of wasted hours: I have been doing practically nothing, for the last four years, but making calls, writing money letters, running around, day after day, day after day. Because Co-op and *Film Culture* and the Tek must continue or else where the hell are we? But everybody acts like these are businesses of some kind that bring money, whereas these are services

and therefore losing propositions from the beginning to the end. But everybody treats me like these are businesses. And then we talk about culture, and we talk about arts, and about the avant-garde. Aren't we confusing something? Either one is willing to put oneself completely behind something or one is going with fashions and playing games, and I have reached the end and I don't like any games. Or maybe I just feel low today because I just came home after twelve hours at the Co-op and I did nothing but begging, trying to solve money problems & I didn't get very far. And it makes me angry. Yes, boy, work boys, if you want to see the new cinema grow. Run, boy run. It's all your idea, after all, who needs it! So I run. Because I am a sentimental midwife who doesn't want this newborn new art die untimely or live on oatmeal, like myself, from day to day. So the midwife becomes also a mother because nobody else wants to do anything but say nice words. But this baby doesn't need any words. It needs money, it needs concrete and material help, not words. That's why we never talked aesthetics during our first meetings, two, three years ago. We spoke only about concrete needs, like the distribution center, so that our movies could reach people, so that we could begin to connect with the people; and about a theatre, a place to show our movies. The only thing I didn't foresee was that it would be me who would have to carry all this on my shoulders, for three, four blasted years. Everyday another bill. Another bill, another humiliation, more begging, more running, and sometimes I feel so tired of it all, like I've been doing it for 1,000 years hoping that yes, yes, maybe tomorrow somebody else will come and take all this burden off me, so that I could fly, perhaps.

There have been reproaches, that yes, one shouldn't pamper the artist too much. But for heaven sake, what are we talking about: Pampering? WHO is really helping the avant-garde film-maker? Nobody is helping the avant-garde artist today. I cannot call the occasional small gifts a real help, no.

Anyway, I don't know, this evening, where to turn to, or what to do, and so I am sitting and writing this black letter. I thought you should know how I feel, sometimes. Because either we are friends and we listen to each other, or we are just strangers.

Literature and Morality, by J.T. Farrell:
"In the case of the audio and film, a major contradiction produced by capitalist economy arises between commodity sales pressure and the needs of art. For a society based on commodity production worrying art becomes commodities." (p. 57)

"...And the function of humanizing our knowledge of the world is one which art can, and should perform. For art can achieve this, it helps increase our awareness of the human aspects of life; it offers us images, representations of the quality of life and the quality of men in different times and places. Today we most urgently need such an expanded awareness. The usual Hollywood picture does not present life as it is lived. The human relationships portrayed in these pictures generally seem false, we cannot confirm them by our own experience or knowledge. The great majority of Hollywood films require us to delude ourselves with the belief that the crisis, the destiny, the feelings of the hero and heroine have a significance for us, socially and emotionally. Usually, the opposite is the case. These films are conceived in terms of naive reverie, and they lack internal conviction." (p. 109)

January 20, 1965
A meeting between Shirley Clarke & myself took place at the Chelsea Hotel. We agreed that something should be done to assist the distribution of the "middle"

At the Coop.

7 N Goodman St
Rochester NY
14607

17 Feb 1965

Jonas —
        Surprise! and thanks
for the Danish Pabst
program — your Cukor
F.C. was a darling —
I've switched from Variety
obits to laughs with
you — Herman has check
Louise Brooks

Geo. Maciunas
Jackson Manor
1321 N 14 St.
Phoenix, Arizona 85

PHOENIX, ARIZ.
9 PM
7 JAN
1965

THIS SIDE OF CARD IS FOR ADDRESS

U.S. POSTAGE
4¢

AIR MAIL

Jonas Mekas
Film Culture
414 Park Ave, So.
New York, N.Y.

Big Boss!
I did not have time to put together the materials for Al's 2 books, but I will do so when
I return by mid-February.
How is the cinematheque theatre? Can we have "concerts" there in April?
If possible we would like to have following schedule. April 4, 11, 18, 25
Let me know if we can plan on this,   May 1 8 15 22
because I must notify far in advance each   June 4 11 18 25
composer who will organize own evening.   July 4 11 18 25
We will not advertise concerts, but send   Aug. 1 8 15 22
announcement—invitations, so it would be   Sept 4 11 18 25
considered as private-show, no occupancy   Oct 1 8 15 22
permit required I suppose. (??)   Nov. 4 11 18 25
Another item: I moved to a new address 349 West Broadway
apt 11. (only a block north of Canal).
On same floor is an empty apartment being remodeled, which
I have reserved. Maybe you are interested. It has 2 rooms.
kitchen with new refrigerator & stove. AND RENT IS ONLY. $56!
It is a very good deal. Easy transportation, near all subway lines.
If you are interested - call Mentasti (between 5 and 5:30 PM)
AL 4-9089 & tell him you are the friend of mine for whom I was
holding the apartment. If you are not interested, let me know, I have
will offer it to someone else, OK?
Ben Vautier wishes to make a film festival in Nice, I have sent him 2
Fluxus movies. Have you any suggestions? Could you send him something?
Ben Vautier, 32 rue Yondutti de l'escarène, Nice.   Best regards, George

From George Maciunas, from Arizona.
His asthma was getting so bad that the
doctors, in panic, sent him to Arizona
where the weather was easier. He managed to survive there only for a month
before rushing back to New York. He
could not stand the boredom, monotony, and "cowboys," it was worse than
asthma, he told me.

cinema (I used that term, but Shirley forbid me to use it again)—films like those of Shirley's, Rogosin's, Morris Engel's, etc.

I accused Rogosin, Shirley, De Antonio for leaving the Co-op in the stages of early formation and going after U. Artists and big money, following "big deal" dreams, when we all agreed at our early meetings to stick together and build our own distribution center. So we went ahead without them and they cannot blame us now for "excluding" them (Shirley blamed me): they excluded themselves by their own free choice. And they failed. Nobody excludes anybody at the Co-op.

Anyway, after couple of hours of arguing, we agreed that we shouldn't hold grudges. Now it's time, we agreed, to do something about the low budget narrative and semi-narrative film. The theaters from across the country keep coming to the Co-op asking for "features" and they mean Shirley's etc. films.

We decided to create the B branch of the Co-op, for the "theatrical" films. We rejected David's proposal to create or be part of his private enterprise. Private enterprises tend to become exclusive and create antagonism.

We decide to invite Lionel Rogosin to join the center, to work together.

We never had money to buy enough socks, or money for laundry.

So I keep washing my socks in the evening, in the sink, and I watch the dirty brown water running into the sink.

Naomi said today: Look, you have hole in your socks. Yes. I said, I have hole in my socks. And my pants are old and not washed and not pressed because I have only one pair of pants. But we have a Film-Makers' Cooperative!

March 1, 1965

Kenneth Brown was unhappy that I filmed *The Brig*. I didn't ask his permission. He said: you can't do things like that! Oh, hell, I said, I didn't film your "play": I filmed my reactions to it. If anyone still wants to make a "real" movie out of Brown's play, to adapt it to cinema—he may as well do it. Brown once told me he had an idea for a million dollar production of *The Brig*, with thousands of prisoners. It should be done. The point of cruelty done by one man to another man can never be overstressed. I, myself, I am not interested in adapting plays, I always said so and I am repeating it here again. *The Brig*, the movie, is not an adaptation of a play: it's not a filmed play; it is a record of my eye & my temperament lost in the play. And then, in the first and last place, *The Brig*, the movie, is my gift to the Becks. My own share in all of this, really, is the pain in the neck from the weight of all that equipment I had on me during the filming, or pain which every *cinema-vérité* film-maker feels most of the time—and, I tell you, pains in the neck can be as bad as those of the heart.

March 15, 1965

Dear Mark [Eden]:

It was good to see you at your own home and with the music of the ocean & wind.

We are back in New York. Alan [Marlowe] will have to spend a day or two helping Diane [di Prima] to catch up with the work at the Poet's Theatre. But he is working at the same time on organizing the materials for the Brussels trip.

(...) Alan [Marlowe] is very much in the clouds most of the time and although clouds are needed too, the firm ground is also needed. That's why Diane is so concerned with her little printing press, and I am concerned with the daily needs of the Cinematheque and the film-makers who are doing the work: for it's their creation that precedes the distribution. For me it's important to have at least one small theatre in NY in which we could do whatever we want—and we are being pushed around, these days. What seems like a small thing—and it seemed to some that it's completely insignificant what the new poets, the new film-makers, the new artists were doing for the last few years—but now it's becoming evident that it's bigger than anyone thought it was, it can be bigger, and maybe is, than any Bomb will ever be. Man's spirit, the strength of the fruits of man's spirit cannot be always measured by the quantity alone, I mean, by the seeming quantity.

Anyway, we are proceeding—or continuing—further with our work and with a growing faith & strength—& we are with you—

March, 1965

So much has been said about the "essence" of things and men, that you'll forgive me if I'll say a few words in praise of the surface. I was provoked by this sentence: "Schneemann abstracts, removes all social context, alters and distorts reality instead of moving toward its essence."—Michael Smith, V. Voice

Nov 26, 1964

Writing on *Meat Joy*

I have been walking with these thoughts for months now, as you can see. So I better get rid of them.

All arts have been revolting against "essence," against "social significance," for those terms mean, imply either the Old (Comfortable, Capitalist) essence & significance (a trick to protect oneself from anything that may upset the status quo) or simply they mean nothing (or nobody knows what they mean.) So the artists junked everything that had been known as essence and significance and began searching for it anew, from scratch.

In painting, in sculpture, for a decade now, the artist has been exploring the new textures, materials, surfaces, junk, garbage, things around him, putting them in/on his canvasses, until they swell (& smell), until they are no longer paintings but surroundings, environments, things.

In cinema: Jack Smith, Warhol, Brakhage, Markopoulos, Rubin, Jacobs are going directly to the surface (impactness) of things, or man, of textures, faces & bodies. Things that surround us, the human body itself has become invisible during last two centuries. Two centuries of industry, rationalism and materialism succeeded in making the material world invisible to our eyes. It was Warhol who demonstrated to us that Campbell soup cans had become invisible. He demonstrated to us that they exist, that they CAN be seen. That the Empire State Building CAN be seen. Smith in *Normal Love*, like a magician, opens to us the world of color and texture in simplest materials around us that we keep seeing every day without perceiving them, without seeing them. Brakhage and Markopoulos are demonstrating to us that there is LIGHT, and that we have EYES, and that there is HUMAN BODY. Ken Jacobs shows us that shadows exist, that film exists, that the grains of film exist. Nam June Paik even shows that DUST exists and falls on everything, including film. Nothing can be taken for granted: man is basically blind. Man sees nothing unless he's shown it. He is like that cat whose nose must be put into its own piss to see it.

Music: La Monte Young goes beyond all melody until his music becomes one uninterrupted sound, until all sounds fade into one, and then you listen to its surface and you begin to discover most fantastic melodies, the greatest music of the Century.

The Happening Theatre, Carolee Schneemann's *Meat Joy* brings us back to the touch, smell, to the surfaces of things and bodies; it accepts, with love, everything that our insistence on ideas (or on certain ideas) kept us away from; even what was "repellent," like "raw" meat, or chicken guts, what we usually dread & fear to touch—glittery, vomity substances (under the excuse of our own "delicateness," the delicateness of our natures…).

Eh, the last walls of puritanism and rationalism and false idealism are crumbling, we are beginning to feel the surface again, although our touch is still numb.

What an irony, we must say, that man has to find himself through the object & surface world, through the phenomenal world. Our pomposity in us still denies this, we still insist on "importance," on "essence" the way we know and understand it; we reject the sensuous world of *Meat Joy* as lacking social "essence". We'd like to go directly to heaven without going through the earth—we'd like to be saintlier than God Jesus Christ Himself. What pompous asses we are.

Yes, Carolee Schneemann removes the social context, or, rather, the familiar social contexts, to break us open, to expose our senses, to bring us back to our senses. I remember my father, taking & mixing cow's dung in a pail and with his bare hands applying the mixture to the roots of young seedling trees. I watched him, with a sort of disgust and wonder, I remember, and although like all other boys I grew up with, I used to step into the hot cow dung in cold autumn days, to warm up my feet—I felt a disgust and a wonder seeing my father working with it so casually as if it were no different from touching corn, or tending horses, or stroking the wheat stems, or looking at an approaching rain cloud.

But now my childhood riddles begin to solve themselves in very different circumstances, and so when I watch *Meat Joy* and I see the performers throwing themselves into the immediate experience of meat and chicken guts and paint and sweat and touch of bodies and grease—I know that this is not an empty gesture devoid of essence, but, just the opposite: touching the very essence; the long held-back desire of man to be one with all things, to return down to earth, down to the surface of matter; man is realizing that he can't look disdainfully at the meat world without somewhere deeper in himself doing the same to his own meat, to his own body, and his own soul. So that from the angle that I am looking from, *Meat Joy* becomes an essay, a philosophical essay on Essence and Matter.

Therefore, Dear Reader, if I may call you so—don't blame Andy Warhol for showing you eight hours of Empire State Building: blame Western civilization for making the reality invisible to you; thank the Artist for making you see the Empire State Building. Praise the Artist for bringing the surface reality and things and all kinds of phenomena that surround us and make us what we are, to our consciousness. Praise the artist for enabling us to see again, to hear again, to feel again: for giving us EYES, EARS, SENSES. We are waking up, and the world around us is waking up together with us.

Or is this only my spring dream? Tell me, Dear Carolee.

March 28, 1965

New York City
Dear Mark:

I received your telegram about sending *Normal Love. NL* is still in the editing stage. Part I, which is 80 minutes long, is completed, the editing, I mean. But the sound is on tape. Jack is working on the second part and he is going his own speed and nobody can speed him up. We held a benefit screening at the Cinematheque last Thursday of Part I, in order to raise money for continuing the work on Part II, and we managed to raise $400. But making a print and putting the sound on, etc., etc., is a big expense (this is only a work print; the original has to be still edited) and that is our immediate concern. Really, not so immediate, since Jack has to complete editing the Part II before the print can be made.

I have no idea if you are in communication with Marlowe, but I want you to know this: it is my simple duty to help any human being who is in need of help, and if that help is within my power. I have given some advice and information to Marlowe, because I believe that his theatre is performing a very important role in New York. But that doesn't mean that I go with Alan's ideas and plans that are outside of his theatre. I completely disapprove his actions and ideas concerning Merrymark, you, and a number of other things. That's why I went to S. Francisco, with Diane di Prima. I had to bring him back to New York before he does more damage to us all. I am only sorry that I didn't come earlier to SF, to stop some of the unnecessary money spending—for, although money is only paper, we know, that even paper can be misused. That's why I was appalled at what I saw in SF.

I prefer to do my simple work for the film-makers, on the practical every day level. I don't want to be on any of the boards of any of the big worldwide or cosmic organizations—that's not my job. My job is right here. The more I think about what happened during the last four weeks the more I have to admit that I have to stick to what I am doing, that is, to help the film-makers to do their work and on a very limited, down-to-earth budget; to bring their work to the attention of others thru the Cinematheque and Film-Makers' Cooperative. My work and my intentions have been disrupted and blown out of proportions during last few weeks by Marlowe's dreams. I permitted myself be distracted and sidetracked from the real work. Say, what would all the big organizations do, if the artists would stop creating? What would they distribute to the people? We are screening Anger's *Scorpio Rising* tomorrow at the Cinematheque and we expect trouble with the police and with the theatre owner. Whatever happens, we are proceeding with our plans to have OUR OWN place. I found one small theatre on 23rd St. and unless something unexpected happens we are taking it on Monday. It will be $1,200 per month, which is within our reach.

All the budgets I sent you, the second batch, could be cut down. Film-makers are beginning to feel that now everybody's with them, that now they can spend more money on their movies, etc. They have been misled by the publicity in the press, by their own success, and perhaps even by me. It's all an illusion. I still don't see anybody with money coming to their assistance.

I thought I'd let you know how I feel. I hope to see you in New York soon.

Dear Mark:
Neither Mister Sharff nor anyone else is going to get a penny from the money that has to go to our film-making. We do not want to work with people who want retainers. That world is gone. Let that spirit go also. In hell there are bags full of gold. I am also getting tired of phony telegrams. We do not want support from people who do not believe in what we are doing. Our work needs money and will bring money but not at the price of selling our soul and our reason. Let us neither overpush or overrush or despair. Both life and time is with us. Our work is growing because angels are our partners and they ask neither contracts nor retainers, only love.
Jonas, on Easter Day

Easter Day, 1965
It's no great pleasure to drink a cup of coffee on an empty stomach, nosireee. Really, I had enough money to order a corn muffin, too—so it wasn't that bad. But there is no great pleasure in looking at someone else's hamburger next to you, not

at all, and particularly not on an Easter day. Oh, my dear Uncle who told me to go and see the Wide World!

April 25, 1965

Andy's farewell party (he is going to Paris for his show). It was sad to see Montgomery Clift, Judy Garland, and a few others from the Hollywood gang, all good people, but now sad and lonely. They disappeared among the new "Underground" stars in Andy's loft. They were standing on the side, nobody even wanted or could talk to them. It was depressing & sad to watch it. Clift was drunk, he stood on the side and watched the crowd. Only Tennessee Williams seemed to be having a good time, dancing and prancing with the nymphets and flooseys, having fun, surrounded by his boys. He came to Andy's studio for the first time a month ago; I met him that evening and he was as sad as Clift this evening, staring with blank eyes into space. Since then he has been coming frequently. I saw him Friday night, watching *Vinyl*, and enjoying himself, not giving a damn any longer about who he was or is, I mean, the fame and all, and nobody seemed to bother him here.
Ah! How the times change!

April 29, 1965

Morbid days of New York.
Shoot the gloom.
The street thru the window, perhaps.
There are gloomy mornings, days, endless.

May 2, 1965

Came home tired like a dog. I had another of my money raising days. We need $500 by Monday to put deposit on 23rd St. place, and $100 for the license, and $100 to pay the City Hall Cinema. I left Frances and George at the Tek, they are mimeographing the Bulletin today, and I said, I'll go out to dig out some money. Had only two tokens with me, so I did plenty of walking. Panna

was home, so I persuaded her to help me with some calls. We both got completely disillusioned, discouraged, after a few calls. So she got some wine and started drinking. Even those who we knew for certain had extra money, they were not interested. Avant-garde cinema, bah! Panna got very angry about it and kept calling. The more wine we drank the angrier we became. But our calls ended in exactly zero. So I bid her good nite and I had another walk along the park, and then I went home and fell on the bed like a sack.

"Jazz was collected among the numerous skeletons the middle-class black man kept locked in the closet of his psyche, along with watermelons and gin, and whose rattling caused him no end of misery and self-hatred. As one Howard University philosophy professor said to me when I was an undergraduate, 'It's fantastic how much bad taste the blues contain!' But it is just this 'bad taste' that this Uncle spoke of that has been the onefactor that has kept the best of Negro music from slipping sterilely into the echo chambers of middle-brow American culture.
And to a great extent such 'bad taste' was kept extant in the music, blues or jazz, because the Negroes who were responsible for the best of the music were always aware of their identities as black Americans and really did not, themselves, desire to become vague, featureless Americans as is usually the case with the Negro middle class." —LeRoi Jones "Jazz and the White Critic"

Isn't it that a similar "bad taste" that keeps the "underground cinema" from disappearing into the polite and nice middle class cinema of the Hollywood etc. independents?

"A 'snake eye' bomb, recently used in action for the first time in Vietnam, is part of a

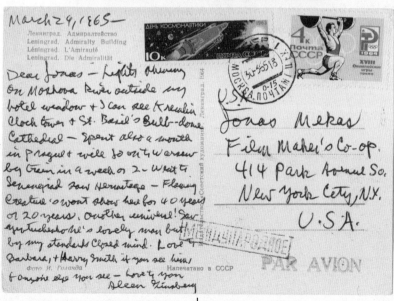

March 29, 1965 —

Ленинград. Адмиралтейство
Leningrad. Admiralty Building
Léningrad. L'Amirauté
Leningrad. Die Admiralität

Dear Jonas — Lights shining
On Moskova River outside my
hotel window + I can see Kremlin
Clock tower + St. Basil's Bulb-dome
Cathedral — spent also a month
in Prague + will do so in Warsaw
by train in a week or 2 — went to
Leningrad saw Hermitage — Flaming
Creature's wont show here for 40 years
or 20 years. Another universe! Saw
Yevtushenko he's lovely man but
by my standards closed mind. Love to
Barbara, + Harry Smith if you see him
+ anyone else you see — Love to you
Allen Ginsberg

фото И. Голанда   Напечатано в СССР

Jonas Mekas
Film Maker's Co-op.
414 Park Avenue So.
New York City, N.Y.
U·S·A·

PAR AVION

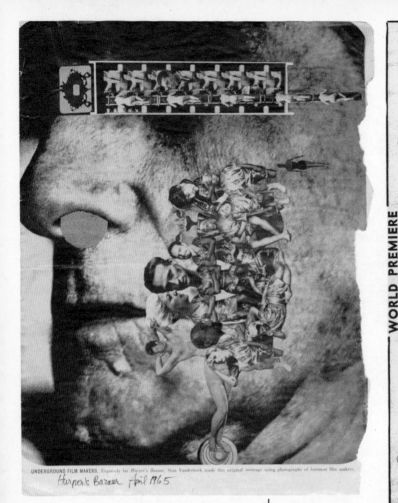

UNDERGROUND FILM MAKERS. Expressly for *Harper's Bazaar*, Stan Vanderbeek made this original montage using photographs of foremost film makers.

Harper's Bazaar April 1965

Panna Grady came into my life during the filming of *Guns of the Trees*. She lived comparatively humbly in a small Greenwich Village apartment and was pretty confused. But she fed us so many times when we were really broke and hungry during those months. I did not follow her life later, but she re-emerged at Dakota Hotel, in 1965, throwing parties for writers and artists that included Burroughs (whom she wanted to marry) and Warhol. That's how we reconnected again. Later she married the writer, Philip O'Connor, and moved to the South of France.

whole new armory of exotic weapons in use or under development for the armed forces."—NY *Times*

Thursday
0.60 tokens
0.50 milk
0.20 coffee & roll
David bought a meal

Friday
0.90 tokens
0.45 food
Harry bought a meal.
Stone bought a malted.

"I feel that I am working (living) moving in a vacuum."
"But isn't that the first condition for arriving at something new, a place where you have never been before? Don't be afraid of a vacuum: vacuum only means that now you are free from whatever tied you down."

"I have to work for higher purposes," he said.
"Just do your goddamn daily duties; the 'higher purposes' will take care of themselves," he answered.

May 4, 1965
Filmed the epileptic on the street.
Filmed the sick woman led by two Puerto Ricans, on 4th St.

Diane Hall came in to show me her discotheque dress she borrowed from Baby Jane.

May 5, 1965
P. Adams Sitney came from New Haven. We walked to the Post Office with loads of mail, talked about this and that. First Spring day, sunny. Filmed P. Adams Sitney's hands. He came to go with Herman & Barbara to apply for Tek's theatre license. They were fingerprinted, like criminals.

"You cut your hair," he said. I told him, I have been trying to raise money for the Tek this weekend, having teas with old mostly rich ladies at the Russian Tea Room, so I had to cut my hair, otherwise no money. But I got no money anyway, sorry I cut my hair.

ULTIMATUM: TO THE NEW YORK ART THEATERS
We are asking you to surrender.
The surrender will be unconditional.

"Bruce's 'art' like that of the shaman in primitive society, depends primarily on his ability to locate and expose the fears and resentments—the demons—that beset and torment his audience. Lacking the elaborate artifices of a Genet, Bruce goes about this exorcism in an intuitively direct manner by violating verbal taboos or offering threats of violence or outrage.
(...) It will be evident from even so simple an explanation as this that Lenny Bruce must be 'offensive' to be effective, and that the test for whether his work possesses 'redeeming social value' lies in a judgment of his success in utilizing obscenity for cathartic effect. Such a judgment could be just only if it were based on actual observation of the comedian's performance, for his words are often only a kind of commentary on what he does."—Albert Goldman in *Censorship*, No. 2, Spring 1965, p. 3 – 4

May 6, 1965
Oh, these sunny mornings at the Co-op, with the sun coming up just above the Belmore cafeteria.
I hope Shep's magazine will ever come out: He is sleeping on a beat up sofa, at the Co-op.
Walked across the park. The old road is black now, and green.

Apple trees are all in bloom. I almost missed the spring again.

I was breathing the air freely and deeply.

Did some filming.

Frances and George said Jack was here. Jack is coming, he is buying a used Bolex for $420. "A used Bolex for $420? He is crazy," I said.

Curtis Harrington called, just came to town.

NY Times quotes Juan Gosch: "The President of Santo Domingo is Johnson," said Joan Bosch bitterly. "He is our chief, our boss."

May 7, 1965
On cinéma-vérité

Not long ago I saw a TV documentary. It showed a "primitive" country in Asia. Its author introduced it as a "cinéma-vérité" film, by which he meant that this film showed truth and nothing but the truth. The film was accompanied by his own running commentary. The commentary was naive, patronizing, and stupid. At first, I thought that this commentary destroyed the "cinéma-vérité" aspect: we heard the film-maker instead of the peoples themselves. But then I thought: Yes, but this stupid commentary is just what the film-maker thought when he was filming these scenes. This stupid commentary is part of the "cinéma-vérité" of this particular film: it records truly and unmistakably the mentality of the man who made the film! It helps us to understand the angle from which he looked at the reality which he chose to film for us, as "film-truth." In other words: everything, no matter how silly, how bad, how unperceptive, how banal this film is, it is still truth. Every reality made by man reflects that man. Camera eye will lie as much as the man behind it, knowingly or unknowingly.

About Art and Truth

If we take a scene from a movie by Hitchcock, one moment of an actress close-up in *Vertigo* may contain as much or more truth or essence of certain human emotions as Cartier-Bresson's famous scene of a Frenchman crying during the liberation of Paris. An emotion can be caught in the street or it may be created by an actor in a studio; an actor's emotions can be richer in truth than the one caught casually in the street, sometimes.

Andy Warhol did not shoot an actress "doing something" in *Poor Little Rich Girl*. Edie Sedgwick was fed lines, was directed, while the shooting was going, and we hear the directions in the actual film; she remained herself but she was very open to the outside directions which challenged her, made the actions richer, made the content richer, demanded from her more than what she would have asked from herself if there weren't any suggestions and challenges; and she reacted to what was said; so that a richness was achieved impossible to arrive at by simply photographing real life, the "real" Sedgwick walking around the room. Various emotions and reactions were provoked and registered that make the film so sadly beautiful and such an insightful statement on the inner state of a rich girl anywhere today.

Art and truth is a very complicated matter. It is very difficult to speak about "truth" or "real" in cinema, it is. I have been seeing a D. W. Griffith retrospective at MoMA. Crude and primitive, as some of his first films were, hamming and exaggerated, they contained deep truths on human passions, on social attitudes of the period, the psychology of the period.

May 8, 1965

Naomi came with her friend, I forget her name, the girl with the Moreau cap and *Elle* under her arm. Naomi said: "Oh, I don't see anybody with whom I could have a good conversation, you know, to dig in, to show my inside."

"You know what's your trouble," I said, "what's our trouble? We are always digging into ourselves, digging in, wallowing in our emotions until we are sick and confused like hell, because the deeper we dig the less we understand anything. Why don't you just stick to the surface for a change? Let's praise the surface of things. That's what I did in my farmer's days."

"O.K.," said Naomi, "come with me, we saw some jewels in the window, buy them for me, I like jewels."

"That's better," I said, "jewels are beautiful." The day is beautiful today, the sun is shining—and you want to dig into yourself, wallow in yourself. A woman should be interested more in jewels than in conversation, anyway," I said.

"I don't believe you, I think you are joking," said Naomi.

"I am not," I said. "I could even add that a woman should be more interested in jewels than in her own soul…"

"Yes?" said Naomi.

"Yes. That would help to clean up this whole emotional mess."

May 10, 1965

I dug out Brussels reel, Barbara's footage, etc.

Got back from the lab the S.F. footage.
Sondra Hoffman reel, 8 mm.

May 11, 1965

Leslie said, Jack called today and was full of bullshit. He said, we stole money from him, etc., etc., etc., etc., the old story of the paranoid, and I was so sick of this bullshit, suddenly, that for a moment I wanted to drop everything, the Co-op, and the Cinematheque, and go to some god forsaken country and do my own work, just for myself. How a man as brilliant as Jack, almost a genius, how a man like that can be so sick, and so fucking paranoid about his pennies (or is it his penis?) to suspect even his friends, Leslie, or me, stealing his miserable pennies! This is just beyond the limits of my brain. I felt so fed up with it, so sick, that I was walking the streets, cursing myself for always forgetting and forgiving, even shit like this—because, really, can really a great and beautiful art come from such a paranoid? Flo Jacobs said this morning: "Oh, but that's how Jack always is." Yes, but why should he? Or why should one approve of that part of Jack?

May 13, 1965

Shot Barbara Stone planting flower seeds on the window sill.
"Oh, look, Barbara has a flower garden."
She was planting the seeds.
Alexandra was looking out the window.
Shot Gregory and Diane on 4th Street.
"I have no school today," she said.
"Why?"
"I don't know why.
I don't have school, that's all."

May 14, 1965

I borrowed $5 from David. But then I met Elizabeth [Krejtejn] and we had to eat something and I have to save something for tomorrow, it should really last til Monday. So we kept walking and walking, and I felt tired and so we sat on a bench in the park and looked at people feeding ducks in the pond. Then we turned back towards the 42nd Street because she wanted to see more of the city so we had malted milk with what was left and kept enough for three tokens and we continued walking since we couldn't stop anywhere without money and her money was stolen in the airport. Later, at home, I found some peanut butter and some bread.

May 15, 1965

Joel came yesterday. Could you give me six dollars, he said. Please, Joel, I said, I can't explain it to you, but I HAVE NO MONEY,

I never have, I am not paid by anybody, and I have no money. It's better for you, easier for you to get to ask for money from others because they take you for a poor broke devil; it is different for me, I can't ask money from anybody even when I haven't eaten for days, like now, because everybody thinks I am a millionaire.

Today at MoMA, Dov comes to me and says: I need $100 for a print of my film, could you? Dov, I said, are you crazy? I know it would be nice to give you $100 but why do you come to me?

The other day Naomi told me she really believes (and some of her friends do, too) that I am a millionaire in disguise who plays a poor man. She says, it's all written in my "countenance" the way I behave. So there I am!

May 16, 1965

P. Adams Sitney came this morning. A friend of his drove him to New York from New Haven. Went to see Bruce Conner's show, was closed. Barbara gave to each of us a can of yogurt.

A hot sweating day. We were walking with P. Adams Sitney and it was so hot we had to stop for a cold malted milk, only that much money we had left, and since we were passing the 10th Street, we decided to bring one for Gregory, too.

Gregory was in the middle of editing. Strips of film all over the place. He was running the film on the projector, from hand, film on the floor, and was cutting pieces out, by eye, against the light. He rented the projector for two days, that's all the money he had, he has to return it tomorrow, he has to do all cutting today. Hasn't been out for two days, not even for eating. We looked at him in amazement as he was cutting the strips just like that, no viewer, and he seemed to know exactly what he was doing…

Whenever I visit Gregory I am amazed how organized he is, how organized his room is, every piece—you can count every piece, you see every piece, not like my own mess. Anyway, Gregory was editing with film strip hanging down from the ceiling to the floor, so that the south side of his room looked like a willow tree, really, with film strips down to the floor. On the table little strips and pieces of film, laid out like some kind of game but it's a sequence really, a scene.

Nothing on the walls, as if he had just moved in… A shelf with some binders and by the door a gift from Brakhage, he said, a strip of hand-colored Cinemascope film. Even as we were leaving, the last image of Gregory was him standing there by the projector with scissors in hand, ready to cut the film as it was just about to appear from the gate.

Later we dropped in to see Maysles, in his renovated fantastic Village apartment, and we had a stout and talked for a while about this and that, and Maysles sat there in a soft chair and a fan was blowing and there was a girl stretched out on the floor, I forgot her name, and the whole atmosphere was full of laziness and relaxation. I was thinking about Gregory's room, which seemed to breathe with intensity and poetry.

We spoke & gossiped about movies (what else but gossip can grow in such an atmosphere?) and sipped our stout.

"What is all this about 'film poetry' that you keep talking about?" asked Maysles [David] at one point, and there was a note in his voice which meant, "I hope you aren't serious? How could you talk about such nonsense?"

"Poetry is the easiest thing to laugh at & about, so better we don't talk about it," I said, and there was dropped the subject.

No date, 1965

I dreamt the following words, I had a feeling it was either a name or ???: KÁLA LÍLA LALIÉS.

P. S. to my last week's *Village Voice* column (Psychedelic Theatre, Coda Gallery, etc):
I may not have made clear enough that my thoughts in the last piece were very indefinite. Those were casual thoughts, personal reactions, gropings. Secondly: I am not against the use of drugs (or LSD). I think that nothing should be forbidden to a normal grown up person. The drug "revolution" is (was) directly connected with the changing attitudes to living, to life. What I am saying, however, is this: The first stage of the drug "revolution" has reached the end. But we got stuck with it. Now we have to get over the drug. The drug has shown us, has unzipped some areas of consciousness (or unconsciousness) that were suppressed, they were sealed off by the age of reason & industrial revolution and etc. The Drug is helping to destroy the Will of History etc. etc. etc. Still: be it reason, industry or drugs: it doesn't matter on what man gets stuck—a hook is a hook, man…

Tuli: "That is always the question, what to do."
Anne: "I will do it, I do it through making love."

P. S. I thought I should add a P. S. to P. A. Sitney's letter. It should be known, I think, that neither the last year's European Exposition of the New American Cinema, nor the Buenos Aires exposition has received any financial support from outside (with one single small exception), despite my constant and desperate efforts. Last year's and this year's Exposition are being pushed into life jointly by the Film-maker's Cinematheque, Co-op and *Film Culture*, because we believe that the American cinema is not really represented at film festivals, that it should be seen in other countries, that our cinema will help to rejuvenate the cinema in Europe and S. America—or simply, that beautiful films should be seen and enjoyed outside of New York.

The sad part of this is that none of the three mentioned "organizations" has money. They remain non-profit and in deficit; and I find myself spending most of my time running around trying to collect some money for the prints, labs, and other work, to keep the "organizations" alive and to pay the Exposition expenses. Nobody has come to our assistance. And to collect money in small miserable sums, is not the most pleasant of pastimes. Not all film-makers have yet understood that most of the work done around the Co-op, *Film Culture* and Tek is voluntary and monastic. I see too much egoism, selfishness, short-sightedness and ugliness among our film-makers, which is OK, only that it is discouraging sometimes. And the real reason for my giving up the Buenos Aires trip is really that I have to stay here trying to patch up the financial trousers which keep falling down…

God bless Sitney who gave up a well-paid summer job (and he needs the money to pay his studies) to work on the Exposition for NOTHING because he too believes in this new cinema.
And neither of us knows why we are doing this, really, but we feel that these things should be & must be done and it is so easy to sit on the side, to criticize, to do nothing so I want you to know this.

Image: blank.
Sound: Beethoven.
Listening to it. It played across the street.
Image: At the window, night, half-open, whatever you see.
I thought: what a dream. Dream of perfection, no end to this dream. Composer after composer seeking the new sound, the new dream.
I thought about Gregory.
Image:
Gregory—how he is going after his dream (or Stan), with what persistence, even at

FRIENDS OF NEW CINEMA, Inc.

TENTH FLOOR • 1776 BROADWAY, NEW YORK, N.Y. 10019

July 7, 1965

Mr. Jonas Mekas
c/o Film-Makers' Cooperative
414 Park Avenue South
New York, New York

Dear Jonas:

As you requested, the following is the current
list of film makers (names and mailing addresses) to whom
the Friends are sending monthly checks. As you will note
the list numbers eleven checks, the choice of the twelfth
being held in abeyance until the Friends have a further
meeting on the subject. When the choice is made I expect
that the stipend will be made retroactive to June, 1965.

Names	Mailing Addresses
Ken Jacobs	25 Ferry Street, New York City
Peter Kubelka....................	Sonnenfelsgasse 11 Wien 1, Austria
Storm de Hirsch	136 W. 4th Street New York City
Jack Smith	89 Grand Street New York City
George Kuchar and Mike Kuchar.......	250 East 207 Street Bronx 67, N.Y.
Carl Linder	254 Waller Street San Francisco 2, Cal.
Bruce Baillie	263 Colgate Avenue Berkeley, Cal.
Andy Meyer	56 Symphony Road Boston 15, Mass.
Bill Vehr	517 East 12th St. New York, N.Y.
Gregory Markopoulos	40 West 11 St., New York, N.Y.
Jerry Joffen	c/o Helen Naihaus 103 W. 75 St. New York, N.Y.

I have not yet finished reading the Berman brief on the
"Flaming Creatures" appeal but so far it seems fine.

With best regards.

Sincerely yours,

Allan A. Masur

AAM:fk

FRIENDS OF NEW CINEMA

RECIPIENT	YEAR
Baillie, Bruce	- 1965, 1966
Beavers, Robert	- 1968, 1969
Brakhage, Stan	- 1964, 1965
Breer, Robert	- 1966, 1967
~~Brooks, David~~	-
Broughton, James	- 1968, 1969
Chomont, Tom	- 1968, 1969
Davis, Jim	- 1964
de Hirsch, Storm	- 1964, 1965, 1966, 1967, 1968
Jacobs, Ken	- 1964, 1965, 1966, 1967, 1968
Joffen, Jerry	- 1964, 1965, 1966
Jordan, Larry	- 1968, 1969
Kubelka, Peter	- 1964, 1965, 1966, 1967
Kuchar, George	- 1964, 1965, 1966
Kuchar, Mike	- 1964, 1965, 1967, 1968, 1966
Landow, George	- 1964, 1965, 1966, 1967, 1968, 1969
Leonardi, Alfredo	- 1967, 1968, 1969
Levine, Naomi	- 1964, 1965
Linder, Carl	- 1965, 1966
Maciunas, George	- 1968, 1969
Markopoulos, Gregory	- 1964, 1965, 1966, 1967, 1968
Mead, Taylor	- 1965, 1966, 1967, 1968, 1969
Meyer, Andrew	- 1965, 1966, 1967, 1968
Menken, Marie	- 1966, 1967
Nelson, Robert	- 1966, 1967
Noren, Andrew	- 1967, 1968, 1969
Rice, Ron	- 1964, 1965
Rubin, Barbara	- 1967, 1968
Smith, Jack	- 1964, 1965, 1966, 1967, 1968, 1969
Stewart, Micheal	- 1969
Sitney, P. Adams	- 1965, 1967, 1968
Summers, Elaine	- 1967, 1968, 1969
Vehr, Bill	- 1965, 1966

In 1964 with Jerome Hill we came up with a humble idea, with a $40 monthly stipend to a dozen of avant-garde film-makers. Forty dollars sounds like very little today, but it was monthly rent money in those days. I changed the list slightly at the beginning of each year. It was pennies from Heaven to some.

the cost of friends, betraying friends, going after his own dream of images.
Image: myself, trying to sleep, but can't; with my hand brushing across the face, eyes,
following my own dreams,
day after day.

at Davidson College somebody described his state of being as:
"lock myself in a black room & wait"
"hang by the feet head down & swing for two hours"

"Lord is my Shepherd."
"I don't see any wool."

June 12, 1965
Roots of trees in the park; a woman walking along the park road with a child on each side; flowers on the roadside.
I walked across the park. There was this fantastic smell in the air of summer noon and flowers. I filmed a few white bells on the roadside. This summer will drive me crazy.

The sun remains our aim. The artist believes in the aristocracy of the spirit—the Establishment of the spirit. Man's spirit is eternally in avant-garde—that is the true avant-garde on which we are meditating these days in the deep Lower East Side silences, with no great rush: avant-garde has no need to rush: It's always on time, it always comes.

LSD, everybody wants to take LSD: to expand consciousness, to know things! And what, when you realize that you don't need all that knowledge, all that learning.
Both LSD and LEARNING are illusions.

June 12, 1965
I dreamt a girl by the name TERENCE KANE

June 13, 1965
Shot windy playground in the park, with P. Adams.
Shot Amy test bits in the office.
Shot Alexandra dancing on the table & other bits.

June, 1965
ANSWERS TO THE QUESTIONS SUBMITTED BY "SPUTNIK OF FILM FESTIVAL" (MOSCOW)

Questions:
"Free-camera," improvisation, "stream of life", Dedramatization, deheroization, documentalism—here are some of the "diseases" of our cinematographic art for a few last years. Do you consider them to be just temporary fashion? Or you think of them as really new trends? What are, in your opinion, the most progressive ways of the cinematic development, in general, and in film directing, in particular.

What are the most outstanding achievements of cinema art in two recent years.

Thank you in advance, we remain sincerely yours,
V. Vladimirov, Editor

Answers:
Neither "free-camera" nor "improvisation" nor "cinéma-vérité" are diseases. A disease takes something away from man, weakens him. All of the above mentioned phases of cinema, styles of cinema, add new knowledge to man and to cinema. It is wrong to call them fashions. Cinema is a very alive art. It is wrong to expect cinema to stand still, static, without any researches or curiosities, when life itself keeps changing. The artist is like a scientist: he never stops researching. Improvisation, cinéma-vérité are such researches, man's look at himself from new angles. Researches are not fashions. To call them fashions is a bourgeois

thinking. Sound thinking (dialectical thinking) teaches us that these are necessary steps in our constant growth. When a cinema in a country becomes static, it means that man's thinking and ways of living have become static, the progress has stopped, at least in those aspects of our existence which are expressed thru cinema. Improvisation, cinéma-vérité, free cinema, etc., are the new ways of seeing, feeling, perceiving, thinking, knowing.

The most outstanding achievements of last ten years have been in two areas or directions: in further development of cinéma-vérité styles, in training our eye to look at reality; to bring to the attention of the novelistic-fictional cinema the new textures of reality, new themes, new faces, to remind the fiction cinema that life is changing. The second major development has been the growth of the non-narrative cinema. The most important film of the last two years, far above the rest, is Stan Brakhage's *The Art of Vision*. Its content has to do with the deepest perceptions and truths of man and not with the passing whims, trite plots, trite feelings, trite problems with which the contemporary "commercial" cinema is replete. *The Art of Vision* is the only recent film I know that is not following man from behind: it is far ahead of man, it is leading him, and when you walk out, after this film, you walk for days full of music, elated you have gained something that directs your life to more perfection, to higher ideals, to more beauty and more truth.

June 18, 1965

Herman in *Le Bon de la Civile* uses "single frame" technique, like Gregory in *Twice a Man*. But he still uses it as a "montage," he succeeds in completely dehumanizing, abstracting the human story, faces, presences. People in his film become mechanical.

In Gregory's case, single frame technique has nothing to do with montage.

He expands humanity of his people by enveloping them in thoughts. He does not abstract or mechanize. He expands, both, his subject and the film language.

June 20, 1965

Visited Beverly Grant. She lives now with Tony Conrad in a small room on Second Avenue and 27th Street, in the back, with a beautiful yard full of trees and shadows. She asked if I could do something to get money for her, to pay for Stella Adler's —she wants to attend summer season. A benefit, or something. And in a hurry. And I can't do anything, nothing. After Mario Montez benefit, Naomi came, she wants a benefit; Joel Markman wants a benefit; Bill Vehr wants a benefit. And, lately, I keep refusing to be dragged into all these projects. I am putting a hard fight to gain some time for my own work, and I have to fight for every minute of my time. Everybody wants something to do for them, to get money or to get equipment for this or that, and I am sick and tired of everything.

Later in the evening I had supper with Romney. I told him about Beverly's troubles. She really needs $220, she said.

Romney said he paid for her Stella Adler's studies last summer, and, he said, he hasn't heard from Beverly since. But he said he will be willing to give $100 to Tony, to help him with his film, he has faith in him.

June 21, 1965

Filmed:
In the park. Apple blossoms.
Frances.
Bibbe & P. Adams in the cafeteria.
—*Walden*, Part I (June 21st).
Ken Jacob's wedding.
Tony Conrad and Beverly Grant at their home.
Women's prison.
In the Park. Baseball players.

June 22, 1965

Filmed Bibbe in the park

for the "Movie Journal"
Andy Warhol: "We need more craftsmen. Soundmen, cameramen."
I have noticed that films fall apart physically during the screenings, our filmmakers do not know even how to splice. Do they consider splicing not worthy of their art? They should read Brakhage's essay on splicing in *FC* 34.

Ken Jacobs: "The trouble with cinema until now was that it was always in focus"— after seeing *Poor Little Rich Girl*. Andy Warhol shot two versions of *Poor Little Rich Girl*: one out-of-focus, another in focus. The first out-of-focus version was an accident. Then he took the first half of the out-of-focus version and the one half of the in-focus version, put them together, and made a third and final version—he felt that the beautiful abstraction of the first complimented the beautiful realistic sharpness of the second. Therefore, in the end, it wasn't an accidental use of out-of-focus.

Jerry Malanga: "When are you going to write about *Vinyl*?" Soon. Anyway, there are no new films. Jack seems to have gotten stuck forever with editing *Normal Love* (my opinion is that *Normal Love* was edited during the shooting, and any additional editing of it wouldn't basically change the film, at worst it may make it arty.)

To see more, to be able to see more with our "real", "physical" eye means only that we are beginning to see more with our inner eye.

No more ONE universe, ONE image, ONE screen.

"When today art communicates, it is not so much a transmitter of ideas and information as it is a sender of energy."—Otto Piene

Abstraction will come to pass, will become concrete (new vision of concrete, deeper reality—new spiritual development stage). Light-movies-strobes etc: realization of / or becoming conscious of LIGHT (beyond the "physical" meaning) (the "physical" is expanded) and realizing again that it could be manipulated by "dark" forces.

June 29, 1965

FOR TINA'S FILM
I read:
"Draw near unto me and I will draw near unto you; seek me diligently and ye shall find me; ask, and ye shall receive; knock and it shall be opened to you."
"Whatsoever ye ask the father in my name it shall be given unto you, that is expedient for you." p. 64
"And if ye ask anything that is not expedient for you, it shall turn into your condemnation." p. 65 (?)—"Pearl of Great Price"

Image:
She alone, full body in the frame, standing a little like da Vinci man's figure.
Voice:
"Here I am, I said, just myself & nothing else is certain. I will start with myself, listening to God."

July 1, 1965

A meeting was held at the Film-makers' Cooperative to determine the present and future ownership and fate of Ron Rice's films. Gregory Markopoulos, Leslie Trumbull, P. Adams Sitney, Robert Brown, Jonas Mekas, Amy Rice's brother, and Howard Everngam.

The following decisions and discoveries were agreed upon:
1. Howard Everngam will evaluate his investment in Ron Rice films.

Mr. Everngam indicated that it may come to $1,500, approximately. Some of this money has been already paid to him by the Film-makers' Cooperative, in rentals from Ron Rice films.

2. All rentals from Ron Rice films will go to Howard Everngam (as they did until now) until the amount (see #1) is paid.

3. After Mr. Everngam's investment is repaid, all Ron Rice films will revert to Amy Rice.

4. After the films are reverted to Amy Rice, it will be up to her to determine whom the rentals will go to—she is free to keep it all for herself and Christopher or assigning certain percentages to those who worked on Ron Rice films, including Mr. Everngam.

5. It was also agreed that a print of all unfinished films of Ron Rice should be made before any editing or organizing is attempted. That included *The Queen of Sheba.*

6. All originals that are now with Mr. Everngam will be placed as soon as possible into storage.

7. It was brought to the attention that some footage by Ron Rice (by Olympics) is in S.F. labs. Bob Chatterton or Taylor Mead is supposed to know something about it.

8. Some technical equipment borrowed by Ron Rice from some of the labs and equipment places, which is at this moment with Amy and other people, will be returned to whomever it belongs.

9. A committee was set up to see that the decisions of this meeting were executed properly. The committee will act as an advisor in all other matters involving Ron Rice films. The committee consists of Jonas Mekas, Howard Everngam, Amy Rice, Gregory Markopoulos, P. Adams Sitney, Ken Jacobs, and Storm De Hirsch.

The Caller & Secretary of the above meeting: Jonas Mekas.

CHAPTER EIGHTEEN

... My dreams...
Coop Memo #547899
... Ken Jacobs,
Naomi... On Barbara
Rubin... Letter
to Sitney (about my
work at 'Tek)...
Letter to Jack Smith
... Letter to Sitney
(about my life and
work)... Beatles
movies... Letter to
Kenneth Anger...
Meeting Carl Theo-
dor Dreyer... Letter
to Markopoulos...
Letter to Naomi
about my style
of living... On Ex-
panded Cinema...
Gregory Marko-
poulos... Letter to
Jerome... Letter
from Ginsberg...
Coop wall Memo...
Film Culture... Stan
comes to town...
Desperate money
letter to Henry
... Letter to Mario
Montez... News-
papers and Under-
ground cinema...

A DREAM:
*I come into the room thru the open door.
I stop. I look around. I can hear a woman
crying. But the room is empty. I look right,
then left. I listen for a moment.
Then I wake up.*

ANOTHER NIGHT: ANOTHER DREAM:
*I am standing in an empty, wide field. Sun
pours down. Idyllic. But I can hear a woman
crying. I look left, I look right—nobody in
sight. Crying is quite loud. Slowly my eyes
move to the ground, to the earth. Is the earth
crying? I wake up.*

July 3, 1965
On my way to Millbrook—
Shep: "This part of the river always re-
minds me of Rhine."
Conductor: "You can't take pictures here."
Me: "Yeah??"
Cond.: "Where are you from?"
Me: "New York."
Cond.: "You can't take pictures here."
Shep: "It's a long time I haven't smelt a wet
puppy."
Leary: "New way of communicating. No
symbols—but direct!"
Me: "Yes, but symbols also. But a new
meaning."

July 4, 1965
Ken Jacobs: "What are we doing here?
Why aren't we all in jail? Our moral duty
today is to be in jails."

July 9, 1965
"People don't understand why I like
watching my own movies. I think they were
made by God." (Harry Smith)
"Critics are like eunuchs, they know who
to do it to, but they can't." (Gil Bradley,
Sydney Film Festival)

A poster says "Communists Always Forwards". They ignore the importance of backwards (heart, blood) movements, & sideways movements.

July 13, 1965

Naomi called. She said, she will never come to the Tek or Co-op. She is very mad. Because I never speak to her. I said, I have nothing to say. Oh yes, she said, you speak to everybody but me.
I went to the Psychedelic Theatre last night and I saw her and all I did was I waved. I did not want to speak to anybody. So now I have a baby on my hands.
I said, I will hang up if she continues like that. But, luckily, she hung up before I did.

July 15, 1965

Mail to Robert Kelly the diary note on the Madison Park.
Read Tolkien

July 21, 1965

The beauty of Barbara's project is not so much the success of the project but the very thought, her belief, the innocence of her belief, the idealism, that such a thing should be possible today and that people are ready for it. Every great missionary and crusader and saint always thought so about what he / she was doing. It seems that despite the seeming failure of the project, of the "mission," of the idea—something was achieved, something came into existence: a little bit more subtle dream took a slightly different course. The concrete, material realization of the idea would have done less than the project's seeming failure. Anyway, success or failure, all great souls keep trying it, and the flight is always too high for the everyday souls.

July 27, 1965

Saw Bertolucci's film. Saw all the mistakes of *Guns*. Saw where I was four, five years ago.

My new film must be personal; about "unimportant" things; about things that are important to me, not the so-called "society"—opposite of *Guns* in a sense.
My new film will be concerned with myself, not with "the world."
The line "I want to be concerned with myself" pronounced by a 10-years-old, by a 20-years-old, by a 30-years-old; by a 60-years-old man.
Frances as she was in *Guns* and Frances as she is today.
8 mm footage: trying to catch people "casually," their essence, their poetry.

July 29, 1965

0.45 Tokens
0.42 Food (coffee & donut & yogurt)
0.20 Papers

(Harry Gantt bought a meal)

The print of *The Art of Vision* came to New York—finally—and was shipped immediately to Buenos Aires. P. Adams Sitney, who is going with our S. American Exposition, left for B. Aires yesterday. Exposition is opening on the 1st of August.

August 15, Sun. 1965

PAS:
It is almost unbelievable but it's August 15th. Last three weeks went like nothing. I didn't even see them. I managed to complete N. 37 and it's now all at the printer and the issue should be out next week. I had no help whatsoever. Louis took a tv job and has no time. Griffith issue came out. We had a mad mailing session, to beat the deadline. The Post Office is after us. But managed to get out on time. Right now I am working on another, mixed issue, which should go to the printer next week —I'd like to free myself from *FC* for a few months. More and more of the Tek's work I'm pushing on Bob & Frances, despite their obstinacy & sometimes laziness (Bob's). It

is beyond my understanding how one can be lazy when there is so much so unbelievably much to do! So much excitement in the living! Even if it bogs you down.

Anyway, I had no time to write to you. There was nothing new to tell. You know everything. Except a few things. Gregory finished his editing, so now he has nothing to do. Jack was arrested last week, together with Piero, got involved in a fight with cops at a screening (Jack was defending a girl and he hit the cop—as any gentleman should). They may be out by Monday.

From what I hear, you are doing a good job in BA. Barbara just came back and brought me up to date. In case you don't know, she managed to sell all her films, last day—they all converged on her last day, how idiotic. David spoke with Kenneth about *Scorpio* and it's OK. It's OK with my own films whatever you want to do with them. But not with the others. Gregory has been particularly "money-minded" lately. He just doubled his rentals at the Coop— He has been also upset about the term "underground" that has appeared lately (last week) again in headlines, articles in *Daily News*, *Show Business*, and he said he doesn't want his name mentioned in any piece that connects him with "underground"—you see, he is trying to get some support from foundations and he thinks he has to build around himself a certain aura of respectability. I think it's nonsense. I don't think we should care at all what newspapers say—but Gregory cares. Gregory always wanted to go to Hollywood. It's pretty hot here and you are lucky you aren't here. Dogs are lying flat on the streets.

I think it is a very good idea that you are dropping postcards to some of the filmmakers once in a while—they are happy, for a change. I heard some good about you, in any case.

But I am getting fed up with all of the filmmakers.

My plans call now for a 3-year retreat— no more 6 months or 8 months. I am burning slowly all the bridges behind me. The coming three years belong to my own film work. Five films. My New York (or American) Testament.

A very complex project. But that's it.

It was hopeless until now. Even if I have had time—I had no money. Yesterday I had my first lucky break—I got $3,000 for myself, with no strings attached, so now I am pulling out the match to light the dynamite box.

I still think *The Art of Vision* should go to São Paolo—even if nothing else goes. Write me if there are any financial problems of sending *The Art of Vision* to São Paolo—maybe Jerome will help me to do something about it. Maybe *The Art of Vision* could be detached from the rest for that purpose.

Sorry that I could send you only 70. Till now. I will have another check by Tuesday, even if it's a small one. I am still licking my financial wounds.

But everything will be OK.

Best to Miguel

& keep yourself SOBER

August 21, 1965

In our "early days" we didn't give so damn much to money: we were happy to have screenings, everybody could come and see our movies. Now we want MONEY.

I thought I will tell you how I feel about it, no use carrying it silently. I think that things are beginning to stink.

Look, Jack: do you really think that those few friends (they are all your friends, usually) whom you prevented seeing your movies by your insistence that NOBODY WILL COME IN FREE, and when you charge $2—will ever support your filmmaking with money? They are poor bastards, poor souls, all your friends. You are directing your revenge on the wrong people. Those who can afford to pay—they pay anyway, that's their way of life. It will be your poor friends who will be kept out, like some of those who were kept out last Thursday, while there were seats empty.

I don't like this type of attitude. I think it is a sick, paranoiac attitude. The damage done by such an attitude is not repaid by the extra money (say, $5.75) that you manage to squeeze out with such an attitude. No other film-maker is that sick about it (about this "everybody's getting free into my screenings," "how I am going to complete *Normal Love* if the Co-op lets people free into my benefit screenings," etc.) and no film-maker yet got richer or poorer from such tactics.

Judging from last screening (Thursday) you had about thirty friends, "stars" etc. who came and whom you let in free anyway. And then, there were five or six who were also your friends, but somehow, temporarily, they have fallen into the second, unfavored, category, so they were kept out. And I just don't see why, I see no logic in your madness.

There are bad things in the air lately, concerning success, money, fame, publicity. And it's not the moon's fault, as you or someone else indicated. It's all our own goddamn fault, our own doing. And if our best film-makers, our best souls let themselves be caught in this shit: how can we blame the others?

I really think it's about time that we begin thinking about this and try to do something about it. We are all becoming petty, small, sick, pompous asses, and no great art can ever come from pompous asses.

I really don't think we have the right to complain that nobody comes to our help with money, etc. I don't see why they should, the way we are. I think we should be dumped out on garbage grounds in New Jersey, with no great losses to anybody. That's my fair opinion, this Friday morning. Outside, it's autumn, and the sun is bright and the air is clear somehow. The only ugliness, the only stink is coming from us.

August 24, 1965

PAS:

Separately I am sending some money, tomorrow morning. I am meeting Harry Gantt early tomorrow, he's lending some money good old Harry—he did the same last time. No one else seems to understand the real needs. I called a number of people trying to borrow some, explaining, that there you are, stranded with the Exposition, for the good of Cinema, for the good of S. America and the North America—nobody seems to care about anything but themselves. I am really getting fed up with everybody. Anyway—Harry is saving us this time again. And I haven't paid my bills yet, and they are big this time—the Griffith issue is out, and the Harry Smith issue is out. I am broke like a willow. Debts on all sides. Tek is still paying the debts incurred by Harry Smiths prints. And we are still readying the 4th Street, extra expenses, and again nobody wants to help, and everybody keeps saying: Oh, fine, what a fine job you are doing, good boys, good boys. And Gregory is running around telling everybody that he's going to withdraw his films from the Coop because he is not underground and because he doesn't like Jack Smith, and etc. etc. Everybody's vision ends with the godamn nose. When Gregory talks thru his films, his speech is beautiful, his content is beautiful; when Gregory talks thru his own mouth, he says stupid things, worse than a child, but he's supposed to be grown up.

As you can see, the scene is pretty fucked up in New York, you don't even have to know the details, you can see from my mood, and I am not so easy to move out of my normal farmer's calm; but I am losing patience. I have managed somehow to

Jonas Mekas and P. Adams Sitney.

To be argued by
No. 34 EMILE Z. BERMAN

New York Supreme Court

APPELLATE TERM—FIRST DEPARTMENT

PEOPLE OF THE STATE OF NEW YORK,

Respondent,

vs.

KENNETH JACOBS, FLORENCE KARPF and JONAS MEKAS,

Defendants-Appellants.

BRIEF OF DEFENDANTS-APPELLANTS

EMILE Z. BERMAN AND
A. HAROLD FROST,
Attorneys for Defendants-Appellants,
100 William Street,
New York, N. Y.

On the brief:
EMILE Z. BERMAN,
DAVID G. TRAGER,
FRANK R. ROSINY.

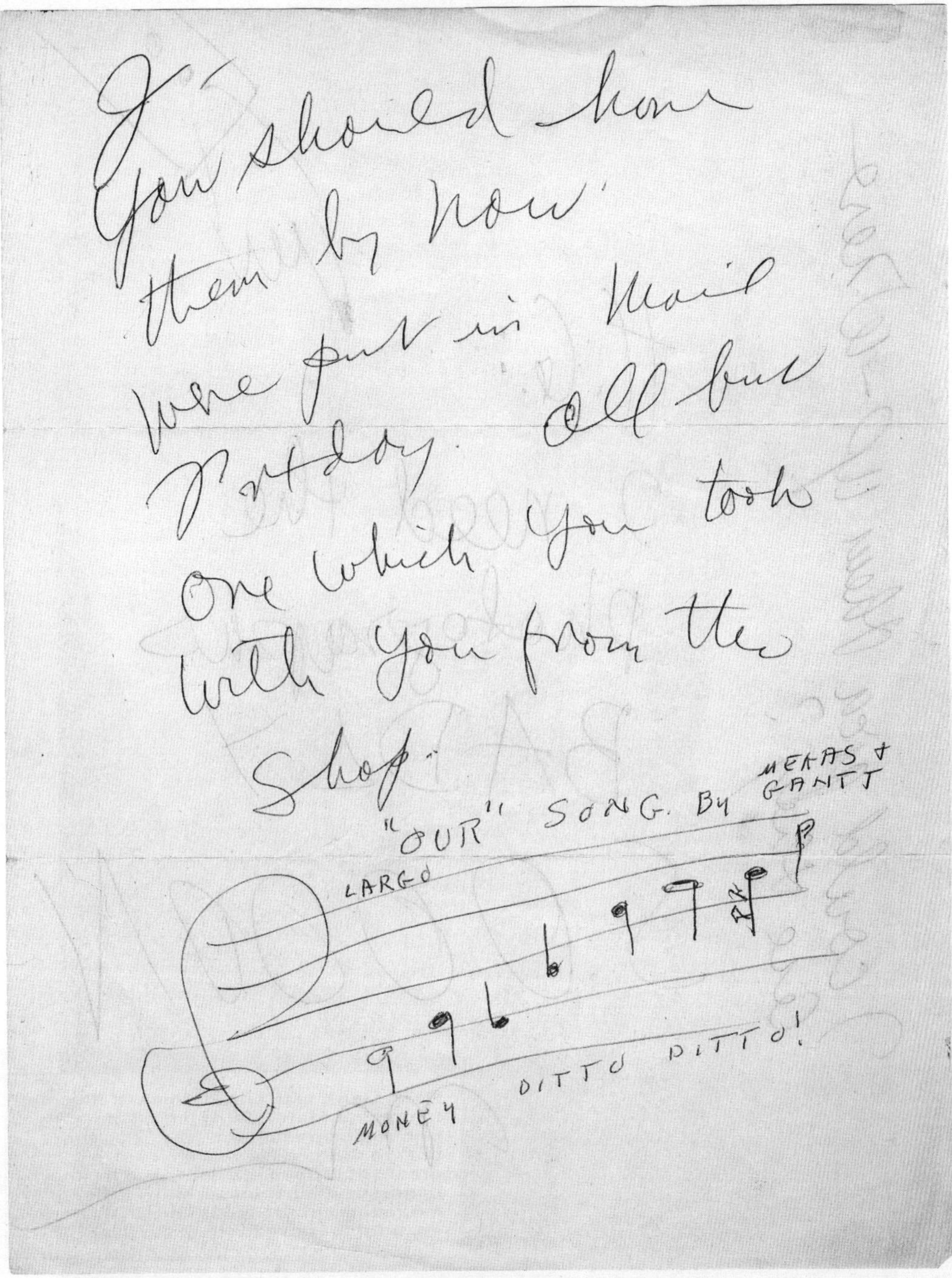

You should have
them by now.
Were put in Mail
Friday. All but
One which you took
with you from the
Shop.

"OUR" SONG. BY MEKAS + GANTT

LARGO

MONEY DITTO DITTO!

Harry Gantt with Lita Hornick of *Kulchur* magazine. Harry Gantt did all my printing beginning with the 5th issue of *Film Culture*. He was an ideal, a dream of little magazines. And he knew hundreds of dirty jokes. Many little magazines of the 1960s and 1970s were grateful to Harry for their survival.

free myself almost completely from the Tek's work, luckily, so I have more time for myself. Frances is doing five men's work, with Bob slumbering as usual; and I put George to take care of the theatre. We had a few good San Francisco programs, with nothing new from New York.

Did some shooting, although most of my time last two weeks went to straightening *F.C.* matters—two issues to mail, and the preparation of the autumn issue.

Ken Kelman came with a truck today to the Tek, he brought Filmwises back—pages are missing he said. Menken is still working on her page, something like that. A slow business.

I hope you are surviving, one way or another. I really promised to myself (as you probably did to yourself) never again embark on any Expositions. We'll stick to our home, more quietly and peacefully. It's too godamn nervewracking, too exhausting. I hope you feel better about it. You, there, at least see some of the fruits of the Exposition. I see only the thorns.

Keep the beard high—
Life is only beginning—
Art is old—Pound is old

September 1, 1965

About a year ago I stopped going to movies. I mean, to the "regular," Hollywood movies and the imported "art" movies. I felt I needed an intermission. I wanted to have some kind of new perspective to the "commercial" cinema.

Last week I started going to the movies again. I am seeing three, four movies every day. I have been reading and hearing from friends all about these new movies, how advanced, even "experimental" they are, and above all, how mature and adult they have become. Listening to their discussions in the Cinematheque's lobby I pictured all these movies, *Pussycat*, and *Knack*, and *Help*, and I couldn't wait to see them.

But now I saw them and I have to say that the commercial cinema has never looked more miserable. *Knack* carried the Cannes awards this year, but the movie is so bad it's embarrassing. *Pussycat*, one of Sarris' favorites this year, is a third rate cinema and a second rate comedy and I thought Sellers was just terrible and the movie sloppy and corny and heavy. We are talking about comedy. But comedy usually has wings and is light.

And what a let down *Help* was. *Hard Day's* wasn't a very good movie either, but comparing with *Help* it was almost a masterpiece.

I will continue seeing them, I hope I'll find something. And I was beginning to think that I was living in my own fantasy cinema, that I was exaggerating the achievements of the "underground." But I wasn't! The most mature cinema is produced underground. Like Brakhage's *Songs*, last Friday: on 8 mm, little movies, home-made, but what a cinema!

I am ready and anxious to see everything that New York Film Festival will have to offer this year—NY Film Festival being the biggest of the "best from all film festivals." But the very fact that the Press and Critics and Directors of the Festival can devote pages in the newspapers and the press releases without mentioning the most vital modern cinema today—Brakhage's *Songs*, for instance—this fact alone makes the festival ridiculous.

September 14, 1965

Dear Kenneth:

I thought it is time for a letter, even if it's a short letter. There are two or three things to communicate to you.

I will start with the one that was bothering me for some time. That is, *The Brig* opening at the Cinema Theater. I thought you should know that I have nothing to do with it. The sad truth about *The Brig* is that as soon as I finished shooting, it was taken from me by the Living Theatre and the playwright's agent, Sterling Lord. I shot it without asking their permission, so they put me against the wall and I said, OK, I shot it, here it is, you can do what you want with it: it is my gift to Becks. The only thing I insisted was that Coop retains 16 mm rights for distribution, to help the Coop. I will be also given 5 % from the rentals. But I have nothing more to do with it. Stone is handling 35 mm distribution for them. I told David that as far as I am concerned I don't want *The Brig* played at the Cinema theatre. He respected my wish, but thought that he should help Becks to make some money anyway, so he booked the film. So I thought you should know it. David has great respect for you and your work, but he doesn't exactly understand the boycott spirit, he lives in another world, and not much use trying to change him.

My own efforts during these two months went into strengthening the Cinematheque and freeing myself for my own work. In connection with that, I had to let Bob go back to his studies. It was too difficult for him to handle some administrative situation. In his place I got John Brockman, a very energetic young man who mastered the whole works in a few days and is running the place by himself. I will be coming in only once a month to do the monthly programming. I hope that finally I found the Leslie Trumbull of the Cinematheque. I hope so. For the work at the Tek kept draining me all summer long, I just couldn't escape it. I don't even know how I managed even to shoot what I shot. And your film came just in time when I had not a single penny for food, not talking about buying film.

Brockman is looking for a theatre where *Inauguration* could be played. You should be hearing now very soon on this subject, he does things fast. For it would be great to see it on three screens. Somebody, I forgot his name, was here from SF the other week and told us about the screening of *Inauguration* you had there.

Finally: There is still one more check to come to you for the last screening of *Scorpio*, etc. and you should receive it in two weeks or so from now, it will be over $500.

Our screenings, beginning October 1st, will be held seven nights a week.

We haven't scheduled anything from you for September. I am working right now on the October program. If you feel that you should have a screening on the regular program in October, drop an air-mail note. The three screen screening would take place before early October. Though, I guess, it would be better to wait until then and have no other screenings. I have no doubts at all that we'll have a proper place for *Inauguration* for the first part in November, and in case you plan to come to NY for that occasion, you could make your plans that way.

I may be going to France for two weeks, a week from now. Anything to be done?

I hope your own work is going OK.

September 17, 1965

Filmed Th. Dreyer, at his hotel. Cold morning, crossed Central Park, filmed some trees. Dreyer, I met him after his films at the New York Film Festival. I said I would like to make a film portrait of him. He got very interested. So we agreed to meet early Sunday at the hotel he was staying, he is very busy, he said, it was the only free time.

The sun was streaming thru the window. What do you want me to do, he said. I said, nothing, just sit there as you are. And I made a few shots, close up, side, front, different takes. I hope it will come out. He was very intrigued, and asked many questions about what I was doing. So I had to tell him about what is happening in the underground. He found it all very interesting, he kept repeating it, "interesting possibilities."

Carl Theodor Dreyer, from *Walden* as filmed on September 17, 1965.

September 24, 1965

You go outside, look at the sun. Then, you return home & you can't work, you're impregnated with light.

Shoot: Amy cleaning dust from books, etc.
I meditated today on all the books ever written, on all wisdom & poets.
I felt their spirit present in my room.
So I cleaned the dust from the shelves.
Humbly I touched the books,
the territory of the spirit.

From Gustav Meyrink:
"The desire of mortal man to see supernatural beings is a cry that wakes even the ghosts of the underworld, because such a desire is not pure; because it is greed, rather than desire; because it wants to 'take' in some way or other, instead of learning to 'give'."

"We know that there is no good or bad; only right or wrong."

"They believe that the body ought to be neglected and despised because it is sinful. We know that there is no such thing as sin; the body is the beginning of our work, and we have come down on Earth to transform it into spirit."

September, 1965

What else is new? Harry got into argument with Naomi and threw out from the fourth floor Co-op window his terrific 16 mm projector. Luckily nobody was hurt, but our window went.

October 1, 1965

Dear Gregory,
I thought I'll write you a letter. Several thoughts bother me when I think about some of your latest statements.
They all concern your anger whenever you see that your name is mentioned in connection with "Underground Films."

I understand the reasons for that but I don't understand *the form* your anger and your attitude take. A number of times lately, on such occasions, and in your arguments with Harry & Jack, you have declared that "this will be the reason for my resigning from the Co-op."
I consider this unwise and hypocritical. Whom are you trying to punish? And whom are you fighting?
Your anger against the press, against the stupidity of the press & other communication media directs itself not against the press, no, (I have seen on many occasions that you LIKE publicity!) but against the film-makers! against the Co-op! I cannot understand this logic & I ask you to explain it to me, in writing. For you cannot say that film-makers themselves write those articles. As a matter of fact, most of our film-makers are illiterates…
Will be waiting to hear from you.

October 4, 1965

A letter to Naomi but also to all film-makers & my friends:
I thought I will take this occasion to go into a subject that I am not always too willing to go into. Really it doesn't exist for me. Only once in a while it comes out. But you provided me with such an occasion, yesterday, and those occasions are becoming a bit too often and too painful.
So I will tell you something about myself. Really, one small aspect of myself: how do I survive. How I live or How I Starve.
As often before, you asked me for money. Not the Co-op, not the Tek. They come and ask ME for money. So I shrug my shoulders, or I say nothing, or I just walk away. Or I just ask why they ask me for money. And they look at me, or get angry, like you, and tell me that they want to spit in my face— and they have spat into my face. I take all this for granted, something I got used to thru the years. But sometimes I am losing my patience.

I asked you, "Do you ever THINK?" Do you ever think more seriously about what Cinematheque, or Co-op, or anything and anybody around you are, how they work and how they survive. How I live or how I survive?

When I came to this country, for ten years I worked in factories, on the docks, in shops, loading trucks, making deliveries, in greasy machine factories, etc., etc., and I used at least to eat decently. But in 1959 I decided to quit. I just had enough. I could not work all day in some stupid factory, come home totally exhausted and still work on *Film Culture*, and *Village Voice*, and see the movies I wanted to see, and etc., etc. etc. So now I have been living from all kinds of part-time freelance jobs. I *should* tell you that I haven't been paid or taken neither from *Film Culture* not the Co-op nor the Tek; just the opposite. I have spent the last ten years of my life trying to bring in money for all these losing products and activities, because I believed and I still believe in their absolute necessity. I kept and I still keep scrounging for them. I have chosen an expensive or, rather, costly freedom, since I have to survive on those few paid lectures that I get a year or a few writings here and there.

I have told you this already once, I remember. Once, when you asked me why I don't eat in restaurants, I told you that that is the price of my freedom. I have never been able to afford to eat in restaurants; I seldom go to paid movies. I have reduced my meals, during the last ten years, to one meal a day, and it is not really a meal but something, say, a hamburger, or an oatmeal, whatever it is. I owe much gratitude to all those friends who have often fed me during these past few years, and there are many of those.

I have learned to be free from food and clothes. I have reduced my wardrobe to one corduroy suit that is my four-season fashion.

When I told you all this that time, a year ago, you told me that I am a fool and that I don't live like a human. That I don't know what pleasure and luxury is.

I tell you it's better to give up certain human pleasures and luxuries than become inhuman. Because your needs of money last night made you inhuman. I really forgive you what you said, no word can harm me, no action. I have gone through my schooling. But it makes me feel bad when I see you or any other filmmaker becoming insensitive because of money and turning against me or their friends. It is this that hurts me, to see you being carried away by this kind of ugliness. I don't say that you should renounce everything, like I have—that is neither easy to do nor sometimes necessary to do. But I would ask you not to lose your human kindness. I would ask you not to get angry, not to release your desperations on wrong people, on your friends.

When I told you yesterday that "I have no money"—and I didn't—there were other times when I had some and then I split with you as I split my money with Harry and with many others—so you said: yes, but you took all that money this evening, give me some.

Should I explain, at this late date, that not a single penny of the Co-op money can be touched by me or anyone else who works at the Co-op, that the Co-op has to account to the film-makers that the money has to go to the film-makers; that none of the money is MINE; that I receive no salary, that I have given years of my life and will be giving more years freely and without ever asking anything in return or imposing any conditions, and that money wouldn't be the condition to do something I really believe in.

Because I respect my freedom, even if I have to take your spit into my face; even if your mind can not work or grasp that someone could spend years of one's life working not because of money but because of faith or madness or I don't know what. It is neither a wise thing nor a smart thing to do anything without being paid, so you can take me for an idiot or fool, if that makes you feel better. But I just wanted you to know my attitude to money and to this whole business.

I wish you luck. Get rich. But leave me alone where I am.

I wish you luxury. Trips. But leave me in my peace right here.

THE EXPANDED CINEMA MONTH AT THE CINEMATHEQUE

Although not seen by the public eye and unknown to the professional movie critics, new and startling developments have been taking place in cinema during the last ten years. Cinema has been going into a number of new directions. The peripheries of cinema have been expanding.

Film-Maker's Cinematheque will be devoting the entire month of November to an extensive survey of these various experiments and developments. The survey will be called the Festival of Expanded Cinema.

What's happening, briefly, is this: the simple one screen, one image, one projector cinema is being complicated by multiple screens, multiple projections; the eye is being challenged by multiple imagery; screen and image shapes change and spin; live performers and screen action merge; multiple exposures cover the screen; slides begin to move; new kinds of projectors bring sculpture and objects alive on the screen in splendorous colors; a shopping bag full of groceries becomes a movie and vice versa; hand held projectors; balloon projectors; balloon screens; video projections; sculptures with built-in movies; robots that take movies; machines that make movies—the idea of cinema, where does cinema really end or begin are completely upset by these new explorations.

We are surrounded, the man is thirsty for a new kind, much more intense sound-light-experience—and that's what's happening.

"Que m'importe que tu sois sage? Sois belle! et soit triste!"—Baudelaire

"Cet homme était si intelligent qu'il n'était plus bon à rien en ce monde."
—Lichtenberg

"Fermez les yeux, et vous verrez"—Joubert

"Der Leser eines Spannungsromans moechte wissen, wie das Buch endet, der Dickens-Leser wuenscht, es moege niemals enden."
—GK Chesterton, HERETIKER, Hyperion V. 1912

October, 1965

Gregory, after watching Andy's *Temptations* at the Cinematheque's Open House screening, declared that he will never show any of his films at the Tek. Andy's film, he said, is pornography, it's ruining the Tek's name. He doesn't want to have anything to do with Tek.

A great film-maker is not always a great critic or a great democrat. He asks me to keep Andy out of Open House screenings —screenings which have been devised to be open to everybody.

Just a few days ago, when Soltero told him that Tek is hesitant about advertising his title *Jerkoff Epic* (I felt it was a stupid way to get cops into the theatre), Gregory said to him he should place an ad in *The Voice* at his own expense. What an inconsistency of thinking!

Earlier today John Cavanaugh told me that Gregory seriously was telling him yesterday that David Stone and myself were using thousands and thousands of the money that is being contributed to the Tek to help film-makers, for ourselves. David showed me a letter he received a couple

FILM-MAKERS' CINEMATHEQUE
434 LAFAYETTE ST. AL4-4060

SPECIAL ANNOUNCEMENT

FESTIVAL OF EXPANDED CINEMA

New and startling developments have been taking place in cinema during the last two years. The peripheries of cinema have been expanding in a number of new directions.

Film-Makers' Cinematheque will be devoting the entire month of November to an extensive survey of these various experiments and developments. The programs will include multiple screens, multiple projectors; multiple imagery; changing screen and image shapes; merger of live performers and screen action; multiple exposures; moving slides; kinetic sculptures; hand held projectors; balloon screens; videotape; video projections; various light and sound experiments; etc.

The Festival will consist of thirty evening programs. Each participant will be responsible (in whole or in part) for an evening program. We hope to have at least twenty different programs.

Among the artists participating in the Festival will be:

Kenneth Anger
Roberts Blossom
Robert Breer
Jackie Cassen
Milton Cohen
Ken Dewey
Ed Emshwiller
Al Hansen
Dick Higgins
Alfred Leslie
Angus MacLise
Klaus Oldenberg
The Once Group (Ann Arbor)
Nam June Paik
Larry Rivers
Beverly Schmidt
Jack Smith
Don Snyder
Gerd Stern
Elaine Summers
Aldo Tambellini
Stan Vanderbeek
Andy Warhol
Robert Whitman

At Adolfas' wedding, with Leonas Letas, Adolfas, and Algirdas Landsbergis, our old gang from Wiesbaden/Kassel Displaced Persons camps days, October 19, 1965.

With Adolfas and Pola Chapelle, on the wedding day, October 19, 1965.

days ago from Gregory. It was one of the most stupid letters I have ever seen.

The strange thing about all this is that then Gregory turns around and shoots tests to get into Hollywood!

October 6, 1965

New York City

Dear Jerome:

I don't know where to start, but I'll start somewhere.

I have been thinking and thinking, and I have come to the following conclusions concerning my trip to Cassis, my present work in New York, and a dozen other matters.

I don't want this to be a disappointment for you—but I had, or I have, to postpone my trip to Cassis to the second part of November.

These are the complex reasons:

I have to be in Berlin, to participate in a Colloquium on cinema, on December 8th. I hesitated accepting it until yesterday. I thought, I cannot afford two absences from New York this year, with two more issues of *Film Culture* to be prepared, and the work at the Cinematheque. Plus, I felt, if I go now—then I have to rush back immediately, to get out *Film Culture*. It has always been in the past few years, that whenever I go somewhere—Mar del Plata, or Cannes, or Knokke le Zoute, I have to rush back immediately. Never one day longer.

I have decided to combine my Berlin journey with Cassis. No doubt, you'll be back in NY by that time, and there will be nobody to show me really the place—but I'll try to look around—if that is possible at all—and get some idea about the possibilities for next summer etc. Then I will continue to Berlin. Stan has also accepted the invitation, so it's possible that we both will travel together. In any case, I find this about the only way I can manage it properly. There will be no rush then. And no rush after Berlin. I decided to spend these three coming weeks in preparing the last two issues of *FC* that I must bring out this year, and thus make myself free for the next few months. I need some peace. I started shooting, last week, something in between, and I had to drop it. It wasn't exactly the film I want to do. What I really want to do is my *Diary* film or films, which I have been shooting these last two years, and the *Walden* film, the one with the 12 years old girl. I looked through all the footage that I have for the *Diary* and I was surprised to see what I managed to collect during the last two years. Now I have to edit it. As for the *Walden*, I have pages and pages of notes and I want to write the script based on those notes. That's why I need some peace. I hope to devote the months of December and January to the *Walden* script.

I feel like I'm letting you down, this time —but I just couldn't figure out any other way without getting myself into a greater confusion than I am in already.

I also had some second thoughts on your next summer project. I don't know to what conclusions have you yourself arrived now when you are back at Cassis and after you have spoken to some of the people. But my thoughts are something like this:

I am a little bit afraid about the Festival. I don't think you should get involved into something big like that. I think it would consume so much of your time, thoughts and energy which, instead, should go into your film-making. These fears perhaps come from my own experiences, since so much of my time is consumed by the Coop, Tek, or *Film Culture*. And now, more than ever before, I feel that it is only through our own creative work we can really reach others (or ourselves) and that all our energy should go to film-making. I think you should make a film this coming Spring or Summer, and everything should go towards it, avoiding any other temptations or side-trackings. The Festival may side-track your film. On the other hand, I have no clear idea what film you have in mind —it is very possible that the Festival is absolutely necessary for the film itself.

One thing remains: whichever way it will be: Festival or no Festival: I will be there with my camera ready to record and assist, as I said before. All that I am trying to say—and this is again, perhaps, only my own personal preoccupation at this stage of my life—to shrink a little bit instead of expanding; not to lose myself in big projects; to make something smaller and more personal but more beautiful. Any kind of Festival now scares me a little bit. That was one of the reasons why I hesitated accepting the Berlin invitation. I joined only to keep Stan company. I did not feel like going there and talking at the Berlin Congress Hall: for who am I to talk about cinema, really? What have I really done? When compared to Stan? So now I am going to Berlin to praise Stan, instead. I may bring *The Art of Vision* with me.

So forgive me again, that instead of coming myself, I am sending this letter. But that's how it had to be.

& thanks for everything. No one has helped me so much, when I needed most, and so generously, and I'll be always grateful for it.

November 3, 1965

Inter-Office Bulletin-Thought-Note
Concerning the matter of who-should-go-in-free.

I have given much thought to this matter, for I think it is a very important matter.

It's connected with the very name, Film-Maker's Cinematheque, film-maker's underlined. Even if the Tek loses money, it is more important to avoid the bad feeling than gain one or two bucks for the Tek. Whom are we keeping out? Five or ten film-makers, that's all. And usually, those ten are the ones who love cinema most.

We are not in business anyway. So what the hell.

My nose can smell plenty of bad feeling around, and I don't like it. It's not doing any good, to antagonize the film-makers, even if only five or six of them, because then we are defeating our purpose: to serve the film-maker. Yes, we are serving the public, too, but not at the cost of the film-maker.

I think the policy from now on, and with no side-tracking, concerning this matter, should be always the same: to any screening, full or not full house, film-makers should come in free. Their friends should pay, no doubt. Unless you can see that they are completely poor, and the house is empty anyway.

Tek's motto should be: the film-maker is always right, even when s/he is wrong.

Not that some of them couldn't afford to pay: this "coming in free" business is their small vanity, small privilege, which they feel they are entitled to. Sometimes that may come from a stupid thought that the Tek is "making money" with their work. No use arguing and telling them, and I wouldn't advise you to try it, judging from my past experiences.

November 4, 1965

I am walking the streets of NY again, and cursing. Reduced to two tokens a day for traveling, and 50 cents for food, I walked all the way downtown, 90 goddamn blocks, when I have so much to do, when I have to bring out two issues of *Film Culture* within two weeks, when my own film is sitting on the table not touched. Again, I spent last three days and today calling for money, writing letters, desperate for the Cinematheque is completely broke, we had the account overdrawn by $800 last night, and we have to return $2,500 loan by next week, and Allen Ginsberg needs his $200 back, and I sunk all $3,000 that I got for my film into the Tek, and there is no help

LITERARISCHES COLLOQUIUM BERLIN

VERÄNDERUNG IM FILM

Programmfolge der Filmbeispiele aus den U.S.A.:

I. BRUCE CONNER

1. Cosmic Ray
2. A Movie

II. CARMEN D'AVINO

1. Pianissimo
2. The Big O
3. The Trip

III. STAN BRAKHAGE

1. Two:Creeley/McClure
2. Dog Star Man: Part 2
3. Mothlight

IV. ED EMSHWILLER

1. Thanatopsis
2. Folge aus "Relativity"

V. SHIRLEY CLARKE

1. Folge aus "Scarey Time"
2. Bridges

VI. STAN VANDERBEEK

Feedback No. I

Diskussionsleitung: AMOS VOGEL

The team of the Literarisches Colloquium Berlin. I had to be part of it, but had to make a last minute cancellation, due to the work at the Coop. Bottom: from left to right Stan Brakhage, Carmen D'Avino, Stan Vanderbeek, Ed Emshwiller. Top: Bruce Conner, Shirley Clarke, Walter Höllerer, Amos Vogel.

Oct 29, 1965

was for making a print of Harry Smith's film emergency fund. City Lights
261 Columbus Ave
S.F. Calif

Dear Jonas:

I have rent paid here for another month & am staying long enough
to continue some work on an mss. for City Lights & take part in Berkeley
fundraising poesy readings & another march this month. Running low on
loot and need back the $200 I loaned you/filmmakers last July 10. I think
I said I'd need it in a month or two from that time but have not run out till
now and have no other income for the next few months so definitely do send
it withing a few days if x possible.
                    Little Stephen Bornstein here too, tell
Barbara Rubin I'll write her soon as can, Sanders here singing with Fugs
much better than I last heard in NY.   Hope you're well & everything
prospering, filmmakers etc. I got Volkswagon camper moveable transistorized
house & will be heading back to NY that way stopping over in the nation
wherever it looks interesting. Spent weeks with Gary Snyder in isolate
northwest Cascades & another while at Big Sur x titanic canyons on Pacific
high on LSD one afternoon very wordsworthean & pleasant. I'd quit LSD
long ago too frightful & nowadays it's all tranquil, I was amazed. Love
to Harry Smith & Joffen if he's around.
     Send the $200 fast as you can please.
                                as ever
                                Allen
                                Allen

from anybody, everybody likes to talk and sympathize, but no real understanding or even wanting to understand; so I am beaten, tired, angry, & hungry. ANGRY & HUNGRY, here is a title for a book, anno 1965. Good I collected some energy in Cassis, it will last a week or two. But to live on coffee and toast—I bought some beans last night—is too draining, too impossible, too maddening. How do you manage? asked Seymour Stern yesterday. "From desperation, we do things from desperation," I said.

Last night I spent two hours with couple people from *Newsweek*, they were doing an article on the "underground." They gave me one small Bourbon and I got drunk. Not from Bourbon but from worries & all those beans. So I left them and walked out into the night, dizzy.

I was told by John today that Rockefeller Foundation just gave a grant to somebody to write a book about us. What a goddamn joke. When we have been asking desperately to help us, when it's such a goddamn stupid struggle just to keep the Tek going—here they give money to somebody to write our necrologue. Money for Death; but not for Life.

November 5, 1965

Dear HR,

I thought I should drop you this note. I have a few things to communicate to you. Since you have been very helpful to us (by us I mean the Coop & the Cinematheque) in the past, I thought I shouldn't keep you in the dark about what's happening.

I have been trying & desperately, for the last two weeks, to raise $4,000 which we need to pay the bills and debts and they are all urgent and overdue—and our account is overdrawn by $800 this very moment—but nobody seems to understand our real needs, nobody cares what happens to us, nobody even responded to my letters and calls. Everybody seems to believe that Coop and Cinematheque should be self-supporting, or even MAKING money. Nobody wants to understand that we AREN'T IN BUSINESS. Our job is to help the new, the unrecognized, the unknown artist; it is a midwife's job; and that by our very nature we'll always remain financially on the losing end. Both, the coop and the Tek have been losing from $600 to $1,000 every month, and it has to be so, and it will be so, for we have to give a chance to the people that nobody else would, and lose money with it. That is the price which we have to pay, if we are really concerned with the avant-garde, with the new artist, with the growth of cinema as an art. Everybody keeps talking about us, writing articles, and nobody wants to do anything that would be of real help. I can't do it alone and by myself. I am tired. I have been beaten, for the first time. And I see no way out. All our attempts to get Foundations interested in helping us; all my letters; all my calls end in nothing. I have even sunk into the Coop & Tek $3,000 that I got to make my film—I was ready to go and shoot my film, finally—but then I had to sink it, everything, into the Coop and Tek, to save them from dying, when we need them most. Even the $10 weekly dollars that I get from the *Voice* I am sinking into the Tek. For the last two years I have been practically living on coffee and toast. I walk downtown to the Tek 90 blocks every day to save a token. BUT I HAVE NO REGRETS. I feel I have to do it, and I act accordingly to what I believe. But I am tired. And angry. I am angry that people who could do something about it; people who have much better contacts than I who wasn't even born here, who came here as a stranger; that people who talk so beautifully about us DO NOT MOVE A FINGER when the help is needed. The apathy is unbelievable. Everybody's concerned about themselves, and nothing else. Nobody will take anything away from himself.

I may sound low, but I am low.

I don't even dare ask you to do anything about it. I don't dare ask anybody to do anything about it. EVERYBODY has let us down. All words of sympathy sound hollow to me.

The only man I respect today is dead. He burned himself in front of Pentagon. The first Saint America has produced. Which is something. So, not everything is so bad, after all.

With Love,
(that's all that's left when everything else collapses)
Jonas

P. S. Yesterday I heard an almost unbelievable, almost macabre news. A man came to the Tek and asked if he could see all the Tek past programs for he just received a grant from a FD (I forgot which one it was, but it was either Ford or Rockefeller FD) TO WRITE A BOOK ABOUT US! And this after all our desperate attempts to get some help to keep us alive. So I told this man: fine, fine. Write your book. We may be closing in a week or two anyway. So that will make a nice post-mortem book.

Everybody's interested in the DEAD, nobody wants to help to sustain the living. That's the most funny joke of 1965.

November 8, 1965

Still working on trying to save the Tek. Amy lent $200, and Kelman, to our greatest surprise, came with $750 loan, which wasn't that easy for him, he has no income. Isabel came tonight to Jack's show. "I got your letter," she said, "and Henry got one, too, but we didn't call because there is nothing we can do." Can't blame them. They are only fashion travelers in the Underground, not the passion partners.

Mr. X: "My brother wrote those surrealist visions, I am translating them—he wrote

them after the shock, after he saw the tortures in Vietnam; they used to put electrical outlets one in the woman's mouth and another in her vagina. That was too much, and he flipped out.

Me: "Who was torturing? The Vietnamese?"

Mr. X: "No, French."

Last night after the screening, Stan, Carolee, Tenney and Kellys, we went, we sat at Stone's until three in the morning, talking, talking, talking.

Kelly said, "This is a good house; there is a kitchen, there is an eating room, and bedrooms—you don't see that anymore, there are no more homes. This is a home." We talked, as we sat around the big heavy wood table.

Today we sat in the kitchen, talking about money. Stan just refused a grant from the Rockefeller Foundation. He feels he can use and needs money, but can not apply and give false promises or promises that he may not be able to fulfill.

We spoke about money.

The green paper.

November 8, 1965

Dear Mario:

I thought I will drop you this note. I have to explain something, or try to explain, if that's possible at all. You asked me for ten dollars last night. You said you asked Isabel, and she said she didn't have any.

It hurt me to say No, and I walked the raining street, home, and I still couldn't forget it. I tried to tell to a few other film-makers, and to a few other people, that I have no money—and it's of no use, everybody expects me to have money for them. When I say that I don't have, they look strangely at me, not believing—and now, as months go, as years go, whenever I am asked for money, I begin to blurt almost automatically, NO; almost with anger. Although I know I have no right to be angry about anything. The anger in my NO seems to be

P. Adams Sitney and our poet/friend, Robert Kelly.

directed towards the one who is asking—in this case, towards you—but what I am really angry about is that with all the money floating around in the world I am so helpless to help those who really need, even if it's one dollar.

Somehow, everybody's confusing me either with the Coop or Cinematheque, as if the money that comes from screenings would go to me. Somewhere, already in the distant, almost distant past, I stopped explaining, I stopped defending myself. Now I let anybody say or think what they want. But to those few who would like to know the truth, I can tell, and I am telling now to you, in my confused way, that I have made my way of life and one of my unbreakable principles, not to use, not to depend, not to use a single penny for myself what I get for the others. I know very well that if I ever got anything for film-makers, a few donations, or loans, for the Coop, for the Tek—and plenty of money was sunk into making the coop into something useful—I had to do plenty of running around these last three or four years—every dollar from the $1,500 that went into the *Normal Love* was collected, borrowed, begged—but I managed to get it, only because it wasn't for me, only because I kept my personal needs outside. I still live on a coffee and a toast most of the time, and I walk 90 blocks downtown because I have no token to take a subway, and very often my legs get weak—for I have no income of any kind, except my weekly $10 that I get now from *The Voice*—and even that very often goes to the others, for I haven't found a way to refuse, until the last penny goes out. But then I have to say NO.

Money should be the last thing to make enemies of friends. Money should be the last thing to make us angry. But it makes us angry so often. So forgive me my abruptness last night. For before you, the same evening, before you asked me for ten dollars, there were two others who asked me, and I got impatient from certain desperation. Coop is not me, and the Cinematheque is not me, and that money is not mine. It all belongs, whatever there is, to the film-makers, not to me. And it all has to be accounted directly to the film-makers, nothing can be taken out like that: for film-makers, like anybody else, are like children. Evil children. I have heard and seen more ugliness, ugly conversations, shouting, at the Coop, and Tek, and all about money, all about money, that's what the film-makers are shouting about. It's money that causes us to shout, to shout at others. How low we can fall, and what art can then come from us.

Since this letter is all about money, I thought I should vomit this out, so that I don't have to say NO to you ever again. I will say YES, even when my pockets are empty.

I have been trying and always almost in vain to pull myself out, to disappear, not to be seen either at the Coop or Tek—it's like I don't exist—so that film-makers could direct their anger and their wants and their requests and their lashes at others. I want to destroy the very idea that there is one place, one center that listens or sometimes fulfills their wants. For there is nobody, really, who really wants to help us, all that there is is plenty empty and beautiful talk, sweet tongued. But nobody comes with help. So then I keep coming to the screenings and helping whatever I can, saying to myself: let them spit at me, let them unleash their anger, and complaints at me, nothing can hurt me any longer—for there is nobody else that wants to take that. Who am I to run away, what's my real function in this life?

Still it's hard, sometimes. We stopped talking to each other long ago, the film-makers. The more that I have never been very talkative. Only the poor angel Barbara keeps telling me (like she is telling all of us): why don't you talk to each other, why are you so locked each one in his own shell, why aren't we communicating, why aren't we loving each other—but the walls run along our lives long as our lives, walls of silences, of misunderstandings, so I said there is nothing to lose if I drop you this note of an attempt, confused as it is, at self-explanation and asking a forgiveness—

No date, 1965

Dear Sirs:

Why do our newspapers and magazines (even the best ones) assign articles on Underground Film to writers completely ignorant of the subject? They keep coming to the Cinematheque, and they say: "I have been assigned to write a piece on the Underground Cinema; I don't know anything about it but I want to know everything." You talk, they listen, but the piece comes out crooked: you can't teach film history and film aesthetics in one hour. Howard Junker's piece (*Nation*, Dec. 27) is one such crooked piece. The Expanded Cinema program was blueprinted not as an indication of what's coming, no, but as a survey of what has been done, what is being done in the field. These people have been working in the expanded cinema areas for years, only nobody gave them a theater or deadlines to execute some of the ideas, publicly. That's what the Cinematheque has provided them with. It's avant-garde, but it's nothing of the future. That's why it's going next to the Lincoln Center.

The author refers mysteriously (why?) to some big moneys coming to the film-makers, "from you know where," he says. Film-makers would like to know where the moneys are available (coming) from: they need money to make films. Very few people are interested in sponsoring the Avant-garde (Underground) Film. That's why we have set up the Cinematheque, to help the avant-garde film-maker with screenings —and it doesn't always work. So, please, don't be so secretive, and tell us more about "from you know where."

Mr. Junker talks about John Brockman and the Cinematheque as about Brockman's private business project, while in reality Mr. Brockman is only a hired servant of the Film-Makers' Cinematheque, which, again, is a servant of the film-makers. It may be impossible to conceive, in a country where a private business enterprise is so highly valued and respected, that the Film-Makers' Cooperative and the Tek are trying to maintain & develop a different, non-competitive working spirit. We are getting impatient with some of the recent attempts to undermine our spirit and our intentions and we intend to strike back at any TV program or magazine article which attempts to destroy us, to commercialize us or on us. Why are the TV programs and magazine articles so replete with distortions, wrong facts? Why are they always done by outsiders, by complete outsiders? Why not go to the sources? Where is your journalistic first-source curiosity? Come to the film-makers: we'll answer any question you want. We'll even write your pieces for you!

Perhaps the most ugly aspect of Junker's article is his attempt to split the artists' spirit by his provincial attitude to bohemia and sex. One of the strengths, and a source of the recent outburst of creativity has been its diversity, its creative freedom, the multiplicity of its views. Junker wants to reduce this to one view, to his view, and he implies that that is the positive way. Yes, we know these positive thoughts! God save us from them. The author talks about "fagotty films," "bohemian paranoia," and "avant-garde incest," but he betrays only his own puritanical and provincial paranoias, fears which the Underground Film-Maker, with his roots in the Beat Generation, has outgrown long ago.

The Cinematheque, despite some recent statements by the press, will remain open to the multiplicity of the diverse directions of the Underground film-makers—and that includes a number of things that neither the writers nor the public will like. Public wheelers & dealers, businessmen and establishment! We know your ways, and your snares, and we won't be caught alive in your wishes. Those are evil wishes: they are wishes to shrink man's spirit and imagination.

Jonas Mekas, Director
Film-Makers' Cinematheque

CHAPTER NINETEEN

December 1, 1965

Opening of the 41st St. Tek tonight.

Before the show, Schectman took me to the 41st corner Longchamps. He bought a beer and took a plate of free tiny sandwiches. He was amazed at how fast they disappeared, so he brought another one. It was the only meal I had today.

Last night Stan, or a day before, we walked and Stan was telling to someone about how little I eat. No, I said, I eat much— but I have no budget for food so I don't eat. In France, at Jerome's, I suddenly realized that in New York I am eating only about one fifth of what I could or should really eat to keep the energy.

At Longchamps, Schectman said: "Oh, I wish I could eat as little as you do, to keep myself in good shape."

December 2, 1965

I had only one token and I used it to come to the Co-op and now I am sitting and waiting until somebody comes and buys me a coffee.

Again, all week long, rumors about Rockefeller Fd. giving us a grant (to Tek) but this has been going for last two months and I am sick and tired, debts right and left. 41st

Theatre cut the rental expenses in half, so we should break even on that.

I gave up the Berlin trip. I sent the ticket back. I couldn't leave things as they are. And Leslie is on jury duty. So I sit at the Co-op answering those millions of calls. I never realized how busy this place has become. And the sun is pouring thru the window, from above the Belmore cafeteria. It is eight thirty in the morning.

Stan Brakhage said one thing at the Cinematheque last Monday. "The term 'art' must be redefined; I am willing to stand behind that term 'art'," he said, "I like that term, I will stand behind that term with my work—art has been always redefined thru the works of art."

Old truths seemed almost revolutionary when restated at a proper time.

December 6, 1965

Dear Kenneth:

I sort of promised, without much thinking, to go to Berlin to participate in some kind of symposium on modern cinema—you must have heard something about it; but on the second thought, I mailed the tickets back, and decided to stay in NY where I really belong, if I belong any place at all. I just don't see what use a symposium can serve. The Museum of Modern Art symposium—which I could not attend, I was out of town—was, everybody agreed, a big joke. But the film series went with a beautiful, almost fantastic success, every show sold out far in advance. The city is still talking about it. The only people who hated it were the film critics.

I have some good news, I think. We (I mean, the Cinematheque) moved to 41st Street Theater, between 6th Avenue and 7th Ave, into a 200 seat theater, we signed one year contract. And we are paying only half of what we were paying at the Astor. The Astor woman, we found out not long ago, was sucking our blood. We used to pay her over $1,600 a month, and we found out that

she herself was paying only $400 a month for the damned place. So we threw a few cursewords at her and moved out in a hurry.

I am doing the programming for the months of January and the first part of February. I should have it ready in a good week. I wanted to check with you, if you know about your movements. The theatre is perfect for 3 screens, has a wide front; and it has a projection booth with seven windows. If you could make an approximate guess, we would keep that week for you—for I think it should run, your program I mean, for at least a straight week. Let me know what you think.

Bleecker St. Cinema, the Fifth Avenue Cinema, and the Garrick Cinema are interested in screening *Scorpio* commercially, but the conditions, I think, are not acceptable, at least not until you have your own show. Bleecker is offering $500 for *Scorpio* and *The Brig* for one week—but that much you could make in one night at the Tek. They would only drain thousands of possible customers.

I hope you are accomplishing what you planned to do in Europe. I myself, I am more free now (I have a new man to help me at the Tek, John Brockman, and he is very efficient) and I am doing some editing on the footage I shot past spring and summer. I am happier, in many ways.

If I don't see you in NY before Christmas—have a good holiday. And give my best to Noel Burch.

December 14, 1965

Gregory:

I feel I have to write you this short note. Because it bothers me too much. To doubt your own friends! To believe a stupid Boston woman instead of Stan! How low we have fallen, how incredible. To think that Stan would ever let you down, and in public, and in such a petty and mean way. What's happening, what kind of paranoias are eating us up? Aren't you, as an artist, who has some duty, if not all duty, to go against such paranoias, to beautify the world? And now, you, yourself, are contributing to it, by doubting your best friends, and for what? You have said yourself, the other day, that some film-makers are using their words too loosely, lately. Now, what about you?

Really, I think something terrible is happening in New York. Please don't contribute to it, but help to fight it, to disperse these vapors of ugliness.

If it would help you anything, at this stage of your mind, check with Andy Meyers who was with Stan in Boston, and at his screenings, or are you going to let Andy down the river too?

We don't have to keep ourselves TOGETHER by force. We have to keep ourselves together by love. And what is this thing, what kind of light-less blind hand that is trying to rip all of us apart?

Almost before Christmas,
Wishing you best
P. S. Trust your friends 77 times even when you hear wrong about them.

December 24, 1965

Visited Naomi, at Bellevue Hospital. Depressing, terrible. Supervisors rude, inhuman. Morbid, dark, dirty. Even if healthy, one could get sick there in a week. Naomi has been there for two weeks. She was lying in bed, she said they pumped her full of tranquilizers, because she shouted about something. I sat on the edge of the bed, talking, and the supervisor shouted at me, rudely, get up from the bed, you have to talk standing, she said, you can't sit on the bed. Naomi buried her face into the pillow not to scream. I stood up, and we talked that way. She did not look well at all, all life and brightness was gone, she barely spoke. Around us the other inmates walked in underwear, baggy sack things, like in a typical, "movie" insane asylum scene. They perpetrate that spirit. This place should be burned down, closed, wiped out from the face of the earth. They have no room for receptions, no privacy, no intimacy, everything like a huge factory or subway station, with coke machines, smoke, and ugly tables, the whole atmosphere sick, inhuman. And they are treating people! They are trying to cure these people by surrounding them with rudeness, sickness, inhumanity. Unbelievable, fantastic, the neglect, the carelessness, the inhumanity. I came to see Naomi with an idea to pacify her, to talk to her, to help her to accept the Hillside Hospital—her only solution—and which she is avoiding —but surrounded with that atmosphere, I could neither communicate to her nor begin to have a real connection, or poetry of two souls—talk of two souls—everything was arranged to destroy this, to keep us in that inhuman atmosphere. How any cure can be possible here, in this inhuman place, if two people aren't allowed to talk in peace, and give some of that peace to the other, who needs it? This is a crime. I wanted to shout in desperation, against the whole set up, but it was no use, I felt. So here I am now, putting all this on paper, at least that much, for these crimes are unforgivable. This place should be made into a human place, colorful, and warm, not like this, not like a slaughterhouse, factory, dirty and lifeless—there should be flowers, and maybe music, and none of the sack bag uniforms that are so sickening to see. I wouldn't keep there even those steel beds, which shout with the steel voices, and clank clank—I saw no human touch, there, all human touch has disappeared from this place. The place which is supposed to help the patients to become again human beings, has become a place that has been stripped of all that is human.

January 24, 1966

We met at 10:30 pm at Lionel Rogosin's place—Shirley and myself. We again explored, now three of us, the theatrical feature length film situation and our immediate needs. We had no disagreements. We said, only the producers disagree: filmmakers always agree.

We decided that whoever has any distribution or theatrical or whatever private business running—it's OK, let them run them. We decided, as of tonight, to create another branch, or division of the N.A. Cinema Group, which will be called Film-Makers' Distribution Center. It will be, in a sense, another, perhaps commercial branch of the Co-op—it will take care of the large area of the theatrical, art theatre, TV etc. distribution aspect which the Co-op hasn't handled till now.

Among the film-makers who could or should be invited to join this branch we listed, besides the three of us, Gregory Markopoulos, Storm De Hirsch, Andy Warhol, Peter Goldman, Robert Downey, Jack Livingston, Adolfas, George Morse, Peter Kass, De Antonio, Maysles brothers, Leacock, Pennebaker.

I was delegated to call Perlman, to proceed with whatever legalities there are, if any, to open a bank account in the new name; to hire a secretary to run the center. We are meeting tomorrow night with Louis Brigante, see if he will do it. Other possibility, we thought is Rudy Franchi.

We figured, that with $10,000 we could push the Center through the first year. The salary of the secretary should be around 125. For the initial fund, Lionel pledges $2,000, Shirley $2,000. I said I will get somewhere $1,000.

Light-movies-strobes etc: realization of/or becoming conscious of LIGHT (beyond the "physical" meaning) (the "physical" is expanded) and realizing again that it could be manipulated by "dark" forces.

Bully is the lonesomest man in the world. Have you seen the sadness in the eyes of animals?

It's the same lonesomeness, solitude.

The form, perhaps, should be that of the heartbeat, or breathing—pulsating in and out (fade in & out—images & sound) day after day burst after burst.

It was long ago, I saw the first images of *Shchors*. Two of us, one winter evening, we stole in through the back door of a small town theatre, silently, and there we stood, hiding in the dark behind the seats, staring at the huge white endless spaces of Ukraine, the breathtaking images of Dovzhenko. And then we felt somebody's hand on our necks, and we were out again, in the dark little streets, with the film's images still falling out of our eyes. And it was a winter, and we walked, and we passed the same wooden bridges, and the same telephone poles, and the same snow—.

"They are singing, they are singing!"

I have never forgotten those lines. We children stood by the road and watched the Red Army passing by as they marched by —that was in 1939—and they were singing too. In the streets, in the markets, they sang. Was it a calculated weapon or was it part of the Russian soul? But the song was there as strong as anything.

January 23, 1966

filmed Adolfas, Pola, Weinbergs in wind and slush, Hudson sleds

January 26, 1966

filmed sparrows, and gave them to Flo. It is clear that I can not guide my actions towards others by their actions towards me (concerning Edouard, for example.)

"My paintings are not an assertion of a kind of 'knowing'; they exhibit no conclusions. I discover myself being here within

FILM-MAKERS' COOPERATIVE
414 Park Avenue South
New York 16, New York
Telephone: MU 5-2210

9. February, 1966

Jonas,

A reminder:

In the next week or so, Cooperative will receive a print each of
PARTs II, III & IV of Brakhage's DOG STAR MAN for distribution.
The invoice, from Western Cine Service in Denver, Colorado, will
amount to approximately $120.00.

I would like to feel fairly sure that I may give you the invoice
the day I receive it, and -- within a very few days -- be able to
write Western Cine that a check has been sent to cover that invoice
by a friend or friends of Brakhage.

When I sppke with Stan last night (asking him to rush through the
above order), he told me that I had been the only caller on that
day, which was Crystal's birthday. I wished her greetings from
everyone in New York City.

He has completed and seen approximately 3,000 feet of his feature
(between 45 and 60 minutes running time expected), most of which
he feels will go directly into the film. The film will require
lip-synchronized track, and he seems quite solidly committed to the
project.

He is reading books on anatomy and books by/on Jung. Jane is reading
"War and Peace." The house is totally snowbound. They raided the
attic for presents for Crystal, and, as a result, they seem to have
created an unusually bounteous birthday.

They send their love and greetings,

FILM-MAKERS' COOPERATIVE IS A DIVISION OF THE NEW AMERICAN CINEMA GROUP, INC.

125 West 41st Street   FILM*MAKERS'   Tel.: 564-3818 (art.3)
Showings nightly: 8 & 10   CINEMATHEQUE   Reg. Adm.: 1.50

FILMS   OF   JOY
In Honour of the Angry Arts Against the War in Vietnam.

Wed., Feb. 1   8 & 10
SPECIAL PREVIEW ... FIRST PUBLIC SCREENING.
THE FIRST WAR FILM HAS BEEN MADE:
"23RD PSALM BRANCH"
by S T A N   B R A K H A G E

Thurs., Feb. 2   The Most Joyous Films of All!!
"Y E S " by Naomi Levine. " LITTLE STABS AT HAPPINESS " by
Ken Jacobs; with Jack Smith. "G E O R G I A" (premiere) by Gordon Ball.
"HARE KRISHNA" & "NEWSREEL: LINDSEY AND HOVING - OLMSTEAD TRAIL HIKE"
by Jonas Mekas.   "CHILD" by Bob Cowan.   "FISTFIGHT" by Robert
Breer.   "MR. HYASHI" by Bruce Baillie.   "VERMONT IN 3½ MINUTES"
by Linda Talbot.

Fri., Feb. 3   B R U C E   C O N N E R
will appear IN PERSON!
He will do nothing.
Films to be shown: NY FILM FESTIVAL 10 SECOND COMMERCIAL (Rejected by the
NY Film Festival as "too fast". This is the film reproduced on the Festival
Poster in 1965.)   VIVIAN with Vivian Kurz. 2½ min.
BREAKAWAY (Premiere Showing) with Antonia Christina
Basilotta. Sound track by Antonia Christina Basilotta. 2½ min.
COSMIC RAY 4 min.   A MOVIE   12 min.
REPORT 13 min.
2 Premiere Showings:
LOOKING FOR MUSHROOMS 8mm, color, 12 min.   Made in
1961 to 1965 in San Francisco and Mexico.
MORNING RAGA   8mm, color, 12 min.
...and maybe something else.

Sat., Feb. 4   Two Extraordinary Film Experimentalists:
J O H N   C A V A N A U G H
and
D A V I D   T H U R M A N
will present their new film works.
"EXQUISITE!" -Barbara Rubin

Sun., Feb. 5   NOTE TIMES: 7:00, 8:30, 10:00

" 2 3 RD   P S A L M   B R A N C H "
by   S T A N   B R A K H A G E
"Stan Brakhage's '23rd Psalm Branch' is the most perfect anti-war film, and
it is right that the film advances from the napalm and hydrogen of 35 millimeter to speak in the husky whispers of 8 millimeter. Brakhage acknowledges
himself as poet on the screen, after the whirl of technique and montage and
trembling exposures of war footage, the author's hand scrawls a message over
and over on the flashing divided screen. The footage is a tortured and
beauteous nervous system... '23rd Psalm Branch' is the Magician, standing at
the table waving his wand, as on the Tarot card, but in the agony that
follows meditation on carnage...as he frees eternity again and guiltlessly."
- Michael McClure (poet and author of "Love Lion
Book", "Poisoned Wheat" etc)

Mon., Feb. 6   P A U L   M O R R I S S E Y
One - Man Film Show.

Tues., Feb. 7   Two by A N D Y   W A R H O L
"K I S S " (1964) —— (1966) " T H E   K I T C H E N"
By popular demand!   "The funniest script in the under-
The most requested underground film.   ground." -Sheldon Renan

Wed., Feb. 8   Films of M A T T   H O F F M A N
"Meter Maiden", "Response", "Monopoly", "Rooftop", "Composition #1",
& "Composition #2"
-and-
" M U R __ 19 "
by MARK RAPPAPORT

Thurs., Feb. 9: NAM JUNE PAIK.
Fri. - Mon., Feb. 10 - 13: ALL PREMIERE PROGRAM ...
"FAT FEET"(RED GROOMS), "SOUL FREEZE"(BOB COWAN), "MOSHOLU HOLIDAY"(GEORGE
KUCHAR), "WATER SARK"(JOYCE WIELAND) AND OTHERS.

MEMO #547899

to the film-makers, members of the Coop:

Let's talk about the problem of theory and practice.
The difference between the suggestions, criticisms,
imaginings; and the concrete situations of the actual
person who does the work. It's easy to throw sharp
criticisms and make suggestions how to improve this or
that, while you drink your beer. Another thing is
actuality.

In actuality, you have people like Leslie and Brigante
who are giving their lives to it, and without getting
paid, only because they believe in it, and they have
been doing it when nobody else believed in it (they
still don't believe in it). And since this thing, the Coop,
grew and developed not according to some carefully
and expensively planned and backed ~~project~~, worked out
by hundreds of BELL employees and engineers and planners,
but came from nowhere, from itself, and through all kinds
of mis eries and pressures, yes, it went wrong here
and there. But you can not walk into the Coop and
shout at Leslie, Look, you, so and so, You no Good,
Things Are Bad, look, this University there did not
receive my film in time; etc. etc.

You just can't do that! These are the people with their
own temperaments and feelings and they are doing everything
they can, so you have to talk to them like to human
beings! And you have to help them to improve things, if
you have any good suggestions. This is, after all, your Coop!
You have to trust their devotion. Because you yourselves
have much less of it! You are just a little or BIG egoistic
person who wants others do things for you... and do it
perfectly... You don't want to do what they do, and for no
money. They provide a free service to you, you damn fools.

February 1966, helping Barbara Rubin to drape the screen at the 41st Street Cinematheque for her *Caterpillar Changes* show. I moved the 'Tek to 125 West 41st Street in January. Velvet Underground and Gato Barbieri did the music for the show. Velvet Underground used the 'Tek that spring as their practice platform.

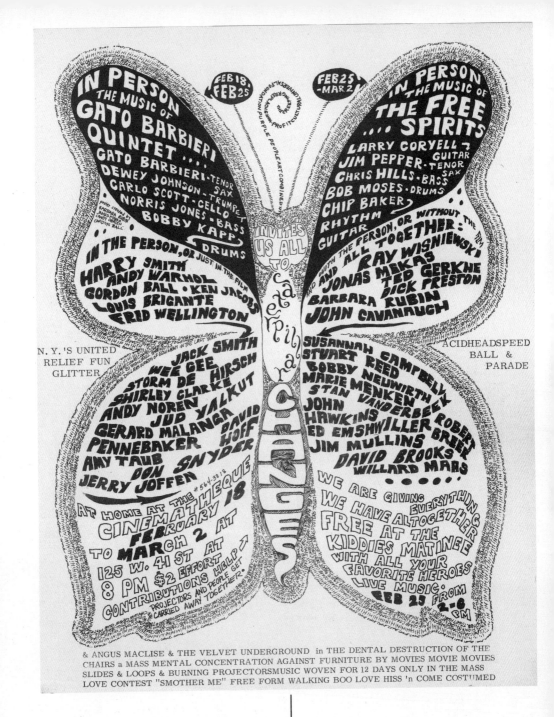

& ANGUS MACLISE & THE VELVET UNDERGROUND in THE DENTAL DESTRUCTION OF THE
CHAIRS a MASS MENTAL CONCENTRATION AGAINST FURNITURE BY MOVIES MOVIE MOVIES
SLIDES & LOOPS & BURNING PROJECTORSMUSIC WOVEN FOR 12 DAYS ONLY IN THE MASS
LOVE CONTEST "SMOTHER ME" FREE FORM WALKING BOO LOVE HISS 'n COME COSTUMED

PRESS
FOR IMMEDIATE RELEASE

The Underground will present a festival of movies, slides, film
loops, jazz, rock, et al. The artists, led by Barbara Rubin, plan to
topple the current concept of theatre and movie house by placing the
musicians in the middle of five screens (one on the floor!) and seating
the audience on large palettes instead of the conventional rows of seats.
Featured are top jazz saxophonist Gato Barbieri and his quintet and the
exciting new rock sound The Free Spirits, plus films by leading underground movie-makers; among them Andy Warhol (responsible for "The Chelsea
Girls"), Jack Smith, Ed Emshwiller, Jonas Mekas, and Miss Rubin.
      It's all part of the radical new programs being presented at the
Film-Makers' Cinematheque, 125 W. 41, under the title "Catepillar
Changes". There will be shows nightly at 8 p.m. from Saturday, Feb. 18th,
thru March 2nd. Tickets, priced at $2, will go on sale each evening
one hour before the performance.
      On Saturday, Feb. 25th, there will be a special matinee (the
"kiddie" show),from 2 to 6 p.m., for which admission will be free.
(Attendance is limited to 200.)

          For further information, call 564-3818 after 3 p.m.

TO THE PRESS
      ON FEB. 18th to MARCH 2nd at the CINEMATHEQUE 125 west 41st STREET
FROM 8PM ON WE ARE HAVING NEW YORK'S FIRST UNITED ACIDHEADSPEED RELIEF
FUN BALL & GLITTER PARADE. IN THE DENTAL DESTRUCTION OF THE CHAIRS
A MASS MENTAL CONCENTRATION AGAINST FURNITURE INSTIGATED BY THEIR
PRESENCE BY ANGUS MACLISE & THE VELVET UNDERGROUND WITH THE CONTRIBUTIONS
OF THEIR MOVIES, SLIDES, LOOPS, PROJECTORS, & MADNESS OF HARRY SMITH
ANDY WARHOL RAY WISNIEWSKI JONAS MEKAS TED GERHKE STEWART REED GORDON
BALL LOUIS BRIGANTE KEN JACOBS FRED WELLINGTON MATT HOFFMAN DICK PRESTON
JOHN CAVANAUGH JACK SMITH PIERO HELICZER SUSANNAH CAMPBELL BOBBY NEUWIRTH
DAVID THURMAN AMY TAUBIN RICHARD FORMAN GERARD MALANGA STORM DE HIRSCH
WEE GEE ANDY NOREN SHIRLEY CLARKE JUD YALKUT PENNEBAKER DAVID HOFF DON
SNYDER JERRY JOFFEN MARIE MENKEN JIM MULLINS ED EMSHWILLER STAN VANDERBEEK
HOHN HAWKINS ROBERT BREER JERRY HYLER WILLARD MAAS DAVID BROOKS BARBARA
RUBIN PLUS IN PERSON THE MUSIC OF GATO BARBIERI QUINTET & THE FREE SPIRITS
& JUST ABOUT ANYONE ELSE YOU CAN THINK OF FOR 12 DAYS IN THE MASS LOVE
CONTEST "SMOTHER ME". WE EXTEND AN INVITATION TO YOU GLADLY THOUGH I
SINCE OUR LAST MEETING AT THE EVENING OF NAM JUNE PAIK & CHARLOTTE
MOORMAN WE WILL HAVE TO MAINTAIN BETTER THE er THE ER OF THE BUILDING
& THE FIRE & THE LICENSE DEPARTMENTS SUGGESTIONS THOUGH AGAIN WE CAN
NOT GUARANTEE WE WILL COMPLETE THIS SHOW EITHER. & PLEASE BRING YOUR
WIFE GIRLFRIEND CHILDREN FRIENDS & ALL TO OUR MATINEE PERFORMANCE ON
FEB. 25 th STARTING AT 2 pm love & kisses ALL OF US

a process. My works are human marks to celebrate my growing and living within this process." (Father Roman, St. Vincent College)

We watch Andy Warhol's, or Walter De Maria's boxes expecting something to happen, some kind of sudden aesthetic wave to grip us. But the boxes do nothing, little movies do nothing: they are there for their own beautiful sake. Little shreds of Ken Jacobs' soul, of Stan Brakhage's soul, nothing really for the "grown-ups" who, after all, are here to do big things!

Empire film is not static. Every 1/24 of a second one frame jumps forward!

BEE-IN—a complex / group as against:
BEING—self
…a twitch of consciousness…

Leo: "I wrote two poems so now I can do nothing."
Jonas: "I made two calls…"

Robert Frank 34 Third Avenue
A / G Gallery, 925 Madison Avenue

Art is not democratic; artworks emerge in clusters in certain places at certain times —it's not spread equally across the country, as NEA would like to see.
Populist as vs. elitist approach in funding of arts has to do with popularization of art, not with the creation, making of art.
You talk about "arts and their economic partners." This is a hell of a partnership…

R. J. Stewart, Earth Light, p. 47:
"The more aligned to royalty, imperial policy and statesmanship, the further away from primal sources."
Talking about religion, but I think the avant-garde film in its essence is the same. Hollywood sides with royalty.

"…stuttering on the brink of eternity…"
where did I hear that?
was it in connection with Jack Smith, Ken Jacobs?…

Overheard: "I used to dream. Now I don't even sleep."

"Diese Kunst verlangt, dass der Kuenstler bewusst handelt und nicht in der Ekstase mit seinem Ich untergeht."—Igor Stravinsky

"Nur wer ein lebendiges Gefuehl und echtes Verstaendnis fuer die Gegenwart hat, kann die Kunst einer frueheren Epoche voellig begreifen und das Leben bei denen entdecken, die tot sind. So sollte man auch beim Unterricht mit der Erkenntnis der Gegenwart beginnen und dann erst schrittweise in die Vergangenheit zurueck gehen."—Igor Stravinsky

We should be like children, said Leslie.
No, I said—at two years old they are already our own mirrors, brats, monsters like us; maybe at six days they are still pure, perhaps.

"What is best in music is not to be found in the notes."—Mahler

Yes, some anxieties come from God, others from the devil; some peace is from God, some from the devil…

No date, 1966
"In art, as in all matters of spirit, ten years are the utmost rarely reached limits of a generation. The new generation follows hard on the heels of the old. Its instincts for change and self-assertion, far from being the same, are naturally opposed, and the newcomers, looking coolly at the achievements of their immediate precursors, and with a feeling of vague but extreme dissatisfaction."—Bernard Berenson, *North Italian painters of the Renaissance*

"Almost immediately a large moth fell at my feet, fluttering wildly. I said, to Jane: 'What's that?' in a stupid voice to which she immediately replied: 'It's a death dance.'

It fluttered for fully twenty minutes before our dog ate it." (Stan Brakhage in a letter to Robert Kelly)

February 6, 1966

Had an argument with Barbara concerning Andy Warhol show. She said, there should be no Press screening because Press aren't people. I said: It is easier to build a barrier and be by oneself and grow "independent" and crooked than to grow together with the rest the world & remain independent & original & true & beautiful.

On the meaning of "esoteric":

Something that must be learned, acquired; something that one can't get without an effort, without changing oneself, pulling oneself up to it.

"Only in this sense is it esoteric, like every profound wisdom, which does not disclose itself at the first glance, because it is not a matter of surface-knowledge but of realization in the depth of one's own mind."—Lama Govinda

March 18, 1966

children talking on the bus: "who can do the nastiest thing" game.

"after the school we go to the Central Park. We found a lobster once. There is a stream. Maybe somebody put it there. It was without one claw."

DIARY OF A COP

Image: a page from the diary.

Text: "After trying everything, and having no other way out, and being hungry, and being not too bright, I decided to take the only job left to me…"

out to:

Image: Taylor Mead as a cop. One morning, instead of dressing in cop's uniform, he puts on his dungarees, worker's clothes. He is either fed up with the cop's job and wants to become a regular worker, or maybe he is still sleepy and he thinks and lives in his past, when he was a worker.

His wife, perhaps, stops him and, against his will, forces the uniform on him and pushes him out to work as a cop again.

Three old "All American" women (60 – 70 years of age?) making fun of Taylor Mead (the Cop) because of his softness ("a softie").

March 27, 1966

Al Leslie: "I had a choice between art and life and I chose art." (Commenting jokingly on why he didn't join the Saturday Vietnam protest.)

"I may change it again. In three months from now I may come back to it and I may see that this line, here, for instance, doesn't work the way it should and I'll redo it. I think painters in general are paying more attention, are working harder on their work than film-makers. Film-makers seldom return to what they had done three months ago. They work without perspective to their own art."

Kelman:

Looking skeptically at the plate of food at Romeo's: "One has to be stronger than the food one eats."

Among the recent film portraits one stands out: Ken Jacobs' *Lisa and Joey in Connecticut*.

April, 1966

Manifesto on Newsreels

The Cinema is *not* doing what it could be doing.

Our poets have brought the cinema and their art to new heights.

What about the film journalism, the documentary film-maker?

He had sold himself to the inanities of TV, of industrial documentary, of *USIS*.

I introduce the first public performance of The Velvet Underground, at the Psychiatrists Convention, Hotel Delmonico, January 14, 1966.

Dear Jonas,   March 7, 1966

I feel much better.

I am fencing, biking,
knitting, dancing etc.

I get lots of attention.
The birds on the trees
are pale green & fuzzy.

I need some clear
16mm sprocketed film - even
though primitive, I want
to do something in this
manner.

I would also like to
see the "Voice".

Spring is coming.
                Love, naomi

A note from Naomi Levine.

Which is O.K.

But there are also cruelties, injustice, stupidity across the country. Let's bring it into the open with our cameras.

Like at no other time in both film history & the human history, we have now equipment available to get into the darkest, most forbidden, hidden corners of man's activities. With our 8 mm cameras we can record the KKK & the life in prisons, cruelty of man to man in Vietnam, genocides and folly-cides & bring it all to the public eye.

Let's not leave it all to the fake reporting of TV alone—it's like leaving all reporting to *Time-Life*. If needed, we should act as spies of Truth for the good of knowledge & truth.

April, 1966

Co-op Newsreel series.
Contemporary Newsreel.
Invite everybody across the country.

April 7, 1966

I asked Barbara when is she going to plant flower seeds. She said, it's still too cold.

April 20, 1966

"Today we have a need for a new language because we have more to say than ever before and the old laws are too confining. We need a language which explains MORE of life than ever before because we are EXPERIENCING more life than ever before because we ARE more than we ever were before."—Mel Lyman

Why am I so preoccupied with fleeting images, with the eye reality, with the surface reality? Desperately holding on to the slowly vanishing disappearing fragments of the gross reality.

I can hear you crying, my soul. I can hear you calling. But I am still going in circles, afraid to look inside, afraid to drop everything.

April 21, 1966

Yesterday I looked at *The Brig*, and, later, in the lobby, surrounded by students, who said they thought it was an immense experience—NO, NO, I shouted, I don't want to make films on violence, on brutality any longer, even if brutality exists and will always exist. I don't want to see that reality even on film. I want to make films that would fill you with a good feeling—the feeling of happiness instead of thoughts of terror and violence: not an empty happiness, but a blissful happiness—that's what I want now and anything less than that makes my heart sick, makes me suffer. So much ugliness around, so much ugliness —why should I contribute still more to it, even if it's through art, even if it's art!

April 22, 1966

What's this emptiness, this feeling of emptiness that seized me suddenly—

After leaving the Tek, we walked for a while through the rain, wet streets, and we talked, and it became clearer and clearer, and sort of sadder and sadder—and, really, emptier. I suddenly felt, I suddenly saw how small, how sickly, how almost disturbingly sickly most of the art, most of the new cinema, is. I wanted suddenly to see something real, or very, or just beautiful— even if it's not a work of art, maybe a tree, a small grass patch in the park, something. But everything seemed to be covered with sadness and dust, with the dust of sadness. Yes, there are Stan's *Songs*—they are close to beautiful in the way I feel this evening. But what else? All that emotional sea! Why do we have to create only within this, or from this dirt to reflect the dirt of existence? Why are we so caught in this net of our own sadness? Oh, how I would like just to sing, or just to listen to something, that would lift out, and up—not by making us "face" the reality, the dirt, but by its own cleanliness, and perfection, and... that's

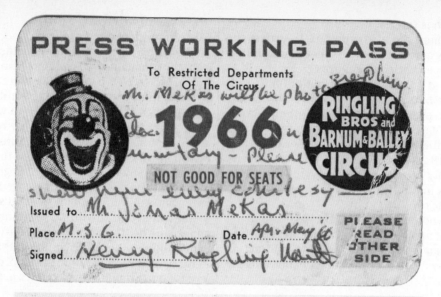

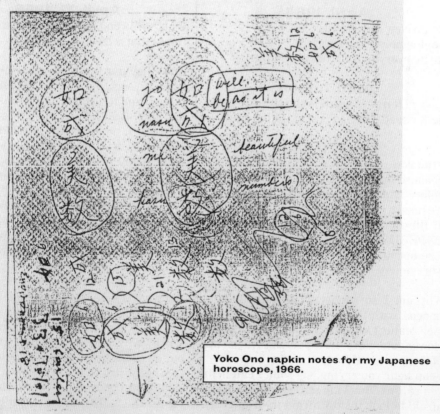

Yoko Ono napkin notes for my Japanese horoscope, 1966.

NEW YORK ETERNAL COMMITTEE
FOR THE CONSERVATION
OF FREEDOM IN THE ARTS

COORDINATOR: PAOLO LIONNI

c/o THE BRIDGE THEATRE
4 ST. MARKS PLACE
NEW YORK CITY10003
TEL. OR3-4600

Formed on April 13, 1966, at The Bridge The atre, in
order to coordinate all action and opinion directed towards
opposing the intim idation, harassment, slander, unfair
treatment or obstruction of creative artists and/or their
sponsors by public officials or the press, and to act as
a source of information and records regarding such treatment.

Artists are requested to report matters in which these
issues are involved to the Committee so that it may advise
and/or act on such matte rs, striving to safeguard the
interests of the creative community in New York while at
the same time keeping an up-to-date account of the official
and media attitudes towards artists and their rights.

The Committee will issue press releases and sponsor
demonstrations when it deems them necessary as means of
reaching the public with the oft-obscured or suppressed
truth and import of such matters.

by
PAOLO LIONNI, Coordinator

ALLEN GINSBERG
Committee On Poetry

ELSA TAMBELLINI
Bridge Theatre

JONAS MEKAS
Film-makers' Cinematheque

LIONEL ROGOSIN
Bleecker Street Cinema

ED SANDERS
The Fugs

ALLAN KATZMAN
The East Village Other

ANDY WARHOL
The Plastic Inevitable

what I long for, and everything else suddenly seems to be insignificant, so empty, so down-dragging, so disturbing.

"For this is Zion—*the pure in heart*."

"and who layeth his life in my cause, for my name's sake, shall find it again, even life eternal."

But HOW? HOW? he asks, what should I do? "Nothing, you can do nothing," comes the answer.

The Spring is here.
Snow will disappear.
Put to the ground your ear
and listen until you hear.

The earth has just shifted again.
Love soon will surround Earth.
What an exciting Spring!

We are that Love.
We are that Poison.
We are that Springtime.
We are that Earth.
We are that Shift.
We are Love's tools
& Love's Fools.

May 2, 1966

$30 in cash to George for licensing fees
$10 to Sitney, travel expenses

for the film
…three times he struck with the stick…
…the form, perhaps, should be that of the heart beat, or breathing—
beat, or breathing—
pulsating, in and out / fade-in and fade-out
images & sound
day after day, burst after burst—

May 4, 1966

Now, perhaps more than ever before, I feel like I am resting on some kind of ground, something that will not sink immediately; some warmth, some clarity, something that I am not clear yet what it is, is touching me, from inside, and I am not so lost, not so desperate. But still, it is so fragile, this feeling. So many years of searching, of desperation, of getting up and falling down on my face again, into the same mud of my own doings, yes, my own doings, in this or that previous lives, doesn't matter.
Will I be strong enough to go further, to strengthen this first basis?

May 7, 1966

…still trying to return to childhood… to the farm…
But the true destination is far out in the future. Free from the past. It still ties me down. Sentiments.
Psychology.

Yoko Ono: "According to the Japanese horoscope, you are the youngest among us, we have to take good care of you."

Still holding onto the last walls, or bits of walls, not letting go completely.
It is painful. I want to be free, but I am holding, against my own desires—they are so strong.
God: Help me break all my walls. Let me crawl like a helpless worm. Let me be naked, completely. Let me be honest with myself, completely.
Why do I hold onto the walls, why don't I crumble?

A STORY
He traveled 10,000 miles and by foot, to see what's at the end of the road, & he found, upon his arrival, that there was really nothing at the end of the road, nothing but a small pile of rabbit shit. So he laughed at himself.
Yes, he has seen the rabbit shit at the end of the road, at the end if every new "change," of every new social philosophy, and he wants

no more part of Final Knowledge and Final Solutions. He prefers the ever-changing knowledge and the ever-changing solutions, and he does his best to let life go by itself. The "useless" artist prefers to do nothing about it, and that is the most difficult action of all life releasing actions.

TO PESARO & WORLD FILM-MAKERS
New York, May 18, 1966

Although I could not be present at the Pesaro Film Festival, I would like to speak to you from a distance, through this open letter. Although some specific feelings expressed in this letter may be personal, I'll be speaking in the name of the independent film-makers of America, who have delegated me to do so.

You don't see us often at film festivals. Very often, the "independent" American films that you see at Pesaro, at Oberhausen, or Mannheim have very little to do with what we are doing. There is a special, festival-minded breed of film-makers, and you find them in every country, who will get their films into any festival, no matter how bad or indifferent their work is. Whereas some of our best film-makers, those who are doing really exciting work, can not afford the festival prints of their films or, simply, aren't interested in film festivals. There is a feeling in the air that film festivals have become commercial & bureaucratic fairs at which we would feel very much out of place. Even the most advanced ones, like Pesaro, are working within the same commercial festival traditions; they do not truly reflect what's really going on in cinema. At least, we know they do not represent or reflect the new American cinema.

Yes, what about Pesaro? To select the new American films for the current festival, it delegated a French film critic to do it. Now this critic, no matter how much we respect him, doesn't know much about what's happening in America: his knowledge of American cinema comes from Paris releases and… from film festivals. So we told him we know best what we have, what's really happening in our cinema, what would really be of interest for a festival of new cinema. This year, for instance, we would have sent Stan Brakhage's *Songs*, Gregory Markopoulos' *Galaxie*, Harry Smith's *Heaven and Earth Magic*, Tony Conrad's *Flicker*, Andy Warhol's *My Hustler*, Bruce Baillie's *Quixote*. But the festival representative seemed to be very clear, in his mind, what kind of films he wanted. He had a very definite conception of what "new cinema" is or should be. He wanted something that already corresponded to that conception. He wanted more "cinema-vérité," for instance. And he didn't even look at the truly NEW AND IMPORTANT WORK DONE IN AMERICA TODAY, the work that would have been a real discovery for the festival. And this happens with a festival whose main aim is to serve the NEW CINEMA.

Or take Cannes Film festival. I was asked, this Spring, by the Festival, to suggest what, if anything, there is that they should consider bringing to the Semaine de la Critique. I wrote to them approximately this:

"When you ask about films suitable for the Semaine de la Critique, you still have in mind the same type of films you saw four years ago. I could suggest a few titles of that kind of cinema—but since our cinema has changed and is still changing, it would be wrong to help you to continue that dream. Yes, there are the other, and truly new films to take to Cannes. But what's the use even suggesting? What's the use telling you that Andy Warhol has taken cinéma-vérité into completely new areas and has produced some of the most important contemporary cinema? Or Brakhage's *Songs*? Cannes wouldn't even consider 8mm films. Or Gerd Stern, or Robert

Whitman, or Nam June Paik? They can't even be previewed. You still think in old terms. You still think, that everything that is really good and new in American cinema can be packed up, wrapped up and shipped to you like any other movie, for previewing. This is no longer true. Very often, you have to bring the film-maker, and one or two technicians, and even equipment. For what they are doing, very often, are *film evenings*, cinema evenings, but no films in the usual, conventional sense. These evenings, like some of the evenings of Gerd Stern (USCO), or Andy Warhol, or Jerry Jofen, or Stan Vanderbeek —with multiple projections and multiple sound systems, and with live participation, would shock Cannes into new visual, kinesthetic perceptions and into cinema of the future. They would realize that there is truly new cinema, that something revolutionary is happening in cinema" etc.

I ended by suggesting six programs to take to Cannes. And what do you think happened? A representative of Cannes came to New York, looked at some familiar work, ignored whatever new and revolutionary was happening, ignored film-makers' suggestions, and went back to Paris, declaring to the Press, before leaving, that he has found no interesting work done here and that, therefore, the young American directors will not be represented at Cannes this year.

Dear colleagues, film-makers and film critics: the conception of film festivals must be changed. Bureaucracy has got to go. Film-makers should decide what should be shown, they know what's happening. Money should be used not for importing stars, or for publicity but for paying for the prints of the films shown, for the shipping of films, or for important film-makers, their technicians, their equipment (for inter-media shows). For instance, even if Pesaro representative would have seen and liked *Songs* or *Galaxie*, the film-makers wouldn't have even afforded to make prints of these films for sending to the festival. Cinema is changing, but the film festivals have remained the same—that's what's wrong.

I went into the film festival aspect in more detail only to show that the new film-maker (and that goes for all countries) cannot trust any commercial (or State; or one that is based on commercial tradition) film financing, film production, film distribution, film exhibition or film promotion set-ups and organizations. WE HAVE TO START EVERYTHING FROM SCRATCH, FROM THE BEGINNING. NO COMPROMISES, HOWEVER SMALL.

Five years ago, the young American film-makers got fed up with what we saw around. We started abandoning all commercial illusions. We started from scratch. We did our work, no matter what distributors or film critics said. The new American cinema grew up like a child, from nothing, not even wanted. Our critics even say that, like children, we don't listen to our parents; we are irresponsible; we use dirty language; we masturbate; we are oversensitive; and other such things of young natural growth. There is much that they don't like about us, there is much that isn't mature or "perfect." We aren't even "beautiful" sometimes. Some of us have pimples on our faces. BUT WE REFUSE TO USE PLASTIC SURGERY TO CHANGE OUR FACES AND OUR SOULS INTO THE FACES AND SOULS YOU WOULD LIKE TO SEE. Take us as we are, or go your own way—we say. We keep seeing attacks and descriptions of our work in French, German, Russian film periodicals—articles usually written by people who have seen only one or two of our films. We stopped bothering about them: we couldn't care less about what they say, because we know that what we are doing is beautiful, is important, is changing the face of cinema around the world, is an expression of the changing times, is coming out of our hearts & out of the needs of our souls, and we have a great responsibility to continue that way, not to compromise it, not to betray it—and the dangers & the temptations are many.

Since all commercial film-distribution and film-financing organizations are set-up on a private business basis and not to help the film-maker to continue making films, four years ago, the independent film-makers of America organized their own film distribution center, the Film-Makers' Cooperative, which is run by the film-makers themselves. We decided not to give our work to any of the commercial distributors. We developed a more human working system. We stuck together, we grew and expanded. Through the Co-operative, we increased our outlets tenfold.

We created a distribution circuit embracing colleges, universities, film societies, art theaters, art galleries and museums. The circuit is still growing. By now we can make a film for $10,000 and get the money back with no great effort. Many of our films have been sponsored by the Co-op, by advancing money from coming rentals. At this moment we are setting up 100 theaters (friendly theaters) across the country for the distribution of our work. For this purpose a new division has just been created—the Film-Makers' Distribution center, which will work in conjunction with the Co-op. Fifteen theaters have already pledged to exhibit all our new work. This new set-up, in about a year from now, should make us free to increase our budgets—if the need arises—to $100,000 or even $200,000 with no great risk involved and with no commercial distributor or investor dictating to us what we should or shouldn't do.

To promote the idea of free cinema, of new cinema, and to assist some of our European colleagues, this July we are opening a branch of the Film-Makers' Cooperative in London. Arrangements are being made for distribution center and for a theatre, through which our work will be easily available and with little unnecessary shipping expense to any place in Europe. Through this London center, we also hope that some of the European new cinema—the European Avant-garde cinema will be able to reach New York.

We want to stress that the Film-Makers' Cooperative and the Center do not divide films into any budget, length, or subject categories. We take cinema as a whole. We are letting all film-makers know that any film-maker who has an extra print of his film (all prints at all times at the Co-op and the Center remain the property of the film-maker) can send it to the New York or London branches of the Co-op and the film will be distributed, no matter how much or little it costs to make. We are not categorizing films. Each film at the Co-op requires special treatment, each film has its own audience, each film has its own life. At this point, we would like to urge you —and I direct this Open Letter to the independent film-makers of the world, to anybody whose life is cinema, who is making and must make films—to create Film-Makers' Cooperatives of your own, in your own countries. There is no other visible solution. There is no other way of escaping the grip of the commercial set-ups. This net of international Co-ops could then exchange among themselves and help each other beyond the boundaries of their own countries. The boundaries are bound to disappear anyway very soon. With the changing times, with the new spirit in the air, with communications and speed increasing, it would be too bad if we were to delay our action. We have to surround the earth with our films, lovingly, like our hands. We have to abandon thinking in terms of budget and sizes and lengths. We have to abandon unnecessary separations and divisions. We have to abandon the commercial distribution methods.

With whom are we competing? With ourselves? The film-makers should set up cooperative distribution centers, co-ops, and eliminate all the competitive and negative spirit that still pervades cinema. Let's not worry about the big commercial success and the audience of millions. If the health and freedom of our art needs it we should be willing to retreat to our own homes, to our friends' homes: cinema as a home movie. The art of cinema cannot be created with money but with love; it can not be created by compromises but by purity of our attitude. Certain simple truths sounds like preaching. But I don't mean to preach. This is an expression of an attitude which I share with many other film-makers.

A note on the Financial Set-Up of the Film-Makers' Cooperative: The film-maker deposits his print with the Co-op. That print is his membership card. During our yearly meetings, film-makers elect an advisory board of film-makers, to supervise and to advise the running of the Coop. The film-maker remains the owner of all his prints. He can take them out whenever he wants to. No contracts of any kind are signed. Trust is the basis at the Co-op. That's the first condition. Income: 75 % of the rentals (from gross) goes to the film-maker, 25 % goes to the Co-op, to cover the running expenses, the shipping, etc. The London branch, the rentals in Europe being much lower, will (at least for the time being) operate on a 50 % to Co-op, 50 % to the film-maker (from the gross) basis. The film-maker is allowed (and encouraged) to distribute the same film through other distributors—as long as that other distributor doesn't object to the Co-op's distribution of the film and works on humanly acceptable terms. We have been trying to break up the monopolistic film distribution idea. It would be ridiculous to try to sell, for instance, a book through only one bookshop, or rent it through only one library. But that is what we still find in film distribution. Films should be distributed through as many different distribution centers as possible. By this coming Christmas the Co-op is placing film prints, on 16 mm and 8 mm for sale in bookshops, in record shops and in general stores. It is time that we revolutionize, bring up to date the methods of film distribution and exhibition. The prints of our films soon will be in every home, on the shelves like books, so that one can pick them up and look at them whenever one feels like doing so.

Film-makers of the world: let's do it now. Let's go home and start from there. Let us not waste time with any of the old-fashioned set-ups; they are not for us. They are ugly, sick leftovers of egoism and competition. They are from another world. They don't wish us any good. They will drag us down. Let's spread the new vibrations of the spirit across the world and keep us growing and keep us in love.

Which brings me to my last point: the social engagement. There is all this talk going about our being irresponsible, about the new cinema (all over the world) being irresponsible, socially disengaged. Don't listen to that. We are the most deeply engaged cinema there is. When the film critics say that we are not reflecting the social realities, they mean we are not reflecting those social realities (or aspects of reality) of yesterday, not today. Film critics and the public go by inertia carrying yesterday's engagements on their backs. Artists, when we are really creating from our hearts, we deal with the changing, new realities, new content of the spirit, and we say that we are closest to the pulse of man's heart, we know where it hurts him and what he needs where he is going or should go. Let's not become weak, let's not give in to the blabber of the press, or film distributors, or film critics, or politicians; we have to do what we have to do.

FILM-MAKERS' CINEMATHEQUE

41st STREET THEATER
125 W. 41st ST. NYC 564-3818

SCORPIO RISING

Inauguration of the Pleasure Dome/Fireworks

AND OTHER FILMS BY

KENNETH ANGER

MARCH 17-27

8 & 10 PM

UNDERGROUND · AVANT-GARDE SHOWCASE

OPEN 7 NIGHTS · $1.50

FOR DETAILS SEE OUR WEEKLY VILLAGE VOICE AD

MURRAY POSTER PRINTING Co. Inc., 221 W. 64 St. NYC

FILM-MAKERS'
CINEMATHEQUE
41st STREET THEATER
125 W. 41st ST. NYC   564-3818

ANDY WARHOL'S

MY HUSTLER
SIN IN THE SUMMER ON FIRE ISLAND

APRIL 3 thru 10
8 P.M. and 10 P.M.

UNDERGROUND · AVANT-GARDE SHOWCASE
OPEN 7 NIGHTS · $1.50
FOR DETAILS SEE OUR WEEKLY VILLAGE VOICE "AD"

* MURRAY POSTER PRINTING Co. Inc., 221 W. 64 St. NYC

During the past two years, Film-Makers' Cooperative has sent Expositions of our work to various places of the world. We are watching what's happening in new cinema around the world. And often we are alarmed. Most of the time, what's called the New Cinema by Cahiers du Cinema or Cinema 66 we find is only another variant of the same old cinema. Beware: Dorian Gray is at large! Dorian Gray, the dandy of the supposed new cinema, will die soon and you'll see his shriveled, dry old body appearing slowly from under the beautiful make-up. Beware of film-critics: with their terms and categories they keep you tied down to certain established idea of the "new." Film-makers: there is very little New Cinema at Pesaro, or Cannes, or Oberhausen, or Karlovy-Vary. Let's not fool ourselves. There will be little new cinema at any film festival unless the festivals change, change immediately and drastically and totally. The feeling is in the air, however, that things are beginning, will begin to move, are moving already, and the movement will increase in speed, until it reaches the speed of light and sparks fire. The commercial, competitive empires are crumbling. Let's not even waste energy fighting them, in kicking them: surely, they will fall by themselves. It is more important to do our own creative work, the work of building, no matter on what budget, on what size of film or how long a film; no matter whether film festivals or theaters will or will not show our work; no matter how many people will see it; we have to do it the way we feel it should be done when we really listen to ourselves, our deepest intuitions. That's the only way of doing it. That's what we (I) wanted to communicate to you. A few facts about ourselves, a few feelings, a few passions. And we hope you are with us. We are with you. There is really no distance between us.

Jonas Mekas

May 18, 1966

Excerpt from a letter to the members of the Film-Makers' Cooperative

In February, the Branch B of the Co-op, under the name of Film-Makers' Distribution center, was created. We have a number of films at the Co-op that are suitable also for the so-called theatrical (commercial) distribution. Theatrical (comm.) bookings differ from the usual Co-op booking in that they require special treatment, special promotion materials (required by the theaters), different financial arrangements, etc. etc. We have been lucky to receive a small grant for one year, to pay the running expenses of this Branch B, with one hired man to do the work (Louis Brigante is that man) & we hope that by the end of the year something will be accomplished. There are three advisors to the Center—Shirley Clarke, Lionel Rogosin, and myself. We meet every Tuesday night & review the progress of the Center & make plans and have some beer. The first project of the Center is the current New American Cinema retrospective at the Bleecker St. Cinema (the program One I am enclosing with this letter), and the theatrical opening of *Scorpio Rising* and *The Brig*, same place. Later this summer, the Center may be preparing a special side-show series of the newest works for the New York Film Festival. A number of other projects are on the table, but we'll talk about them as they become more real.

There maybe some questioning, why the Center, why not do it thru the same Co-op? But a number of good heads have discussed this already & have come to the conclusions which we have followed. Eventually, in a year or two, or three, both branches should become one again—who knows. Or we may split into one hundred different branches. I myself I always prefer some confusion & nothing can be more confusing than two Co-ops in one—that's pretty confusing, you have to admit it.

"Midway upon the journey of my life I found myself in a dark wood, where the right way was lost. Ah! how hard a thing it is to tell what this wild and rough and difficult wood was, which in thought renews my fear! So bitter is it that death is little more."—Inferno, Canto I, *The Divine Comedy*

May 20, 1966

A DREAM

I had a dream. There was a huge surge of water. Everything was being covered by water. As I saw the waters coming over everything, I tried to understand, why. And then I saw, in that huge ocean by now, that used to be Manhattan, I saw or I was shown a little white mouse, a small white mouse playing with a snake, and I saw millions of drops of water—now the ocean consisted of individual drops—rushing towards the mouse and the snake, and a voice was telling me: the white mouse doesn't know what dangerous game she is playing with the snake; the white mouse is part of us, and we are rushing to save her—said the water drops or something behind the water drops.
I woke up.

May 30, 1966

And again I asked I prayed as I asked to indicate to me what to do.
I prayed & tried to come closer, deeper,
But the voice inside said: Where are you trying to escape, into what depths, when your work should be here on earth & thru the love of others! Believe, believe, believe in me, & love, & everything else will be given.
& I felt warmth descending upon me
& I knew what I had to do.

I remember the morning I passed Avignon. The Nice express was speeding across France. I woke up, I looked at the window, and I saw the morning. It was the most pastoral, most peaceful morning I had seen since my childhood. Oh, the lost peace!— I thought,
then I fell back into sleep, a tormented, bad sleep, painful, with bits of broken dreams.

Taylor Mead (in Cassis): "I'd like to play Mary Pickford in 1920 in a movie called *World War 2½.*"

Taylor Mead: "My movies are contrived. Andy's movies are so much anti-contrived that they are too contrived again."

Something should be said about the cliques, coteries, groups. The Underground film-makers, the New York film-makers, they say, are split into cliques. That is supposed to be very bad. But it is not! Cliques are really groups of people who feel very passionately about something, and whose passions and aesthetics coincide. The friendship feelings, the bonds grow between them, and they constitute a wall that protects them from the public's arrows. The public never appreciates the passionate heat of the front lines of the arts: it bothers them, and perhaps, deep inside, it embarrasses them, the heat of their passions; perhaps they feel guilty of not being capable of that heat themselves. Not even older artists understand it.

July 12, 1966

To the yogis and others:
Yes, it's good to sit and meditate. It's good to run out of town. You think it's safer, there, you have more control of things, the little devils won't find you there, in your castle! But God doesn't test you in your castle: he catches and tests you in your little daily activities, in your little meetings with people, when you are in the FIELDS, not in your castle. It's in the fields that

```
                                        LONDON FILM MAKERS' COOPERATIVE
                                        (temporary address)
                                        c/o Paul Francis
                                        9 Gilbert Place
                                        London, WC1, England
                                                  Phone: HOL 1817
                                                  July 1, 1966

Film Makers' Cooperative
414 Park Avenue South
New York, NY 10016
Att: Jonas Mekas

Dear Jonas,

We have held off sending you information regarding the London Film-
Makers Cooperative until now, because prior to this point we had
little to say about the specifics of our cooperative.

Two weeks ago we sent out a call for a meeting, an organizing meeting
of the cooperative -- 21 film makers attended -- and several others
pledged support altho they could not attend the meeting.

The letter you had written to MILES along with your mimographed statement
were read, and there was a general agreement with all the aims and
principals of the New York Cooperative.  The lines of the London
cooperative will follow most closely those of New York.  There are
a few minor points which may differ from New York, but those are necessary
in order to comply with  the law here in regard to non-profit organizations.

At first this first organizing meeting a sub committee was set up (composed
of filmmakers) to draft a constitution and general statement of purpose.
The committee has held two meetings, and we are now prepared to have
the first general meeting (Tuesday July 12, 1966) at which time
the governing board of film makers will be elected, and we will be officially
established.

We are in the proces of getting space for the cooperative, and will
for the time being use the above address as the headquarters, in that
Paul Francis will be most active, and the address is centrally located
for the film makers.  We decided not to use Indicia or Better Books
as our addres, in that we feel that the cooperative must be free of any
ties with outside sources such as book stores and theatres which
have other vested interests.  However, both Indicia and Better Books
have offered us facilities for screenings. Indicia at the moment is
not set up for film screenings, and it will be a few months before they are,
and Better Books is set up, and in fact at present they have regular screen-
ings.  In addition to the two bookshps, the Jeanetta Cochrane Theatre, a
large modern avante guarde legit house, has offered us their facilities for
late night screenings which we will be able to use starting in September.
The other reason for not wanting Indicia as the Hq. for the cooperative,
in that they are competitive with Better Books, even though it is a
friendly competition, we believe that it could be a disruptive factor
in the coop set up if either one of the bookstore was played against
the other, and at this point we need both of them as an equal and stble
factor not fighting one another at the expense of the cooperative.

                          SIGNED,
                                R.E. DERGERAT
                                PAUL FRANCIS
                                R. HARTLEY
                                HARRY MATASON
                                J.  KEEN
                                LEONARD FOREMAN
                                R. HUDSON
```

LONDON FILM MAKERS ' COOPERATIVE
(temporary address)
% Paul Francis
9 Gilbert Place
London, WC1, England

Phone: HOL 1817

Film Makers' Cooperative   July 1, 1966
414 Park Avenue South
New York, NY 10016
Att: Jonas Mekas

Dear Jonas,

We have held off sending you information regarding the London Film-
Makers Cooperative until now, because prior to this point we had
little to say about the specifics of our cooperative.

Two weeks ago we sent out a call for a meeting, an organizing meeting
of the cooperative -- 21 film makers attended -- and several others
pledged support altho they could not attend the meeting.

The letter you had written to MILES along with your mimographed statement
were read, and there was a general agreement with all the aims and
principals of the New York Cooperative. The lines of the London
cooperative will follow most closly those of New York.   There are
a few minor points which may differ from New York, but those are necessary
in order to comply with the law here in regard to non-profit organizations.

At this first organizing meeting a sub committee was set up (composed
of filmmakers) to draft a constitution and general statement of purpose.
The committee has held two meetings, and we are now prepared to have
the first general meeting (Tuesday July 12, 1966) at which time
the governing board of film makers will be elected, and we will be officially
established.

We are in the process of getting space for the cooperative, and will
for the time being use the above address as the headquarters, in that
Paul Francis will be most active, and the address is centrally located
for the film makers. We deceided not to use Indicia or Better Books
as our address, in that we feel that the cooperative must be free of any
ties with outside sources such as book stores and theatres which
have other vested interests. However, both Indicia and Better Books
 have offered us facilities for screenings. Indicia at the moment is
not set up for film screenings, and it will be a few months before they are,
and Better Books is set up, and in fact at present they have regular screenings.
In addition to the two bookshops, the Jeanetta Cochrane Theatre, a large
modern avante guarde legit house, has offered us their facilities for
late night screenings which we will be able to use starting in September.
The other reason for not wanting Indica as the Hq. for the cooperative,
in that they are competitive with Better Books, even though it is a
friendly competition, we believe that it could be a disruptive factor
in the coop set up if either one of the bookstore was played against
the other, and at this point we need both of them as an equal and
stable factor not fighting one another at the expense of the cooperative.

— x x x x —

everybody sees what little petty and pompous asses you are. You can't stand this, you can't stand that, everything seems to interfere with your goddamn personal salvation. I don't know why I am letting myself to become angry about it, but I guess, I have been contaminated by such "yogi" attitudes myself and I'm desperately trying to free myself from that crap, to spit it out of my stomach. My personal salvation is zero if it's achieved by unconcern with others; it's zero, if I walk the streets without even noticing the bums.

July 27, 1966

Rehearsing the 1st act.

Malina: "We are making a movie collage. We are creating all the scenes from movies —the workers automation scene (idea) is from Chaplin. There are scenes from avant-garde movies. *Frankenstein*, of course."

Me: "I am looking and thinking how a theatre—your theatre—is equipped better than cinema, to present certain multiple collage ideas. Because of the human presence, I think."

Malina: "There is nothing in art like human presence for dramatizing ideas, in art. This is a huge collage of ideas."

Malina: "The degree of liking *Frankenstein* will be measured by the degree of our own human development."

July 28, 1966

Yes, yes, the actors are in town! The theater is coming!

The people stood in the shadows of the hot noon and looked at them from a distance and there were whispers and their whispers went around the town, like in the *Barber of Seville*, and within minutes the whole town knew: the actors are in town!— Like they know that a calamity had struck at the other end of town, a fire, or some other such fearful event.

Yes, The Living Theatre was in town, and they meant business, they meant theater, and they were not normal people, they couldn't be normal, they have to be something else, outside of the normal reality, outside of the normal—

And they will always remain mysterious, and mystery is always both tantalizing and fearful, mystery of the conditions of creation, the conditions an artist must embrace in order to be able, when the time comes, to descend as deep into himself or step out of himself, herself, and become as much the part of what he's doing, be a part of it as much as it's humanly or inhumanly possible—to switch almost at a finger flip into the state of the utmost seriousness which is the condition sine qua non of any creation—

—all these thoughts suddenly came and ran through my mind as I watched them, the members of The Living Theatre, that last Saturday, in Cassis—as I watched them, now on stage, sitting in a circle, in the utmost concentration and seriousness, just before the very beginning of the performance itself—half gods, half humans, unlike any of us—yes.

"Actors are divinities, and one must be patient with them," said Ms. Chaliapin at Les Roches Blanc, as we were eating, with Jerome.

Cassis 1966

Taylor (Mead) says his next movie will be *Clattered Harmony*...

Taylor Mead: "Thank God for the Jungles" (we were talking about Vietcong)

Myself, eating in NY 1/3 of what I am eating in Cassis, and surviving

Taylor Mead: "Fellini needs more vagueness; like Jack Smith. Now he is so clean."

Taylor Mead: "You make me think now. I haven't thought in years."

We walked that night, three of us. Cold wind was blowing from the Seine, & Ken [Rubin] asked, suddenly: "Why are we here?" I said nothing for a moment, then I said, "Do you want a farmer's answer, or an intellectual's answer? We'll never know the answers. Now we are here, cold, walking, wet, asking questions. We'll keep asking questions. But you know by now that answers are given equally to those who ask & to those who do not ask. I am going thru a stage when I ask a question, I feel, is pretentious. But then, not to ask questions can be pretentious also."

He saw me to the station, and I saw his bold monk's head from the window, a little bent down, from height or from thinking.

Tertullian (born 155):
"Any waters on earth are susceptible of sanctification because all waters generally were hallowed by the spirit of God brooding over them at creation."
Alec Wilder: "Jerome is always doing something, like a professor. I feel so guilty when I do nothing."

The smell of Blood is the Landscape of Provence
Three fundamental attitudes:
jubilation (joy)
la douleur (suffering)
la meditation (contemplation)
Taylor:
"He has a great sense of orgasm"
Visited cemeteries of Bonnieux.
Ganagobie monastery.
"Mohammed, great conqueror-to-be, became armor-bearer for his uncle, and was dishonorably discharged. At the first sight of blood he became sick at his stomach."
Jerome just walked in and told that the area which we visited three days ago and which I filmed will be closed soon as the French atomic testing grounds.

August 28, 1966

You keep calling yourself a goddess.
If you are a goddess than you are a fallen goddess or a goddess under a punishment, undergoing a punishment. Otherwise you wouldn't have that craving for recognition: a god or a goddess is recognized—even on earth—immediately. You are a suffering goddess, if you are a goddess, and we can only have a compassion for you, but no adoration...

There are film-makers in the avant-garde lines who are very careful (I call it paranoiac) about where their films are being shown. I remember two years ago, getting into arguments with Ken Jacobs, who wanted to check the identity, the politics, the occupations etc. of everyone who wanted to show his films. He didn't want, for instance, his films to be rented to Madison Avenue people—on moral grounds. Until it became impossible to control. It was easy to keep track of such things when there were only two or three people renting films. But things changed fast, so that now films sit on the shelves at the Co-op and anybody can rent them, same price, King or Bum, Fascist or Saint. Film-makers gave themselves to the fate of all other artists: film-maker's responsibility and his control ends with the completion of his film. To demand further control, who will show it, how it will be handled: that is a full time job. Few are willing to do that; nobody— including me—knows how to do that.
Still, Stan Brakhage last year withdrew all his films from the distribution, in his own attempt to square things with the world and himself and to put a question mark next to all kinds of dissemination, its methods and processes, of works of art. Then, in another dramatic gesture, he placed his work back into the Co-op and entrusted the development of humanity to the angels. Bruce Conner, the other day, instructed me to withhold his films from

In the railroad station of Marseille, 1966.

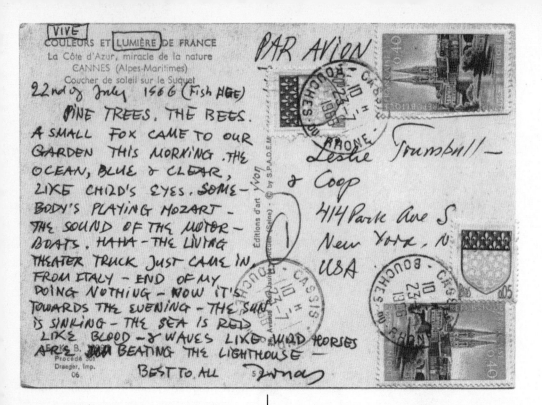

22nd of July 1966 (Fish Age)
PINE TREES. THE BEES.
A SMALL FOX CAME TO OUR
GARDEN THIS MORNING. THE
OCEAN, BLUE & CLEAR,
LIKE CHILD'S EYES. SOME-
BODY'S PLAYING MOZART -
THE SOUND OF THE MOTOR-
BOATS. HAHA - THE LIVING
THEATER TRUCK JUST CAME IN,
FROM ITALY - END OF MY
DOING NOTHING - NOW IT'S
TOWARDS THE EVENING - THE SUN
IS SINKING - THE SEA IS RED
LIKE BLOOD - & WAVES LIKE WILD HORSES
BEATING THE LIGHTHOUSE -
BEST TO ALL

PAR AVION

Leslie Trumbull —
& Coop
414 Park Ave S
New York, N
USA

By the lighthouse of Cassis, with Taylor Mead, 1966.

In Lacoste, Provence, by the castle of
Marquis de Sade, 1966.

the European Exposition on the grounds that a) some of the screenings are organized or take place in "communist" institutions, b) he is afraid that the screenings may undercut his future income in those cities…

I have always considered that to want to restrict the showings of one's films has more to do with paranoia than money or morality. Also: the more you show a good film, the more demand there is for it. And nothing can be done for the bad film. There is this curious thing, introduced by the Co-op four years ago, these simple principles: a) no film is rejected by the Co-op, b) no value judgment is passed. There was such fear of this principle, here and abroad. I had to defend it with my teeth. What will happen to the art of the film, they asked. What happened is that every film found its own audience, according to its own merits. Darwin's law applied to art, that's what we have now. In the old-fashioned, commercial distribution system, any film, no matter how bad, can be pushed into success by million dollar promotion. Not under the Co-op system. Under the Co-op system, which doesn't advertise films, good films grow, bad films trail behind.

Knowing how paranoid most of the film-makers are about keeping track of their work, I was very curious to see new Aspen issue, 20,000 copies, which included prints of Richter, Moholy-Nagy, Vanderbeek and Rauschenberg films. I think it's fantastic, revolutionary, to throw 20,000 prints of *Rhythmus 21*—still the masterpiece of the abstract cinema—into the people, with no fears that now I'll lose the audience. I happened to drop in, I was visiting someone, the other day, a stranger, in Ohio, and when the evening came, they pulled out their 8 mm projector and they screened, for the 100th time, they said, the Aspen package of films. The whole family was arguing about what record to play, what music, for the soundtrack. There were discussions, which music goes and which not, or maybe no music at all, they had seen the films silent, many times, etc. etc. I can just see what this kind of beautiful dissemination of film through families will do to the level of *Film Culture* in these coming years.

So, dear film-makers—let your films go into the world, don't cling to them.

SCRAPS

"…for however great the good, one may never do anything wrong however small, to bring it about."—St. Teresa of Ávila

"There was a time when I trusted the world's aid; I see clearly now that all that is worth no more than a few sprigs of dried rosemary…"—St. Teresa of Ávila

We are bringing this message to you as a public service. At this point, please turn the volume of your TV set down and listen, see if there is no shooting on your street, in your ghetto.
(short pause)
If all quiet, please turn the sound on again. This is a public announcement.

This is an unpaid advertisement.
This is what you have to do:
a) take over the government
b) declare war
c) declare peace
d) declare war again
e) disappear

When on a plane, I never eat their chicken dinners. I just can't take the chance. Imagine, the plane crashing, and me falling down, with a badly done piece of chicken stuck in my mouth. It would simply be too ridiculous for words to go down into the depths of all eternity in such a stupid way.

The long sitting in the room results in false sensations.

We need more Puerto Ricans to destroy the efficiency.

JUST A DREAM

They keep telling us there is nothing new happening in cinema…
The Underground is a product of Jonas's imagination…
that nothing is really happening… it's all wishful thinking…
Yes, it was wishful thinking.
It was a dream.
And we kept repeating it and repeating it and the word became matter, it became true.
We knew it would become true.
We fought your skepticism and your inertia of past memories by our projections of our dreams, our wishful thinking.
Yes, yes, yes, many other things that we are talking about excitedly aren't here yet. They are still projections, dreams, ideals that came to us in our sleepwalking seconds—our seconds of contact with the Dream—
But they all will come thru.
We'll keep repeating it and repeating it until the word, the wish will become matter.
That's our weapon!
Our passion and our faith is our weapon.
Our dream will wash away all the soot and all the bad memories,
and what are you going to say then,
what are you going to say then.

SCRAPS

It's a great idea to dismiss all yesterday papers with morning!

Three times he struck the stone with the stick…

I don't understand why you are graduating. I have been hearing about your kind. I mean, about guys who go to college for years and years and graduate, and all that. I have never been able to understand it, I have always been very suspicious of anybody who can take all that stuff that is given in schools, and play the student, a goddamn student, ridiculous.

"The film-makers who have banded together under the auspices of the Film-Makers' Cooperative have each and every one of them that divine fire and confidence which the ancient Greeks called *thrasos*. That is to say, insolence. But insolence of a divine nature. For them, cells, air bubbles, atoms, rays, film frames are the flame of their continued existence. Like the ancient priests of Egypt who sang hymns to their gods by uttering the seven vowels in succession, the sound of which, says Demetrius of Alexandria, produced on their hearer as strong a musical impression as the flute and lyre, just so, the film-makers today are experimenting to a degree where the images, symbols, sounds are as if unknown." *F.C. 32*

"A radio is not a louder voice, an airplane is not a faster car, and the motion picture (an invention of the same period of history) should not be thought of as a faster painting or more real play.
All of these forms are qualitatively different from those which preceded them. They must not be understood as unrelated developments, bound merely by coincidence, but as diverse aspects of a new way of thought and a new way of life—one in which an appreciation of time, movement, energy, and dynamics is more immediately meaningful than the familiar concept of matter as a static solid anchored path to a stable cosmos."—Maya Deren

Received: Sept. 9, 196~

Canyon Cinema Co-operative
1748 Haight Street
SanFrancisco, Calif, 94117

Film-Maker's Co-operative
414 Park Avenue South
New York, N.Y. 10016

To the Directors:

At a meeting on Wednesday August 24 of 17 Bay Area film-makers and many
interested friends, it was agreed to organize a co-operative distribution
office to be known as Canyon Cinema Co-operative.

This move has been in the offing for some time and was finally realized
because we have, at least temporarily and hopefully for some time to come,
virtually rent free space in commune with the Straight-Ashbury Viewing
Society. The other hurdle was personnel, and now with one full-time
volunteer and several part-time volunteers we are able to function.

We are presently holding benefit film showings to raise money for printing
a catalog, mailing, advertising, etc. You will receive a copy of the first
mimeographed catalog shortly as a supplement to the Canyon Cinema News.

We hope that a symbiotic relationship between yourselves and us can be
achieved. The Co-ops must certainly co-operate, even if no one else can.

At this point however, we must ask for largely unreciprocated aid. We
ask for your general mailing list and your mailing list of member film-
makers. Non-member film-makers too, for that matter. Certainly all
known (and unknown) film-makers should know of our existence.

The Canyon Cinema Co-op is organized on the basic principles you have set;
75% of rental to the artist, 25% to the Co-op. Perhaps, in the future,
to speed mailing and save postage, we could split the country in two and
refer orders back and forth. For instance, if we got an order from east
of the Mississippi, or the Rockies, or whatever, and you had prints of the
films ordered, we could send you the request by air mail, and the films
would be shipped from your office. And vice-versa.

But for now we will simply thank you in advance for whatever assistance
and advice you can give and close with

Regards,

Bruce Baillie, Robert Nelson, Ben Van Meter, Directors, Canyon Cinema Co-op

September 2, 1966.

- 296 -

**With Gideon Bachmann, in New Jersey,
filming for German television, 1967.**

CHAPTER TWENTY

... Tired... Searching for money for 'Tek and Film Culture... Intermedia issue of F.C.... My childhood... My daily working schedule... America Today series... Valéry on poetry... A letter to the Mayor of New York... Searching for a secretary... How to copyright films... Notes from Rome... Notes from a N.A.C. agitator... On screening movies in Italy... Pesaro... The Art of Vision... Climaxes in cinema... My films seized at the NY airport... A trip to Ávila...

October 12, 1966

It seems sometimes, you don't do much. But the concentration drains you out completely. I remember, when three weeks ago, in one single day I managed to raise six thousand dollars, to pay back debts of *Film Culture* and some of the Cinematheque bills, and guaranteed the next year's publication of the magazine, and worked out grants for 12 film-makers— it was all done very easily, in a way, everything was ready for it, in a way—but I was almost dead, by the time the day ended, I was completely dead, drained out. Somebody asked me, what did you do today, and I couldn't explain, because all that happened was that I left the house in the morning and I came back home in the evening, and so much happened, and I didn't move a finger, I just moved from place to place, said the right words, almost in a trance, and everything happened by itself. But it drained me somewhere deeper, much deeper—with my mouth dry, and my ear drums ringing, for two days, for three days I was drained out, completely drained, it took me time to come back to normal.

October 13, 1966

Yesterday (12) and today (13), two very busy, important days. Many things have come together, that it's amazing. Like yesterday. And it continued today. I took Kubelka to Jerome, he wanted to see his work. But then everything led, all forces came to some kind of focus, and I think I succeeded in assuring a money grant for Kubelka, which should come thru any time now, and a grant for Kenneth Anger, which also should come thru. Today, I called a meeting at Shirley's place, with Louis and Schectman. In a sense it was a historical meeting. And I think we put the basis for acquiring a theatre of our own. I proposed that we buy an old building, or an empty lot, and build a theatre of our own, really, we should ask Buckminster Fuller to drop one of his domes on the lot. The idea, once proposed, had an electrifying effect. The room was already full of energy. And now everybody felt, that that was the thing to do. It was clear, suddenly, in our minds, that that was what we needed; Buckminster Fuller's dome.

INTRODUCTION

The purpose of this special issue of *Film Culture*, INTERMEDIA, READYMADES, ETC. is twofold: a) to give our readers an idea about what's going on in the avant-garde arts today, and b) to serve as a sort of catalogue or index to the work of some of the artists involved. There is no one name to describe the work done by these artists. The most frequently used terms are "mixed media," "intermedia," "expanded cinema," "happenings," "events," and "readymades." The term "readymades" is defined by George Maciunas in the Fluxus section of this Catalogue; the term "mixed media" (or "media mix") has been frequently used by USCO group; the term "intermedia" has been defined by Dick Higgins in the first issue of The Something Else Newsletter; under term "events" see section on Yoko Ono. On "happenings" read the interview with Ken Dewey. As for the "Expanded Cinema," I coined the term to describe the by now historical survey of these marginal areas, or the avant-garde areas, at the Cinematheque, autumn 1965. I knew the amount of work done on the borders of each of the arts involved, and I was aware of the impossibility of covering the entire ground in one single survey. The primary purpose of the Cinematheque being to serve the cinema, I had to limit the survey to those artists and to those shows where, despite the long and often unpredictable arrows shooting into various directions, the cinema predominated. In other words I had to exclude most of the expanded painting and sculpture (although not completely, as in the case of Carolee Schneemann's light sculptures or Bob Whitman's Make-Up Table), expanded dance (although dance came in numerous ways thru the work of Emshwiller, MacLise, Blossoms, Snyder and, practically, thru most of the shows), etc.—I had to stick to the Expanded Cinema. I felt it was time to pull all this research into the open in one huge survey, and see what holds the light and what not—to gain a perspective to the whole range of new explorations. On the other hand, there was a need, I felt, to bring some fresh wind into the numbed atmosphere that was surrounding the New York film-making scene in the Spring and Summer of 1965. To assist me with the execution of the Survey I pulled into the Cinematheque the young John Brockman, at that time with the St. Mark's Church, and he proved to be just the perfect man. The rest is history.

October 26, 1966

I am sitting alone. It's raining. I search for a Chopin record, & I sit and listen to it.

October 27, 1966

Instead of trying to put God back into man's life—it's too late for that—now man has to make an attempt to put himself into God.

"Augustine's constant contemplation of God, his all-absorption in Him, was something actually kinetic, calculated to move mountains."—Robert Gordon Anderson, *The Biography of a Cathedral*

"If an infidel or barbarian really does what is in his power, God will reveal to him what is necessary for his salvation, either by inspiration from within, or by sending a missionary. God does not refuse grace to anyone who does what he can."
—Saint Thomas

I looked at the flowers, leaning on an old stone wall, & they told me, that the shower of sound & light of mixed media is nothing but the showering of us with particles of concrete matter.
the flowers told me also: my disquietude when I am in nature is because it's my childhood that is pulling me back & I can't go back—

CO - OPERATIVE

Phone: COV2161

94, CHARING CROSS ROAD, W.C.2

November 23, 1966

Dear Jonas,

As you can see by the above letterhead, we are finally in business. In the past ~~week~~ three weeks we have had an "opening festival" of films, and have screened over seventy (70) new films. Over half of them had never been seen before here in London.

The Cooperative has over fifty active members, mostly young film makers. There are about four films in progress this moment with about ten more to start soon. Of the film shown they were evenly divided between NY Coop films (The Brig, Scorpio etc.) and films made here by London Coop members. Within six or eight weeks we chould have our catalogue out, and in it we hope to have about 35 London made films.

I have been elected chairman of the Co-op, Paul Francis and Bob Cobbing are joint secretaries. Our address is above, and we have a rent free, good size office. Within two weeks we will have an editing room set up for all film makers use here in London.

We are working toward a permanant theatre here in Soho and the chance of it coming thru is extremely good, and it should be soon. I was told that you were sent CININ, our new film magazine. The second issue will be out by February.

But, more on our exhibitions. We have weekly screenings at Better Books, and will have the Chelsea College available for weekly screenings also sometime after the first of January.

We are now concerned about when you plan your trip, the one you thought you'd make in late November? We have over one hundred requests for film programs from all over England...Do you have any news for us on the possibility of our getting Films.

All your emmesaries who arrive in London, go to Miles at Indicia Bookstore. That's nice, but he's not in the co-op, has never come to a meeting, has never been at a screening, etc, and he isn't involved in the film world. I don't know why you constantly send people to see him about film activities.

We would appreciate your answer to the availability of the films etc..

Till...

Harvey Matusow
Chairman,
London Film Makers Cooperative

(Home address 6, Aubert Park
London N.5.
Phone DIC 1514

- 300 -

Brakhage crossing Central Park, 1966.

in the nature I seem to fall back into that happy silence—while in truth my place is in the city & working forwards, never backwards—

"I have to work for higher purposes," he said.

"Just do your daily duties; the 'higher purposes' will take care of themselves," said the voice. (or "Fuck you—just do your fucking daily work; the higher purposes will take care of themselves.")

Even the highest lives today are pretty low when we think about the real glow that human life could be, or some lives have been.

"I was always alone as the other boys considered my activities sissy-ish and girlish although I have yet to find a girl or a sissy who loved NATURE as I did. I was deemed positively ECSTATIC by flowers and birds and all such delicacies."
(Mel Lyman)

November 24, 1966
I filmed P. Adams, early morning, in New Haven.

November 26, 1966
AM: Worked on the *Diary* film
At the Co-op
PM: MS delivered for N. 42
working on Barbara's tapes for the film
Session with De Grazia and Barney Rosset on *Shoot Your Way Out*, etc.

November 27, 1966
11 AM: Session at the Co-op
12 NOON: Session at Shirley Clarke's, with De Grazia
Shoot Your Way Out
1 PM: Meeting with Schectman at the Maidman Theatre
2 – 4 PM: At the Cinematheque, made a decision to take Cinema Rendezvous theatre for *Chelsea Girls* at the Village Theatre,

inspecting the projection for AMERICA TODAY
7 – 9 PM: At the Cinematheque, Monday Meeting
Stopped at the Co-op to pick up MS for the new catalog
10 – 11:30 PM: Proofreading catalog
11:30 – 1 AM: Session with Jacques Ledoux of the Cinematheque Belgique
1:30 AM: home

November 28, 1966
I filmed Stan in Central Park.

November 29, 1966
8:15 AM: Session with G. Maciunas at the Co-op re. *Film Culture*, Mixed Media catalog, etc.
9:30 – 12:30: Working on the Mixed Media catalog
12:30 PM: Co-op—splicing titles to the AMERICA TODAY program; other business
2:30 PM: Press screening of AMERICA TODAY, at the Tek. Arrangements made, contracts signed with the Ackerman for the Rendezvous theatre for *Chelsea Girls*
5:30 PM: reception for Ledoux at the Museum of Modern Art (meeting about money in Museum's back room, Shirley, Louis, Schectman, myself, Storm)
7:30 PM: Back at the Tek advertisement prepared for the *Chelsea Girls*
12:30 AM: back home

November 30, 1966
10:30 AM: Ad placed in the *Times*
session with Vincent Canby
11 AM: At the Ackerman's office, details about the projection, money delivered
12:30 PM: Session with Schectman about money for advertisement and projectors
2 PM: Co-op
3 PM: Home
7:30 PM: The Village Theatre, AMERICA TODAY premiere

AMERICA TODAY
Program One, December 1966
Introduction:
The cinema has developed many and complex forms of story telling. More lately, the avant-garde, the "underground" film-maker has made cinema into a subtle tool of poetry. The multimedia shows are exploring the far frontiers of light and motion. It's the journalistic cinema, with all its multiple directions, that has been almost totally ignored. This at the time when the motion picture camera has become the most subtle tool of creating and reflecting the life around us. This at the time when new techniques enable the film-maker to observe the reality and comment upon it as freely and as unobtrusively as does the poet and the writer.

The AMERICA TODAY series has been conceived to serve at least three different ends. First, it will provide the film-maker with an outlet for journalistic expression. Secondly, it will provide the theaters with carefully put together programs of contemporary cinema that a theatre otherwise wouldn't know what to do with. Thirdly, by cutting through the various levels of America today—its thoughts, its feelings and its events, the series will help us to know each other better. On one hand, the series will expand the conception and forms of cinema; on the other hand, thru these forms and thru this content it will expand us. In one simple sentence we could say that the AMERICA TODAY series will bring the journalistic cinema up to date with other forms of cinema.
AMERICA TODAY programs will be issued to theaters across the country over three months. The series are programmed by the Film-Makers' Cinematheque and are distributed thru the Film-makers' Cooperative and the Film-Makers' Distribution center.

PROPOS SUR LA POÉSIE
"We know that the word "poetry" has two meanings, that is, two quite distinct functions. In its first meaning, it designates a certain genre (kind) of feeling, particular state of feeling which may be evoked by a variety of objects or circumstances. We can speak about a landscape being poetic; we my call poetic a certain moment of life; or we can describe a person as poetic.
But there exists a second usage of this term, a much wider usage. Poetry, in this second meaning, refers us to an art, to a strange occupation the purpose of which is to reconstruct that feeling, that emotion that designates the first meaning of the word 'poetry'."—Paul Valéry, p. 1362
Oeuvres, Tome I Bibliothèque de la Pléiade, 1965

April 5, 1967
An open letter to the Mayor of New York City:

We, the Underground, the Independent film-makers of New York, we read the Mayor's statement printed in the Festival program, and we listened to the Mayor's speech at the opening Dinner; and we have come to the following conclusions:
1. The Mayor's office is completely surrounded by the so-called "motion picture industry," that is, by that part of the film-making community the sole aim of which is to make money.
2. The motion picture industry, by posing or postulating itself as the only important part of the film-making community, is misleading the Mayor, and through him, the people of this city about what's really happening and about what's really important in cinema.
3. By reducing film-making of this city to the economics alone—and what's more, to the multi-million dollar economics alone—the motion picture industry is engaging in a vast activity of replacing

At the Film-Makers' Cinematheque, December 1966. Jack Smith, Mario Montez, Piero Heliczer, Jonas Mekas, Andy Warhol.

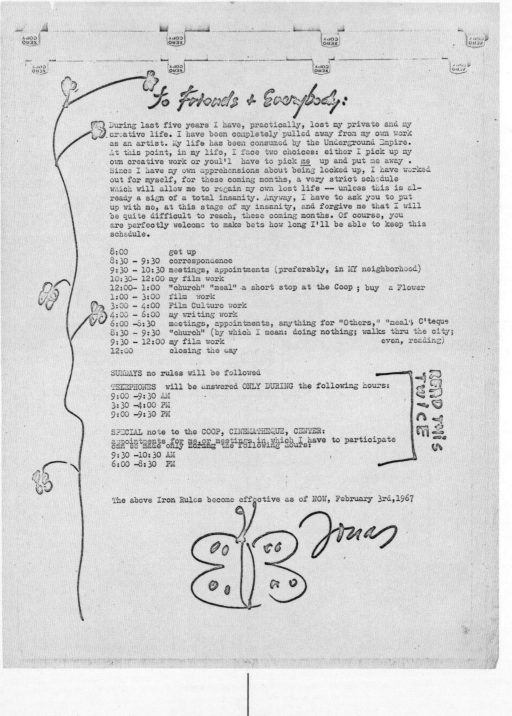

To Friends & Everybody:

During last five years I have, practically, lost my private and my creative life. I have been completely pulled away from my own work as an artist. My life has been consumed by the Underground Empire. At this point, in my life, I face two choices: either I pick up my own creative work or youl'l have to pick me up and put me away . Since I have my own apprehensions about being locked up, I have worked out for myself, for these coming months, a very strict schedule which will allow me to regain my own lost life — unless this is already a sign of a total insanity. Anyway, I have to ask you to put up with me, at this stage of my insanity, and forgive me that I will be quite difficult to reach, these coming months. Of course, you are perfectly welcome to make bets how long I'll be able to keep this schedule.

```
8:00           get up
8:30 - 9:30    correspondence
9:30 - 10:30   meetings, appointments (preferably, in MY neighborhood)
10:30- 12:00   my film work
12:00- 1:00    "church" "meal" a short stop at the Coop ; buy  a Flower
1:00 - 3:00    film  work
3:00 - 4:00    Film Culture work
4:00 - 6:00    my writing work
6:00 -6:30     meetings, appointments, anything for "Others," "meal'; C'teque
8:30 - 9:30    "church" (by which I mean: doing nothing; walks thru the city;
9:30 - 12:00 my film work                               even, reading)
12:00          closing the day
```

SUNDAYS no rules will be followed

TELEPHONES will be answered ONLY DURING the following hours:
9:00 -9:30 AM
3:30 -4:00 PM
9:00 -9:30 PM

SPECIAL note to the COOP, CINEMATHEQUE, CENTER:
appointments for me or meetings in which I have to participate
can be made only during the following hours:
9:30 -10:30 AM
6:00 -8:30 PM

READ THIS TWICE

The above Iron Rules become effective as of NOW, February 3rd,1967

Jonas

Sponsored by the Greenwich Village Peace Center
N.Y.U. Students for a Democratic Society / Artists
and Writers Dissent / Committee of the Professions

224 West Fourth Street, New York 10014 / AL 5-1341

WEEK OF THE

ANGRY ARTS

AGAINST THE WAR IN VIETNAM

January 29—February 5, 1967

Dear Fellow Film-maker,

We invite you to participate as a film-maker in the Week of the Angry Arts. The Angry Arts program, covering a full week of exhibitions and performances, takes in painters, poets, dancers, musicians, film-makers, etc. It is intended to give an opportunity to artists to express their opposition to the war in Vietnam.

Therefore, the film committee has devised the following plan. We invite you to join us in making a communal film under the tentative title, We Believe . . . Personal Declarations by American Film-makers for Life Against the War. (We would like to receive other suggestions for the overall title.)

We are asking you and other film-makers to make and contribute a 16mm film, black-and-white or color, silent or sound, of up to but no more than 100 feet in length. (All film must be 24 f.p.s.; sound film must have optical track.) The films of the contributors will be assembled by the committee. Each film will be separated from its neighbor by a length of leader. There will be a title card at the end listing the names of all contributors to this historic document. Each contributor may, if he wishes, have his name appear with his film.

While the film represents a protest against the war in Vietnam, it is not necessary for any film-maker to restrict his contribution to the subject of war per se. Having said this, we leave it to you to infer from the title how broad the scope of the film is.

The premiere of this unique film will take place at the Village Theater, which seats 2600. Additional screenings will be held at other theaters during the Week of the Angry Arts. While all films submitted will be joined in the initial screening, the film committee reserves the right to assemble a final version for further distribution. It will be the property of the Angry Arts committee, and will be exhibited wherever and whenever possible after the first Week of the Angry Arts. Any money received from the exhibition of the film will go to the cause of ending war.

Your film should be sent to Week of the Angry Arts, Greenwich Village Peace Center, 224 West Fourth Street, New York, N.Y. 10014. It must be received by January 22, 1967.

We urge you to state as forcefully as you can in your own filmic terms your feelings about this war.

Sincerely,

Shirley Clarke, Hilary Harris,
Ken Jacobs, Jules Rabin, *Richard Preston*

For those who would like to contribute a film but cannot, money contributions to the overall work of the Week of the Angry Arts would be welcome.

Please Post

Please Post

On Jan. 14, 1967 in the golden Gate park in San Francisco there will
be he ld a day of peace manifestation, organized by the League of Spiritual
Discovery as an inaguration of the S.F. chapter, incorporated
presnt will be
tim leary
a llen ginsberg
Peter orlovsky
Ala n watts
independently but in   cooperation with the League of Spiritual Discovery
Cary Synder master minded the day
with Zen Roshi Suzuki, Zen master of Soto Zen Temple in S.F.
contact for information Martinez Algier & Michael Bowen 415- 431- 4093
there will be dancing poetry rock n roll mantra singing & 10,000-20,000
people are expected
towards the cooperation of all creeping kreplachs, spiritual, Rock n roll
the laegue of spiritual disvcovery & Soto Zen, painters writers poets movies
makers, budhist tantreks & everyone in buying over 100 acres of land near
tassagaro hot springs, near Big Sur, as an isolated shangrala, to set up
a hugh ashrum under the ownership & authority of the Zen Zoto Temple for
meditation & open to all with a communial kitchen with Ca ry Synder & alan watts
in residence

also on Jan 28 Or 29 allen will introduces Swami Bhaktivananda all night at
avolon Ballroom S.F.

Also Allen Ginsberg will give a poetry rock n roll reading sometime in
mid jan at the filmore auditorium backed by the music of on e of the several
S.F. rock groups like QUICK SILVER MESSANGER SERVICE & THE GREATFULL DEATH

the spiritual values of this city with the economic values. And the industry is trying to make the Mayor part of this activity, or conspiracy.

4. We are afraid that, the way we see it, the Mayor has already become a victim of the motion picture industry's schemes. His dinner speech sounded as if it was coming, as if he was speaking through the brains of the industry: he wasn't speaking from his own heart and mind.

5. As a consequence of this, instead of speaking of cinema in New York—which this Festival is all about, its nine programs reflecting the wide variety and scope of film-making in New York—the Mayor was speaking only about the Industry. Instead of speaking to the film-making community which is right there in front of him—he spoke about the industry and to the industry.

6. When some members of the wider film-making community, specifically, Shirley Clarke, Al Maysles, Adolfas Mekas, Lionel Rogosin, Andy Warhol and myself asked the Mayor why he spoke to the Industry (which, he told us proudly, had six—I repeat, six—films shooting, in New York) instead of speaking to the entire film-making community which he had right there and which, we told him, has thirty films in shooting if not more—all that our Mayor could say was to admit that he was wrong and therefore—I quote—"I should go and hang myself," before he was pulled away by the Industry and Mayor's Motion Picture Department employees.

7. But we don't think that the Mayor should hang himself. It's the industry that should hang itself.

8. When the Motion Picture Department of this city pushes a small minority of film-making community into the prominence, and, specifically, a minority the sole aim of which is to make money, it means that it's equating culture and spiritual values with money. And we are beginning to be concerned with the consequences of this perversion of values that is being imposed upon the Mayor's office and upon the thinking of the motion picture Department of this city.

9. We are concerned with it, for the suspicions are beginning to arise that if this is happening in New York, than, on a larger scale, this must be also happening in Washington, in the Government's film offices. The list of people who surround the so-called American Film Institute looks too suspiciously like Who's Who in the Film Industry.

10. Our fear is that this perversion of values, of putting the monetary values on cinema before all other values, has taken root all over the country.

11. What a sad irony. Or is it a joke? For a long time now the better minds of this country, artists and educators have been deploring the fact that there is no support, neither from the State nor the foundations for the Independent film-making in this country. We hoped that some day it would come. And, indeed, it came. But before we managed to reach the cashier's window, the Industry was there before us.

12. So now we feel that it's all up to us. It's our responsibility, the responsibility of the underground film-makers to tell you what's happening, before it's too late. Because there is still time to correct it.

13. We are here to tell our Mayor that we are with you, that the Underground is watching over the motion picture affairs of this city, and that we see what's happening. We see that the Industry, while pretending to be with the City, in truth is selling the city away. But we are not going to permit the Industry to do this even if we have to

act as the Motion Picture Department of New York City in exile.

14. We have to do this because the world is changing and it's changing fast and we can not permit ourselves to stand by quietly when we see that the Industry is blocking the cultural growth of this city, and its people.

15. Some of the most beautiful cinema in the world today is being created in this country, and in New York. And not by the Industry, but by the Independents, by the Underground. If anybody anywhere is talking about the American cinema, or about New York cinema today, it's because of the Independents and not because of the Industry.

16. Does our Mayor honestly think that he has to push Industry because the City needs money? Isn't our Mayor considering, ever, the deeper welfare of the people of this city? Surely, the city, the economy of which is built on the death of spiritual values, is doomed.

17. But we don't want our city to sink. We think this city can be the greatest city in the world and the most beautiful city in the world.

18. But the greatest city in the world has to be pure at heart. The economy of the Greatest City in the World must be governed by the spiritual values and concerns.

19. So we are saying to you: The people who surround you are corrupt to the roots. Turn to the younger generation, to the teenagers of America, to the Underground of America. We are with you. We are keeping our eyes on our city. And we are going to help you. That's what we want to tell you, on this occasion.

P.S. This text was read at the festival of New York City Films, organized by Department of Cultural Affairs. Mayor Lindsey was present.

May, 1967

Penalty system to those who treat us like little children.

Idea: how to copyright film prints
The copyrighting of individual prints could be done in the following manner:
At the end of the films, on the original, there should be blank frames left. The lab should be instructed when the print is ordered to write in the empty frame the number of the print, and in the other empty frame (blank frame) they should write the name of the owner of the print (to whomever you are selling it). After the print is made, the markings on the original (or master—whatever) are wiped off. The film-maker keeps in a book the track of who has what number of print. Those who want to steal, to make dupe etc. prints from some other print, instead of ordering it from the Film-maker, will not be able to do so because of the number and the name.

May, 1967

For a film:
Interviewer talks to a black man. You can hear the Interviewer's questions but the black man's voice is not heard although we see him speaking. But you can guess his answers from his face.
The irregularity of some of the Gr. Village streets—but the best example is Rome—allows even to a smaller part of the city to develop and live in privacy, to build small villages within the City.

May 8, 1967

Stopped at the Cannes Film Festival. The air is full of endless sales talk. This is a place where all proportions and perspectives get completely mixed up. What's more, Cannes is not technologically equipped to show the newest works of cinema. The 16 mm equipment is primitive and the two screen (double screen) projections are not possible.

JONAS MEKAS IS LOOKING FOR A SECRETARY

devote a few hours every day * ready upon call *
must be completely devoted * like a monk * must have
transcended the Beat * that is, must believe in being
on time on the dot * personal needs sacrificed to the
needs of others * doesn't have to like movies * I wouldn't
like to work with one who thinks she IS or should be an
artist * it's balloney * must know how to spell perfectly *
French knowledge preferable but not essential * 4-5 hours
a day * in a way I need an ideal secretary, but that's
what I need*

May 25, 1967

Rome
The visitors of this city clicking with their cameras seem to radiate with a silent admiration for all the bloody ruins. I would blast the Coliseum, with powder. Why should humanity keep the remnants of bloody monuments? They do not uplift, they drag us down, they drag all the tourists down, you can see it from their faces, full of phony admiration. In those stones is embodied the new Roman spirit and it reaches after us with a vengeance and it continues doing its ugly work even today. The new Roman architecture is as ugly as the Mussolini architecture. I would really extend this and I'd say that we should destroy all the bloody monuments of New York. The monuments of New York are about the ugliest monuments in the whole world. I want to create an Underground Anarchist Organization for the Destruction of the Monuments of New York.

May 26, 1967

There is much talk about a cinema of protest. But our cinema, I mean films like those of Stan Brakhage, Bruce Conner, or Barbara Rubin or Landow are films in anticipation of celebration, not protest.

From The NAC Agitator's Notebook
Question: How is your cinema opposed to Hollywood?
Answer: Our cinema *is not opposed* to Hollywood. We are not fighting Hollywood. That is a wrong notion. We are simply different from Hollywood. We are two different animals, one could say, like a horse and a cow. A horse and a cow do not deny each other, do not oppose each other: they are two different animals grazing in the same meadow, serving different purposes.

From The NAC Agitator's Notebook
Question: What is the meaning of this film?
Answer: There is no ONE meaning to a film.

The correct question should be: What does this film mean to you? There is no meaning applicable to all people equally. Each one of us sees a film in a different way, sees different things in it on different viewings. To ask for *the* meaning of a film is a merchant's approach to art. A merchant always wants to know the exact price, the exact amount of everything, he wants to know it's *one* dollar, *two*, *ten* dollars.

Michel Fontaine: "When I watch the NAC film I completely forget about theater." (Fontaine is a very fine theater director from Marseille.)

In Italy, and in the rest of Europe, there is much talk these days about the film language. Pasolini has contributed much to this discussion with his essays. Pesaro film festival had two seminars on the subject, with very intelligent international linguists and aestheticians digging into the meanings and definitions of the filmic language.

What I wanted to say, in connection with these discussions, is that the words "new" and "language" have been so stressed and over-emphasized lately, that the meaning of the "new" has been confused. I noticed this in Europe, but it's true in New York, too.

May 27, 1967

The Art of Vision opened Pesaro Film Festival this afternoon. From approximately 150 film "critics" and newspapermen only 12, I repeat (for the curiosity of the future writers): only 12 (twelve) stayed to the end. That is the true state of the film criticism in Europe anno 1967.
Just a week ago, I screened *The Art of Vision* in Torino, at the Galleria dell Arte Moderna. It was also an afternoon. 200 people came to see the film (no film critics,

but people). 150 people stayed to the end. That's what I mean by Film Festival audiences. Bored scribblers, paid to see films, sat there thinking (that is, if they are able of that faculty called thinking) about the beach and gossiping, with no interest and no patience for cinema, not willing to put any effort into it.

May 28, 1967

At Pesaro, the "critics" who walked out of the *The Art of Vision* (over 100 of them) stayed during the whole of *Der Findling*, a mediocre film by George Moorse. Not a single one walked out! There cannot be a better, or more cruel condemnation of these film critics than this simple fact.

One of the differences between the young film-makers of NY and those of Italy or France or Germany is that the latter are still trying to adapt themselves to the old distribution and production systems while we in America we are developing our own systems and methods of dissemination and production.

June, 1967

From The NAC Agitator's Notebook
Question: What is a New Cinema?
Answer: The New Cinema is that cinema which, when the movie critics see it, they cry: "It's terrible! It says nothing! It's not cinema!"
The New Cinema is that cinema which is created without the approval of the critics; it's correct to say that it's created *despite* the critics.
The New Cinema is that cinema which produces new critics and kills the old critics.

From The NAC Agitator's Notebook
If anyone says to you, at a screening, that "Oh, nobody can understand this film," "nobody can see or like anything in this film," "this film does nothing but make our eyes hurt"—don't try to answer it, it's a trap question. Instead, turn to the audience and ask: "Is there anyone who *liked* the movie? Whose eyes were *not* hurt?" Etc. The audience will answer it for you, the audience will take care of the hecklers, it always works.

From The NAC Agitator's Notebook
In Torino, after Guido Aristarco reduced the NAC to cubists, Dziga Vertov and Buñuel, I ended the discussion by proposing to the panel and to the audience to accept and sign the following resolution: "We the panel and the Audience (place & time) we have found nothing new in the New American Cinema. We therefore propose that the Italian cinema remains where it is." The audience rejected the resolution with a stormy shouting: *"No No No!"* That took care of Aristarco. Fadini turned to me and said to the audience: "He is just an instigator."
True, this was an agitator's trick on my part. But it was the only effective way of fighting Aristarco indirectly, to reveal the absurdity of his statements by pushing the situation to the extreme. It was no use going into long detailed arguments.

June, 1967

The technology of cinema in France and Italy is at least five years—maybe more—behind. At Cannes they were unable to project *Chelsea Girls*, they could not work out the double screen problems and sound problems on 16 mm. In Torino they almost never got the films in focus. Jerome Hill's *L'Anticorrida*, a two-minute film was over by the time they got it in focus. I had to drag down the projectors from their booth into the middle of the auditorium to increase the light power, to project *The Art Of Vision*: they would have continued projecting it with washed out colors as they did till I came to Torino. To find a 16 mm projector in Rome or Torino or other places is a tremendous problem. In Pesaro,

With Robert Kramer, at the University of Iowa, 1967.

when they discovered that Cavanaugh's film was 8 mm, they had to get an 8 mm projector all the way from Milan.

After seeing European cinema & talking to the European artists, I get into the mood of criticizing & analyzing, away from celebration. Like a poison rising from the past.

June, 1967

The Underground Film-Maker is going to cover with single frames every inch of this earth, every face, subways, prisons, madhouses, wars, armies, banks, White Houses, poor homes, rich homes. We are going to free 7,000,000 cameras, we are going to give them a voice, so that we could see right in front of our eyes, one step removed "from reality," but still knowing that it's reality, not Hollywood or Cinecittà—We are going to look at ourselves almost face to face and see how primitive and ugly we are: we'll give ourselves a tool with which we can see ourselves.

Yesterday I passed a store and I shot a few single frames of the inside of the store through the open door. Immediately the owner rushed out protesting, *You can't do this*. That's what's going to happen when all the Underground film-makers will start buzzing with their 7,000,000 cameras: all the egos will start protesting: You Can't do That to Me, You are Invading MY Private Property, etc. etc.

The cop in Pesaro forbade me to film the railroad station. The soldier in Falconara forbade me to take pictures of the tiny one-plane airport. A big military secret… We have so many things to hide, to keep secret from our fellow men, so much bad conscience. And that's what the Underground film-maker is going to reveal.

The New Cinema is made with and for love; the old cinema is made for and with money.

At Pesaro, each time a film—a short film!—ended, they kept shouting *Light Light Light!* Adrienne Mancia characterized this correctly, I think, as "a lack of tradition of viewing." That is, they are not able to accept the darkness from which the images emerge, to wait in silent expectation. They can't stand the silence and darkness of a movie theater. During the silent films they were making noises, they were creating funny soundtracks, etc.

One could say that the film festivals, from what I have seen, have become festivals of film "critics," or should I say, "scribblers." They sit there and they measure everything against their little petty egos, they can't stand anything on that screen that contradicts them. So they whistle, they make noises, they crave recognition, not cinema.

June, 1967

Both in Torino and Pesaro the Fluxus films were among the ones that provoked most controversy. But also they were among the few which were really liked by a small minority. They pointed out that they liked them primarily because there was in them something mind-clearing, something happy and life-approving—without any usual psychological muddlings. Fluxus films, like *The Art of Vision* are life-celebrating films, not life-analyzing films.

At one of the discussions someone quoted Aristotle saying approximately "What is possible to the eyes of *public opinion* is not what is possible to the eyes of philosophers"—which is to say, that there are different depths to reality, different eyes will see deeper or shallower.

Also, during the discussions of the linguists a difference kept coming in between the figurative and non-figurative arts, the difficulties in discussing, using musical or literature terms in discussing cinema. There will never be exact likenesses.

June, 1967

The old cinema *knows* what cinema is (which means, it likes to *look back* at itself; that is, it's all *cooked*). When the Old Cinema tells us, What Cinema Should Be (or Is), it tells us what cinema *has been til now*. The New Cinema begins where all such knowledge and certainty end.

The best way to end the New Cinema is to agree about what a New Cinema is. The old film-maker always has a clear aim, purpose in front of himself (his mind). He cannot conceive of going ahead without a purpose. But that is what the New Film-maker is doing. He is going ahead without any clear idea of what that future holds for him or his art. All that we know is this: We all agree that we don't want to remain where we are. Even if we don't know where we are going *we want out of here!*

June, 1967

Film festivals are places where films are being shown on the screens so that the film critics could properly and loudly exercise their craving for recognition. Festivals are for the critics, not for the films.

At Pesaro, like any other film festival, the audience of "critics" was like any low developed audience. Only those of NAC films were "appreciated" which had pop music soundtracks (Harry Smiths *Early Abstractions*) or had something "funny" (like *Oh Dem Watermelons*) or fast motion coupled with fast pop music (the work of Bruce Conner). (The same I have noticed in New York. Europe is no different in that regard.) So that the above mentioned films are really "appreciated" for wrong reasons. They are listening to music. During the screening of Harry Smith's films at Pesaro there was a bunch of teenagers in the back of the auditorium who kept singing Beatles soundtrack all during the show and it was going well and everybody applauded. It was a discotheque sort of happening. Which is OK. What's bad, is that this kind of criteria is then applied to watching Brakhage and *Bardo Follies* and they say these movies do not swing, and they start booing. You see, no Beatles music in *Bardo Follies*.

June, 1967

Take a paragraph from prose or a poem and analyze it "as film," by crossing out the words which the popular opinion of cinema (critics) would exclude; cross out all "and"s and other "meaningless" words leaving only nouns, only the "meaningful" words.

June, 1967

I have come to the conclusion, I don't know why I haven't come to it sooner, that the middle class can not produce cinema, or any interesting cinema. At Pesaro, I saw films in which petty middle class film-makers were using Resnais cutting and Markopoulos editing, and overexposed frames and disjointed structuring, and were doing it well, but nothing came out of it, nothing of consequence was produced by it. Because it's nothing but a technique. The content is the same old middle class petty content, petty preoccupations, petty emotions, distorted emotions, petty fears, ideas, etc.

The techniques of the new cinema, as illustrated by the work of the Italian Underground, have become universal. It's the content that makes all the difference, that gives special, particular nuances and touches to these techniques, so that they really speak and vibrate. I keep repeating that the techniques ascribed to the NAC are not *American* but belong to the new generation, to the new cinema in general, internationally.

THE ART OF VISION
Notes for Pesaro screening.

One way of measuring the importance of an artist is by his influence on other artists. Stan Brakhage has exerted more influence on the new generation of American film-makers than any other contemporary artist (next in influence are Ricky Leacock, Gregory Markopoulos, Jack Smith and Andy Warhol.) Beside his films, his book *Metaphors on Vision* (1964, *Film Culture*) is the best summation of the new film aesthetics.

The Art of Vision, with its first screening in 1965, became a manifesto and the masterpiece of the new way of seeing and the new way of expressing that seeing through film. *The Art of Vision* could be also looked at as a Lesson in Seeing. It is constructed in such a way that it leads the viewer deeper and deeper into the subtleties of vision until, by the time you reach the midway, you have no way back. No matter how you resist or dislike the film, by the time you are through, you are one lesson further in seeing and your appreciation of the new cinema will never be the same.

No use going into interpretations of this monumental work. My experience shows that each of us will see it slightly differently. To me, personally, it is an epic film. And it tells a very "simple" story: A man goes and goes and goes all his life towards something—and no matter how much effort he puts into his journey, he is just where he started. But the way Brakhage tells this one-sentence story it becomes a story of Miltonian proportions, in his ambition and in the greatness of his fall. Guy Davenport once compared this film in greatness to Melville's *Moby Dick*.

It is wrong to look at *The Art of Vision* as an abstract work. It is a "realist" work. All its details, all its materials have been taken from "actual reality"—be it sun explosions, blood vessels, the birth (he filmed the births of his own children) or the Colorado mountain slopes (where Brakhage lives)—all is real, all is there. But these particles of physical reality become words and metaphors in an epic language of utmost precision. After all, the teachers of whom Brakhage speaks with most respect are Gertrude Stein, Ezra Pound, Charles Olson—although he made his first film, *Interim*, inspired by Rossellini and it was a "regular" neorealist movie.

What else could or should I tell one who is about to see this film for the first time? That it took Brakhage four years to make it? That he has made approximately 30 other films before he came to this one? That Brakhage lives on top of a 9,000 feet mountain in Rollinsville, Colorado, together with his wife and four children? And that since *The Art of Vision* he has turned all his love and attention to 8 mm cinema and has made 23 most beautiful film songs—short lyrical film poems.

June 13, 1967

Climaxes in cinema presuppose solutions. Only when you propose a solution you have a climax leading to it. The New Cinema is a cinema without climaxes. It doesn't propose any solutions, doesn't give one answers. That doesn't mean that there is no construction, or orchestration. But this orchestration is not based on climaxes. It's based on variations on a theme—many subtle climaxes.

There is no one center of consciousness. Or maybe, truer, some thoughts come from other centers.

I am having also sentences coming to me, conversations between two different of my personalities. Storm said: "You are lucky, you have only two personalities. I have seven & more, all conflicting."

All religions and politics that are based on working towards tomorrow's Paradise, are immoral. They commit all kinds of crimes in the name of tomorrow. *Paradise Now* doesn't permit you any postponements (chess moves) of morality & obligations.

Pier Paolo Pasolini in his Roman apartment, July 1967. He came to most of the 20 programs of the American avantgarde cinema I brought to the Centro Sperimentale.

Customs Form 6051
TREASURY DEPARTMENT
10.21, C. R. 1943
Nov. 1942

RECEIPT FOR MERCHANDISE OR BAGGAGE
RETAINED IN CUSTOMS CUSTODY

Nº 274028

United States Customs Service

District No. _II_, Port of _New York_ _June 26_, 19_67_

Ex _TWA 905_ Arrived _6/2~_, 19_67_ Dec. No. _CF 6059_

The following packages have been received from _Jonas Mekas_

and have been retained for _Screening_ _(Name)_

(State reason for retention)

Trunks _____, Cases _____, Bales _____, Hand pieces _____, Packages _2_ TOTAL PIECES _2_

Contents said to be _#1 – 11 Reels undeveloped Film #2 6 Reels Film_

G. O. No. _____

Roy Johnson 3671

Inspector.

INSTRUCTIONS.—Prepare IN TRIPLICATE. *Original* to be given to passenger and presented to Deputy Collector at Customhouse when claim is made for the package(s), or for purpose of securing necessary shipping permit. *Duplicate* to be attached to package(s) as an identification tag. *Triplicate* to be used as a record of package(s) retained.

Baggage will not be shipped in bond unless passenger arranges with transportation company to do so.

16—32071-2 U. S. GOVERNMENT PRINTING OFFICE

Do The Right Thing Now. It's now that matters. Only the right actions of Now will create a Right tomorrow.

June 23, 1967

Returning from Madrid. At JFK, they check my passport against the Big Fat Book. The official makes a note on my Declaration Card. I move my suitcases to the customs man. He looks at the Declaration Card and asks for my passport. He goes into his office, come back. "Hm," he says, "I see that you had some trouble in California. Do you have any of *those* films with you?" "Yes," I say, "I have some films." "Are they obscene?" "No." "Are any of them commercial?" "I don't know. I wish they were."

After good twenty minutes of scrutiny, including my monologue on the necessity of changing the custom laws, the films, like books, should travel free through all the borders—the officer told me that I was giving him "a talk," and he made up his mind to take all my films "in," which he did, taking all my exposed and undeveloped footage I shot in Europe, and all my developed footage, my six reels of DIARIES, which I had with me.

"When are you to give it back to me?" I asked.

"You'll get it back," said the officer.

June 27, 1967

I called the Customs Office. Miss Suske said my films hadn't arrived yet from the airport & please call tomorrow.

June 28, 1967

Miss Suske is on vacation. I was connected with Miss Pushkin. My footage hadn't arrived yet.

June 29, 1967

Spoke with Miss Pushkin. The film hadn't arrived yet.

June 30, 1967

Noon. Miss Pushkin's secretary said Miss Pushkin is out. (Is she writing poems?) Please call in the afternoon. Can give no info.

Expenses on calls:
From N. York: 0.20
Newark: 0.40
From N.Y. 0.60
$1.20

FRIDAY
11 AM. Spoke with Miss Pushkin. The films arrived, she said. Please call in the afternoon.
3 PM. Long distance call. Disconnected in the midst of conversation. Second call brought me to Miss Pushkin. She said they looked at all developed film & I could pick it up. I asked if they screened my "undeveloped" originals. She said no. They are developing it, they will screen a print. Will they pay for the print? I asked. Because I don't need a print. I was connected with her boss, Mr. Fishman. He assured me that they will not screen originals— but the developed film must go from the Criterion directly to the Custom House. I said, O. K. I said that the only thing I allow is to screen the print, not originals.

July 1, 1967

Dear Paul Adams Sitney and Julie:
I was told that the Italian mailmen are on strike. I hope this letter will reach you this year (what year?).

We are somewhere in New Jersey, in a very lyrical green place, just after the rain, and there is Thoreau's *Walden* on the table, someone has been reading, and we have been shooting for last five days Adolfas' movie—I haven't seen much of New York since I came back.

As you know, I proceeded from Cassis to Madrid. Arrived there Tuesday evening, and slept in a small place, somewhere in

Madrid, and had a strange dream. Usually, my dreams are very simple, down to earth, farmer's dreams—I have no "strange" dreams, no symbolism, no surrealism. But this time I dreamt I was trying to tame a DRAGON. I was riding it, and I was in a complete mastery, I had no fear of any kind, and someone was telling me, that in the old days they used to kill dragons, but that today we should try to make the dragon work for us, we shouldn't kill the dragon, and that my (and our) function really is to teach people how to make the dragon work for them. WORK, WORK, WORK, was the message given to me by someone, WORK WITH PEOPLE. I know very little about the ancient symbology and the unconscious, really, about the sub-conscious meanings of dragons. I told the dream to Richard (& Amy) and Kelman and Storm and I got different interpretations. Dragon as Europe (Old Continent); Dragon as Wisdom (Storm). Etc.

Next day, very early, at seven o'clock, I took a train to Ávila. We crossed the craggy, stoney hills and mountains (Ávila is 9,000 feet high), the landscape rained with stones—and after a three hour ride there it was, it said: ÁVILA. I had with me only my camera bag, I left all other belongings at the airport, so I swung it across the shoulder and proceeded to walk into town. The day was clear and blue and it was very hot. I tried to find a map of the town, but nobody had one. And since my Spanish was practically nil, I decided to rely just on chance, intuition, and the guidance of St. Teresa. I immediately found myself in a beautiful square full of blue wild flowers, and I picked up two of these blue flowers and I put them into my camera bag. (Later I discovered that there were roses and roses around the houses, further in the town.) There were two churches, two very old churches around the square and there were children playing around them and I took a few frames of them, although I

didn't go into the churches. I proceeded walking deeper into the town, and soon I came before the gates of Alcázar, one of the many gates in the walls that surround Ávila's heart. I saw no tourists, and practically no cars, only the donkeys loaded with baskets of bread stood on the sidewalks, and the faces of the people were good and there was a feeling that I was in a different century. The rest of the world disappeared somewhere behind that railroad station and those hills and the fields —I was completely somewhere else. I hadn't eaten since I left Cassis, thirty hours ago, and I felt I shouldn't. I felt I should not speak to anyone or ask for anything from anybody, that whatever there was for me in this city will come to me by itself. And when I asked someone where St. Teresa's house was the man didn't know either, and he told me to continue going. Soon I found myself in front of the Cathedral of Ávila, and it was completely empty—it was still too early for the tourists if there were any—and I walked in and as I stood there looking around, a very very old eleventh Century church—I saw a small note which said to the effect (it was in Spanish, of course) that here, it was in front of this little altar that Santa Teresa de Jesus was first visited by St. Mary. So I took out the two blue flowers from my camera bag and I put them on the altar, beside a few roses that someone had placed there, in front of a statue of St. Mary. There was a very good peaceful feeling there, and I sat on the bench for a while, resting, as if giving my regards to St. Teresa and to St. Mary from all the avant-garde film-makers of New York, and from both of you who couldn't be there.

As I then continued my journey through the town, I came to another church. In truth, it was a pretty drab "modern" church, and I walked in and it was the church built upon the spot where St. Teresa was born. There was a room with a statue of St.

Teresa, it was a small room, exactly (a note said) on the spot where Saint Teresa was born. It was one of the most silent spots I have ever been. In fact, it was so silent, so silent, that the silence became like a matter, you could go deep into it, and there was no end—it was leading you into somewhere very very deep, very deep. Again, the room was completely empty, I was the only visitor there, and I sat in the room for a long while, with an unmistakable feeling of the presence of the Saint in the room, and I didn't know what to do or what to say although I knew St. Teresa was there. And then I proceeded further.

I walked out through the gates of St. Teresa. I left the old heart of Ávila and I descended into the tiny streets of the suburbs of Ávila most of which in the days of St. Teresa was just a plain field but which now was covered with tiny streets that ran down by the steep hill and into the fields. On my way down the hill I saw a girl by a house which was practically covered with roses. I asked her for two roses, and she gave me two, and I gave her five pesetas, and she didn't refuse them, and I continued further down the hill to where I guessed the old convent of St. Teresa stood, the one she built secretly and in great difficulty, her first one—and when I arrived to it, the gates were closed. I walked around it, to the other side, and I found a small door, used by workers, so I walked into the yard. I saw a nun walking in, so I followed her and I found myself in a long dining hall, in which there was nobody not a soul but there was a long table where the nuns—it seemed so—ate. At the end of the room there was another table, a small one, and since I didn't want to go further and disturb the good nuns, I placed the two roses on the little table, and I walked out of the convent and out of the yard, the same way I came in—and soon I was in the fields where the rye was in full growth, full of red poppies and blue flowers the name of which I don't recall in English but In Lithuanian they are called "rugiageles," the "rye-flowers." The fields were full of sun and heat. By now I had walked for several hours and I was hungry and thirsty—but the whole field, the whole slope was like the essence of summer. Really, it was also the essence of my own childhood, so I stood there looking at the fields and breathing the perfume, the whiteness, and the greenness of the rye fields.

I kept climbing up the hill, and kept walking along the wall surrounding Ávila. The hot white dust of the sandy field covered my feet and I was getting dizzy from the brightness and Ávila. But I felt that I had to continue walking. I went back to the Saint's birth chapel and I sat in the solitude and rested so for another while. I thought I was all alone. But I wasn't. There was a girl in the corner of the chapel, sixteen or seventeen, kneeling. I could see only her back. Later she stood up and left the chapel and I could see her face, it was a very sad and intense face and a very beautiful face and our eyes met for a second and I was alone again in the chapel.

I continued walking the streets of Ávila the rest of the afternoon and the evening. I felt like retracing, like crossing every street that St. Teresa walked, I was walking the streets for her, again, crisscrossing the traces left by the Saint. I came upon a little plaza, called plazuella de la vacas, the little plaza of the cows—it was the old field where the cows, the cows plowed by themselves while the farmer, St. Teresa's friend, prayed in the church with the Saint. Now the field was a plaza with a tiny monastery on the side and little houses and streets all around it. The plazuella was full of children and I sat there for a good hour, surrounded by children, click-clacking my single-frames, and I have never seen anywhere such beautiful children, they were like angels.

Filmstills from *Song of Avila*, 1967.

It was one of the things that amazed me in Ávila, the children, how angel-like they looked, the children of Ávila.

I felt here no presence of the sadness of the Western Civilization. The town was still in another century, the faces, the eyes of the people, the streets were in another century, and there was something very sober and maturely serious about their countenance. Eternity was hovering over the city. While I was walking down the hill, an elderly woman with two children joined me for a few streets, and she kept saying "chalor," or "colore," which I understood meant HEAT, heat—and I said, si, si, chalor, chalor—and the children laughed. The woman was dressed all in black, very beautiful black (the beauty and the properness of the black was another thing that struck me in Ávila—before I never really believed that black could be so alive and so beautiful)—and her face was like you see only in some old books or some of the faces that I saw later, next morning, in the early Spanish paintings, and in Goya, at El Prado.

The evening came and I shot the setting of the sun as it slowly sank behind the gates of Alcázar and behind the walls. I went back to the place where St. Mary appeared to St. Teresa de Jesus, and next to the Cathedral I found a third rate hotel called Roma and I took a room for the night. Then I went back into town. I stood in front of a small restaurant, completely tired, trying to make up my mind to have a beer or not, and as I stood so, looking at my feet and the dust on my shoes, looking back at the day, I kept asking myself: why did I really walk and walk and walk like that— I probably walked every street of Ávila and I walked around the town twice, and all the fields around Ávila. I didn't exactly notice it, when I did it, but it all came into my consciousness now, as I stood there, and I had no explanation and it didn't make much sense. There must be a mean-

ing in all this, I thought. And as I stood there, thinking like that, a small dog came from somewhere and started licking my feet and the dust from my shoes, the little dog, and he licked all the dust from my shoes and I didn't move, I took this as a message from St. Teresa—I felt that St. Teresa sent this dog, as if she were thanking me for my walking, for all the streets that I walked for her, and she was taking back the dust from my shoes—although I didn't deserve it at all, because it wasn't me who was really walking the streets of Ávila—not consciously so—it was some other "reason" doing it—and this dust, there was a feeling that this dust was a closer bond between us than anything else I could have done.

So I went back to the hotel and I slept in peace and I dreamt nothing, at least not that I know—it may come back to me some other time, perhaps, if I dreamt anything. I left Ávila at six in the morning. The entire city was sleeping. The streets were completely empty in the dawn. I was in the church of the Dawn, alone. I was walking towards the gates of the city, and my steps were making a sound that seemed to echo across the entire city—the city was so silent. I was walking with one thousand feet, the stone pavement went clink clink clink, a sharp clinky stone bell sound and as I walked behind the gates of Alcázar, and I kept walking, with my camera bag on my shoulder, from one end of the city to the other, to the East, where the railroad station stood. The train was just pulling in into the station and I jumped in and then I went to the window to look at Ávila and I leaned out—but it wasn't there. I looked but I couldn't see it—it was behind us, directly behind the train line, in time and in space, all I could see was the rising sun, so I took my camera out of the bag and I started shooting the sun, click clack click, as it was slowly rising above the stoney landscape of Castile.

I should add here a footnote to my Ávila trip. At the JFK airport, upon my arrival in New York, late the same day—after spending seven hours at El Prado—the custom officials seized all the film I had with me, all my New York diaries, and all my undeveloped film shot in Italy, in Vienna and in Cassis—they snooped thru all my luggage and even thru my papers and I was getting all angry and pepped up about it—some welcome home, I thought. Only next morning, at home, when emptying my suitcases and bags, I discovered that the custom men had overlooked two rolls of film. After looking closer, I discovered that these were the two rolls that I shot in Ávila. And as I looked at them, with some amazement, thinking about the amazing coincidence, suddenly the room was filled with the smell of roses—a brief gust of roses, very strong—and it lasted a few seconds, and then it was gone. At the same time all my anger was gone too.

Another postscript: In the little church built where St. Teresa was born, in the church, there is a sign, I don't know where it came from, was it something St. Teresa wrote or said, or someone else wrote, but the sign says: "Despues de mi muerte hare caer un alluvia de rosas." And I suddenly realized that St. Teresa and roses were inseparable. I stood in front of that sign and I read it more with surprise than amazement. Because nothing really amazes me any longer. Miracles are realities like all other realities around us. The two roses* on the Third Avenue, remember, they didn't really amaze us: we took them as if they were two drops of rain or anything else daily and casual. Or the book

at the Lyon's. Or our conversation with Jerome on 42nd Street, or the roses that Storm brought to your farewell party.

JEROME'S BOOK: Ever since I bought the three volumes of St. Teresa's writings, last Summer, it seemed, somehow, that wherever I went I kept meeting St. Teresa. When I arrived to Cassis, last August, the first book I found on Jerome's table was a very rare volume of letters of St. Teresa. Then, months later, in New York, one evening we were walking, Jerome and I, from the Cinematheque, where he had just seen Stan's *Songs*, and we were talking, and somehow, maybe because we had just seen *Songs*—everything seemed so beautiful and even the drabness of New York looked more happy—it seemed like somebody was pouring blessedness upon New York, and, caught by that mood, I started telling about St. Teresa, about what I was reading —and about my vague plans to make a film either on the life of St. Teresa or in honor of St. Teresa. And then we went home, each our own way.

Next morning Jerome calls me and leaves me a note to come. I come, and he shows me a letter, written around approximately the same time, last night, when we were talking about St. Teresa, written by an old good lady and a friend of Jerome's, to the effect that she was going through her books and she found this old book that she had no use of and it's a book on St. Teresa, a volume of her collected writings, a very beautiful old edition, and I am sending it to you, maybe you can use it— said the letter.**

TWO ROSES ON THIRD AVENUE: Just before I left for Italy, early in May, it was 7th or 6th of May, we stood, Sitney and myself, under a canopy (it was drizzling) on the Third Avenue and 28th Street, on

---

* I put a star above. Since this letter is becoming a "full" account of at least one chapter of this experience, I should put down here, not so much for you, since you are familiar with most of what I am going to record here—but for those few of our friends to whom I thought I should send copies of this letter—I will record here the incidents or occurrences mentioned above.

** I still have this book.

the East side of the street, in front of a small oriental restaurant, called I think Izmir, where we had just eaten, and, as I said, it was drizzling, and we were sort of saying goodbye and making last plans about how we were going to meet and where—Sitney supposed to come to Europe in July and take the New American Cinema Exposition from me, so that I could return back to New York—and we asked ourselves, where are we going to meet? In Rome? "We should meet in Ávila," I said, and Sitney immediately said, "Yes, sure, in Ávila." And as we said this, suddenly we became aware that there were two roses right under our feet, one red and one sort of paler red (Sitney's memory is that it was white)—right there, by our feet, from nowhere. And as we looked at the roses with sort of surprise, we knew clearly where they came from, we knew they were from St. Teresa—there was not even the slightest question or doubt in our minds —but we looked up, like everybody would do in such a case, although we knew we were only enacting the looking around action—we looked at the windows above us, and nobody was there, and it was impossible for the roses to fall from a window because we were under the canopy. As we were looking thus, a passerby, a man, came along and he looked at the roses and he said to us, "This must be an omen," and he continued walking. At the same time we became aware of an old man who appeared as if from nowhere, a very old man, and he stretched his hand—I didn't see him approaching but I saw him right there as he stretched his hand, picked up the two roses from the ground, said something to the effect that "they belong here," and he placed them on the steps of the house in front of which we stood. We remained for a moment there, contemplating this occurrence, then we continued down the Third Avenue as if nothing unusual had happened—we took it as a very natural occurrence, somehow. Only later, really days later the miraculousness of this occurrence struck us in its full clarity and beauty.

STORM'S ROSES: Storm just related this to me last night. The night Sitney left for Italy, Shirley held a small farewell party for him. Before coming to Shirley's, Storm had to stop at a friend's birthday party. On leaving the friend's house, this friend suddenly, upon the moment's whim, took a bouquet of roses that someone had brought to her, and insisted that she take them to Sitney. Now, what happened is that although Sitney and myself had made plans to meet in Ávila, all the circumstances came together in such a way that it became impossible for Sitney to do so. We decided that we should meet, therefore, in Rome, and then I'll go to Ávila by myself, and Sitney will come to Ávila at some other date, by himself. We both felt pretty bad about it. So you can imagine Sitney, looking at Storm handing him a bouquet of roses. Storm knew nothing at that time about our Third Avenue experience.

THE LIFE OF ST. TERESA: At the last footnote on our changed plans, I should relate here another small incident. We met in Rome, Sitney, Julie and I, and we were sort of feeling guilty about not meeting in Ávila. Next morning, Sitney took Julie to the Lyon's bookshop—Julie wanted to buy an English book to read. She came to the table, she stretched her hand and picked up the first book she found—and the book was "The Life," by St. Teresa. Now the peace descended upon us. Suddenly we both felt relieved. It dawned on us, suddenly, and I said it in words: "This must be the sign that St. Teresa is really everywhere. We shouldn't pin her down to Ávila alone. She is with us wherever we are."

Dear P. Adams Sitney and Dear Julie: I am writing all this down, and it is strange, when I sit here in this New Jersey house,

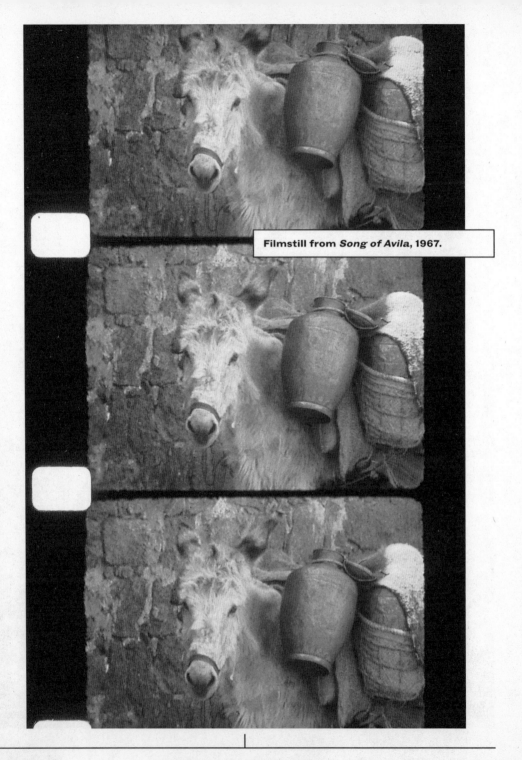

Filmstill from *Song of Avila*, 1967.

looking at the wet green trees—I suddenly am, like on several other occasions since my coming back to America—suddenly I am surrounded by the presence, by the feeling, by the atmosphere of the little room, the little chapel of Ávila, and I can feel the presence of St. Teresa here—I brought it all with me here, or, probably more correctly, it all followed me here. And the feeling that surrounds me when that happens is so strong and so real that I look with certain amazement back at my stay in Ávila and I am surprised that I couldn't perceive that feeling and that atmosphere with similar precision and sharpness when I actually was there—but it's only here that it presents itself so vividly, so unmistakably something new on this very very new continent called America—like nothing that I had ever felt here before. So that I feel at moments that I have been or I am nothing but, in a certain sense, a servant of St. Teresa, someone who carried her on my shoes across the seas to this continent—because I do not dare, I do not deserve to say that I carried her here in my heart and in my mind—a small particle of St. Teresa experience—one needs a much purer mind and a much purer heart for that.

Love—and give my love to John Cavanaugh wherever he is— Jonas

July 3, 1967
Went to the Custom House, Bowling Green. Picked up the NY *Diaries.* Had to sign a paper that I got it, that's all. They said they will call when the European footage is developed.

July 10, 1967
Called Miss Pushkin. She said the film was sent to the lab. Not back yet.

July 11, 1967
I called Criterion. Spoke with Harold. He said footage came back and they made a print & the Customs People are coming tomorrow to check it. He said they always make a print, when it's original.

Friday, July 14, 1967
Called Miss Suske. She said the film was cleared & ready to pick up at Criterion. Went to Criterion, found that they had made a print for the Customs People and that I'll have to pay for the print. I got the bill.

Developing 11 rolls of 7242 Ekta	93.50
print	120.36
waste	3.61
total	$217.47

I told Criterion that I didn't order the print that I didn't need the print that I can't and don't want to pay for Customs People's prints. Customs People should pay.
After talking with Criterion, it became clear that to get any money from Customs People will be a very very long hassle. I need the originals immediately. The only way to get them is to pay the whole thing. So I held the teeth tight and paid and took the film.

4 PM. I called Miss Suske and asked why aren't they paying for the prints they made. She said: "We gave the film to the lab, and told them to print it for screening." She said, call Mr. Fishman tomorrow, if you want to talk more about.

July 18, 1967
Mr. Fishman is not in.

July 19, 1967
"Mr. Fishman is not in. Will be back next Monday."

July 25, 1967
4 PM. Reached Mr. Fishman. Fishman: "They (Criterion) made the print on their own. We didn't order it."

Myself in Cassis, as painted by Jerome Hill, with Julie and P. Adams Sitney in the background, summer 1967.

Decided to give up. You can never win with them. They have one million loopholes to escape through.

Among the many Saints usually pictured with dragons:
St. Michael
St. George
St. Margaret
Pope Sylvester
St. Samson (Archbishop of Dol)
St. Donatus
St. Clement of Metz
St. Romain of Rouen
St. Philip the Apostle
St. Martha
St. Florent
St. Cado
St. Maudet
St. Pol
St. Keyne of Cornwall

The Greek word *drakon* comes ultimately from a verb meaning "to see" "to look at" and more remotely "to watch" and "to flash".

CHAPTER
TWENTY
ONE

July 7, 1967

Bardo Matrix light Show (at the Cinematheque) with live music by the Burning Bush. Earlier in the evening, we were talking with Richard Foreman and Amy Taubin, about the general slump of creativity in New York during last year. Amy noticed, that the way she sees, there were so many painters and photographers and musicians who threw themselves into the light shows, a year ago. But what happened was that each of them had ideas only for one program. So they did that program, whatever it was worth, and again slumped back. Or kept repeating the same. So that after a while you begin to have *déjà vu*.

The only change in the light show character during the last three months was caused by the import of the S. F. ideas. The Bardo Matrix's image show I saw at the Tek tonight must be among the most beautiful in that respect. Charles Levine was jumping up and down and repeating: "This is about the best light show I saw since SF. This is as good as the SF light show."

What I saw was very beautiful. Very colorful, subtly colorful, not just like most of the other shows. And I saw here about the best integration of the old newsreel footage (which every light show now uses) with the abstractions, and colors and superimpositions produced by dry or wet slides and movies (in this case, *Valley of the Cosmic Flower*, a movie by Jack Coke.)

Talking about light shows: I saw a few light shows in Italy. At the Piper Club. They were patterned, approximately, to the Dom or Gymnasium show (Warhol). They were very loud, very noisy, full of gadgetry for moving and turning and flickering lights and gelatins, and there was always a pretty bad rock and roll group—and everybody was swinging and dancing but in general they lacked subtlety and, as Taylor Mead noticed, "the Europeans do not know how to dance rock and roll…"

As John Cavanaugh put it, they look like they are imitating somebody dancing, they are not really fully out of their skins, they are holding back too much "form" which they don't want to drop yet.

July 14, 1967

ABOUT SCREENINGS OF OUR MOVIES
We don't really have such a great need for all those millions of people. Our films are not made with millions of dollars.

The commercial theatrical system has been devised for commercial films ("products"), that is, Hollywood. To want to use that system for our work means to change our work into Hollywood work.

Which, as a matter of fact, some of us are beginning to do. During last few months I have been running around for money, for the Cinematheque, meeting people from all kinds of walks, and many from the industry, and I was amazed how many of our film-makers have been there, at the United Artists, at the MGM, at the Universal, at the Warners, peddling their scripts, peddling themselves and peddling their films.

Why don't we have enough faith in what we have started, in the Coop? Something beautiful was started six years ago, but we keep wanting to get back into the SYSTEM.

Oh, what honor to screen our films on 42nd Street, at a Trans-Lux theater!

A film-maker will give his films to a lousy commercial theater where the prints will be run 50 times a week, where the prints will be completely butchered, and he gets no money—but he still feels that it's prestige & honor of some kind to have his films shown at a commercial theater.

I think it's a very bad state of things, practically, mentally and in all other ways. Our aim should be, if anything: to have our own 16 mm showcases in all major cities, very carefully and objectively programmed and run. I think that with all the energy today wasted in trying to CHANGE the existing theatrical system, it would be much easier to simply build our own system from scratch and on completely different, non-competitive principles, like we built the Cooperative.

I don't believe any longer that it's worth spending any energy in changing the old order & systems. I am for abandoning them all. I am for building our own order from the very center of our own energy. This is the end of July 14th Memo.

No date, 1967

INTEROFFICE MEMO
Concerning commerce.
This has mostly to do with the Film Distribution Center but it applies also in other places.

Like, we are trying to be like the others, like the Big Boys, trying to beat them on their own terms: by advertising, big ads, clever ads. We sit and we think about clever lines, "what will bring the people in," etc.

A feeling is beginning to develop in me, the way I see things, that somewhere we have been side-tracking, that a few correctives are needed. The aims may be still correct, but the methods we are using may never take us there. I don't know why we are trying to win on commercial terms.

MOVIE JOURNAL
by Jonas Mekas

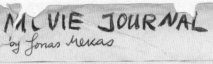

THE MORAL CLARITY OF ANDREW SARRIS
(demonstrated in three chapters)

Chapter One

"THE POINT BEING MADE IS UNCLEAR. IT'S ALL FRENCH PROPAGANDA"

> A column I did for *The Village Voice* in 1967 but I never submitted it for publication.

Relaxed, far from Vietnam, Andrew Sarris has a political revelation [see last week's review of "Far From Vietnam"]

Chapter Two

"By contrast, the Vietnamese peasants are neat, alert, and dedicated"
A. SARRIS ibid.

Chapter Three

"How curious this cult of the peasant abroad"
A. Sarris

Lionel Rogosin and Louis Brigante.

The Underground between 1960 and 1966 grew and caught everybody's imagination only because it grew out from its own center. We didn't dissipate, we didn't go OUT, we simply remained there, in our own center, among ourselves, and thus we generated an immense energy which then by its own force spread out and took over the imaginations of the film-makers, the people, newspapers, media, etc. etc.

WE DIDN'T HAVE TO DO ANYTHING ABOUT IT. It just worked by itself. Because we have something that is of a unique order.

Now, it seems, we are beginning to reverse this. We are beginning to get caught by the ways of the world.

I feel that it's time to seriously think about our present position and methods and make drastic correctives.

We shouldn't advertise: we should INFORM. We shouldn't try to sell ourselves: let them come to us, those who need our work.

We shouldn't compete with others: if what we create is really of importance, it will win out by its own force, why waste energy. We should stay away from all commercial, theatrical methods and continue working out and strengthening the cooperative methods and alternative film screening places around the country.

We don't really have such a great need of all those millions of people. Our films are not made with millions of dollars.

The commercial theatrical system has been devised for commercial films ("products"), that is, Hollywood. To want to use that system for our films means to change our films into Hollywood films, which, as a matter of fact, some of us are beginning to do. During the last few months I have been doing a lot of running around, searching for money for the Coop and the Cinematheque, meeting people from all kinds of walks of life and business, and I was amazed how many of our film-makers have been there, at the United Artists and MGM, the Universal, Warners, peddling their scripts, trying to sell themselves.

A film-maker will give his films to a lousy commercial theatre where the prints will be run 50 times a week, where the prints will be completely butchered, and he gets no money—but he still feels that it's a prestige & honor of some kind to have his films shown at a commercial theater...

Something beautiful was started six years ago but we keep wanting to get back into the system.

Our aim should remain to have our own 16 mm showcases in all major cities. I think that with all the energy wasted today in trying to change the existing system, it would be much easier to simply build our own system from scratch and on completely different, non-competitive principles.

This is the end of the Memo.

Jonas

No date, 1967

I keep hearing criticism of the Center and the Coop. Which is O.K., it's just like it should be. What bothers me is the form of the criticism. Oh, they say, look at that or that distributor, look how efficient they are, look how they are pushing that film, look how much they do for a film, look at those full-page ads. Look, they say, I wonder if we'll ever be that strong. And they say it with a sort of tone of envy and a tone of "realism," and nobody can rebuke them, because what they say is true. But what that truth amounts to, it's equivalent to saying: "Oh, look, how corrupt and unscrupulous they are—isn't it a pity we aren't like them?"

Yes, they are pushing films, but they are pushing them like sharks, they are eating each other's throats and they are shoving something down the people's throats. They are pushing their films with no considerations and no scruples. That's where your choice comes in, that's why the Coop was created. If there is no difference in our approaches and our methods, in human quality, from those of the BIG companies—then we better pick up our bags and go home.

August 4, 1967

TYPEWRITERTELEGRAMTOEVO
SUBJECT: POLICE
I AM GETTING TIRED OF READING ATTACKS ON POLICE STOP POLICE ARE PEOPLE LIKE EVERYBODY ELSE STOP POLICE DO BAD CRUEL THINGS AND SO DO WE ALL STOP THE BAD DOINGS OF THE POLICE ARE VISIBLE BUT OUR OWN BAD DOINGS ARE VERY OFTEN HIDDEN STOP WE HAVE TO LOVE POLICE LIKE EVERYTHING ELSE TO CHANGE THEM STOP LET'S END ATTACKING POLICE IN GENERAL STOP IF ANY COP BEATS SOMEBODY LET'S NAME THIS COP BY NAME THIS SPECIFIC COP PERSONALLY STOP CHANGE CAN BE ACHIEVED ONLY ON PERSONAL LEVEL STOP POLICEMEN HAVE NAMES LIKE EVERYBODY ELSE STOP NO HUMAN BEING SHOULD BE GIVEN UP AS HOPELESS THAT'S NOT LOVE'S WAY STOP POLICEMEN ARE ALSO HUMAN SO WE CAN NOT GIVE UP POLICEMEN STOP WE SHOULD HAVE LEARNED THAT MUCH BY NOW ABOUT THE WAYS HUMAN STOP IF YOU HATE A COP YOU ARE WITH THE POWERS OF HATE STOP

August 4, 1967

Breakfast at David Stone's. I am trying to reorganize *Film Culture* publishing aspect, so that we wouldn't be delayed for no great reason. Stopped at Everngam. Picked up a print of *Chumlum* for the Dickinson University. They are establishing a library of avant-garde film, for University study purposes, so I arranged to make one print for them. Strike Coordinating committee 280-3602 called (Columbia University), I need to show some films there, to help the strike, later this week.

Stopped at Tek. Shirley in the middle of shooting a film on Coltrane. They are using the Tek on free days.

Letter from Leonardi. He is touring Germany with his films. "Situation of German Co-ops is pretty mixed up."

Warren Sonbert, telling about Hiler's film, by now mythical—how beautiful it is—and Warren's own new film, which he is editing, trying to reduce one hour of footage to six minutes. He never edited, till now. "It's time that you begin to get interested in sound, also—aren't you getting enough of pop music background?" "I am," he said. "But on the other hand this period that I was in, the films of this period seem to be just that, with the music."

Stopped by the Methodist Church, Peace Center, to see some "political" documentaries. Offered a plan to David and Gottlieb: all "revolutionaries" should invest in stock, go into Wall Street there is no other way. Or hit the businessman where it hurts him: scare the consumer away from stores. Saul [Levine] was sitting on the steps of the church, nursing the wounds he got at Columbia University.

August 8, 1967

Dear David [Stone],
It would be very easy for me, with my kind of nature, to get into arguments with you about every sentence of your letter, about what really matters today—but I have no time for it, and I feel it would be quite useless at this time. All I can do, these days, is to scribble some very personal notes, at the end of the day, and they are too fragmentary, I'm too tired. My interests, my time, and my energies are going somewhere else. For instance, I could not react these past ten days to any of your actions or statements, because to me it was much more important these last two weeks to do everything so that Willard's and Marie's

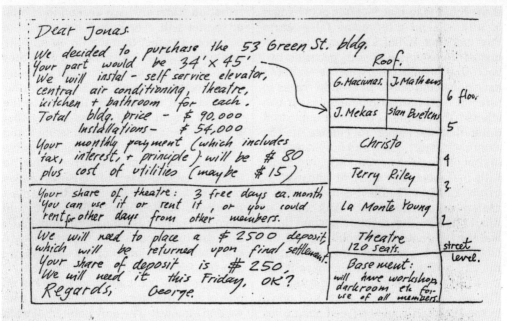

Dear Jonas.
We decided to purchase the 53 Green St. bldg.
Your part would be 34' × 45' —
We will instal - self service elevator,
central air conditioning, theatre,
kitchen + bathroom for each.
Total bldg. price - $90,000
        Installations - $54,000
Your monthly payment (which includes
tax, interest, + principle) will be $80
plus cost of utilities (maybe $15)

Your share of theatre: 3 free days ea. month
You can use it or rent it, or you could
rent for other days from other members.

We will need to place a $2500 deposit,
which will be returned upon final settlement.
Your share of deposit is $250,
We will need it this Friday, OK?
Regards,   George.

Roof.		
G. Maciunas.	J. Mathews	6 floor.
J. Mekas	Stan Bvetens	5
Christo		4
Terry Riley		3
La Monte Young		2
Theatre 120 seats.		street level.
Basement: will have workshop, darkroom etc for use of all members.		

4¢ U.S. POSTAGE

THIS SIDE OF CARD IS FOR ADDRESS

Jonas Mekas
P.O.B. 1499
New York 10001

show could take place—after many years of waiting, and after many false starts. The fact that Willard managed to force himself to complete for this occasion two new films which otherwise he wouldn't have done, and Marie put sound tracks to three of her films and made tapes for two others—this, to me, is the most important thing that happened to cinema in the month of August, 1967, and not Stan's pulling out of the Coop or your own arguments with me about who is right and who is wrong and I can't afford going into such useless arguments. That's why, when to you it's politics that is the important thing, and the international Revolution, and the fact that the Movielab is the richest lab in the city and that we shouldn't give it our work—to me it's more important that the film-makers of the three films tied down by the Movielab would be freed, their films should be freed, and the Co-op should be strengthened so that such things wouldn't happen again, in the future, where labs keep you by the balls because you had to play their commercial games, you had no other alternatives. I am interested in building & strengthening that other alternative, and fuck the Movielab, I didn't give a damn about it. I feel my time will be better spent trying to raise the $500 that the Cinematheque lost on the Maas-Menken retrospective—yes, the Cinematheque lost again, but Cinema gained new works, so I don't regret that we lost $500 and that I'll be running my ass off for the next few weeks trying to get that money somewhere—because such is the state of things of art in this country (as in all the other countries too) and hard work and a few fools like me are needed to keep it going. You see, I have no big principles and it's difficult for me to get involved into your principles, as in those of Stan's—it's all so abstract, so unreal, and so beyond me.

You seem to make a very big point of the fact that you know more about film distribution "than anybody around the Co-op or Center will ever know," but you seem to ignore the fact that the Co-op and the Center are cooperative bodies and they are NOT private businesses and you can't push everybody aside and do just your game even if that game is the best in the world. I would go as far as to say that it's more important to work together and fail, to work in our own unbusinesslike way and make small progress than to follow someone else's big business ideas, patterned on the most competitive, most inhuman business methods around, and become another Big Business and FAIL, because that would be a failure. We are not after Big Business or big success. We are not for becoming a BIG BUSINESS, which you say you know how to do but no one else at the co-op knows, and it's true, we don't know it. The only point is: at what price that knowledge, and to what end? And you may ask: What do we want, then? What kind of distribution center should the Co-op eventually become? And I have to answer: we don't know, I don't know. But I believe that there must be, there is a possibility of a more human, less shark-like way of disseminating works of art, of cinema, and dealing with film-makers, and assuring that they can continue making films—than all the organizations that exist for that purpose today. And it's no use of staying on the outside and criticizing. We all must contribute ideas, and work, and our actions, they must be PURE, and selfless, and nothing to do with COMPETITION, and etc. and etc.—and little by little we can build up something beautiful that works. It has to remain a process, a thing in progress. We must have enough faith to go forwards without any very definite idea in front of us, only a direction where everything, what tomorrow will be, depends on the attitudes (morality) of the actions of today, right here and now. What makes me wonder is why, why, when you see something beautiful beginning to develop, and when some mistake in it hits your eye or your mind: why, instead of coming to help, to help to eliminate that mistake (or misdirection) so that the thing could grow healthier—why do you turn against the ENTIRE thing, instead of the sick part?

Once there lived a farmer. One day, during the season of strong rains, he noticed that there was a hole in the roof and that it was beginning to rain inside. So the farmer took an ax, tore down the house, and started building another house, with no hole in the roof...

So many film-makers, because of a little thing, one or another, some mistreatment, circumstance or mistake, get all angered and upset and begin to demolish the Co-op instead of thinking about the ways of changing such things, so that they wouldn't happen again.

Always mistrusting, even at the Co-op which is owned by nobody, which belongs equally to everybody: even here we find somebody on whom we can put the blame, never on ourselves. Why haven't THEY improved this or that; why haven't THEY done this or that. I have some news for you: THEY may have never thought of that, limited and busy as we all are. So TELL it. YOU ARE THE CO-OP, we all are, goddamn, and we'll either work together or we'll fall together—and you'll be responsible for it, you, Stan, as much as I, Jonas, and you, David, and you. Responsible for everything. That's why I am scribbling this.

RE: CENSORSHIP

It's a fallacy to think that members of the Co-op, the film-makers, or myself, think and feel about, for example, censorship (it could be some other thing) the same way as we (or I) did five years ago. These were busy and important years, and we all grew up a little bit, and learned something. Very important changes took place.

So now it's easy, and not only for you, but also for us, to say: "Oh, the way we handled *Flaming Creatures* wasn't the best way, we made mistakes." The case of *Flaming Creatures* was handled at that time the way it was because we were not ready (and you were not ready) to handle it any other way.

(from an unfinished letter to Stan):

Isn't it a little bit strange that while you seem to be much concerned with the dangers of war and the progression of fascism in this country, that instead of cutting into the roots of it, THOSE WHO ARE IN POWER, you turn all your attacks exactly at those forces or little fledglings that are opposed to the growth of fascism in this country (or anywhere). You attack the most liberating, consciousness expanding parts, the artists, the religious movements, Timothy Leary—the people and the movements which remain the only islands—no matter how imperfect—of anti-war and anti-fascism in this country. You don't turn against Dean Rusk: you turn against the underground film-makers. You don't turn against Hollywood your anger: it's the Underground that's getting the brunt of your anger, not Hollywood. And you play dumb, in your anger when you exclaim: "From what do they want to be FREE, the free love people? Haven't they always been FREE?" What kind of cynicism is this? Do you really mean that?

SCRAPS

..."the men who contracted this disease were exclusively those in whose subconsciousness, for some reason or other, there never arose any impulse of faith in anybody or in anything..."—Gurdjieff, "Beelzebub in America"

we are scrounging only through the remnants of past religions and bits of thinking without any knowledge what to do with it and what to keep and what to drop.

Walking through the streets. Stopping to contemplate scenes which remind me of my childhood. Knowing all the time that there is no way back.

I sat on the steps of the Pentagon and I looked at the grass. That would be nice, I thought, if the day will come, when one will sit on the steps of the Pentagon and will be able to contemplate the grass, and forget the blood.

For PBL film:
"we interrupt this program to remind you to listen if there is no shooting in your ghetto"
"have you been robbed today?"

La Camparaita, tango record

Meher Baba: "An extension of consciousness consists in being conscious of that which was formerly a part of the unconscious."

August 9, 1967

ON COMMUNICATION, EDUCATION, AND ART
(Conference on Education and Training, Americana Hotel, Aug. 9, 1967)

This is a message from the Underground WHAT'S AT.
The other word from the Underground is avant-garde.
I am speaking about the avant-garde of the arts,
I am speaking about those who are in the first lines.
In the first lines of humanity.

We are all there, with our bodies. But we aren't there with our minds and spirit.
The rules of the society in which we grew up and in which we live keep us behind the REAL TIME, behind the PRESENT.
We are behind HERE AND NOW, we are behind the REAL TIME by at least one generation.

The artist, with his finer sensibilities, escapes the feeling, the thinking, and the living patterns of the society.
He doesn't merely reflect the INERT, or the PERSISTING reality—as the popular arts do; he gives us insight into the HERE AND NOW reality, where it's really at.
We have to study the work of our artists, or perhaps it's more correct to say we have to BE with the work of our artists to see not so much what's coming but what's HERE ALREADY.
And to see it seems to be there ourselves.
Content of all art is our BEING.
Our Being in progress.
A constant upsetting of our status quo.

But it's here that the society and all its education and communication institutions fail.
It's this that is the most neglected area today: the being exposed to, and the understanding of the deeper meanings of art.
We look at the works of art but we can't READ them.
All our talks about the education and art are reduced to the discussion of tools, of media, how to produce more of it. That is, the physical aspect of art.
We look at a film and we completely fail to READ the message and the knowledge that the artist locked into it, be it a poetic work like Brakhage's 23rd Psalm Branch, or a realist work like Troublemakers.
Sometimes we ban the works of art by force, as we did with Flaming Creatures, one of the most poetic works of art of our generation.
We do everything to remain with the superficial, second-rate knowledge, second-hand experience.
In our media, with the help of the huge promotion and publicity and advertising

CLOSING STATEMENT

CECILE K. MILLER TO FLUXHOUSE CO-
OPERATIVE II, INC. -- Purchase of
Premises located at 80-82 Wooster
Street, New York, New York

Place: Offices of Wein, Lane, Klein & Malkin, 60
            East 42nd Street, New York, New York.

Time: August 9, 1967 at 10 A.M.

Present: Cecile K. Miller, Seller.

            William Miller, adviser to the Seller.

            John Loehr, Esq. of Wein, Lane, Klein &
            Malkin, attorneys for the Seller.

            George Maciunas, President of Fluxhouse
            Cooperative II, Inc., Purchaser.

            David Antin, Secretary of Fluxhouse Co-
            operative II, Inc., Purchaser.

            Arthur M. Siskind, Esq. of Squadron &
            Plesent, attorneys for the Purchaser.

            Arthur Hull of the Title Guarantee Company,
            title closer.

            Joseph H. Woolwich of Helmsley Spear, Inc.,
            broker.

            Lee Schoenfeld of Don Liebermann Organi-
            zation, broker.

1.   The Seller delivered to the Purchaser a
Bargain and Sale Deed, with Covenants Against Grantor's
Acts, dated August 9, 1967, conveying title to the Pur-
chaser of a parcel of land and building located at 80-82
Wooster Street, New York, New York. The Deed was delivered
to Mr. Hull for recording, and return thereafter to
Squadron & Plesent.

2.   The following adjustments were made and
credited to the Purchaser:

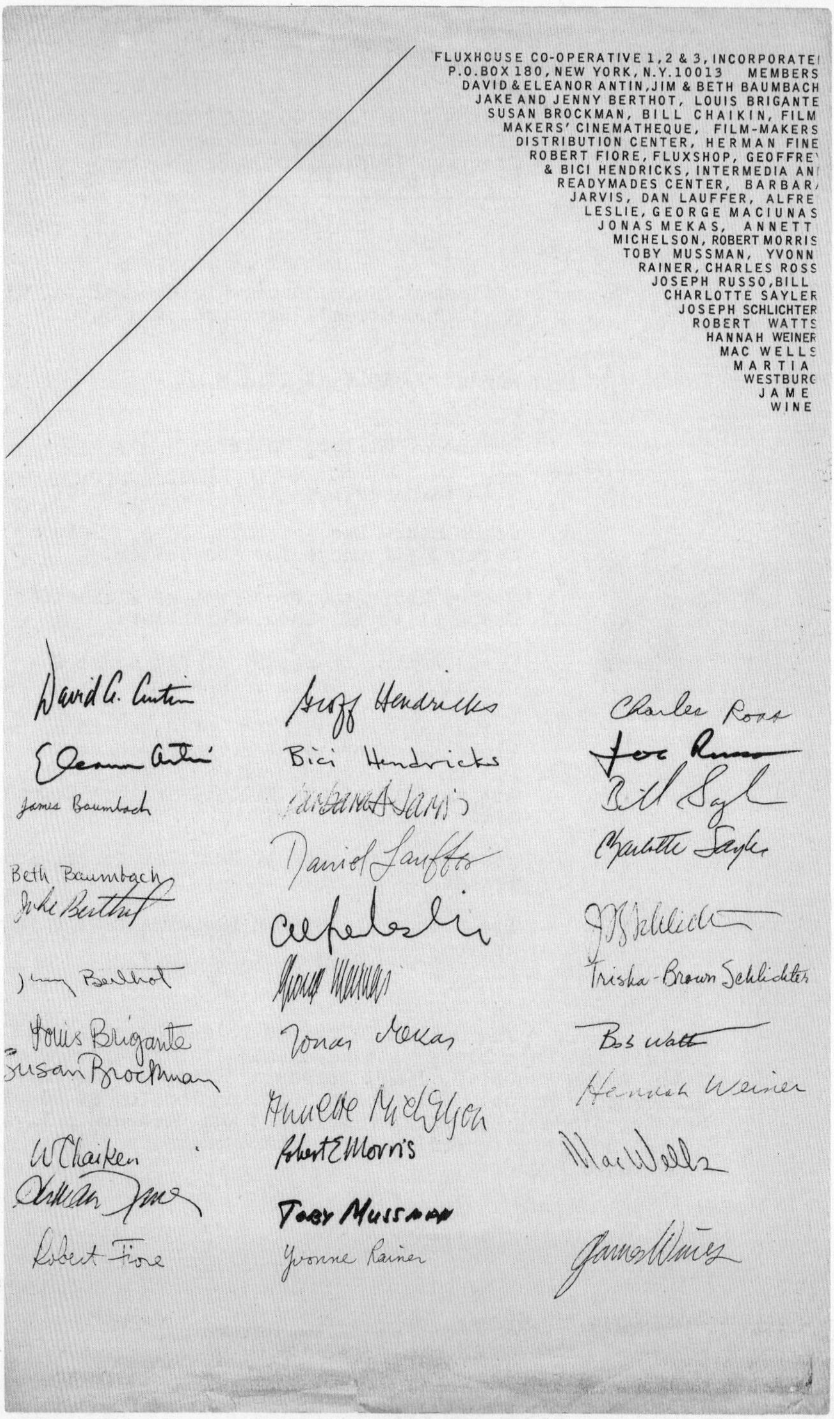

David C. Antin

Eleanor Antin

James Baumbach

Beth Baumbach

Jake Berthot

Jenny Berthot

Louis Brigante

Susan Brockman

W Chaiken

Robert Fiore

Geoff Hendricks

Bici Hendricks

Barbara Jarvis

Daniel Lauffer

Alfred Leslie

George Maciunas

Jonas Mekas

Annette Michelson

Robert E. Morris

Toby Mussman

Yvonne Rainer

Charles Ross

Joe Russo

Bill Sayler

Charlotte Sayler

J. Schlichter

Triska-Brown Schlichter

Bob Watt

Hannah Weiner

Mac Wells

James Wines

machinery, we keep rehashing the second-rate experiences.

But the message from the Underground is this:

MAN CANNOT LIVE BY MELODRAMA ALONE.

The sad thing is—he lives, or he thinks he lives.

A huge gap has developed between art and society.

Art is completely useless in the contemporary society.

It's so useless, we are so blind to its meanings and doings that even our artists find a pleasure in describing themselves as "useless" artists—not to make a paradoxical point, but to express their true attitude. We say that Stalin's Russia condemned modern art as escapist and backed only the social realism.

In America today, we tolerate modern art but we ban it by our ignorance of it.

Not that we do it according to a conscious plan: it's our way of life, it's the whole way of thinking. It's the whole attitude to art that has gone wrong. Art is not part of our life. No art classes in schools!

When I am talking about art, about the art of cinema, I am not talking about the Hollywood cinema or the European art film. I am not even talking about those marginal works or aspects of works which you know today as Underground Cinema.

I am talking about the art of Stan Brakhage, of Gregory Markopoulos, of Robert Breer, of Marie Menken, of Kenneth Anger, of Bruce Baillie, of Peter Kubelka, of Jack Smith, and I am talking of Dreyer's art.

I am not talking about that cinema which comes out of, and reflects only the temporary preoccupations and obsessions of the society.

I am talking about that cinema which comes from the deeper streams of our intuitions and which is not merely a reflection of WHAT IS but which keeps alive the subtlest ideals of man, the art which keeps alive the dream of Eden.

The worst thing is not that we have been driven out of Paradise but that we have lost our memories of Paradise.

We have to proceed to immediately correct this.

The millions that we spend on all kinds of conferences and analyses produce nothing but more of the same.

We have to create special bodies, organizations and foundations to completely re-orient the society concerning the interpretation of art, the meaning of art, the attitude to art. We have to bring back art classes to schools.

We have to reestablish the supremacy of man's spirit over the matter, over the tools, over the means, over the media so that the media could really be media, because not all is medium that looks like medium and not all that sounds like a message is a message.

For instance, this is not exactly a message that I am reading…

It's a warning…

Medium is a message. But not all messages are food for man. A green landscape, to look at a green patch on 8th Avenue and 25th Street is much more nurturing for man's spirit than all the transmissions on all the media in New York City on August 9th, 1967.

We live surrounded by garbage and our own ashes.

And the only station in which the important message is clicking is not on our way. We'll never arrive there, the way we are going.

I'll tell you a secret, why:

some fool has pulled the railroad switch and we are on the wrong tracks. We have been derailed! Ha Ha Ha!

To get back on the right track we have to do the following:

a) to stop the train

b) to go way way back

or c) to go across plenty of uncultivated fields.

But since nobody knows any more how to stop the train, we'll have to jump out of the running train, some of us, even at the danger of breaking a bone or two.

(from a note to Peter, never completed, not mailed)
The policy that the Co-op shouldn't reject ANY film or ANY film-maker—this, when I was only working it out, five years ago, wasn't introduced as the Co-op's way to protect bad films. No. Bad films need no protection within any set-up. You have to remember, that it was Stan's *Anticipation of the Night* that was rejected by "highly" selective taste of Cinema 16, and not just any bad film. And it was this case, the case of the *Anticipation*, that made it clear to me, at that time, that we have 1) to create our own distribution center, and 2) that the decision which films to include or to exclude in such a distribution center can never be entrusted to anybody. Didn't we all trust Amos? or Parker Tyler? But how long did it last? Art changes, tastes change: "critics" do not... We can trust no organization to act as a critic (selector) of art works. It's therefore, for the protection of the GOOD films, that the decision was made not to reject any film. Bad films will come and go and will disappear, but works of quality will remain—as long as they are not dumped into the toilet when merely born, by the distributors. You know what they told me in Vienna, the young film-makers there? They said: "Oh, you are distributing Peter's films? We wish you'd reject him, then he'd know how we felt when he was rejecting all of us. He is an enemy of cinema." That's what they were telling me.

(from a letter to Stan):
It was one thing to say to Shirley, "You are not an artist," as you said to her when you were at her home last time; and again another thing was the attitude, the tone of your voice, the way you said it. We all know that some films are not "art" (or are "lesser" art); some paintings are not art—most of them aren't very good art; but it comes to why, WHY we decide, and when, for what reasons, to pronounce, suddenly, that they are not art, that somebody is not an artist, what point we are making. And the point you were making to Shirley was black, your reasons were ANGER, and they hurt Shirley, and you had no right to do so, you had no right to hurt Shirley, because it makes no difference how you hurt one. You hurt her for no reason at all, for your own "aesthetic" pleasure. It did not do any good to the art of cinema or to the humanity but I know that it did something bad: there was some black energy produced, it hurt somebody, and I am not the one who insists that one should never criticize a work or that one should never tell the truth. It comes always down to the reasons, to how you say it, and the context. And I know it was a sheer blindness, you falling to pieces in New York that time that made you lose all perspective and proportions and sense. You were INSENSITIVE to Shirley as a human being. Now, from your letters, it sounds that you are PURE REASON, that you are reasoning something out, very clearly—but I don't think it's REASON because the tone of your letters is full of bitterness and anger against everything and everybody that isn't "clean," there is no clear thinking there and there is no reason in your letters. Last letter, as a matter of fact, was full of pins and thorns, your tone had them, and they were not directed towards you: they were directed towards others, those were not thorns of the cross: these were thorns that you were giving a birth to, like the voodoo pins— voodoo pins into the Co-op, voodoo pins into the dummy of the Co-op (a dummy because your image of the Co-op is not real, your image of the Cinematheque is a distortion—still, they serve the same purpose

as the dolls serve the voodoo magicians): some will take them for real and the destruction will start its work, breaking through into the Co-op blood vessels.

August 14, 1967

Dear Peter and Minnie:
Here I am, back in New York. It's drizzling. Sort of grey. And only now I realize how much I got during these two days in Newport. I can walk now along this greyness and keep sort of smiling, inside. The sun is inside, bits of sun that I caught in Newport where there was no sun, but it was shining anyway. There was something good that happened, and that made all things shine. You were too busy with the wedding to care about anything else, but there was something else anyway. Your wedding —despite what you may think about the people, the hundreds of people who were at the wedding—no matter what you said into the ear of your tape recorder—there was something happy about your wedding.

August 23, 1967

Co-op cannot engage itself in politics or aesthetics. It's a booking center, it doesn't program, curate, it doesn't advise. It's Stan who is introducing, or who wants to introduce politics and aesthetics into the Co-op by his proposal (as does Peter) to make the Co-op into a selective distribution center, to keep certain film-makers out. In truth, this would mean giving in to very narrow politics. For in its essence, every work, and every act of man (no matter of its aesthetic qualities) is political anyway.

August 26, 1967

I have to put down some notes on the subject of Shirley. I have to do so because it's going too far. Poor Shirley, she is taking it bravely, and even with humor, all the blame and even dirt—but she shouldn't really, she shouldn't. It's people's stupidity that she is trying to take, patiently. She lost patience only once, three weeks ago, at the directors meeting, when Willard walked in and started cursing her. She started trembling and walked out into the other room without saying anything. But she came back, 10 minutes later. What the stupid people are saying, is that Shirley is guilty for the 41st St. theater becoming "commercial," that Shirley has "private "interests" to defend the 41st St. theater. You see, we are the avant-garde artists! Shirley is a "commercial" artist, a commercial film-maker... Stan said it, last time he was in New York, he said it right there, in Shirley's place and in presence of at least 10 people: "Shirley, your films have nothing to do with film art," or something to that effect. Which Shirley swallowed, and so did we all. There was no arguing. But now this is going too far, when this is being repeated and repeated in new variations.

Not that Shirley's films are being attacked here, *The Connection*, or *Portrait of Jason*; I wonder if Stan has even seen them, as a matter of fact. What's being attacked here is the narrative Cinema. Which is such a nonsense that I, whose life began in literature and who knows what prose and what poetry is, I have to protest this stupidity and have to do something to stop it. I have seen too often in my life the poets condemning the prose writers, this is taken as a good, traditional joke, a humorous fight. That makes the attitude of Peter and Stan look still more provincial. I am a poet, therefore poetry must be the only valid form and no other form of cinema has any value... Which is chopping out, with the knife of human vanity and stupidity, huge chunks of man's existence, man's experience, because the laws of life are such that to grow harmoniously to a greater perfection, all the centers of man must move forward equally, and that's why we all have all the different arts, and that's why we have all the different genres and

Monday   either at the   Gideon Bachma
Ellen: co-op or at   Dracula n U of
         your house   Film 28.66 +1

1. Ellen or Louise or both: The "contributors"
   mailing (materials in "Louise: Look in" Box)

2. Pick up from Filmtronics originals of "Diaries"
   (NOT THE PRINT, which will be ready only
   tomorrow) — this is for latish P.M.

3. iF Na   Naomi Levine calls for me, inform f her that her "originals"
   will be here late today or tomorrow mmmm •[Do Not Mention Filmtronics pickup !]

4.   make four copies of each of the new Voice column pages

5.   the "enclosed"( ) manuscr pt by Kelman should be xeroxed, one copy
      (this week)
6.   I'll be back here at 3PM

7.   Payments to you: I hope by thxxm the second half of this week to catch up
      with the avordrawn account. so mmmmmm you'll be paid by the end of this
      week for the first stretch.   Box 4191
                                                               Naivobi
8.   Call JU-28930 and talk to anybody xxxyxxxx, for me, find out what's the
      current address of PETER BEARD   kenya
              find out: can one get the new B.Dylan record wrapped for air-mailing   africa
              to send to Africa -- (that's where P.Beard is, somewhere) -- I'll
              leave money tomorrow for the record amdm -- but don't mail it yet

9.   I have to INCREASE the strictness of my life routine if I want to finish
      my film. I'll be here at the "office" only between 8:30 A M-10AM
      Chxxmmx At Chelsea I don't answer calls, they take only messages
      As your involvement in my "business" becomes greater, we'll have to set
      up early meaatings at the Chealse, on your way here, or something
      like that -- to review the day's progress   letterheads
                                                        brown envelopes

10. George Maciunas, Cinematheque's "designer" "artist" etc etc -- is printing
     all kinds of materials mnhmmmmmm for sending with the Foundation letter.
     Check mmmmmmim with him (925-0274) about the progress of printing, he knows
     it's urgent, and get them leaflets here when they are ready   This Wk

11. Richard Foreman SC-41581 is familiar with all our money raising compains
     and the Foundation Book (he got it for us) and he will be working with you
     on this specific, foundation project -- meet with him (he comes often to
     the coop) and see what advise he has for you on this project

12.
      Mail the letters

During a weekend I spent with Minnie and Peter Beard in Newport, Peter thought I should try for an hour or two to pretend I was a dog. I tried. I tell you, those were two very hard hours. It was especially hard to keep up with chasing the cars!

Nairobi, a frequent haunt of his, where Minnie Cushing and the other members of her safari had gathered for the traditional farewell dinner, and since her return to Africa the following winter, the two had been together for seven months. Now that they were finally back in the fold, marriage seemed inevitable, at least according to one of Peter Beard's current versions: "We never went through tacky proposals or anything like that. Everyone just assumed it was going to take place and of course we were both perfectly chuffed to go along with it. It was all part of the milk-fed lava flow of molasses down the avenue of life and we just followed the flow."

The milk-fed lava flow of molasses led to the misty afternoon of August 12th, when a small motorcade with police escort pulled up before the crowd that had assembled in front of Newport's historic Trinity Church and the bride, wearing a long, white organdy dress, entered the church with her family. Canon Lockett F. Ballard presided over the ceremony and within seven minutes had pronounced the couple man and wife. Afterward, the wedding party adjourned to the Cushing family estate, where the bride and groom stood side by side to receive the congratulations of their 416 guests, fed each other the first slice of cake to unanimous applause, and awaited the musical flourish of Peter Duchin's orchestra that would herald their solitary turn on the dance floor.

It was an impeccable enactment of the ritual except perhaps for the fact that the groom, who had asked his friend, avant-garde filmmaker Jonas Mekas, to record the event, was busily engaged in supervising the production, directing scenes and wandering through the crowd eliciting ironic comments for the soundtrack. When the moment came for him to dance with his bride, nobody could find him. He was later discovered out on the rocks in conference with Jonas Mekas, devising a plan to induce the bride to dive with him into the sea so that the film would climax with them swimming toward the horizon. "I'd never been in a wedding before," Minnie Cushing said later with an ingenuous smile, "but I felt a sense of obligation to what was supposed to happen." This, presumably, did not include plunging into the sea in your wedding gown, or having your husband disappear at the moment when everyone was waiting to see you dance with him, nor did it include his telling you, after all the Polaroids he'd taken at the wedding came out black, that it must be some sort of sign.

The couple had planned the next two years of their future together. After a short vacation in the Bahamas, they would cross the Atlantic on the Queen Mary's final voyage, spend some time in England and France, and then go on to Kenya where they'd first met and where they intended to make their home on a forty-nine-acre stretch of property in

Rolling Stone, Nov. 16, 1978

Press clipping on filming Peter Beard's wedding, August 1967, *Rolling Stone*, November 16, 1978.

From: THE FILM-MAKERS' CINEMATHEQUE
FILM-MAKERS' DISTRIBUTION CENTER
FILM-MAKERS' COOPERATIVE

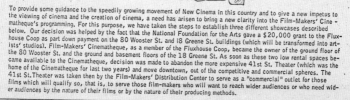

August 20th, 1967

To: ALL FRIENDS OF CINEMA

To provide some guidance to the speedily growing movement of New Cinema in this country and to give a new impetus to the viewing of cinema and the creation of cinema, a need has arisen to bring a new clarity into the Film-Makers' Cinematheque's programming. For this purpose, we have taken the steps to establish three different showcases described below. Our decision was helped by the fact that the National Foundation for the Arts gave a $20,000 grant to the Fluxhouse Coop as part down payment on the 80 Wooster St. and 18 Greene St. buildings (which will be transformed into artists' studios). Film-Makers' Cinematheque, as a member of the Fluxhouse Coop, became the owner of the ground floor of the 80 Wooster St. and the ground and basement floors of the 18 Greene St. As soon as these two low rental spaces became available to the Cinematheque, decision was made to abandon the more expensive 41st St. Theater (which was the home of the Cinematheque for last two years) and move downtown, out of the competitive and commercial spheres. The 41st St. Theater was taken then by the Film-Makers' Distribution Center to serve as a "commercial" outlet for those films which will qualify so, that is, to serve those film-makers who will want to reach wider audiences or who need wider audiences by the nature of their films or by the nature of their producing methods.

FILM-MAKERS' DISTRIBUTION CENTER	FILM-MAKERS' CINEMATHEQUE	
41st ST. THEATER During the month of September the 41st St. Theater will be transformed into a regular First Run moviehouse. Because of its low (when compared with other arthouses) cost, it will, finally, fill the long overdue need of a first run showcase for the independently made features. The theater will be owned and programmed by the Film-Makers' Distribution Center. It will be used to premiere or simply run all those films or programs of films which have a need of wider audiences, be it by the nature of their content or their producing methods. The Theater will open on October 1st with the premiere of Shirley Clarke's new film, "The Portrait of Jason."	**CINEMATHEQUE I (80 WOOSTER ST.)** This will be our experimental showcase open to anyone who has a film or a mixed media show, happenings, events, etc. with no strict "quality" control over the programming. The audiences will have to take chances with new artists and with new works of established artists. This will be our workshop, our testing ground where anything goes. It will premiere all new Coop works. Cinematheque I will open September 30th with the First Annual N.Y. Film-Makers' Ball which will inaugurate one month Festival of New Cinema and Events.	**CINEMATHEQUE II (18 GREENE ST.)** In a sense, Cinematheque II will be our Academy. The films at the Cinematheque II will be carefully selected. Although the emphasis will be on the Avantgarde cinema, other classics of cinema will not be excluded. This will be a place of CINEMA. This will be the first Repertory Cinema Theater. The programs will be designed so that during a period of one year a film student would have a chance to see the best that there is in cinema. Every addition to the repertory will be carefully considered. The 18 Greene St. building will also house the Millenium Film Workshop, the Cinematheque Archives, the Film-Makers' Coop archives, lecture rooms and private film viewing rooms for film students, visiting University film teachers, and others.

To put all three showcases into working conditions we need your immediate assistance. This is what's needed:

41st ST. THEATER $12,000 is needed for putting proper projection, the marquee on 42nd St., the entrance to the theater from the 42nd St., to change the lobby, to put in new seats, to paint the theater. After this work is done, theater will be able to operate on approximately $1500-$1800 weekly expense (as against the $2500 weekly rental of the lowest price theater available today to the film-maker in midtown area).	**CINEMATHEQUE I (WOOSTER ST)** Total of $16,000 is needed before October 1st. Expenses are devided as follows: Clean-up, painting -- $500; electricity -- $700; seats -- $600; plumbing, bathrooms, toilets -- $1500; front of building -- $400; flooring of theater -$3500; projection room $1700; projection and sound equipment -- $4000; down payment on the building (needed by September 1st) -- $3280. Monthly rent will be $250.	**CINEMATHEQUE II (GREENE ST.)** Total of $16,000 is needed before November 1st. (The breakdown of expenses is similar to that of Cinematheque I). The down payment on the space is $3050 and is due on September 15th. Additional $5000 will be needed to put the workshops and lecture rooms in shape. Monthly rent will be $250.

ASSISTANCE CAN BE GIVEN IN THE FOLLOWING WAYS:

a) donations -- written to Film-Makers' Cinematheque (tax deductible)
b) loans -- to the Film-Makers' Cinematheque for the Cinematheques I & II, and to the Film-Makers' Distribution Center for the 41st St. Theater.
c) co-signing bank loans with the Film-Makers' Distribution Center (which has by now a good standing with the banks but not quite enough to take loans for the amounts needed to bring all three showcases into existence).
d) there may be other ways we haven't thought of.

FILM-MAKERS' CINEMATHEQUE, G.P.O., BOX 1601, NEW ... , N.Y.
FILM-MAKERS' DISTRIBUTION CENTER, 175 LEXINGT... YORK, N.Y.

**Fundraising for the Film-Makers',
August 1967.**

ESTIMATED MATERIAL AND LABOR COST FOR 80 WOOSTER ST.

		Material cost	Labor cost	Our labor
SCHEDULED FOR AUGUST				
Clean up and wrecking and removal:	industrial vacuum	$ 50.		)
	wrecking			) 1 man week
	removal	30		
Scaffold		35		1 man day
Electrical wiring:	1000' 30amp wire	160		
	2500' no.14 wire	100		
	1/2" conduit, 500'	35		
	1.25" conduit, 500'	130		20 man days
	reducers, connectors, etc.	100		
	80 outlet fixtures	100		
	80 switches	30		
240 seats (4 seat benches)	steel frames, 120	120		
	wood seats & backs	480		2 man days
Plumbing	Public toilets:			
	8 w.c., 3 urinals, 4 sinks	300 (Sears)	1000	
*	6 bathrooms (1 per floor)	600 ,,	2000	
*	new plumbing system	1000	2000	
Painting:	sprayer (compressor & gun)	100		3 man days
	white enamel 20 gal.	80		
Front of building, entry:	new door & photo laminate	60		
	window panels (photo lam.)	300		
	TOTAL FOR AUGUST:	8810 (5600 available from Fluxhouse		
		3210 needed by Cinematheque		
SCHEDULED FOR SEPT.				
Electrical AC main wiring:	*1000 amp. AC from street			
	*100 amp. per floor,	2000 (mtl. & labor)		
	*200 amp. ground floor			
Flooring for theatre (alternatives)	8x8 asphalt block	2000	3500	
3500 sq.ft.	abrasive ceramic tile	2000	2600	
	glazed brick	3500	3500	
	terra cotta tile	5000	3000	
	terrazzo	2000	3500	
	wood gym floor	2500	3000	
	seamless plastic (Sancoura)	4000 (mtl. & labor)		
Mezzanine floor 600 sq.ft.	precast conc. slabs	1200		
for projection and control booth	block partitions	300		
	extra stair	200		
bathroom and toilet partitions	* wood studs and dry bd.	800	800	
(wd.stud, careamic wall & floor)	* 8 doors	400	400	
4000 sq.ft. partitions	*ceramic tile 3000 sq.ft.	1500	2300	
3000 sq.ft. tile (wall & floor)	**TOTAL FOR SEPT.**	9900 (4400 available from Fluxhouse		
		4500 needed by Cinematheque		

* for items marked with (*) Fluxhouse coop. has the following amounts:

For plumbing:	5600
For electrical:	2000
For partitions:	2400
TOTAL	10000

80
45
480
320
36 10

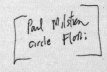

Paul Milstein
circle Floti:

forms and styles—we have this amazing variety. And I am not saying that they are all equally important to all men at the same time. No. It all depends on where we are, each of us, and our growth, at this moment, and what nourishment we need. It's therefore that it's evil to cut other people's food, at this moment—other people's films—when that is the only thing they need at this moment on their way to another step.

There is also this "commercial" crap, this terminology game. "Commercial," "theatrical," as opposed to "non-commercial," to "nontheatrical." Which is only a game. To call commercial anything that in number of heads or seats surpasses your usual expectations, to count only the audience of say 100 as the "art" audience, is nothing but snobbishness. A theater, located on 41st St., is commerce, we say, because it's not a crummy loft. What kind of thinking goes into this, I have no idea. Films can be equally exploited "commercially" on the university campuses as in the so-called "commercial" theaters. And I have seen films treated with love by many commercial theater owners and I have seen films butchered in many universities.

Even I have to blame myself for giving in, occasionally, to Stan's idea of the "select few." But I am regaining my balance. I cannot abandon my intuitions and wisdom in place of rationalizations that come from some kind of pompous stance that's crying for attention: "look here, look here, I am an artist!" Because I know that a true artist is so much above the rest of his contemporaries, in his work, as in his humility, he doesn't have to do so. He doesn't have to step on the others, or kick the others away by force. If you are the light, you shine no matter where you are.

August 27, 1967

Another Co-op meeting. With all the bad prophets pulling now to one and now to another direction. All the energies wasted! Everything is bad. Don't do this, don't do that. All these negative attitudes, these egos, mistrust. We think we are really realistic, we call this negativism realism, that's how low we have fallen! Now, they say, the location [80 Wooster St.] for the new Cinematheque is bad; the theater is terrible; it will never work; you'll never get the money; they will close you up. Et cetera et cetera. Thus, from Colorado to New York. The mentality that I'm facing now every day, and much of this is reflected in Stan's letters and Peter's critiques, is that you can't move into something until that something is ready, until the conditions are ready for us there. But it's artists who create conditions. We are the frontiersmen, we can change things, we can create conditions. By moving the Cinematheque downtown, to Wooster Street, we are automatically creating an entirely new borough, the South Village. No manufacturer, no businessmen can do that. Art can.

In any case, I am tired. I was walking with Amy, down to 23rd St., and I said I need all the strength I can get, tomorrow, so I'll just walk for an hour and I'll let the wind blow out all these wrong energies that got into me during the meeting, all those negative attitudes. I need a good windy cleanup job.

Unless the United States becomes a socialist dictatorship country, I don't see any other way that the dissemination of films can take in the future but that, which has already been established by the tradition in painting, literature, or music. I don't see where cinema differs, in that respect, from the other arts. It will develop its own natural (and unnatural) selection, and with the distortions and academies. A sort of Darwinian law of the arts. Like, how do you go about getting a book published or buying a book? We trust certain critics and certain publishers. And it always comes down to the authors, to the individual authors, it simmers down. Many books that we buy we throw out. We stick to the few (not so few, sometimes—even Stan's shelves are bulging with books). We can't even trust the histories of literature. We have to recheck the classics and we have to recheck the discards, too, and we sometimes come up with revelations, rediscoveries. We can establish for cinema, and we are going to establish them anyway, academies, and it will keep high standards for a generation, and then they will be taken over by academics or by idiots or fools and they will discard our classics and they will stuff our Academies with junk. That has always happened. So that one is left to one's own choice, on the very end.

With the new methods of film dissemination and reproduction coming closer and closer, with films sold like books and like records and screened in our homes, new ways of distribution will develop naturally and inevitably. There will be private salesmen, there will be co-ops, there will be many other ways.

Stan puts himself in the role of a prophet, but that stance is totally unnecessary. Because such are the laws of life that things grow and change, no prophecy is needed here. The role of the co-ops will change, as the home movie library situation grows. Even if the co-ops would end today, they would have done their job anyway. However, we can go to the next stage also and do the job there too. We'll be changing with the changing technology of cinema, of reproduction. We cannot make rules going by the standards of a primitive technology that we have today. All this will change soon, the cinema will become part of every home, and the co-op is only one stage of that development. There will be at least something beautiful about this transition period, some ideal. The transition from the commerce to the home didn't happen in a jump and by itself: in between there had to be this underground cinema, this cooperative period, a human touch, disorganized as it may be, some human element, some ideal involved that made this transition into something warmer than what it could have been. We had to do it, or someone did it thru us, some angel. And only a bad pig eats its own offspring. You spit at the past without which you wouldn't be where you are.

I begin to see that Stan has missed the point and the humor of all my references to the establishment and art with the capital A. I have no enemy. Co-op has no enemy. It's all play of words and paradoxes. We say that we are anti-art in order to make others aware that what's called Art today (in schools, etc.) has really very little to do with what art really is or could be. By doing so we (I) do not deny art: by doing so we assert art.

Willard stopped by briefly at the Co-op today and got angry and wrote more curses on the wall next to Andy's name, and next to Gregory's name. After everybody left for home, late at night, Storm and Shirley got some colored pencils and began drawing flowers to cover the curses. They worked hard, for Willard wrote it in big splashy letters. They covered the curses with flowers and the wall looked again happy.

Somebody has to atone for the evil and foolishness of others—so the world won't catapult into insanity.

It was a long, rambling directors' meeting and everybody left, the place is full of smoke and cigarette butts and empty coffee cups. It's 9 o'clock. Only Louis is still behind his table, and his eternal cigarette (unlit) hanging down his jaw. He looks quite unperturbed. Later at the Charlies, Shirley speculated about what keeps him so undisturbed in all this bustle and heckling. "It must be the gravity of his body, the weight of his body. "

RE: 80 WOOSTER STREET

If the Cinematheque will ever open, it will be thanks to St. Teresa who raised all the money, sometimes in most ingenious and unpredictable ways—such patience, despite all our foolishness. No matter what, I know that by Friday the bills will be covered, money came very last minute, like that Pacific Railroad train, in the movies—she is the hardest worker. Then, Richard [Foreman], who undertook the work, and stuck with it, who ripped off the plaster from the walls, all black, and dusty, and dirty, dragging junk out of the place, and looking after all the workers, and keeping all under control, somehow, through all the disasters of money and labor—who decided, with Barbara, and Amy, three months ago, that they will devote one year of their lives, to this cause, to create the new home for all of us—and stuck to their promise. And Louis who endorsed our most hopeless efforts with his silence. And Shirley, who sat with me through all the coffee cups, through many money huntings, rambles, senseless conversations with business people, for money—making those calls and taking all kinds of crap thrown at us. And poor Louise, trying to maneuver all those bank books, loans, and bouncing checks, and overdrawn accounts, trying to put together all the ends that do not stick together no matter what you do. And George, laying now sick with the 104° temperature, after one million trips to the building department, never giving up, and still keeping a smile.

"I'm not saying that such prophecies always just fulfill themselves, because that would be a manifest absurdity. But what I'm saying is that your own beliefs about the outcome of any social situation of which you are a part, are a factor in the outcome." S. I. Hayakawa, *Contact*, vol. 1

REVISIONS OF STAN VANDERBEEK

Attended session at the international Congress on Religion, Architecture and the Visual Arts. McLuhan had to be there too, but he didn't show up. Stan Vanderbeek showed up and gave one of his usual visionary talks and then proceeded with the *Panels For the Walls of the World* show which surrounded the Congress with multitude of images. Images on the ceiling, images on the walls, images on the people. I have seen the panels a number of times before, in various different places and in many different versions. One thing bothered me, suddenly, this time. And I'll tell you why.

Stan insists that what he's doing is "information gathering," "information feeding," "information explosion." I wonder what the word "explosion" means, in this case. This barrage of images, this mixture of movie clips, newsreel footage, and freshly filmed field, sky and city images, instead of becoming information which we are supposed to absorb instantaneously and simultaneously and which is supposed to make us much more knowledgeable, does the exact opposite: it devalues all information, it transforms all images into meaningless and senseless patterns. All images become part of the huge wallpaper—Stan's title, Panels for the Walls, is aptly chosen. In other words, "information" truly explodes into grains of light.

One could reason, that this is the true way of learning: first you wipe everything out. But I wonder if Stan means what I mean. He keeps talking and writing about the technology which will enable us to store all the existing images and will re-create them by pushing a button. And surely, that will come. We know that there can be vocabularies of images as there are vocabularies of words. The schoolteacher even today can produce for his pupils any picture, any tree, any fish, any flower. But what are we going to learn from a random barrage of images, à la Stan's own *Dome*? Historically, Stan Vanderbeek's work (and the work of others working in that direction) is just where it has to be. It's part of our effort, at this time in history, to free ourselves from all past meanings given to the things we see, to the thoughts we think, to the emotion we feel—so that we could have another fresh look or try at it all. So we have this leveling and this reevaluation. But that's also why I'm beginning to feel fidgety during Stan's (and similar others) shows (or, often, reading the underground newspapers): it was all good and worthy and necessary and, as a matter of fact, inevitable till now. These were the first steps we had to take. But to keep repeating the first steps from now on will mean that we are stuck where we are and we are not able to go further into where the next step of our work is, whatever that work is.

One thing that is preventing us from getting out into the clear is that we are still stuck on Buddhism, many of us. It would be a mistake to look at all the current excursions into Buddhism as anything but transitory rechecking of the past. Man cannot go back, man cannot stay for very long in past religions or past schools of thought. One has to come back to one's own time and do the job here and now, hippie or no hippie—unless somewhere on the road one becomes a spiritual megalomaniac concerned only with one's own "salvation," which is a sure way to go to hell. The same applies to image megalomaniacs.

September 4, 1967

RE: ESTABLISHMENT

A little more on the "establishment" theme. Now, they tell us, we are the establishment. This is just another trick to kill us. We are not the establishment! The real establishment is as strong as ever. They call us establishment to deceive us, to lead us to imagining that we have power, that we can influence the life of our country. It is not quite so! But there is some truth in it: we are beginning to be an influence. That's why they want us to die at this beginning because the establishment, the real establishment has eyes and sees danger even in our beginnings.

We ourselves are fooled by it. Fooled by the little bit of visibility. As if our films screened in three or four theaters is a big deal. As if we were really reaching the people that we should be reaching. Even Stan writes now that the Co-op has become a big business. The reality is that we haven't even done one thousandth of what we should be really doing. The art of cinema, and really it's the same for any art—is still an unwanted thing in this country as it is in other countries. The industry is still in all its power. And we are still struggling, lonely and powerless. So why do you, Stan, think that we are that big when we are practically nothing. We are only a small island of people who decided to work together without competing with each other. No doubt we make mistakes, we are often dragged into ways of business talks—it's hard, so hard to resist it when it's practically the air we breathe— we are still in the midst of the wolf society. Let us not be fooled by the sweet songs of Establishment or those who have dreams of becoming Establishment.

September 18, 1967

I went to see *Bonnie and Clyde*, came back two hours later to the Center, and Shirley and Barbara were still talking. "You are still here?" I said. "Yes, we are discussing the FUGS film," said Shirley. "Everything is fine, the only thing is we can't figure out the God problem. Where do you start? How do you get to God?" "I don't know," I said, "maybe you should drop everything. You can't get to God. You can only search for him. He either comes or he doesn't." We were standing in the street, the three of us, and they were still talking about

16 Greene Street building was the first
building in Soho that George Maciunas
was negotiating to purchase, as Fluxhouse I. 80 Wooster Street, the purchase
of which he was also negotiating,
was designated as Fluxhouse II. But the
16 Greene Street deal fell through. It's
thus that 80 Wooster Street became the
first Soho cooperative building established by Maciunas. In the photo above,
I am being filmed by Bachmann's TV
crew. My plan was to open Cinematheque
II in that building.

Stan Vanderbeek and Prof. Gerald O'Grady.

**I SEEM TO LIVE, VOL. 1
CHAPTER TWENTY ONE**

God. Waiting for taxi. Shirley said, "There were days when I used to scream in my room, alone, bad days, and I used to shout: Come, God!—and he didn't come."

October 2, 1967

NOTES PRESENTED AT THE SYMPOSIUM OF NEW DIRECTIONS, ORGANIZED BY THE NEW YORK CULTURAL SHOWCASE FOUNDATION, WALDORF ASTORIA HOTEL

Avant-garde Cinema, the Underground
I represent Film-makers' Cooperative and Film-makers' Cinematheque which embrace 238 independently working film-makers. We are also known as avant-garde film-makers. Some call us Underground film-makers.
There is the commercial cinema—it gives to the people what they want, what they are trained to want. It's cinema as "public expression." We have nothing to do with it. But the Mayor's office seems to be very much concerned with the cinema as industry in this city. Which is fine…
But man cannot live by melodrama alone. It is here that the Avant-garde film-maker comes in. A new cinema movement started in New York, seven years ago, and it has liberated cinema. Now everybody can make movies, we say. There is a completely new attitude to Cinema. Cinema has reached maturity of the other arts. And the techniques, the aesthetics, and the major works of this new cinema have been produced within the walls of the city. It has brought to the American cinema an international prestige comparable only to the prestige brought to American painting after 1945.
Everybody started speaking about New York as the city of cinema. And soon, the businessmen came to exploit it, Hollywood moved East, and the Mayor's office joined them, and the avant-garde film-makers who made New York into the movie city,

we're brushed off. Worse than that: the press and other communication media, who like to concentrate only on the sensational aspects of everything, made us look like a freaksville. So here I'm talking to you from the freaksville.
But there are 238 of us around the Film-Makers' Cooperative, and there will be many more. We have rejuvenated the cinema, we have brought life into American cinema, and we have some right to insist on certain matters.
It should be noted here that although in all other countries the organization and promotion of the new cinema is done by various civic groups, in America this is being done by the film-makers themselves. No foundation, no civic organization has given a cent to help us in our work. In truth, the city has often disrupted our work. At this very moment, the District Attorney's office is holding over $2,000 worth of our equipment, taken away from the Film-makers' Cooperative under the pretext that an obscene film was shown with that equipment! We're still being treated like criminals, not as artists. We want this attitude to change! We appeal here to District Attorney: return to us our tools, our screens and projectors. Films are not criminals, and our projectors are not guns. Or are they?

It's important that the city, the Mayor's office begins to make a difference between cinema as commerce and industry, and cinema as an art. All we see at this moment is industry. I propose to establish a committee consisting of film-makers and film critics, to see that the work and the problems of the avant-garde film-maker are taken into consideration whenever cinema is discussed at the Mayor's office.

SHOOT YOUR WAY OUT WITH THE CAMERA
(Teenagers' Underground Film Project)

Introduction:

SHOOT YOUR WAY OUT WITH A CAMERA* film program is being organized by the Film-Makers' Cinematheque and the Film-Makers' Cooperative.

We urge you, all those who'll receive this Outline, and who'll agree with its basic directions, to proceed with the work in your own communities immediately and in your own way. Much or most of the success of this Program will depend on you, on the regional, local film-makers. You should feel completely independent. We don't want too centralized a program. Where the Cinematheque and the Cooperative will try to come in is with the cameras, the film stock, the developing, and later, after the films are completed, with the showings across the country. We are working patiently trying to raise the necessary moneys for this project. If money will not come we'll do it without it.

Jonas Mekas, Shirley Clarke
For the Film-Makers' Cinematheque and the Film-Makers' Cooperative

The General Purpose of the Program:
The purpose of the *Shoot Your Way Out With the Camera* program is to provide at least 200 youths, age 14 – 20, primarily the black people (in some cases, though it may be other minority groups) with 8 mm (sometimes 16 mm) cameras—boys and girls who can not afford and would like to use

---

* A note re. the SHOOT YOUR WAY OUT WITH THE CAMERA project:

May 20, 2013
Regretfully, this idealistic, almost utopian project, as described in the above Manifesto, presented by Shirley Clarke and myself at the Citizen Initiative Conference, organized by Lindsay, Mayor of New York City, in early December 1966, never got off the ground. Despite all the good will of many friendly organizations and individuals, Shirley's and my efforts to raise monies for the project, and our attempts to persuade Kodak to contribute cameras and stock to the project, ended all in a lot of wasted time and frustration. But it was a beautiful idea, I still think so.

---

them; instruct them how to use cameras (through local underground film-makers, film workshops, etc.) (one can learn how to run a camera in one afternoon) so that they could use them to make diary-like, journalistic or poetic films about their own lives, how they feel, how they live, what they see. In short to give them, through this Underground Film Program, a new voice, a third eye.

Why do we direct this program "primarily to the black people"? It's because among the 230 film-makers in the Film-Makers' Cooperative there are only two black film-makers.

It has to be stressed, however, that this is not an ANTI-POVERTY or REHABILITATION or PROFESSIONAL TRAINING program: this is an UNDERGROUND FILM-MAKERS' program. This is a program of the underground film-makers who would like to share with others, with those who were deprived of it, the excitement of the new language of the new art. We are not interested in Politics or Profession: our politics is cinema. We want to surround this earth with millions of buzzing 8 and 16 mm cameras and see what happens.

No doubt, some people will say that we are engaging ourselves in a "useless" and "romantic" project. Let them think so. We consider that "usefulness" of most social programs is very superficial. We want something less "practical" but more essential: the excitement and joy of discovering one's world through light and motion, through the camera.

Until the arrival of the Underground cinema, cinema was either a profession or an art: it was never (or very very seldom) the game, a joy. The film was too expensive, the cameras were too expensive, and one felt that it needed all the Training and all the Knowledge to do anything in cinema. The cinema remained in the studios. The underground liberated the cinema, it brought it out into the sun, and it took it into the streets, and into the subways, and into the Lower East Side, and into the homes. Statistics show that we have seven million cameras floating around somewhere in the United States. Where are they? They are, no doubt, in our homes but we don't see them. By giving 200 cameras to the black youth (200 against 7,000,000) we are making an attempt to plant into the people's mind, to liberate an idea of a new and free use of the camera. In a sense, perhaps, we want to dramatize the idea of the Underground Cinema, and to liberate the SEVEN MILLION CAMERAS, give them a new meaning and a new life. We want to WAKE UP SEVEN MILLION CAMERAS.

At the same time we want to give a new voice to 200 black youths—a voice that can be used to sing, to shout, or to cry, or to attack, or to defend oneself and one's people. This is what we say to you, to the black youth and to the teenagers of America today: we are not interested in social programs, we are not politicians, we are underground film-makers. But if you yourself feel that this new voice (through the 200 or through the 7 million cameras) should be used to criticize or to attack local or higher politicians so that your life could be improved—if you want it to be improved—DO SO, criticize, attack, reveal —make your film frames into bullets of truth. What's important is that you say what you want to say and what you feel; you can become an instrument in changing your own and other people's life. If you like, however, you may film the flowers, and the babies—that's O.K. too. That's the beauty of the Underground Cinema: anything you do is O.K., as long as you do it from your heart. The flowers are also politics.

How the Program Will Operate
The overall program will be guided by the Directors of the *Shoot Your Way Out* with the Camera program, appointed by the Film-Makers' Cinematheque and the Film-Makers' Cooperative.

The program will raise money enough to acquire at least two hundred 8 mm cameras (some should be sound cameras); twenty 16 mm cameras; 500 hours of 8 mm film; 100 hours of 16 mm film; 10 tape recorders; coverage of all lab expenses (developing and printing) of the above footage. Attempt will be made to have most of the equipment and stock donated to the Program by the equipment and film stock companies and stores. Regional committees will be asked to raise, on their own initiative, extra money to acquire more equipment for their own communities.

SUPPLEMENT I
The following organizations and individuals have pledged their support to the SHOOT YOUR WAY OUT WITH THE CAMERA (Teenagers' Underground Film Program):
- Millennium Film Workshop
- United Planning Organization, District of Columbia, Washington DC
- Canyon Cinema Cooperative, San Francisco
- Film-Makers' Cooperative, New York
- Film-Makers' Distribution Center, New York
- Flaherty Seminar
- International Society of Krishna Consciousness
- Grove Press
- Director of the Metropolitan Museum of Art, Mr. Hoving
- Allen Ginsberg, poet
- *The East Village* Other, Newspaper
- *Village Voice*, Newspaper
- Boston Film-Makers' Cinematheque
- The Underground Press Syndicate
- Elia Kazan, film-maker
- Shirley Clarke, film-maker

film program:

MING GREEN, by Gregory Markopoulos
GALAXIE, Gregory Markopoulos (excerpt)
SCHWECHATER, Peter Kubelka
CASTRO STREET, Bruce Baillie
WARHOL ANTHOLOGY (excerpts from HAIRCUT, EAT, SLEEP, and
        EMPIRE), Andy Warhol
THE CIRCUS NOTEBOOK, Jonas Mekas
THE FLICKER, Tony Conrad

80 minutes of film

followed by comments by Jonas Mekas: ... What's meant
by "new" in the new cinema... The new cinema constructs,
builds -- doesn't destroy... The failures today are the
critics, not the artists... When the critics and the educators of the society loose understanding of the meaning
of art in man's life -- art becomes "meaningless" in that
society... There is no meaningless art... The preoccupations
of the avantgarde film-maker today... the directions... the
crossroads... the dangers... The meaning of "avantgarde"
in art and in life...(which is the same)... The avantgarde
artist as the only religious artist today... which also
means he is the only political artist today, the only
comitted artist today... committed to things that really
matter in the real progress of man... that is, the soul
of man... and what does it mean to have 8,000,000 movie
cameras in U.S.A. today...

CHAPTER
TWENTY
TWO

... My day schedule Oct. 9, '67... Meeting Warren Beatty... Letter from Helen Adam... to Amos Vogel... Kenneth Anger escapes from London... Meeting Otto Preminger... With Shirley Clarke we go to NY World Fair grounds... Meeting Robert Duncan... Policemen lie also... Hunting for money ... Drinking on empty stomach... Broke again... Coop Wall Memo on whom to blame... Plan for a Spring Festival ... Coop meeting... Beauty of New York morning... On Norman Mailer... We are in Times Square... Intro to the traveling Film Exposition... On *Nude Restaurant*...

Warhol movies... interoffice memo... On commerce... Creation of NEWS-REEL... Notes on Dec. 21 Newsreel meeting... Letter to Sitney... On Newsreel & avant-garde... On finances...

October 9, 1967

9:30 delivered file to Criterion, Wendy's wedding, yesterday.

10:00 paid visit to Cultural Office, Department of Parks.

Submitted an application for a grant, for the Cinematheque. Miss Truder was scaring me that there is no more money left this year, all used up. Hannelore said she'll arrange a meeting with the head of the department.

Autumn in C. Park, gloomy, leaves falling. Called Preminger. Made an appointment for Friday.

Called Warren Beatty. Made an appointment for Thursday.

2 PM Saw short Yugo films at MoMA. Couple not too bad.

Decided to separate Center from the Co-op. 6 PM Co-op director's meeting.

Decision to separate from Co-op announced. Assistance to Leslie discussed.

Raising of funds discussed.

Millennium Film Workshop discussed. Listened to Ken's grievances. Linder reported on Newsletter's progress.

The construction works on 80 Wooster St. are moving slowly. NO money. The bills are mounting from all sides.

During the last two weeks, we have spent all our time, Shirley and me, meeting and calling people for money. Nothing.

The other day we saw Lloyd, at Rockefeller. He said, yes, but you are an *Urschleim*, and we can't help *Urschleim*. The foundations are set up to help things only after they begin to grow, not at the original, first, *Urschleim* stages. So there we are!

October 13, 1967

13th must mean something. By Monday we have to cover $6,800 bill for the 80 Wooster work—the floor, the lights, plumbing, etc., one million little things. Preminger just canceled his appointment. We counted on him. Sent a telegram to Kazan, S. O. S. By the evening, all pooped out, we gave up, and Shirley decided to borrow some from her mother, by Monday, for two or three weeks.

Wednesday we spent three hours with Warren Beatty. We couldn't understand each other, nothing. He said, point blank, that he wasn't going to help anybody, any film-maker whose work doesn't make money. He said, we are fools. He said, maybe, though, he could sell us to bigger companies, if we want to be sold by him—he may even produce himself a film with Shirley, me, Jean Renoir, and somebody else—there should be four—a segment film in which he could act, and may even direct one segment himself. Three hours of tiring rambling leading nowhere. What's more, he got sort of insulted when I referred to *Bonnie and Clyde* as Penn's film. "What do you mean?" he asked, "It's MY film, not Penn's. How do you know it's Penn's film? What about me? Where do I come in?" So that lead into a very long discussion and rambling on the function of the actor, cameraman, director, etc. etc., in *Bonnie*, but we couldn't come to any agreement about any of it.

Borrowed again a dollar from Shirley. Last two months Shirley has been saving me every third day with a dollar. The irony is that I can't even spend it on food—I get stuck with fast appointments, for money which I never get, and very often I have to spend it all on subways or even taxis, with no time for walking.

A LETTER FROM HELEN ADAM
223 E. 82nd St.
Oct. 11th

Dear Jonas,

It was such a pleasure to meet you again at Barbara and Howard's.

I enclose your Tarot reading & hope it will come true. It is one of the best anyone I know has had for a long time.

I was fascinated by your wonderful story of St. Teresa and the mysterious roses. It is wonderful to feel the goodwill of a great being from the supernatural world.

Very best good wishes always.
Helen

P. S. Your most beautiful & haunting M.S.S. has just come. I was enthralled by it. The strange ritual of the long walk in the foot-steps of the Saint, & the little dog licking the dust of your boots, & the bells echoing through the empty city early in the morning! It is like an eerie & magic poem.

I do indeed hope you will truly make a film about St. Teresa. Only you could do it as beautiful as it should be done.

About the dragon dream. The oldest dragon of all is the Worm Ouroboros who bites his own tail, & is one of the mighty symbols of Eternity. My own favorite dragon is "Smaug" in Tolkien's "The Hobbit"! an adorably awful creature.

Thank you again for your lovely & inspiring story. Helen

Helen Adam.

LETTERS

☞ to the editor ☜

TO THE EDITORS:

This is my answer to Amos Vogel's "Thirteen Confusions."

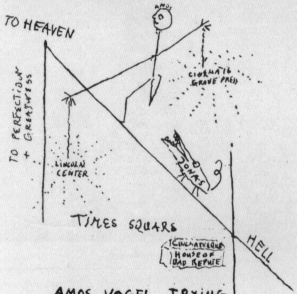

AMOS VOGEL TRYING
TO WALK ON A
TIGHTROPE OF THE
NEW AMERICAN CINEMA

(Ed. Note: Jonas Mekas was among a number of leading filmmakers and critics we asked to comment on Amos Vogel's "Thirteen Confusions" in Evergreen No. 46, but his answer arrived too late to be included with the other replies in the last issue. An excerpt from his response is printed above.)

In Memoriam

KENNETH ANGER

FILM MAKER

(1947-1967)

October 1967

Jonas, Tarot reading

1. First card. THE SIGNIFICATOR. The basis of things in both the Astral world and on the Earth. THE LOVERS. The greatest love card in the pack. Love, beauty, trials overcome.
2. The card that covers. This means the atmosphere in which all the other currents work. THE STAR, another great major card. The angel is pouring forth the waters of life and blessing.
3. The card that crosses. The opposing forces, but this card is also wonderful. THE WORLD. Fame, travel, success, happiness, great good fortune.
4. The best that can be expected in the circumstances, ACE OF SWORDS (reversed). A card of great force used ruthlessly. You are capable of taking the Kingdom of Heaven by storm with your own strength, or of snatching the crown of triumph by sheer will power. But because this card is reversed the sword could be two-edged and you yourself could be hurt by using it.
5. The base of things in the past. THE EMPEROR again a major card, meaning you have an Emperor's strength, & royal power.
6. The more immediate past. VII SWORDS. Blindfolded among swords. Difficulties & not knowing just what way to turn. But not defeated, still on your feet.
7. The influence which is coming into play in the near future. VI CUPS. New & happy relationship. Cups filled with stars & talents. The only problem, which to choose.
8. Yourself as the Tarot says you are now. V CUPS (reversed) a card of hesitation, having drunk of many cups & exhausted them, you are not yet turning round to taste two more.
9. Environment. THE HIGH PRIESTESS. The great Queen of the world of mysteries. She could indeed be Saint Teresa, as you suggested. Anyway she is watching over you.
10. Hopes & Fears. VII wands. Struggle, but with blessening wands, which means the struggles are somehow good.
11. The culmination of the reading. VI wands (reversed). Riding in triumph & covered with laurel. But because it is reversed this triumph, though sure, will be long in coming.

Altogether a splendid reading, all sort of powerful beings of love & magic raining blessings on you.
Helen Adam

October 14, 1967

Saturday morning, I came to the Co-op, to do some work, Louis also. Around 1 PM we decided to leave, and we were waiting for a taxi, when we see a taxi coming with someone waving at us from it. Kenneth Anger. So Louis took Kenneth's taxi and I with Kenneth walked back to the Co-op. He was just coming from the airport, just dropping his things at One Fifth Avenue, where, he said, Melina Mercuri is staying. It's difficult to describe how beaten and shook up he looked. His hand was bandaged. Blue streaks on his face. He said, his left (I think he said left) ear broken, inside. He showed his leg, under the knee—all swollen and blue. He kept saying that he is no longer Kenneth Anger. The film-maker Kenneth Anger has died, finished. His name is now Nimo. Nothing. From Latin. He may be a film-maker, this Nimo, but maybe not. He dumped his things on the table, all kinds of pills and a few magazines he bought at the airport, horoscope magazines, etc., Berkeley Barb. He said the Co-op door has to be repainted. Now it looks too dark, he said, "poisonous green," very bad. At first he hesitated walking through that door. "Amos, Cinema 16," he said, "very evil people." [A year ago we had moved The Coop from my 414 Park

Ave South loft into the former offices of Cinema 16, on 175 Lexington Avenue.] I said something to the effect that we have cleared the air, we have forgiven certain things or forgotten. He said, "I hope you're not forgiving Johnson." He said he's planning to do something about the war. Something that may cost him an arrest. He may go to Washington. He kept talking, quite irrationally sometimes, a shook-up way. So we decided to go and eat somewhere. I took him to the Izmir restaurant. He will repaint the door himself, he said. He made it a study of his life, the color. He knows colors and their meanings. Anyway, he said he will sell all his belongings, at an auction soon—do I know a good large place where he could hold an auction? And he'll give all the money that he'll get from the auction, to Greece. "Because it's horrible," he kept saying, people are being put in jails there, even his friends. He has to make this symbolic "magic" gesture; he said he'll talk to Mercuri about it.

He had no good hopes to retrieve any of the stolen and lost film, footage of *Lucifer Rising*. And he didn't want to increase the price for finding it, whoever will find it. Thieves, he said, do not deserve more than $100. He said he may shoot Willard Maas, and Rogosin, for they're bad people. He blamed Rogosin for misusing *Scorpio*, for whatever he did with it.

As we ate, and also had something to drink —I drank retsina, Kenneth drank soda— he began to relax a little bit, became more silent. And started living again a little. He came up with a plan of holding a screening of *Inauguration*—he said he brought the three screen version and he'd like to have a show of it. Also, a show of what's left of *Lucifer Rising*. He kept talking about how the hippies are misusing love, and how all the terrible forces are encroaching upon the cities. Cities should be abandoned, he said. He said he may just go to some distant quiet country, or just a coun-

try town, someplace, and start his life from zero. Everyone, by seeing *Scorpio*, everyone thinks, he said, what a terrible man Anger is. He doesn't want that Anger any longer. That's the public image of Anger he doesn't like any longer. That Anger is dead, he said. He never lived, he said, he was a public creation. He said he'd like to make some documentaries, newsreels about the SF scene, hippies, to really show what it's all about. Plans kept coming up, as we walked back to the Co-op…

October 16, 1967

Early this morning we settled a bank loan from the bank, cosigned by Rappaport, shortstop of $6,000, for the FD center. I wrote letters to Avon Foundation, asking for a grant for the Co-op catalog. Delivered a letter to Vera List, asking for help.

The day was beautiful again, because we pushed things a little bit further, with this morning loan. I had a feeling, when I got up, that it will be a good day. I told Shirley that St. Teresa won't let us down.

6 PM Shirley and I went to see Big Otto [Preminger]. He apologized for having canceled the last Thursday's meeting. He said he took LSD and forgot our appointment, lost all sense of time. It was his first trip, and Tim was there. He thought it was only 9 AM but it was really 3 PM, he said. He said that was the only thing he lost control of, during the trip: the sense of time.

Anyway, he sat there behind his long huge table, a tremendous and good table, a good feeling—it was very good feeling about him. Otto kept talking, telling stories. Chuck Wein came in with a friend. There was no long talk about money, he understood everything perfectly, he said he'll give $5000 this week. He said, any director who's getting older wants to be with younger people. It would be good, he said, if he could teach cinema two months out of 12 every year. He liked the Russian system of teaching cinema. As he rambled,

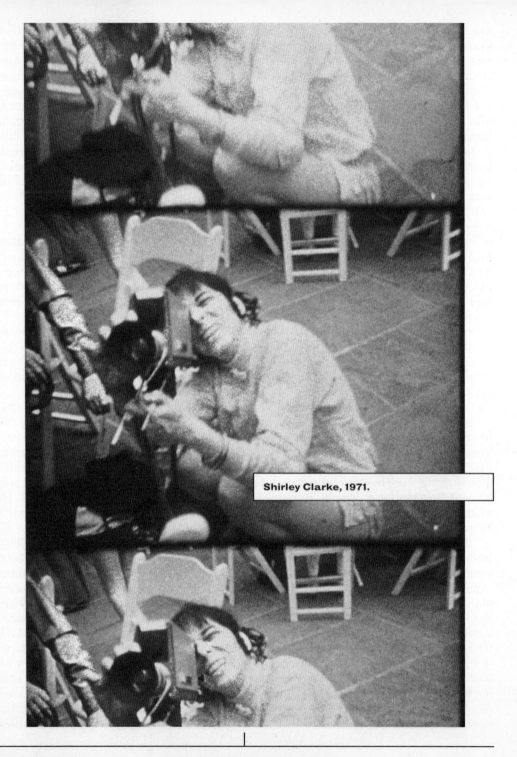

Shirley Clarke, 1971.

**I SEEM TO LIVE, VOL. 1
CHAPTER TWENTY TWO**

With Otto Preminger.

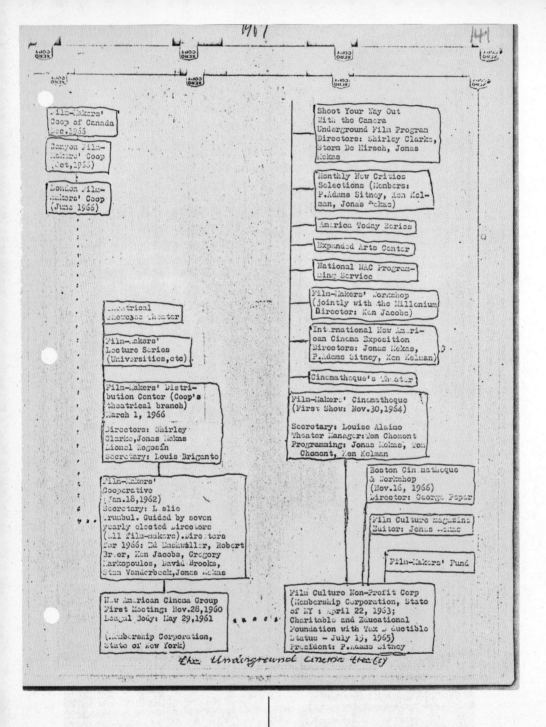

he said he didn't like to edit films, it comes from his stage background. When he shoots he avoids too many different angles. He gives only one choice, one angle, so that there is no choice in editing, so anybody can cut it. Because of this too careful self protection from editors, he said, sometimes he himself gets stuck: it would be good to have a closer shot, but he didn't shoot any closer shots. Shirley said she could sit all day and all night in the editing room. She shot *Jason* in 20 or so shots, but then spent months in the editing room...

We left Big Otto and the day was good and shining. It was good, we thought, that he remembered us under LSD, didn't forget us even under LSD, even if he couldn't make the appointment, he saw us from very very close, probably, without knowing it himself.

We were talking, and I was telling about David Wise and all the children who were making films. "How old is David Wise," asked Otto, "and when did he start making films?" "Oh," said Shirley, "David Wise was making films when he was five." "When I go home this evening I'm going to beat my kid," said Otto. "Why should you do that?" we wondered. "He is seven and hasn't made a single film yet," said the Big Otto.

October 17, 1967

Shirley plodding across the morning grass, all wet, with red shoes, lagging behind me. Her shoe was pressing—"those net stockings," she was complaining, with our hearts half broken about all the unused buildings and stupidity of man. We visited the old New York World's Fair grounds, in Flushing. The city's Cultural Affairs office called and said maybe we could do something with the New York State Pavilion. So very early this morning Shirley and I we proceeded to Flushing, by subway. The desolate place, with only three or four structures left. We had to walk for a good

mile to the New York State Pavilion, and when we arrived, we couldn't get in. After we finally located a guard, he had no light, and the electricity was disconnected, or didn't work. We checked the projectors in the auditorium by lighting matches. Later a flashlight arrived. Six huge modern 35 mm projectors sitting without any use. And the round auditorium. We couldn't figure out what we could do with it. Best for music jam sessions, or Stan's Dom. Only it's all 35 mm, what a pity. They build those structures without thinking how they would use them after the Fair is over. Incredible. How damned stupid, we thought, all that money. Just for upkeeping alone. The guard said, they have to raise 120 flags on the festivities days, and there are flags that need six men to raise them. We could run the whole Cinematheque just on flag money. Anyway, we looked at it, then we had a frankfurter, and back we came.

3 PM we had a session with the Ford Foundation, it was O.K. The man was very attentive, took many notes, expressed some hope, and said will visit the Co-op and the Tek on Friday 2 PM, to see how we operate, how we look.

Preminger's assistant called and gave info on the B&H xenon projectors. Very very nice, I thought, not to forget us small Ottos.

October 18, 1967

Had a session with Doris Freedman at the office for Cultural Affairs. Reported on World's Fair visit. Had lunch with Hannelore, some good cheese, some good bread, two good apples, the most solid meal I've eaten in a long time. My meals have been reduced to pennies these days, to chance, to friends' homes. Mostly, Stone's.

Managed to pass through the barricades of Joe Mankiewicz. I think it was his daughter, some person like that—sounded very sweet, young 17, and with some sense of humor (that made me wonder who she really was, she had an unusually good sense of humor)—anyway, I spoke a minute or two with JM and he said he may help us, asked us to send all info to his office, about the Tek & Co-op. He said, "I'm not as rich as the writer Kazan is, so don't expect to match his contribution." K hasn't come thru yet but he signed a bank loan for the Center, for $6,000.

A letter came from Helen Adam inviting me this evening to her home, Robert Duncan is in town. I opened her letter, and I had a feeling that fairies light and happy surrounded the letter and me. I saw it very very clearly. Later, at Adam's house, I saw all the miniature sculptures, frames, everywhere, with fairies. There must be something there, they must be all around her. She is one of the most beautiful human beings I have ever met, and her sister, too—there is that bell-ringing of happy voices, greeting everybody, the room full of their voices, such a good feeling. They, too, are like two fairies, so beautiful. I was wondering why Robert Duncan doesn't look at people's eyes, at least not for the first hour or two. At first I thought he was blind or something, he kept looking 45 degree angles or say 30 degree angles to the side, not directly at you, and it was a very strange feeling to talk to one who is looking somewhere else completely. Like guarding himself from something until he is really sure who that other is. Or looking at one from the side vision—like when you look at the sprites and ghosties…

November 7, 1967
Yesterday in the *New York Times*, I read that 2,000 policemen called in, didn't show up for work, and paid as an excuse that they were sick. Now, for Christ's sake, how could 2,000 healthy cops suddenly fall sick? No doubt, they were lying. How stupid of us to entrust our justice, our law and order to the people who lie!

I do not believe that you have to HATE things in order to change them or get rid of them. I do not believe that HATE must be the source or at the bottom of human development, human progress.

November 9, 1967
Some luck lead me to one good call & Mrs. Auchincloss said, come & I'll help you what I can. I went and I was hungry and tired and she treated me with a vodka and I was almost drunk. I don't know what I said, but she was very kind and interested and gave a $500 check to push things forward. I walked out and I was really drunk, just with one vodka. This will teach me to drink on an empty stomach. The streets looked like Christmas, and all women in subways looked full of desire and love. I stopped at the Charles to have some chili & was still dazed.

These last two weeks have been so exhausting and I have no idea how I pulled through or how I am pulling through all the bills & George calling all excited, and Richard with his pessimistic scares and Davis writing from Boston fearing that SF Mimes won't be able to open in time.

Anyway, for two months, really, we were going with Shirley after big shots, with no results. Two weeks ago Shirley gave up and I retreated into guerrilla warfare—for small, $200, $100, $50 buck donations, loans from friends, film-makers, strangers, anybody. Yesterday I had an inspiration and I went into skirmish attack—infantry, "pechota,"—and I'm mailing a sort of chain letter, asking for one dollar. By hook or crook the Cinematheque will be completed.

By placing the idea that everybody can make movies we want to liberate cinema. Which has nothing to do with politics or aesthetics of cinema. It's by keeping cinema in the studios that cinema is all politics and nothing else. We want to liberate cinema from politics by putting it in

With Allen Ginsberg and Richard Roud at the New York Film Festival.

**I SEEM TO LIVE, VOL. 1
CHAPTER TWENTY TWO**

Rona Page, who made Ondine lose temper, in *The Chelsea Girls*.

Rona by Shirley

the people's hands. Cinema of the people, that's what the Underground Cinema really is.

10 PM: On my way home, tired like a dog, with my mouth dry, my ears sounding, I could barely hear my own voice, talking to Ed Sanders, and we went to visit Shirley, and found Barbara there too, and I almost fell on the floor, and Shirley gave me some orange juice. Some strength regained, I continued to my room. Found a thanks note from Kenneth, for last *Voice* piece, and a package of his SF relics; also, a letter from Stan to Kenneth in which he says, "I realize now I had hoped my threat to withdraw would have caused them to create some additional situation some highly selective branch of distribution," and he continues, how we are betraying him, etc... Tired as I was, I couldn't feel any anger about it. He's talking about "additional situation" when I can't keep one single situation going and am running with my tongue out and nobody's moving a finger to help, not Stan, on his mountain top, and I am sick and tired and I wish I could run somewhere but I have strength only to reach my bed and collapse on it.

November 16, 1967
I tried to work on my film diaries, I couldn't. I had to drop it and go for a walk. It was cold and windy.
I am avoiding George's calls. It must be about money. Every call today is about money. This afternoon I passed Central Park and stopped to see Hannelore. But she had no money either. I am on a guerrilla warfare now, for small sums, anything goes, skirmish tactics, dollar by dollar. All my sources have been exhausted. No response from anybody. Whomever I call, is either broke or not interested. Best of luck, they say. Like the Foundations: it always ends with "best of luck." Like nobody really needs the Cinematheque. But then, who needed the Co-operative, five years ago? It's always the same. So, may as well, I'll push for another few months, even against the current, and see what happens, if for no other reason. Because I have no reasons, I have stopped reasoning long ago. Cold wind in my face, that's what happens, cold wind and the grey night of New York. And Harry [Gantt] keeps calling. He got stuck with $9,000 for the Co-op catalogue. So Harry keeps calling and dropping SOS messages.

November 17, 1967
A FEW NOTES ON THE SPRING FESTIVAL
EXPLORING AREAS: SEX, MORAL TABOOS IN ARTS; REVOLUTIONARY POLITICS; SHOULD WE BAN ART? AND WHEN?
This should be the most comprehensive one week gathering of art "facts" to illustrate and demonstrate those explosive areas. This should be done by presenting the works themselves, and also through a series of high-level inter-university (including government offices) panels and conferences. To cover the legal aspects, what it really involves.

THEATER: Michael McClure's play *The Beard*; either the original Evergreen Theatre (NY) production could be brought for one (Monday, when the theatres are closed in NY) day or a special production could be put on. Shirley Clarke is very interested to produce a special staging, with Carl Lee (one of the best black actors today) as Billy the Kid. It could be done for $1,000.

MOVIES: Films like Jack Smith's *Flaming Creatures*, Barbara Rubin's *Christmas on Earth* could be presented, with discussions following the films.

SAN FRANCISCO MIME TROUPE could be brought. They are the furthest out mime group in the country, banned from many states and many cities because of their sexual and political explicitness.

NAM JUNE PAIK and CHARLOTTE MOORMAN could represent happenings and music (Moorman is known for her nude solo performances.) Both are top artists.

WYN CHAMBERLAIN, the painter could organize a small portable exposition of erotic paintings and sculptures. Or ask Gregory Battcock to do it. Or Andy Warhol.

CAROLEE SCHNEEMANN could come and give a dance evening, a dance piece called *Meat Joy*, a tremendous sensual dance piece, happening—one of the best of that kind.

KENNETH KING could come and perform his dance piece with the snake—I do not recall the title of that piece, but I will dig it out some material on it. *New York Times* was shocked.
As plain experience, nothing to do with sex, but revolutionary enough to include in the festival would be LA MONTE YOUNG performing one of his 3 or 4 or 6 hour music pieces—greatest music you can hear anywhere today.

Really, if you'd bring the people mentioned above, you'd already have a tremendous festival. I forgot, THE FUGS, too. But you never know where they will be by April. Sanders said he would be willing to come. I also spoke with Paik, La Monte Young and Kenneth King, they said O.K.
more notes to follow
Jonas

One political film, *The Edge*, a feature film, could be included: about a group of people planning to kill Johnson... a panel discussion to go with it: Should We Kill Johnson?...

November 17, 1967
FILM-MAKERS' CO-OP MEETING
Charles Levine, smoking, smiling like a wet cat; Carl Linder having a very serious discussion with Louise, he just wiped his nose, picked up Galinger's beer, had a sip; now they are very serious, with Louise making steno notes, in any case she looks like she's stenoing sort of; Robert Breer keeps pointing his finger to the floor as if he's trying to explain something to Naomi, back to me—both in heavy winter coats, and Naomi plenty of brown hair dripping down her back (by brown I mean her coat), Willard just put a cigarette in his mouth, sits very relaxed, and sort of skeptical about all the bustle that Jack Perlman and Shirley and Storm seem to be going in the other corner, next to be huge (eight pieces, that's huge) bouquet of flowers that Willard brought from Marie and "a beautiful Puerto Rican (or did he say Spanish?) girl" or something like that and here is Fred Wellington coming in, pushing carrying a chair in front of him, and he went all the way back, as usually, picked up a pack of cigarettes—really, he's still searching for them—now he put his coat on and is leaving, which means he didn't find cigarettes. Robert is now lifting both of his hands up in the air, his fingers spread out, illustrating something very mysterious, and I am getting curious, "operating on the spur of the moment," Shirley said, the connection unknown. Larry is fixing the Xerox again and Willard lit Carl's cigarette, "I've been quiet," said Willard, context unknown, missed. "Never," said Shirley, context unknown. "What's a nice girl doing like you going to jail," Shirley. Storm now sits peacefully with her arm resting on the chair. "That smug glowing look," Jack P, context unknown. By now there are too many speaking at the same time, and outside, behind the windows, cars are making plenty of racket. Fred is back, with cigarette (unlit) hanging out

from his jaw. Willard stands up, "excuse me," he says, walks toward the xerox, turns back, "when do you think they are going to start?" I shake my head to four directions, and Willard does the same, and walks to the left—Naomi has a huge warm "muffler" if that's the name of the thing in which you stick your hands in cold weather. "Let's have a meeting," Shirley. "Let's get over with the meeting," Jack. "O.K." Jonas. Naomi: "I am voting for and against," and she walks out. I count: Six present. 250 invitations (Jack calls them "proxies") went out. "I went from Houston to Austin by bus." "I don't know Geography, I know geography of the body," says Maas. "I am doing a billion things already. Hustlers are great people." "I'll be making money." "BULLSHIT," Maas. "I'm just talking about decoration." "I can yell too, but it's pointless," Storm. "I will write a letter. I am also a writer, you know. I know about Aristotle." "I don't have to account to anybody." "For Christ's sake I've been up for 24 hours." Shirley is cleaning the place, and everybody's rambling and walking back and around the room, excited voices, meeting is over. "Peter is arguing in an insanity ward." "I reached a karma," Carl, context too complicated. "An issue which one has to understand in a very broad sense," Shirley. Positive proposition: "No, why couldn't a center try to force a theatre to accept the same rentals as the Co-op and to have fewer showings perhaps on Saturdays." Louise: "It's being done, in other areas of the country. They are paying full rentals." Storm: "I think so much depends on the individual film-maker. The representation means more than the economics." Shirley: "It's not fair for some film-makers to carry others." Storm: "I see a vision of development." "A co-op whatever it is, a factory or whatever, is always less effective than a really greedy shark," says Peter, "because there is nobody who drives it so bloodily." Shirley: "I'd endorse

Charlie's idea to expand the percentage from 25 % to 30 % or 34—we need more personnel but we are going to get money." Peter: "There are film-makers who could have large audiences, like Shirley and there are others, like Stan or me and ..." (lost too much and too fast)..." That's why we are talking here: WE SMELL DANGER," said Jonas. "Now we are more positive, I like this kind of talk much better." "Books, not sex..." "For example, B&H"... "I just tell you that B&H went into business"... "What about Getz"... "He's got a good job..."

November 27, 1967

7:30 AM, walking through the waking up city, the air is still clear and clean. It's cold, the cold is clean and sharp. The smoke is outlined clearly against the sky. Cold winter morning. But there's something good about it, it makes you feel happy and good. The clarity of nature. Not a "monumentalist" sort of kind, this clarity, but one that has something to do with original things as they are, before they are surrounded by all kinds of emotions and psychology. There is a good energy in this clear morning air—I don't feel in it yet the bustling petty occupations and worries of people— the night cleans the air out of it, until again during the day it becomes thick with all kinds of crap. This smoke, this wind is clear and good.

The instrument communicates with the song.
Old violins are very much sought after.
The audience dances, inside, goes thru all the motions of the dancer on the stage without knowing it.
The Vienna Philharmonic auditorium helps the musicians. They say, even bad musicians sound good at the Vienna Philharmonic. The walls communicate with the musicians.

There are deep laws of the energy interactions, interrelationships, there is always a communication, touching each other both ways, acting upon, we see it or we don't see it, we admit or we don't.

Continuing on the subject of Norman Mailer (see last week's *Voice*) I could sum it up like this:

Mailer comes out a winner, in his film work, because he is willing to make a fool of himself. He is willing to work in the new medium right on the edge of the avant-garde—the avant-garde of the narrative cinema—instead of trying to imitate, to work within the vein of the official, classical cinema. He is willing to blunder his way through. Robbe-Grillet is also in the avant-garde of the novel, he is not in the vanguard of cinema. Basically, maybe, because there is no contemporary avant-garde film tradition in Paris.

NOTES FROM THE UNDERGROUND IN TIMES SQUARE:

You may be wondering sometimes, what we are doing Uptown.
Why don't we stay downtown...
But we are in the very heart of this black, sad city.
We are in Times Square.
And we are here to stay.
Until the blackness changes into color.
We are in the very heart of this city with our *Home Movies*
to remind you—right next to Radio City Hall:
that there is also the private, the small, the subtle, the
almost invisible...
We are the dust in your eye reminding you of Home...
where you talk heart to heart...

INTRODUCTION
The current exposition represents a cross cut through what's being done in what has become known as the New American Cinema.

As any introduction, this introduction has to be brief, therefore I can only very approximately indicate what this cinema is all about. We know, that every art has two poles, two extremes. On one hand, man expresses himself in art through narratives by telling stories (we have this in music; painting; literature; etc.); on the other hand, as he goes into more subtle areas of his experience, he begins to express himself less directly, by suggestion, and through metaphors, through poetry, moving into the abstract, and the decorative.

The main contribution (and preoccupation) of the New American Cinema—if we simplify it a little—is that its working area is this second, poetic aspect of self-expression. During last six or seven years the American film avant-garde has developed, created an entire body of non-narrative cinema. It has developed its syntax and its language. So that the cinema, which until seven years ago was half-an-art has freed the film artist to create as freely as in any other art. If we want, we can tell stories, or we can write essays, or we can write with our cameras three-minute lyrical poems. The sensibilities which until now have found an outlet only in written poetry or painting, now, in America at least, are finding an outlet in Cinema, through this new filmic vocabulary and techniques.

This, no doubt, at least partly, conditions the viewing of this cinema. The audience must realize that this cinema differs essentially from narrative cinema. The audience has to learn to respond with their own sensibilities to the sensibilities of this cinema. The audience has to physically change the eye to learn to see, to really appreciate this cinema. Those who are facing this cinema for the first time, should consider this exposition as a seminar in seeing. That way both the film-maker and the viewer will come out of the show richer. One has communicated something, a new vision of the world; the other has gained something: new vision of the world.

The only other thing that I should mention, probably, is that these techniques and this cinema didn't come into existence as a trick: it came, it had to be invented as the only way through which a great part of modern content could be expressed through art. These films reveal the new generation of America. And since the new generation of America is part of the world's new generation, this cinema somewhere in its essence expresses also you, even if it may not be clear from the first viewing, how and which part of you it expresses. Like all poetry, film poetry is "written" in a more condensed language than the language of prose, it requires a number of different viewings to really begin to get into it. But then some of you will go right into it very first time.

There is a tale according to which after God created the world, he looked at it and he thought it was great. So he created Cinema to record and celebrate that world.

But the Devil did not like that. So he put a money bag in front of the camera and said: Why celebrate reality if you can make money with this instrument.

And believe it or not, all film-makers ran after the money. So God, to correct the mistake, created the independent film-maker, and said: You'll make movies and you'll record and celebrate life and all my creations, but you'll never make any money with it.

So now for over fifty years or so, we have home movies, independent film movements all over the world. In 1964, in the United States alone there was over 8,000,000 amateur, home movie cameras. I have no doubt that the number of cameras all over

the world has doubled since then. It may be God's work, or maybe the devil's, I don't know. But these millions of cameras are recording fragments of reality. Vacation trips, birthday parties, weddings, unseen places, little joys, fooling around after a few glasses of wine or vodka.

I do not have to tell you what an incredible source, what a document of present civilization is recorded in those millions of film frames.

December 8, 1967

When reviews came out, in the big press, on the *Nude Restaurant*, I was wondering. They all, for the first time, had something to praise. They said it was Warhol's most professional film. They also said there was, finally, a real "star," somebody that will go, probably, to Hollywood, they said and who had something to say, not like those others who have nothing to say. So I was suspicious, right there. I knew something was wrong there. So it didn't come as a big surprise that *Nude Restaurant* is among Andy's least interesting productions. It is true: Viva is telling clearer and better stories than any other Warhol star in any other Andy movie, and sure she'll go to Hollywood—but there is this one levelness in the stories. While in all other movies, and the *Chelsea Girls* remains the best of all—there is this ambiguity, this fragmentary talking, not too interesting, as a story, but sometimes interesting—a talking that is a reflection of something more than a story. Now, in the *Nude Restaurant*, everything becomes just words, word story. Not much more than that. There is nothing beyond. You walk out and little is left although you are quite entertained while you watch it. But *Chelsea Girls* lingers with you, much more was revealed through the "boring" and "unprofessional" talking than in all the stories of Viva.

I got a similar impression from Ludlum's piece, at the Bowery. Like it was interesting

INTEROFFICE MEMO from Jonas
Dec. 14 1967

concerning commerce
this has mostly to do with the Center but it applies
also in other places
like we are trying to be like the others, like the Big
Boys, trying to beat them on their own terms: by advertising,big
and ads, clever ads, we sit and we think aobout clever lines,
"what will bring the people in" etc --
        a feeling is beginning to develop in me, the way I see things,
that somweher we have been sidetracking, that a few correctives are
needed in our work. The aims maybe still correct, but the methods
may never take us to those aims, nmthnymmmmm I don't know why so we
we are trying to win on the commercial terms? cotteetttcoot
        The Undeground between 1960 and 1966 grew and really
exploded upon the people only because it grew out from the center.
We didn't dissipate, we didn't GO OUT, we simply remained there,
in the center, among ourselves, and we thus we generated an immense
energy center which then by its own force spread out and took
over the imaginations and fanatsies of the newspapers, people,
media, etc etc. WE DIN'T HAVE TO DO ANYTHINGABOUT IT. It just worked
by itself. Because we have something that is of substa nce.
        Now, it seems, we are beginnihg to reverse this. We are
beginning to get caught by the ways of the world. Andmm
        I feel that it's time to seriously reeeprojeetiottty
so consider our present posotion and methods and make drastic
correctives.
        We shouldn't advertise: we should inform.
        We should try to sell ourselves: let them ask for us.
        We shouldn't compete with others: oumm if our substabce
is better than THEIRS, it will win out by its own force, why waste
energy?
        We should stay away from all the commercial theatrical methods
and continue working out and so strenghtening the cooperative methods,
the flat renati methods.
        We don't really have such a great need of all those millions
of people. Our films are not made with millions of dollars. oo
mm meroraorormrre
        The commercial system theatrical syste m has been devised for
a very commercial product, that is Hollywood. And to want to use that
system for our work means to change our work into Hollywood work.

        Which, as a matter of fact, some of us are beginning to do.
"During last few months I have been running for money, for the Cinemathec
taaxing meeting people from all kinds anf walks, and many from the
industry, and I was amazed how many of our film-makers have been there

at the United Artsist, at the MGM, at the Universal, trying to sell themselves
out, peddling scripts and peddling the films.
     Why don't we have enough faith in what we have started, in the Coop?
     Something beautiful was started six years ago, but we keep wanting
~~kumanelaxing~~ to get back into the SYSTEM.

     The Center was started from a need. To serve the film-maker who wanted
to ~~much~~ show his films in theaters. ~~T~~ That's how the Center started. As
long as there is one film-maker at the Coop who wants his films shown ~~commercial~~
theatrically, that need has to be considered ~~by the Coop (center)~~. But that
doesn't mean that we shouldnt ~~consider~~ ~~something~~ try to changing ~~of~~ that
sitiation.
     Our aim should be really working out a commpletely different attidute
     Oh what a honor to screen your film on 42nd St!
     A film-maker will give his films to a lousy 42nd St theater, ~~the~~
whwre the prints will be run 5o times in a week, where the pirnts will be
completely buthscher, and he gets no money -- but he still feels that it's
prestige of some Kind to have his films shown on 42nd St
     I th8nk it's a very bad state of things, spiritual and mental, and
ih any other way.

     Our ideal ~~strrl~~ should be, if anything: to have our own 16mm shocases
in all major cities, very carefully and objectvively p programmed and run
~~With the~~ I think that with all the energy today wasted in ~~try to~~ changing the
existing theatrical system ~~into what we want or~~ it would be much better if
we would simply BUILD OUR OWN SYSTEM from the scratch and on completely
different principles. ~~and Sxxior~~
     I don't believe any longet that it's worth ~~p~~ spending any energy
in changing the old order. I am for abandoning it.
     and building our own order from the very scenter of our own
energy.

     This is the end of the Dec. 14th MEMO

                                   Jonas

for a moment, while you watched the play, but like nothing remained after you left the theatre. Like we have seen all this so many times before, in Jack's movies, in Bill Vehr's movies, in many other productions. An absurdity and "ridiculousness" that evaporated right there, and nothing remains.

December 22, 1967
ON CREATION OF NEWSREEL
At the Film-makers' Cinematheque, 80 Wooster St.
A meeting of about twenty people was called to order by Jonas who also did the inviting:

Jonas: We are here... I guess... to discuss and practically establish... we don't know what to call it, and it's up to you what to call it, and, really to develop it and define it, what it will become, what it will be. But, vaguely, very vaguely, maybe we could understand what we are talking about if we'd call it a CONTEMPORARY NEWSREEL. That is, that footage that many of us pick up every day at demonstrations and pickets and, sometimes, at some more quiet moments... and it's there, and something is happening, and we think that it should be seen across the country, and in other countries, and very often it's sitting, that footage, it's sitting and nothing is happening to it, nobody sees it, and time passes and it becomes just history. But it could, really... these... I'd say, to begin with...
I'll speak now just for myself, that those of you who consider right now that something like that, the organization, the centralization of such material is not necessary, those could leave right now because I don't think it's time to discuss, to go into any arguments... and only those, I'd say, those who really think that something like that is necessary, should stay and we then should talk together. In other words, only

those who really believe that such footage should be organized and made available and should be distributed—
I go very often to universities and colleges and many of you go, and we face the situation that there is this interest and need there and there is no place to get that kind of material. The students... and now, before the election, week by week, this need will intensify...
You know, yesterday the Universal Newsreel Services closed. So I think it maybe... Just yesterday we sort of came together at the Film-makers' Cooperative, and without knowing that the Universal Newsreel Service was closed, we decided... all interests came together... because many of us have been thinking for a long time now that something like that should be done. So that now, I think, we should combine our forces and do it.
So now I said my say and so now anybody else who...

December 27, 1967
Meeting, to sum up:
On December 21st a meeting was called (at the Cinematheque, 80 Wooster St.). The purpose of the meeting was to establish a contemporary newsreel service. It was a coincidence of some significance that the same day, daily press announced the closing of the Universal Newsreel Service.

About 20 people showed up, mostly cameramen, film-makers, and a few in between stragglers. We thought that it was a shame that all (or at least most) of the footage taken during demonstrations, events, happenings etc. etc. simply going to waste. It seldom reaches the people, nobody knows who has what and where. The footage sits there with the film-maker until it becomes history. It was agreed that some of this material should go to the people, to the universities, colleges, and towns. It should be seen, people should be informed about what's going on in the country, so that things could be changed. And we aren't talking about the info that's clogging our TVs—we are talking about some real happenings, some real information.

A RADICAL NEWSREEL, so to say.

The meeting was informed that the Film-makers' Cooperative is open to the newsreel distribution across the country. The theatrical—or special task—branch of the Co-op, the Distribution Center has offered to the newly formed Newsreel Service a corner of its office, and a table, and the basic organization set up. Melvin volunteered to do the basic work. He will serve as liaison and can be reached around noon at the center.

By the way: nobody should try to give a definition of what we mean by "newsreel." Let's not waste time on it. Let things take their own course. The "radical" or "new" newsreel will define itself according to how deeply we'll get into what's really happening in this country and all around the globe. All our discussion at this initial stage should center around the practical, down to earth, and immediate (not those of the future and problematic) matters. Let's not get stuck in verbiage.

During the first few months we should not go after perfection of our newsreels. There could be three or five-minute reports going out almost next day after the shooting, with no sound, just basic identifying titles, or with some sound tapes. In another week or two more polished version, and maybe with optical sound, could be ready for more delayed situations. Once every month much more complete monthly America Today reports could be prepared from all the daily and weekly materials. There should be an advisory committee (elected?) to coordinate all the projects, to make the decisions and policies, to assign people to prepare all the above-mentioned versions of newsreels, etc.

February 3, 1968

Dear P. Adams Sitney (and Julie, too):

I found time to write a letter! Now. Only because Gideon is shooting something right now, and he wanted to shoot me typing. So here I am. I said, I'll take this occasion to at least START a letter to you, even if I may be interrupted by some other nuisances or emergencies and I may never be able to complete it. Plus, a Dylan record is going in the background. Plus, I am not so sure where you are. You said you'll be in Amsterdam until approximately the 15th, so I am taking chances.

Stan visited, just by surprise, the city, stayed for a few days and then went back. He is still going thru whatever he's going, but it's on a different plane now, so he made peace with the film-makers and with the Co-op, he put his films back, had a show to some friends of the first installment of *Scenes from under Childhood*, which is very very beautiful, met some of the old friends, spent nights arguing about politics—and then went back.

The Minister of Finances is still having the same difficulties, the same problems, but the things begin to look brighter. The people are beginning to find the Cinematheque even on Wooster Street, which is (I don't know how well you know the city) quite difficult to find, when you don't know; so things are beginning to stabilize there. The only problem is that the building work is still going on and more money is needed for materials and workers. Also, our huge back debts are breaking our back. On top of all this, I have a March 1st deadline to complete at least a part of the *Diaries*. Knox gallery, in Buffalo, is sponsoring it, and they have a show on March 7th, so I have been pushing quite hard, day after day, and I am keeping a monk's schedule. I appear at the Co-op at 8 am and at 11 am I call it quits and I disappear to work on my movie, until 6 pm. Then it's time for me to go to the Tek. Tek operates on limited

January 3rd 1968

To the Seven Directors of the Film-Makers' Cooperative
   and to the hard workers of the Coop & the Center

This is to let you know that a directors' meeting will take place this coming Monday Monday, January 8th at 6PM at the Film-Makers' Cooperative. It would be good if all seven of us could get together, for once.

Basically, these are the things to discuss and to decide:

1. Should the Film-Makers' Cooperative and the Film-Makers' Distribution Center be (or are they already?) TWO legal bodies or one? If these are two legal (independ- end) bodies then the relationship between the two should be discussed and defined.

2. In the case we decide that the Film-Makers' Distribution Center is part of the Film-Makers' Cooperative, I propose that we drop the name "Film-Makers' Distribut- ion Center" and that we call it a more functional name, say, Cooperative's "Spe- cialized Bookings Office." In other words, the Film-Makers' Cooperative will have two clearly defined working offices : a) Flat Rental (Booking) Office (Dept.), and b) Specialized Booking (Rental) Office (Dept.).

                    this would be an approximate plan
                     of the Coop:

FILM-MAKERS' COOPERATIVE
"your film is your mem -
bership card"; "no film
is rejected"; "every film
grows or dies on its own
merits"

supervised by the Seven
Directors elected yearly
(actual work done by hired
workers)

FLAT RENTAL OFFICE
(approximately what
Leslie's office is
now)
(theatrical and non-
theatrical -- any flat
rental bookings, as
listed in the catalog)

SPECIAL RENTAL OFFICE
(approximately what Louis'
office is now)
(theatrical and non-theatrical -- anything that deviates
from flat rentals)
(film-makers's permission
needed to deviate)

FILM SHIPPING &
STORING OFFICE

SPECIAL ASSISTANCE
OFFICE (programming
assistance, info.

This is the basic outline. As you can see, the outline doesn't permit much anything outside bookings of the regular or irregular bookings. Which means, we have one more problem to solve. What do we do if a film-maker comes and with what he thinks has "wider" "theatrical" "possibilities" and he wants "an opening" in a "regul- ar theatre," so that his film could have its "proper" "audience."

During Gideon Bachmann's filming trip to New Jersey, 1967.

**I SEEM TO LIVE, VOL. 1
CHAPTER TWENTY TWO**

NNNN

ZCZC RWU281 FTC4236 1404

USNY HL ITRM 055 01920730

ROMA 55 8 1810

59.4

8893820   1968 JAN 8   PM 1 28   8893848

LT

MEKAS FILMAKERS COOPERATIVE

175 LEXINGTON AVENUE NEWYORK

F MD-

AFTER MANY EFFORTS OF OUR LAWYER CAVANAUGH NOW FREE STOP

BUT ABSOLUTELY WITHOUT WINTER CLOTHES AND MONEY DOESNT

WANT COME BACK STATES STOP WE CANT FOLLOW GIVING MONEY

AND WE AFRAID WILL PUT HIMSELF IN SOME OTHER TROUBLE

STOP PLEASE SUGGEST WHAT TO DO STOP BEST

LINO   1968 JAN 9 AM 10 51

TIME TELEPHONED

COL 175

John Cavanaugh, a young film-maker in his twenties, was brought by Pesaro Film Festival to show his 8 mm films. While in Rome, on his way back to New York, got into the drug scene and into a lot of trouble. When months later Italian police sent him back, his mind was so destroyed that eventually he ended up in the Islip hospital for the mentally ill. My recent research into his fate brought no results. All his films were stolen and never recovered during his brief stay at the Chelsea Hotel. One of his short films is in Fluxfilm Anthology. While in New York, he walked the streets carrying a huge Samurai sword (he was of comparatively tall height).

personnel, just the manager, projectionist, and myself, so very often I have to be either manager or the projectionist, depending who wants to take off. So that my work on the *Diaries* is constantly interrupted, broken to pieces. There are all kinds of indications that some money may be coming in, from Foundations maybe, very soon, but the river is dry right now and the bones are showing.

I spent some time with Standish Lawder, we went together to St. Louis, to some conference, and he's trying to find something for you, when you come back. If he can't find anything, we may find something for you in NY, because by that time things should improve.

Cavanaugh just came back, completely out of his mind, and destroyed in prisons and madhouses. I hope he will get out of it. I have no idea how he'll end up this time, it's beyond the point of help, or normal help. It happened what we told you will happen, also happened exactly what I told in the beginning of this letter will happen, that is, I was interrupted in my writing of this letter, and now this is a different typewriter, different time (Monday morning instead of Sunday PM) and different place (Co-op), a very Aristotelian situation with a non-Aristotelian spelling different spacing, too.

Enclosed is a bit of History: The Swedish Scrolls were dug out by our scientists. See if you can dig out some gold now with those scrolls.

Meanwhile, try to survive somehow. Friends should be sending another check soon.

Should we plan for autumn your ONE MAN show at the Tek? This was a joke seriously meant.

—Jonas

February 12, 1968

Question: Why are you interested in Newsreel? How do you reconcile your interest in Avant-garde Film with your interest in Newsreel?

Jonas: For a number of different reasons. The Newsreel genre of cinema, the fact film is the most neglected, most underdeveloped aspect of cinema today. And a neglect of a large area of cinema means that the film artists are neglecting a large area of life. The film-makers, as many other artists today, have gone far in creating of contemporary, personal art, art as "self-expression." But now some of us, and I am talking about film-makers, are turning our cameras on reality around us. The more that the camera now has become, during the last ten years, a penetrating all-seeing eye that can be brought into unpredictable situations without being an intruder—streets, prisons, battle fields, courtrooms, public offices and homes— and show how the things really are, not as poetry but as facts of daily occurrence. I believe that a society before it can really go one step forward must know goddamn well where it stands today and I don't have to tell you that not everybody yet realizes that we are standing on a big garbage heap. The newsreel should help us see that.

Almost automatically, it should be understood that in order to really fulfill it's function, in 1968, Newsreel film will have to adapt, develop, find its own modern, contemporary, up-to-date form, techniques, shape. Cinema has undergone a revolution, during last ten years, and the Newsreel can continue that revolution. We can not reveal, we can't see things in a new, revealing way, by looking at them the same old way. Old forms, old styles, old techniques perpetuate old content, old ideas, old status quo. It's here that the main challenge will be, for the film-makers who are concerned with the Newsreel film or should I say with Reality.

As for the second part of the question, that is, how to reconcile my interest in avant-garde film and the Newsreel film, it's like this:

I see no difference at all between the Avant-garde Newsreel—and the avant-garde film, because a real Newsreel, a newsreel which can help us to get out of where we are, MUST BE AN AVANT-GARDE NEWSREEL, must be in the avant-garde of humanity, must contain and be guided by our highest and most advanced dreams: One World, One Humanity. No frontiers, no borders, no customs fees, tariffs, no exploitation of man by man, no more armies, no more passports, no more guns, no more rich, no more poor, no hate, no money, none of that shit that is being fed today to us as our Way of Life.

Dear Shirley:

Two things:

a) George was trying to reach you to tell you that Ornette could move in tomorrow, temporarily, to another floor, his own floor will be ready soon. George said, he could give him keys tomorrow.

b) Louis is spreading FALSE propaganda against me & Tek, as far as the rumors are reaching me, his references about how "Shirley is upset" that Center didn't get the promised money. THE CENTER GOT THE PROMISED MONEY, with only three or four hundred difference, which I needed to pay the accountant. If Louis can't straighten out his budgets that's one thing, but to put blame on me or Tek is another. Eight thousand is eight thousand, no matter what marks we make IN OUR BOOKS (I had to designate it as "rentals"). More than that. Tek accepted all of Center's $14,000 bills without arguing. That means the Tek will eventually give a $3,000 "grant" to the Center, because at least $3,000 of those $14,000 was spent by Tek to pay rentals for the 42nd St theatre when Center was using it as its showcase. So I want these facts to be taken into consideration. Instead of $14,000 the center is getting $17,000, at the very end. In short: TEK PAYS ITS BILLS, sooner or later. But will the Center pay its bills? That's the thing to worry about, if there is anything to worry about at all.

Hope to see you soon—

P. S. I think that $5,000 should be returned

CHAPTER TWENTY THREE

March 13, 1968

INTRODUCTION TO BUFFALO PREMIERE OF *WALDEN*

Next to the main title of *The Diaries*, there is another, smaller title which says: The First Draft. And then, I remember Maya Deren, who used to say: Works of art are never completed: they are just abandoned. Anyway, I intend to continue polishing my *Diaries*, and I consider this version the First Draft, even if my wishes to complete them the way I really want may never come through, the way I am, involved in one million things. As a matter of fact, my diaries would have been still sitting sealed in film cans for I don't know how long if the Buffalo Festival of the Arts wouldn't have come to my assistance with a devil-break-neck-deadline. So here I am, and I am mightily grateful. I hope that the example of Buffalo will set a precedent for other art and education institutions to come to the assistance of other avant-garde film-makers. Film remains a costly art: while the commercial film-maker has banks and commerce to help him, the avant-garde film-maker has nothing to sell and nothing to bargain with but his own art, and needs YOUR kind support and is grateful for it. I want to make this point.

P. S. *The Diaries* were shot during last three years, almost every day, bit by bit. For me, so badly and desperately distracted by my other activities—as Minister of Finances of the American Film Avant-garde, and as the Minister of Propaganda, etc.—this was the only way to keep my brains in one piece—by keeping such a diary. This First Draft contains only one third of the footage —mostly those notes, those daily sketches which lent themselves to a fast "deadline" completion.

As I said above—I have no idea when I'll come to editing other footage. I hope you'll find something of value or interest for your eye in these first Chapters that I am unveiling here for the first time, for whatever they are.

April 3, 1968

Cincinnati

We have been working for last three days preparing Hermann Nitsch OM Theatre event. We got some blood from the butcher, we drove with Hermann to a farmer in the suburb of Cincinnati, and got a slaughtered pig. We returned tired but happy and ready for the performance. Steve Gebhardt met us as we arrived. He looked all shook-up.

"Hermann," he said, "we just heard on the radio that Martin Luther King was killed."

We were dumbfounded. Hermann looked at the ground. We stood for a long minute with no words. Then Hermann looked at me and said:

"Should I still do my performance?"

He meant his Ritualistic OM Theatre performance at the University of Cincinnati, which was scheduled to begin in about an hour.

"Yes, you have to do it," I said. "Dedicate it to Martin Luther King, and all the innocents, and do it. Nothing more fitting could be done for such an occasion. I think you have to do it."

I had to catch a train an hour later. Hermann began his performance by dedicating it to Martin Luther King. I watched first few minutes then left for the train station.

AN INTERVIEW
(confidential)

INTERVIEWER: (who would like to remain anonymous): You have been interviewing other film-makers. I thought the readers of the *Voice* would like to know something about yourself. So, permit me to ask you a few questions. First: Lets face it, the secret is coming out, it has been all your invention, all this Underground business, right?

JONAS: Since there is nothing much to lose now, it's time that the world knows the real truth about the underground. It all started then years ago, when a few of us in New York, realizing that we want to make films and that we can not get our hands on the Hollywood studios or their equipment, one day we came up with a brilliant idea which we immediately proceeded putting into practice. It was a fantastic idea, based on our knowledge of Hollywood psychology.

INTERVIEWER: What was the scheme, exactly?

JONAS: We decided to concoct a few obvious kooky techniques, gimmicks, like hand-help cameras, out-of-focus shots, shaky camera work, amateur (non-actor) casting—other kinds of such way out, far out things. Knowing the Hollywood psychology, we knew that if we give enough publicity to it, it will be only a question of a few years of insistence, on our part, some clever publicity, and Hollywood would pick up our bait. And would you believe it, our plan worked! Our plan really worked. Today, in Hollywood, they have picked-up our "techniques," they are running around the studios with hand-held cameras, they are shaking the cameras, while all the dollies and tripods and Mitchells rot in the storage rooms. Next week a truck-load of tripods is arriving from Hollywood to New York; also sputniks, and Mitchells, they will sell them for nothing, just to get rid of them. Hollywood took our bait and is rushing to "underground" techniques, and we are finally free to take and use any equipment we want, and rent

August 25th 1967

To:
Norman N.Holland
State University of NY at Buffalo
College of Arts and Sciences
Annex A
Buffalo, New York

Dear Mr.Holland:

Thanks for clarifying what you meant by "Buffalo premiere."

About my own proposal:

I should be more specific, perhaps. Really, when I proposed myself
to make a film specially for the Buffalo Festival of the Arts, I had something
specific, a specific film in mind, and that is, to edit my NEW YORK DIARIES
film. The shooting is practically completed. But I need two or three
thousand to edit it and put sound to it. With money available the work
can be done in four months. An excerpt, 3o minutes of it, unedited, was
shown at Pesaro film festival, outside of the main Festival, and it was
thought by many leading critics as the best thing shown there. Another
excerpt of same lenght was shown at the Festival of Film on New York,
last Spring, and it was the most successful show there. There is nothing
for censroship in this film. It is all New York, its people, its streets,
its winters, and summers, and its spring — and it's not a documentary,
it's a film made in a diary form, my own diaries. That's what it is,
approximately. As it is now, with the little money I get now and then,
it will take me two years to complete it. So, I thought, Buffalo could
perhaps help me. Whatever. Up to you to decide. I am at your disposal.
I'll inform you about other possibilities, if I hear about any.

Sincerely,

G.P.O., Box 1499   Jonas Mekas
New York 1, N.Y.

Dec.25th 1967

To:
Mr.Gordon M.Smith
Albright-Knox Art Gallery
Buffalo, New York 14222

Dear Mr.Smith:

I was very happy to learn that the Buffalo Festival Committee has
decided to underwrite the completion expenses of my new film, "The
New York Diaries." With the $2000 that you have put aside for this
purpose I should be able to complete the film on time, that is, for
your March premiere.

I am collecting some useful information for your Press department,
including some photographs. I hope I have one more week time for it.

Meanwhile, here, in one paragraph, this is what the film is all
about:
"The New York Diaries" were shot during the last three years -
from Summer 1965 to Summer 1967. Almost every day I kept shooting
scenes close to my own life, the surroundings, the weather, the
changing seasons. It's very difficult to tell now, whether this is
a portrait of me or a portrait of the New York City. What I was (and
still am) trying to do in this film, is to develop a new genre of
film, the diary film. If it's perfectly legitimate for a writer to
sit and write down his "diaries," it's perfectly fine to do the same
thing for the film-maker. So that's where everything started, from
that idea, and it went and it took its own course and it pulled me
along.

Once more I'd like to thank you for your help. I really belive
that this grant will establish a very important precedent. The
avantgarde film-maker doesn't have yet, as it is now, any place to
go for help. You are providing a key to the solution of this problem.

                                  Sincerely yours,
                                  and Happy (Busy) New Year
                                  Jonas Mekas
                                  Jonas Mekas

Jonas Mekas
G.P.O., Box 1499
New York 1, New York

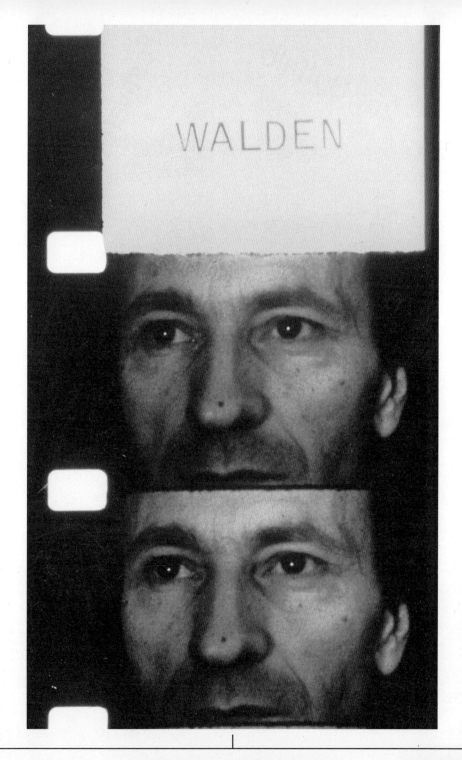

THE NEW YORK DIARIES
1950–1969

689

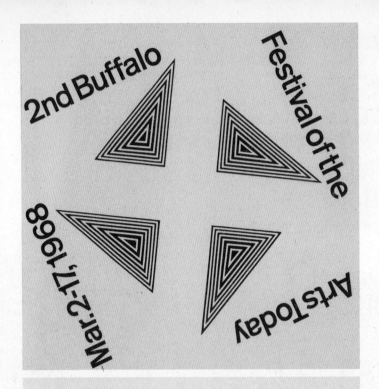

THURSDAY, MARCH 7

4:30 p.m.	Theatre Panel Discussion "Playwrighting" Edward Albee Richard Barr Alan Schneider	
	Studio Arena Theatre	No. 9 $1.00
8:30 p.m.	Films: World Premiere "New York Diaries", by Jonas Mekas	
	Gallery Auditorium	No. 10 $1.00
8:30 p.m.	Plays by Albee continue at	
	Studio Arena Theatre	No. 11 $2.75, $3.25, $3.75

FRIDAY, MARCH 8

2:30 p.m.	Music Panel Discussion John Cage, Lukas Foss, Alfred Frankenstein	
	Gallery Auditorium	No. 12 $1.00
4:30 p.m.	Theatre Panel "Stage Design" Jo Mielziner, Ming Cho Lee, Eugene Lee	
	Studio Arena Theatre	No. 13 $1.00
8:30 p.m.	Merce Cunningham Dance Company	
	Upton Auditorium	No. 14 $3.50, $2.00 Student†
8:30 p.m.	Plays by Albee continue at	
	Studio Arena Theatre	No. 15 $3.00, $3.50, $4.00

†Student tickets are available only at 218 Upton Hall, Buffalo State
University College, and Norton Hall Ticket Office, State University.

large studios for nothing, even some of the big stars are offering themselves to act in our movies just to be in them. The plan worked 100 percent! So now we'll begin making our movies.

INTERVIEWER: What about the press? How come they didn't figure you out?

JONAS: It seems they swallowed our bait too. Some of them we bribed. Or we placed our own people in strategic positions. Some openly suspected, I have to admit this, that the whole Underground Film thing is only a big publicity gimmick. But they never guessed how true they actually were! It was just too good to be true… as they say.

INTERVIEWER: Don't you feel any conscience pangs about it? About misleading the people and the film-makers?

JONAS: Not at all. We, that is, those few of us who participated in this plot (and I can't reveal their names yet) we consider that it's perfectly all right. We consider that an art generation that has lost its sense of humor is simply no good anyway. If any "artist" got hooked on our scheme, then he wasn't an artist to begin with. He was a no good fool, following fashion hooks. Therefore, no big loss! After all, there are only one or two artists in each generation anyway and nobody can mislead them!

INTERVIEWER: You sound like a very unscrupulous bunch of people. I wonder about your politics. Would you say something about your political beliefs? Like Vietnam, for instance?

JONAS: Of course, I have nothing to hide. For instance, I am very outraged about the complete inefficiency of our army in Vietnam. I consider it a complete waste of people's money. I see no reason at all why each of our boys there can't kill one Vietcong per day. After all, aren't they hired to do the job? Aren't they paid? And all the stories about the bombs dropped on the empty fields? Who cares about the fields! Dump them on the people, on Vietcongs. I think a thorough investigation of the army is needed. Somebody's sabotaging our war! Are we becoming a nation of sissies? We need two soldiers for one Vietcong, they say. How many soldiers shall we need if the Chinese move into the war? It's ridiculous.

INTERVIEWER: What do you propose?

JONAS: The soldiers have proved their inefficiency to deal with this situation. They can't kill properly. They aren't worth the money. So why not send them all home and use the money we spend on them to hire Mafia to do the job? The job would be done faster, cheaper, and with more efficiency. What we need is real professional killers, that's what we need. Let's go to the source of the matter.

April 25, 1968
Dear P. Adams and Julie:
Someone from Amsterdam sent me a batch of pictures, from Knokke, and I see P. Adams Sitney with his beard in the camera. And Julie is there too, standing by, watching. The pictures are lying on my table, right here.
Anyway, greetings from the rainy New York—I just came back from the Cinematheque, and my shoes are full of water, shlurp, shlurp. We are showing *The Illiac Passion*, it's almost Holiday.
Before I go to some good news, I want to remind you of the importance of *l'affaire Smith*. Any progress? Any News?
The good news here is that Ford Foundation came through, believe it or not, with $40,000 grant. Specifically, it's for the completion of the Cinematheque, construction

work. Practically, the money went out in three days, and we are empty again. We had $32,000 of urgent debts, so we returned them, and people were quite surprised to see their money back. Another $8,000 went to Maciunas for completion work on the Tek. So that we are as pure and happily empty as before, but with two differences: most of our debts have been wiped out, and the Tek will finally completed, so that we can relax for a little bit—this goes for the Ministry of Finances—and concentrate on the shows themselves. The third good thing that is now, with the endorsement of one official foundation, it will be much easier to get some additional funds to continue the shows. For all further fund raisings we hired (with Ford money) a professional fundraising firm.

So that much on that.

Here is something else, much more important, really. During the last six months, the attitude to the Avant-garde film in NY has changed tremendously. Ford grant is the proof of that change. The idea of the second showcase for the Avant-garde film in New York—the idea of the Two Cinematheques, one for the experimentation, where anything goes, and another for very carefully selected programs, an Avant-garde Film Academy, sort of—something that I kept pushing all winter long, but failed to get any support—as a result of which I gave up the second building and concentrated on 80 Wooster St—this idea now dissolved into something else.

Jerome came up with an idea to put such an Academy into the Shakespeare Festival (Joe Papp & Co) building. They have a very beautiful building on Lafayette St and 8th St corner. What they want to do there is something like Village Lincoln Center. They have a legit theater there going (Yakov Lind's play, or something like that), they will have a concert hall for music, another one for dance. And now, Jerome persuaded them to have one special auditorium for cinema. While Peter was still in town, we all went to the building, and we decided that it is the place where Peter's old dream of the EGG theatre could come to reality. So that's what it will be. The work is going already, and the theatre should be ready by the first of January, 1969.

Peter gave all the instructions of his dream to the architects, and left for Vienna. Jerome is supervising the construction. The idea is to make this theatre (120 seats) into the First Avant-garde Film Repertory Theater. There will be a board of say, five or six film "authorities" (say, Kelman, Brakhage, Kubelka, Sitney, and myself) who will decide which films should be admitted to such a repertory theatre. Once we decide on films, the prints will be acquired and kept in the library, for the repertory screenings. There will be one director, one coordinating director, who will do the programming, prepare notes, and guide the promotion—in close cooperation with the five program directors. Our first idea was to invite Peter to be the coordinating director. But we gave up the idea. It would be too difficult for Peter himself, knowing how choosy he is. And then, he has to make his films, he shouldn't be tied down. Third reason: Stan said that if Peter would run such a place, he wouldn't have anything to do with it. Otherwise, Stan is completely behind the idea. So we sat and we sat thinking about this matter, and we decided that YOU are the best man to run such an institution. So Jerome delegated me to write to you and inquire about your plans. This will be a foundation & City etc. sponsored project, Cinematheque will come in only indirectly, probably as Information Department or Library Department or Advisor. So that there will be enough money to run it properly, to pay everybody properly, and you'll be getting a good salary, no worry there. Also, you will have proper assistance. David may do some of the business managing, temporarily. My fair opinion is that the role that this Avant-garde Film Repertory Theatre will play, is much more important than some of the people who are now involved with it, I think. Universities, colleges, etc. etc. from across the country will be watching its programming and guiding themselves, their own programming, and also making decisions on what films to purchase (this is breaking open, this whole field of purchasing films for Universities—a very new development, you'll have all kinds of surprises when you come back)—

Now, this will affect your travels. You'll have to make up your mind. We may simply cut our Exposition and call it quits. You'd have to come back a few months before the opening of the theatre, so that you'd have enough time to prepare the whole thing. Ideally, you should start working in July or August, not much later. So I'm enclosing $100 which is to go out and drink plenty of Irish beer and take your time and make up your mind and send a telegram to: Jerome Hill, 1860 Broadway, New York, NY. We'll continue from there.

There are other developments. Like, David Brooks has a 55 minute film which is very very very beautiful. Ken Jacobs has a two hour long film which is even more beautiful than David Brooks' film, really it's tremendous.

Kelman wants, very badly, to go to India. Maybe he should take the Exposition from you?

Film-makers are very anxious to have any program notes in which they are listed —particularly like the one printed in Amsterdam, a copy of which they can see at the Museum of Modern Art, but not at the Co-op! You don't have to send them with your own money—tell, or ORDER— make it part of the arrangement, that the Museums in which the shows take place, would send at least 20 copies of the program brochure to NY, to the film-makers. Because that piece of paper is the only thing they get from it, and they are rightly vain. So please understand them and do something about it.

Jerome is leaving in another 10 days for Cassis. You may go and visit him there and talk about the theatre plans there. Jerome wants to be deeper involved in it. Really, it wouldn't exist without him—and I'm not talking about his money: I am simply talking about his inner involvement with it, he believes in it as much as we do.

End of page, end of letter. Beginning.
Love to both,
Jonas

May 7, 1968

Dear Norman:

I thought I should drop you this note. It was too crowded to say anything understandable or even hearable last night. But I was drinking my vodka and I was milling in the crowd and I was listening and arguing and then I went home and I thought I should write you this note.

There will be all kinds of very literate people around you who will be very skeptical, openly or deviously, of your "film work." DO NOT LISTEN TO THEM.

There will be those who will say that all you are doing is splashing your god damned personality across the screen like a god damned exhibitionist. Don't listen to them. Some of them are simply fools, but most of them are too close to you (personally or thru your writings) to know what your film work really is and those who will be helping you with your films—cameramen, editors, etc. etc—they will tell you (and they will sincerely feel so, god damn idiots) that THEY are the FILM-MAKERS, and you are a WRITER, and that although they may not be as good film-makers as you are a writer, they, nevertheless, at this stage, they KNOW more about WHAT CINEMA IS, than you, a poor beginner!

DON'T BELIEVE THEM. You wouldn't make a big mistake if you'd take for granted that ALL PEOPLE WHO ARE HELPING YOU ON YOUR FILMS know NOTHING, GOD DAMN NOTHING about what cinema IS. Follow this rule, I am telling you this as a good uncle… from my life experience, and from listening to the party ramblings last night, and from watching your work. Your film work is fresh and solid and real and earthly humorous and the best thing that has happened to narrative cinema since Andy Warhol and Godard. And whatever & wherever it goes wrong, I can almost detect some of the "filmmakers'" fucking fingers.

Anyway, your both films are tremendous. There is no other work I can think of in cinema—and certainly not *Bonnie and Clyde*—which gives so much insight into the character of the criminal & the cop, and on such essential, not melodramatic, levels. There are no such complicated & multifaceted characters in any of the Hollywood films, no such characters as your Sargent Pope is, with his Dostoyevskian obsessions, inspirations, and fuck ups. Don't worry that your films lack traditional, professional "touch." That could only ruin the best part in them, at this stage. The inconsistencies of your films are as essential as their consistencies. Cinema has been so dull, character-wise, that it's important even at the cost of a few formal technical bumps to throw oneself into the depths, to throw oneself out, so that something of substance would be caught, revealed, provoked, so that cinema (or the narrative) could expand, and bloom. So that you shouldn't give a damn to that kind of criticism. I read Kazin's piece, last Sunday, on *The Armies of the Night*, and here was a conservative literary critic seeing value and function of the form you took for the expression of that specific content —but I doubt if a single conservative or even MODERN film critic would have as

much intelligence and sense as Mr. Kazin had—at least they haven't shown it for *Wild 90*. So that I thought I should put this down, on paper, both as a forewarning and an advice—although you do not need any, you have gone thru it, you have had enough of it with your books. I just don't want you to get any kind of thoughts of inferiority, only because you are NEW in cinema, or because you are so deep in the Arts of Letters. If you are NEW in cinema, those, who are helping you, they haven't even born yet, for cinema. As for the scribblers, the film reviewers, it will take them a good ten years to realize—some may never come to it—what you are really all about, what your film work is all about—they will wait until it becomes history, when they can talk about it as history…

I hope I am exaggerating. Whatever—both, *Wild 90* and *Beyond the Law* are now part of that modern American narrative film which is here to stay. You are in the vanguard of it, and there are very very few others, either in front or behind you. I can tell you this with some authority, with an old mid-wife's authority, one who has helped all kinds of babies, some ugly some beautiful, so that now I can recognize one, for what it is, with the first rays of light.

If there is any occasion when you need anyone to come in defense of your film work publicly—against one or against million—here I am, at your services—
Sincerely yours, Jonas Mekas

May, 1968

The time has come for some men to shift the evolution one step further: to the international matters. Science, technology and our nervous systems have outdistanced all our social, racial, revolutionary radical movements. As far as the necessities of man today go, all contemporary radical movements remain narrow, nationalistic, ideological, racist, and not really revolutionary.

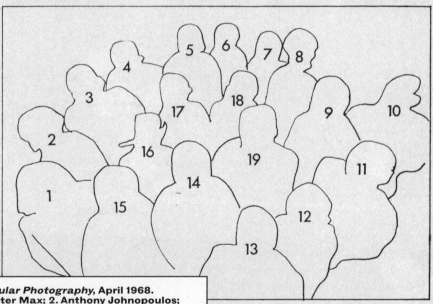

Popular Photography, April 1968.
1. Peter Max; 2. Anthony Johnopoulos;
3. Richard Leacock; 4. Ken Jacobs;
5. Robert Downey; 6. Andy Warhol;
7. Nico; 8. Paul Morrissey; 9, 18, 19. USCO,
anonymous; 10. Cyril Griffin; 11. Jacques
Katzmacher; 12. Paul Kim; 13. Jonas
Mekas; 14. Stan Vanderbeek; 15. Don
Snyder; 16. Barbara Rubin; 17. Jerry
Brandt.

200 East 57th Street, New York 22, N. Y.   PLaza 5-3448

January 13, 1967

Dear Jerry:

It was a delightful surprise to be informed of your generous Founder's gift to the New York Shakespeare Festival. Please accept my informal thanks as well as that of our Board of Trustees and Joe Papp.

With the conversion of the Astor Library Building (a commodious Victorian Renaissance landmark) into a multi-purpose complex of theatres and other recreational areas, we have many exciting plans to make the building a vital part of the new excitement in both Greenwich and East Village as well as for the entire city.

If you are not off on a ski slope, would love you to visit the building with me (perhaps after a Luchow lunch). We've no concrete plans for film showings, as yet, although we are hoping to be able to have a suitable projection booth in one of the two main theatres. I need your advice on this.

With all good wishes for the coming year to you and Alan (whom I shall call early in the week to be posted on your whereabouts).

Sincerely,

Burt

Joseph B. Martinson

Mr. Jerome Hill
1360 Broadway
New York, N.Y. 10023

Mekas at 80 Wooster.

Maciunas at 80 Wooster.

Jonas filming Maciunas, Yoshi Wada in background.

FILM-MAKERS' CINEMATHEQUE, 80 WOOSTER STREET. TEL.: 925-2250. TICKET: $1.50; STUDENTS: $1.00

JULY 1, MON. 8 P.M. KEN KELMAN: EXERCISES IN FILM HISTORY, LECT. 29: DEAD OF NIGHT BY CAVALCANTI, DEARDEN, CRICHTON, AND HAMER, DEREN'S MESHES OF THE AFTERNOON. A COMMERCIAL FILM AND AN AVANTGARDE ONE, BOTH DEALING WITH DREAM AND LEVELS OF REALITY.

JULY 2 & 3, TUESDAY & WEDNESDAY: CLOSED, NO SCREENINGS.

JULY 4, 5, 6, 7, THURS. FRI. SAT. & SUN. 8 P.M. FILMS OF LARRY JORDAN: NATURE TUNES, PICTOGRAMS (THE LEFT EYEBROW OF THE HERMIT, THE SOCCER GAME, THE 40 AND ONE NIGHTS OR JESS'S DIDACTIC NICKEL-ODEON), DUO CONCERTANTES, PETITE SUITE (SHOMÍO, THE DREAM MERCHANT, PINK SWINE, BIG SUR: THE LADIES, RODIA-ESTUDIANTINA), EIN TRAUM DER LIEBENDEN, JOHNNIE, JEWELFACE, HAMFAT ASAR, THREE MOVING FRESCO FILMS (ENID'S IDYLL, PORTRAIT OF SHARON, HYMN IN PRAISE OF THE SUN).

JULY 6, SATURDAY, 10 P.M. NEWSREELS.

JULY 8, MON. 8 P.M. KEN KELMAN: EXERCISES IN FILM HISTORY, LECT. 30: DEREN'S RITUAL IN TRANSFIGU-RED TIME, HARRINGTON'S FRAGMENT OF SEEKING, BRESSON'S DAMES DU BOIS BOULOGNE. VERY DIVERSE APPROACHES TO RITUAL CINEMA.

JULY 9 & 10, TUESDAY AND WEDNESDAY: CLOSED, NO SCREENINGS.

JULY 11 & 12, THURSDAY & FRIDAY, 8 P.M. FILMS BY CARL LINDER: DEVIL IS DEAD, OVERFLOW, SKIN, WOMANCOCK, DETONATION, CLOSED MONDAYS.

JULY 13, & 14, SAT. & SUN. FILMS BY GREGORY MARKOPOULOS, PROGRAM I, EARLY WORK: FLOWERS OF ASPHALT, CHRISTMAS CAROL, PSYCHE, LYSIS, CHARMIDES.

JULY 13, SATURDAY, 10 P.M. NEWSREELS.

JULY 15, MON. 8 P.M. KEN KELMAN: EXERCISES IN FILM HISTORY, LECT. 31: STAUFFACHER'S SAUSALITO, MARKOPOULOS' PSYCHE AND LYSIS, ANGER'S FIREWORKS, THEVENARD'S GLIMMERING. VARIOUSLY SUC-CESSFUL WAYS TO GIVE MATERIAL SUBJECTIVE TREATMENT.

JULY 16 & 17, TUESDAY & WEDNESDAY: CLOSED, NO SCREENINGS.

JULY 18, THURSDAY, 8 P.M. OPEN HOUSE. OPEN TO ALL FILM-MAKERS, FIRST COME FIRST SCREENED. COMP-LETED FILMS AND WORKS IN PROGRESS.

JULY 19, FRIDAY, 8 P.M. & 10 P.M. FILMS BY NORMAN BERG, BUD WIRTSCHAFTER AND ANDREW NOREN (KODAK GHOST POEMS).

JULY 20 & 21, SATURDAY & SUNDAY, 8 P.M. FILMS BY GREGORY MARKOPOULOS. PROGRAM II: SWAIN; TWICE A MAN.

JULY 20, SATURDAY, 10 P.M. NEWSREELS.

JULY 22, MON. 8 P.M. KEN KELMAN: EXERCISES IN FILM HISTORY, LECT. 32: MAAS' IMAGE IN THE SNOW, BROUGHTON'S MOTHER'S DAY, PETERSON'S PETRIFIED DOG. 1948 SYMBOLISM, AND SURREALISM.

JULY 23 & 24, TUESDAY & WEDNESDAY: CLOSED, NO SCREENINGS.

JULY 25 & 26, THURSDAY & FRIDAY. 8 P.M. EVENING FOR BILL KATZ AND THE LIBRARIANS: BLONDE COBRA BY BOB FLEISHNER, KEN JACOBS), PRELUDE BY BRAKHAGE, WAVELENGTH BY MICHAEL SNOW, HOLD ME WHILE I'M NAKED BY GEORGE KUCHAR.

JULY 27 & 28, SATURDAY & SUNDAY, 8 P.M. FILMS BY GREGORY MARKOPOULOS, PROGRAM III: MING GREEN, THROUGH A LENS BRIGHTLY, HIMSELF AS HERSELF.

JULY 27, SATURDAY, 10 P.M. NEWSREELS.

JULY 29, MONDAY, 8 P.M. KEN KELMAN, LECTURE 33. IN THE STREET BY LEVITT, LOEB AND AGEE, MEYER'S THE QUIET ONE, HARRINGTON'S ON THE EDGE, PETERSON'S LEAD SHOES. A NEW DEGREE OF CANDID, IN-FORMAL DOCUMENTARY; ITS CONSOLIDATION IN STORY FILM; THE PERFECTION OF SYMBOLISM AND SURREALISM.

JULY 30 & 31, TUESDAY AND WEDNESDAY: CLOSED, NO SCREENINGS.

NOTE: BECAUSE OF THE EXPENSIVENESS OF MARKOPOULOS FILMS, ALL 3 PROGRAMS OF MARKOPOULOS WILL BE $2.00 WITH NO STUDENT DISCOUNT.

**I SEEM TO LIVE, VOL. 1
CHAPTER TWENTY THREE**

So, I am proposing the Tenth International. We shall skip at least five internationals, just to indicate how big a step we have to jump to catch up with ourselves.

We should create in all countries all cities all places groups of people endorsing the following:

To abandon all armies.

To do away with all forced conscription.

To do away with all borders and separations dividing one country from another.

We are for nations and countries as traditions, as languages, as cultures, but not as separating, dividing political units, separated by passports and borders.

To do away with all passports and borders.

To eliminate all prisons.

This is a global party, a global movement. Until now, all radical movements have been national, separatist. Groups in every country, at least in the most progressed countries, should organize mass burnings of passports, to help man to begin to realize that the separations of the world into countries is outdated.

Groups and individuals in every country, students should organize mass crossings of borders and frontiers of countries, to indicate their stupidity and their invalidity, outdatedness, silliness.

Groups of people should massively ignore the customs and walk through the lines of customs with packages of all kinds of goods and things.

Mass sit-ins and takings-over should be organized in the custom houses, frontier houses & stations, border houses, to invalidate their anti-human restrictive dividing functions.

All kinds of dividing signs, slogans, indicating frontiers, should be dismantled, burned, destroyed.

Congresses and governments should be urged by pickets and sit-ins to abandon dividing, separating laws and go into international co-ops.

All money should be burned publicly.

All kinds of spying should be encouraged and exercised to bring to consciousness the fact that no knowledge should belong or is property of one country or one agency. We are ONE HUMANITY. National secrets should be pulled into the open, secret documents published in the press, televised, in order to break down the secret myth.

All Military and police services should be boycotted, ignored, abandoned.

Publishing houses of the One Humanity literature should be opened—given out for free—Buckminster, McLuhan, Wilhelm Reich, Einstein, Alice Bailey, B. Russell, H. Miller—

Petitions to the UN should be filed by groups and individuals demanding introduction of an International Passport for those who do not wish to belong to any country, any division—as a temporary means of traveling passport and as a revolutionary tool of the New Action.

Newspapers should be started for publishing for everybody's use all knowledge, any available information, national secrets, information about the movements of the armies, to analyze all the chauvinistic thinking patterns, policies.

We appeal to all the Teenagers of the World. Youth of the world. The Grown Up Generation. Scientists. Artists. Educators. Listen to yourselves. Listen to the dreams of humanity. We are here and we can all join together and make this world beautiful before it's totally destroyed by madmen, politicians, dictators, businessmen, and our own passivity.

Start your chapter of CIA (Central International Agency) now…

RE: RESPONSIBILITY TOWARDS OTHERS

While in Buffalo, during one of the television interviews there, on John Corbett show, John Corbett was telling me how Allen Ginsberg, who appeared there before me, was almost violently disavowing from any responsibility towards others. I have no idea what was the real context, what Allen meant when he said that he is not responsible for others. But when I was told this, it set me thinking. Does Allen really believe that when he reads there, in front of 2,000 students, nothing happens between him & them? Whatever we do, we affect others. Allen affects. The mind of one man affects the mind of the other. It is true, that each of us is a soul and each of us is responsible for his soul: that is God's contract and God's gift. But what happens, sadly, too often—an idea, a book, a film, anything can take over the liberty of a soul and keep it in a dream, in a state of hypnosis, for days, for months, for years. It's this that I'm thinking about. It's here that the responsibility comes in, & it's here that Allen has to answer to himself: do I open them to their own liberty or do I pull them into my own orbit.

And then, there is this other aspect to this, the law which simply makes one's own growth impossible, after a certain degree of progress, without lifting others higher. One has to pull oneself up by himself—but someone has to be there, higher, & to throw some light on that next, higher—& here we are tied together, one man to the next, inescapably, & without any choice—one soul tied in brotherhood of the journey to the other.

LETTER FROM NEW YORK
Where do I start?

1. We have three active Film-Makers' Co-operatives by now. In New York, we have the mother Film-Makers' Cooperative (175 Lexington Ave., New York, N.Y.). In San Francisco, there is the Canyon cooperative (7556 Union Street, San Francisco, Calif.). In July, the third cooperative was born in Chicago (c/o Lawrence Janiak, 540 Cornelia St., Chicago Ill.). All three co-ops follow the basic rules of the co-ops: a) no film is rejected, b) film-maker gets 75 % of all income, c) it's governed by a board of film-makers, d) your film is your membership card to the co-op. There is also the Film-Makers' Distribution Center, in New York (175 Lexington Avenue), which is engaged in commercial distribution, but its status is not defined at this moment, it's not a co-op yet.

Incomes from the distribution thru the co-ops have been still growing. We feel that beginning with this autumn, the universities and colleges will come in increasing numbers.

With all kinds of sharks trying to exploit our work, one of the main concerns is to avoid any kind of sensational advertising, promotion, etc. We want to be factual, and stress is on the author, not on the subject matter.

2. A few new works appeared during last few months which should remain part of our repertory. One of the most important new works is David Brooks' new film, *The Wind is Driving Him Towards the Open Sea*, a 52 minute film. (His other films: *Jerry; Nightspring Daystar; Winter 64/65*). Brooks describes it as "a film in numerous realities, including those of image, news, myth, philosophy, documentary, mythopoeia." Basically, it's a narrative film, but with all the subtitles and complexities of an epic poem. Stan Brakhage has a new film, *Scenes From Under Childhood*, 25 min. You may be interested in the fact that it's a sound film. Two new film-makers were introduced at the Film-Makers' Cinematheque and should be seen by everybody: Ernie Gehr (films: *Eyes* and *Moments*), and Joyce Wieland (Films: *1933; Catfood; Untitled; Sailboat*). Both have great interest in form. Gehr explores the stop motion and light (in the tradition of Michael Snow's *Wavelength*); Joyce Wieland is interested in orchestration of repeated shots and in minimalism.

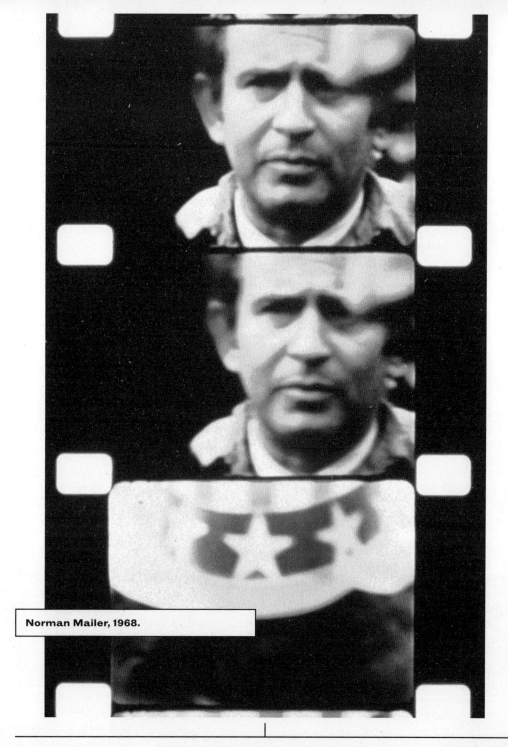

Norman Mailer, 1968.

142 Columbia Heights
Brooklyn, New York 11201

May 20, 1968

Dear Jonas:

     Your letter was fine and generous and splendid as you
always are with your open reception, nay, your incredible
sensitivity to what is new and valid in everyone's work. And I
hope the picture is as good as you say it is--there are times when
I think it is. You know I never told you this but one of the ten
reasons why I got into making films has been reading your columns
over the years and as a result slowly connecting to some of the
ideas--for I missed many of them--in avant garde film which loosened
me up. So this is not only to say that I will be quick to call on
you if there's need, but that I look forward to us finally having
a conversation some day, not an easy matter for either of us, for
so many conversations are disappointments, but maybel we'll have
the opportunity to take a crack at it. Will you be on the Cape
this summer? If so, please come by to visit. The phone number
is 487-9325, and if not, I'm sure we'll see each other in the fall
on that movie board of which we're both, bless us, members.

     Yours and best,

     Norman

I should also mention Warren Sonbert (whose *Where Did Our Love Go* was included in Sitney's Exposition) and a double screen film by Storm De Hirsch, *Third Eye Butterfly*; and new works by George Landow.

As it is now, I think that if you could send to us 100 minutes long programs of films, say, from Italy, or Germany, or Austria, we could give them exposure, through the system of our three co-ops. Still, we haven't solved the money problem, that is, co-ops barely manage to cover their running expenses, there is no extra money to send say to Leonardi $300 or $400 for making prints for such a program. But if the Italian, or German, or Swiss, etc. film-makers can afford, by hooks or crooks, making one set of prints, and send such a program to either the Canyon Co-op or to the N.Y. Co-op, we could get your money back in two or three months with no great problem. Best, if you want to do something like that, is to notify us in advance, so that we could set up bookings even before the prints arrive.

We do not know yet about Chicago, both the Canyon and N.Y. co-ops are by now pretty well organized.

We have one big question which nobody has been able to answer and maybe some info could be provided in your bulletin, and it's concerning the London Co-op. We have such contradicting reports on the London Co-op and Arts Lab that we have been staying away from both, we don't know whom to trust. By the way, we have a close contact with the Canadian Film-Makers' Cooperative, which is called Canadian Film-Makers' Distribution Center (Suite 11, 719 Yonge Street, Toronto, Canada) and they are well organized by now and we have good experiences with them.

That's about it, this time.

P.S. I am enclosing Cinematheque's program notes on Landow which you could reproduce, if you have space. Landow is VERY VERY good and not enough people know his work.

Description of my course at Yale University
The following thoughts and comments will be elaborated:
What is meant by "new" in the new cinema … The new cinema constructs, builds, does not destroy… The failures today are the critics, not the artists… When the critics and the educators lose understanding of the meaning of art in man's life, art becomes "meaningless" in that society… There is no meaningless art… The preoccupations of the avant-garde filmmaker today… The directions… The crossroads… The dangers… The meaning of "avant-garde" in art and in life… (which is the same)… The avant-garde artist as the only religious artist today…which also means he is the only political artist today, the only committed artist today… committed to things that really matter in the real progress of man… that is, the soul of man… and what does it mean to have 8,000,000 movie cameras in the U.S.A. today…

A NOTE ON CINEMA AND POLITICS IN ITALY
Despite my complete approval of Sitney's handling of the Exposition (nobody's perfect—and I am more interested in Sitney's "perfections" than in his "imperfections"; I firmly believe that P. Adams Sitney is still the best man to guide this kind of Exposition)—there is one area in which I completely disagree with P. Adams Sitney, and that is, the subject of "politics." P. Adams' attitude to politics is purist to the point of paranoia. Whenever he hears the word "politics" he thinks about political parties, Marx, I don't know what. He goes all the way out to stress the point that the New American Cinema, the avant-garde film has nothing to do with politics. I, just the opposite, believe that you can't open your mouth, you can't make a movement

without revealing your politics. To me, politics has nothing to do with political parties, with Marx, L.B.J. I insisted, in all places I went, in Torino and Pesaro, that our Exposition, our films could be considered really political films. This, no doubt, was such a preposterous statement, I was immediately attacked and challenged by both, communists and rightists: yes, what the hell this has to do with Marx? Or war in Vietnam? Your films are pure escapist crap!—More or less in that spirit. Which immediately led into the subject of what are we really talking about when we say politics; it caused long and hot discussions, and I told in no vague terms that what they call politics is just politicking and propaganda, and that the true politics are locked in Art, and they better try to get this into their heads. Now, this was quite a shock to some, in most places, this kind of statement, in the very heart of the Italian Communist Party, in Torino, and it left the intellectuals of Torino and Milano arguing and fighting on this subject long after I was gone. What Sitney failed to see, is that the Italian left intelligentsia is the most advanced, the most open to new ideas, to changes, of all groups in Italy. And when Sitney says that Italian communists mistook N.A. Cinema for some kind of radical movement—my God, we should only rejoice that at least someone sees in our art something real and radical. Who else takes us seriously? But Sitney preferred to continue playing the old game of "avant-garde"—art relegated to hothouses. The way I see, all art is political in the deepest sense of that word. And I consider that it's my duty as an artist to resist the wrong, harmful propagandistic mafia & power politics as well as the avant-garde hothouse politics.

No date, 1968

To keep the Cinematheque going, to keep the European Exposition going, and to keep the *Film Culture* magazine going, and to keep the screenings at the Cinematheque going, we need money. We operate on a $3,000 a month deficit. Plus to these expenses, during last six months, we have been trying to build our own theatre on 80 Wooster Street—we got tired of running from place to place.

How are the Cinematheque's deficits covered?

Here is how it survived thru January and February: A friend of the Tek's projectionist sold his car and lent all the money to the Tek; Ellen Hirst donated all the money she made on... what? Jonas contributed all the money he made on his lecture tours of those months, plus the money of his *Voice* column; Amy Taubin, an actress pledged a weekly donation, and keeping the pledge until the building of the Cinematheque is completed. Robert Breer contributed his films free for a two-day show at the Tek. Other contributors during the months of January and February were: Mitch Miller Foundation, George Plimpton, Howard Wise.

Dear Stan, Jane, and children:

With the usual delay I want to thank you for your beautiful tapes—sounds, including the donkey—which I received in time. As was expected, I didn't complete my *Diaries* in time. So I took to Buffalo the first draft. I hope I didn't let them down too much. No more such deadlines for me. EMERGENCY REQUEST: I completely forgot something. Only now, sitting in Jacksonville, Ill.—from all places—I remembered that I scheduled *Song 15* for March 21st and *23rd Psalm Branch*. Could I order one print of each, for the Cinematheque? So that our set would be complete. It will be carefully guarded and well used. I wonder if there is enough time for *Song 15* to get made for March 21st? Should I ask for Jerome's copy? Money for both, *Song 15* & *23rd* will be shipped as soon as you let me know how much.

Peter, no doubt, informed you about the "Academy" developments (or, as I call it, "The Concert Hall of Cinema") (The Chamber Series??? Maya?)

Meanwhile this beautiful person Nitsch was dropped in my lap in N.Y. Not enough that I have to be the Minister of Finances of the avant-garde film—I have to be the Cultural Attaché of Austria. I have to do the Austrian job. Peter & I agree that it was very timely and necessary to give Nitsch this chance—but Peter never thinks what it involves. So I got stuck with a good $1,000 expense and only God knows where the money comes from—it comes thru my blood—almost literally—or thru the blood of my crying, unfinished films—it will cost me three lecture trips to cover THAT.

Meanwhile, we are still trying to complete the Wooster place. While all the PURE eyes are directed towards the Future Academy, I have been left alone, and with impurity, to struggle with the problems of NOW, with finishing our little miserable poor 80 Wooster Cinematheque—this insignificant stepping stone for the Future Academies of the Avant-garde film—So you can understand how I appreciate your giving your *Songs* to screen at the Tek, as a benefit. The only other film-maker, besides you—who understood our needs & problems—is Breer who donated his films for a free show. Emsh loaned some money. All the others would be sitting by your door next day, if you don't pay. I can't blame them. They are undernourished physically & spiritually.

I'm scribbling this, but I have no idea if you'll be able to read my scribbling.

The sun is climbing higher and higher, I can see the roofs of Jacksonville, Ill. & it begins to look like Spring will be coming soon. I am sitting here in a motel room waiting for some students to come & to fetch me—we have a noon show at the College—so I'm taking this pause to drop you these notes—unreadable as they are —with my best regards to all of you—and to let you know that I'm thinking about you very very often—these days—and all other days—

Jonas

P.S. I just went thru my "File" of letters etc. & was reminded—I found your letter—that you are sending *23rd* thru Grove. I'll call Grove as soon as I'm back in N.Y. In that case, only *15* is missing. Unless in the CI-16 set? I can't check this until next Sunday.

June 2, 1968

Received the first issue of a British film mag, *FIBA*, edited by George Paul Solomos. Magazine carries a by-line: *A Critical Bulletin of the New Professional Cinema.* Throughout the issue runs a very bad chauvinistic arrogance, directed against the American Underground, against the London Co-op (which supposed to be clandestinely sponsored by the N.Y. underground, etc.).

Down with the barriers, borders, national interests, national parties, national movements! Technology has already outdistanced us, and we are having a hard time to pull ourselves by the ears. The co-ops, the film-makers of the world, working in the most advanced medium, must abandon all the national, separating, dividing attitudes. With a jet, we are in New York today and in the evening we are in Tokyo. The TV images span the entire earth. We keep making dividing lines. We keep them by force, by inertia. And they hold us, by inertia. Let's free ourselves from borders.

June 8, 1968

"I guess, some people are unreasonable," said Laotze.

"Some people are sometimes reasonable, sometimes unreasonable," added Confucius. "Some reasonable people are sometimes unreasonable," said Buddha, but he never finished or didn't want to finish or didn't know how to finish, he couldn't or he wouldn't, and that's why this saying isn't reported in any of the usual books.

June 10, 1968

At the symposium, at the Donnell Library, I asked the following questions:

Question: Why do all libraries carry books but not all libraries carry films?

Question: Why do all libraries carry newest books, but film libraries which carry films carry only OLD films?

Question: Because of the development in the communications and dissemination technology within these coming years separation between books and films will be narrowed, the dissemination aspect, that is. How are the libraries preparing to make this change?

Question from the audience: Do you have any censorship etc. pressures?

Answer (me): Yes, we have them, but we have them as a result of us pressuring THEM to free themselves. Our pressuring provokes them, and before they open themselves, they exert an opposing "pressure," for a while.

REPORT FROM THE CO-OP
(NEW YORK):

June 10th, the directors of the Co-op held their routine bi-weekly meeting. Present: Robert Breer, Ken Jacobs, Jonas Mekas, Ed Emshwiller, Charles Levine, Leslie Trumbull, Jack Perlman (attorney). Brief report was made by Jack Perlman on the status of the new name. For the last three months or more we have been trying to detach Film-Makers' Cooperative from the New American Cinema Group, Inc., to make it into an independent non-profit cooperative. Legally, being part of the New American Cinema Group, Inc., it makes Co-op into a business (profit) organization, which it's really not. The second reason for the separation is that some film-makers do not want to have much to do with the Film-Makers' Distribution Center, which is also a division of the New American Cinema Group, Inc. So that now, when the Co-op got detached from the N.A. Cinema Group, it got also automatically detached (legally and in many other ways) from the Distribution Center. Anyway, the Co-op is going thru the last stages of becoming a completely independent body. It will be registered in all legal books as Film-Makers' Cooperative.

Most of the meeting time was devoted to the discussion of the conditions under which the film-maker should sell his prints to the libraries, universities, etc. From several discussions of this subject it's becoming clearer and clearer that the film-maker shouldn't sell his prints at all but should LEASE them for the lifetime of the print. Leasing simplifies the legal aspects of the deal. As for the price, for how much to lease—each film-maker should decide for himself. The general consent was that no film-maker should lease his prints (for the lifetime of the print) for less than two or three times the lab cost of the print. There are many universities and public libraries approaching film-makers these days. Film-makers should make clear to them certain basic conditions: a) the print is being leased to the University for the lifetime of the print, b) University is not allowed to make copies from that print, c) the print can be used only within the boundaries of the University and only in the classrooms, for study purposes, d) the print shouldn't be used for any paid, entertainment purposes, e) the print can not be used on televisions, etc. In the case of Public Libraries, the Co-op directors felt that the film-makers should insist that the print should NEVER leave the premises of the Library. It's time that the libraries begin to think seriously about the ways of solving certain problems of film lending. Too often, films are being screened under terrible conditions, etc. etc.

Libraries should have screenings rooms on their premises to serve the film-viewer. Until the price of the film prints goes down (which may happen soon, if the new reproduction methods come into existence) there is no other way of controlling the traffic of prints, EXPENSIVE prints. I attended a gathering of Public Library execs and they were complaining that the avant-garde film-makers do not want to sell them their films. I explained to them some of the problems of the film-makers, I told them that the film-maker depends on his rentals, that he can not give his expensive prints to the libraries until the libraries solve simple and basic problems of lending and handling the prints. The reaction of the library execs was very slow, I felt like I was trying to drive a nail through a concrete block.

Leslie made a note that the new edition of the Catalogue is being prepared and that the end of June is the last time to send in any new information, new entries, or changes in the old entries.

Co-op has a problem with the new films. Since it's impossible to issue a new catalogue more than once a year (mailing alone costs almost $2,000), films which came to the Co-op after the last catalogue went into print, that is, a year ago—practically nobody knows about their existence. To print monthly or quarterly supplements is a solution which the N.Y. Co-op intends to seriously consider.

It was decided that within one week from today's meeting yearly election sheets will go out to all members of the Co-op. They should be sent back to the Co-op by July. Film-makers' meeting is being called at the Film-makers' Cinematheque, 80 Wooster Street, on July 23rd, 6pm, during which the envelopes will be opened and the votes counted, the new government announced.

June 12, 1968

Polanski, in this week's *Variety*, makes fun of Truffaut and Godard, calls them "kids who play revolution," and brags that he participated in "real" revolution. Polanski, like many others who are laughing at Godard and student demonstrations, are all those who call all these events "kids revolution," they long for "real," old fashioned blood baths. They want to see blood. They do not realize that without any blood, in a completely different spirit, with passive resistance, the students, these "kids" have already changed the world by at least a dozen chapters, and they have done that without a single drop of blood. If there was any blood, it was not spilled by the "kids": it was spilled by the police. Yes, Polanski is very very happy at Cannes, a very happy funny capitalist he is, but…

Glauber Rocha came by. Complained that they can't see NAC in Brazil. Rocha says, Rio is the capital of the New Cinema, and São Paolo is the Brazilian Hollywood. Nuovo Cinema makes 5 – 7 features every year; the Industry—close to one hundred. But the young Brazilian cinema, he says, is full of gusto and is directed to the people and is being shown quite widely through Brazil. Can you say whatever you want in your films? No, he says. He said, last night he stopped in a place, in the Gr. Village, where a young man was lecturing on the S. American situation, and he really knew the situation. But there were only eight people listening to him. Thousands of hippies in the streets of New York, but they don't want to listen when somebody has something to say.

He said, the Brazilian films can't be shown in New York: they aren't Spanish, they are Portuguese. And I always thought they spoke Spanish. What about Argentina? I asked. "Oh, we are a colonial country, so we are closer to France than Argentina," he said. "It's true. I keep going to Paris. I am going to Paris now."

June 14, 1968

The New York Post, today:

The student revolt which started with an attack on Springer newspapers in Berlin last spring has now swept around the world. Did it result from an international *conspiracy*? Is there a student underground linking the ivy halls of Columbia in New York with the crowded Communist universities of Belgrade, Warsaw, Cracow and Prague?

This column, after extensive research, is able to report that there is an international student conspiracy. Mark Rudd, who for a time closed down Columbia University, visited Fidel Castro in Cuba shortly before he brought anarchy to Columbia. A delegation of Latin American students visited the U.S. this spring shortly before trouble broke out on American campuses. Daniel Cohn-Bendit, the French-German student revolutionary, also visited the U.S. shortly before trouble erupted here. (Drew Pearson and Jack Anderson)

Did *Post* really need any research to know this?

From the beginning of human history, from the earliest dreams from Eden, man has been longing to become One Humanity again. No boundaries, no custom agents, no passports, no frontiers, no wars. The International Conspiracy the public media are talking about could be also called, because that's what it is, Man's Longing for the Paradise on Earth. The Youth of all countries, despite all the silly national separations, they feel it very strongly, and they understand each other, and they work together and they'll do so, they will keep their Conspiracy work until humanity becomes one again. Theirs is the positive, the heavenly conspiracy.

The Governments, on the other hand, are engaged in the evil conspiracy of nationalism, of separations. It's not the International Conspiracy that the people should be afraid of: it's the National Conspiracy of governments that is People's Enemy. The public media have perverted the truth and now nationalism has become a virtue and they call the International Conspiracy bad names!

June 16, 1968

Dear P. Adams Sitney:

Your last letter, your hassle with Gregory, has a smell of New York. You have only one Gregory to cope with, and you sound exhausted and pissed off—what about me, who has three dozen film-makers to cope with? Just a touch of reality... As you know quite well by now, whatever you do, if you do something that is tailored to suit or do a job for many film-makers, a larger project —be it Co-op, or Tek, or *Film Culture*, or now Exposition—there will always be individual film-makers on your neck, sometimes with blood on their fingers, fighting against you, and most of the time justly, when you look from their personal, single, that is, egotistical view. So that someone is always hurt, and I have given up trying to make everybody happy at the same time. I try to make everybody happy at different times, if possible. It's enough to make you sick, as Confucius used to say.

Anyway, as you see from the enclosed text (Letter to Film-Makers), I have informed all the film-makers whose films are included in the Expositions about the termination of the Exposition. You are right (in your letters) that the Exposition stayed a bit too long in Europe. Not much too long —but perhaps by two or three months, that's all. You no doubt are tired like a dog and all you can think about is your novel and the stillness of some hidden village in Spain. And so do I. I swear with both my hands lifted never again to engage myself into any Expositions, or into any projects where thirty film-makers stand behind you with logs lifted above your head, if you make one wrong move. I really had enough.

I think they had me. They managed to discourage me, which is a pretty hard thing to do. But I intend to go into the shrinking period. I intend to close myself at 80 Wooster Street and become a monk.

I wouldn't be so discouraged if it wouldn't be all because of money. It always goes back to money. Bruce Conner thinks that the Exposition robbed him or is robbing him of his European Money Potential, can you imagine that? I have a pile of angry letters on my table, all about money. Some indirect, and not very honest money scheme is also noticeable behind some recent Gregory activities—including his pulling out of the Exposition. I used to say that a film-maker is always right, even when he is wrong; he is still RIGHT—but, God, is he STUPID, too. One can be right and stupid at the same time, I guess.

I am writing all this nonsense because I feel pretty low today. (Larry Jordan cancelled his show, refuses to send his films from SF, because Cinematheque hadn't yet paid $120 bill to the Canyon Cinema Co-op) (More Stupid News.) And I have to raise over $2,000 this week to pay the workers at the Cinematheque, for installation of air conditioner, etc. etc. I can't get any money anywhere these days, everybody thinks we are RICH, we received $40,000 from Ford Foundation. I can not explain to them, that that money was spent before it came in, the expenses of buying two floors, the construction work are over $60,000—and although Ford money cleared most of our debts, we'll need another $5,000 or so to complete the place. It will be a hot long summer, I can smell it.

Since even to you may not be clear (being far as you are, and this Tek project came after you left) why I am going thru all this trouble to build our own place, our own theatre—all I can tell is this: When you'll come back you'll notice a few sad discoveries, changes. One of them is that while the reputation of the Avant-garde film grew, books are coming out, and now maybe even the Academy (Papp) will come into existence—the places where the avant-garde film-maker could screen his films, the audience for the avant-garde film, has SHRUNK to a small core of true film lovers. There are so many places which "show" UNDERGROUND FILMS—like Gate Theater, two or three theaters on 42nd Street, even Bleecker St Cinema—but they are not showing avant-garde film. You know what they are showing. And that's where the people are going. Two years ago, both the film lovers and the sensation seekers used to come to the Tek, and we did well. Now, we lost all the sensation seekers. It started happening about a year ago. That's when I caught the first signals of what was happening. It's at that time that I started thinking about a long range plan, about moving out of expensive theaters and having some cheap place of our own—like a cellar with some dried bread and a bottle of water, and a few roots, for DRY TIMES—and that's where we are. I went thru the most exhaustive year of my life, to build the Cinematheque and I still see one more long hot summer— but I am ANGRILY HAPPY, and I am beginning to be ANGRILY RELAXED, most of the time—because despite the money problems this week, and a few more weeks to come—we are holding our screenings every day, with no financial considerations of any kind, and we don't give a damn even if not a single sensation seeker will come—we have a place where we can see films for ourselves, and with those few who really care about film. The audience at the Cinematheque is very seldom over 40 people (it swells to a full place, we can seat over 200, when there is at least 1% of sensation in the name or title, that happens)—and the feeling is very good. So that I am willing to go thru another summer of money hunting, dollar by dollar, and I am willing to take plenty of crap from film-makers and anyone who has extra free crap available—

The Avant-garde Film Repertory Theatre will compliment the Cinematheque, and it will act as a quiet, independent and constant wedge into the uptown spheres. It will afford even better programs than Cinematheque, as far as the classical avant-garde goes—because A.F.R. Theatre will be free of money. Cinematheque has to devote more time, proportionally, to the new films than to classics and established avant-garde artists, only because the rentals of films are becoming too high. Imagine, Gregory charging $200 for one screening of *Twice a Man*, forty people watching? I booked a complete retro of Gregory's work at the Cinematheque, for July and August, with full knowledge that it will eat up all my lecture and *Village Voice* column moneys for at least two or three months, sixteen hundred bucks. A.F.R.Th. will have no such worries or considerations, in its programming. That's where your job will be easier. Although the fact is that the audience for the serious avant-garde film has shrunk to a minimum—it is also true, that from now on, this audience will start growing, with no fake & sick pumpkin swellings that come and go, but with a steady & "healthy" growth of true film lovers, something permanent, something on which the avant-garde film-maker will be able to depend, this small core of film lovers. So you can see, I am very optimistic... That's why I am a little bit worried about Gregory when he writes that he thinks he's discovered his real audience—in Europe! He's pulling out of the Co-op (not withdrawing, but just taking out the prints) all his prints and is sending them to European Archives, etc. Europe will be going through the same UNDERGROUND film swellings, now, as US went during last five years. Europe is up for grabs, friends, film-makers...

I am reaching the end of the page, and I have no idea what I am writing here, so I better stop. Andy is improving and will pull thru. The day he was shot I went to the Hospital, and there, in the waiting room, everybody was crying and being pretty low, and I said, what the hell is this, a funeral? Don't you know that people of weak and hungry constitution like me or Andy do not die that easily, you just can't kill them that easily, he'll pull thru... He'll be O.K.

I may have to go to Venice in August, around 25th. What's your Spain schedule? We could still meet at Ávila. After all, St. Teresa built the Cinematheque, not me. Let me know your schedule in advance.
Love to you both,
Jonas

June 17, 1968

STAN, JANE and CHILDREN:
I know, it is hardly forgivable, my last letter —laziness, I should converse with you more often, because the city is pretty grey and one gets tired seeing the same faces, and the faces one sees here, these days (and not only these days) are as grey as the city itself—so that I sit here, tonight, this late evening, and have a longing—don't laugh— to see the face of your kind good serene and humorous donkey (I think, when I think back, that Roscoe—is that the donkey's name?) has more sense of humor than most of the people I know or meet— and the sense of humor goes together with wisdom and serenity)—
anyway, you can't imagine how happy I would feel if tomorrow, walking uptown, Eighth Avenue, to the Post Office, I'd meet the DONKEY!

As you can see, this city isn't doing any good to me if I am beginning to have such strange wishes... But I am a city man now, or one who wants to be a city man, to prove some kind of point, just despite of everything, to prove that man is marching forward, that he cannot go backwards, to his village—to MY village,

yes, I stick to this godforsaken city probably because ALL I WANT, REALLY, I want to go back to my village—which, by the way, doesn't exist, practically, any longer— there are long wide fields of collective farms stretching now along the brooks and rivers where my little village was—and this complicates the matter still more, that it's no longer there—but I want to go back to the village, particularly now, when the summer is here because I have to get up early, before the sunrise, to go fetch the horses in the fields, barefooted, through the cold dew, leaving long wet patches in the grass—and the day will be long, the more that we didn't go to sleep until two in the morning, we were walking along the road, from one end of the village to the other, a dozen of us, singing, all evening, and deep into the night, and the song was floating like milk across the sleeping fields, and through the white mist hanging around the river—and then you are deep in your sleep, and you hear mother's voice, GET UP, GET UP, THE SUN WILL BE RISING SOON, and you rub your eyes and they begin to open only by the time you reach the middle of the field, when you begin to hear the horses shnurrping and you begin to look around, and you see the sky red like a huge explosion of morning coming up, right there behind the trees, and the horses, peaceful, and quiet, eating wet green grass—eh–

bless you all but it's really me who needs blessings

Jonas

June 21, 1968

I called the building department, Mr. McGinnis (Inspector McGinnis) 566-3130. I said, we think we've completed everything, we would like someone to come and inspect the place, we would like to apply for proper licenses for 80 Wooster Street Theatre. He said, call on Monday, will assign inspector.

Brakhages, 1963.

CHAPTER TWENTY FOUR

... Notes on Coop meeting... Letter to Joyce and Ken re. George Landow... Beginning of work on licensing 80 Wooster Street... Meetings with Building Department... Letter to the Avignon Film Festival... Letter to the Canyon Cinema... More trips to the Building Dept.... Letter from Brinkmann... Lunch with Rossellini... Coop meets... Courts... Trips to the Building Dept... Completion of the European Traveling Exposition... Postcard from Ginsberg & Yoko Ono... About serving on film juries... On FM Distribution Center... Letter to Barbara, Ginsberg, Gordon... Letter from Kenneth Anger... Depressing letter to Sitney... Policemen ask for bribes... The Hell is the Court... I begin to hallucinate...

June 24, 1968

FILMMAKER'S COOPERATIVE
Director's Meeting
Present: Ken Jacobs, Ed Emshwiller, Robert Breer, Jonas Mekas (directors); Charles Levine (Guest Director); Louis Brigante (FM Distribution Center), Charles Hoag (Director of Filmmakers' Lecture Bureau); Leslie Trumbull (Secretary of the FM Co-op); Jack Perlman (attorney of the Co-op).

Charles Levine reported on June 21st benefit for Civil Liberties to which filmmakers contributed films (K. Anger, Jonas Mekas, Ken Jacobs, Newsreel, Charles Levine) and Levine acted as projectionist. Levine said, "films were a smash success, more so than the rock and roll group they had on the boat" (the benefit show took place on a Hudson boast...).

Charles Hoag reported on the progress of the Film-makers' Lecture Bureau. He is meeting film-makers, collecting information and ideas and preparing information sheets on each film-maker. The Lecture Bureau is being sponsored by the Distribution Center, but it's being structured in such a way that it could become an independent co-op on its own when it becomes self-supporting. Ken Jacobs and Breer raised the question whether 25% wasn't too much to keep from the lecture fees to run the Bureau. It was explained by Louis Brigante and Mr. Hoag, that for the first year the 25% is a must, because the Bureau has no funds, and the Center is only helping through the first stages—the

Center has no money, either. What's more, most of the initial expenses, preparing catalogues, information folders, photographs, etc., etc.,—will fall on the first year's budget. The second year will be easier, and it will be up to some smaller percentage. The Lecture Bureau will be owned by the film-makers and by no one else.

Jonas made a report on a complicated animation set-up that someone is considering donating to the Cinematheque, if we can assure that it will not be misused, that we'll take good care of it, and that it will serve film-makers' needs. It was decided that yes, let's have the machine and see that we take good care of it. More details on the machine will be next week.

A complaint was made by Ken Jacobs about bad projection lately at the Cinematheque. Jonas explained that he has a weak heart and can't fire film-makers (film-makers are projectionists at the Cinematheque), but that he may have to fire George Landow. He also said that at least 75 % of the bad projection can be blamed on film-makers themselves who do not provide leaders for focusing, whose splices are sloppy and make projectionists lose loops, who do not clean their films, who keep long leaders with all kinds of scribblings on them which make the audience laugh where seriousness is needed, who bring to screenings "green" prints (they stick), etc., etc., etc. But he said he may have to fire George although he may die of hunger... Part of the problem (he said) was that Tek can afford only $40 a week for the projectionist, and only George is willing to work for it.

Millennium workshop was briefly discussed. Emshwiller said he was very impressed with the dedication of the people around it. Ken Jacobs, and all the others, exchanged a few sad remarks about the fact that Millennium workshop has no equipment. Jonas made a categorical statement (Ken disagreed but he said he wouldn't shout) that he has come to the conclusion that film schools and film workshops attract wrong untalented people, and film schools and workshops are totally unnecessary. He said that this will be his stand from now on. But, he said, film-makers need a pool of equipment, a kind of free rental service. Ken said that's what Millennium ideally hopes to be.

Secretary of the meeting, Jonas Mekas

To the film-makers: Joyce, Ernie, Ken, etc: Yes, I am going to fire George, so that your films could be projected nicely and properly by someone else. You can sit and watch them, nicely,

But there is something that is bothering me, and I have to unburden myself, and try to look into it, as it comes out.

There are several things. There is Joyce, angry, grumpy, coming to the Cinematheque, on Monday, to pick up her tape, not saying anything to me, and leaving without a word, turning her back, angrily, and walking out sulkily. "THIS IS IT. I don't want to talk to you. You are no Good." And then Leslie's note which says: Joyce told me she will never show her films at the Tek. And Ernie, sitting there high, in his seat at the Tek, and then walking out. A terrible thing happened: "I AM RIGHT! There can be no question about my being right: The other is always guilty, not me. Here was my precious little work of art being destroyed by dust in the gate, by five seconds of sound omitted." And similar disasters.

Not that I want to diminish the unproperness of the projection. Not at all. What bothers me is the attitude that we, film-makers, take towards those who work with us. Instead of coming to George and telling, look, maybe I could help you— see, how this or that mistake could be avoided—let's see what we could do so that this wouldn't repeat again. No, we don't talk, we don't even think in those terms of togetherness. Instead, we act like insulted GODS, because our ART is so important, and we walk out angrily, and we declare war, this is it, this is the end, fire him, get rid of him like he is our enemy.

And there stands George on the platform, and he makes mistakes, and he isn't perfect, and nobody is, but some are more perfect than others, of course—but I do not remember anyone perfect—Ken says, hire Bob, because Ken saw some of Bob's projections, and he saw some of George's projections. But I have seen many many of Bob's projections and many many of George's projections, and I know how many times I ran upstairs to Bob and focused the lens myself, exactly as with George— maybe a few times less, but what does it mean, nine or ten, or ten or seven—even seven and five, ten and five proportions, what does it mean, it's not perfect, and the imperfections of George, which is number ten, is not very much more devastating than that of Bob, which is number five— depends on when it hits you, whom it hits, Ernie or Jack or me etc.

But this precious little ego, this precious inhumanity to one who is projecting your work, because he was asked to do so, and he is trying, because nobody else would do it for $40 a week—we sit there, and we are still trembling, like birds, because there is our precious art on that projector, and nothing else means anything but the god damn dust there in that frame, and that out of focus image, and we declare war on the man up there on that platform, because what right does he have to do THAT to OUR baby?

But I feel, shit, all your babies are shit if you can treat human beings like that, if you put your work above human beings, if you can take such stance only because someone is trying and failing—no pity, NO PITY—you walk out sour and cold and inhuman, or if you don't walk out, you sit there all cramped inside, full of unspeakable silent anger. My God, not even people, they didn't even get enough people to see my film, the place is almost empty—no doubt, this is another blunder they made, and they think they are doing something for cinema! Sure there must be many more people who want to see my work, only that they don't come because who wants to come into a place where this kind of thing is being done, where films are tortured like this...

But I am going to fire George it seems.

Yes, the wheels of INDUSTRY are turning, they have caught up with you, George. The automation, the capitalism, the economy, the perfection, efficiency, and the PURITY, Madame Purité. Let's not have any of these human frailties and mistakes displayed right there in front of us, when we want to sit there and just watch the WORKS OF ART. Out you go, George. Get new glasses, and go take a few lessons in concentration, and efficiency. Come back in a few months, maybe the COMPANY will rehire you, maybe YOU'LL MAKE IT yet after all—but now, I don't think so, George. You see, the PEOPLE are rebelling, they want perfection, they are using pressure, they are banding together, playing politics in BLOCK pressures—so that we have to give in, I don't think we can keep you that easily, just think about our reputation, St. George, and forget the dragons.

You see, art is more powerful than human relations.
Art is more important than your neighbor. Or let me say MY art is more important than human relations.
MY art is more important than my neighbor. Love yourself like you love your ART...

I am a moralist, I guess, moralizing, a fucking moralist, trying to make a big deal out of nothing, nothing... So I am going to fire George and make things REALLY GOOD, to please your precious butterfly egos, so that they could grow and blossom, despite EVERYTHING. EVERYTHING. ORDNUNG MUSS SEIN.

Yours Worriedly, Jonas

June 24, 1968
9:30 AM. I called McGinnis. He said an inspector has been assigned, will come today. I waited all day long at the Cinematheque. Inspector didn't come.

June 25, 1968
9 AM. I called McGinnis. He said, I really have to talk to the inspector Pero. Call tomorrow.

June 26, 1968
9:15 AM. I called Inspector Pero. Pero said 80 Wooster is not his zone. Call Mr. Burns, Inspector Burns. I called Inspector Burns. He said will come before noon today. Burns came. A nice elderly man. Said "O.K.", he sees no problems, no objections. He said, now we have to call the "construction inspector." Inspector Burns approved only... I was not too sure what, but he certainly approved something.

June 27, 1968
9:15 AM. I called the building department, explained our needs. They said, speak to inspector Pero. Pero said, he will come tomorrow.

June 28, 1968
Inspector Pero came. Found three objections. One door too narrow by three inches. Lights missing in the fire passage. Elevator must be blocked. Otherwise, he said, he had no objections. The only thing, he said, the only problem is in the basement, which is not completed. I said, we are interested only in the ground floor, in the theater. Basement will take another year to complete, we have no money. He said, it's possible. Such a permission, to approve the ground floor alone without touching other floors can be given by the borough superintendent, Isadore Cohen. See him and get the permission, and it's fine with me. We said, okay, we'll see Mr. Cohen. After the inspector left, George [Maciunas], who is working on the construction, asks me: "did you give him any money?" "No," I said. "That was a mistake. Now he will find some more problems. They always do that. Everybody pays. Everybody told me to pay. I can tell you right now: next time when he comes you better have some money or you won't get the theater approved." I laughed it off. "You want to bet?" I didn't take the bet. "How do you know he won't object the money? I would feel stupid offering money to inspector," I said. We ended right there. George said, this is no place for idealism.

Later in the afternoon I stopped at the Cultural Affairs office, in the park. I spoke to Miss Truder, a friendly soul there. I asked her how one gets to the borough superintendent. He sounds very big to me, the title and all that. Miss Truder called Mr. Cohen right there and made an appointment for next Monday 10 AM.

June 28, 1968
Dear Jacques Robert: (Festival d'Avignon & Jean Vilar):

Vous êtes fou, dear Jacques Robert.

J'ai reçu votre lettre—de la lune—parce que votre lettre n'est pas de cette terre—votre lettre est aussi fou—

Now let's be serious. And permit me to speak in plain English—with a few typewriter mistakes—

From your letter one would think that you confused UNDERGROUND with HOLLYWOOD. You are asking us to send 20 hours of film, and IMMEDIATELY—and provide you with all kinds of information—and you *completely forget to enclose* FIVE THOUSAND DOLLARS to make prints and pay the mailings and prepare materials... You see, Hollywood has plenty of money and they have money there to make hundreds of prints for their lousy films and they ship them to festivals (that's why we have no respect for any of the festivals) and they have staff to prepare written garbage materials, etc. etc.—but we, in the UNDERGROUND, we barely manage to make ONE MISERABLE PRINT, and this one blessed miserable print is the only thing we have and so we put it in the Film-Makers' Co-op so that people could rent it, so that we could get a few dollars back and if we are lucky, sometimes, we manage to make another print—and now you want us to send this print to you! Who do you think you are? I wonder sometimes what kind of people run the festivals if the only thing they can think about is THEIR needs, and never those of the artist. I don't give a damn who organizes, who pays for your Festival d'Avignon: next time you plan one, include in your budget money necessary to pay for the prints and for the shipping of the prints.

Forgive me if I sound a little bit mad, and I'm tired, this is a late hour of the day, and your letter happened to be only one of at least twenty that I have received this spring asking THE UNDERGROUND to send many hours of film for their "very very important" film festival—but not one, NOT A SINGLE ONE of them bothered to put himself in the shoes of the film-maker and see what it all means.

Yes, sure we want our films to be seen in Avignon. I have been in Avignon, I have seen even the sunrises of Avignon, and I love Avignon—but please change your ideas about the American avant-garde film. We are not the most loved people here; our films are not filling the houses; we are doing much better than ten or even five years ago—but it's one thing when Hollywood is doing well and another thing when avant-garde is doing well.

When Hollywood does well, it counts its millions; when the underground does well, it buys another roll of Ektachrome. As for other services: info etc.: we do not have any money to keep a central office of information, we are all film-makers, we are disorganized as far as printed info goes, and we aren't even too interested in that aspect too much. I try to fill this gap, by myself, whenever I can—but I am getting crazy, between my film-making and my functions as Minister of Propaganda (and Defense) and Minister of Finances—and now you want me to become even the MINISTER OF EXPORT & FOREIGN RELATIONS... Visitez moi dans la maison de fous, demain... avec quelques rouleaus d'Ektachrome... Je suis Le Pape de la lune...

The truth is: WE ARE SURROUNDED. We are surrounded here, in this beautiful and wide America, by the commerce, by the fascists, by Hollywood mentality, and we have to be constantly on our watch, and work hard to continue making films the way we want. If we have done what we have done—no matter how little that is— even that little was done, literally, by going HUNGRY. Things haven't changed too much.

So forgive me that I can't do anything for the Festival d'Avignon. Nothing, absolutely nothing.

Someone else has to do it: YOU. It's time that we begin to think how to change Film Festivals so that they could serve the art of cinema, not the commerce. But to do that, some festivals will have to work for the artist—and not the artist for the festival. All festivals think that they are the MOST necessary things in the world, and that the film-maker should be very very happy that they are kindly invited...

The word is: BULLSHIT. MERDE.

I'd like Monsieur Jean Vilar to see this letter too, so that he wouldn't think that we are not participating because of bad intentions. Our good intentions wouldn't pay even for one print even if we put all the good intentions together... But we are with you. J'espere, cher Jacques Robert, que vous comprendrez notre impuissance, our HELPLESSNESS which is quite BOUNDLESS... sans limites... please explain this to the people of Avignon—with our apologies—Sincerely, Jonas Mekas

June 29, 1968

The cop came into our office. He looked like a captain. He said, he has eighteen or so men under him. Once a month he will send someone to collect money. It's up to us to decide how much we want to pay every month. If we don't pay, we will be closed. He said he will be back on Monday to get our answer. We said, we have to talk this thing amongst ourselves.

Now, this is a little bit closer to reality.

July 1, 1968

Dear Robert:

About money. Where to begin. I'll say, first, there is hope. Minister of Finances never gives up. "The train will arrive." The good thing is, at least for this Minister of Finances, that the train has always arrived. But waiting periods are becoming longer and longer.

About Friends: there won't be another $1,000 from them. You see, that $1,000 was never promised. Actually what I mean is that it was ME who promised, not the Friends. And the other $1,000 which was sent to you a year ago, was really earmarked for *Film Culture* magazine. Something happened with the Friends during last year, they cooled off towards us, a little bit. Main reason for this, no matter how hard it is to name it, is Stan's pulling out of the Co-op. Meanwhile, Stan is back. But the things that his pulling out caused will never be corrected. Two largest backers of *Film Culture* mag & co-op practically pulled out because of Stan's pulling out.

That's why there haven't been *Film Culture* mag—practically—since then. We are reorganizing our resources, somehow, but it takes some time. Because there is one thing that was like a secret of my own and one or two friends around me mostly, and that is, that it was with the *Film Culture* money that the Co-op was put on its feet, mostly, and I was planning to peel another thousand from *FC* and send it to you. But now that's gone. Another big blow was —and the cause was the same—that the money promised for the Co-op catalog never came through and whatever I could scrape around went to the printer. Later, I managed to work something out with Friends, and they're finishing their payments for the catalog, in monthly installments, and this will drag for some time— still it's a great help. But I lost the printer which did all the work on *Film Culture* till now. He can't take other chances.

Before I go into the good news and aspects, let me continue for a while with the bad aspects.

It became clear, about a year ago, a month or so before Stan pulled out, that the audience for the avant-garde film in New York had dropped to an alarming minimum. Putting my feelers together—my business sense, my intuition, my close involvement, and my experiences as Minister of Interior —I came to the following conclusions at that time—and now, a year later, I see that I was completely correct—that one of the main reasons for the success that the avant-garde film and the Underground film enjoyed in LARGE cities was that the large cities contain so many snobs. The publicity that avant-garde film was getting, no matter, for good or bad reasons, good or bad publicity—brought to us both, the lovers, the true lovers of cinema and the sensation seekers. This success immediately brought the SHARKS into the game. The sharks opened theaters all around the big city, and whatever they play now, no matter what crap, their advertisements say that they play UNDERGROUND FILMS, and even AVANT-GARDE FILMS. What's more, the SHARKS, being more clever and richer than, say, the Cinematheque, managed to get theaters in most accessible, most crowded places. This dragnet of the commerce got all the sensation seekers, all the tourists, all the floaters, one-timers. The Cinematheque got what was left: the true film lovers. Now, seeing that that's what was coming, a year ago I made the decision to move to a cheap place downtown, to 80 Wooster Street—to spend energy on raising money to fix up the place, no matter what it costs—so that we could have our own place, at least one place where we can show what we want. My analysis of the audience dip, by the way, will soon apply to SF, and LA—unless it's there already—and a few other large cities. It will apply also to a large number of universities. But I'll be back to the subject a little bit later. Meanwhile, we are back at the Cinematheque. It was a bloodily exhausting struggle to build it. I'm not exaggerating, but this was probably the most exhausting and frustrating year of my life. Most of the old money sources became closed to us, I had to hunt constantly for new people, I still cannot cross the street without bumping into someone I owe (Tek owes) money. If the Tek was completed, and I'm happy to report now, that it has been completed—this week we are going through the last stages of licenses and permits—it was completed against the grain of almost everybody, including film-makers, who did not show even the smallest understanding of what we are doing or what we are going through—Stan who indirectly carries so much blame for some of our bad luck, proved, later, also to be the only one—or really the FIRST one who understood what we were doing, and donated his *Songs*, I mean, permitted us to screen *Songs* without RENTALS. Other film-makers will sit on our doorsteps, almost with lawyers, to get every penny's worth.

Now, I'll go into the better aspects of the report.

Good thing number one: more serious organizations and foundations, during last year or so, began taking the avant-garde film more seriously. It took several years to sink in, to reach their little brains—but now it's there. So that it will be easier and easier to get grants for the avant-garde film. The Ford grant to the Tek was one such breakthrough (all the money went immediately to pay some of the urgent construction bills—it didn't cover all; construction work was $55,000 and that's what we asked for—but we were cut to $40,000 which is fine, we bless Ford, but which still keeps us in the hole). There will be others. I don't want to go into the distribution aspect, which you know very well. It's clear that for another year or two the distribution aspect will grow and it will grow because the avant-garde film is only beginning to sink into the backlands. For instance, the NY Co-op won't need any outside help to bring out the new catalogue this year. When I am talking about the dip of the audience I am talking mainly about the big cities and the key universities —and as far as the distribution goes, big cities are quite insignificant.

I have been working, for last few weeks, on a few foundations. I am trying to pull into the Cinematheque (the only tax deductible organization we have) enough money to pay the remaining debts (over $20,000) for the construction works, and work out some kind of continuous in-flow of money which would guarantee the continuation of *Film Culture* mag, the running of the Cinematheque (after the construction is completed, there will be other expenses—the personnel, projectionist, manager, secretary, accounting, $200 per week, the total will run at $200 – $300 weekly deficit), and helping the Millennium Workshop, and also some money for grants to Canyon Cinema and Canyon Cinema News, and any other such undertakings. The prospects at this stage look OK, we hired a professional fund raiser, and we hope that beginning with August our situation should begin to improve. I know it will improve. I have long fingers in those kinds of things, I am almost never wrong. So that, as Minister of Finances and Minister of Propaganda (and sometimes, Defense) I can do nothing, at this stage, but leave you on this optimistic note, the train is coming in. Meanwhile you'll have to struggle longer. The first three years of the NY Co-op were much worse than that, believe me. At least, now, the bookings are coming in every day.

I wanted you to know where I stand, myself, with my endless projects and problems so that you wouldn't think that we have milk and honey—which is not a bad idea, to have milk and honey, I may do it right now—the only thing is that my ice box is empty—and it's hot like hell, the sidewalks are steaming, cats are sticking to the walls, the leaves are drooping (where the hell you see the leaves?)—

with best regards,
Jonas

July 1, 1968

10 AM. With George, architect's assistant, we go to see Mr. Cohen. Cohen listens, calls in the inspectors, looks through the plans, says O.K. to get a temporary C.O. for the ground floor, and says "don't leave this place until you have everything filed." We file for C.O., for 290 seats, the clerk (inspector?) scolds us angrily for going to Mr. Cohen, why didn't we go directly through him. I say, Inspector Pero told me. The clerk (?) is very unhappy. He keeps looking at the plan and finally finds one door too narrow. Nothing doing until that door is fixed. I say, "But, Sir, Mr. Cohen…" Nothing doing. We go home.

I set up hidden cameras all over the Tek to cover our meeting with the "money" cops. It would make a perfect film for the N.Y. Film Festival… The cop doesn't show up. Instead, another cop comes, in the evening, during the show, and writes us another summons.

We fixed the door. We covered the elevator. We fixed the lights. George filed the necessary amendments, filed the applications for the Public Assembly permit and C.O.

July 2, 1968

Having a beer in a Christopher Street bar, Rossellini, Annette (Michelson), someone from *EVO* paper. Rossellini arguing that there is no really new cinema in Italy. But he is completing a twelve-hour movie on… nutrition. Really, he said, on survival.

Three steps of the Revolution: the young Christians; the Troubadours; and the student revolution. All three revolutions, he believes, were conducted by, primarily, young people. He is producing his film himself and he doesn't care how it will be shown: in installments, or in longer or shorter parts—like he doesn't care how he reads a book, in 30 or 50 or 10 page sittings.

He still remembers last Christmas, the screening we had for him at the Cinematheque. I tried to tell him that there is a budding film underground in Italy too, but he said there is nothing in Europe like Brakhage's *Window Water Baby Moving* or Bruce Conner films or Nelson's *Oh Dem Watermelons*. Films like these, this type of film aesthetic and style and content are completely revolutionary in cinema, he said. He said, there is too much of the old, empty style in European avant-garde film-making. But in Brakhage the form and content merge totally and produce a totally new cinema. He is for this cinema, he said. "If I wouldn't be making the films I make now, I think I'd be making films like Brakhage."

Rolf Dieter Brinkmann
Engelbertstrasse 65
5000 KÖLN
West-Germany

28.6.68

Dear Jonas Mekas,

together with a friend of mine I'll soon be editing
quite a big anthology: ACID - Underground and the New
American Scene. This anthology will be published by
Melzer Publishers, Darmstadt and is a kind of READER
which will contain the new cultural transition in
literature, art and related subjects. We have already
essays by McLuhan - who writes about The Future of
Sexuality also Tuli Kupferberg on Social Engagement
and William Burroughs's essay about tape recordings
The Invisible Generation; John Clellon Holmes writes
about The New Girl and Seymour Krim about Newspapers
as Literature. Poems are by Ted Berrigan, Ed Sanders,
John Perrault, Gerard Malanga and Paul Blackburn as
well as some Stories by Burroughs, Donald Barthelme,
Hubert Selby jr., etc. All this will be arranged with
a lot of pics and comics.

Thebook is due for publication this autumn and looking
through it all again we noticed that we left out an
article about Underground Movies. Please, could you
cooperate here - it is urgent - and contribute an
essay for the anthology. We dont neccessarely a new
essay because as I said before the wholematter is
somewhat urgent. We were thinking about an essay as
previously published in Film Kulchur or Village Voice
and if at all possible could you please add some
interesting pictures! However, we trust your selection
as far as the theme is concerned. It could be something
about the Underground Movie Scene generally, a sort of
Introduction or just as well an article about a certain
film or a film-maker. It might be a good idea to send
a small selection of your articles?

We have to submit the anthology at the middle of July
and would be very pleased if you could send your essays
by Air-Mail! and of course as soon as possible. The
publishers will refund any expenses.

It surely is unusual to make such a request though
we hope it is not alltogether in vain and we are
looking forward to hear from you.

Love and Peace -

Rolf Dieter Brinkmann

Dont let the continent rot!

Roberto Rossellini in Central Park.

I SEEM TO LIVE, VOL. 1
CHAPTER TWENTY FOUR

July 3, 1968

Dear Stanley A. Bennett:

It took me some time to answer your letter, but here it is:

ANSWERING FIVE QUESTIONS POSED BY STANLEY A. BENNETT:

1. What has been the greatest assistance to me in my "career" so far? Answer: God.
2. Which film directors (if any) do I admire and why? Answer: Lumière, because he is so beautifully real; Brakhage, because he is so really beautiful.
3. Which films (if any) do I consider to be outstanding and why? Answer: All films by Lumière, and all films by Brakhage, for the reasons already given: Lumière's —because they are beautifully real, Brakhage's—because they are really beautiful.
4. Is there a film I particularly want to make? Answer: Five, or six, or more.
5. Have I any advice for the amateur filmmaker who wishes to produce films that can be judged alongside the professionals? Answer (advice): Drop all wishes to produce films that can be judged alongside the professionals— because such a wish is a very very low, uninspired, draggy, wings-clipping wish—unless you like ducks.

Sincerely yours,
Jonas Mekas

P. S. Both Lumière and Brakhage are amateurs, home movie-makers.

July 3, 4, 5, 6, 7, 8, 1968

WAITING.

We begin to realize that nothing will go that fast. We decide to go ahead and finish our July screening schedule but we are announcing the closing of all screenings beginning August 1st, to get the proper license.

Cops started coming every evening, sometimes twice. Summons every night. Sometimes twice. We collected a pile of them. The cops told me that they would appreciate a few bucks. They stand in the dark corridors and wait. Eventually I make them understand that I am not going to pay them. So they laugh and write another summons.

July 8, 1968

Present:

Ken Jacobs, Ed Emshwiller, Jonas Mekas, Charles Levine (guest), Leslie Trumbull (Secretary of the Co-op), Jack Perlman (attorney of the Co-op), Louis Brigante (Director of the F.M. Distribution Center). Where are the other directors? Peter Kubelka is still in Vienna (coming back at the end of the year); Shirley Clarke just left for S. Francisco for two months teaching job; Stan Vanderbeek is in Texas teaching for a month; Robert Breer, no information.

Jack Perlman informed us that we didn't have a "quorum." All we can do is ramble. Ken Jacobs again raised the question of why the Lecture Bureau is charging 25% for its services. Jonas said that for its first year he has no objections to 25% and, anyway, the Lecture Bureau is a co-op and nobody's going to buy houses with leftover money if there will be any left over from the 25% retainer. Since it's a co-op, its member and directors can easily reconsider the percentage after the first year. Jonas raised the question of the catalogue supplements. He said there should be a supplement coming out every three months. Leslie reported that Supplement No. 1 is at the printer and will be mailed out next week or so. Seven thousand copies (there was one printer's mistake in my last Co-op letter. It said the mailing of the catalog cost $2,000. The right figure is $4,000, and we mail 12,000 copies for about 35 cents per copy. Because of such a high price for the Fall catalogue, it's clear that new editions cannot be brought out just like that.

The Supplement No. 1 will be 16 pages, and won't be mailed to absolutely all but only to about 6,000, and the mailing shouldn't cost more than $400 – $500.) It was decided that in order to speed up the preparations of the new supplements, the Co-op will invite Suni Mallow, Editor for the *Film-maker's Newsletter*, to undertake the organizing of the new materials. She'll see what new films come into the Co-op, she'll prepare the necessary information materials which she would then print in the *Newsletter*, the way Canyon Cinema does. Every three months a new supplement will be brought out using these monthly prepared materials as the basis. Somebody brought up the question of additional mailing pieces on individual film-makers. Some film-makers would like to mail more extensive promotional sheets on their work and use the Co-op's mailing lists. Since the Co-op's mailing list is very, very large, it's too expensive for one film-maker to put it to any use. It was suggested that film-makers should group themselves in larger numbers, let's say five, six, or more, and enclose their leaflets in one mailing. Charles Levine said he is willing to be the coordinator of such mailing projects. Film-makers who want to do additional mailing, please contact Charles. All expenses of printing the materials and mailing must be covered by the film-makers themselves, since the Co-op policy is not to engage in any activities or expenses which are directed to individual film-makers' promotions; Co-op only engages in those activities and expenses which are for the promotion of ALL the film-makers. Louis Brigante suggested that if the Co-op could sponsor the lecture Bureau then even the 25 % retainer could be dropped: the film-maker would receive all the money that comes from lectures. (At this stage the Center is sponsoring the Lecture Bureau's activities.) This matter will be discussed in next meeting(s).

July 9, 1968

Spent the morning in Court. Paid $100 fine for the summons. Called building department. Inquired about the status of our C.O. and P.A. The secretary said, nothing new on it. Inspectors didn't turn in their reports yet.

July 10, 1968

In Court. Summons. $100 fine.

July 11, 1968

Spoke with inspector Pero. Asked him when is he going to turn in his report. He said, he can't give an approval to our floor because there are violations on other floors. I said, "But, Sir, Mr. Cohen said..." Inspector Pero said I should talk to the Inspector McGinnis, tomorrow. He can't do anything.

July 12, 1968

Called McGinnis. Told me to call tomorrow.

I called Isadore Cohen, the Borough Superintendent. He remembered me and expressed surprise that we didn't have the license yet. He said, he already gave his permission to license the ground floor before the other floors are completed. He said, come Monday and don't leave the building until you have all licenses in your hands.

July 15, 1968

8:30 AM, brave and confident, I go to the Building Department. I see McGinnis. He calls Pero. What's what, he asks. I say, ask Pero. Pero explains him that he can't approve the ground floor because there are violations on other floors. He leaves me alone with Pero. Pero says he has to inspect all the floors this afternoon. I say, it cannot be done, I have to contact all the people, get the keys. He doesn't understand that, gets angry. He is under impression that I own the entire building and

July 12, 1968

Mr. Isadore Cohen
Borough Superintendant
Department of Buildings
Municipal Building
Room 2003
New York, New York

Dear Mr. Cohen:

My assistant, Miss Cader, informed me of the
assistance you gave Mr. Jonas Mekas in ironing out the details
of the occupancy permit for the Film-Makers Cinematheque.

A prime goal of this department is to bridge the
gap between the city and the artistic community. I am sure you
will agree that we must begin to meet the needs of this community
for its vitality and richness are important to the life of our
city.

It is gratifying to know that you share our
concern, and I thank you for your help.

With best wishes,

Sincerely,

Doris Freedman
Director
Department of Cultural Affairs

I can do whatever I want. I try to explain that it's a cooperative building, that we, the Cinematheque, we only own the ground floor & the cellar and that to arrange the inspection of the other floors is a big project. He says, come back after you arrange such an inspection.

I decide to talk to Cohen again. I go to Cohen's offices. While I sit there, waiting, McGinnis comes in and asks me what I am doing there. I say, I had enough of this game, I want to talk to Cohen. McGinnis says, come back into my office, let's try to straighten this thing out among ourselves. He calls Pero. I try to explain to McGinnis that I was told by Pero to go see Cohen, two weeks ago, and that Cohen, who is higher than they, has already approved the ground floor. Pero insists that I am inventing, that he never told me such a thing, that is, to go to see Cohen. I stop arguing, I see that I am not getting anywhere. They scold me for pestering them and ask me to arrange inspection of the other floors. I said, I will.

It became clear to me, today, by watching both inspectors, that it was not a duty that they were doing, no: they were playing some kind of game. I saw all this today, in the Building Department, and I was walking home pretty depressed and my head was full of all kinds of very pessimistic thoughts. I still could not believe it, but my trained eye told me that it was true: there was a game being played: I WAS BEING TAKEN FOR A RIDE. But the sun was bright and I was walking briskly towards Wooster Street, and my faith in Man wasn't shaken a bit... I mean, I began recovering it as soon as I was out of the Building Department, out in the sun.

Co-op has become commercial? By just issuing a catalogue and mailing it to universities?

Eh, but the rebellions are always tragic and futile...

The rebel is, obviously, always in an alarming minority. He is told this wherever he goes, ten times a day.

Since the majority can never see further than one day, the actions of the rebels are always crushed, silenced, they are always doomed to failure...

There are 200,000,000 people in the United States. Only one million, at most, are participating in acts of peace. That makes half a percent...

Humanity is like a pyramid and the rebels are on the top of the pyramid. The nation constitutes the bulk of the pyramid and it cannot be shaken that easily, it will take some time for the vibration to reach the lowest stones.

Luckily for the pyramid, the rebel cannot be frightened by its size.

Rebel cannot be frightened because he is not reasoning.

Rebel is an inevitable reaction, not a reason.

The riots, the shoutings, the burnings, they all come and we should be joyful about it, about the fact that the rebel is not a reasonable man.

The spiritual laziness, the inertia is unbelievably attractive.

In a sense, you cannot choose to become a rebel.

Rebellions are blessings from heaven, to wake us up, to give us another chance.

To the Film-Makers
Subject: TRAVELING AVANT-GARDE FILM EXHIBITION
Last May, Film-Makers' Cinematheque sent to Europe ten (approximately) programs (over 70 titles) of "recent" (last four years or so) avant-garde films. I opened the Exposition myself, in Italy, then P. Adams Sitney came to take it from there. Films went to Austria, Switzerland, Sweden, Denmark, France, Germany, Yugoslavia, Finland, England, Belgium, and are now on their way to Spain, our last stop. Films

were shown in approximately 20 cinematheques, cultural centers, and universities. Complete information, with dates, places, program notes, press clippings and Sitney's reports from each city is being prepared and should reach film-makers in another few weeks.

I said, the library is going to its last stop, because Sitney and myself we both agree that the job of the traveling avant-garde film library in Europe has been completed. A tremendous interest has been created throughout Europe in avant-garde film. Many misconceptions about the American avant-garde film have been dispelled. Film avant-gardes are budding all over Europe. Film-makers cooperatives have been organized or are in stages of organization in Italy, Switzerland, France, England, Germany. A new Cinema movement is on its way in Europe. Not that the American film avant-garde should take too great a credit for it: it would've happened anyway. What we did was we sped it up, we provided some directions, we gave some confidence.

The second reason is financial. A year or two ago, it was still a big hassle to organize a show in Europe. There was a fear and resistance and nobody wanted to spend any money helping bring the exhibition— until just a few months ago or so—(most of the transportation of films, Sitney's lodging and food was paid from New York —not even the Cinémathèque Française paid Sitney's transportation). Every dollar I had to hunt in New York to keep the traveling avant-garde film library going. It was a headache and a nuisance. This situation began changing during the last few months. Now they want us. So now we consider that whoever wants us, has to put some work into it. The shows until now were our gesture of friendship to the young European film avant-garde—they were our main audience. But now the wider audiences and institutions are beginning to be interested, and there we stop, our job ends here.

The third reason is more difficult to explain, but one can call it a "political" reason. My own feeling is, that with the United States using all kinds of "power" to influence other countries, good power and bad power, for good reasons and bad reasons— even the avant-garde film library could be misinterpreted—by some very good people—as America's long fingers to manipulate the film avant-garde of other countries. The less we impose on others, these days—even with good things—the better, I consider. Therefore—home we go, even with art. We know, the armies won't follow our example—but they may.

As for the question marks and in some cases pettiness of some of our film-makers who feel that they may have lost money, that Sitney should have charged money everywhere he went—we know that wasn't possible. First the ground had to be prepared. Film-makers who think so (that is, about money) they judge by the situation which they find now and, naturally, the situation IS different than two years ago. That's why we say our job is done and we go home. From now on the work will be continued by the European film-makers' cooperatives.

One last thing: traveling with the Exposition from country to country, P. Adams Sitney has collected all kinds of useful information, contacting people in every corner of Europe. If any of the filmmakers are going to Europe, it would be advisable to get the contact addresses from Sitney (through the Cinematheque, 80 Wooster St. NYC) and take your films with you when you go, so that you could be in touch with the local cooperatives and you could organize screenings of your work wherever you go and thus keep yourself alive.

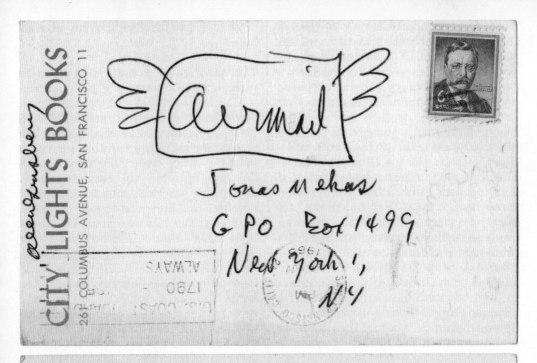

Airmail

Jonas Mekas
GPO Box 1499
New York 1,
NY

Dear Jonas —
Thanks for Prompt $ — what a relief,
you came through.
Spent last weeks with Hell's angels +
Berkeley Vietnam Day Committee. Stephen
Bornstein here, + tell Barbara, also, Bryden
settled down, clean, working at Stained
Glass Company + his wife soon having calm
baby.
Bunch of Berkeley + cristal folk just
poached on door. Leaving here for LA + zigging cross
country home after Dylan Concerts — Dec 15 — love Allen

The traveling avant-garde film library should be back in New York sometime in August.
Jonas Mekas
for Film-Makers' Cinematheque

July 16, 1968

Made all arrangements with the owners of the floors upstairs. Other floors of 80 Wooster are owned by painters, sculptors, dancers etc. who come occasionally to work there, to rehearse, etc. Got the keys to all the floors. Called Pero. He isn't in today! I returned all the keys, I go thru the whole business of rearrangements, backward.

July 16, 1968

Dear Mr. Eipidos (& The Underground Film Center):
Concerning the first Montréal Experimental Film Festival that you are in the process of organizing in said town for the week of October 24th to 31st and to which you were inviting me as one of the "judges" I have three following things to state:
I will come, under the following conditions:
a) I should be given the chance to see ALL, absolutely all films submitted to the festival (although you may restrict the number of films shown for the public, for time reasons). "Jury" screenings, unless they are the public screenings with the wide audience participation—should be totally private with no outsiders present.
b) I will not participate in any voting of one or two or three best films of the festival, that is, in the old-fashioned system of price giving. No matter how many judges, two, three or five or any number—even if they are all film-makers—the tastes and the backgrounds of each of the judge is so different from the next judge that any such voting of the best is nothing but a game in randomness and chance. I will support, that is, I will only participate in a "prize giving "system which is based on personal selections, that is where each of the judges will name his own selection and will give his own reasons for why he made the selection the way he made.
c) No film should be excluded from screenings because of its length or width. That is, 8 mm, 16 mm, 35 mm films, single screen, double or triple screen projections should be invited. I wouldn't make any demands beyond this, however, since your finances might not be able to afford cineramas, etc.—but I would wish that all such technical limitations would be announced in advance in your invitations or regulations, to avoid misunderstandings and bitterness later.

If you can meet these three basic commands, I will participate in the jury. Only one thing bothers me: how the hell are you going to decide which film is experimental film and which is not. However, since no film will be rejected the problem will solve itself: the film-makers themselves will decide it for you: the right people will gravitate to the festival. Darwin's law applies in art like it applies to the development of species…

Wishing you the best of luck with the project.

Sincerely, Jonas Mekas

July 17, 1968

Again, I make all arrangements, get all the keys, I call & reach inspector Pero. He comes at 1 PM, very hot, sweating. Pero looks thru all the floors, every room. (Last Monday, he said: "How can we give you a license for the ground floor. On the second floor they may be making bombs!") He finds no bombs, makes many notes. He leaves abruptly, with no word, neither hello nor good-bye, he just walked away. My mouth was left half open. Have no idea what to think. Smells very bad.

July 18, 1968
WAITING.

July 19, 1968
George wants his bet money (see June 28th). I say, wait wait, not yet. I call inspector Pero to inquire about what he thought he found. He's not in. Call on Monday.

July 22, 1968
9 AM. I go to the Municipal Building to see inspector McGinnis. McGinnis says, tomorrow, we'll come, both of us, inspector Pero and I, for another inspection. I say, I have to be in Albany, at the University of Albany, I won't be present at the inspection. He says, they'll come anyway. I make arrangements with Richard to give them a tour.

To the Film-Makers' Distribution Center: There is one thing that is bothering me, and it's this: whenever I feel like checking if there is any money for me (rental money, I mean) at the Center, I swallow my words, and I say something else, I can go into the Co-op anytime I want and ask for whatever there is for me and there are no problems. From the very first days of the Co-op, the tradition was established that whatever happens—film-makers' money is not touched, it's there for him whenever he feels like asking for it. It took for the Co-op a long time to grow, but it grew without impinging on the film-makers. Now, the policy at the Center seems to be to push for faster growth, and since there is no money for a fast growth, all available monies are used up, including the money of the film-maker, and even this doesn't do the trick. I see a basic mistake here and as one of the directors, no matter how small my voice is, I have to voice a warning, and opposition, a disagreement. I don't think that the Center should push for fast growth. Let it grow slowly, with the monies that are available. WE ARE IN NO COMPETITION, and therefore we have all our time. The future is ours. We are the film-makers. So why the hell the rush? I am opposed to all expansion on new projects. I'm for shrinking of the Center to the basic distribution activities that can be done with the basic available monies. Film-makers' money should never be used, film-maker should always know that the money is there for him, no matter how little that may be. Co-op's karma is clear and transparent. It's time to begin to think about the karma of the Center before it's too late. Let's put bridles on our ambitions. Let's not reduce everything to money—the success or the failure of the Center is not in money but in the administrative wisdom, the relationship with filmmakers, and un-ambitiousness of the Center's policy (which means, I consider it now too ambitious—at this stage). Jonas

July 23, 1968
Dear Barbara, Allen, Julius, Peter, Gordon, Candy, and I don't know who else (and the trees and the flowers and the animals that run and creep and jump) (and don't forget the insects that bite and suck and run away):

it's strange to write to you, in the country, from the city—here I am, the real farmer, sitting in the city, and you all there sissies trying to become farmers. But I guess that's how the things always go: every farmer boy wants to go into the city and every city boy and girl dreams of the flowers and the streams in the morning dew... So, good luck. I will meet you in 15 years, when the Megalopolis or whatever the name of that city will be that will fill the space between New York and Chicago, I'll meet you in 15 years on one of the streets of that future city—probably on your way to the shrinker, because by that time you'll have so estranged yourselves from the city life that you'll have all kinds of re-orientation problems—luckily, there will be a period of transition, because it will be five years from now when the first Megalopolis streets will appear visibly out of your windows, just behind the flowers and brooks and cows and chicks—so you'll have a period of transition from your farmer's life to the life of the Megalopolis. Still—good luck.

Now after I've scared you a little bit (just a little bit, because you're not taking me too seriously) I can go into other things. Like: It's pretty hot and smoggy here and I can feel some kind of black stuff going down my nose & my throat, it's called the AIR. Yesterday bumped into Jerry Jofen, almost bumped, because he was walking with his usual absent-minded eyes looking somewhere five blocks ahead or behind, I have no idea which, & his jumping kind of walk, half on the ground, half in the air sort of—and I said Hello and he said how is Barbara and I said she's OK but they don't let her out of bed or something so she has to go to the outhouse to write a letter, it sounds like a concentration camp, I'm afraid, but they will be all right—and Jerry Jofen went his way and I went my way—downtown, to Wooster Street, where we have a garden outside, with raspberries and mimosas and they are blooming and so I got some water and I poured the water on their hot leaves and on their roots and I was talking to them and excusing myself for the heat, but they said, it's OK, what can you do about it, although mimosas seem to be less happy about it than the raspberry bush and half of her leaves are on the ground, I guess that's why they call them mimosas. And then we looked at the movies, like all city people do—regretting all the time, somewhere in the back of my mind, that I can't have a horse in our little garden, nor sheep—a farmer boy will always have such dreams, even on the 80th floor of the Empire State Building—those strange visitations from the past—like, for instance, you, that is me, you (me) walk along Broadway, cars, people, smog—and suddenly I stop like nailed to the sidewalk: hell, where is this smell coming from: the smell of a bark from a willow tree! Really. So I look around, for a second, some people look at me, they think I am crazy or something—and then I continue walking. They keep coming back to me like that, every smell, every sound, every touch, back from the past, and they materialize, right there, by my nose, in the very middle of Times Square they keep trailing me—so what can you do—the same way the City is or will be trailing you, in the middle of a beautiful summer day in the wide fields you'll suddenly feel: garbage cans! a cockroach wall! street noise!

Oh but I am wasting paper I have no idea what I wanted to tell you—I guess, nothing —just to say HELLO to all of you and let you know that I am still here—Love to all

July 24, 1968

I come back from Albany, late at night. I call Richard. Richard says McGinnis and Pero came, looked thru, made many many notes, were very very unhappy, found everything wrong. He said, according to the inspectors, we'll have to tear down the building and put another one in its place.

I don't sleep all night. I have all kinds of terrible dreams. McGinnis and Pero play a big role in them.

July 24, 1968

Dear P.A.S.:

I am on a train and far from the typewriter. I hope you'll be able to read my handwriting.

Your last postcard is pretty depressing. I hope you are not letting yourself get bogged down by the army notice. I think you should simply forget it for another month & take it easy and devote your time to your novel and Spain, and trust that everything will work out OK when you come back. We'll put all our ingenuity to keep you out of the militarists' jaws. Trust your angels. You have—the card said—sixty days to appeal. As soon as Jerome comes back—he dropped me a note—we'll plan some kind of help—letters of support from Shakespeare Festival, Cinematheque and Museum of Modern Art, and a few others. And only if all our requests will fail, only then you'll have to start worrying and make proper decisions—to do whatever you feel you should be doing. Canada is always there, as they say. But I certainly wouldn't waste Spain worrying about it.

I hope you received my letter I sent to San Sebastián (it seems that one or two other letters—the one I sent to Frankfurt & Cassis—missed you. Have you made forwarding arrangements? There were other letters and checks in my envelopes. From your postcard it's not clear if you got the letter which I mailed to San Sebastián, including your A-1 army letter, and in which, among other things, I said that it's OK to ship COD films to the Museum of Modern Art, on the name (personally) of Willard Van Dyke. Include *Flaming Creatures*, without listing it though, and mail him a complete list of films (*FC* not to be listed).

I still haven't decided about Venice.

Definitely I'm not going to sit on the jury—the only thing I haven't decided is this: should I just send them a letter, informing that I'm not coming—OR: to come & announce that I'm not going to sit on the jury—make the announcement in the airport & depart for, say Spain. But this may be last minute decision. I'm supposed to be in Venice on the 25th of August. There is so much hypocrisy & playing games going around that I am becoming more and more Calvinistic about these matters. These past 12 months have been quite eye-opening for me, and many illusions have broken to pieces, many dreams—only a few are left & I can not betray them—we are entering a period where much will depend on our strength and, let me say, purity to the very end—& sometimes, there are days, and very often, lately, when I say here to myself, like I said to Annette Michelson the other day: Oh, if only P. Adams Sitney was here!—because all kinds of sharks have infested the avant-garde pastures, & the hippies have all gone to pot, megalomania, petty selfishness; LBJ has driven all the radicals and politically desperate to violent thoughts and propagandistic distractions—the others to apathy—there are all kinds of bad things in the air—and it looks like "everybody for himself" is the guide line—like hippies—(Ginsberg, Barbara Rubin moved to a farm, upstate)—leaving towns, and when I brought Larry Jordan's films for practically the first time to NY, two weeks ago—I didn't see a single film-maker at the screening (yes, Ken Jacobs came)—But what I am saying here, and I sound pretty depressing myself, after scolding you for being depressed—I shouldn't scare you away from settling down here. Despite all the bad things one could say about things down here, I have a feeling that a MOUNTAIN can be done by two, three people with strong beliefs. The material is here, the people are here, misled, confused, like sheep, & even tired. Even if we stick to our own area, the avant-garde film, a lot can be done, a word here, a word there—& it would affect other areas of life—but I feel completely & totally alone these days, and a little bit beaten down myself—but I am trying to hold, until I'll begin to see some light—and another man at this period would be like that cavalry in the Westerns that appears the last minute—

Anyway, it's raining, I'm watching a wet landscape running past the windows, from the train, on my way home, from Albany—thinking about myself & both of you there

KENNETH ANGER   S.F. March 16

Dear Leslie —

       Just a note to thank you for the check &
confirm that the four prints have been mailed to you
today via special handling-special delivery.

       Had my last show last nite on the Berkeley
campus
as a benefit for the Fuck Defense Fund — legal fees for
the kids that got arrested on campus on the four-letter
word basis. They're all very nice kids. I've read the
N.Y. Censorship recommendations you sent me a copy of
to that group & a few other student groups I've had
showings for recently & it's a guaranteed laughgetter.

       The <u>fourth</u> print I've sent you is another
print of Scorpio as Bob Brown wrote you had everything
booked for a playdate he had in May. So hold the new
print for his use at that time. After Bob's show, you
can hold it & see if you need it. Also have the print of
Scorpio you're going to send to Boulder <u>returned</u> to you
as I've decided I'd rather have the Coop have enuf prints on hand to
avoid, if at all possible, the hang-ups like Bob's show
in May. That'll make 5 prints of Scorpio with the Coop.

       Will send 2nd print of Fireworks to you
shortly.   BEST,

                                K

PS Somebody told me they'd seen Scorpio on a "ten
best" list for 64 published in The Voice. What's the
chance of getting a copy? Am always glad to see things
even like the silly ref. in Look (thank Jonas for me)
but most stuff that appears in the prints about my
work is so far off beam it's not funny. Then what one
Kritik writes is so often picked up by other lazy
writers later, so misconceptions are multiplied ad
infinitum. An example is enclosed from student paper
which picks up Knight's dreary errors. Hardly anyone
except Carolee S. have gotten even close to what the
film is all about. Do you keep a file of clippings on
my work? I'll send you clips that appear on the west
coast if you do tho its just for the record, most don't
have too much to say. Let me know.

                                        All best, K.

Richard Foreman and Kate Mannheim. Richard and his team helped me to clean up the 80 Wooster Street space, it was stacked to the ceiling with junk. He worked with George to make the space usable. During the following several years it was the stage for his Ontological Hysteric Theatre.

P. Adams Sitney showing ink on his hands. As a signer of legal papers to register *Film Culture* Non-profit Corporation, he was fingerprinted. As a man with a "criminal record," I could not act as a signer.

far far away—& I said to myself, why don't I drop a few words—even if they are unreadably scribbled—
Love to you & Julie

July 25, 1968
Early, 9 AM, I walk along the street and I have a new plan... I call McGinnis, I tell him that sure, everything's wrong, but what if instead of applying for 290 seats we apply for 75? After all, we don't need 290 seats. McGinnis says, Oh, sure, if you'd apply for 75 seats or less you wouldn't have to go through any of this, you wouldn't need any of these things. You don't even need the P. A. permit. Thank you, I say, that's exactly what I am going to do.

July 25, 1968
The other night, when the cops came, we had a long conversation with them. We even talked about old age, how one will feel, say, he, as a cop, when he will be very old, with his hair all grey, and when he'll look back at his life, and will remember all that he has done in his life...

I consider that I should put everything that is in my power and in my capabilities into 80 Wooster Street, even if THE WHOLE WORLD IS AGAINST IT—and only then, after I do ALL that is in my power, I should retreat—but retreat with a clear consciousness that I have done what I had to do and help me God—because we never really do what we HAVE TO & CAN DO, we only do one hundredth of it and we retreat, and we say: Oh, it was impossible... or, oh, God didn't want it... that must be the will of God... The truth is: It's only the way of our cowardice, the way of our excuses, or simply our god damned laziness. That's why the whole world is in pieces, because those who could act with wisdom and strength have abandoned it after a few attempts, to those who act—

The Beatles, making now disappointing statements about Maharishi... Like pigs, trying to get fat on meditation, on correct breathing, power of concentration... for what? Always starting from the opposite end. The right human actions will do that. Do not worry about the SOUL: The soul is divine. You can neither improve nor change it, it's too deep and out of your reach. Do what's by your nose: love your neighbor and serve him. Then you'll breath well too.

July 26, 1968
George goes to the Building Department and changes plans, from 290 seats to 72 seats. He files: 1. revised approved plan, 2. revised specification sheet.
Myself, with Richard, we go to the Criminal Court, Part 6B or Part 6—I don't remember which. I notice that PART, when one reads through the glass door from inside, it reads TRAP. Richard has a batch of summons and I have four or five. We sit there, on the bench. Ten or fifteen other people sitting. Silence. A green tree behind the window! Hollow steps. Judge comes in. He sits down. Doesn't look very happy. Bad news. And it shows. He seems to want to do something today. He wants to act as the straightening hand of the City. Of course, it doesn't matter that in this Part (Trap) he has to deal only with small offenders. He will show them how to respect the law! He lifts his voice, he talks to a tall black man, a worker. He scolds him about something. I try to listen, I try it very hard, I am curious, but the hollowness of the place eats up the words before they reach me. I try to listen, but all I hear is "Thirty days in jail, and no suspension," and "to set an example." To set an example? Who the hell will know that you sent this man to thirty days in jail? How can you talk about setting an example when even I, who is sitting here, in the court, have no idea why he is going to jail? Next, he scolded a black woman, and gave her

a $50 fine or one day in jail. His mood gets worse and worse as the day progresses. Our turn comes, and we stand there, and he looks at us, and then he says, he will call us again. We sit down. He manages to send a few more people with fines. ONCE, he smiled. I didn't catch what was behind it, what kind of smile that was. Our second call comes. We stand there and he begins to shout, literally, to shout. "How did you dare commit all these crimes? I should put you on bail right now, I should send you to prison! How dare you commit all these crimes. How did you dare to run a theatre without a license!" Jack Perlman, our attorney, he tries to say something. "Your Honor… Your Honor…" He is sweating it out, he says something about how we are working hard, etc., but His Honor is in a bad mood, and we are two perfect victims, intelligentsia, and Richard has a mustache, and I look a perfect criminal type, a sly fish, no doubt, a smarty who runs probably a huge theatre, maybe like Paramount, another one of those clever guys who wants to steal millions from the city. So we stand there, and our legs are shaky, and His Honor concludes: "If you dare run the theatre again this evening, I am going to arrest you." So I say, "No, Sir. I give you my word. We are not going to run the theatre tonight." He expresses some doubts about my "word" (in his mind an image: CINERAMA pictures, secretly, without the theatre permit, on 80 Wooster Street, 2,000 people!) (Image in my mind: Three months in jail; cops kicking my ass.) Anyway, Jack gets it postponed to September 12th. We didn't even dare mention other summonses. The Judge said: "$100 for the first offense. There is no rule how much you have to pay for the second." Since I have seven or eight summons on my name, and Richard has seven or eight on his name, we have a good ten years of jail coming… or $100,000 in fines… So I said to myself, I should be quiet like a mouse. I clenched my teeth, I swallowed whatever I felt like saying, and I kept my teeth and my blood until I was out in the street. I looked at the sun, trying to get back my faith in humanity. I failed. I still felt like a louse. The judge, in his bad morning mood, splashes shit on people, and then it's up to the people to clean it up. There were at least three lawyers present in the court but not a single one expressed any surprise at the judge's moods, none of them protested. It was all very normal! But people should walk out of the courtrooms, and ask for another judge, when a judge walks in and begins to display his moods. They should ask for their money back, so to speak.

I was angry, as I walked uptown, to Wooster Street. I thought the ground will open and swallow the whole city, any second. But it didn't. So I continued uptown.

July 27, 1968

8:30 AM we go, with Richard, to "work," to the Building Department. I change the C.O. to 72 seats. We suppose to withdraw the Public Assembly Application. It's not needed any longer, for 72. They send us to the room 2012. Room 2012 sends us to R. 2007 or 2017. The room 2017 sends us to the room 20000 or 50000000. And so we go through five or six rooms until we end up at the table of a certain Zaccobachi, or something like that. He says, yes, your Application should be here. He searches and searches: can't find it. I say: We don't need it anyway—why look for it. We decide to let it die. I have a vision:

In twenty years from now they'll find it and they'll APPROVE IT!

We go to see McGinnis. I say, please, I beg you, how could we speed it up? I am sure, now for 72 seats, there shouldn't be any problems. We are interested in speeding it up, Sir. Mr. McGinnis says: "We are not interested in speeding it up." He goes back and brings a list of violations, his notes taken on July 24th. Two pages... He says they have to retype them. "But, Sir," I say, "these violations were for 290 seat theatre. Doesn't it make any difference, 290 or 72?" I receive no clear answer. He keeps pointing at the list.

On our way out, I have an inspiration... We stop to see the chief Engineer. Engineer isn't in, but one of his assistants, Engineer Kent is in. He is sitting alone in a dusty grey room and looks very lonesome and sad and bored. We inquire, we say, Sir, we need your advice: WHAT IS OUR CATEGORY? We are showing these movies, to 30–50 people. And we have these lectures. And we are publishing a magazine. And we have these archives there. What is our CATEGORY? Are we really a THEATRE? Maybe we are a workshop, or a school? Maybe we are having these troubles because we have the wrong category... This word THEATRE, this strange word... What are we, Sir? Sir?

Engineer Kent listens and says nothing. He doesn't seem to be in a very talkative mood. The morning is pretty depressing and grey. Finally he says. He says, he isn't sure. We could also be a trade school, he says. He says he doesn't understand what the troubles we are having. He stopped talking. He didn't seem to be able to get interested in us. His mind was somewhere else, certainly on some huge problem. The whole room was so depressing that I couldn't blame him for not being able to get interested in us. So I looked at Richard, and Richard looked at me, and we left. The engineer Kent was still sitting alone, by his huge table, looking into the grey emptiness in front of him.

At this point I should introduce the Dear Reader into some other confidences and details of my current daily life.

I consider now that I am working for the City. I am working at the Municipal Building. Every morning, practically, every morning, at 8:30 AM, like all other workers,

I take the subway downtown. I walk to the Municipal Building with the stream of other "small" workers (some of the bigger workers come around 10 AM, I noticed), and I go to "work." I go up to the 20th floor. After a few weeks of "working" at the Building Department I began to know the newspaper man, and I greet him, and some people began greeting me in the elevator (maybe they think I am an inspector?)— I get out on the 20th floor, where the Building Department is. I have my coffee and a doughnut, and I talk to a few other people who pass by and who know me by now. Some of them are like me, we are all members of a sort of Kafka Club, they have been coming for the same reasons, for some stupid detail, week after week. If I have to wait, I kill some time by going to other floors. I have made friends on several floors already, and I go to visit them. Because, practically, I have been "working" in this god damned place, in this building longer than I have worked in some of the factories, in my Brooklyn days, and people are beginning to think that I am really working here, and I am beginning to feel a little bit like home. Next time, I may even leave some of my belongings here. Anyway, the sad truth is, I am trying to get this god damned C.O. for the Cinematheque, this god damned C.O. Last night I was thinking. I was trying to guess what new violations will they invent (they say, "find") next time. It is becoming a game with me and Richard. I train my imagination powers that way. It's a kind of Yoga. But while the imaginations of the Building Department inspectors run into most unpredictable directions, my imagination stays grounded. For instance, at 7:30 AM I jump up and go to "work." Or I stand there, in the middle of the theatre, and I kick a wall, and I say to Richard: "Don't you think THIS is TOO WEAK?" Or I see a crack in the floor and I say to Richard: "Don't you think this could become a DANGEROUS SPLIT by

next week?" Sick things, unimaginative. But the Inspector stands there, in the middle of the theatre, on 80 Wooster Street, at the Film-Makers' Cinematheque, ("Go South, where the sun is") (Where the Spring St & Wooster St meet"), he stands there, and sees 5,000 people locked up, watching a Brakhage film, and suddenly huge tongues of fire engulf the entire building and these poor 5,000—maybe more—these people are TRAPPED. They are trying to escape, and they can't! Obviously they can't, because the fire is coming not ONLY from the burning street (...inspector continues his fiery vision...) but ALSO from ALL THE OTHER SIDES at the same time, including THE ROOF. And how the hell could he give us a license? Don't you see the fiery vision? Next morning, a headline in the *NY Times*: 5,000 PEOPLE BURNED TO DEATH AT THE FILM-MAKERS' CINEMATHEQUE WHILE WATCHING BRAKHAGE FILM SCENES FROM UNDER CHILDHOOD DEPARTMENT BUILDING MCGINNIS PERO BLAMED LINDSAY IS CALLING FOR STRICTER LICENSING CONTROL MEKAS ESCAPES TO CUBA
—Eh, friends, should I tell you something? There is one thing that is very strange in this story. Don't they realize if? Not even the *NY Times* headline says anything about it? THE ATOM BOMB FELL on the Film-Makers' Cinematheque! Don't they realize that?

July 30, 1968

9 AM I arrive at the Court. One more summons, from last week. I wait for my call until 11:20. Get adjournment to Sept. 12. The judge was normal (not the same as the other day) and treated everybody sort of as a lawyer would or should, which was surprising to see.

7:45 AM: UP
8:15 AM: Post Office, breakfast

9:00 AM: Court (summons)
11:20 AM: finished with Court.
To the Tek. Answering mail, organizing archives, other daily business, sessions with George on building problems. Carla.
1:30 AM: At the Co-op
2:30 AM: Chelsea Hotel. Completed letter to Chiarini, Venice.
Completed letter to National Council of the Arts, asking for a grant.
5:00 AM: Working on the retyping of MS.

July 31, 1968

Called McGinnis. Asked about the list of violations, when are we getting it. He said, it's being typed by Mr. Mandel, X-2390, Room 2015. I reached Mandel, it's not typed yet, there is no girl to do it, he says. I said, when do you expect you'll have a girl to do it? He says, sometime next week, we hope. Wow, I said, but it's urgent that we know what's wrong, so we can go fix the violations. Maybe we could come and type it ourselves, or just have a look at them, untyped? Mandel says O.K., come and look. Richard says he'll go and will make a copy. N. stopped at the office. Haven't seen him for some time. He says his father is in construction business and he knows everybody in the Building Department. He says, we are fools if we think we can do it ourselves. We need an Expeditor, he said. What's an expeditor? I ask. He says, It's a man, it's a professional negotiator between the Building Department and the constructors. He's also known as the Payoff Man. He will do the whole legalizing business, he knows all the ropes, he knows the price of everybody. He said we are fools and know nothing about America if we think that we'll get the license without paying off. He said, a building a few blocks away from ours had similar problems, but $1,000 did the trick and everything went smoothly to the happy end.
A few other people dropped in. We argued about idealism, and principles. They said,

FILM CULTURE NON-PROFIT CORP.
80 Wooster Street
New York, N.Y. 10012

(212) 677-2460

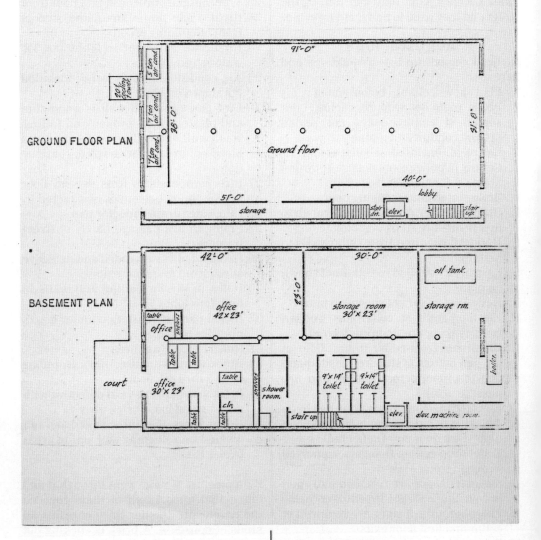

GROUND FLOOR PLAN

BASEMENT PLAN

fine, fine, stick to your principles, but you'll have to abandon the building, you are not going to win. I said, if that's the price of the principles, I'll give up the building, I'll give it to Mayor Lindsay as a Christmas present.

Two cops at the theatre this morning. Asked, where are we showing the movies now. I said, find out, I'm not going to tell you. Later Richard said, they met him in the street and they tried to find it out from him.

August 1, 1968

Richard copied the list of violations and here it is:

1. Plan shows cellar to be basement
2. Boiler room not properly enclosed nor sealed at ceiling—holes not sealed around conduit and piping
3. Gas meter enclosed in boiler room
4. Ceiling in boiler room not fire-retarded
5. Steel vault angles corroded
6. Boiler room housekeeping poor
7. Holes in boiler room ceiling through to first floor—fire stops inadequate
8. Handrail required from cellar steps to boiler pit
9. Partitions installed in cellar not shown on plan
10. New wood cellar not shown on plan
11. Elevator shaft at cellar has wooden ramp making fire-door ineffectual
12. Headroom from cellar to first floor at top and bottom of stairwell inadequate due to piping across bottom and fire passage at top
13. Elevator machine room door has been cut at top to circumvent piping and conduit—Fire door now ineffectual
14. Toilet drop ceiling stringers supported with ban iron
15. Sprinkler heads are recessed into opening cut into ⅝ Firecode ceiling covering
16. Phosphorous exit signs are required at cellar and first floor exits
17. Duct work for toilet ventilators not fire retarded in public hall
18. Iron stairs from first floor fire escape to rear yard has defective treads and stringers
19. 4'0" wide metal stairs required at rear exit of first floor to fire escape
20. Skylight at first floor rear is rotted and defective
21. Skylight at first floor rear is not shown on plan
22. Transom glass broken at first floor front
23. Right angle now illuminated sign at front of building (wood)
24. First floor exit door to lobby not 3'8" wide as required
25. Air conditioning unit being installed not shown on plan
26. Fire passage north wall is wood stud and plaster and is broken and falling; south wall and ceiling is of terra-cotta block—plan calls for concrete construction
27. Fire escape stairs from second floor to mezzanine balcony is obstructed by rain water drain collector pan
28. Piping in fire passage partly obstructing egress
29. Diamond plates corroded and defective at required first floor exits
30. Holes in plaster ceiling and walls in first floor lobby
31. Illegal partition installed under mezzanine fire passage
32. Holes in rear yard area
33. Holes in walls and ceilings in public halls 2 thru 6th floor
34. Brick walls at rear yard defective with missing and loose brick work
35. Upper floors illegally occupied and subdivided into sleeping and eating areas by A.I.R.'s

It's a nice list. George went through it and found that almost half of them concern the basement. Another third contains all kinds of nonsense. A brick is sticking out in the wall of a building across the yard! A hole in the garden where we are planting flowers! Things like that. George only found three legitimate things and all three are easily fixable. Then, there are only five or six "violations" which in architect language belong to the category of "existing conditions," that is, the basic structure of the building as it was found, and to correct them would mean to tear down the building and construct another one in its place. We were surprised that the list didn't include any violations from the buildings across the street, or even further away, say, from the 14th Street, or even from the Municipal Building. Because, since no man is an island, no building is an island either. Where do you draw the line? Where does one building really end and another begin? Think about the deep philosophical implications of the list above and reflect on the meaninglessness of your miserable life in the larger context of the Building Department Cosmos.

We looked at the list, we shook our heads one way, then other way. We couldn't transcend it. We felt small and insignificant and we felt guilty about endangering the lives of citizens, and for all the other wrong things we have done today. We decided to sell our two floors and buy an island in the Bahamas.

"Cinema is 1,500 years behind the sight."
—Kubelka

CHAPTER
TWENTY
FIVE

... Letter to Fred Camper re. Warhol movies... Letter to the Millennium Film Workshop... About myself, money, 'Tek... Letter to Chiarini re. film festivals... On artists... More trips to the Bldg. Department... My hallucinations resume... Letter to the Commissioner of Buildings re. Soho, artists, 'Tek... "Shoot" or "film"... I am told to bribe the Building Department officials... Letter to Liberation Press... Letter to Carla Liss in London... Meeting with Larry Kardish... A trip to Roxbury, Boston... More on bribes and the City...

August 2, 1968

Dear Fred Camper:

I read your letter to Andy Warhol Films. I have read a few other similar letters before, from other people. The situation is ridiculous, the reasons are sad. The way I see it, these are the reasons:

Until about two years ago, the Underground film was left alone. Newspapers & magazines exploited the Underground Film for their own corrupt reasons, to sell a few more copies of their lousy papers, but the theaters and distributors kept out: Underground was too dirty, too amateurish, for them, money gains too questionable. But about two years ago, with changing attitudes to sex, and with some of the Underground films beginning to make money here and there, the sharks moved in. First, they began making all kinds of offers to buy some films out, to buy the distribution rights, particularly those films which could be exploited on the sex angle. Rogosin bought *Scorpio Rising* & Downey films, Gate theatre tied down a few films, and there were a few others. Andy stuck with the Co-op. Janus. Sloan, Grove. Bell & Howell. They all moved in. A number of large companies wanted to buy *Chelsea Girls*, *My Hustler*, but Andy stuck to his, what one could call, position of solidarity with other film-makers. But some of his more "business" minded advisors, publicity people and promoters kept coming up with dreams of big money, big deals, big openings—and about fifteen months ago, somewhere there, beginning from there, very often, the commercial, "shark" methods began creeping in. Very often, instructions were given to the Co-op and the Center to keep certain films out of university or film society "small" shows because such shows may damage the chances of bigger screenings in that city—be it theatrical, commercial opening, or a big university screening. This kind of thing always happens when one begins to think about big money. Shirley Clarke did the same (or gave permission to the Center to do it) with some of her films. David Stone forbade the University of Berkeley to show *The Brig* (as the "producer" he had the right to do it, at that time), for two days before the show, because he was making a deal with a local theatre for a bigger screening (which didn't come through). These kinds of considerations prevented your own screening of Warhol films in Boston. Film-Makers' Distribution Center, of which I am only a powerless advisor, I have noticed, is using the same tactics of withholding films from film societies or universities when they feel that they may have a larger commercial booking in that city. It's all very ugly and stupid, as far as my knowledge— and principles—of the distribution goes. Nobody can prove to me that a university, a film society, or any other limited screening can harm the unlimited, the wider presentation. It's just the opposite, it always helps. This has always been my position, tested and triple-tested at the Cinematheque. No doubt, if the film is a stinker, then even a screening to five people may damage its further "exploitation." And I wouldn't give a damn how one should sell it. But the better the film, the more it gains by more exposure, it grows like a flower from rain and sun. And since I consider the majority of Andy's films GOOD and VERY GOOD, nothing, absolutely nothing can stop the growth of his audience. SO that this stupid policy, whoever is the architect of it, cannot be excused. But I have given up arguing with business "geniuses," nothing can change them on that point—unless you hit them on the head with a bag of money.

Oh, these money considerations, how much bad feeling they have brought in, during these last two-three years. Money has split friendships, money has kept films from the public, money has brought in ugly advertisements, distortions—money has increased the rental prices of some of the films to the heights unreachable to true film lovers—the dreams of money (or illusions) have even undermined the creativity of one or two very talented film-makers. When the publicity reached its crest, two-three years ago, some of our dear film-makers began thinking that they are darlings of the people, that now, surely, there won't be any problems of getting any money they want to make their films, etc. etc.—and they kept making demands, like children—some are in that illusion even today—I have spent many many hours arguing this point, trying to show some of the reality—that is, that nobody is giving a damn about the avant-garde film, it's all public media bit, all fashion and no passion. Lately, the dream has changed its direction: now they have finally realized that nobody will come with bags of money to sponsor their little movies (although one illusion remains: Am. Film Institute! Naomi almost cried—really she was very angry that AFI didn't give her money to make her beautiful movies!)—yes, but THEY WILL COME AND BUY THEM when they are finished, they will come running with money jingling, and the theaters, yes, they will come! Until this dream will die too. Still, for instance, the most commercial film-maker of the underground, Andy Warhol, is ten miles from the borders of the commerce. And that is where all his advisers are making their biggest mistake. That's where Shirley is making her mistake. My own brother is making that mistake. We went through this almost ten years ago, in 1960, 1961, in the beginnings of the co-op, and Rogosin and Shirley and De Antonio and a few others didn't believe us and they went the way of commerce, trying to work and sell their work to big companies. Seven, eight years passed, they failed completely, but still didn't want to believe the real reason which I told them at that time and I'm repeating now, only that now this affects a larger number of people, including Andy, and even Gregory, and Rochlin, and really a good dozen, and the reason is:

With Andy Warhol at The Factory.

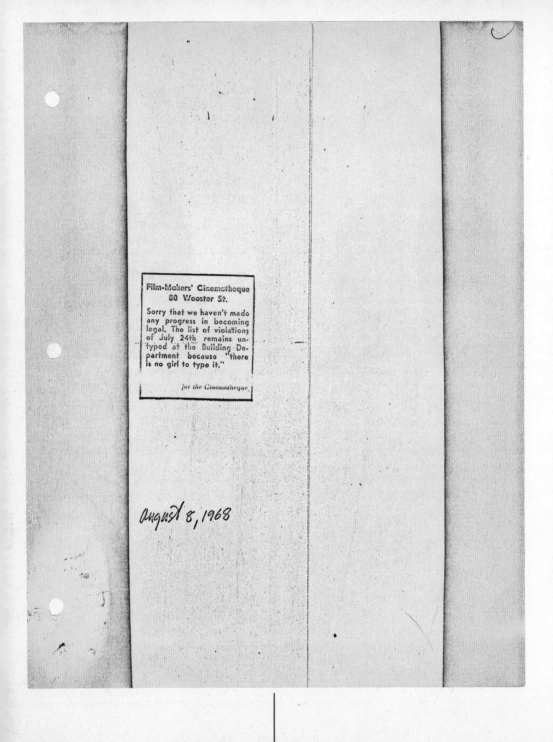

Film-Makers' Cinematheque
80 Wooster St.

Sorry that we haven't made
any progress in becoming
legal. The list of violations
of July 24th remains un-
typed at the Building De-
partment because "there
is no girl to type it."

for the Cinematheque.

August 8, 1968

GOD DAMN, WE ARE DIFFERENT AND WE ARE MAKING DIFFERENT FILMS, and our audience is not the same, and our sales methods must therefore be different. NOBODY WILL EVER BUY US. If such time ever comes we should begin really worrying. But those who do not accept this they go through all kinds of sales contortions, a lark trying to pass for a peacock.

Little by little, Film-Makers' Distribution Center is duplicating all the methods of the bigger distribution companies—and everything is fine, except one thing: it won't work. Sooner or later the "masses" begin to see that this little, sensitive bird is not the bird they want to buy: their bird knows only two or three notes to sing, and that they understand—and our bird is clever, and he sings many notes, he is a foreigner.

As the old saying goes: don't try to jump (or: you can't jump) higher than your own belly button.

Basically, I believe that any scheme, any scheme is immoral, all calculations are immoral, and they are punished, sooner or later—and to keep the film from somebody because you want to make more money with it at the local movie theater, is immoral, ugly, is anti-film, and the film cries hot tears and those tears, yes, no tear remains unpunished.

Sincerely yours, Jonas

August 2, 1968

To: The Millennium Workshop & The Film-Makers' Newsletter

The week has been bad enough for me, with the closing of the Cinematheque and with another bare escape from the Tombs, and one million in unpaid bills. But I have to write this letter now.

I am "informing" both, the Millennium Film Workshop, and the Film-Makers' Newsreel, that this will be the last time (that is, this month) that I'll be able to pick up the rent bills ($285 for the Millennium) and printing bills ($260 for the Newsletter). Not that I have any idea where I'm going to get the money even for this month. But I'll get it somewhere.

It's part of my bad nature that I don't know the word "no." I get entangled in helping all kinds of outside projects, and then I waste all my time, and all the money that I get for my lecture trips, and from the Co-op, from my films. And here I am, breaking into pieces, not knowing what to do, my unfinished films sitting around the table, around the room. I haven't been able to touch them for many months now, because all I have on my mind these days, these weeks, these months—yes, these YEARS—is money, money, money.

Everything came together, and the building of the Cinematheque, downtown, has strained the last drops of my patience, all my money, all my connections, and even my faith, very often. We still have no place to show our movies, any movies. I thought that 80 Wooster will be such a place, and I put all my weight behind it, and many other people put their energies behind it. Eight hard months of work, these were hard months, we wasted plenty of energy, life and faith, on Wooster Street. The whole thing cost us $70,000, and it's completed, but now they say we are not legal, and I have $30,000 of debts to pay, for construction work and to the film-makers, for the shows that we kept holding—we kept screening films, even as the construction was going on—we were so hungry for films, just to see some films—

But now the police and the Building Department have clubbed us, and they told us either to stop the screenings or they'll send us to jail. So we said, fine, no, we don't want to go to jail, who wants to go to jail! So there we are, we are closed again. The reasons for our closing are not very graspable, and we are still trying to understand them, I hope we will. It has to do

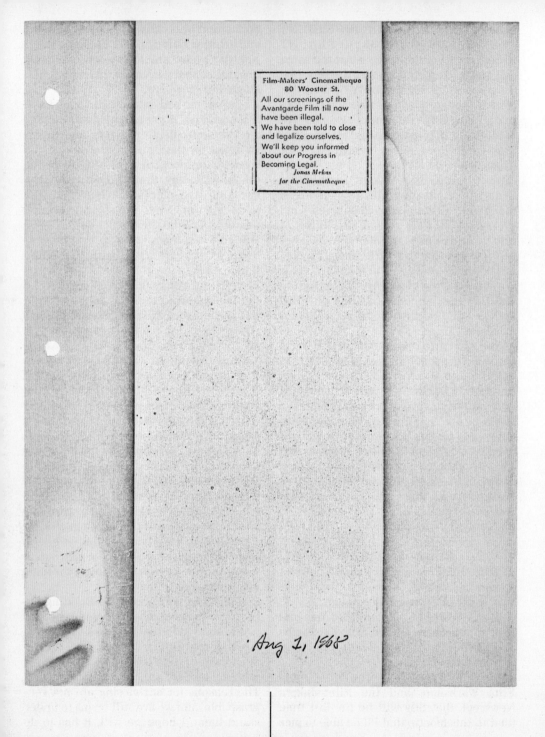

Film-Makers' Cinematheque
80 Wooster St.

All our screenings of the
Avantgarde Film till now
have been illegal.

We have been told to close
and legalize ourselves.

We'll keep you informed
about our Progress in
Becoming Legal.

Jonas Mekas
for the Cinematheque

Aug 1, 1968

with getting proper licenses for screenings, and if you think we spent all that money on construction work just for the fun of it—I wish it could be so—you don't know the city. Whatever we did was required by the city, in order to get the licenses, and we did everything they told us to do—close to the impossible—but now they seem to be playing some kind of game. What kind of game—that we are trying to find out. One thing is clear that it may take weeks perhaps months until we can open the theater again. And some more construction work will be needed, although not too much. Meanwhile, we are down to our last shirt. We are working on all kinds of straws, anything to grasp, very often it slips—but we never give up, we are not going to give up. Still, for some period of time, we have to put ourselves on a very strict regime. We have no choice at all. We will trim whatever we can trim. We will arm ourselves with patience for long waits in the Building Department corridors. We have more than two dozen summonses coming, they'll be as big as the judge will feel that day or other day—the first one is $100, but there is no rule on how high they can go on the second, that's what they told me in the court—how did you dare to commit such a crime, to show movies without a licensed theater permit! The judge was fuming in anger, and our legs were shaking as if we had killed somebody, or something.

Anyway, I am sitting now, in my room, far away from the judge and the cops and even far away from 80 Wooster St.—and I'm thinking how to solve my own life problems, how to get back to my films which are sitting right here on the floor, by my feet, creeping around my feet, begging me to work on them—so I'm thinking, how to work on them, and how to have the theater opened, and how not to go out of my mind —because I do not intend to give up, I won't play the Building Department game

—and I am all exhausted and burned out —I have no idea how I'll collect enough energy to start another day, tomorrow, to face the god damn city officials, and the black streets.

So forgive me that I am coming to you with this bad news. I don't know what else I can do. I have no more friends to whom I can turn for money. And I don't expect any money of my own soon: I have no lectures coming, no nothing. I was much luckier in the spring, and that helped us all. Wherever I go now, I meet people to whom I owe money, and the equipment, and advertising and etc. etc. companies are writing us angry letters and are threatening us with courts. I've come to the end of my rope and that's it, I can't go further. If I go further, it will be pure luck. It's still very unbelievable that we've come this far. All of the last six, seven years have been chance, luck, and circumstances, as far as money goes. I can tell you that with some authority, as the bankrupt Minister of Finances. But at least the Co-op is now on its own and is going fine. So that at least something will be left and will go. But I really cannot even care, at my present low state, what happens to the Millennium or the Newsletter, I simply don't have any energy left even to care about them. So it's all up to you. And if there is really nobody else who can or wants to care about them that much that that person will go out and use his own money, no matter what he has, and beg from others in order to pay Millennium and Newsletter—than what the hell, nothing matters anyway.

The window is black (it's really still grey, but it looks black to me), it's evening, it's in New York, it's the beginning of August, there is a Republican (Democrat?) Convention going on in Florida, it's hot, my icebox is empty, there is a strange buzz in my head, in my ears, the strips of film are hanging on the door (they have been hanging like that for the last six months), there

is somebody's pledge pasted on the wall in front of me which says "come March 1968 I'm coming out" (he never came out), the sound of the trucks in the street,
Sincerely yours,
Jonas Mekas

August 2, 1968

To: Professor Luigi Chiarini,
Il Direttore Mostra Internazionale d'Arte Cinematografica
La Biennale di Venezia
Venezia, Italy

Dear Mr. Chiarini:
Forgive me that this letter is coming so close to the festival date. But, after lengthy considerations, I have decided to decline your kind invitation to serve as a judge at this year's International Exhibition of Cinematographic Art. Here are some of my reasons.
First of all, I do not want to get into the middle of political fights I know nothing about. I am of the opinion that this wouldn't have happened, what's happening with the film festivals, if the film festivals would have followed a road of open acceptance of cinema, of all cinema, instead of becoming showcases of certain kinds of cinema. If Cannes is a Festival of Propaganda For the Commercial Melodrama, so Venice has become a Festival of Propaganda for the Serious Commercial Melodrama, and the difference is not a big one. Venice may not be as lavish in its sales decor as Cannes; nevertheless, through its more puritan and spartan style, it serves the same end. It doesn't serve cinema (and I am not interested in exceptions): it serves a certain kind of cinema under the pretext of The Cinema. All Major film festivals, in that sense, are Whores of Cinema, and, as the tale goes, sooner or later, their teeth will fall out.
Already two years ago, in my letter to Cannes Film Festival and to Pesaro Film Festival I have pointed out the main objections to the film festivals as they were then, and I called for immediate and drastic revisions. They can't say they haven't been warned in advance! But nothing has changed since. So what I said then remains true today: Film Festivals represent neither the "new" cinema, nor the "now" in cinema, nor the Art of Cinema. Film Festivals, and this includes Venice, represent only the tastes of their Directors and those of film industries. The fact that some of the film industries this year are boycotting Venice means absolutely nothing, it's just an internal quarrel, like one between the Democrats and the Republicans in the United States, but it doesn't matter much which one is officially in.
You invite me, Henri Langlois, and Peter Weiss to come judge films at the Venice Biennale. But we'll come and we'll find that we are only figurines in a game: our choices are predetermined. You have already preselected the ten or eleven films which will be shown at the festival, "in competition." Our judgment will operate only within the sphere of your personal taste. How and where does our authority and our taste and knowledge, as jurors, come in, in regard to the world cinema anno 1968? I do not feel like playing such a game.
Consider another inconsistency, or, rather, absurdity that one finds today at all major film festivals. You invite one playwright, one film archivist, one film-maker, one film critic, one producer, one writer—people from completely different areas of interest and authority, and you want them to agree upon one film, to name one film the BEST film? Have you seen anything like that in the competitions of, say, musical works? Or poetry? Do we have, then, to argue the randomness of such agreements and decisions of such hodgepodge juries? Why do we mislead the people, then, with such chance choices? As some kind of enter-

tainment, similar to the lottery? Only film-makers can be judges of film. And even so, it would still be ridiculous and absurd to ask five or six filmmakers to vote upon one best film, to agree upon one film: at best, they can only point out their own PERSONAL preferences, with an explanatory note, how and why did they choose the way they chose, with no attempt to clash one judge against another. Instead of announcing the Winners, festivals should announce the personal preferences, choices of each juror film-maker.

Consider the third point, which, in a longer run, is even more damaging than the first two. By the very fact that Cannes, Venice, Berlin, Karlovy Vary and the other "major" film festivals have become such publicized commercial markets, the real place, in the proper context of Film Art, of the films shown at those festivals is blown completely out of proportion by the publicity and the salesman. As a result of this misleading irresponsible publicity, people tend to accept the festival winners as truly representative of the best films made this year in the countries represented at the festivals. Do we have to argue that the truth, most of the time, is very different, that the festival films only occasionally actually represent the best films made in those countries? That these are only the films which either you, as Director of the Festival, chose, or some official motion picture organization or government chose; that none of the films, say, either by Brakhage, nor Markopoulos, nor Jack Smith, nor Warhol—just to mention the four most creative film-makers in America today—the names without which you cannot talk about American cinema today—none of them have been shown at any of the so-called "major" or "official" festivals of d'Arte Cinematografica? It may be indicative of something, no? I cannot even begin to tell you how much damage has been done by film festivals to the proper growth and education of cinema as an art. The state and the true values of the art of cinema are being distorted by the film festivals. It's the COMMERCIAL FILM MELODRAMA that is the Queen (what a curious case of transvestitism...) of all official film festivals, not the art of cinema, and not the new cinema.

What do I suggest, then?

I really have no suggestions. My feeling is that no great damage would be done—really, it would be a blessing, as far as the art of cinema goes—if we'd drop all existing film festivals, with their systems of selection of films, systems of prizes, categories, and their social, publicity and sale systems. It would be wrong to try and fix a sick tree by fixing its branches when the thing has to be changed from the roots: the wrong tree, or, rather, a WEED is growing in the Garden of Cinema. Get rid of it. Let's get rid of all official film festivals and see what comes in their place—nothing much worse can happen, that much is certain. We do have, for instance, readings of poetry, and international premieres of new works of music. There could be similar international premieres of films, too, perhaps, where more respect is paid to the work itself and less to the film industry and sales aspects. Individual films could be brought to the attention through world premieres—not on a competitive basis, but presented simply and fairly and from sheer joy that there is a new work by Chaplin, by Godard, by Rossellini, by Brakhage, and that it should be brought to everyone's attention; not to clash them AGAINST other works of art; not submerge them in a stock market of shouting salesmen but to present them peacefully and beautifully by themselves. Bresson. Markopoulos. Mizoguchi. Marker. Resnais. To introduce an element of competition in art and in such gross and hodgepodge ways, as we have today at the film festivals, is really not doing any good service to the art of cinema, but the opposite, to put it mildly. To point out a few films or a few good directors who HAVE BEEN helped by the festivals even as they are today, is to engage oneself with hypocrisy.

It's for these and a number of other similarly important (to me) reasons that I have decided to say no to your kind invitation. One may think—the same way that many are reasoning about the Black Rebellion and the Student Cultural Rebellions—that "let's not take extremes, let's sit and discuss, there must be a middle road." I feel that such an attitude at this stage of the Overblown Importance of the Film Festivals would only mislead people (and ourselves) about the real (bad) state of things, and about the real urgency for drastic and immediate changes in the film festival system: not by way of evolution, but by way of revolution.

To sum up: festivals as they are today promote wrong understanding of what art is—the art of cinema in our case—and they spread distorted and wrong relations (separations) between man and man. The change is needed so badly that the relative rightfulness of some of the institutions (in this case, Venice Film Festival) as compared with others—is completely irrelevant. We cannot argue about parts and details when the entire thing is wrong. I intend to boycott all official film festivals and will urge other film-makers, film critics, and anyone concerned with the art of cinema, to do the same. Once more I apologize for this late communication of my views.

Sincerely yours,
Jonas Mekas

No date, 1968

Those who have watched the growth of the New American Cinema, the Underground Film, should know by now that our attitude, our spirit is TO BUILD, TO CREATE, not to destroy. We didn't waste energy on destroying Hollywood film industry: we directed our energies towards creating a new kind of cinema, a more personal cinema, toward the liberation of the camera; we didn't waste any energy on destroying or fighting the competitive, commercial film distribution set-ups and systems: we created our own, Cooperative Distribution Center, Film-Makers' Cooperative, based on noncompetitive human relations; we didn't waste energy fighting censorship: we created a cinema that is changing the censorship laws; we aren't even wasting energy on fighting the corrupt public information media—we created our own, Underground information film, the Newsreel.

I am for changes. I'm for the new. We must always be in the avant-garde. But I part ways with those—no matter under what name, under what radical disguise or slogan they go—who attack festivals because, they say, festivals promote "art" and that "art is part of capitalism, "and therefore, art must go." etc., etc. These people have been taken by the film Festival propaganda machinery: they believe that what is shown at the film festivals is art! Number two: they have been taken also by capitalism. They consider art just is another commodity. Radicals of the world! Do not make these mistakes! To the real vanguard of Humanity—and the artists are in that Vanguard—art is not a commodity and art is not the melodramas you see in film festivals. In art, like in science, all the knowledge, experiences, and dreams of man are summed up, traced, forecasted. Man cannot live by melodrama alone. It's not "art" that you—radicals of the world—revolutionaries and rebels of the world—should be fighting but the wrong ideas about art, wrong understanding of art. There is no film art at film festivals today. And if you think that to be anti-art is radical or revolutionary—you should begin worrying: because life has already outdistanced you and you will find yourself soon among the retrogressive forces. The true revolution is somewhere else, the true revolution is in the spiritual Vanguard. And if you want to know where that is—put your ear close to the art of your times and listen, until you hear it.

New York Times, June 21, 1968
Grace Glueck (reporting on the disruption of the Venice Biennale by students): "'the artist belongs to the bourgeois world," said the architectural student, leaning out of the ground floor Academy window. "They are directly tied to the process of producing capital.'"

August 2, 1968

Richard called Building Department, to check if the list of violations is being typed. He was told they still haven't got a girl to type it. Maybe next week. Richard said again: could I come and type it for you? No, it's not done so. Call on Monday or Tuesday.

It's Friday evening now. I'm sitting at home, alone. I'm already beginning to save my patience and energy for next Monday. Trust to the end. Trust to the end. I repeated twice. But I am calm I am not banging my head against the wall. I seem to be perfectly normal. I am not crazy, believe me. My nose just twitched. But that's normal. I stare at the wall in front of me for three minutes without thinking anything, without seeing anything. That's normal too. The dragon went back into the wall just as it came. I just peeked at myself, in the mirror. The face, I admit, it has a few suspicious lines. I have seen faces like that in paintings of Munch and Van Gogh. Both sources could cause alarm. But I'm trying to be calm. I am really beginning to look at the whole thing as some kind of modern and 100 % pure American yoga system. If I succeed going through this exercise, even if it takes five years—I should gain

complete mastery over myself. Better than spending time with Maharishi. Unless, that much I have to admit—unless I crack up before it's over. But one has to take that chance. The floor just squeaked. The beams are too weak, must be changed. I must do something about it on Monday, before McGinnis finds out.

August 5, 1968

In the afternoon, Richard went to the Municipal Building. The list wasn't ready yet, not typed, "no girl."

August 6, 1968

9:30 AM I meet Richard at the Municipal Building. We have our coffee on the 20th floor, like every morning, and then we go to see the Borough Superintendent Isadore Cohen. In three sentences I present him with our problem. I show him a page with 35 violations, (Richard's copy; Building Department hasn't typed it yet). He says: "So what are you going to do about it? You have to comply with it, no?" Without even listening to our explanations, he takes for granted that the Building Department is ALWAYS RIGHT. The Building Department can never be wrong. He says he can't do anything for us. We should go see Engineer Clark.

Engineer Clark is very kind to us. He goes down the list, one by one, he listens to explanations. Finally he says: "You should never argue with the Building Department. Do you think you can win an argument with us?" "No," I say: "No. I don't want to win an argument: I want to find out the facts." Anyway, he went down the list, he dismissed some, placed question marks on others. He came up with three or four real violations. And even these three didn't have anything to do with the theater; they had to do with the basement and other floors.

At this stage, feeling quite optimistic, I decided to leave Richard alone to continue the "work" in the Building Department, and I went to my other business. Richard came back late in the afternoon. He looked black. He said, "We can sell the building now. It's all finished. Engineer Clark went to engineer Jaccobachi who approved the plans last fall, before we started construction. Jaccobachi flatly declared that he made a mistake approving the plans, and that he's revoking his approval. He said our building needs a larger fire passage, and that is not in the plans." I asked George how much the passageway may cost. He said, over $20,000 maybe more. This is not the end of the disaster: facing Engineer Clark and Engineer Jaccobachi with their disaster report, Isadore Cohen decided to revoke his permission to let us go ahead with the ground floor before the rest of the building is completed. Disaster is complete. The Building Department made an amphibious (is that the expression?) assault on us and smashed us victoriously. Bravo, bravo! We are wiped out.

August 9, 1968

I am making plans to announce the formation of a new political party, the aim of which is to close the Building Department and free the people. I called the director of WNYC, Seymour N. Siegel, whom I had met during one of my "working" trips to the Municipal Building. I reported our miseries. He listened. But I had a feeling I sounded stupid. How am I going to explain to anybody the real reasons? The real reasons? No doubt, we SHOULD comply with the building Department Regulations... Mr. Siegel said he will try to find out what's what. But I have a feeling there will not be any good results. The Building Department will simply tell him that we have 35 violations. Of course, they aren't going to tell him that practically all of those violations have been dismissed by their chief engineer, Larry Clark...

Last Tuesday, on my way out, I stood there, leaning against the wall, when McGinnis passed by. I felt like saying something. "Sorry that we seem to be such nuisances with this thing. But it's important to us. This theatre is the only place where we have where we can show our movies." He looked at me, smiled, and said: "Yes. I have seen some of your MOVIES, I understand what you're talking about. When I come to see your MOVIES I don't go with my wife—I bring my girlfriend..." That's what they think about us. Is that why they are doing it? Maybe even with the police instruction? Keep your city clean...

August 14, 1968

Oh, how I am tired of all of this!
I saw R.S. He is an architect and does many big constructions for the city. I told him our story. Asked for advice. He said he knows the Building Department too well and he hates their guts and he understands us perfectly, and he advises us to get an expeditor as soon as possible.
Went to see Truder, at the Cultural Office, brought her up to date. She said she'll try to do something.

August 15, 1968

The Office for Cultural Affairs arranged a meeting between the Cinematheque and Robert J. Malito, Secretary to the Department of Buildings. I told him our story. He listened kindly. He expressed a genuine wish to help us. He called Engineer Clark. I could see it from Malito's face, that Engineer Clark was pushing him into the corner. He was telling him about all the violations. Malito used expressions like, "If nothing can be done then nothing can be done... but let's see..." Anyway, an agreement was reached for him to visit the Cinematheque next week and familiarize himself with the problem.

HOUSING AND DEVELOPMENT ADMINISTRATION
JASON R. NATHAN, *Administrator*

Department of Buildings
2 LAFAYETTE STREET, NEW YORK, N. Y. 10007

JOHN T. O'NEILL, *Commissioner*
JOSEPH FERRO, *Deputy Commissioner*

October 7, 1968

Miss Nancy Kendall
325 East 5th Street
New York, N. Y. 10003

Dear Miss Kendall:

    Thank you very much for your recent correspondence
concerning Film-Makers Cinematheque. We are most appreciative
of your taking the time to give us the benefit of your views
of this group.

    While this department understands the nature of the
work of Film-Makers Cinematheque and sympathizes with the
difficulties of the sponsors of this group, we cannot set
aside specific provisions of law which have been enacted to
provide for the safety and welfare of the public, nor authorize
a variance that this department is forbidden to grant.

    Within the bounds of our laws and with the safety of
each and every member of the public in mind, we are more than
willing to cooperate with and assist Film-Makers Cinematheque
and any other group in our City.

    Thanks again for your interest.

Sincerely,

Robert J. Malito
Secretary to the Department

August 19, 1968

Mr. Malito and Engineer Clark inspected the theatre. They went through the list of violations. Engineer Clark agreed, in front of Malito, that none of the objections were too serious. He dismissed most of the violations; others, he admitted, could be easily corrected. The second door, to which there was so much fuss given before, was not found necessary at all, for the 72 seat theatre: one door is enough. Why, I wondered, didn't he tell me that before, motherfucker. The only real objections, was agreed, were two, or rather three:

1. Some of the artists were living (having studios) in the same building as the theatre.
2. One of the fire exits—the one which was AGREED WAS NOT NEEDED for the 72 seat theatre—was too low, in one spot, by four or six inches, and should be corrected: it was needed for the other artists working in the building. When I said that this passage was approved in the construction plans as is—Engineer Clark said that the Building Department was free to change its mind whenever it's "necessary." Even after we had spent all that money on construction? Yes, he said.
3. Engineer Clark said that for a 72 seat theatre we have TOO MUCH space and we should build partitions and separate the theatre from the rest of the space. I told him that the experimental nature of our theatre requires all the space—the walls and ceilings are being used as projection surfaces. I told him that his thinking was fifty years behind. Of course, this had no impact on the Engineer Clark. Both, Engineer Clark and Mr. Malito agreed that the objections were not too important. The Building Department, they said, is permitted to make exceptions in special cases. The fire passage, in our case, could constitute such an exception. Mr. Malito said I should call him in a few days.

August 21, 1968

Upon the advice of Mr. Malito, I wrote the following letter to the Commissioner of Buildings:

The Honorable Commissioner of Buildings: I am writing to you on behalf of the Film-Makers' Cinematheque, located on 80 Wooster St. N.Y.C. I am doing so after discussing the matter with Robert J. Malito, Secretary to the Department of Buildings, and the office for Cultural Affairs, Department of Parks.

We are asking you to issue us the Certificate of Occupancy so that we could use the ground floor of the said building for lectures, exhibitions, and film screenings (application for 72 people), and the basement for office space and workshop rooms. It seems that there is a small problem, concerning the granting of such a Certificate, and only you could make the proper decisions. The problem has to do with the nature of the building and the location.

At this point I have to give you some background information on the building.

The 80 Wooster St building was purchased in the Autumn 1967 by the FLUXHOUSE Cooperative. The Kaplan Foundation and the National Foundation of Arts loaned $20,000 to the Cooperative to acquire the building.

What is the FLUXHOUSE Cooperative? I don't think I could do better but to quote from the text prepared by the Cooperative:

THE ARTIST'S PROBLEM

While it has been recognized for some time that New York City is one of the leading arts centers of the world, with probably the largest artist population, it is considerably less well known that the city suffers from a severe shortage of economical working space for artists. In part this shortage is due to the moderate means of the average professional artist and the artist's special space requirements. Normally the artist requires large unbroken spaces with high ceilings and adequate illumination, and these needs can only be met by commercial lofts. At the same time these lofts, which are relatively expensive, are rarely zoned for living or require considerable alterations to make them suitable for dwelling, so that the artist is often forced to pay double rent—one for living and one for working—which he can ill afford. Moreover the fluidity of the artist's work regime, demanding periods of concentrated activity, make the separation of living and working spaces very undesirable. Both the city and the state, at the urging of the Artist's Tenants Association and various other sympathetic groups have attempted to alleviate the problem by making certain concessions in zoning requirements. These attempts, though well motivated, have been insufficient. The artist is put into considerable expense in improving the property, even to comply with relaxed requirements. What is more, his investment is unprotected, since there is nothing to prevent his landlord from even doubling the rent on the now more valuable property when the artist's lease has expired. The result is that the improved loft is removed from the class of economical working spaces.

THE ARTIST'S PROBLEM IS PART OF A LARGER GENERAL PROBLEM

But the scarcity of economical working spaces for artists is part of the general problem arising from urban obsolescence and decay. Large areas of the central city, zoned for commercial and light manufacturing use were constructed sometime ago. The narrow streets and old buildings are usually not suited for the demands of modern commercial usage. Because of this and the fashion that dictates the location of the more flourishing businesses, the more profitable enterprises tend to compete for space in a few favored areas. The older sections are left to house the more marginal businesses; the buildings are rarely in more than partial use, and are hardly profitable to their owners. In many cases they've been allowed to fall into disrepair. These areas, frequently abutting low income or slum residential areas, become foci of urban blight. Up to now significant attempts at urban renewal of these areas involving costly clearing of the areas and new construction, have not been made. And the process of obsolescence and decay here continue without obstruction. Nevertheless there are many buildings in such areas that are architecturally sound and potentially valuable is considered from the point of view of radically altered use.

A STEP IN THE DIRECTION OF A SOLUTION

With the artist's problem in mind FLUX-HOUSE was formed as a non-profit co-operative corporation consisting solely of professional artists seeking adequate combined work and living space. Its aim is to purchase, renovate and maintain suitable buildings for artist occupancy. A comprehensive survey led FLUXHOUSE to select the area of Manhattan between Houston and Canal known as "Hell's Hundred Acres," as the most suitable because of economy and location, and because it contained a number of very sound, though underused buildings. This area is the site of precisely type of obsolescence described. Moreover it abuts on lower income residential areas immediately to the East and West. FLUXHOUSE's immediate plan is to purchase three buildings, already selected, within this area as the site of an artistic community. These buildings are to be renovated as work-residences which will not only comply with zoning

Film-Makers' Cinematheque, 80 Wooster Street, 1968.

Jackson MacLow and John Cage at Film-Makers' Cinematheque.

requirements but also conform to the specific living and working requirements of the individual artists. Renovation, which has already been thoroughly planned will, include in each building a self-service elevator, a central air heating and cooling system, new flooring, kitchens, bathrooms, plumbing, lighting fixtures, walls, partitions, doors, closets etc. Moreover two of the buildings will house theaters for the performing arts, which will be used for film exhibitions, dance recitals, concerts etc. They will also house wood and metalworking shops, photo darkrooms, a film processing and editing laboratory, a sound studio and offset printing press. All of these facilities will be available to all the artist members of the cooperative. But FLUXHOUSE intends to go beyond this to become an integral part of the adjoining community by making available to the children of the area workshops in the various arts under the supervision of the artist members of FLUXHOUSE. In view of the wide range of special competences of the artist residents of FLUXHOUSE, these local workshops can include, depending upon the needs and desires of the neighborhood, work in painting, sculpting, filmmaking, dance, printing etc. It is our belief that introduction of an artistic nucleus as FLUXHOUSE into such an area can pave the way for other similar projects and perhaps initiate the conversion of a marginal and deteriorating commercial district into a cultural center with value extending far beyond the immediate bounds of the community.

Film-Maker's Cinematheque joined the artist's Co-op and acquired the ground floor and the basement of the 80 Wooster St building.

The artists in the 80 Wooster St building and their renovation expenses till now:

- JOE SCHLICHTER & TRISHA BROWN
  dancers & choreographers $11,000
- MARTIAL WESTBURG
  sculptor
  $10,000
- ROBERT WATT
  artist (objects, events)
  $9,000
- CHARLES ROSS
  sculptor (plastics, lenses)
  $7,000
- BETH BAUMBACH
  weaver
  $5,000
- SHOEL SHAPIRO
  architect, designer
  $7,000
- JOEL McGLASSON
  designer
  $5,000
- MELVIN REICHLER
  painter & sculptor
  $10,000
- CINEMATHEQUE
  workshop & experimental theatre
  $55,000
total: $120,000

(other artists' cooperatives in which renovation work is going on are:

16 – 18 Greene St	6 members
64 – 70 Grand St	20 members
131 Prince St	8 members
465 West B'way	9 members
451 West B'way	10 members

AND HAPPY SHOULD BE THE CITY WHERE THE ARTISTS ARE SOLVING THEIR OWN STUDIO & LODGING PROBLEMS.

Now, we come to the Film-Makers' Cinematheque.
Film-Maker's Cinematheque was established four years ago. It was approved by the Government of the United States as a

tax-deductible educational Foundation. Its main purpose is to serve the independent, the avant-garde film-maker, and to assist the beginning film-maker. The Cinematheque serves as a center for showing and promoting their work; it publishes books and magazines dealing with the avant-garde cinema; assists with grants to the avant-garde film-maker; conducts film-maker's workshops; sends expositions to other countries; assists universities, museums, galleries, state and city cultural offices in programming films and lectures.

(For a more detailed description of the Cinematheque's activities, and the statements by Otto Preminger, Arthur Mayer and the Office for Cultural Affairs, Department of Parks—see the Supplements to this letter.)

In the past, the Cinematheque has been using various other buildings, where there were theatre and office facilities. However, the rental costs became too high for a non-commercial organization. In autumn 1967 we decided to join the FLUXHOUSE Co-operative and construct our own theatre, much cheaper to operate and of a more suitable design for the needs of an experimental film-maker. Such a theatre was constructed on 80 Wooster St. All work but a few minor things have been completed July 1968. The construction of the Cinematheque theater has been paid by grants from the Ford Foundation, Kaplan Foundation, Avon Foundation, and individuals such as Jack Valenti, Otto Preminger, Elia Kazan, Joshua Logan, Celeste and Armand Bartos, and others.

WHAT DO WE NEED FROM THE HONORABLE COMMISSIONER OF BUILDINGS?

There seem to be at least two obstacles blocking our Certificate of Occupancy:

The old rules of the Building Department require that for the number of people that we are applying (72) the space is TOO LARGE, and it should be cut down by enclosures & walls. But we consider that dividing of the space would defeat the work we are going to do in the place. WE NEED ALL THAT SPACE. The nature of the contemporary film experimentation is such that often two, three, and more projectors, and two, three or more screens are used; plus, the ceiling and walls are used as projection surfaces. The Cinematheque has been a pioneer in modern projection techniques and it intends to remain so. (The first Expanded Cinema Festival which the Cinematheque organized in 1965 has since revolutionized the entire theatre-discotheque style and technology.) It's important to stress the fact that although many of our films are open to the public, the Cinematheque is not a theatre but AN EXPERIMENTAL FILM-MAKERS' WORKSHOP.
That is one.

Another obstacle seems to be the fact that this EXPERIMENTAL THEATRE-WORKSHOP is housed in the artist's co-operative building. But what could be more proper and more wise than that?
If I understand it right, the objection centers around the by now outdated clause that some of the artists are not only working in their studios, but also sleeping; and that is against the law. Our contention (and our appeal to you) is twofold:
a) four or five artists living or working above the theatre-workshop can not constitute any possible danger or be endangered themselves, in case of fire (unless the atom bomb falls...) (only a few weeks ago, the artists working at night on 80 Wooster St noticed and timely prevented a fire in the neighboring building).
b) it's about time that the City reconsiders some of its attitudes and regulations con-

cerning the lodging and working spaces of the artists living in New York City. The Building Department should extend all possible help to the artists' cooperatives which are taking much of the City's worry away without much of the City's help. Artists should be permitted to live where they work, if they want. An artist doesn't work according to the clocks and punch cards. He works twenty four hours and his studio, very often, is also his bed. It just can not be any other way. The unreasonable regulations force the artists into breaking the regulations and wasting everybody's time and energies.

I am asking the Honorable Commissioner of Buildings to give to this matter a serious and careful consideration. We need your help. The artists of New York need your help. If New York City wants to remain in the lead of artistic researches and creation, a few readjustments here and there could do a lot. And forgive me that I went into such great lengths concerning this matter.

Sincerely yours,
Jonas Mekas
Film-Makers' Cinematheque

Copies of this letter are being mailed to: Robert J. Malito, Secretary, Department of Buildings; Roger Stevens, Council on the Arts; Joan Davidson, Kaplan Foundation; W. McNeil Lowry, Ford Foundation; A. A. Heckman, Avon Foundation; August Heckscher, Department of Parks.

No date, 1968
MOVIE JOURNAL (unpublished)
We say, we "shoot" a picture. There's this connection with the gun somehow. But you could also imagine, if you want, that the camera is sending you 24 kisses per second. The camera eye is like the eye of a baby, it looks at you and it makes you ashamed. That's why the cops are smashing cameras. Many cameras were smashed by the cops at the Grand Central Be-In and during the Columbia University Truth-In. The cops must have plenty to be ashamed of, why else smash cameras? They do it very casually, their sticks "slip." If this continues, we may have to call a Film-In and surround every cop in the city with ten movie cameras, watching their every step. Mind, I am not interested in waging any special complaints against COPS, to me they are no more corrupt than the rest of the public servants. It's just that they are putting themselves so unnecessarily on the spot. We can use cameras to get rid of some bad traits of our public servants. The eight million cameras that we have in this country today are eight million walking mirrors. So let's behave.

September 4, 1968
Almost three weeks passed since Mr. Malito and Engineer Clark visited the Cinematheque. No news. Mr. Malito said, he already twice planned to meet with the Building Department and the Borough Superintendent to discuss our case, but was interrupted by other urgent business. Supposedly, they are holding a meeting today, I was told.

September 10, 1968
I called Mr. Malito. He informed me that they held their meeting. The Building Department is preparing a letter to us, everything will be explained. Mr. Malito indicated that they couldn't come to any good decision. I'll wait for the letter.

September 22, 1968
Still waiting for the letter.
I had a conversation with a certain R. He gave me the name of a professional Expeditor.
I met the Expeditor and told him our story. The Expeditor said sure, he could do it for

us. We were fools to wait that long, he said. Everybody bribes, he said. He used to work for the Building Department and he knows it inside out. Now he works for big constructors, he's expediting BIG. "But we wanted to do it the legal way," I said. "Our mistake was that we by-passed the Inspector. That was our first bad mistake." "You really went higher than the inspector?" asked the Expeditor, a little amazed. "That was a bad mistake. With just the Inspector I'd have done it for you for $200 or $300. Now you'll have to pay another $500 to their boss," he said. "Oh, no," I said, "we went even higher than that... We went to the head of the Construction Department too..." "Oh, no," said the Expeditor, shaking his head, "how foolish can you be? Now it will cost you another $500." "Hmmm, hmm..." said I, "but the Borough Superintendent knows about it too..." "That's too bad. That will cost you another $500. Still it can be done, I hope, the whole job for $2,000." At this point I had to admit that I made another booboo: our case is known in the Mayor's Offices by now... At this point the Expeditor gave up. He said, he'll look into it, he'll speak at the Building Department, but he can't help fools who do not follow the established procedures.

September 24, 1968

Still waiting for the letter from the Building Department.

I told Mr. H about our conversation with the Expeditor. He was appalled by the very idea of speaking with an Expeditor. His sense of justice was trembling. "But look," I said, "every large company has an expeditor—it's a perfectly legal procedure ... What's legal? Legal is what the People do. And they do it, no? So, it's legal... You have to admit that, things being as they are, the system being totally corrupt, it's for the good of the citizens of this town to have a Cinematheque open instead of closed. To insist on an abstract morality

point, in this particular case, would make the Building Department the winner: by keeping the Cinematheque closed, they'd succeed in their plot of depriving the City of its proper spiritual growth and thus make it into a better place for their own corrupt schemes. It's obvious, therefore, that even if we have to bribe, we have to keep our spiritual institutions going. It's like the famous lie of Joan of Arc." Thus spoke I...

September 26, 1968

TO LIBERATION PRESS
Dear John:
Four, maybe five times during the last three months I've promised to write you a report on our troubles. Our troubles are complicated, they involve the Administration of the City of New York. They also involve the police of the City of New York. If I put down on paper all the things that have happened to us during the last three months, with all the names involved—a good number of civilian servants would end up in jails. Or at least I hope so. My diary of these last three months reads like a chapter from the new novel by Kafka. But, mind—even in my diaries I couldn't enter all the cases and dates and names of the civilian servants, particularly the policemen and the Building Department employees, who approached us, and insisted that we should pay them, like everybody else does. And these people are so cocksure about their business and about their untouchable positions, that they are not afraid to give the names and addresses of the bribe-collecting contacts. They know perfectly well that nobody will squeal, there are machine guns to shut up the squealers. Our trouble started only because we were such blue-nosed idealists. We couldn't believe, couldn't believe that it was all true, not some kind of gangster movie. So we said no, we are not going to pay, we ain't got any money. Sometimes

Hannelore Hahn, New York City's office for Cultural Affairs, 1958.

they didn't say anything, just looked, and we were supposed to know what their looks meant. But we refused to read their faces.

Still, I decided that I should remain silent. You know my reason? It's like this. During the last two years I've come to detest the public media. That includes the underground press. I've seen, in the underground press, and the BIG press, everything being exposed. Everything becomes a "press case," headlines. I've also seen everything, later, disappearing back into the darkness of apathy and time. Everything is being used, milked, manipulated, as NEWS. Not as things to correct, to overcome, to change —but as NEWS, that's all. I've come to the conclusion, or, rather, I'm getting to it—I am in a sort of transitional period—where I feel that if one can really cause any real changes, it can only be by one's own hard work. I have wasted hundreds of hours dealing with small bureaucrats, I have been treated like a village idiot; I've seen how other people are being treated by them; and I still have hopes... Every day I'm dealing with people who have no idea what our films are. All they are interested in is money, money, money. And I consider that a dozen more of these bureaucrats in jails wouldn't make the smallest dent in the system. I really mean it. Before I undertook the construction of the Cinematheque, I had no idea the degree of corruption within the city administration. I always thought it was only outsiders' paranoia, suspicions, slander. So I learned my lesson. Now I know that I'm dealing with a corrupt system, with an immoral system, with inhuman system, ugly system, an unjust system. Call it whatever name you will, it's all those names and more. But I do not believe I should waste my energy combating it. I am basically a farmer, I "grow" things, that's what I am best at. And I know that I should conserve my energy for that purpose. I therefore decided to work quietly and persistently at least as long as it's humanly possible—reopening of Cinematheque. A few months one way or another doesn't matter at all. We are always too god damned rushed... So that our work, our real work of changing the system should begin right there, in the Cinematheque, THROUGH OUR FILMS. That's where our real power is, if we have any, or if that can be called power at all, this building of an island of beauty and truth through our art in the middle of the city of Gold, yes, of Gold...

Because, really, I cannot blame the City administrators for their corruption, for their love of money, for their completely moral perversion and irresponsibility. They came to it all like into an inheritance. It's perfectly normal for them to treat others the way they are treating: they don't know any other way. They are sleepwalking through the system. Where does one begin the re-education? I guess the Chicago gathering was some kind of education. I hope so, I don't know. Next time it may not work. You can't cure overnight an inhuman system perfected through so many thousands of years. The corruption is not only in their souls and their minds: it's in their very flesh, in their bones. That's why I consider that it would be inhuman, on my part, to turn in the cops and the inspectors who have asked for bribes: it would only show that I haven't transcended the real situation of things. Because where it's really at, it's somewhere else, completely somewhere else.

Those few of us who have some vision of a better humanity, we cannot allow ourselves be distracted or detracted from our real work; we cannot allow that. I believe more in the silent work, at least that's where I am now. Tomorrow I may scream. Sometimes I feel like screaming, very often, as a matter of fact...

So I thought I owe you this explanation. Because, believe me, it's not easy to be silent these days. The corruption makes you want to scream ten times every day. So I clench my teeth and continue living. This is the Age of Living with Clenched Teeth…

Love,
Jonas Mekas

September 27, 1968

Hannelore called. Asked me to call Mr. Rosen, in the Mayor's office. He called Miss Friedman's office asking for info on Tek. Apparently he received a letter from somebody complaining why the Cinematheque is closed. People have been writing letters to the Mayor's office on our behalf.

I spoke with Rosen. Miss Friedman had already briefed him about us. I gave him more details. He said, he'll look into our story. Meanwhile, I am still waiting for the letter from the Building Department in answer to my letter.

Dear Carla:

Your letter came. I have a feeling you are doing better in London Town than in N.Y., the way the things are here these days. Stay put. Things are confused and as bad here as they were when you left. The City is still leading us by the nose, promises, meetings, wasting time, more paper and more confusion and not a bit of progress. Day after day, week after week, month (yes!) after month. I hope it won't become "year after year." Everybody promises, and always bounces back, whenever the Case reaches the small bureaucrats: the small bureaucrats of the Building Department are like a Barricade of Corruption, firm, unmovable, eternal, like Hell itself. Temporarily we had to stop all screenings. The Methodist Church screenings became too draggy. I had to let Richard go, he works now for *The Voice*, for bread, and I can't waste my life dragging projectors back and forth. Since there is no money coming from anywhere, I keep piling the bills on the corner of the table, without opening the envelopes, let them rest in peace. George [Landow] got a job (paid) with Scientologists, he is in that bag, got hooked. There was a call from Washington last week, they said they may consider our application for a grant in about three weeks from now, so there is a glimmer of hope there. So better stay put…

Indian summer is killing us here. Hot, humid, smoggy. It takes plenty of courage to breathe this air. The sound of the cars is coming through the windows. Hot. I am editing my film diaries, at least I have more time now… And I am watching TV on your set—that was most unfortunate, to leave it with me, because I got completely hooked on it, terrible, I watch for hours any kind of crap.

Just thought, that is, remembered something. I am going through the last stages of negotiations with the Jewish Museum to start an Avant-garde Film Series, a Flying Cinematheque program, once a week (Thursdays) at the Museum, I will know by Monday if it's definite. If it comes through, I may not be able to get away without you. I think the series will be well attended. I am putting much hope into it. We should be able to reach a different audience, and to correct their image of the avant-garde film, or, truer, to implant an image, the right image—I don't think they have the vaguest idea what we are all about, the vast midtown and uptown population. This series should be our "campaigning" program, politics of the Art of Cinema, a beachhead, an arrow. When I know more about it, I'll write to you, to come or not to come.

Meanwhile, have good time. The Future is Ours, inevitably. The Sun is a Big yellow Flower. Give love to Yoko Ono. And give love to the Beatles, and tell them, give them the message from their older brother, that's me: it's about time that they make one Serious (Mature & Serene) choice

ON WHOSE SIDE ON WHICH SIDE OF THE FUTURE DO THEY STAND? It's time to stop playing games with businessmen, movie exploiters, commerce: it's time to join the Co-op, the non-competitive, the life-freeing forces. On which side do they stand? It may be too late already—this is the last call…

Anyway, let the Beatles buzz their own way—the road is wide—and we'll buzz our own way—I hope you are buzzing happily yourself—I see no reason why not—and please DO NOT FORGET TO SEE THE TURNERS WHILE IN LONDON—TURNER IS FANTASTIC.

Love, Jonas

October 14, 1968

This is a week later. Just back from Canada, where I had to be juror at the Canadian Film Competition, at the Gallery of Ontario, in Toronto. One week of Canada did me good. When I read the Building Department letter to Mr. Heckscher, a week ago, I was so mad that now I am glad that I didn't write anything at that time. Not that I am any less mad now! What hypocrites! What a misuse of their positions as Civil Servants! They sent to Mr. Heckscher the same old 37 violations list without even mentioning that they themselves dismissed practically the entire list. Isn't their primary concern TO HELP THE PEOPLE, to serve the people, to help us to overcome our difficulties? Outrageously and insultingly they insinuate, in their letter, that the Cinematheque shall break the law and permit 420 people in a 72 seat theatre. TOO MUCH SPACE for the Cinematheque. What a nerve! What a way of applying power, what a crooked way! They also lie about informing me in advance about it, it's all so hopeless. How can you search for any justice when they can block you so easily with the words & acts of hypocrisy and nobody can do anything about it. It's all in the system. Law & Order. It's all

in the books. After all, whom should Mr. Heckscher believe, me or the Building Department? Really?

October 15, 1968

R. reported to me today about some of the New York real estate underground activities. He's in those circles, it's in the family. He said, there is a big uproar, a big angry uproar in the real estate circles about the artists moving downtown. They expected the small businessmen of that area to slowly disappear. They wanted to take over those real estate properties, and with little money. But now the artists discovered the same. The artists started moving in, buying lofts, buying buildings, joining into co-ops. By doing so, they immediately increased the value of properties in that area. So now the real estate moguls are very upset. R. said, the Building Department and the City Administration are working very closely with these moguls and are doing their best to keep the artists out, by means of one law or another. That's what you are facing, he said, that's what is behind all your troubles.

October 16, 1968

With the work piling up, with my duties at the Cinematheque, at the Film-Maker's Co-op, *Film Culture* magazine, and now, the Jewish Museum series, I have to get up very early, usually around 7 AM, in order to get any time for myself. And then all these god damn people from all over the world, wanting this and wanting that, and the Cinematheque is closed, I have nobody to help me now, and Carla left for London, it's really really bad.

Anyway, I thought today about doing something about the licensing of the Cinematheque. Film-makers keep calling me, asking, when are we going to open. I thought maybe I should write a letter to Heckscher, explain everything point by point.

I stopped at the Museum of Modern Art, and Larry Kardish showed me a letter he received from the Building Department as an answer to his inquiry why the Tek was closed. It was full of the same bullshit and sweet excuses, Oh, how good we are, Oh how much we'd like to help them but sorry, their building is collapsing. That's what Larry said. He looked at the enclosed list of the famous 37 violations and he was sure, he said, by the time I go back to 80 Wooster St, I'll find the building caved in. What a great power of such a list! What a clever & devilish invention!

"What are you going to do about it?" asked Larry. "Oh," I shrugged, "what can you do about it?" I suddenly felt so tired of the whole thing, so tired. I have so much other work to do. Where and in what place of my head & my heart will I keep and nourish the Fight for the Cinematheque? I felt so drained out, suddenly. Finally I understood what Engineer Clark meant when he said, "Do you think you can win against the Building Department?" That's it. They don't look at their work as a service to the people: they look at it as WIN or LOSE. They won, I have to admit it, at least today. Their tactics are the same as in Stalin's prisons or in KZ camps: they exhaust you, they drain you out. After all, they have hundreds of employees to put their time and their energy against your own miserable time and energy. They are invincible. Somewhere, at some point you reach the line when a feeling of futility of it all begins to take over you. The absurdity of the whole thing, the absurdity of the system, wins over you. They are invincible. Nothing will be SERVICED to you, no: you have to CONQUER it all, you have to virtually rip out from their iron claws every little thing that actually belongs to you, always belonged to you. These hired civil workers, paid with your own fool's money—they are there, an invisible iron wall, the ENEMY, an IRON FORT, and you are only a little

Indian, maybe with a bow and a few arrows (and I don't even dip my arrows into poison)—and you try to climb their wall, THEIR wall. You climb and you climb, and they keep hitting you right on the head, plump, plump. Your head is all bloody, the poor head. And you keep doing so, because your Mamma told you that there is Justice. The idealist, ha ha ha... Until, suddenly, you realize that it's ALL VERY REAL. They took it for real, they are doing it for real, THEY ARE OUT TO WIN. You realize the absurdity of your struggle for "justice," "truth." Your faith finally collapses and they WIN again as they have always won before you, me boy.

O.K., St. Teresa de Ávila. I give up. I suspect, the whole thing was to bring me to the realization of the absurdity & vanity of my belief that the Cinematheque can be constructed by Human Power... In reality, this whole thing is beyond the Human Reason and Human Endurance. I give up. I declare my unconditional capitulation. The way I feel today, this may be the last entry into this Diary of a Man Who Wanted to be Legal. What a waste of human energy, what an outrageous waste! I am even losing my sense of humor, which is really bad. Tomorrow I am going to buy a Gun Manual, I saw one today in the window on Park Avenue & 28th Street. I am going to buy a gun for myself. For hunting ducks...

November 3, 1968
Came to Roxbury, to visit Mel, Forth Hill, with an intention to film the Hill people, as an example of the pre-Aquarian community, for PBL film. Then I soon realized, that it's impossible, that it's not such an easy matter to catch on film without destroying the buds of new life, & I gave up and brought back only fragments of faces, voices, children—
Oh, all you beautiful people wherever you are—lead your lives, & your real work is

where you are, where neither radio nor TV is watching you.

November 27, 1968

For over a month now, Miss Joy Manhoff, from an office close to Mayor Lindsay, has been digging into our case. No great news.

As Confucius informs us… Miss Manhoff, like Mr. Heckscher, the only way she can check our case, is by going back to the same people who originally fixed us up… So that the goodhearted and well intended inquirer-investigator will get the same answers as the victim. Thus the Inquirer himself becomes a victim. This is the crux of the matter.

As long as things run smoothly, I mean, as long as nobody complains (or as long as nobody complains too loud)—everything is fine. But once a complaint comes, there is no way, absolutely no way for the superior of finding out the truth, because the superior has to get his facts from the same people who, according to the complainer, committed the abuses and misuses of power. Therefore, I swear, I'm not going to ask any of Mayor's people to investigate our case any longer. It's a useless effort for both sides.

How does the old saying go? You can't win against City Hall… Please write it on your wall. The above sentence is so true that I believe it was probably uttered by God himself, in one of his humorous moods, and you better take God's word literally, me boy. I think people like me should be locked up for bothering the City Hall, for wasting everybody's time. It's me who is guilty. The finger of justice will strike me sooner or later…

November 28, 1968

Two boys uptown—I can't disclose their names nor the location—they are opening a small theatre, uptown. I asked them today point blank: "Just for my own curiosity —did you get it CLEANLY, I mean, the license…" "Oh, no," they said, "we had to give some 'dirt'. You have to do it as proof of their manhood. This exchange of 'dirt' from hand-to-hand is a proof of their manhood, to these people. It is a must, it is a sexual fluid. Taking bribes obviously indicates that they're human, not some kind of office machines. It's all sexual, it has to do with hands, with a certain 'privacy' between the two. 'From hand to hand, it's all sexual.'"

November 29, 1968

Two prominent wheels of the showbiz just bought a church, Midtown, and they are going to make it into a theater. We looked at it to see if we couldn't move the Tek there. The two wheels wondered why 80 Wooster closed. I said, we are having these licensing problems… "Who is dealing with the building department, who is your man?" They asked. "It's me. I'm handling it myself," I said, in all my innocence. At which point both big wheels of the showbiz took another look at me. Then they shook their heads and started laughing: "That's why. That explains everything!" said one. "They'll never give you a license. You can't go as you are and expect to get a license. I see where your problem is."

I left them and I was walking home, and the streets were dark and gloomy. Of course! Why didn't I think of it myself! I am a marked man. There must be some mark on my forehead that I haven't noticed. The Building Department stamped me while I was sleeping. Here goes the Man Who Never Got His License. People! Romans! Look at the face of a man who will never get a license! I tried to look at myself, in the glass window. I saw a gloomy, dark figure, a character from the darkest pages of Dostoevsky, a social aberration. I thought I shouldn't stay on the street, I should go where all such dregs go. So I descended into 42nd St. subway network, that dark abode where you can hear the heart and the sadness of all humanity throbbing… And I stood there, looking around, for a while, I listened to the noise upstairs, the distant noises of the city, of the street. Then I stepped into one of those 25¢ "get your photo now" booths, I took my last quarter out of my pocket and I took these pictures: I wanted to look at myself closer. I also wanted to provide you, dear reader, with some concrete evidence, so that you know how a face of a Man Who Never Got His License looks. So here it is, for your scrutiny—as I retreat deeper and deeper into the sewers of the greatest City in the World, the city where 10 million people work and live in… (unreadable)…

December 3, 1968

I left the sewers to make a telephone call. I became lonely in the sewers. I suddenly felt like making some contact with humans. I kept thinking whom I should call. I couldn't remember any names, I couldn't remember any of my old friends. The only names I could remember were those of Mr. McGinnis, of Engineer Clark, of Mr. Malito, of Miss Manhoff. I decided to call Miss Manhoff because I long for a woman. Even the sewers cannot kill the sex, dear reader. Anyway, I telephoned Miss Manhoff. I asked her—I have no idea why, I have no real explanation why, but I wanted to know if "there was any progress on our case." She said, sorry, there's not much new to tell you. The city has been having so many problems these weeks, there is so much to do. "Very sorry to hear it, very very sorry," I said, "I am very sorry that you have so many problems, very very sorry." I felt really guilty about it. I kept apologizing for a minute or two. Then I suddenly completely forgot what I really wanted to know from her, why was I really calling? I hung up. On the subway floor there was a scrap of the *New York Times* quivering. I picked it up, kindly, and started reading it.

CHAPTER TWENTY SIX

... FM Coop meets... On London FM Coop... Confusions in film terminology... The Real is Beautiful... FM Coop as a Process... On FM Distribution Center ... Memories... Dragging the projectors... Brakhage explodes at MoMA ... The American "radicals" as part of the "capitalist" system... Coop Chronicles... On New Canadian Cinema... Letter from Louise Brooks... Gallery of Modern Art censors Brakhage... Child molesting and Brakhage... I get fed up with it all... The Chelsea Hotel elevator... What's an "underground" move... A letter to Jerome re. Anthology... Letter from Antonioni... Sitney clashes with Brakhage...

NOTES ON THE NOVEMBER 28TH MEETING OF THE FILM-MAKERS' COOP DIRECTORS
Place: Film-Makers' Coop, 175 Lexington Ave. Present: directors: Ed Emshwiller, Stan Vanderbeek, Shirley Clarke, Jonas Mekas; guests: Carla Liss, Jimmy Vaughan, Charles Levine; Jack Perlman (attorney); Leslie Trumbull (Secretary of the Coop)

Stan briefed us on his trip to Mannheim Film Festival, and to England. He said he found friendly and bustling undergrounds wherever he went. He also found that the "commercial" movie disseminators, particularly TV, are very eager to get our films. Stan thinks, and we all agreed with him, that it's about time that we get more facts about how to handle the foreign TV offers and bids, so that we could help the film-makers who want such info, so that we wouldn't get caught by the exploiters, swindled out of our films, etc. Since we were on the subject of the international TV scene, we decided to invite to our meeting Jimmy Vaughan, who happened to be in town. He grabbed a taxi and joined us a few minutes later. Vaughan has an office in London and he has been specializing, for last few years, in European TV sales (he has made a few sales for Shirley Clarke, Kenneth Anger, Scott Bartlett, myself, and a good number of other film-makers). He said, it's true, the European TV people are beginning to dig underground. But it is also true that it depends much on whose film and what kind of film. Vaughan agreed to serve as our TV sales adviser in London (12 Fouberts Place, Regent Street, London W1). He also agreed to try to sell programs of films approved and selected by the Coop directors. He stressed that he is not interested to sell every film but only those which he likes (or those which the Coop Directors will select). So that please do not swamp him with films. He has strong tastes…

Carla Liss, who has been working with the Cinematheque, until its unfortunate closing, went to England, in August, and spent some time with the London Film-Makers' Coop. She is back now, in New York, but she is going to London again in two-three weeks, and for good: she will be working with the London Coop. She says (Stan Vanderbeek and Michael Snow said the same) that the London Coop is a legitimate Coop, governed by film-makers, and by now is quite well organized. Their income doubled during the last year, and the number of films is growing. They would like to have more of the American underground. London and the rest of England is hungry for films. Jonas made the following proposition, at this point of discussion: All the film-makers who participated in the Traveling Avant-garde Film Exposition (which Sitney was taking across Europe) should deposit the Expo prints with the London Coop, for distribution. The prints are back in N.Y., but Carla could take them very easily to London, in a big batch. The prints are no longer "new", they went thru the European drill, and it wouldn't do much good to return them to the film-makers—they would do more good in London where they could make some bread for the film-makers, as long as they can. The film-makers whose prints are with the Exposition, and all other film-makers who have extra prints to go to London should CONTACT CARLA LISS or JONAS (c/o Coop) IMMEDIATELY IF NOT SOONER. Carla is ready to buy her London ticket, and is getting rid of her car—so do not delay.

P.S. FROM CARLA LISS concerning the above: The London Coop can arrange many bookings and most probably lectures for film-makers travelling to England with their films. We ask only that you give us fair notice of when you plan to arrive. One month's notice would be ideal—to arrange bookings, proper pub(licity) (this word crack belongs to Jonas), program notes, etc. Another service the London Coop can provide is the programming of packages of films to travel to Coops throughout Europe who will organize screenings in their own CAPITALS (this letter crack belongs to Jonas). All film packages leaving England are accompanied by a member of the London Coop to ensure safekeeping. In the future we'll keep American film-makers up to date about the scene in England/Europe through the Film-Makers' Newsletter in NY. And you can write to us: THE LONDON FILM-MAKERS' COOP, c/o David Curtis, 126 Longacre, London W.C.2, England.

Continued, by Jonas:
A NOTE ON THE NOV. 29TH MEETING AT THE FILM-MAKERS' DISTRIBUTION CENTER: Louis Brigante made a report on the progress of the Film-Makers' Lecture Bureau. Charles Hoag, who put the foundation to the LB, went back to the Columbia, to continue his studies. Ange is in charge of the LB now. The materials for the brochure are now being finalized, polished, almost ready to go to the printer. If any film-makers are still making up their minds, come to some decision fast, if you want to be in the catalogue.

A question was raised by Jonas concerning the terminology. The terminology used by the Coop and the Center, I said, and here I am repeating, is inaccurate, is misleading, is at the bottom of many of our misunderstandings. Primarily, at this point, I am concerned with four words: "commercial,"

Carla Liss, my assistant at the Cinematheque 1966–68. In 1968 she went to
London to help get on its feet the
London Film-Makers' Coop. She was
also an active Fluxus artist. In the
later years she worked as a professional
psychiatrist.

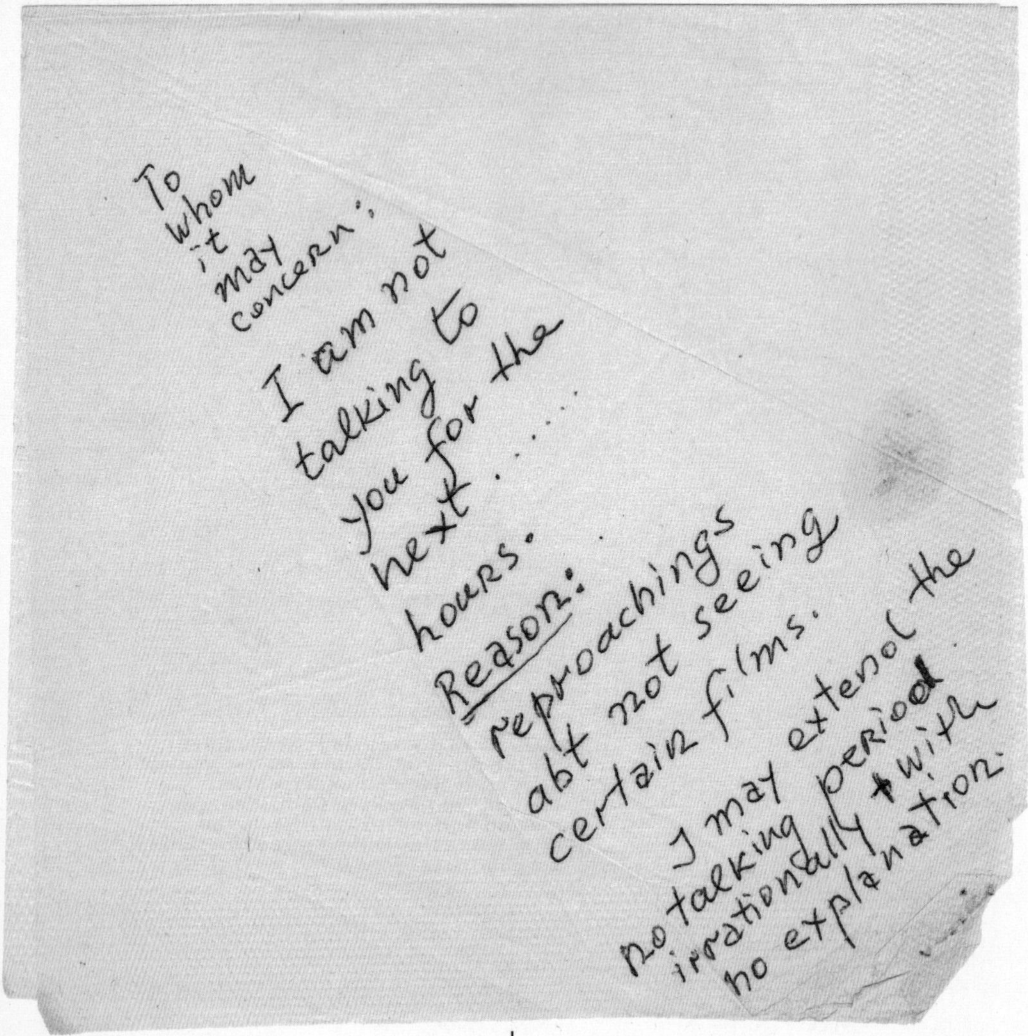

To whom
it
may
concern:
I am not
talking to
you for the
next ......
hours.
Reason:
reproachings
abt not seeing
certain films.

I may extend the
not talking period
irrationally + with
no explanation.

"non-commercial," "theatrical," and "non-theatrical." None of these four terms is accurate or real. But our reactions to them are very real indeed. Much antagonism between independent film-makers has been produced by the continuous use of these terms. Even the working methods and policies of the Coop and the Center have been contaminated by the use of these terms. My position is this: A film is a film is a film; a screening is a screening is a screening. I have seen shows at film societies and colleges which were more "Theatrical" and "Commercial" (in their numbers of people and handling of publicity) than some of the most "commercial" "theatres" and the opposite. The only real terminology, the only difference that I see is the following: 1) flat rental situations (with a properly worked out sliding scale of rental fees), and 2) special rental situations (you can imagine anything here). And that's about all. Every Coop, sooner or later, will have to face both situations and will have to handle them. Every Coop, therefore, has to have two tables, or divisions. In New York, when we faced this problem, we created the second Table, the Second Division, and we called it the Film-Makers' Distribution Center. But something went wrong. Soon we began to look at the Coop and the Center (and this was reflected in their operations) as TWO different things—not as TWO DIFFERENT ASPECTS, SERVICES to the same ONE film-maker. The split occurred, now I have no more doubts about it, after thinking and thinking about it for months now—the unfortunate split occurred only because we kept using the WRONG TERMINOLOGY, the terminology inherited from the competitive, corrupt distribution systems. And so we got caught by it. This is the very time to begin to correct it. I suggest, that one way of beginning the correction is to spend some time—at the NY Coop, at the Center, at the Canyon Coop—and everywhere—discussing the above FOUR terms and their implications—and thus, gradually, to move out into some clearer waters. I really don't like where we are now.

Jonas

P.S. Just in case: by "a film is a film is a film" and by "a screening is a screening is a screening" I do not mean that all films are the same or all screenings are the same: what I mean is that each film and each screening is a case in itself.

December 3, 1968
I keep criticizing the life around me, there is so much wrong done by man to man —but my camera refuses to criticize, my camera wants to celebrate life, my camera refuses to film anything that isn't a celebration of life, so I have this problem—as I go thru life, frame by frame—

December 7, 1968
Interview with *L'Express*, M. Bizot (?).
Coming home, from Post Office, I saw Joel Markman, slumped, unshaven, sitting in the lobby, completely down. He asked for some change, to make a telephone call to his brother, he said, and I gave him my last quarter, that's all I had left. The stars of the New American Cinema!

James Stoller had a very correct word for the film *Revolution*. It is a dumb film. A commercially minded film-maker "full of good intentions" wants to make a true to life film about the hippies, about something he doesn't know, something he doesn't really belong to or doesn't really believe in. To really present in cinema or any other art a subject without distorting it you must either love it or hate it. No phony neutrality. The director of *Revolution* seems to have tried to show hippies positively, because he thinks that's the thing to do—but everything comes out dumb. All sensitivity, intelligence, all the flowers become stupid, dumb, vulgar, everything dies in front of his cameras. Even the underground film techniques which are used in this film seem out of place, artificial, they don't work. Films which have caught some of the essence of the flower generation were made by the underground film-makers themselves. They will remain as the true documents of the period. Amongst the most successful attempts from outside, I would point out here Andy Warhol footage (some 70 minutes or more) in *Four Stars*, which he shot in S. Francisco. That footage is like nothing else that Warhol has done. There is a group of San Franciscans, in a room, doing nothing, with children, and babies, and music, and later, on the ocean shore —that footage has more truth about the *Revolution* than all of Jack O'Connell's film. Good intentions failed him. There was no heart in it. There was mind in it, but the mind was dumb.

I was reminded again, & very kindly, that I had promised, in one of my weak moments, to do a column on movies for AVATAR. So I sat down by my typewriter and was ready to start clacking with one—really with two —fingers. But there I stopped again. I saw the AVATAR paper before my eyes. A paper that preaches and teaches. A paper full of revelations. Like all Underground papers these days. And I have nothing to reveal. In my heart, I remain a farmer. Things for me are real, down to earth. Don't take me seriously when I begin to preach or "spiritualize." Because it means I am talking about things I do not know. But I could tell you something about the fields just before the sunrise. Say, when you walk barefooted across the wet fields. The feeling of cold clear dew on your feet, as you walk. And the sound of the snorting horses, a little further.

Oh, movies. I don't know how I got into them. I don't know what I am doing here, in this huge America, the furthest outpost of humanity. Maybe I got into the movies because I am a farmer and I miss my morning walks. Because I miss reality. Nothing is real here to me. I walk along the Eighth Avenue, to 34th Street, to pick up my mail, or to the Cinematheque, and suddenly I stop. Suddenly I have to look around. Because suddenly the air all around me smells like wet morning fields, and the scent of certain flowers is present in the air. But I see nothing but cars passing by and buildings crowding the sky. So I continue walking. I don't know what I'm doing here. Just killing time, I guess. The only reality that is important to me here is not real, is a mirage, I can't film it. I have no idea what my real work is. So I fool around with my camera. Just follow the end of my nose. Maybe, maybe, maybe I'll catch it. And there is nothing spiritual, it's all concrete. The lens. The film. The crank. The light that falls upon that building. The movement of the hand, the camera. Everything is down to earth and real. Developing the film. Printing the film. Projecting the film. And then, the image on the screen, the screen, the light bouncing from the screen; the eye. It's very discouraging sometimes, to know that while all your friends are so deep in spirit and LSD and Beyond, here I am, with my nose and my eyes in reality, in the pursuit of reality. Not enough that I step on it, walk thru it, no—I have to look at it thru my viewer, to register it on film, and then project it again, again and again. A tree on the street. Then, the same tree on the screen. Like I look at a dirty corner of a street, and it looks beautiful on film & then I catch myself thinking, it must be pretty miserable to live in that dirt, that dirt is... But on film it's beautiful, the textures of misery. I celebrate reality. Even the reality of misery can be celebrated. It's strange, how every ugly thing is beautiful, if you can detach it from suffering, cruelty.

What's this in my pocket? Two chestnuts from Paris.

Yes, I am wandering thru this city, obsessed with reality, looking for the reality of my childhood. Meanwhile, there is this huge gap in the walls of reality, *an sich*, between the time I was born and the time I found myself wandering thru the streets of New York. The difference between the morning dew, the snorting of the horses, and the life & the experiences reflected in the faces of today which are caught by my lens—oh, there is no difference, really, all is just falling away, and I seem to be somewhere else already, beyond the dew and beyond the emotions and motions of yesterday.

But the farmer is still looking for his morning dew, the arrow of the childhood in his chest, broken.

Excerpt from a letter to FDC:
Permit me to ramble.

To begin with, it's important to state one basic principle which has been part of our work for last six years, and that is: we always considered, or at least I have always considered our work only as a process, a direction. That's why we have been avoiding, from our very first meetings, theoretical and aesthetical discussions. The reason for this is that such discussions are always taken over & monopolized by people who have very definite and final opinions and believes. Now, we always guided ourselves by very concrete day-by-day, problem-by-problem matters, and they changed as time went.

So that when early in 1966 the theatrical film distribution began to open itself for us, because of all the publicity we were getting, there was a very concrete and immediate need to do something about that matter. The question of "theatrical," "commercial" distribution kept coming to the Coop Directors' Meetings. As the theatres kept coming to the Coop, it became clearer and clearer that they were not yet ready to book our films on a flat rental basis, that we faced a completely new area of audience.

As this situation was getting riper and riper, one day, I sat at Chelsea Hotel and rambled with Shirley Clarke about the very first meetings of the New American Cinema Group and the very first days of the Coop. It wasn't really a rambling—it soon became a very hot arguing. Because my position was that some of the film-makers who participated in our early meetings had betrayed us, and I said, Shirley, you are one of them. It was in 1961 when we saw this situation coming. It was in 1961 when I insisted that we have to create a distribution center with two arms, the non-theatrical and the theatrical. But everybody said: Oh, what can we do, how can we poor things compete with the big distribution companies? So nothing happened—I mean, nothing happened with the theatrical branch—Rogosin, De Antonio, Shirley, Allen, etc. etc. continued their wolf-eats-wolf existences. Only the non-theatrical branch was created. And that's how the things started happening —thru the people who stuck together, weak as we were, and poor. So we broke the field for the others, too.

As we were arguing about this, Shirley said: So why don't we do it right now? Do you think it's too late now to do what we didn't do six years ago? Five years ago? No, I said, probably not. So, why don't we do it right now? said Shirley. Let's get some more help, I said, like Lionel Rogosin. We need money, I said. So next day we met Lionel and told him what was on our minds. Rogosin said O.K. It was decided that Shirley will put up $3,000, Lionel another $3,000, and I'll pull in some borrowed money, $2,000. We had a few more general rambling sessions and started looking for a man who could run the theatrical branch of the Coop. We decided that for a year or two we should keep a very close eye on it, the three of us, acting as sort of advising directors to it. After checking with a few possible candidates for running this new branch, we came to a stop. We couldn't find anybody to run it, someone who wasn't too contaminated with the usual commercial film distribution methods, and someone whom we could trust. Until, suddenly, one day, a thought crossed our mind: LOUIS. So we got together again, Lionel, Shirley, and myself, and this time we also invited Louis [Brigante]. Louis listened with his cigar dangling down his jaw, and said nothing. Give me two weeks to decide, he said. And two weeks later he said O.K. And that's how the Film-Makers' Distribution Center was born, with the official March 11th (1966) announcement.

George Landow: he says he wants to make litany films. *Bardo Follies* is an attempt at litany. Medieval quality.

What's called "speed" in cinema is very often the amount of content, compactness of different contents—like poetry is more compact than prose or music... Messiaen more compact than Tchaikovski.

"Don't underestimate these kooky groups like the Citizens for Decent Literature; when they get on to something they will bug and bug and bug their Congressmen, or they'll telephone. One old bag will notify another, and like there's a thousand notified in five minutes via the telephone. They jam the phone either to the fuzz or whoever they're bugging, or the public library if they want a book removed, or a theater if they want a picture taken off. A hell of a lot of the time, people give in to them and think they're basically, you know, like good people. But they ain't."
(source unknown)

February 3, 1969

This morning, walking crosstown, along 23rd Street, I suddenly was stopped, I was stopped dead, by the color of a small, red, tiny flower that I saw suddenly before my eyes, and it was so very real, on a sunny hill, and it was so red, so red. And I stood there, like an idiot, remembering, a little red flower of my childhood, of which even the name I have forgotten—but not its color, its little leaves imprinted upon my eyes, upon my memory. Then I recollected myself again, and I continued walking.

Yes, yes, this Dziga Vertov is a sick man, a man without a home, busying with everything and anything, but deep inside always longing for home. I wonder what the Jews must really be. I think they are all knots and gangrenes, centuries and centuries of suppressed longings & needs of HOME. You can't be from nowhere. You can't belong everywhere—there is no such culture yet. It may be coming—but the Jews never supported that, they were always Jews. So now they are all sickness, like me. That's why they say, a Traveling Jew. Every traveler is a Jew. I am all sickness.

No date, 1969

We have 400,000 marines in Vietnam. I figure that each of them should kill at least one Vietcong every day—else, what are they doing there? Aren't they paid to kill? If we cannot wipe out three million Vietnamese, what are we going to do with 800,000,000 Chinese? I accuse the USA army of sheer inefficiency. I suspect that USA are dropping the bombs on plain fields, just to keep the production going. "Dropping a greater tonnage of explosives on it last year than our Air Force expended on the whole Pacific Theater in the last war." (From a newspaper)

Cineaste says that art is not necessary if it doesn't serve millions. I say that a society is not necessary which ignores art.

February 18, 1969

Dear Adrienne, Larry, and Willard:

Late this evening, after I was through with the Jewish Museum screening—after dragging the projectors, film boxes, acting as a pick up boy and projectionist and door boy and light switch boy and ticket taker—there was a small handful of faithfuls who came to see Emshwiller films—after walking the street, breathing in some fresh air and contemplating the state of the avant-garde film-maker in this town—or any other town—seeing how little support the avant-garde film-maker has—so little, that even after all these years I still have to drag the projectors across town, and do all other little things to have at least one weekly miserable screening of AVANT-GARDE FILM in this town—I dragged my tired legs—and I hadn't eaten since early morning's coffee—and because I had no money left after paying for the films—I dragged myself to Sitney's place, sat down by the kitchen table, and started eating my doughnut which I had bought on the way—

As I was eating thus my miserable doughnut, Sitney described to me some of the events that took place at the MoMA's screening earlier this evening, at the Canadian show, about how Stan stormed on you, HOW DID YOU DARE, HOW DID YOU DARE to show these stupid films! How did you dare! Are you out of your minds, dear Adrienne, Larry, Willard, to show those young, confused beginners? You are ruining the museum! Why don't you stick to art, good art, accepted art! You are undermining CINEMA! More or less in that line—as I have been told—I don't want my films to be shown here, in such company!

I tell you, I am sitting home now, and I had some bread and some honey so I have something in my stomach and I can take it better now—but when I sat there and listened to it all, it was so INCREDIBLE, so unbelievable, the behavior of our respectable AVANT-GARDE FILM-MAKER(S) that it left me speechless and sick. I understand, that the order of the films on the program could have been improved. I also understand that Bob's film was added to the program, which made it worse. But there is a way of talking constructively and positively about it. But our Great Artists are like drunk cowboys. They are out to shoot the young film-maker, and always in the name of art. How incredible, and how stupid. I guess, this is just another proof that great artists can be stupid and cruel to LIFE, to anything BUDDING that is a little foreign to their own tastes. They can lose all perspective on things. They would like to see the young born with beards. How incredible. I am sorry that you had to take the brunt of Stan's OUTRAGEOUSNESS towards his younger colleagues. I am also sorry that I was the chooser of the films—I am not sorry that I chose what I chose from what there was—but I am sorry that you had to take the brunt for my choices. My choices represented the MOST ALIVE branch of the Canadian cinema—doesn't matter how fragile that branch may look in comparison to DWG, and Dovzhenko, and Eisenstein, or Brakhage and etc. etc.—there it was, the most alive part of the Canadian cinema, lifting itself towards the light—honestly, sincerely, and beautifully—and the drunk cowboys of the American Avant-garde walked in and started kicking with their boots all over the poor fragile heads of the young Canadian film-makers—and over the Museum itself—KILL THEM, KILL THEM—KILL THEM IN THE NAME OF ART! As if the avant-garde film wouldn't have enough enemies yet!

It's very late, and I am dead tired to go longer with this—I need some sleep—but I wanted to drop you this note and let you

Continued from page 10

a separate print on deposit with the Center so that it could be used for theatrical distribution should the print at the Co-operative be out on a booking.

In any event, unless the Center has permission from the filmmaker it cannot distribute the film on a theatrical basis. So if you would like your film to be made available to theaters through the Center, you can do so simply by informing either Leslie Trumbull at the Cooperative or James Lithgow at the Center.

Should any filmmaker have further questions on how the Center can assist him to distribute his film, he may contact James Lithgow who will be pleased to help in any way he can. Address: 175 Lexington Avenue, New York, N.Y. 10016 (Phone:(212) 889-3848).

Coop Chronicles

I have beeen so busy with the moving of the Cinematheque screenings to the Gallery of Modern Art, and with raising money to pay the rentals for the shows, that I have completely forgotten to report on two meetings of the Coop. By now everything is so far back away that I do not remember the dates.

At the first unreported meeting Miss Johnson from Aspen magazine presented to us Aspen's plan for selling films, on 8mm & 16mm, in bookshops and through the mail. Aspen is going to announce its plan publicly very shortly. The idea is to establish a series similar to, say, some book clubs, where a certain number of carefully selected titles is offered to the public each month. The Aspen film series will cover all genres of cinema. The selection committee of the Aspen Film Library consists of Annette Michelson, P. Adams Sitney, and myself. First thirty titles will be annouced as soon as the terms with the filmmakers are worked out. And that was, specifically, the purpose of Miss Johnson's meeting with the Coop. directors: to work out, together, the rules, the methods, and the conditions of such a project. I do not recall all the ideas and suggestions thrown at her (by Ed Emshwiller, Ken Jacobs, and myself) but she made notes, and the gist is that her attorney will meet with the Coop's attorney, Jack Perlman, and will try to prepare a workable contract. Emsh felt that there is much to learn here from the book publishers' contracts, where the author is paid a certain advance and then gets a percentage from the copies sold. The same should be done with the filmmaker.

Miss Johnson attended our second meeting. two weeks later, which was more a conclave than a directors' meeting with James Broughton, Stan Brakhage, Peter Kubelka Robert Breer, Emsh, Ken Jacobs, Charles Levine, Suni Mallow, Storm DeHirsch and countless others present and the Aspen project was endorsed. We'll be waiting for the fruits. Most of the second meeting was devoted (it's all on tape, four hours of it) to the discussion of the University, etc. film festivals. It's beyond my powers and talent to figure out what was really suggested or agreed upon for every suggestion and statement there was immediately an anti-suggestion and anti-statement coming from a different corner (physically, aesthetically, practically, emotionally, politically, etc.). University film festivals are very damaging. University film festivals are very good. Festivals in general are bad. Festivals in general are o.k. We should

28

do something about film festivals. No, we should leave film festivals alone. And etc., and etc. One thing was really agreed upon (there was even a vote on it), a proposal by Ken Jacobs to hold some kind of continuous informational screening, one in N.Y. and one (we thought) in S. Francisco, where ALL new films would be shown once, to a small audience and to the self-appointed or invited (by whom?) writers on films. These "writers" or "critics" (mostly filmmakers themselves, but also anybody) would look at all new films and scribble down their impressions, their enthusiasms, their cirticisms, personal as they may be and all these scribblings will be then collected by an appointed (or self-appointed?) editor and published, as part of a special bulletin or magazine (or part of some already established publication) so that news and info on new films would go into the world. That will be the main function of this eternal film festival (or screening) to provide some written info on all new films. This matter, it was decided, will be picked up at our next meeting, to work out practicalities of the idea. It was suggested that Canyon Cinema Coop should discuss this proposal also.

Self-appointed chronicler of the Coop. meetings

Jonas Mekas
March 19th 1969

Jonas at work on the Coop chronicles

know how SICK SICK SICK I am about the state of ARTISTS in CINEMA—how petty, small, pompous, inhuman they can be sometimes! I hope their behavior won't discourage you from continuing the support of the young film-makers. I do not understand—how stupid one can be to think that the case of the avant-garde film has been won, that now we can begin to kick each other—when the truth is just the opposite: the avant-garde has as few true friends as ever ever before—Love, Jonas

P. S. This note in the morning. Basically, I think, what this is, it's the lack of proper traditions in cinema, that is, among the film artists. I grew up with poets, I spent the first part of my life with poets, and among poets, and particularly in Europe (but same applies to Ginsberg) there is this old tradition, that the best of the recognized, older poets, really, all good poets, they have always been the protectors of the younger ones, no matter how fragile the up-comer may be—the good poet is sure enough of himself, of his art, and of ART in general, he is not embarrassed to help the young poet, he feels it's his duty. That is the tradition I grew up with. But I don't see that in cinema yet. It betrays the lack of trust in the art itself, this constant putting down of the young film-makers, this paranoia for… for… I don't know what —this paranoia of looking for perfection where one should look for love, and give love.

February 18, 1969
Dear Jeffrey:
You ask me if I know any good schools of cinematography "or where I can find data in this vein."
All data of/on cinematography and cinema is locked in your own veins and your CAMERA, waiting for you. Get a roll of film and a cheap camera and start shooting.

Remember at all times: Every dollar you waste on film schools you steal from your unborn films. Jonas Mekas

P. S. There are no "good" schools for cinema. There are no good schools.

No date, 1969
The Underground Film (The Avant-garde Film) is the only film today that is concerned with the art of cinema.
The Underground (Avant-garde) Film is the only revolutionary cinema today.
The radicals and revolutionaries keep writing and seeing only Hollywood (including European Hollywoods) movies produced and distributed by imperialist companies.
The radicals never go to the Underground (Avant-garde) movies.
The radicals are supporting the imperialist cinema and ignoring the revolutionary cinema.
To call oneself a revolutionary or a radical and at the same time to pay money and support capitalist-imperialist cinema while ignoring the revolutionary cinema, is an act of collaboration and an act of betrayal.

To be a traitor to the revolution means to be an ally of the imperialists.
The radicals and revolutionaries of America are really allies of the imperialists and capitalists.

March 31, 1969
TO THE DIRECTORS OF THE FILM-MAKERS' COOPERATIVE AND TO ALL FILM-MAKERS

Sunday, March 30th, Shirley Clarke and myself, we had a brief meeting during which we came to approximately the following decisions:

The Film-Makers' Distribution Center, as it's known today, should be closed.

In a drastically revised form, the present FMDC should become a "special task" division of the Film-Makers' Cooperative, acting under the direct supervision of the Secretary of the Cooperative. Its functions will be determined by the Directors of the Film-Makers' Cooperative and the Secretary of the Cooperative.

What authority do we have to bring up this proposal?
It was Shirley Clarke and myself who met on January 20th, 1966, and came to the decision to establish the Film-Makers' Distribution Center. Our reasoning went something like this:

In 1960 and 1961, during the early meetings of independent film-makers in New York, there was much discussion of the need of such a center. But in reality, the feature length narrative (and documentary) film-makers kept trying to get the attention of the established film distributors and didn't do much about establishing a distribution center of their own. The non-commercial, the Underground film-makers, however, stuck together and established the Film-Makers' Cooperative. The Cooperative gathered them together, gave them a sense of solidarity, and provided a stable —and constantly growing—income. Based on simple, open, and noncompetitive principles, the system of the Cooperative was later accepted by the film-makers in other countries.
In 1966, however, both myself and Shirley thought that despite the work done by the Film-Makers' Cooperative, there was one area of "independent," "low budget" film-making that was not sufficiently helped within the Cooperative, non-commercial set-up. Some films, in order to get back their production money, needed "premiere" openings, press reviews, cross-country theatrical releases, etc. etc.

The Film-Makers' Cooperative wasn't set up to do all that. So that we felt, at that discussion, in 1966, that we should make another attempt to establish a distribution center for the more theatrically minded, higher budget film-makers.
January 24th, 1966, we met Lionel Rogosin and presented him with our plan. He agreed with us and said he had been thinking along similar lines for some time. He agreed to be the third member of the Center. All three of us pledged to put up a certain initial amount of money to start the Center, which we did (total of $6,000, I think). After a few weeks of scouting for who could run such a Center, we came to Louis Brigante. After some hesitation, he agreed to have a try. We three remained as the advising and governing directors, until such time, we said, as the Center will be ready to become a coop on its own.
As it happened, very soon we clashed with Lionel. The basic problem was again the same in 1960: soon he lost interest in the Center. At the same time as we were putting the ground stones for the Center, Lionel was organizing his own, private, distribution company for the independent cinema which went into direct competition with the Center. As a result of this, without any "fight," but with a clear and friendly understanding of the situation, Lionel gradually withdrew from the active support of the Center. Shirley and I remained.
Louis did a good job in guiding the Center through its initial stages. I should make it clear that the failure (that's how we see it) of the Center is not the failure of Louis. The failure is completely somewhere else, and I'll be getting into it immediately. As far as Louis goes, our opinion is that he did a heroic and impossible job.

What went wrong with the Film-Makers' Distribution Center?

First of all, it's the failure of the film-makers themselves. The facts of the last ten years show, and the years of the FMDC reconfirm this, that as soon as the film-maker becomes more successful publicity-wise or theater-wise, he's immediately looking for greener pastures, bigger pastures. Or if he isn't successful enough—again, he follows the rumors of greener pastures and leaves the Center at the first greener occasion. Sometimes these run-aways come back into the Center, disappointed—but the occasion comes again and there they fly off again. No real solidarity, no real trust. Now, this isn't so at the Film-Makers' Cooperative (exceptions are very few there). The non-narrative, avant-garde film-maker in general is more stable, as far as the distribution goes. The non-commercial, non-theatrical distribution doesn't offer too many temptations, there are few to pull him away, to mislead him. There have been cases, lately—lately there have been approaches to non-commercial film-makers by private individuals and groups, who try to tie down their films with all kinds of projects and promises—but very few film-makers follow them. But when we come to the feature length (or sometimes short) narrative films, or to more publicly minded film-makers, this running away & around has been and still is the pattern. In case of the Film-Makers' Distribution Center, such running away becomes particularly damaging when the Center puts up moneys for openings of films. Sums going over $5,000 have been put up by the Center for opening films which later ran away. There is no way for the Center to get the investment back. The sad irony of all this is that, the way things stand, it's the non-theatrical film-maker who really supports and keeps alive the Film-Makers Distribution Center, the theatrical distribution branch.

In cases where the films remain with the Center even after New York opening—an example could be Shirley's own *Portrait of Jason*—it takes a year or two just to repay the "opening" expenses; whereas a film without any "premiere" opening, placed into the Film-Makers' Cooperative, brings money to the film-maker with the first screening. It's becoming clear—and the thought is not new at all, we discussed it already in 1959 and 1960—that for a low budget independent film-maker neither the New York openings nor the press reviews are really needed. Or, if needed—then the price is not worth paying. There are many other ways of introducing a film, if the film is good. In the cases where the film is bad, the premiere openings later can be used in very distorting and misleading ways to push the film across the country.

I am using the word "push," because that's another thing that we both, Shirley and I, find unacceptable. The pushing involves the use of established publicity methods, the competition with established distribution and exhibition set-ups, programming according to certain "commercially" attractive topic lines, using overblown advertising, etc. etc. Sometimes the Center has gained (by persuasion or other methods) a commercial theater, a new outlet: but the New Cinema has suffered a blow from the publicity campaigns of that theatre.

The division between the Film-Makers' Cooperative and the Film-Makers' Distribution Center has contributed to the growth of a dualistic concept of the New American Cinema. Those around the Cooperative supposed to be more "artistically" or more "underground"-minded; those around the Center supposed to be more "for the people." We are for healing this split.

Further: Our feeling is that with the upcoming new film dissemination methods (sales of prints and EVR systems) the entire present theatrical distribution system will have to go, and, therefore, we feel that we shouldn't waste much energy in trying to establish something that is outdated and doomed to begin with.

Whatever we find good about the Center could be done within the existing Film-Makers' Cooperative—with minor additions. So that instead of the present Film-Makers' Distribution Center we propose the creation of a special division at the Film-Makers' Cooperative. The present FMDC will be revised drastically and will form the basis of such a division. Its personnel will be under the direct supervision of the Film-Makers' Cooperative. It will run the Film-Makers' Lecture Bureau, it will assist in film programming those who will request it, it will handle some of the "foreign" relations (programs to other countries) and whatever the Secretary of the Coop will feel is "out of the usual" run of the Coop (previews of films for visiting film bookers, for instance).

With this letter, we are informing the Secretary of the Film-Makers' Distribution Center, Louis Brigante, about our decision. We would like Louis to supervise the gradual transformation of the Center into a division of the Film-Makers' Cooperative. The idea of the Film-Makers' Distribution Center was a fine idea, we thought. And maybe it really was. But since it has become unworkable—for the reasons outlined above—and since to make it workable we do not have enough energy (nor money)—it's much wiser, we feel, to make these timely corrections.
—Jonas Mekas

P. S. I think we should emphasize that the experience of the reality of the Film-Makers' Distribution Center made it clear to us that if you have to deal with the Establishment (in this case, the Exhibitors) (a horrible bunch for the most part—who sell "Art" films because their theaters were too small to turn into supermarkets —or else are riding the crest of the popular European "Art" Films—"why can't Americans make such nice, simple, intellectual, artistic, sexy, lyric, human, etc. etc. films as they do in Europe?") & that to deal with these people—rather than university or museum people who show films because they truly love them—to deal with these people, we ourselves have to behave like "pros," meaning that they only understand their methods of selling & buying (PUSH is the word you used) & that these methods of the HARD SELL are distasteful, repellant, and below the very images that our films contain.
—Shirley Clarke

No date, 1969
AUDIO TAPE MAILED TO THE MONTREAL CONFERENCE ON CINEMA, INDUSTRY, AND CENSORSHIP

(Gong, à la British wartime gong):
This is the Underground speaking. This is the Underground speaking.

There is a New Canadian Cinema and it's not like any other Canadian cinema. The New Canadian Cinema has a finer vibration, is made of a finer matter.

The heavy vibrations of the Old Canadian Cinema and the heavy vibrations of the New Canadian Commercial cinema are dragging us down.

The Old Canadian Cinema deals with dead matter.

The matter of the Old Canadian Cinema has become so stiff with age that it doesn't bend with the movements of life any longer; it resists the rhythms and forms of life. It sits heavily on the ground like a duck.

The cinema of Dewdney, of Michael Snow, of Joyce Wieland, of Larry Kardish, of Lee Nova, of John Hofsess, of John Chambers, of Les Levine, of David Rimmer, of Michael Hirsch dances and their cameras sing.

I am not coming to Montreal because the whole Seminar is one big mistake.

It's a mistake for an independent, avant-garde, underground film-maker to sit at the same table with businessmen, commerce, industry, unions, censors. There is completely nothing to gain from it. It could only lead to compromises in which the Commerce would gain and the Art of cinema would lose. The Commerce is ruthless. Unions are ruthless. The censors are ruthless. But the artist is a kind man, a peaceful man, and it's easy to drag him into kind compromises: he doesn't want to hurt anybody.

It's much better to stay away.

Take my word for it: there can't be anything in common between Industry and the Art of Cinema. If you find something in common, then please re-check your arithmetic: there is a mistake somewhere.

There can't be any discussion between the independent, underground film-makers and the Unions, Censors, NFB, CBC or ABCDZ.

You state in your leaflet that "Others will discuss censorship (and what to do with it now that nobody wants it)."

Nobody wants it and you still want to talk about it? You can still take it seriously! Please, forget about it, wipe it out of your minds. A film-maker should forget all about censorship. *Censorship* doesn't exist!

If you go into any talks with censors, you may find yourselves, at the end of the talks, believing in censorship. There is always that possibility. Don't underestimate the persuasive powers of the censors!

You also say in your leaflet that during these seminars "it will be your chance to view the winners of the 20th Annual Canadian Film Awards." Thanks a lot! You are planning to perpetuate the Commerce, you are planning to impose hours and hours of poison upon the eyes and minds of people and you are talking about it as if you were doing something very nice.

The best thing you could do, as a Seminar —as the only correct and positive and instructive action, is to close all the Annual Canadian Winners into a casket and dump them into the closest river.

I'd like you to vote on this proposal.

(period of silence on tape)

Next, in your leaflet you raise a question, as a topic for a panel discussion: "CAN a Canadian film Industry be started? Was one started and lost?"

Oh, for God's sake! If the Industry was lost, say a prayer and let it rest in peace. You cannot talk about the Film Industry and the Free Cinema, or the Art of Cinema, at the same time.

I propose right now that this meeting stands up and remains standing in silence for exactly one minute in memory of the Film Industry of Canada which should rest in eternal peace and never rise again. One minute silence please.

(funeral march music on tape)

And now after we have put the Old Canadian Cinema to eternal rest, let's go home, get our cameras, and make home movies.

But do not let yourselves be fooled! There is no happy ending here. The Industry is not dead. The Commercial cinema is not dead. It's stronger than ever. As a matter of fact, we are surrounded! There is only one way to survive, for an independent film-maker: through uncompromising purity of our attitude to our art. Do not go into any talks with the enemy.

Those of you here in this auditorium who are with the New Cinema, your revolutionary duty is to leave this place immediately. This place is an enemy camp. You have nothing to gain by bargaining with the

Dear Jonas — As an editor you fascinate me even more than your divinely crazy magazine — How do you keep your head clean of the muck that makes most film magazines the work of silly show offs who write nonsense totally unconnected with anything they see on the screen — If they ever _do_ see anything on the screen — you must come to see me so that I can stuff you with roast chicken and pick at your brain.—
Love Louise

Thanks for returning my photo —

A note from Louise Brooks, 1969.

enemy. All he wants is your soul. He wants you to become part of the Industry. I go and I leave you to your own existential decisions.

(Gong, à la British wartime gong of BBC)

April 20, 1969

Dear Burton Rubenstein:
Let distributors distribute
let the exhibitors exhibit
let the lovers love
let the artists createfilm-makers make films
let the leaves come & go
let the stars move
let the critics criticize
let the films come & go

SEEING and BELIEVING are two totally different things (sometimes they are not)
SEEING is not the same as BELIEVING (sometimes it can be)
SEEING is not OPPOSED to BELIEVING (sometimes it is)
BELIEVING is not opposed to SEEING (".")
SEEING YOURSELF and BELIEVING YOURSELF are two different things.
They are neither opposed nor not opposed (sometimes they are both)
(sometimes it's rubbish anyway)

BEING SEEN and BEING BELIEVED are two independent things and are neither the same not opposed nor not opposed (but they could be)
(most of the time it's VANITY)

EFFORT TO SEE and EFFORT TO BELIEVE are two independent efforts neither opposed nor not opposed (sometimes they are both)
(both are WASTED efforts)

P.S.: I NEVER WANTED TO ABANDON TRIPODS. I only discussed the contemporary and fleeting usages & inhibitions & usages of tripods and meanings of those usages—all temporary and in flux.

The FREEDOM OF THE EYE CANNOT BE EXTENDED because the eye HAS NO FREEDOM.

ARE THERE ANY ANTINOMIES?

Whatever you'll do with your footage will be PERFECT if you'll do it with innocence —or passion—or anger—or disgust—personal shows—shows to friends—shows to festivals—shows to snobs—shows to nobody—

nothing can be reasoned out

Without having seen your work I believe it's PART OF YOURSELF
SHARE YOURSELF WITH OTHERS
WHY ALL THE HAIR SPLITTING
WHY FORGETTING
WHY DO THE STARS MOVE
WHY THE LAKE IS THERE
WHY BIRTHDISEASEDEATH ETC

some people do
some people don't
Sincerely,
Jonas Mekas

April 30, 1969

Naomi, on subway: "Jack came. We had a good talk. He looked at my film, how I'm working. I said to him: what I really want to do is to have children. There was a long pause. Then Jack said: I don't want to have children with you…"

Stan previewed part II of the *Scenes*, at P. Adams.

May 12, 1969

To: The Gallery of Modern Art
Columbus Circle
New York, New York

Dear Dr. Samartino:
This letter is to inform you that beginning June 2nd the Film-Makers' Cinematheque will terminate its screenings at the Gallery of Modern Art. Here are some of the reasons:

1. The Cinematheque cannot allow its screenings to be censored by the Gallery. We do our own pre-screening and films which fall into the category of commercial sex exploitation have no place in our programs. Whatever is screened at the gallery has value either as art or as a student's work. And since the main function of the Cinematheque is to assist the beginning film-maker, and to provide an outlet for the serious Avant-garde Film, we cannot allow you to stop our programs only because of the squeamishness of some of your employees. During my last conversation with Mrs. Samartino I received a strong impression that the case of Stan Brakhage—the show of his new works was stopped without advance notice—may very easily repeat again.
2. The $2.00 price is too high for most of the serious film students. The $2.00 price limits our audience to a few film lovers, and to all kinds of sensation seekers who can afford it.
3. The building itself, the tradition of bad art in the Galleries exudes a very stifling and bad atmosphere not suitable for presentation of any living art.

Sincerely,
Jonas Mekas, for the Film-Makers' Cinematheque

No date, 1969

Text for Toronto Star for Brakhage show:

THE ART OF VISION
Note to the audience: Stan Brakhage's *The Art of Vision* is the absolute masterpiece of the New American Cinema. At the same time, it's one of the most attention- and love-demanding films. The film is silent and is 4½ hours long. Usually, people are asked to come to see films. I ask you not to come unless you have enough loving attention to see a silent and 4½ hours long film, the only entertainment of which is spiritual.—Jonas Mekas

May 14, 1969

Announcement:
Jonas is closing all his businesses
is (has) moving(ed) out
location & direction unknown

Bulletin says:
Am fed up. Had enough.
Taking time out

may want to look around
won't be home

do not write do not call do not bother with
any "interesting" or "useful" things

totally useless

have good time & good luck

have resigned as minister of Finances,
Propaganda & Defense
the offices are for grabs

all powers and forces have been relinquished

have joined the secret order of
the guerilla monks

very unpredictable & irresponsible

may be dangerous

anyway, he ran away

& is on the loose. Bulletin says, film-makers
drove him out of his mind. But there may be
other reasons too. We are prone to simplifying

things. Our analysis may not be final.
doctor in charge
/signed/ Bellevue Hospital

No date, 1969

Good films live through the scratches.—
Ken Jacobs

IN DEFENSE OF THE CHELSEA HOTEL
ELEVATOR

Dear Traveler:

Please do not speak badly about the elevators of this House. The elevators are doing their best to serve you.

You say, the elevator stops at the wrong floors! But this is the elevator's way of telling you that it loves you, that it treats you kindly: it's trying to show you every floor, the elevator wants you to feel home. You say, the elevator's door closes too slowly. So you keep pushing buttons & knobs! But the elevator sees this and has pity on you, wretched & nervous creatures that you are, with your hearts beating fast, in a hurry, rushing, trying to "save" every second. The elevator sees all this. The elevator is trying, in its own best way, to slow you down, to relax you. Instead of taking you straight down, the elevator will take you first up, to the tenth floor, and it will stop at every second floor on its way down for no apparent (to you) reason. But the elevator has a reason: the elevator is trying (in the only way available to it) to put some patience into you, to slow you down a little bit, so that you'd begin to look at yourself, and at the other people in the elevator, you may even say Hello to your neighbor. The elevator is trying to break us out of our expected Routines. The elevator is introducing us to a few irregular twists & rhythms, disrupting our mechanical habits.

The elevator may not always be right. It may slow you down when you REALLY have to rush somewhere (seldom as it may be)—so forgive the elevator. For the elevator should have a right to a few mistakes. After all, the elevator is on a slower Evolution level than you who should know it better.

Be kind to the elevator. It's doing everything it can to help you to change yourself, to reach for the Second Birth.

Sincerely yours—

Friend of the Elevator

No date, 1969

The function of Andy's *Eat* is to bring down our blood pressure... to slow down the heart rhythms into those of meditation—it is an antidote to the protracted, anxiety, sick rhythms of our civilization.

To feel beauty one needs a certain humility.

No date, 1969

QUESTION: How would you describe an Underground movie?

ANSWER: An underground movie is a movie which drags one down to the ground and under the ground. It deals with simplified reality, it simplifies and banalizes all experience, all feeling. It seeks temporary and shallow escape and avoids reflection. It drags one down from any subtler experience. No doubt, I am talking about Hollywood, about 99.99% of it. It's the Hollywood, it's the Commercial Art Film that is the true Underground.

Happening evening: suspense evening with things on the verge of falling down

SOUND FILM:
a chair pulled
street scene: cars etc.
someone walks into the frame, feet sound in sync, you can hear every step.
But no other sounds of the streets.

May 27, 1969

Dear John [Schofill]:

After closing the Gallery of Modern Art screenings, that is, June 1st, I'll need a long period of catching up with one million debts. But as soon as I begin to see the light of sky again I'd like to bring to New York the six or seven missing programs of the SF Retrospective. Could you send me the list of films (or programs) which you think should compliment the ones shown at the Gallery? I'd do the booking myself, directly, to save you more trouble, whenever we are ready. I am not too clear, really, why in your last letter you got so upset that one or two films fell out or were shown on another day. Haven't you ever run any showings yourself? Don't you know the problems involved in running screenings like this, and not just one a week, but fifteen shows a week, which we have? I hope you have relaxed by now. Because it's no use spending your energy on little things like that. Those few of us who attended all programs of SF Retro are very happy and we are not worried about one or two films missed—we are going to bring them here anyway, soon—We have a much better idea of what's going on in SF. As soon as we resume our screenings I would like to bring back a few selected programs, the best of what we saw, for another look, because I know that there will be much talk here about all the missed films.

There is no way to compensate you for all the work you did, and for all the worries. I am enclosing 15 bucks to cover some of the cash expenses. If that doesn't cover it, let me know.

One thing: Lenny Lipton's film (sound), we started screening it, but we gave up after ten seconds. Projector stopped, one frame was burned. Since the fool sent his original, I didn't want to take any chances with it, and decided not to screen it, after one mishap. However, a check went to him for one show. I haven't noticed any other disasters during the Retro.

Thank you for everything
Jonas

No date, 1969

"wir wissen von den Dingen nichts, was wir nicht selbst in sie hineingelegt haben." —I. Kant

"…the reader should be carried forward not merely or chiefly by the mechanical impulse of curiosity, not by a restless desire to arrive at the final solution, but by the pleasurable activity of the journey itself."—Coleridge

July 1, 1969

Dear Jerome:
Remembering the peace and quiet of Cassis only occasionally interrupted by the sound of a motor boat, barking of a dog, a bird chirping, a splash of piano notes (Julia, the Rubinstein…) or music from Taylor Mead's portable radio (Taylor isn't there but his spirit walks around) —remembering the noon walks to Roches Blanches, the hot dust of the road, and the crickets on the slope, just before turning into Roches Blanches—etc. etc.—remembering all this I do not want to disturb your quiet rhythms with any letter from New York. A New York letter, even when it's peaceful, is impregnated with vibrations of Rush, of Trouble, of Worry, of Smog.
Anyway, here I am. Since by now you may have received reports on our progresses and our retrogressions, from P. Adams and Stan, I thought I should drop a few words myself. I haven't seen P. Adams' & Stan's letters, so I have no idea what you know or what you don't know about where the Anthology Cinema stands right now. There has been so much tension, and explosions, war cries mixed with vows of peace, during the last two months here, that I thought a report is due from me.
I'll try to be brief, although the heat (it must be 150 degrees) doesn't let me concentrate properly. The main problem, the main cause of the tension through which

~~xxxxxxxxxxxxxx~~ the underground movements:

0. Open House screenings at the Charles Theater, 1961-63

1. Screenings at the Bleecker St.Cinema, February 4th,1963 — April 8th,63.
   Saturday midnights. The managers of the theater, Marshall Lewis and
   Rudy Franchi ordered the screenings discontinued, because the low quali-
   t of the Undeground is ruining the reputation of the theater, they said.

2. Gramercy Arts Theater, 138 East 27th st : July 1st 1963 to February 15th
   1964. The owner of the theater threw us out on the grounds that we are
   screening unlicensed and obscene movies.

3. ~~xxxxxxxxx~~ New Bowery Theater, St Marks 4 — from February 24th to ~~xxxx~~
   March 3rd,1964. Closed by the police after seizure of "Flaming Creatures."

4. The Fourth St Theater, 4th St   — March 7th, 1964 — closed/after one   by the police
   screening of Genet film, film seized.

5. Washington Square Art Gallery, 530 West B'way. From July 16,1964 to
   September, 1964. Gallery closed, we had to leave.

6. New Yorker Theater, Monday nights, Nov.30th 1964– Dec 21st 1964.
   Had to move out, because New Yorker decided to use Monday nights for
   "rare classics".

7. Maidman Theater, 416 West 42nd St — January 18,1965– Jan 26,1965.
   Moved out after the owner or manager of the theater, seeing huge
   crowds coming to our shows, started lifting the rental price.

8. City Hall Cinema, 170 Nassau St — January 25th,1965 to May 31st ,1965.
   Three days a week. Had to move out after the City decided to tear down
   the building.

9. Astor Street Playhouse, Lafayette St — June 4th to November, 1965.
   Four days a week. Then daily. Moved out when the owner, seeing the
   crowds of customers, increased the price to the impossible.

10. 41st St Theater — Dec.1st 1965 — August 30th 1967. Daily screenings.
    Moved out after the rent of the theater was raised too high.

11. 80 Wooster St   Dec 18,1967– July 30 1968. Daily screenings. Closed
    by the police and Building Department "to complete the licensing" of the
    theater.

12. The Methodist Church, 4th St. August 1 to August 25 1968. Temporary
    arrangement didn't permit us to stay longer. Mondays only.

13. Bleecker St Cinema, August 25th — moved out because of improper union
    projection/ of 16mm films.

14. The Jewish Museum, 1109 Fifth Avenue — Nov.12 1968 — still continuing,
    every Tuesday evening

15. Gotham Art Theater, 43rd St — January 31 1969– Feb 28,1969
    Temporary arrangement. Not thrown out! (weekend screenings)

16. Elgin Theater, 8th Ave & 19th St   — Jan 26th 1969 – March 23 1969.
    Temporary arrangement. Temporarily disconitnued by us, but we may
    pick up the screenings later. Sunday 11:15 AM only. Not the happiciest
    time.

17. Gallery of Modern Art, Columbus Circle — March 1st,1969 — still going.
    Daily screenings (except Monday and Tuesday).

To the Editor. Motion Pictures.

RE: CHILD MOLESTING AND STAN BRAKHAGE

Dear Editor:

    One unfortunate mistake managed to sneak into last Sunday's piece on
the Avantgarde Film scene in New York. I feel it needs correction. The
screening of Stan Brakhage's film "Love Making" was cancelled by the
Gallery of Modern Art not because there actually was a scene of child molesting in it; it was cancelled only because the Gallery thought that there
was such a scene in the film. In actuality, the scene which is in discussion
is a simple and beautiful scene of children playing in a room and jumping
up and down on a bed. It couldn't be more innocent an occupation. Brakhage
is known for his documentary studies of life around him. Since he lives
on top of a mountain, 9000 feet high, he has no distractions, and the sick
preoccupations and perversions of the rest of humanity are far below him.
He can concentrate on reality around him with a naked and innocent eye.
His eye becomes an x-ray camera, a microscope. Everything that happens
on the top mountain gains a heightened importance, be it a cloud passing
by, remnants of a dead animal in the snow, or his own children. Roberto
Rossellini, on his recent visit to New York, saw Brakhage's work and thought
it was not only the most revolutionary cinema he has seen, but also a cinema
that is closest to his own work. The work of both directors is marked by
the intensity of their realism, and by their directness. Both directors have
almost mystical love for every little thing and every creature. In short:
if you hear the word "obscene" used in connection with the Avantgarde Film,
be on your guard, check the work of the artist in discussion for yourself.
Obscenity can be found only in the commercial cinema. In the Avantgarde you
can find only celebrations, adorations, and loving songs. There is a big
difference between singing of nakedness, and pushing nakedness into people's
eyes to blind them to get their money, money, money.

New York City   Jonas Mekas
May 19th 1969

the Anthology Cinema is going at present, is that the idea, the project itself is about the most demanding the people of cinema have ever undertaken anywhere. So it would be silly to even want it to go smoothly. The more, that to do this "most ambitious" project we have pulled or pooled together in one room six most unusual people. It's all for the good. All clashes, at this stage, are for the good. The unfortunate thing here is only this: While the project involves some of the most complicated and delicate organizational work, at least two people, who are deeply involved in this work, that is P. Adams and Stan, have very little or not enough experience in group work, where, in order to make any decent progress one has to give in, to listen to the neighbor, to give in to the neighbor, when needed, to sound certain notes and certain tones so that there would be a harmony. Still worse, both Stan and P. Adams are, to a great degree, hysteric personalities, with totalitarian touches—jokingly one can call them fascists, as we do, among ourselves. Sitney, at least has had experience with the Exposition, etc. Stan is all bundled into himself and round himself, as he is when he creates: his word must be the LAST. He applies the same principle to our gatherings as to his creations, which means, it's either Stan, or it won't go. Now, Peter, he is as great an artist as any, with all the temperamental problems. But by his character, he is sort of a gregarious perfectionist. Plus, he has been running the Austrian archives, he knows what it means to work with people. And he could go nights without sleep consuming barrels of wine for the sake of friendship. Kelman? As irrational as he is, as an artist, during our sessions he has been patiently rational, unshaken, calm, like some unmovable rock there, often, who just by being there brought us back to some sound basis. Broughton: this gentle poetic soul, he could

not understand, why all this voice raising all the time.

Anyway. Where was I? Yes, organizational experience. So that every normal clash is interpreted and is transformed into Tragedy, End, That's It. At the end of last session, Stan, beating incessantly like a stormy wave upon the shore, managed to beat out of P. Adams all his humor, all his patience, and all his energy, and P. Adams ended in a "nervous breakdown" which ended in an ultimatum: it's either me or Stan. Stan now blames his whiskey, he was sort of drunk, that last evening—but they clashed even when Stan was sober, in exactly the same way, and for the same reasons. Basic reason: Stan sees an ideal in front of his eyes, the ideal of the Anthology Cinema—but refuses to look into the room, by his nose, and realize that the idea can be achieved by all of us, step by step, brick by brick—and he keeps attacking P. Adams for anything that isn't yet exactly like the ideal. He doesn't see, he can't differentiate between a thing in progress and the final thing, final ideal. As for Sitney, Sitney has no choice: he has to do first things first, he has to do all the dirty work first. It's easy for Stan to say that the film-maker should get ten times the price for his prints (this was the main thing that brought the last crash on P. Adams that evening)—but Sitney has to think about the moneys for that purpose, and has to keep in mind what's available, and for what, and at what stage. So he says, "Stan, please trust me. Do you think, Stan, that I'll be working, that I'm working *against* the film-maker? Don't you trust me?" And Stan shouts, without even listening: "I always suspected that this will end up by becoming another project where the film-maker will be robbed." "But Stan," says Sitney, "trust me, leave those matters in my department." And Stan shouts: "No! I want to know everything that will be going in Anthology Cinema!" Yes, like he has to know every frame of his film. Sitney: "If I have to check about everything with you, then I quit." Etc. Etc.

I just read something in Berenson's *Aesthetics and History*: "Institutions, no matter how well intentioned and laudably initiated, no matter how admirable the ideas and principles they wish to promote, can be put in practice through individuals alone."

The session ended. Stan went back to Colorado. He sent in his resignation letter. Sitney agreed to continue. Now, the rumor has reached me that Stan wants back. Which means, Sitney would have to go. P. Adams has made up his mind about that. He doesn't think that he can take another session or another portion of Stan. If Sitney resigns, no doubt, I'd have to take it over. I can handle the personalities involved, they can grind their axes on my head as much as they want, it's neither hot nor cold to me—after all, I am a veteran of many weathers, storms and wars. The only problem is that during last year or so I have been fading out all my Barnum & Bailey activities and fading in into my film-making. Either I do it now or never. The last ten years have exhausted me, drained me, I have reached my end, as far as my public activities go. Now I am retreating, shrinking into myself. All I can afford, is to assist Sitney. Secondly: Anthology Cinema without Sitney wouldn't be what we wanted it to be. From the very beginning of the idea I saw it only with Sitney. I know there was no other way of pulling it through, at least not what we thought it should be. Sitney has enough energy to put the whole thing on a working basis, all departments of it: the repertory theater, the publications, the library. If I'd be running it, my energies would be split between my film-making and the Anthology. Everything would suffer. Plus, if Sitney would leave, half of Kelman's soul would be gone too. Kelman is immensely important in the whole project. I have a great trust in his taste, in his intelligence, and his wisdom. He will be very important in organizing the written materials on films, that part which will have a tremendous impact on universities, colleges, etc. The way I see the Anthology Cinema, I see no great essential change in its actual shape and its IDEA without Stan; but I don't see, I just can't see it without Sitney. Whatever Stan may say or feel at this stage, it's all question of an ego, sorry to say so, and his ego is as big as his art, and that's the main problem. It's all personality, personality clashes. I insist, it's ego, and not ideas, not ideals. As far as the ideals go, as far as the idea of the Anthology Cinema goes, we all want the same, and we are going to pursue that ideal. What Stan is afraid of, and he keeps accusing Sitney, is that the IDEA will be betrayed. What's worse, he says, the idea has already been betrayed. It comes to a paranoiac care of an unborn baby, six paranoiac mothers in one room, oh boy oh boy.

Solomon had a problem with TWO mothers and ONE baby. We have ONE baby and SIX mothers (You're a father...) But the solution must be the same, as Solomon's. I don't want it to die, no I'm willing to give it to Sitney TOTALLY & COMPLETELY. I would give it TOTALLY & COMPLETELY to Stan, too—but he DOESN'T WANT IT, he has his films. I can't give it to Kelman; I can't give it to Broughton; I can't give it to Kubelka: THEY DON'T WANT IT, on any conditions. Even I tremble. I would take it, but I'd give to the baby only half of my milk. I'd take it in bad faith. SITNEY is the only one who is willing to throw and is throwing HIS WHOLE LIFE for this baby. So I say, Sitney has to stay, Sitney has to stay even if all the others go. But it's Stan who will have to go, or is going. I trust Sitney completely. And so does Stan, whatever he says. It was in the middle of the emotional outburst, it was in the middle of

Dear JS:

Bad news: with June, we are leaving the Gallery of Modern Art.
They are beginning to censor us, they hate us, we are in enemy's
territory. Beginning June, I'll have to cut the screenings to one
(maybe two) shows every week, mhm All screenings will be at the
Elgin theater, one of the few friendly thaters in town, Sunday
11:15 AM and probably Thursday midnight. I am not sure yet. I may
find another place. In any case, don't do any bookings, stop everything,
and cancell if something was booked, until further notice. I'd like
eventually to see the rest of the Retrospective. I say, I'd like,
because basically I am the only viewer. None of the shows had more
then 20 people in the audience. It's beyond my understanding.
New York audience for the Avantgarde film is dead. We could fill
any place if we'd show films for nothing. All the hip and yip community likes things free and wouldn't pay a penny for Avantgarde Film.
But they pay to see commercial movies, that I know for sure. Anyway,
that's the sad truth. And I am selling my shirt. Probably shoes, too,
but they have holes.

Wait for my further notices on this subject... Thanks for all
help.

Jonas

WAR, during one brief pause of truce, during the last session, when Stan said to Sitney, almost crying: "Do you know, P. Adams? When I sit there, on my mountain, day and night, day and night working by my editing table—why do you think I spend so much time and put so much of myself into it, trying to achieve the utmost perfection? I do it, because I know that P. Adams, that there is at least one person somewhere, P. Adams Sitney, who will notice this ONE frame, that this frame here is right—so I struggle for that one right frame, for you—because if it would be for others, I wouldn't go through that torture of finding the right frame, they wouldn't notice it, I'd say to myself." That's what Stan said, approximately. So he knows that if Sitney cannot keep the standard of Anthology, then NOBODY can. And whatever Stan may say, no matter how he may rationalize the necessity for being with Anthology, it's only a rationalizing of an Ego, an ego that is hurt—but not an ego that is necessarily RIGHT or JUST. Hurt has nothing to do with being right or just.

Anyway, who knows who is right or just. But we have those practical, down to earth processes, needs, steps, situations. And decisions must be made. As things stand now, Stan, after resigning, wants back again, as far as I know. I don't think Sitney should take decision on this matter by himself. He can't and he doesn't want. What we are going to do is this. When Broughton comes to New York in two weeks from now (his play is opening in New Haven), we are going to hold here an Emergency Session concerning Stan's situation. We'll sit together, Broughton, Sitney, Kelman, myself, and we'd like you to be with us—and we'll have Kubelka on telephone, from Vienna, and we'll have to come to a group decision and then let Stan know our decision, one way or the other. That's about it. I see nothing else we can do about it until then.

Meanwhile, since the work has to go, we are proceeding with the acquisition of the films, with the library, with the program notes.

So I thought that much you should know, if it's any good.

And forgive me again the interruption of the Cassis quiet which is almost unforgivable (I mean, the interruption, not the quietude…)

Best regards to Julie. And who else is there? Canaries?

And yes, Ophelia, if she is in Cassis, give best regards from Saint Jean… And I hope you are doing plenty of painting.
Jonas

SCRAPS
Dreams are not poetry!

Q: Why do you show all kinds of films at the Tek?
A: You can allow ALL FILMS only when you know the difference between a good film and a bad film.

Living Theatre open style & wanting actual experience comes from loss of faith or knowledge of what art is & how it works —I mean, people lack that knowledge.

"Whosoever shall keep the whole law, and yet offend in one point, he is guilty of all."—St. James

Bruce Conner says, "Tek's projection booth is open to all comers": Just try! The booth is under a strict key supervision. The art of stealing has nothing to do with doors and locks, as we all know: the art of stealing is older than the art of film-making. And then, we are not that fussy about a few pieces stolen. God gives—film-maker takes. Why is Bruce so worried about the poor thieves? We aren't.

Dear Jonas,

you asked me for a letter saying why I thought
the work of Filmakers should be helped.

Actually I am astonished that you need a letter
of this kind. What can I possibly add about the work of
your extraordinary group, which is famous all over the
world.

It is incredible that you should have to fight
against these economic difficulties.

I believe that the success of many commercial
films to-day is because they have been influenced by
underground movies.

Anyway, I feel that you should absolutely have
all the help you need, in order to continue your experiments and researches, without which cinema could not continue to *evolve* in the way it has so far.

Yours
Michelangelo Antonioni

5th July 1969

And I am particularly
mindful of what you
once wrote in the
VOICE.

Again, it would
facilitate matters for
me in my semi-re-
tirement if Mr. Sitney
would contact me.

Thanking you again
for your fine lines.

Sincerely yours,
Joseph Cornell

FL. 8-9099

Dear Tomas Mekas,

I have called
the office a couple of times
hoping to catch Mrs. S.—
Key in case there be
anything to know the time of

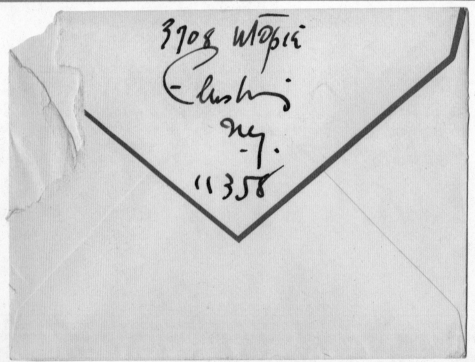

3708 Utopia

Flushing

N.Y.

11358

① inclination to visit again with regard to the proposal in your letter of July 10.

Thank you for your most thoughtful and elaborate sending. I do not feel that my efforts in film-making are really deserving of all that you have written but I do regret that I never had the experience wherewithal to make them so deserving.

Jackie Kennedy and Caroline Kennedy at their Fifth Avenue home. The fate brought us together. For some time I acted as a film tutor for Caroline and John Jr. *Walden* was Jackie's favorite film.

September 16, 1969

To Stan, Peter & P. Adams:

I am amazed, I am deeply amazed, that you could go through all the sessions & meetings, & all those arguments; that you (like Stan) write mountains of letters, without even ONCE asking, mentioning: BUT WHAT ABOUT THE NEW FILMS? What could we do about helping the new filmmaker to show his films? Anthology, Anthology, all day long Anthology, all week long Anthology. But you never asked me how the Cinematheque was doing, or what will happen to the Cinematheque. Do you really think that we can really open and run Anthology, for longer than one day, without being confronted with that problem? Do you really think that Anthology is enough, no showcase for new films is needed any longer? I consider that you are a pretty inconsiderate bunch of artists. One can find things like this only in cinema. Poets would never act like this. They would always think about the new poet. They are not afraid of the new. Classics will take care of themselves! It's the new artist that needs assistance. We end our session, and I run to the Jewish Museum, to project films—and you look at me as if I were crazy! Yes, I am crazy. And I hope I will always remain so.

AFTER-WORD

Anne König
Leipzig, September 5, 2019

In September 2016, Jonas Mekas copied a document to my hard drive that comprised over 1 GB of material. It contained his diaries *I Seem to Live, 1950–2011*. All the other books we had published together up until that point had arrived in the post in blue ring binders, with texts and pictures already organized by him, meaning that our graphic designers in Leipzig needed no further explanations. His *New York Diaries*—the first part of which, covering the period from 1950 to 1969, is now appearing posthumously in the year that also marks its author's death—was too big to fit in any folder. The digital document consists of a total of more than two thousand pages, some eight hundred of which are pictures.

The first chapter of *The New York Diaries* begins with a question: "Was I born a Displaced Person?" In his diary *I Had Nowhere to Go*, published in 1991 in New York by Black Thistle Press, he hadn't yet experienced the displacement thrust on him by fate as a hand that might have been dealt to him at birth. In the book he describes his escape from Lithuania, together with his younger brother Adolfas, and their internment, en route to Vienna, in the forced labor camp in Elmshorn near Hamburg, followed by years of being shifted between DP camps in Germany at the end of the war. The Mekas brothers were among the last displaced persons to board ship for North America in 1949. They planned to head for Chicago, but New York—the first port they arrive at in the New World—was so overwhelming that they decided on the spur of the moment to stay. The last chapters of *I Had Nowhere to Go*, documenting Jonas's arrival in New York, overlap with the beginning of *I Seem to Live*, but they are not identical. The feeling of being alone in the big city, the irretrievable loss of the home he grew up in—the small Lithuanian village of Semeniškiai, where Jonas was raised as part of a large family—the displacement, and the sense of being no longer rooted run like a basso continuo through the early entries in his *New York Diaries*. On December 27, 1954, he wrote, "Like so many times in the past, I'm trying again to organize my confused life… Looney or lonely. Anyway, …" The 1950s were about struggling to make ends meet, bad neighborhoods in Brooklyn, his initial forays into filmmaking with the Bolex, and the painful effort of learning the language. Jonas forced himself to read and write English as a means to find his feet in the vibrant metropolis. Together with Adolfas, he founded the magazine *Film Culture* in 1954, which he established as one of the first independent US American film journals outside of Hollywood. It was his mouthpiece, and he used it to build a bridge connecting the cinematic avant-garde in Europe and expressionist film in Germany with the burgeoning underground scene in New York, which he was personally involved in seeding.

Writing, committing ideas to paper, was one of his daily routines, whether it was film reviews, manifestos, love letters, or poems. "So I'm writing again. But it has always been so in my life. My writing is part of myself, an inseparable part of my existence, it's all in the stars," he wrote in 1957 in an undated entry. Jonas made no distinction between private and public—he was an author on multiple levels: he could be a filmmaker, critic, frontman of the Film-Makers' Cooperative, which he founded in 1962, fundraiser, film projectionist, ticket seller, poet, lover, and a great deal more. All these voices found their way into his notes, which he would not edit until right at the end of his life, assisted by Charity Coleman, who transcribed his handwritten texts, and by his son Sebastian. It was a job that was evidently right up his street, a routine task. As editor-in-chief at *Film Culture*, he had compiled texts and images for the magazine for decades.

His diary resembles a work journal, the kind of literary montage we know from Brecht, pieced together from contemporary notes and documents. In the first chapters, when he launches *Film Culture* together with Adolfas and the two of them try their hand at filmmaking, he cuts together unpublished diary entries written by his younger brother, which we have permission to print here for the first time with the consent of Adolfas's widow Pola Chapelle Mekas. The cluster of material comprises newspaper articles, published and unpublished pieces for "Movie Journal," the column he penned for *The Village Voice* from 1958 on, letters, photos, film stills, and notes on napkins and envelopes—a bunch of scraps in other words that now read as a moving and subjectively concentrated chronology of the New York underground. Jonas is a New American Cinema maniac, who scrimps and saves for everything: the printing costs for the magazine, film equipment for his colleagues, the rent for movie theaters, which he tirelessly trawls the city looking for. He negotiates with greedy landlords and with the Mafioso authorities in New York. He is desperately looking for a place where he can plant the tender seedling he is cultivating, the Film Makers' Cinematheque, founded in 1964. He goes to jail for screening his colleague Jack Smith's *Flaming Creatures*, which has been banned. He supports Andy Warhol, who shoots his first films with Jonas's help. He is sometimes at his wits' end when faced with the grueling task of obtaining money to produce and distribute new films in the world. On December 7, 1968, he moans, "Oh movies, I don't know how I got into them." But Jonas was tough and not easily thrown off

track. On June 16, 1968, after radical feminist author Valerie Solanas had shot Andy Warhol, severely injuring his spleen, liver, and esophagus, he wrote, "The day he was shot I went to the Hospital, and there, in the waiting room, everybody was crying and being pretty low, and I said, what the hell is this, a funeral? Don't you know that people of weak and hungry constitution like me or Andy do not die that easily, you just can't kill them that easily, he'll pull thru… He'll be O.K." Jonas was amazingly healthy despite his poor diet, the result of not having enough money for food. He had an endless supply of energy and the gift of being able to do many things at once, although he was not always sure he was on the right path. His private and professional life merged inextricably. At times, the Film-Makers' Coop was in his loft in Manhattan, and he had to find somewhere to sleep at night. In the 1960s, he fought doggedly for a while to make his own movies. He produced idealistic schedules, which he presented to his colleagues at the Co-op, but which were repeatedly thwarted by the incursions of everyday life. Despite the many tasks he set himself, he found the time to keep a record of his life. His diary was the place where he bore witness to himself, where he attempted to put his thoughts and ideas in order. The first volume of *I Seem to Live* concludes with the entry written on September 16, 1969: "It's the new artist that needs assistance. We end our session, and I run to the Jewish Museum, to project films—and you look at me as if I were crazy! Yes, I am crazy. And I hope I will always remain so."

While Jonas was still alive, we barely discussed the genesis of his diaries because we were busy publishing five other books: *Scrapbook of the Sixties* (2015), the second edition of *I Had Nowhere to Go* (2017) and the first translation of it into German, *Ich hatte keinen Ort, 1944–1953* (2017), *Conversations with Film-Makers* (2018), and *Film*

Culture 80: The Legend of Barbara Rubin (2018). In 2011, Christoph Gnädig—who like so many young European enthusiasts of New American Cinema conducted research for his master's thesis at Anthology Film Archives in New York—stayed with Jonas for several months in Brooklyn. He looked over Jonas's shoulder while he was working on his diaries and reported that Jonas, who was almost ninety at the time, was still typing out his handwritten texts using two fingers—he is said to have been a very quick typist—before transferring them to computer. In the process of editing the texts, he would comment on events that had happened decades before. On May 20, 2013, he annotated an entry dated October 2, 1967: "A note re. the SHOOT YOUR WAY OUT WITH THE CAMERA project. Regretfully, this idealistic, almost utopian project, as described in the above Manifesto, presented by Shirley Clarke and myself at the Citizen Initiative Conference, organized by Lindsay, Mayor of New York City, in early December 1966, never got off the ground. Despite all the good will of many friendly organizations and individuals, Shirley's and my efforts to raise monies for the project, and our attempts to persuade Kodak to contribute cameras and stock to the project, ended all in a lot of wasted time and frustration. But it was a beautiful idea, I still think so." Jonas worked with his long-time ally Shirley Clarke to develop the project, which involved giving 8 mm and 16 mm cameras to over two hundred teenagers, most of them black, who were to capture their daily lives on film. Clarke, one of the few female filmmakers on the underground scene, was often targeted by her white male colleagues. Jonas frequently pitched in to help mediate the cock fights in this fragile social milieu, and his defense of Clarke was heroic. His unpublished 1962 "Movie Journal" column about her film *The Connection* should be regarded as a satirical piece. The text was "prefaced" by a slugfest in *The New York Times* and *The Village Voice*, where Jonas defended her film as the best of the year and trampled all over the deaf and insensitive film critics of one of the city's biggest newspapers. This entry and the fictional secret interview he recorded with himself on April 3, 1968, in which he ranted about the inefficiency of the US Army in the Vietnam War, are pastiches. In these texts, he adopts the attitude of his opponents, lampooning them with their own arguments.

In the editorial work on the diaries, in which I was supported by Christoph Gnädig, Charity Coleman, and Sebastian Mekas, no changes were made to the text. It was not shortened, rewritten, or supplemented, and the chronological sequences, of the kind that occur in chapters Twenty Five und Twenty Six, where there are slight shifts in the ordering of events, were not corrected retrospectively. These sections are more revealing of Jonas's own editorial process. He must have been working on it to the last, arranging, assembling, and moving events, notes, and images until he was happy with the dramaturgy of the text as a whole, amounting to more than two thousand pages—or sixty-one years, to put it another way. His own spellings of words— like "thru" and the many variations of the key terms such as "film-maker," "avant-garde," "Film-Makers' Co-op," or "Coop" for short—have remained in the text as he probably often jotted them down when time was pressing. The different spellings are not simply a reflection of his mood, they also shed light on changes in the way that American English is used. Misspelled names and minor orthographical mistakes, on the other hand, have been silently corrected. Meanwhile, the neologisms that came out of his process of language acquisition have not been touched, nor have the quotations written by the author from memory, which do not always correspond to the original. Montaged quotations like those by the medieval mystic Agrippa von Nettesheim, where several passages are nested in a single quotation, have not been re-edited. Sometimes surnames appear in square brackets after a first name. These additions were inserted by the author himself, although this practice is not consistent throughout the diaries. The second volume, covering the period from 1969 to 2011, will contain an index of persons to help navigate this two-thousand-page diary. It is without question Jonas Mekas's literary masterpiece and will henceforth rank on a par with his cinematic work, rounding out our image of this important author, filmmaker, and underground organizer.

Translation: Simon Cowper

IMAGE CREDITS

pp. 15, 20, 23, 29, 34, 36, 40, 57–58, 67, 79–81, 84, 88, 92, 95, 103, 104 (bottom), 107–08, 110, 114, 118, 120, 127, 139, 146, 154, 156, 159 (top), 160–62, 177 (bottom), 178–79, 184, 192, 195–96, 205, 241–42, 258, 261, 267, 272, 295, 303, 312, 316–18, 321–22, 325–27, 328 (bottom), 329–30, 332, 339–40, 345–46, 349, 359, 363, 366–71, 375, 379, 383–4, 386, 390, 396–98, 400, 403–5, 409–10, 413, 429–30, 433–37, 441–42, 444, 449, 451–52, 455–57, 465, 473–74, 478, 488, 492–93, 499–500, 507–8, 520–21, 529, 534, 536, 549–51, 553–54, 558, 560–61, 567–68, 571–72, 576, 581, 582 (bottom), 587, 592–94, 597, 613, 616, 623, 627, 631–32, 636, 638–40, 650, 656–57, 662, 666–67, 673–74, 677, 679, 687–88, 690, 696, 700, 704, 725, 729, 732, 737–38, 745, 754, 756, 763, 784, 791 (bottom), 792, 798, 803–04, 807, 809–11
Credits: Author's archives

pp. 13–14
Still from *Lost Lost Lost* (1976) by Jonas Mekas, Williamsburg, 1952

p. 16
Author's archives, Brooklyn, 1950

p. 19
Still from *Lost Lost Lost* (1976) by Jonas Mekas, Williamsburg, 1950

p. 24
Author's archives, Stony Brook, 1952
Credit: Pranė Lapė family

p. 25
Author's archives, Stone Brook (top);
Author's archives, Adolfas Mekas and Nėlė Lapė, 1952 (bottom)

p. 26
Still from film footage by Jonas Mekas, Stony Brook, 1952

p. 30
Author's archives, Queens

p. 33
Author's archives. Photo: Adolfas Mekas, Brooklyn, 1951

p. 35
Author's archives. Photo: Pola Chapelle Mekas, Brooklyn, c. 1975

p. 39
Author's archives, 1950s

p. 41
Author's archives, 1952

p. 42
Author's archives

p. 45
Author's archives, 1951

p. 46
Author's archives, Brooklyn

p. 47
Author's archives, 1950

p. 48
Author's archives

p. 51
Author's archives, Brooklyn, 1952

p. 52
Author's archives, Brooklyn

p. 55
Still from *Lost Lost Lost* (1976) by Jonas Mekas, 1952

p. 56
Author's archives, 1952

p. 57
Author's archives. Credit: George Maciunas, 1953

p. 63
Author's archives, 1953

p. 64
Author's archives, Manhattan, 1953

p. 71
Author's archives. Photo: Adolfas Mekas, 1953

p. 72
Author's archives

p. 83
Author's archives, 2013

p. 86
Author's archives. Photo: Adolfas Mekas, 1954

p. 87
Author's archives, Manhattan

p. 91
Author's archives

p. 92
Author's archives

p. 104
Author's archives. Photo: Eve Arnold, 1960. © Eve Arnold, Magnum Photos

p. 109
Author's archives. Photo: *Film Culture* magazine, 1957

p. 113
Author's archives

p. 128
Author's archives. Photo: Edouard de Laurot (top);
Author's archives (bottom)

pp. 129–30
Author's archives. Photos: Edouard de Laurot

pp. 133–34
Author's archives. Photos: Gideon Bachmann

pp. 137–38
Author's archives

p. 140
Author's archives, 1957

p. 142
Author' archives. Credit: Postcard from Carl Theodor Dreyer to Jonas Mekas, 1959

p. 159
Author's archives, 1957

p. 166
Author's archives

pp. 169–70
Author's archives, 1958

p. 173
Author's archives, 1958

p. 177
Author's archives, 1958

p. 183
Author's archives. Photo: Fred W. McDarrah, 1966. ©Fred W. McDarrah, Getty Images

p. 191
Credit: Sam Shaw, 1957. ©Shaw Family Archive

p. 197
Author's archives. Photo: Alexander Hammid, 1943

p. 201
Author's archives, c. 1959

p. 206
Author's archives, 1959

p. 209
Author's archives. Photo: John Cohen, 1959

p. 219
Author's archives, 1959

p. 222
Author's archives. Photo: Unknown, 1958

p. 225
Author's archives,
New Jersey, 1960

p. 226
Author's archives,
New Jersey, 1960

p. 229
Author's archives.
During the
filming of Robert
Frank's *The Sin
of Jesus*, 1960.
Photo: Robert Frank

p. 230
Author's archives,
1960

p. 238
Author's archives,
1960

p. 245
Author's archives,
Harlem, 1960

p. 246
Author's archives.
During the filming
of Jonas Mekas'
Guns of the Trees,
The Bronx, 1960

pp. 256–57
Author's archives,
1960

p. 268
Author's archives,
1960

p. 271
Author's archives.
Photo: Dan Talbot,
1960

p. 277
Still from *Guns of
the Trees* (1961)
by Jonas Mekas

p. 293
Author's archives.
Photo: George
Maciunas, 1961

p. 294
Author's archives,
1961

p. 299
Still from *Zefiro
Torna or Scenes
from the Life of
George Maciunas*
(2002) by Jonas
Mekas, Great Neck,
1970

p. 315
Author's archives,
1961

p. 324
Stills from film
footage by Jonas
Mekas, New York,
1960s

p. 328
Author's archives
(top)

p. 331
Author's archives.
Photo:
Cue magazine

p. 335
Author's archives
(top); Author's
archives. Photo:
Herald Tribune,
New York, 1962
(bottom)

p. 342
Still from *Lost
Lost Lost* (1976) by
Jonas Mekas,
Manhattan, 1960s.
Photo: Barbara
Rubin

p. 350
Still from *Lost
Lost Lost* (1976) by
Jonas Mekas,
during the filming
of *Hallelujah
the Hills* by Adolfas
Mekas, 1962

p. 353
Author's archives,
1962

p. 372
Still from *In
Between* by Jonas
Mekas, 1978

p. 380
Author's archives,
1960s

p. 392
Author's archives,
1960s

p. 399
Still from *Lost
Lost Lost* (1976) by
Jonas Mekas

p. 414
Author's archives,
1964

p. 418
Photo: Anonymous
Credit: Author's
archives

p. 421
Still from unedited
film footage by
Jonas Mekas, 1963

p. 422
Still from a Happen-
ing by Salvador
Dalí filmed by Peter
Beard, 1964

Author's archives,
1963

p. 471
Author's archives,
1963

p. 477
Still from *Award
Presentation
to Andy Warhol* by
Jonas Mekas, 1964

p. 487
Author's archives,
Manhattan, 1965

p. 491
Author's archives.
Photo: Lawrence
Lipton, 1963

p. 501
Author's archives.
Photo: David
McCabe, 1965

p. 519
Author's archives.
During the
shooting of Adolfas
Mekas' *Double-
Barelled Detective*.
Photo: Louise
Alaimo, 1965

p. 522
Author's archives

p. 525
Still from *Walden*
(1968) by Jonas
Mekas, 1965

pp. 530–31
Author's archives,
1965

p. 535
Author's archives,
Berlin, 1965;
Courtesy: Amos
Vogel

p. 539
Still from film
footage by Jonas
Mekas

p. 552
Author's archives,
1966

p. 557
Author's archives,
New York, 1966

p. 575
Author's archives,
Marseille, 1966

p. 577
Author's archives.
Photo: Jerome
Hill, Bouches-du-
Rhône, 1966

p. 578
Still from film *Notes
for Jerome* (1978)
by Jonas Mekas,
Lacoste, 1966

p. 582
Author's archives,
New Jersey, 1967

p. 588
Still from *Walden*
(1968) by Jonas
Mekas, Manhattan,
1966

p. 591
Author's archives.
Photo: Matt
Hoffman, 1966

p. 600
Author's archives,
Iowa, 1967

p. 604
Still from *The Song
of Assisi* (1967)
by Jonas Mekas,
Rome, 1967

p. 609
Stills from *Song of
Avila*, 1967

p. 614
Still from *Song of
Avila*, 1967

p. 624
Still from *Walden*
(1968) by Jonas
Mekas

p. 637
Still from *Birth
of a Nation* (1997)
by Jonas Mekas

COLOPHON

Jonas Mekas
I Seem to Live.
The New York Diaries,
vol. 1, 1950–1969

Editor:
Anne König

Editorial assistance:
Charity Coleman,
Christoph Gnädig,
Sebastian Mekas

Graphic design:
Fabian Bremer,
Pascal Storz

Typesetting:
Hannes Drißner
(Spector Books)

Lithography:
Scancolor,
Reprostudio GmbH,
Leipzig

Copyediting:
Charity Coleman,
Christoph Gnädig

Proofing:
Anne König

Printing/Binding:
Kösel GmbH &
Co. KG, Altusried-
Krugzell

Acknowledgements:
Nick Bennett,
Phong Bui, Charity
Coleman, Christoph
Gnädig, Christian
Hiller, Jim Jarmusch,
Jonas Lozoraitis,
Hollis Melton, Pola
Chapelle Mekas,
Sebastian Mekas,
Benn Northover,
Nathlie Provosty,
Remigijus Rubinas,
Chuck Smith

Further publications
from Adolfas
Mekas: *The Adolfas
Diaries* and *The
Personal Observa-
tions and Insights of
Adolfas Mekas,
from Lithuania to
Brooklyn (1941–1951)*.
Published by
Hallelujah Editions,
hallelujah
editions.com

Published by:

Spector Books
Harkortstraße 10
04107 Leipzig
spectorbooks.com

Distribution:

Germany, Austria:
GVA, Gemeinsame
Verlagsauslieferung
Göttingen
GmbH & Co. KG,
gva-verlage.de

Switzerland:
AVA Verlags-
auslieferung AG,
ava.ch

France, Belgium:
Interart Paris,
interart.fr

UK:
Central Books Ltd,
centralbooks.com

USA, Canada,
Central and
South America,
Africa, Asia:
ARTBOOK | D.A.P.,
artbook.com

South Korea:
The Book Society,
thebooksociety.org

Australia,
New Zealand:
Perimeter
Distribution,
perimeter
distribution.com

First edition
Printed in the EU

ISBN
978-3-95905-288-7